Research and Development in Intelligent Systems XXVI

Max Bramer · Richard Ellis · Miltos Petridis
Editors

Research and Development in Intelligent Systems XXVI

Incorporating Applications and Innovations
in Intelligent Systems XVII

 Springer

Editors

Prof. Max Bramer
University of Portsmouth
UK

Richard Ellis
Stratum Management Ltd.
UK

Miltos Petridis
University of Greenwich
UK

ISBN 978-1-84882-982-4   e-ISBN 978-1-84882-983-1
DOI 10.1007/978-1-84882-983-1
Springer London Dordrecht Heidelberg New York

British Library Cataloguing in Publication Data
A catalogue record for this book is available from the British Library

Library of Congress Control Number: 2009938630

Printed on acid-free paper

Springer is part of Springer Science+Business Media (www.springer.com)

PROGRAMME CHAIRS' INTRODUCTION

M.A.BRAMER, University of Portsmouth, UK
R.ELLIS, Stratum Management Ltd, UK

This volume comprises the refereed papers presented at AI-2009, the Twenty-ninth SGAI International Conference on Innovative Techniques and Applications of Artificial Intelligence, held in Cambridge in December 2009 in both the technical and the application streams. The conference was organised by SGAI, the British Computer Society Specialist Group on Artificial Intelligence.

The technical papers included new and innovative developments in the field, divided into sections on Knowledge Discovery and Data Mining, Reasoning, Data Mining and Machine Learning, Optimisation and Planning, and Knowledge Acquisition and Evolutionary Computation.

This year's prize for the best refereed technical paper was won by a paper entitled "Coping with Noisy Search Experiences" by Pierre-Antoine Champin (Université de Lyon, France) and Peter Briggs, Maurice Coyle and Barry Smyth (University College Dublin, Ireland). SGAI gratefully acknowledges the long-term sponsorship of Hewlett-Packard Laboratories (Bristol) for this prize, which goes back to the 1980s.

The application papers included present innovative applications of AI techniques in a number of subject domains. This year, the papers are divided into sections on AI and Design, Commercial Applications of AI and Further AI Applications.

This year's Rob Milne Memorial Award for the best refereed application paper was won by a paper entitled "Corpus Callosum MR Image Classification" by Ashraf Elsayed, Frans Coenen, Chuntao Jiang, Marta Garcia-Finana and Vanessa Sluming (University of Liverpool, UK).

The volume also includes the text of short papers presented as posters at the conference.

On behalf of the conference organising committee we would like to thank all those who contributed to the organisation of this year's programme, in particular the programme committee members, the executive programme committees and our administrators Rachel Browning and Bryony Bramer.

Max Bramer, Technical Programme Chair, AI-2009
Richard Ellis, Application Programme Chair, AI-2009

ACKNOWLEDGEMENTS

AI-2009 CONFERENCE COMMITTEE

Dr. Miltos Petridis University of Greenwich	Conference Chair and UK CBR Organiser
Dr Frans Coenen University of Liverpool	Local Arrangements Chair and Deputy Technical Programme Chair
Prof. Adrian Hopgood De Montfort University	Workshop Organiser
Rosemary Gilligan	Treasurer
Dr Nirmalie Wiratunga The Robert Gordon University	Poster Session Organiser
Professor Max Bramer University of Portsmouth	Technical Programme Chair
Richard Ellis Stratum Management Ltd	Application Program Chair
Dr. Tony Allen Nottingham Trent University	Deputy Application Programme Chair
Dr. Alice Kerly University of Birmingham	Research Student Liaison
Dr. Kirsty Bradbrook	Research Student Liaison
Rachel Browning BCS	Conference Administrator
Bryony Bramer	Paper Administrator

TECHNICAL EXECUTIVE PROGRAMME COMMITTEE

Prof. Max Bramer, University of Portsmouth (Chair)

Dr. Frans Coenen, University of Liverpool (Vice-Chair)

Dr. John Kingston, Health & Safety Laboratory

Dr. Miltos Petridis, University of Greenwich

Prof. Alun Preece, University of Cardiff

Dr. Nirmalie Wiratunga, The Robert Gordon University, Aberdeen

APPLICATIONS EXECUTIVE PROGRAMME COMMITTEE

Mr. Richard Ellis, Stratum Management Ltd (Chair)

Dr. Tony Allen, Nottingham Trent University (Vice-Chair)

Ms. Rosemary Gilligan

Prof. Adrian Hopgood, De Montfort University

Dr. Richard Wheeler, University of Edinburgh

TECHNICAL PROGRAMME COMMITTEE

Alia Abdelmoty (Cardiff University)

Andreas A Albrecht (Queen's University Belfast)

John Atkinson (Universidad de Concepcion, Chile)

Ali Orhan Aydin (Macquarie University)

Roman Belavkin (Middlesex University)

Yaxin Bi (University of Ulster)

Mirko Boettcher (University of Magdeburg, Germany)

Max Bramer (University of Portsmouth)

Krysia Broda (Imperial College, University of London)

Ken Brown (University College Cork)

Frans Coenen (University of Liverpool)

Bruno Cremilleux (University of Caen)

Madalina Croitoru (University of Montpellier, France)

Ireneusz Czarnowski (Gdynia Maritime University, Poland)

Marina De Vos (University of Bath)

John Debenham (University of Technology; Sydney)

Stefan Diaconescu (Softwin, Romania)

Nicolas Durand (University of Aix-Marseille 2)

Anneli Edman (University of Upsala)

Virginia Francisco (Universidad Complutense de Madrid)

Adriana Giret (Universidad Politécnica de Valencia)

Ole-Christoffer Granmo (University of Agder, Norway)

Nadim Haque (Accenture)

Nick Hawes (University of Birmingham, UK)

Arjen Hommersom (University of Nijmegen, The Netherlands)

Zina Ibrahim (University of Windsor, Canada)

Piotr Jedrzejowicz (Gdynia Maritime University; Poland)

Rasa Jurgelenaite (Radboud University, The Netherlands)

John Kingston (Health & Safety Laboratory)

Konstantinos Kotis (University of the Aegean)

Ivan Koychev (Bulgarian Academy of Science)

T. K. Satish Kumar (Institute for Human and Machine Cognition, USA)

Fernando Lopes (LNEG-National Research Institute, Portugal)

Peter Lucas (University of Nijmegen)

Michael Madden (National University of Ireland, Galway)

Daniel Manrique Gamo (Universidad Politecnica de Madrid)

Roberto Micalizio (Universita' di Torino)

Lars Nolle (Nottingham Trent University)

Dan O'Leary (University of Southern California)

Nir Oren (Kings College London)

Alun Preece (University of Cardiff)

Juan Jose Rodriguez (University of Burgos)

María Dolores Rodríguez-Moreno (Universidad de Alcalá)

Thomas Roth-Berghofer (Deutsches Forschungszentrum für Künstliche Intelligenz, Germany)

Fernando Sáenz Pérez (Universidad Complutense de Madrid)

Miguel A. Salido (Universidad Politécnica de Valencia)

Rainer Schmidt (University of Rostock, Germany)

Sid Shakya (BT Innovate and Design)

Evgueni Smirnov (Maastricht University, The Netherlands)

Simon Thompson (BT Innovate)

Jon Timmis (University of York)

John Tobin (Trinity College, Dublin)

Gianluca Torta (Università di Torino)

Andrew Tuson (City University)

M.R.C. van Dongen (University College Cork)

Graham Winstanley (University of Brighton)

Nirmalie Wiratunga (Robert Gordon University)

Fei Ling Woon (SDG Consulting UK)

APPLICATION PROGRAMME COMMITTEE

Hatem Ahriz (Robert Gordon University)

Tony Allen (Nottingham Trent University)

Ines Arana (Robert Gordon University)

Mercedes Argüello Casteleiro (University of Manchester)

Kirsty Bradbrook (University of Hertfordshire / Vtesse Networks Ltd)

Ken Brown (University College Cork)

Simon Coupland (De Montfort University)

Sarah Jane Delany (Dublin Institute of Technology)

Richard Ellis (Stratum Management Ltd)

Lindsay Evett (Nottingham Trent University)

Rosemary Gilligan (University of Hertfordshire)

John Gordon (AKRI Ltd)

Sergio Grau (Nottingham Trent University)

Elizabeth Guest (Leeds Metropolitan University)

Chris Hinde (Loughborough University)

Adrian Hopgood (De Montfort University)

Alice Kerly (Selex Systems Integration Ltd)

Shuliang Li (University of Westminster)

Lars Nolle (Nottingham Trent University)

Miltos Petridis (University of Greenwich)

Rong Qu (University of Nottingham)

Trevor Runcie (Agile Knowledge Management Limited)

Miguel Salido (Universidad Politécnica de Valencia)

Roger Tait (University of Cambridge)

Wamberto Vasconcelos (University of Aberdeen)

Richard Wheeler (Human Computer Learning Foundation)

Patrick Wong (Open University)

CONTENTS

Research and Development in Intelligent Systems XXVI

DATA MINING AND MACHINE LEARNING

OPTIMISATION AND PLANNING

KNOWLEDGE ACQUISITION AND EVOLUTIONARY COMPUTATION

SHORT PAPERS

Applications and Innovations in Intelligent Systems XVII

Research and Development in
Intelligent Systems XXVI

BEST TECHNICAL PAPER

Coping with Noisy Search Experiences

Pierre-Antoine Champin, Peter Briggs, Maurice Coyle, and Barry Smyth

Abstract The so-called *Social Web* has helped to change the very nature of the Internet by emphasising the role of our online experiences as new forms of content and service knowledge. In this paper we describe an approach to improving mainstream Web search by harnessing the search experiences of groups of like-minded searchers. We focus on the HeyStaks system (*www.heystaks.com*) and look in particular at the experiential knowledge that drives its search recommendations. Specifically we describe how this knowledge can be noisy, and we describe and evaluate a recommendation technique for coping with this noise and discuss how it may be incorporated into HeyStaks as a useful feature.

Experience is the name everyone gives to their mistakes. —Oscar Wilde

1 Introduction

The now familiar Social Web reflects an important change in the nature of the Web and its content. The development since 1999 of blogs, as a simple way for users to express their views and opinions, ushered in this new era of *user-generated content* (UGC) as many sites quickly began to offer a whole host of UGC alternatives including the ability to leave comments and write reviews, as well as the ability to

Pierre-Antoine Champin
LIRIS, Université de Lyon, CNRS, UMR5205, Université Claude Bernard Lyon 1, F-69622, Villeurbanne, France, e-mail: pchampin@liris.cnrs.fr

Peter Briggs, Maurice Coyle, and Barry Smyth
CLARITY: Centre for Sensor Web Technologies School of Computer Science and Informatics, University College Dublin, Ireland, e-mail: {peter.briggs,maurice.coyle,Barry.Smyth}@ucd.ie

Acknowledgment
Based on works supported by Science Foundation Ireland, Grant No. 07/CE/I1147, the French National Center for Scientific Research (CNRS), and HeyStaks Technologies Ltd.

M. Bramer et al. (eds.), *Research and Development in Intelligent Systems XXVI*,
DOI 10.1007/978-1-84882-983-1_1, © Springer-Verlag London Limited 2010

rate or vote on the comments/opinions of others. The result has been an evolution of the Web from a repository of information to a repository of experiences, and an increased emphasis on people rather than content. In combination with social networking services, this has precipitated the growth of the Social Web as a platform for communication, sharing, recommendation, and collaboration.

Web search has continued to play a vital role in this evolving online world and there is no doubting the success of the mainstream Web search engines as a key information tool for hundreds of millions of users everyday. Given the importance of Web search it is no surprise that researchers continue to look for new ways to improve upon the mainstream search engines. However, new tools are also needed to gather, harness, reuse and share, in the most efficient and enjoyable way, the experiences captured by UGC [4, 18]. One particular line of research has focused on using recommendation technologies in an effort to make Web search more personal: by learning about the preferences and interests of individual searchers, personalized Web search systems can influence search results in a manner that better suits the individual searcher [3, 21]. Recently, another complementary research direction has seen researchers explore the *collaborative* potential of Web search by proposing that the conventional *solitary* nature of Web search can be enhanced in many search scenarios by recognising and supporting the sharing of search experiences to facilitate synchronous or asynchronous collaboration among searchers [14, 8]. Indeed, the work of [16, 1] has shown that collaborative Web search can lead to a more personalized search experience by harnessing recommendations from the search experiences of communities of like-minded searchers.

Our recent work [17] has led to the development of a new system to support collaborative Web search. This system is called HeyStaks (*heystaks.com*) and it benefits from providing a collaborative search experience that is fully integrated with mainstream search engines such as Google. HeyStaks comes in the form of a browser toolbar and, as users search as normal, HeyStaks captures their search experiences and promotes results based on their past search experiences and the experiences of friends, colleagues, and other like-minded searchers. HeyStaks introduces the key concept of a *search stak* which serves as a repository for search experiences. Users can create search staks to represent their search interests and they can share their staks with others to create pools of focused search experiences.

The key contribution of this paper is to focus on an important challenge faced by HeyStaks and to propose a recommendation solution to meet this challenge. The challenge concerns the basic stak selection task: prior to a search, a HeyStaks user must select an *active* stak so that their search experiences can be correctly stored and so that they can receive appropriate recommendations. Many users have built this into their search workflow and HeyStaks does contain some simple techniques for automatically switching to the right search stak at search time. However, many users forget to choose a stak before they search and, as a result, search experiences are often mis-filed in an incorrect stak. Ultimately this limits the effectiveness of HeyStaks and contributes significant experience noise to search staks.

In what follows we will briefly introduce the HeyStaks system. Then we will describe the development of a stak recommendation technique as part of HeyStaks' *stak maintenance* features, which allow stak owners to review and edit stak content. In brief, our stak recommender is capable of highlighting potentially mis-filed experiences and offers the user a suggested target stak that is expected to provide a better fit. We will describe an evaluation on real-user search data to demonstrate the effectiveness of this technique.

2 HeyStaks: an overview

HeyStaks is a collarative search systems, similar to those presented in [12, 9]. Our primary goal in designing HeyStaks is to help improve upon the search experience offered by mainstream search engines, while at the same time allowing searchers to search as normal with their favourite engine. In this section we will outline the basic HeyStaks system architecture and summarize how result recommendations are made during search. In addition we will make this discussion more concrete by briefly summarizing a worked example of HeyStaks in action.

Concepts and Architecture. HeyStaks adds two important collaboration features to any mainstream search engine. First, it captures users' experiences in using the search engine, and store them in *search staks*. Staks are a type a of folder that users can create to store search experiences related to a given topic of interest. Staks can also be shared with others so that their own searches will also be added to the stak. Second, HeyStaks uses staks to generate recommendations that are added to the underlying search results that come from the mainstream search engine. These recommendations are results that stak members have previously found to be relevant for similar queries in the context of this stak, and help the searcher to discover results that friends or colleagues have found relevant, results that may otherwise be buried deep within the engine's result-list.

HeyStaks takes the form of two basic components: a client-side *browser toolbar* and a back-end *server*. The toolbar allows users to create and share staks and provides a range of ancillary services, such as the ability to tag or vote for pages. The toolbar also captures search result click-thrus and manages the integration of HeyStaks recommendations with the default result-list. The back-end server manages the individual stak indexes (indexing individual pages against query/tag terms and positive/negative votes), the stak database (stak titles, members, descriptions, status, etc.), the HeyStaks social networking service and the recommendation engine.

Running Example. To make things more concrete, consider the following example. Pierre, Maurice and some colleagues are using the LaTeX typesetting system on a regular basis, and Web search as a source of information about how to use it. Pierre created a search stak called "LaTeX" and shared this with Maurice and colleagues, encouraging them to use this stak for their LaTeX-related searches.

Fig. 1 shows Maurice selecting this stak as he embarks on a new search about the tabular environment, and Fig. 2 shows the results of this search. The usual Google

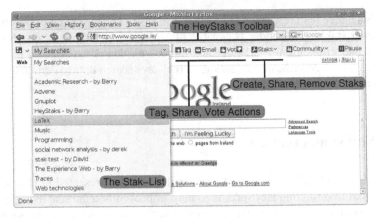

Fig. 1 Selecting a new active stak.

results are shown, but in addition HeyStaks has made one promotion. This was promoted because other members of the "LaTeX" stak had recently found these results
to be relevant; perhaps they selected them for *similar* queries, or voted for them, or
tagged them with related terms. These recommendations may have been promoted
from much deeper within the Google result-list, or they may not even be present in
Google's default results. Other relevant results may also be highlighted by HeyStaks,
but left in their default Google position. In this way Pierre and Maurice benefit from
promotions that are based on their previous similar searches. In addition, HeyStaks
can recommend results from Pierre and Maurice's other staks, helping them to benefit from the search knowledge that other groups and communities have created.

Fig. 2 Google search results with HeyStaks promotions.

Separately from the toolbar, HeyStaks users also benefit from the HeyStaks *search portal*, which provides a social networking service built around people's search histories. For example, Fig. 3 shows the portal page for the "LaTeX" stak. It presents an activity feed of recent search history and a query cloud that makes it easy for the user to find out about what others have been searching for. The search portal also provides users with a wide range of features such as stak maintenance (e.g., editing, moving, copying results in staks and between staks), various search and filtering tools, and a variety of features to manage their own search profiles and find new search partners.

Fig. 3 The HeyStaks search portal provides direct access to staks and past searches.

Generating Recommendations. In HeyStaks each search stak (S) serves as a profile of the search activities of the stak members. Each stak is made up of a set of result pages ($S = \{p_1, ..., p_k\}$) and each page is anonymously associated with a number of implicit and explicit interest indicators, including the total number of times a result has been selected (*sel*), the query terms ($q_1, ..., q_n$) that led to its selection, the number of times a result has been tagged (*tag*), the terms used to tag it ($t_1, ..., t_m$), the votes it has received (v^+, v^-), and the number of people it has been shared with (*share*).

In this way, each page is associated with a set of *term data* (query terms and/or tag terms) and a set of *usage data* (the selection, tag, share, and voting counts). The term data is stored as a Lucene (*lucene.apache.org*) index, with each page indexed under its associated query and tag terms, and provides the basis for retrieving and ranking *promotion candidates*. The usage data provides an additional source of evidence that can be used to filter results and to generate a final set of recommendations. At search time, recommendations are produced in a number of stages: first, relevant results are retrieved and ranked from the stak index; next, these promotion candidates are filtered based on the usage evidence to eliminate spurious recommendations; and, finally, the remaining results are added to the Google result-list according to a set of presentation rules.

Briefly, HeyStaks uses a number of different recommendation rules to determine how and where a promotion should be added. Space restrictions prevent a detailed account of this component but, for example, up to 3 *primary* promotions are added to the top of the Google result-list and labelled using the HeyStaks promotion icons. If a remaining promotion is also in the default Google result-list then this is labeled in place. If there are still remaining promotions then these are added to the *secondary* promotion list, which is sorted according to TF*IDF scores. These recommendations are then added to the Google result-list as an optional, expandable list of recommendations. The interested reader can refer to [17] for more details.

It is worth noting that, unlike many other recommender systems, HeyStaks does not filter information from a search stak in order to personalize recommendation results. Personalization does however occurs in HeyStaks (unlike other systems such as Google's SearchWiki) by *chosing the active stak* from which recommendation knowledge will be used. The focus is therefore on the task or context of the user, rather than an ever-valid user profile that would not account for the diversity of their search activity.

3 Stak recommendation

With the current version of HeyStaks the focus is very much on the recommendation of results during search. However, in this section we will argue the need for a second type of recommendation – the recommendation of staks to users at search time – as a way to help ensure that the right search experiences are stored in the right staks.

The Problem of Stak Noise. One problem faced by HeyStaks, and many other systems relying on users' experiential knowledge, is that of reliably collecting that knowledge. Explicitly requesting information from the user is often considered too intrusive, and discourages many users from using the system in the first place. On the other hand, implicitly collecting this information is error prone because in order to interpret users' actions in terms of reusable knowledge, the collection process must be based on some idealized expectation of user behaviour.

For example, HeyStaks relies on users selecting an appropriate stak for their search experiences, prior to selecting, tagging or voting for pages. Those actions are therefore considered as evidence that the page is relevant to the stak currently active in the HeyStaks toolbar, and to the query, in the case of a selection. The relevance to the query is not guaranteed, though, since the page may prove less interesting than its title suggested. More important for HeyStaks, the relevance to the selected stak is not guaranteed either, for it is common occurence that users forget to select a stak those actions. Many pages are then filed by default in the users "My Searches" stak (which is not shared with other users), or even in an unrelated stak. The point is that this limits the quality of search knowledge contained within the staks, hence the quality of the recommendations made by the system.

Coping with Stak Noise. A solution to break that vicious circle would be for HeyStaks to automatically select, or at least suggest, the appropriate stak when the user starts a query. This is a meta-recommendation problem [15] (selecting the stak from which search results will be recommended). We therefore face two challenges: using a repository of recommendation knowledge (search experiences) for another purpose than the one it was designed for (meta-recommendation), and using it despite the significant amount of noise it contains. Should we succeed, the quality of the collected experiences would increase thanks to the stak recommendation, which in turn would itself be improved.

We envision two different uses of the stak recommender system. The first one, the *on-line phase*, has already been described above: at query time, in order to ensure that the selected stak corresponds to the focus of the user's search. The second use is an *off-line phase*: whenever they want, the owner of a stak can visit a maintenance page, where the system will present them with *a)* pages in that stak which could be moved or copied to one or several other staks, and *b)* pages from other staks which could be moved or copied to this stak. Though the off-line phase is more demanding, we believe that some stak owners will have an incentive to improve the quality of their staks (or "curate" them); e.g. for staks shared by a community of knoweldge workers with a strong need for accurate experience sharing. In the rest of this paper, we will focus on the off-line phase.

4 Noise-Robust Classifier

We consider the off-line stak recommendation problem as a *classification* problem: our goal is to train a classifier to find the "correct" stak for each page stored in the HeyStaks repository. More precisely, the recommender system will use this classifier to find the three most likely staks for each page, and submit them to the stak owner for validation.

The problem is of course to correctly train and evaluate that classifier despite the noise in the available data. Since manually tagging a significant set of pages as relevant or noisy is not feasible, we first propose a measure that we will use as a proxy for relevance. Then we will show how this measure can be used to evaluate and improve our classifier.

In the following, we will represent the search experience stored in each stak S as a *hit matrix* h^S where h^S_{ij} is the number of times that term t_j has been related to page p_i, either as a query term or a tag. Since we use pseudo-terms to represent votes, this matrix captures in a synthetic way all the term and usage data used by HeyStaks. Each line h^S_i of the hit matrix, the *hit vector* of page p_i, is how that page will be represented in our classifier.

Predicting Relevance with Popularity. An immediate approach to predict the relevance of a page or a term to a particular stak is to consider its popularity, *pop*, measured as the total number of hits accounted for by this page or term in the stak's hit matrix h^S:

$$pop(p_i) \doteq \sum_j h_{ij}^S \quad pop(t_j) \doteq \sum_i h_{ij}^S \tag{1}$$

The rationale is that a page or a term may be added to a stak once or twice by accident, but if it has been repeatedly selected for that stak, it is probably relevant to it. The problem with these two measures, though, is that they are independent of each other. We would also like to take into account the fact that a page may benefit from the popularity of the terms for which it was selected: hence, we propose a second measure of popularity, pop_2, for pages, defined as follows:

$$pop_2(p_i) \doteq \sum_j pop(t_j) \times h_{ij}^S \tag{2}$$

This is illustrated by Fig. 4, which shows that a page like $p1$ with a high number of hits will still be popular, but a set of pages sharing the same terms will "inherit" the popularity of that term, even if each one of them has a low number of hits (see $p2, p3, p4$).

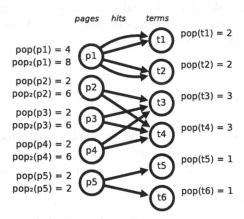

Fig. 4 Popularity measure pop_2 illustrated.

We now want to normalize this popularity measure, in order to make it comparable across staks, regardless of the span and skew of their popularity distributions. First, we bring it between 0 and 1 (addressing the span problem), then we center the mean popularity to 0.5 (addressing the skew problem). The normalized popularity np is computed as follows:

$$np(p_i) \doteq \left(\frac{pop_2(p_i)}{\max_j pop_2(p_j)} \right)^{\frac{\log 0.5}{\log \text{mean}_k pop_2(p_k)}} \tag{3}$$

In order to evaluate the validity of our popularity measure as a predictor of page relevance, we performed a small user evaluation. We limited our study to the 20 biggest shared staks (smaller staks having potentially not reached a critical mass for efficient recommendation). For each of those 20 staks, we picked the 15 most popular pages and the 15 least popular pages. We presented them to the stak owner in a random order, and asked them if each page was relevant or not to that stak. Since other stak users are supposed to join a stak because they share the stak owner's interest in its topic, we assume that the owner's opinion is representative of the user community of that stak.

The results of this evaluations are shown in Fig. 5. We see that pages with a high popularity are almost always considered relevant by users. Unpopular pages, on the other hand, are uncertain: about half of them are relevant, while the other half are not. This is not a big surprise since our popularity measure relies on the number of times a page has been selected; an unpopular page may be relevant but too recent to have become popular yet. We are however encouraged to consider that the noisy experience is located in the unpopular part of our experience repositories.

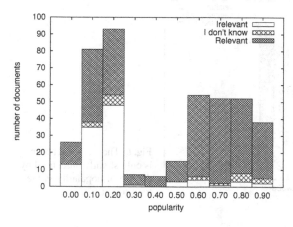

Fig. 5 Poll results. For each stak, the 15 most popular pages and the 15 least popular pages have been manually evaluated by the stack owner.

A Weighted Stak Classifier.   Confident in our popularity measure, we have decided to use it for training our classifier. The popularity measure can be used to *weight* the training instances, so that the classifier learns more from popular pages (more likely to be reliable) than from less popular ones. This weighting is also used to compute the accuracy of the classifier: indeed, the fact that the classifier disagrees with the experience repository for a page with a low weight (*i.e.* considered unreliable) should not have the same importance as a disagreement on a highly weighted (hence reliable) page. The *weighted accuracy* that we use is then computed by dividing the sum of the weights of the "correctly" classified[2] pages by the sum of the weights of all the pages.

Our first training set comprises all pages from the 20 largest shared staks in HeyStaks. Each instance represents a page p_i from a stak S by its hit vector h_i^S, its class is the stak identifier, and its weight is $np(p_i)$. We use three classifiers: a ZeroR random classifier (always predicting the more frequent class), a J48 decision

---

[2] Where "correctly" actually means "in agreement with the available data", which is known to be partially inaccurate.

tree [13] and a naive bayesian classifier. We tested those three classifiers with a standard 10-fold cross-validation. The resulting weighted accuracies are 17%, 74% and 66% respectively.

These first results were encouraging. However, we wanted to measure the benefit of weighting the training instance with our popularity measure. We did the same test, but with unweighted instances. The results are only marginally worse: 17%, 73% and 64% respectively. We then trained the classifiers with boolean vectors instead of hit vectors (i.e. replacing any non-null number of hits by 1), thus removing even more information about the popularity (np is computed using the number of hits). The results are still very similar (and even slightly *better* for the NaiveBayes), as shown on Fig.. 6

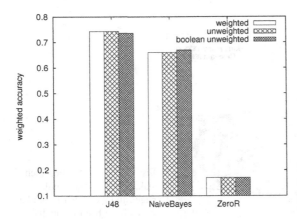

Fig. 6 The weighted accuracy is only slightly influenced by the use of popularity in the training set.

This surprising result may be explained by considering how the accuracy varies for pages with different weights. This is shown in Fig. 7, where each point represents the accuracy of the classifiers (trained with unweighted boolean vectors) when considering only their results for pages with a minimum np. We see that both the J48 and NaiveBayes are better at classifying popular pages, and that this is not a bias in the data, since the random classifier does not share this property[3]. We suggest that there is a correlation between popularity and purely structural similarity, which may account for the fact that weighting the instances does not significantly improve the accuracy – since this is information that the classifiers learn anyway.

Stak Kernels. Another interesting thing that Fig. 7 teaches us is that the evolution of the accuracy against popularity is not linear. Accuracy first stagnates when considering pages with $np \geq 0.3$, then increases steadily until around $np \geq 0.6$, then stabilizes again. This seems to indicate that $np = 0.6$ is a threshold below which

---

[3] As a matter of fact, the random classifier performs worse when considering only popular pages. This indicates that the popular pages are not distributed within staks like other pages, or conversely, that the distribution of popularity is not the same in all staks. This should be investigated as an indicator of stak "maturity".

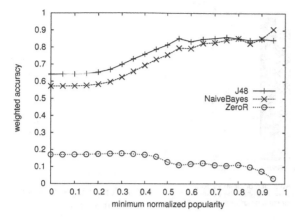

Fig. 7 J48 and NaiveBayes classifiers are better at classifying popular pages.

pages are harder to predict, hence presumably also harder to learn. Since we already know from our user evaluation that pages above this threshold are highly reliable, we might expect to improve the accuracy of the classifier by training it only with them. We call this subset of reliable pages in each stak the *stak kernel*.

We compared the accuracy (computed with 10-fold cross-validation) of kernel-trained classifiers (using unweighted boolean vectors) with some of our previous classifiers, trained with the whole set of pages. More precisely, we compared it with the less informed (*i.e.* using unweighted boolean vectors) and the most informed one (*i.e.* using weighted hit vectors).

The results are reported in Fig. 8. We see that NaiveBayes becomes better when kernel-trained. The outcome is not as definitive with J48, where the kernel-trained classifier is essentially equivalent to the most informed whole-trained classifier. Our intuition here is that J48 manages to learn from the unpopular relevant pages. The loss of those pages, in kernel-training, is not compensated by the lowering of the noise. This is not the case for NaiveBayes, however. Although this difference needs to be investigated, the fact that NaiveBayes outperforms, when kernel-trained, all of our previous classifiers (including J48) makes us confident in the value of kernel training.

Off-line Stak Recommendation. The accuracy of the kernel-trained NaiveBayes classifier makes it the best candidate for implementing the off-line phase of our stak recommendation system, as described in Section 3. In this phase, unpopular pages will be candidates for moving or copying to the the three most likely staks according to the classifier. Those pages will also appear as candidates for inclusion on the maintenance pages of those three staks. It is worth noting that in the cross-validation test, the correct stak is present in the top three guesses in 97% of the cases, which makes us very confident in the relevance of this phase for stak owners.

Furthermore, assigning a page to a stak during the maintenance phase is an *explicit* indication from the user that this page is relevant to the stak, unlike the implicit actions mainly used by HeyStaks to fill its experience repository. Such pages can then be considered as part of the stak kernel, regardless of their popularity –

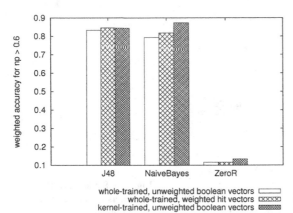

Fig. 8 Comparing kernel- and whole-trained classifiers.

recall that unpopular pages are still relevant in 50% of the cases, according to our user evaluation. This may in turn improve the quality of the classifier, reversing the vicious circle introduced in Section 3.

5 Related works

In this paper, we have focused on one kind of noise that we call *mis-interpretation*: experience is incorrectly filed, mostly because it is implicitly collected and because the user's behaviour is not always consistent with the idealized behaviour on which the collection process is based. This problem has long been studied in the case-based reasoning literature [19, 20], where experience is also collected in a more or less implicit way. With case-base maintenance, however, existing techniques are usually designed to manage case bases with relatively low amounts of noise and work best when relying on an objective measure of when a case can be used to correctly *solve* some target problem. The same kind of approach, applied to recommender systems, is used by [11], using the predictions of the system itself as a measure of likelihood. Hence, it relies on a "pristine" system, not *yet* polluted by noisy data, to train the initial classifier. [10], on the other hand, introduce a notion of trust to cope with noisy data (associated in this case with untrustworthy users).

Another kind of noise is *malicious noise*: unscrupulous users try to lure the system into recommending items for their own benefit [6]. Our notion of popularity is vulnerable to this kind of attack because hits in HeyStaks are anonymous: the popularity of a page can not be traced back to the (potentially malicious) users who selected it. It would seem safer to limit the influence of an individual user on the popularity of each page (even more in the standard workflow of HeyStaks where pages, not staks, are recommended).

A third kind of noise is *opinion drift*. Over time, people may change their mind about their experiences [5, 7]. Furthermore, in HeyStaks, once-relevant pages may become outdated, or be modified in a way that makes them less relevant. The problem with our popularity measure is that, once it has become popular, a page will be considered relevant for ever. This can easily be changed though, by applying ageing to our measure: the popularity of a page fades out as its last selection becomes older.

6 Conclusion and discussion

As the Web evolves to accommodate *experiences* as well as pure *content* it will become increasingly important to develop systems and services that help users to manage and harness their online experiences and those of others. In this paper we have focused on experience management in Web search by describing a case-study using the HeyStaks social search engine. HeyStaks is a browser toolbar that works with mainstream search engines such as Google and that allows users to create and share repositories of search experiences (search staks) which then act as a source of search result recommendation.

The main contribution of this work has focused on the nature of the search experiences that HeyStaks harnesses. We have argued that these experiences can be noisy and that this limits the effectiveness of its search recommendations. As a solution we have argued the need for a meta-recommender system which is designed to recommend search staks, and we have argued that such a recommender can play a key role in supporting stak maintenance and selection. We have described a technique for identifying so-called stak kernels, as the non-noisy essence of stak knowledge – and described and evaluated a classification-based approach to stak recommendation that harnesses these kernels to make accurate stak recommendations.

We have shown that our kernel-trained classifier can be used to implement the off-line stak recommender system described in Section 3. The problem in the case of the online phase, on the other hand, is that we have to deal with *queries* rather than full term vectors. A query is similar to a term vector describing a page, but is a boolean vector (no number of hits, each term is either present or absent), and much sparser (vectors describing pages in HeyStaks combine all the queries used to select the page). Our classifier is already trained with boolean vectors, but we need to perform more tests to determine how well it deals with sparsity, a common problem for recommender systems [2].

We believe that our approach, although quite specific to HeyStaks, can be generalized to other recommender systems facing the problem of a noisy knowledge base. Transposing the notion of kernel may not be trivial, since many such systems have a knowledge base reflecting diverse points of view —while in HeyStaks, each stak is relevant to a given topic. However, as each stak has a single kernel, other recommender systems could have, for their single knowledge base, one kernel per user or group of users, allowing them to classify noise in a personalized way.

References

1. P. Briggs and B. Smyth. Provenance, trust, and sharing in peer to-peer case-based web search. In *ECCBR*, pages 89–103, 2008.
2. R. Burke. Hybrid recommender systems: Survey and experiments. *User Modeling and User-Adapted Interaction*, 12(4):331–370, 2002.
3. P. A. Chirita, W. Nejdl, R. Paiu, and C. Kohlschütter. Using odp metadata to personalize search. In *SIGIR '05: Proceedings of the 28th annual international ACM SIGIR conference on Research and development in information retrieval*, pages 178–185, New York, NY, USA, 2005. ACM.
4. A. Cordier, B. Mascret, and A. Mille. Extending Case-Based reasoning with traces. In *Grand Challenges for reasoning from experiences, Workshop at IJCAI'09*, July 2009.
5. I. Koychev and I. Schwab. Adaptation to drifting user's interests. In *Proceedings of ECML2000 Workshop: Machine Learning in New Information Age*, pages 39–46, 2000.
6. S. K. Lam and J. Riedl. Shilling recommender systems for fun and profit. In *Proceedings of the 13th international conference on World Wide Web*, pages 393–402, New York, NY, USA, 2004. ACM.
7. S. Ma, X. Li, Y. Ding, M. E. Orlowska, B. Benatallah, F. Casati, D. Georgakopoulos, C. Bartolini, W. Sadiq, and C. Godart. A recommender system with Interest-Drifting. *LECTURE NOTES IN COMPUTER SCIENCE*, 4831:633, 2007.
8. M. R. Morris. A survey of collaborative web search practices. In *CHI*, pages 1657–1660, 2008.
9. M. R. Morris and E. Horvitz. SearchTogether: an interface for collaborative web search. In *Proceedings of the 20th annual ACM symposium on User interface software and technology*, pages 3–12, Newport, Rhode Island, USA, 2007. ACM.
10. J. O'Donovan and B. Smyth. Trust in recommender systems. In *Proceedings of the 10th international conference on Intelligent user interfaces*, pages 167–174, San Diego, California, USA, 2005. ACM.
11. M. P. O'Mahony, N. J. Hurley, and G. C. Silvestre. Detecting noise in recommender system databases. In *Proceedings of the 11th international conference on Intelligent user interfaces*, pages 109–115, Sydney, Australia, 2006. ACM.
12. J. Pujol, R. Sanguesa, and J. Bermudez. Porqpine: A distributed and collaborative search engine. In *Proc. 12th Intl. World Wide Web Conference*, 2003.
13. J. R. Quinlan. *C4. 5: programs for machine learning*. Morgan Kaufmann, 1993.
14. M. C. Reddy and P. R. Spence. Collaborative information seeking: A field study of a multi-disciplinary patient care team. *Inf. Process. Manage.*, 44(1):242–255, 2008.
15. J. B. Schafer, J. A. Konstan, and J. Riedl. Meta-recommendation systems: user-controlled integration of diverse recommendations. In *Proceedings of the eleventh international conference on Information and knowledge management*, pages 43–51. ACM New York, NY, USA, 2002.
16. B. Smyth. A community-based approach to personalizing web search. *IEEE Computer*, 40(8):42–50, 2007.
17. B. Smyth, P. Briggs, M. Coyle, and M. O'Mahony. Google? shared! a case-study in social web search. In *Proceedings of the 1st and 17th International Conference on User Modeling, Adaptation and Personalization (UMAP '09)*, Trento, Italy, 2009. Springer.
18. B. Smyth and P. Champin. The experience web: A Case-Based reasoning perspective. In *Grand Challenges for reasoning from experiences, Workshop at IJCAI'09*, July 2009.
19. B. Smyth and M. T. Keane. Remembering to forget: A Competence-Preserving case deletion policy for Case-Based reasoning systems. In *IJCAI*, pages 377–383, 1995. Best paper award.
20. B. Smyth and E. McKenna. Competence models and the maintenance problem. *Computational Intelligence*, 17(2):235–249, 2001.
21. J.-T. Sun, H.-J. Zeng, H. Liu, Y. Lu, and Z. Chen. Cubesvd: a novel approach to personalized web search. In *WWW '05: Proceedings of the 14th international conference on World Wide Web*, pages 382–390, New York, NY, USA, 2005. ACM Press.

KNOWLEDGE DISCOVERY AND DATA MINING

Text Classification using Graph Mining-based Feature Extraction

Chuntao Jiang, Frans Coenen, Robert Sanderson, and Michele Zito

Abstract A graph-based approach to document classification is described in this paper. The graph representation offers the advantage that it allows for a much more expressive document encoding than the more standard bag of words/phrases approach, and consequently gives an improved classification accuracy. Document sets are represented as graph sets to which a weighted graph mining algorithm is applied to extract frequent subgraphs, which are then further processed to produce feature vectors (one per document) for classification. Weighted subgraph mining is used to ensure classification effectiveness and computational efficiency; only the most significant subgraphs are extracted. The approach is validated and evaluated using several popular classification algorithms together with a real world textual data set. The results demonstrate that the approach can outperform existing text classification algorithms on some dataset. When the size of dataset increased, further processing on extracted frequent features is essential.

Chuntao Jiang
The University of Liverpool, Department of Computer Science, Ashton Building, Ashton Street, Liverpool, L69 3BX, United Kingdom e-mail: c.jiang@liv.ac.uk

Frans Coenen
The University of Liverpool, Department of Computer Science, Ashton Building, Ashton Street, Liverpool, L69 3BX, United Kingdom e-mail: coenen@liv.ac.uk

Robert Sanderson
The University of Liverpool, Department of Computer Science, Ashton Building, Ashton Street, Liverpool, L69 3BX, United Kingdom e-mail: azaroth@liv.ac.uk

Michele Zito
The University of Liverpool, Department of Computer Science, Ashton Building, Ashton Street, Liverpool, L69 3BX, United Kingdom e-mail: michele@liv.ac.uk

M. Bramer et al. (eds.), *Research and Development in Intelligent Systems XXVI*,
DOI 10.1007/978-1-84882-983-1_2, © Springer-Verlag London Limited 2010

1 Introduction

The most common document formalisation for text classification is the *vector space* model founded on the bag of words/phrases representation. The main advantage of the vector space model is that it can readily be employed by classification algorithms. However, the bag of words/phrases representation is suited to capturing only word/phrase frequency; structural and semantic information is ignored. It has been established that structural information plays an important role in classification accuracy [14].

An alternative to the bag of words/phrases representation is a graph based representation, which intuitively possesses much more expressive power. However, this representation introduces an additional level of complexity in that the calculation of the similarity between two graphs is significantly more computationally expensive than between two vectors (see for example [16]). Some work (see for example [12]) has been done on hybrid representations to capture both structural elements (using the graph model) and significant features using the vector model. However the computational resources required to process this hybrid model are still extensive.

The computational complexity of the graph representation for text mining is the main disadvantage of the approach, which prevents the full exploitation of the expressive power that the graph representation possesses. The work described in this paper seeks to address this issue by applying weighted graph mining analysis to the problem. The intuition behind the approach is that in standard frequent subgraph mining all generated subgraphs are assumed to have equal importance. However it is clear that, at least in the context of text mining, some subgraphs are more significant than others.

The rest of this paper is organized as follows. In Section 2 a brief overview of previous work is presented. The graph representation of document sets is then discussed in Section 3. In Section 4 the weighted subgraph mining is defined. The proposed Weighted graph mining algorithm, a variation of gSpan called Weighted gSpan (W-gSpan), is introduced in Section 5. A set of evaluating experiments are then presented in Section 6, followed by some concluding remarks in Section 7.

2 Related Work

Much early work on document graph representations for text classification was directed at Web documents. Geibel et al. in [7] demonstrated that it is possible to classify Web documents using document structure alone; however we shall demonstrate that a much more powerful approach is to combine structure with linguistic and semantic information. For example Schenker [16] proposed a number of methods to represent Web documents as graphs so as to include the structural information of the Web documents. The typical approach is to conduct classification using some similarity-based algorithm. However, approaches that operate using graph similarity measures are computationally expensive (for example computing the "maximum common subgraph" between two graphs is a NP hard problem [5]). Hybrid representations have been introduced to resolve the computational overhead associated with pure graph representations, see for example [12]. Such hybrid representations are reported to have better performance than pure graph based methods. However the computational resources required to process these hybrid model are still very high due to: (i) the extremely high number of nodes and edges, low number of edge labels and high repetition of structural node labels, encountered; and (ii) the consequent exponential complexity of the search space.

The use of graphs for representing text has a very long history in Natural Language Processing (NLP). However the work in NLP has focused on language understanding techniques such as Part Of Speech (POS) tagging, rather than text classification. Previous work [13, 20] has looked at the collocation of terms and their frequencies as graphs, rather than the linguistic structure of the sentence. One other study [6] has represented linguistic information as well as word order in a graph for text classification, however the work was limited to very small texts of between 8 to 13 tokens such as the titles of works. As such, we adopt the usage of of linguistic information, structure and semantics in a graph for text classification at a full text scale. In order to achieve this scale of processing, the use of frequent subgraph mining is essential.

Frequent subgraph (and sub-tree) mining, using various approaches, has been extensively studied [9, 10, 22, 8, 2]. However, the main bottleneck is the number of unnecessary candidate frequent subgraphs generated. A substantial amount of work has been undertaken focusing on developing efficient graph mining algorithms using elegant search strategies, data structures or their combinations. Some authors have suggested the use of constraint based frequent subgraph mining to remove unwanted patterns. The weighted subgraph mining approach advocated in this paper integrates the weight constraints into the frequent subgraph mining process to reduce the search space by generating only the most significant (interesting) patterns.

The frequent subgraph mining approach described in this paper is also influenced by work on weighted pattern mining, especially Weighted Association Rules Mining (WARM), see for example the work of [19, 17, 23, 24, 25]. A significant issue in WARM is that the "Downward Closure" (DC) property of items sets, on which many ARM algorithms are based, no longer holds. One solution (for example [19]) is to handle the weights as a post-processing step after mining frequent itemsets, however the weights are then not integrated into the ARM process. Tao et al. [17] proposed a model of weighted support, which satisfies a weighted DC property. Yun et al. [23, 24, 25] introduced a series of concepts such as "weight range", "weight confidence", and "support confidence" for WARM in order to maintain the DC property and push the weight constraint deeply into the mining process. Although the ideas espoused by WARM cannot be directly applied to weighted frequent subgraph mining; the research described here is, at least in part, influenced by this body of work.

3 Graph Representation of Text Data

The graph representation advocated in this paper is described in this section. The representation serves to capture a range documents aspects: (i) word stem, (ii) word Part Of Speech (POS), (iii) word order, (iv) word hypernyms, (v) sentence structure, (vi) sentence division and (vii) sentence order. There are four different types of nodes in the graph representation:

1. *Structural*: Nodes that represent sentences (S) and their internal structures of noun (NP), verb (VP) and prepositional phrases (PP). (Represented by triangles in Figure 1.)
2. *Part of Speech*: Nodes that represent the POS of a word, (eg. DT, JJ, NN). (Circles.)
3. *Token*: Nodes that represent the actual word tokens in the text. (Rectangles.)
4. *Semantic*: Nodes that represent additional information about the word such as its linguistic stem and other broader concepts. (Ovals)

Note that each node has a unique identifier and a label. There are also five types of edge in the graph:

1. *hasChild*: Edges which record the structure of the text such as a sentence having a noun phrase and a verb phrase or a noun phrase containing an adjective. (Unlabeled in Figure 1 for reasons of space.)
2. *isToken*: Edges which link the part of speech of a token to the token itself.
3. *next*: Edges which record the order of the words and sentences in the text.
4. *stem*: Edges which link to the linguistic stem of the word.
5. *hyp*: Edges which link to a broader concept.

An example of these node and edge types is depicted in Figure 1, using the first 6 words in a well known English sentence. Employing the above graph representation each sentence in each text is encoded and linked together with "next" edges to form one graph per text. Content based weightings were then attached to each node in the graph. The Structural elements, being intuitively unimportant to classification, were given a static low weight of 1. The Part of Speech nodes were given a static weight of 10, Token nodes were weighted according to their frequency in the dataset using the $TF \cdot IDF$ method. Stems were half the value of the Token and Hypernyms one quarter the value.

4 Weighted Frequent Subgraphs

In this section the weighted subgraph mining problem is formally defined. As with standard transaction graph mining approaches [9, 10, 1, 11] we commence with a set of *transaction graphs* $D = \{G_1, G_2, \cdots, G_n\}$ and a function $\tau(g, G)$ for arbitrary graphs g and G. $\tau(g, G) = 1$ (resp. 0), if g is isomorphic to a subgraph in G.

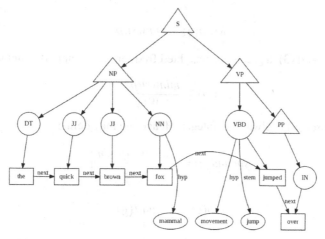

Fig. 1 Graph-based Text Representation Example

Definition 1. The support count of a graph (pattern) g with respect to a database $D = \{G_1, G_2, \cdots, G_n\}$, is the expression $sco(g) = \sum_{i=1}^{i=n} \tau(g, G_i)$. The support of g with respect to D, $sup(g)$, is the ratio of the support count over the size of the dataset D. Then:

$$sup(g) = \frac{sco(g)}{n}. \tag{1}$$

It should be remarked that $sco(g)$ and $sup(g)$, like most terms defined in this section depend on the dataset D. To avoid cluttering notations, such dependence will always be left implicit.

Definition 2. Given a graph g, if $sup(g)$ is greater than or equal to some user defined minimum threshold θ, then g is said to be frequent (in D). The frequent subgraph mining problem is to find all the frequent subgraphs in the database D.

Since the purpose of this paper is to study weighted graph mining in the remainder of this section we define this concept precisely. From now on we assume that graphs come with weights associated with either their vertices or their edges. Let W be a function assigning a weight to any graph g in terms of the given weights for its vertices (resp. edges). In our work, in particular, W will always be a sum of the vertex (resp. edge) weights, but the definitions in this Section hold in a more general setting.

Definition 3. Given a graph g with the weight $W(g)$, the weighted support of g with respect to D, $wsup(g)$, is:

$$wsup(g) = W(g) \times sup(g). \tag{2}$$

Definition 4. A graph g is said to be weighted frequent if and only if its weighted support is greater than or equal to a given minimum support threshold (minwsup),

$$wsup(g) \geq minwsup. \tag{3}$$

From (1), (2) and (3), a graph g is weighted frequent if its support count satisfies:

$$sco(g) \geq \frac{minwsup \times n}{W(g)} \tag{4}$$

Note that $sco(g)$ is always an integer. Hence we may define

$$sbound(g) = \left\lceil \frac{minwsup \times n}{W(g)} \right\rceil \tag{5}$$

and we have

$$sco(g) \geq sbound(g). \tag{6}$$

5 Weighted gSpan

The operation of the proposed weighted subgraph mining algorithm (W-gSpan) is described in this section. The section commences (Sub-section 5.1) with a discussion of support-bound candidate subgraph pruning. This is followed in Sub-section 5.2 by a description of a number of different weighting mechanisms that are used in this study. Sub-section 5.3 then gives the pseudo code of pruning algorithm and briefly decribes how W-gSpan is integrated into the classification process;

5.1 Support Bound based Pruning

Use of the DC property in any frequent set mining algorithm can greatly reduce the search space. However, in the context of weighted frequent set mining the DC property no longer holds. The W-gSpan algorithm therefore makes used of an alternative concept to prune non-interesting candidate subgraphs early on in the generation process.

Let the maximum possible size of a subgraph be mL and the weight for a subgraph be defined as the sum of vertex weights (similar definitions may be given if the graph is edge-weighted). Given a k-pattern g_k with weights $\{\omega_1, \omega_2, \cdots, \omega_k\}$, any future n-pattern containing g_k is denoted by g_n, where $k < n \leq mL$. For the additional $(n-k)$ verticies, if the upper bounds of the weights are estimated as $\omega_{a_{k+1}}, \omega_{a_{k+2}}, \cdots, \omega_{a_n}$, then the upper bound of the weight of the n-pattern g_n is given by:

$$wbound_n(g_k) = \sum_{i=1}^{k} \omega_i + \sum_{i=k+1}^{n} \omega_{a_i} \tag{7}$$

We may then define a lower bound of the support count of a k-pattern included in g_n as

$$\underline{sbound}_n(g_k) = \left\lceil \frac{minwsup \times n}{wbound_n(g_k)} \right\rceil \tag{8}$$

of course the definition can be extended to $n = k$ by setting $\underline{sbound}_k(g_k) = \underline{sbound}(g_k)$ as defined in (5).

Definition 5. A k-subgraph g_k is *workable* if $sco(g_k) \geq \underline{sbound}_n(g_k)$ for some n with $k \leq n \leq mL$, and *unworkable* if $sco(g_k) < \underline{sbound}_n(g_k)$ for all n, with $k \leq n \leq mL$.

Lemma 1. *If a subgraph g_k is workable then it is possible for g_k to be a subgraph of some weighted frequent n-subgraph. On the contrary, if a subgraph g_k is not workable, then g_k has no possibility of being a subgraph of any weighted frequent n-subgraph.*

Proof. Let n be given with $k \leq n \leq mL$. If $sco(g_k) \geq \underline{sbound}_n(g_k)$, then due to $sco(g_k) \geq sco(g_n)$, it is possible that $sco(g_n) \geq \underline{sbound}(g_n)$. So pattern g_n has a chance to be weighted frequent in the future.

On the other hand, if $sco(g_k) < \underline{sbound}_n(g_k)$, then due to $sco(g_k) \geq sco(g_n)$, $sco(g_n) < \underline{sbound}(g_n)$. So pattern g_n will not be weighted frequent in the future.

The Weighted gSpan algorithm will then use a simple condition to decide whether or not to prune a particular k-pattern (in what follows mL is the maximum length of a pattern):

if $sco(g_k) \geq \underline{sbound}(g_k)$, g_k is workable; otherwise we compute $\underline{sbound}_{mL}(g_k)$ (this gives a lower bound on $\underline{sbound}_n(g_k)$), if $sco(g_k) \geq \underline{sbound}_{mL}(g_k)$, then g_k is workable, else g_k is unworkable and pruned.

5.2 Weight Calculation

Given the notion of a weighted bound of a subgraph, as defined above, methods for calculating the weighting for a given subgraph are required. We can identify three approaches for determining subgraph weightings: (i) **structure based**, (ii) **content based** and (iii) **structure and content** based. The distinction between the two is that the structure base weighting approach does not require any advanced knowledge of the potential significance of subgraphs. Each approach is discussed in more detail below.

5.2.1 Structure Based Weight Calculation

In the structure base weighting approach weightings are derived purely from the "structure" of subgraphs. The approach advocated here is based on the frequency

counts of individual nodes and edges per graph in the graph set. Using these frequency counts we adopt Pearson's Correlation Coefficient [15], PCC, to measure
the weight of the edge (considering the nodes making up a 1-edge subgraph as two
variables).Thus for two nodes A and B, let the number of occurrences of A equal
ϕ_A, the number of occurrences of B equal ϕ_B and the number of co-occurrences of
A and B equal ϕ_{AB}; and let the total number of transaction graphs within the dataset
be equal to n. The support values will then be $sup(A) = \phi_A/n$, $sup(B) = \phi_B/n$, and
$sup(A,B) = \phi_{AB}/n$. Using PCC the edge weight (ω_{pcc}) can be derived as follows.

$$\omega_{pcc} = \frac{sup(A,B) - sup(A)sup(B)}{\sqrt{sup(A)sup(B)(1 - sup(A))(1 - sup(B))}} \tag{9}$$

Many other measures of association exist, such as the Chi Squared, cosine or
Jaccard measure, that could equally well be used to determine edge weighting in a
structured based context.

5.2.2 Content based Weight Calculation

In the content based weighting approach advanced knowledge of the nature of the
input set is utilised. The nature of the advanced knowledge can take two forms: (i)
weights that have been predefined (by for example a domain expert), or (ii) class
labels associated with individual graph records (documents).

In the first case user supplied weightings can be attached directly to either nodes
or edges. Thus given a set of user defined node weights $\omega_1 \cdots \omega_n$, the weighting for
a subgraph can be calculated by $\sum_{n_i \in g} \omega_i$. A similar calculation can be used in the
event of user supplied edge weights. We later refer to this mechanism as the "Node
Weight" method.

Alternatively we can calculate edge weights, given user defined node weights,
as follows: if the nodes connecting edge e_i are a with weight w_a and b with w_b;
the probability of a's occurrences is ρ_a, the probability of b's occurrences is ρ_b and
the probability of edge e_i's occurrences is $\rho(a,b)$. The mutual information metric
between a and b can then be defined as $mu(a,b) = \rho(a,b)\log_2(\rho(a,b)/\rho_a/\rho_b)$. The
weight for edge e_i can then be calculated as:

$$\omega_{e_i} = \left(\frac{2 \times w_a \times w_b}{w_a + w_b}\right) \times mu(a,b) \tag{10}$$

The weight for the subgraph is calculated in the same manner as before. We refer to
this mechanism as the "Mu" method.

Alternatively knowledge of the class label can be used to determine the weighting of a given subgraph. There are a number of *feature selection* techniques that can
be utilised for this purpose, examples include Information Gain (IG), mutual infor-
mation(MI), and χ^2 testing. For the work described here the χ^2 statistic was adopted
to apply weightings to subgraphs according to their association with a given class
label. Using the two-way contingency table of an edge e and a graph's class label

y_c, let a denote the number of times e and y_c co-occur, b denote the number of times the e occurs without y_c, c denote the number of times y_c occurs without e, d denote the number of times neither e nor y_c occurs, and n is the total number of transaction graphs. The edge-goodness measure is then defined to be:

$$\chi^2(e, y_c) = \frac{n(ad - cb)}{(a+c)(b+d)(a+b)(c+d)} \tag{11}$$

The χ^2 statistic has a value of zero if edge e and class y_c are indepedent. For each class y_c, we compute the χ^2 statistic between each edge and that category, and then calculated the average value of χ^2 statistic for each edge. Let $c = \{c_1, c_2, \cdots, c_m\}$ denote the set of categories for the transaction graphs dataset, $P_r(y_c)$ denotes the probability of y_c, then:

$$\chi^2_{avg}(e) = \sum_{c=1}^{m} P_r(y_c)\chi^2(e, y_c) \tag{12}$$

After estimating edge weights for each generated subgraph, the actual significance of the subgraph is calculated in the same manner as before. We refer to this mechanism as the "Chi Squared" method.

5.2.3 Combined Content and Structure Based Weight Calculation

It is possible to combine the two approaches, content and structure based weight calculation. For example given a user defined weight for node n_i of w_{n_i}, then the probability of n_i's occurrences is ρ, and the entropy for node n_i is $entropy(n_i) = -\rho \log(\rho) - (1 - \rho) \log(1 - \rho)$. If we also make use of the "degree" (the number of edges incident to the node) of n_i the weight for n_i can be calculated as:

$$\omega_{n_i} = w_{n_i} \times entropy(n_i) \times degree(n_i) \tag{13}$$

Thus, we refer to this mechanism as the "Entropy" method.

5.3 The Weighted gSpan Algorithm (W-gSpan)

The above weighting considerations were built into a variation of the well known gSpan frequent subgraph mining algorithm [22], Weighted gSpan (W-gSpan). However, the proposed weighing framework can equally well be applied to other frequent subgraph (or sub-tree) mining algorithms. The pseudo code for the pruning algorithm employed in W-gSpan is given in Algorithm 1.

After the W-gSpan algorithm is applied to identify weighted frequent subgraphs, these subgraphs are then used to generate a set of binary feature vectors(one per document). A standard classifier generator can then be employed using such vectors.

Algorithm 1 subgraph-mining(GS, s, c, F)

Require: Input: c = DFS code, GS = graph database, s = support;
Ensure: Output: F — weighted frequent subgraph set;
  1: $G \leftarrow$ a set of candidate subgraphs;
  2: **if** $c \neq min(c)$ **then**
  3:    **return**
  4: **end if**
  5: Insert c into F;
  6: $G \leftarrow \emptyset$;
  7: Scan GS once, and find every edge e that c can be right-most extended, and save $c \cup e$ into G;
  8: Sort G in DFS lexicographic order;
  9: **for all** $g_k \in G$ **do**
 10:    **if** $sco(g_k) \geq sbound(g_k)$ **then**
 11:       subgraph-mining(GS, s, c, F);
 12:    **else if** $sco(g_k) \geq min(\underline{sbound}_n(g_k))$,where $g_k \subset g_n$ **then**
 13:       subgraph-mining(GS, s, c, F);
 14:    **else**
 15:       $G \leftarrow G - \{g_k\}$;
 16:    **end if**
 17: **end for**
 18: **return**

---

6 Experiments and Results

In order to evaluate the performance of the proposed graph based text classification method experiments were conducted to:

- Investigate the performance of W-gSpan, in terms of execution time and number of frequent subgraphs detected.
- Investigate the overall performance of the graph based classification process for text classification.

Note that the experiments were all run on a 1.86GHZ Intel Core 2 PC with 2GB main memory.

6.1 Description of Text Data Set

The experimental data consisted of three sets of documents(D1, D2, and D3) split evenly between two classes. The documents were extracted from the Medline dataset by their Medical Subject Heading (MeSH) fields, so that a two class ("polymerase chain reaction" and "magnetic resonance imaging") set was produced. The text was divided into sentences using a regular expression based tokenizer and then each sentence was POS tagged using Tsuruoaka and Tsujii's "geniatagger"[18], producing a sequence of "word/POS" tokens plus the lemma (stemmed form) of each word. This tagged output was then fed into a structural parser which produces a tree with noun, verb and prepositional phrases. The nouns and verbs are then "looked up" in the WordNet thesaurus and up to five broader terms added into the graph. The properties of the (graph) data are given in Table 1.

Table 1 Graph Data Description

	Text Dataset		
	D1	D2	D3
No. of graphs	200	400	1000
Maximal edge count	3002	2917	4047
Average edge count	1141	1131	1135
Distinct node label count	10069	16456	26540

6.2 Performance of W-gSpan

The performance of the W-gSpan algorithm was evaluateded using the four different weighting methods introduced in Sub-section 5.2 above:

- Pearson Correlation Coefficient (pcc-w) for structure based weighting.
- Node Weight (node-w) for content based node weighting (Edge weighting would operate in a similar maner)
- Mutual information (mu-w) for content based edge weighting.
- Chi Square (chs-w) for content based class label discrimination weighting.
- Node entropy (entro-w) for combined structure and content based node weighting.

Experiments were also conducted with no weighting, but this was found to be extremely inefficient with poor outcomes, and thus are not discussed further in this evaluation.

The results of the performance experiments are presented in Figure 2. The runtime values corresponding to different minimum support thresholds are presented in Figure 2(a). The number of identified frequent subgraphs (features), corresponding to a range of minimum support thresholds, is presented Figure 2(b) and (c). There is, naturally, a correlation between support threshold and the number of identified subgraphs: as the support threshold is increased, the number of identified subgraphs decreases. There is also a natural correlation between runtime and the number of identified frequent subgraphs: runtime increases with the number of identified frequent subgraphs. From Figure 2(a) it can be observed that Mu weighting and node weighting seem to work well in terms of run time efficincy, however node weighting finds very few frequent subgraphs. The pcc weighting is the most effective in terms of computational efficiency, and works well in terms of number of features generated. Entropy weighting suddenly increases the runtime when the threshold is below 10%.

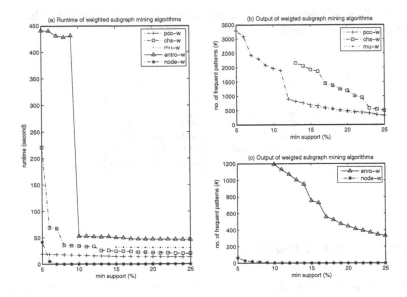

Fig. 2 Performance of weighted frequent subgraph mining on D1 dataset

6.3 Classification Accuracy Comparison

Three different classifier generator paradigms were use to evaluate the graph-based text classification process: (i) a classification association rule miner, TFPC [3, 4], (ii) a Naive Bayes Classifier (NBC) [21], and (iii) a decision tree classifier, C4.5 [21]. Table 2 shows the accuracy figures obtained using a range of support threshold values (for the generation of frequent subgraphs), for the three classification paradigms (with 10 folds cross validation) and using the five different weighting strategies. Experiments conducted with no weightings at all (on D1, D2 and D3 datasets) produced very poor results indicating, beyond doubt, that the proposed weighted graph mining approach provides genuine benefits.

Using no weighting on D1 dataset, it was not possible to obtain results with a support threshold below 85%. When comparing the different weighting schemes, pcc produced the best overall accuracy. Using a standard 'bag of words' approach with TFPC gave a best accuracy of 89%.

If the three classifier generators are compared, NBC performs significantly better than the other two, however C4.5 did not work well with any of the permutations of weighting and support threshold. If the three classifiers are applied on D2 and D3, the classification performance degrades. For example, using PCC weighting with support 10%, the accuracy of NBC on D2 is 76.5% and the accuracy of NBC on D3 is 72.3%. In order to get better accuracies, further processing on extracted frequent features is indispensable and how to model text data as more efficient graphs with less nodes and edges is also crucial.

Table 2 Classification accuracy by different weighting methods on D1 dataset

Classifier	Method	Support Threshold(%)										
		15	16	17	18	19	20	21	22	23	24	25
NBC	pcc-weight	96.5	96	94.5	95	94	93	92	93	91.5	91.5	91.5
	chs-weight	91.5	91.5	89	87.5	86.5	86.5	90	91	90.5	92	91
	mu-weight	97	96.5	94.5	94	94	93	92	93	91.5	92	91.5
	entro-weight	76.5	75	95	95	94	92.5	92	92.5	92	93	92.5
	node-weight	80.5	80.5	80.5	80.5	80.5	80.5	80.5	80.5	80.5	80.5	80.5
TFPC	pcc-weight	91.5	91	88.5	89.5	86.5	84.5	83.5	84	84	84	84
	chs-weight	90.5	90	87.5	88.5	85.5	83.5	82.5	83	83.5	83	83
	mu-weight	92	91.5	89	90	87	85	84	84.5	84.5	84	84
	entro-weight	92	91.5	89	90	87	85	84	84.5	84.5	84	84
	node-weight	54	54	54	54	54	54	54	80.5	80.5	80.5	80.5
C4.5	pcc-weight	88.5	88	89.5	89	91	86.5	86.5	86.5	87	89	88.5
	chs-weight	87.5	87	89.5	89	91	86	86.5	86.5	87.5	89.5	89.5
	mu-weight	88.5	88	89.5	89	91	87	87	87	87	89	88.5
	entro-weight	88.5	88	89.5	89	91	87	87	87	87	89	88.5
	node-weight	80.5	80.5	80.5	80.5	80.5	80.5	80.5	80.5	80.5	80.5	80.5

7 Conclusion

An approach to text classification using a graph based representation has been described. The graph representation of text allows both the structure and content of
documents to be represented. Key constructs to support text classification can then
be identified using frequent subgraph mining. The disadvantage of standard frequent
subgraph mining is that it is computationally expensive, to the extent that any potential advantage of the graph representation of text cannot be realised. To overcome
this disadvantage a weighted subgraph mining mechanism is proposed, W-gSpan. In
effect W-gSpan selects the most significant constructs from the graph representation
and uses these constructs as input for classification. Experimental evaluation demonstrates that the technique works well, significantly out-performing the unweighted
approach in every case. A number of different weighting schemes were considered coupled with three different categories of classifier generator. In terms of the
generated classification accuracy pcc-weighting outperformed the other proposed
weighting mechanisms. PCC-weighting also worked well in terms of computational
efficiency and therefore represents the best overall weighting strategies.

References

1. Cai, C. H., Fu, A. W., Cheng, C. H. and Kwong, W. W. Mining Association Rules with
Weighted Items. In *Proceedings of International Database Engineering and Applications
Symposium*, August 1998.
2. Chi, Y., Nijssen, S., Muntz, R. and Kok, J. Frequent Subgree Mining An Overview. In *Fundamenta Informaticae, Special Issue on Graph and Tree Mining*, 66(1-2), 161-198, 2005.

3. Coenen, F. The LUCS-KDD TFPC Classification Association Rule Mining Algorithm. `http://www.csc.liv.ac.uk/~frans/KDD/Software/Apriori_TFPC/ aprioriTFPC.html`, Dept. of Computer Science, The University of Liverpool, UK, 2004.
4. Coenen, F., Leng, P. Obtaining Best Parameter Values for Accurate Classification. In *Proceedings of International Conference on Data Mining*, Pages: 597-600, 2005.
5. Garey, M. R. and Johnson, D. S. Computers and Intractability - A Guide to the Theory of NP-Completeness. *W. H. Freeman and Company*, New York, 1979.
6. Gee, K. R. and Cook, D. J. Text Classification Using Graph-Encoded Linguistic Elements, In *FLAIRS Conference 2005*, pp. 487-492.
7. Geibel, P., Krumnack, U., Pustylnikow, O., Mehler, A., et al. Structure-Sensitive Learning of Text Types, In *AI 2007: Advances in Artificial Intelligence*, Vol 4830, pp. 642-646.
8. Huan, J., Wang, W. and Prins, J. Efficient Mining of Frequent Subgraph in the Presence of Isomorphism. In *Proceedings of the 2003 International Conference on Data Mining*, 2003.
9. Inokuci, A., Washio, T. and Motoda, H. An Apriori-based Algorithm for Mining Frequent Substructures from Graph Data. In *Proceedings of the 4th European Conference on Principles and Practice of Knowledge Discovery in Databases*, Pages: 13-23, 2000.
10. Kuramochi, M. and Karypis, G. Frequent Subgraph Discovery. In *Proceedings of 2001 IEEE International Conference on Data Mining*, 2001.
11. Lee, S. D. and Park, H. C. Mining Weighted Frequent Patterns from Path Traversals on Weighted Graph. In *IJCSNS International Journal of Computer Science and Network Security*, VOL.7, No.4, April 2007.
12. Markov, A., Last, M. Efficient Graph-based Representation of Web Documents. In *Proceedings of the Third International Workshop on Mining Graphs, Trees and Sequences*, Pages: 52-62, Porto Portugal, 2005.
13. Markov, A., Last, M. and Kandel, A. Fast Categorization of Web Documents represented by Graphs, In *Advances in Web Mining and Web Usage Analysis*, Vol 4811, pp. 56-71, 2007.
14. Mukund, D., Kuramochi, M. and Karypis, G. Frequent Sub-structure based Approaches for Classifying Chemical Compounds. In *Proceedings of the Third IEEE International Conference on Data Mining*, 2003.
15. Reynolds, H. T. The Analysis of Cross-classifications. *The Free Press*, New York, 1977.
16. Schenker, A. *Graph Theorectic Techniques for Web Content Mining*. PhD thesis, University of South Florida, 2003.
17. Tao, F., Murtagh, F. and Farid, M. Weighted Association Rule Mining using Weighted Support and Significance Framework. In *Proceedings of ACM SIGKDD International Conference on Knowledge Discovery and Data Mining*, USA, Aug. 2003.
18. Tsuruoka, Y. and Tsujii, J. Bidirectional Inference with the Easiest-First Strategy for Tagging Sequence Data. In *Proceedings of HLT/EMNLP 2005*, pp. 467-474.
19. Wang, W., Yang, J. and Yu, P. S. Efficient Mining of Weighted Association Rules(WAR). In *Proceedings of ACM SIGKDD International Conference on Knowledge Discovery and Data Mining*, USA, Aug. 2000.
20. Wang, W., Do, D. B. and Lin, X. Term Graph Model for Text Classification, In *Advanced Data Mining and Applications*, pp. 19-30, 2005.
21. Witten, Ian H. and Frank, Eibe. Data Mining: Practical Machine Learning Tools and Techniques (2nd Edition). *Morgan Kaufmann*, San Francisco, 2005.
22. Yan, X. and Han, J. gSpan: Graph-based Substructure Pattern Mining. In *Proceedings of 2002 International Conference on Data Mining*, 2002.
23. Yun, U. and Leggett, J. J. WFIM: Weighted Frequent Itemset Mining with a Weight Range and a Minimum Weight. In *Proceedings of the Fifth SIAM International Conference on Data Mining*, Pages: 636-640, April 2005.
24. Yun, U. and Leggett, J. J. WIP: Mining Weighted Interesting Patterns with a Strong Weight and/or Support Affinity. In *Proceedings of the Sixth SIAM International Conference on Data Mining*, 2006.
25. Yun, U. WIS: Weighted Interesting Sequential Pattern Mining with a Similar Level of Support and/or Weight. *ETRI Journal*, Vol. 29, No. 3, Pages: 336-352, June 2007.

A Sliding Windows based Dual Support Framework for Discovering Emerging Trends from Temporal Data

M. Sulaiman Khan[1], F. Coenen[2], D. Reid[1], R. Patel[3], L. Archer[3]

Abstract In this paper we present the Dual Support Apriori for Temporal data (DSAT) algorithm. This is a novel technique for discovering Jumping Emerging Patterns (JEPs) from time series data using a sliding window technique. Our approach is particularly effective when performing trend analysis in order to explore the itemset variations over time. Our proposed framework is different from the previous work on JEP in that we do not rely on itemsets borders with a constrained search space. DSAT exploits previously mined time stamped data by using a sliding window concept, thus requiring less memory, minimum computational cost and very low dataset accesses. DSAT discovers all JEPs, as in "naïve" approaches, but utilises less memory and scales linearly with large datasets sets as demonstrated in the experimental section.

1 Introduction

Trend mining is a data mining technique directed at the identification of hidden trends in time series data. There are various approaches to trend mining, many of them founded on time series analysis techniques, but also other established approaches such as Association Rule Mining (ARM). ARM, in its most standard form, is concerned with the identification of patterns (known as frequent itemsets) in data within binary valued attributes. The most common framework for ARM is the "support-confidence" framework [1]. In this framework "support" is the frequency with which an itemset appears in the input data and "confidence" is a measure of the reliability of the identified Association Rules (ARs). An itemset is said to be frequent if its support exceeds some user defined support thresholds.

[1] Department of Computer Science, Liverpool Hope University, L16 9JD, UK email: {khanm,reidd}@hope.ac.uk

[2] Department of Computer Science, University of Liverpool, L69 3BX email: frans@liv.ac.uk

[3] Transglobal Express Ltd. Wirral, UK email: {reshma,lawson}@transglobal.co.uk

M. Bramer et al. (eds.), *Research and Development in Intelligent Systems XXVI*,
DOI 10.1007/978-1-84882-983-1_3, © Springer-Verlag London Limited 2010

In Temporal ARM the attributes in the data are time stamped in some way. One category of Temporal ARM is known as Emerging and Jumping Pattern (JEP) mining [8]. An Emerging Pattern (EP) is usually defined as an itemset whose support increases over time according to some "change ratio" threshold. A Jumping Pattern (JP) is an itemset whose support changes much more rapidly than that for an EP. EPs and JPs are distinguished by their change ratio threshold and thus for many purposes can be considered to be synonymous. The discovery of JEPs entails a significant computational overhead due to the large number of itemsets that must be identified to facilitate comparison. To avoid this overhead most JEP mining approaches concentrate on a subset of the potential frequent itemsets such as the set of *maximal* itemsets; that is, the itemsets that show the greatest negative or positive change in value. The computational cost of comparing all items sets across all time stamps tends to render this approach to be, computationally prohibitively, expensive. In this paper we present the Dual Support Apriori Temporal (DSAT) algorithm, an approach to JEP mining that utilizes the entire "data space", but avoids the computational overhead, by using a sliding window mechanism.

The main novelty of the proposed approach is in the adoption of a dual support mechanism in which each itemset holds two support counts, called $supp_1$ and $supp_2$, that benefits: (i) efficient memory utilization, (ii) few IO overheads and (iii) less computation cost. Under the dual support framework $supp_1$ holds the support counts of itemsets in the "oldest" data segment that disappears whenever the window "slides" and $supp_2$ holds support counts for itemsets in the overlap between two windows and the recently added data segment as shown in Figure 1.

The dual support mechanism utilises the already discovered frequent itemsets from the previous windows and avoid re-calculating support counts for all itemsets that exists in the overlapped datasets between two windows, this is illustrated in section 4. Moreover it only required databases access for the most resent segment, thus less IO operations and less memory utilization.

The paper is organized as follows. In section 2 the related work and the problem domain are described in more detail. Section 3 provides a sequence of definitions. To facilitate understanding of the dual support framework a worked example is presented in Section 4. The DSAT algorithm, in its entirety, is then presented in section 5 and evaluated in section 6.

2 Related Work

There are many commercial applications that produce significant amounts of temporal data collected and stored electronically on a daily bases, examples include: web server logs; supermarket transactional data, and network traffic. There are many studies directed at the efficient application of temporal forms of ARM to time stamped data sets [2, 3, 4]. The main issue in temporal ARM is the high computational cost of the processing of the data so as to take account of the temporal dimension. Jiang and Gruenwald [5] compare the temporal data processing models found in temporal ARM, such as: Landmark, Damped and Sliding Windows and their usage depending on the application area. Jiang and Gruenwald also discus issues related to memory management, data structures to store frequent sets and various modified ARM algorithms for temporal ARM.

One category of temporal ARM, as noted in Section 1 above, is Jumping and Emerging Patterns (JEPs) mining as first proposed by Dong and Li [8]. In common with many subsequent JEP algorithms Dong and Li compared maximal itemsets generated using a Max-Miner style of algorithm [19]. A maximal itemset is a frequent (supported) itemset whose supersets are all infrequent (i.e. their support value is below the user specified support threshold). By identifying only maximal itemsets all frequent itemsets can be found by virtue of the DC property (although only the precise support values for the maximal sets are known). The advantage of identifying only maximal itemsets is one of computational efficiency. This is particularly important in the context of JEP mining because of the large number of itemsets that must be identified across time stamps. In addition, to facilitate comparison of itemsets, a low support threshold must also be used hence adding to the magnitude of the problem. However, the maximal frequent set approach does not guarantee the identification of all JEP.

Many JEP mining algorithms have been reported in the literature [6, 7, 9, 10, 18]. Most of these algorithms adopt a maximal frequents itemset approach as first proposed in [8]. For example Tseng et al. [18] extends the work of [8] and proposed EFI-Mine (Emerging Frequent Itemsets) algorithm that discovers JEPs using the technique similar to data streams [4]. The main issue with these existing approaches to JEP mining is that they tend to use only maximal frequent itemsets to identify JEPs. Thus, although efficient, they do not guarantee to find all JEPs.

Our proposed DSAT algorithm differs from the previous work in that we consider all identified frequent itemsets across time stamps. The computational overhead that is normally associated with this approach is avoided by using the dual support concept together with a sliding window approach that requires less memory and data access than would be required otherwise.

3 Preliminaries

In this section a number of formal definitions are presented to facilitate understanding of the rest of the paper. Firstly it is necessary to define the concept of classical ARM. Given a set of items $I = \{i_1, i_2, ..., i_m\}$ and a database of transactions $D = \{t_1, t_2, ..., t_n\}$ where $t_i = \{Ii_1, Ii_2, ..., Ii_p\}$, $p \leq m$ and $I_{ij} \in I$; where $X \subseteq I$ with $K = |X|$ is a k-itemset or simply an itemset. Let a database

D be a multi-set of subsets of I as shown in table 1. Each $T \in D$ supports an itemset $X \subseteq I$ if $X \subseteq T$ holds. An AR is an expression $X \Rightarrow Y$, where X, Y are itemsets and $X \cap Y = \phi$ holds. Number of transactions T supporting an item X w.r.t D is called the *support* of X, $Supp(X) = |\{T \in D \mid X \subseteq T\}| / |D|$. The strength or *confidence* for an association rule X => Y is the ratio of the number of transactions that contain $X \cup Y$ to the number of transactions that contain X, Conf (X → Y) = Supp (X U Y)/ Supp (X).

Emerging patterns, as noted above, are itemsets whose support increases significantly from one data set to another i.e. from w_i to w_{i+1}. An itemset X is called an emerging pattern if the $supp(X) \geq \sigma$ and $GR(X) \geq \delta$ where σ *and* δ are user specified support and growth rate thresholds respectively. *Jumping patterns* are the specialized case of emerging patterns where $GR(X) \rightarrow \infty$ and this is when $supp(X, D_1) \rightarrow 0$. The growth rate of an itemset X from D_1 to D_2 is defined as:

$$GrowthRate(X) = \begin{cases} 0 & if (supp(X, D_1) = 0 \ and \ supp(X, D_2) = 0) \\ \infty & if (supp(X, D_1) = 0 \ and \ supp(X, D_2) \neq 0) \\ \dfrac{supp(X, D_2)}{supp(X, D_1)} & otherwise \end{cases} \quad (1)$$

Time series databases contain data collected over a period of time and can be processed by a sliding window. Each window w_i represents some sequence of time stamped data $w_i = \{t_1, t_2, ... t_w\}$ where t_i is a single time stamp. The amount of data contained in the window may therefore very as the window is progressed along the time series.

Table 1. Super market database

Tid	Items		Tid	Items	
T_1	A, B, C		T_5	A, B, C, D	
T_2	B, C, D, E	D_1	T_6	A, B, C, D	D_2
T_3	B, C, E		T_7	A, B, C	
T_4	B, E		T_8	A, D, E	

Suppose we are given a retail dataset covering two days, D_1 and D_2 respectively. The growth rate of an itemset X from D_1 to D_2 is denoted as $GR(X, D_i, D_{i+1})$ and is defined as in [8]:

$$GR(X) = \frac{supp(X, D_2)}{supp(X, D_1)} \tag{2}$$

As data in different windows is un-evenly distributed, it is necessary to correct the above equation by multiplying it with $|D_1| / |D_2|$, otherwise a bias will favor the EPs process for the dataset with large number of transactions as mentioned in [17]. Thus equation 1 will become:

$$GR(X) = \frac{supp(X, D_2)}{supp(X, D_1)} \times \frac{D_1}{D_2} \tag{3}$$

Given $\sigma > 0$ as support threshold and $\delta > 1$ as growth rate threshold, a frequent pattern X is said to be an emerging pattern from D_1 to D_2 if $GR(X) \geq \delta$. For the data in table 1, if we set $\delta = 3$, then ABC is an EP and ABCD is a JP from D_1 to D_2 because $supp(ABC, D_1) = 1$ and $supp(ABC, D_2) = 3$ and by using equation [2] the $GR(ABC) \geq \delta$, similarly $supp(ABCD, D_1) = 0$ and $supp(ABCD, D_2) = 2$ thus $GR(ABCD) \to \infty$. But $supp(BCD, D_1) = 1$ and $supp(BCD, D_2) = 2$ and by using equation [2] the $GR(BCD) \leq \delta$ thus neither JP nor EP.

In the proposed dual support framework for discovering JEPs, transactions in each window are logically partitioned into three segments as $w_i = \{p_1, p_2, p_3\}$ except w_1 because it only consists $w_1 = \{p_1, p_2\}$ where $p_i \leq D_i$ as shown in figure 1.

p_1 holds data that disappears in the next increment, p_2 holds data that is overlapped between two windows w_i and w_{i+1} i.e. $p_2 = D_i \cap D_{i+1}$ and p_3 consist of data that is added to w_{i+1} after the increment or window slide as shown in the figure 1, where $p_1 = \{t_2\}$, $p_2 = \{t_3, t_4, t_5\}$ and $p_3 = \{t_6\}$ for w_2.

The itemset support counts are denoted as: S_{i1} and S_{i2}, where $i = w_i$. For the first window support count of itemsets in p_1 are recorded into S_{11}, i.e. $S_{11} = |p_1|$, and support counts of itemsets in p_2 are recorded into S_{12}, $S_{12} = |p_2|$. After the window is incremented, from w_1 to w_2, S_{11} is set to zero because the support it holds does not contribute in the next window. S_{12} from the first window is copied into S_{22} in w_2, and the support count of itemsets from w_1 is decremented by p_1. Itemsets from p_3 are generated using S_{22} and then integrated into the already generated itemsets from w_1. Also, S_{22} of any itemset from w_1 is incremented if it exists in p_3.

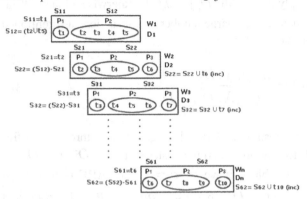

Figure 1 JEPs with dual support framework

The dual support framework therefore uses less memory, features limited IO operations and fewer computations (by utilising the already discovered frequent sets from previous windows), and avoids re-calculating support counts for itemsets that exists between overlapped windows.

4 Dual Support Framework Example

In this section we present an example to illustrate the proposed dual support framework using a sliding windows technique. Table 2 shows five datasets D_1 to D_5 for days starting from 1 to 5. We used days for simplicity but in real applications this could be any temporal interval. For this application we set window size to 3, window slide to 1, support threshold to 25% and growth rate threshold to 2.

For w_1, data sets $D_{1,2,3}$ will be used because $|w|$ is set to 3 as shown in figure 2a. The supports for an itemset is calculated in such a way that $supp_1$ under w_1 holds the number of occurrences of an itemset for D_1 and $supp_2$ holds the number of occurrences of an itemset for the rest of the datasets in w_1. Applying DSAT algorithm following 2-frequent itemsets are generated {(A, B), (A, C), (A, D), (B, C), (B, D), (C, D)}.

Table 2. Example transitional data for 5 weeks

Tid	D_1	D_2	D_3	D_4	D_5
	Day 1	*Day 2*	*Day 3*	*Day 4*	*Day 5*
T_1	A B D	C D	A B C D	C D	A D
T_2	C D	A B E	C D E	A B C E	B C E
T_3	B C	A C D	A C	A C	A C D E
T_4	B D	B C D	A E	A B C D	C

After generating frequent itemsets the window slides (w_2); D_4 is added and D_1 is removed as shows in figure 2b. Itemsets generated in w_1 are cloned in w_2 to avoid itemset re-generation. $supp_1$ for the cloned itemsets in w_2 is set to zero as it no longer contributes to the current window.

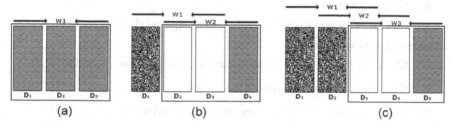

Figure 2 Sliding Windows for table 2 datasets

Frequent itemsets are generated using only D_4 and $supp_2$, consequently the rest of the itemsets are adjusted. $supp_1$ is then calculated for all generated itemsets in w_2 from D_2 and is then subtracted from $supp_2$ so that the accumulative support $supp = supp_1 \cup supp_2$ of itemsets gives the total support count. 2-Frequent itemsets generated for w_2 are {(A, B), (A, C), (A, D), (A, E), (B, C), (B, D), (C, D)}. {A, E} and {A, C} are the discovered JEPs from the frequent sets for w_1 and w_2. This is shown in equation 3. The same procedure is repeated for w_3 as shows in figure 2 where the only JEP discovered from w_2 and w_3 is {C, E}.

Note that if we have a high support threshold there is an option to eliminate an emerging pattern in w_{i+1}. This means that a potential frequent itemset in w_i is no longer considered. If we do need to consider this itemset then a lower support threshold can be used without adversely affecting the efficiency and memory of the system. This is demonstrated in the experiment section.

5 The DSAT Algorithm

Our DSAT algorithm was developed using tree data structures, in a fashion similar to the Apriori algorithm [1], and comprises of two major steps:

1. Apply Apriori to produce a set of frequent itemsets using the sliding window approach.
2. Process and generate a set of JEPs such that the interestingness threshold (Growth Rate) is above some user specified threshold.

Steps involved in the DSAT algorithm are as follows:

For the initial window

1. Load the initial dataset $D_{1-\backslash w\backslash}$ into the memory (w_i).

2. Apply ARM algorithm using sliding windows.

3. Use dual supports for each itemset, $supp_1$ for p_1, $supp_2$ for p_2.

4. Generate frequent sets.

5. Slide window and carry forward all the frequent sets from $w_i \rightarrow w_{i+1}$.

For the sliding window

6. Clone the frequent sets from window w_i to incremented window w_{i+1} .

7. Decrement $supp_1$ of itemsets using p_1.

8. Update itemsets' $supp_2$ as described in section 4.

9. Load only the incremented transactions p_3 into memory.

10. Calculate the $supp_2$ for all the existing itemsets and generate any new itemsets by only considering the incremented time stamp p_3 .

11. Calculate the growth rate of itemsets using both windows w_i and w_{i+1} .

12. Those itemsets with growth rate $\geq$ the threshold are emerging patterns and the itemsets those support approaches to zero in w_i and have support $\geq$ specified jumping threshold in w_{i+1} are the jumping patterns

13. Store JEPs' for the current window w_{i+1} .

14. Go to step 5.

6 Experimental Evaluation

In this section the proposed DSAT algorithm is evaluated with different datasets in order to asses the quality, efficiency and effectiveness of our approach. In the experiments, synthetic and real datasets (with binary and quantitative attributes) are used.

6.1 Datasets

Table 3 overviews the evaluation datasets. It should be noted that the datasets contains both sparse and dense data, since most AR discovery algorithms were designed for these types of problems.

Table 3. Real and Synthetic datasets used for experiments

Dataset	Type	Time Duration	Number of Transactions	Distinct Items	Max. Trans. Size
Server Logs [14]	Real	11/04/08–15/04/09	49,577	1,372	16
Point of Sale [15]	Real	28/09/07–27/09/08	92,685	3,736	19
Transglobal [16]	Real	12/09/07–08/05/09	8,000	3,000	5
T10I4D100K [13]	Synthetic	Not specified	100,000	1,000	29

The first three datasets comprising transactions recorded for almost one year. All the datasets are time stamped and partitioned, except T10I4D100K, so that the number of transactions varies in each partition. T10I4D100K is divided into ten equal partitions of size 10K for experimental purpose. The Transglobal dataset contained quantitative attributes and we discretised the quantitative attributes to binary ones according to the technique proposed in [21]. All the raw datasets were cleaned and filtered to make them suitable for temporal ARM analysis.

6.2 Comparisons with Apriori

Two sets of experiments were conducted to demonstrate: (i) the efficiency of the proposed approach and (ii) the temporal effect on the itemsets (JEPs) as an outcome of the ARM analysis. The experiments demonstrated that the proposed approach was a useful form of trend analysis. All the experiments were conducted on a P4; 1GB, 3GHz machine with windows XP installed using jdk1.4.2.

6.2.1 DSAT Performance

To compare the performance of DSAT we modified the classical Apriori algorithm to deal with temporal data in a conventional manner i.e. process each sliding window and compare it with the proposed DSAT algorithm. The comparison illustrated that DSAT outperformed the Apriori naïve approach for temporal ARM.

6.2.2 Effect of Varying Data Size and Support Threshold

Figures 3, 4, 5 and 6 show the execution time for Apriori and the DSAT algorithms on four real and synthetic datasets with quantitative and binary attributes.

In the figures T1 represents the execution time for the modified classical Apriori ARM and T2 represents the execution time for the proposed DSAT algorithm.

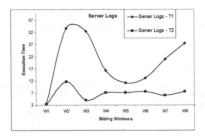

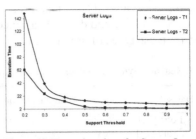

Figure 3a Execution time for Server Log data by varying windows

Figure 3b Execution time for Server Log data varying support thresholds

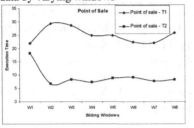

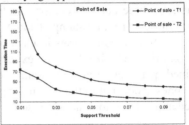

Figure 4a Execution time for Point of Sale data by varying windows

Figure 4b Execution time for Point of Sale data by varying support thresholds

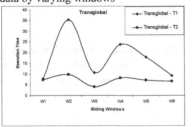

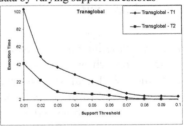

Figure 5a Execution time for Transglobal data by varying windows

Figure 5b Execution time for Transglobal data by varying support thresholds

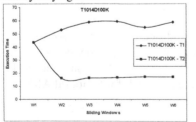

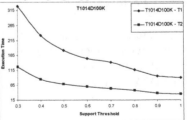

Figure 6a Execution time for Synthetic data by varying windows

Figure 6b Execution time for Synthetic data by varying support thresholds

For figures 3, 4, 5 and 6 (a), the x-axis represents the varying sliding windows and y-axis represent the execution time in seconds for the algorithms for different sliding windows. For figures 3, 4, 5 and 6(b), the x-axis represents the percentage support threshold for the datasets and y-axis represents the cumulative execution time in seconds for the support thresholds. Support thresholds were selected so that the Apriori algorithm could generate frequent itemsets within the given memory constraints so that execution time statistics could be obtained.

Two figures, for each dataset, are displayed in order to show that the DSAT outperforms the naïve Apriori approach not only on the cumulative execution time but also for each sliding window, regardless of various data sizes.

The figures demonstrate that DSAT outperforms the modified Apriori ARM algorithm because DSAT uses already generated frequent itemsets from the previous windows and thus only needs to generate frequent itemsets for the "most recent" transactions. The execution times in figures (a) are not linear because of the varying data sizes in different windows, but near linear in figures (b) as the accumulative windows execution time varies with the support thresholds (the result also displays the ARM property that by increasing support the execution time decreases and vice-versa, algorithm completion time increases[12]).

Moreover the classical ARM algorithm utilises more memory, compared to DSAT, because the use of very low support thresholds leads to the generation of a high number of frequent itemsets. In contrast, DSAT runs more effectively (because DSAT utilises already generated frequent sets from the previous windows, updates their support count for the current window, and only generate the frequent sets from the incremented time stamp as illustrated in Section 4).

6.3 Temporal Effects of Varying Windows and Threshold

The experiments described in this section show how the varying sliding windows affect the overall ARM analysis in discovering JEPs. Figures 7, 8 and 9 show the number of Emerging Patterns discovered (figures a), Jumping Patterns (figures b) and frequent itemsets (figures c) respectively for three different real datasets. The JEPs and the frequent itemsets in the figures are generated by varying support thresholds. As before the support thresholds were selected so that the classical Apriori algorithm would be able to generate large numbers of JEPs so that statistical comparison data could be obtained.

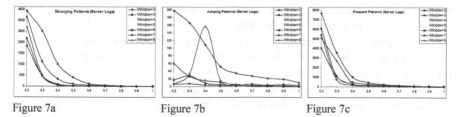

Figure 7a   Figure 7b   Figure 7c

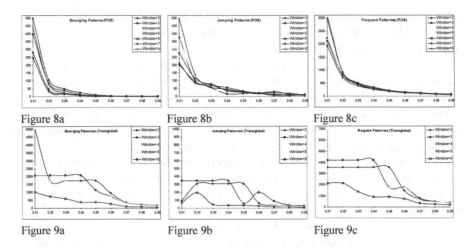

Figure 8a   Figure 8b   Figure 8c

Figure 9a   Figure 9b   Figure 9c

In figures 7, 8 and 9 the x-axis represents various support thresholds and the y-axis the number of EPs, JPs and Frequent items in figures a, b and c respectively. Each curve represents a window from 1 to 8.

From the figures, the numbers of JEPs generated are not linear and there are abrupt differences in the numbers generated due to the number of transactions varying in each window and that the number of transactions changes as the window slides. However there is some linearity for frequent items (Figures 7c, 8c and 9c).

It can be seen from the figures that more JEPs are generated at lower support thresholds as compared to higher ones where in some cases the number approaches zero. The major issue in finding the JEPs is that they are normally generated at low support thresholds because an itemset could qualify as a JEP once its support at w_{i-1} is low as compared to w_i. A JEP can only be discovered once it becomes frequent, or at least is generated in the previous window.

6.4 Trend Analysis

The proposed approach can be usefully employed in trend ARM analysis where data is gathered for fixed or continuous time stamps. For example, the support of an itemset can be monitored over a period of time and it can help end users determine the causes any increment or decrement.

For example, figure 10 shows the support for eight different itemsets, i.e. users' clicks (hits), in web log data that has been monitored for almost a year. Each curve represents an individual itemset in terms of its support for one year from April 2008 till April 2009. The x-axis in the figure represents time in terms of sliding windows and the y-axis the number of time users hits the web pages (itemset).

The website was launched in March 2008, and it can be seen from the figure that the support for the itemsets is low at start up. However, the number of hits increased as more users visited the website, thus increasing the itemsets' support count. From the figure, the itemset {318, 375} has support zero in the first two windows and it emerges as a Jumping pattern at the third window slide; the support kept increasing till the seventh window until it once again disappear in the eighth window. That is because initially page 375 did not exist in the website but was later added (as evidenced by the "jump" in support in the third window). However, later (in the eighth window) it was again removed from the site and the support returns to zero.

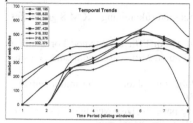

Figure 10 Varying itemsets supports over time

The JEP technique described in this paper is relevant for trend analysis because it not only explicitly highlight trends, but also gives an indication about what factors are influential in boosting or decreasing the relationship between items.

7 Conclusions and Future Work

We have presented a novel approach to efficiently extract JEPs in temporal data by using a sliding window coupled with a dual support mechanism. The advantages of the framework are less memory utilization, limited IO and fewer computations by utilising the previously computed frequent sets. This avoids recalculation of support counts that already exist in between overlapped windows.

The approach has been realized in the form of the DSAT algorithm. The evaluation of this algorithm has produced some very encouraging results. Future work will involve enhancing the efficiency of the algorithm by adopting a T-Tree data structure [11] that uses indexing to further enhance the computational efficiency. Furthermore larger datasets and parallelisation of the DSAT algorithm will be investigated. We anticipate that a stream processing technique [20] would be particularly suitable for this purpose.

Acknowledgement: we would like to thanks Dr. Maybin Muyeba for his valuable feedback and contribution in the research. Also, we would like to thank Michelle Verity and the team at LearnHigher, Mr. Ikram proprietor of the News Agency for providing the Server Logs and Point of Sale data respectively.

References

1. Agrawal, R. & Srikant, R., 1994. Fast algorithms for mining association rules. In Proc. 20th Int. Conf. Very Large Data Bases, VLDB. 487-499.
2. Li, H.F. & Lee, S.Y., 2009. Mining frequent itemsets over data streams using efficient window sliding techniques. Expert Systems with Applications, 36(2P1), 1466-1477.
3. Lee, C.H., Chen, M.S. & Lin, C.R., 2003. Progressive partition miner: An efficient algorithm for mining general temporal association rules. IEEE Transactions on Knowledge and Data Engineering, 1004-1017.
4. Chang, J.H. & Lee, W.S., 2004. A sliding window method for finding recently frequent itemsets over online data streams. Journal of Information Science and Engineering, 20(4), 753-762.
5. Jiang, N., 2006. Research issues in data stream association rule mining. ACM Sigmod Record, 35(1), 14-19.
6. Imberman, S.P. and Tansel, A.U. and Pacuit, E., 2004 An Efficient Method For Finding Emerging Frequent Itemsets,3rd International Workshop on Mining Temporal and Sequential Data, 112-121.
7. Bailey, J., Manoukian, T. & Ramamohanarao, K., 2002. Fast algorithms for mining emerging patterns. Lecture notes in computer science, 39-50.
8. Dong, G. & Li, J., 1999. Efficient mining of emerging patterns: Discovering trends and differences. In Proceedings of the fifth ACM SIGKDD international conference on Knowledge discovery and data mining. ACM New York, NY, USA, pp. 43-52.
9. Rioult, F., Mining strong emerging patterns in wide SAGE data. In Proceedings of the ECML/PKDD Discovery Challenge Workshop. Citeseer, pp. 484-487.
10. Grandinetti, W.M., Chesnevar, C.I. & Falappa, M.A., 2005. Enhanced Approximation of the Emerging Pattern Space using an Incremental Approach, Proceedings of VII Workshop of Researchers in Computer Sciences, Argentine, 263-267
11. Coenen, F., Leng, P. & Ahmed, S., 2004. Data structure for association rule mining: T-trees and P-trees. IEEE Transactions on Knowledge and Data Engineering, 774-778.
12. M. Sulaiman Khan, Muyeba, M., Tjortjis, C. & Coenen, F., 2007. An Effective Fuzzy Healthy Association Rule Mining Algorithm (FHARM). In Proc. 7th Annual Workshop on Computational Intelligence UKCI 2007.
13. IBM Synthetic Data Generator, http://www.almaden.ibm.com/software/quest/resources/index.html
14. Server Logs data set is the courtesy of LearnHigher: http://www.learnhigher.ac.uk
15. Point of Sale data is provided by a News Agent/Grocery Store in Walsall
16. Freight forwarding enterprise data is provided by Transglobal Express Service http://www.transglobalexpress.co.uk
17. Cremilleux, B., Soulet, A. & Rioult, F., 2003. Mining the strongest emerging patterns characterizing patients affected by diseases due to atherosclerosis. In proceedings of the workshop Discovery Challenge, PKDD'03. 59-70.
18. Tseng, V. S., Chu, C.J. & Tyne Liang, 2006. An Efficient Method for Mining Temporal Emerging Itemsets From Data Streams. International Computer Symposium, Workshop on Software Engineering, Databases and Knowledge Discovery.
19. Bayardo Jr, R.J., 1998. Efficiently mining long patterns from databases. ACM SIGMOD Record, 27(2), 85-93.
20. Kapasi, U.J. et al., 2003. Programmable stream processors. Computer, 54-62.
21. M. Sulaiman Khan, Muyeba, M. & Coenen, F., 2009. Effective Mining of Weighted Fuzzy Association Rules, Rare Association Rule Mining and Knowledge Discovery: Technologies for Infrequent and Critical Event Detection, Advances in Data Warehousing and Mining (ADWM) Book Series, IGI Global. ISBN: 978-1-60566-754-6, 47-64.

A Classification-based Review Recommender

Michael P. O'Mahony and Barry Smyth

Abstract Many online stores encourage their users to submit product/service reviews in order to guide future purchasing decisions. These reviews are often listed alongside product recommendations but, to date, limited attention has been paid as to how best to present these reviews to the end-user. In this paper, we describe a supervised classification approach that is designed to identify and recommend the most *helpful* product reviews. Using the TripAdvisor service as a case study, we compare the performance of several classification techniques using a range of features derived from hotel reviews. We then describe how these classifiers can be used as the basis for a practical recommender that automatically suggests the most-helpful contrasting reviews to end-users. We present an empirical evaluation which shows that our approach achieves a statistically significant improvement over alternative review ranking schemes.

1 Introduction

Recommendations are now an established part of online life. In the so-called *Social Web*, we receive recommendations every day from friends and colleagues, as well as from more distant connections in our growing social graphs. Recommender systems have played a key role in automating the generation of high-quality recommendations based on our online histories and/or purchasing preferences. For example, music services such as Pandora [6] and Last.fm are distinguished by their ability to suggest interesting music based on our short-term and long-term listening habits.

Michael P. O'Mahony
CLARITY: Centre for Sensor Web Technologies, School of Computer Science and Informatics, University College Dublin, Ireland. e-mail: michael.p.omahony@ucd.ie

Barry Smyth
CLARITY: Centre for Sensor Web Technologies, School of Computer Science and Informatics, University College Dublin, Ireland. e-mail: barry.smyth@ucd.ie

M. Bramer et al. (eds.), *Research and Development in Intelligent Systems XXVI*,
DOI 10.1007/978-1-84882-983-1_4, © Springer-Verlag London Limited 2010

Indeed, online stores such as Amazon, iTunes, and BestBuy have long established the critical role of recommender systems when it comes to turning browsers into buyers.

Recently, information in the form of *user-generated reviews* has become increasingly important when it comes to helping users make the sort of buying decisions that recommender systems hope to influence. Many sites, such as Amazon, TripAdvisor and Yelp, complement their product descriptions with a rich collection of user reviews. Indeed, many of us use sites like Amazon and TripAdvisor primarily for their review information, even when we make our purchases elsewhere. In the world of recommender systems, reviews serve as a form of *recommendation explanation* [2, 5, 10], helping users to evaluate the quality of suggestions.

The availability of user-generated reviews introduces a new type of recommendation problem. While reviews are becoming increasingly more common, they can vary greatly in their quality and helpfulness. For example, reviews can be biased or poorly authored, while others can be very balanced and insightful. For this reason the ability to accurately identify helpful reviews would be a useful, albeit challenging, feature to automate. While some services are addressing this by allowing users to rate the helpfulness of each review, this type of feedback can be sparse and varied, with many reviews, particularly the more recent ones, failing to attract any feedback.

In this paper, we describe a system that is designed to recommend the most helpful product reviews to users. In the next section, we motivate the task in the context of the TripAdvisor service, which we use as a test domain. In Section 3, we adopt a classification approach to harness available review feedback to learn a classifier that identifies helpful and non-helpful reviews. We then describe how this classifier can be used as the basis for a practical recommender that automatically suggests the most-helpful contrasting reviews to end-users. In Section 4, we describe a comprehensive evaluation that is based on a large set of TripAdvisor hotel reviews. We show that our recommender system is capable of suggesting superior reviews compared to benchmark approaches, and highlight an interesting performance asymmetry that is biased in favour of reviews expressing negative sentiment.

2 Towards Recommending Helpful Reviews

Insightful product reviews can be extremely helpful in guiding purchasing decisions. As reviews accumulate, however, it can become difficult for users to identify those that are helpful, thereby introducing yet another information overload problem. This signals a new and challenging recommendation task—to recommend reviews based on *helpfulness*—which complements the more traditional product recommendation scenarios. Thus the job of the *product recommender* is to suggest a shortlist of relevant products to users, and the role of the *review recommender* is to suggest a small number of helpful reviews for each of these products. We address review recommendation in Section 2.3, but first we consider user-generated reviews and review helpfulness in respect of TripAdvisor reviews, which form the basis of our study.

Fig. 1 A TripAdvisor review

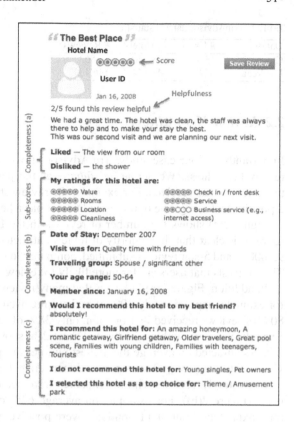

2.1 TripAdvisor Reviews

Figure 1 shows a typical TripAdvisor review. In addition to the *hotel ID* and the *user ID*, each review includes an overall *score* (in this example, 5 out of 5 stars), a *title* ("The Best Place") and the *review-text* (in this case, just three lines of text).

Optionally, users can specify what they *liked* and *disliked* about the hotel, and can provide *sub-scores* on certain aspects of the hotel (e.g. *Value, Rooms* etc.). Further, users can provide some personal information (*Your age range* and *Member since*) and details relating to the date and purpose of visit (*Date of Stay, Visit was for* and *Traveling group*). Finally, users can respond to set review-template questions such as *Would I recommend this hotel to my best friend?* and *I recommend this hotel for*.

For the study described in this paper, we created two large datasets by extracting all TripAdvisor reviews prior to April 2009 for users who had reviewed any hotel in either of two US cities, Chicago or Las Vegas. In total, there are approximately 225,000 reviews by 45,000 users on 70,000 hotels (Table 1). For both datasets, the median number of reviews per user and per hotel is 7 and 1, respectively. These distributions are, however, significantly skewed; for example, the most reviewed hotel in the Chicago and Las Vegas datasets has 575 and 2205 reviews, respectively, while the greatest number of reviews written by any user is 165 and 134, respectively.

Table 1 TripAdvisor dataset statistics

Dataset	# Users	# Hotels	# Reviews
Chicago	13,473	28,840	77,863
Las Vegas	32,002	41,154	146,409

2.2 Review Helpfulness

Importantly for our case study, TripAdvisor allows users to provide feedback on review helpfulness. We define *helpfulness* as the percentage of positive *opinions* that a review has received. For example, the review shown in Figure 1 has received 2 positive and 3 negative opinions and thus it has a helpfulness of 0.4.

Figure 2(a) shows the number of reviews in the Las Vegas dataset versus user score. It is clear that the majority of reviews attracted high scores, with more than 95,000 4- and 5-star reviews submitted, compared to less than 10,000 1-star reviews. This suggests that users are far more likely to review hotels that they have liked.

In addition, Figure 2(a) indicates that many reviews attracted very few opinions; for example, approximately 20% of reviews received no feedback and, while some 80% of reviews received ≥ 1 opinion, only 38% of reviews received ≥ 5 opinions. Excluding reviews with no feedback, Figure 2(b) shows that the most poorly-scored reviews attracted on average the highest number of opinions (almost 11), while reviews with scores of ≥ 2-stars received on average between 6 and 8 opinions.

Interestingly, reviews with lower scores were perceived as being less helpful by users (Figure 2(b)). For example, on average 63% of opinions for 1-star reviews (approximately 7 out of 11 opinions) were positive, with 4 out of 11 opinions being negative. In contrast, of the 7 opinions attracted by 5-star reviews, 87% were positive; thus, only about 1 of 7 opinions attracted by such reviews were negative. In other words, 1-star reviews attracted on average almost 3 times as many negative opinions as 5-star reviews, indicating that users were far more divided in their judgements about the helpfulness of reviews with low scores compared to those with high scores.

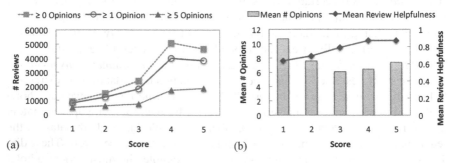

Fig. 2 Las Vegas dataset trends. **a** number of reviews versus score. **b** mean number of opinions per review and mean review helpfulness versus score. Similar trends applied for the Chicago dataset

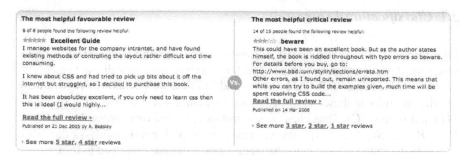

Fig. 3 Review ranking: an example of the Amazon.com approach of listing the most helpful poorly-scored and highly-scored product reviews side by side

2.3 Review Ranking Schemes

The above findings indicate that relying on review feedback alone to recommend and rank reviews is insufficient, given that many reviews fail to attract the critical mass of opinions that would permit reliable helpfulness assessments to be made. Currently, TripAdvisor ranks reviews either by date or by user score, but there is no guarantee that the most recent or highly-scored reviews are the most helpful.

In other domains, more sophisticated approaches to review ranking have been explored. For example, Amazon now suggest the most helpful poorly-scored and highly-scored reviews alongside summary product descriptions (Figure 3). From a review recommendation standpoint, we believe this is a step in the right direction, as it enables users to rapidly assess product quality. Again, however, this approach is limited to cases where sufficient feedback on review helpfulness had been amassed.

The main objective of this paper is to develop a classification approach to identify the most helpful product reviews. Our approach, which is detailed in the next section, seeks to train a classifier from reviews that have attracted a critical mass of helpfulness opinions, such that the classifier can then be used to classify the helpfulness of arbitrary reviews, including those that have received no feedback on review helpfulness. Indeed, such a classifier may be generalisable to domains where review helpfulness data is not collected; although this question we leave for future work.

3 Classifying and Recommending Reviews

We adopt a supervised approach to classifying the most helpful reviews. Review instances are labeled as *helpful* or *non-helpful*, and a review is considered *helpful* if and only if at least 75% of opinions for the review are positive. In this way we focus the classification task on the prediction of the most unambiguously helpful reviews.

3.1 Classification Features

Prior to classification, each review is translated into a feature-based instance representation. Review instances consist of features derived from four distinct categories which are mined from individual reviews and from the wider community reviewing activity. We refer to these categories as *user reputation* (R), *social* (SL), *sentiment* (ST) and *content* (C). Thus each review instance, I_j, can be expressed as follows: $I_j = \{R_j, SL_j, ST_j, C_j, class_j\}$, where $class_j = \{\text{helpful, non-helpful}\}$ as described above. In the following sections, the feature categories are described in turn.

3.1.1 User Reputation Features

These features are designed to capture a user's reputation with respect to the set of reviews that the user has authored in the past. The features are:

R1: The mean review helpfulness over all reviews authored by the user.
R2: The standard deviation of review helpfulness over all reviews authored by the user.
R3: The percentage of reviews authored by the user which have received a minimum of T opinions; in this work, $T = 5$ (see Section 4.1).

These features capture the intuition that users who authored helpful reviews in the past are likely to do so in future. As such, we expect reputation features to be strong predictors of review helpfulness. Given that many reviews, however, receive only limited feedback on review helpfulness, we explicitly evaluate classifier performance when reputation features are excluded from review instances in Section 4.

3.1.2 Social Features

These features are concerned with the degree distribution in the bipartite user–hotel review graph. We mine six such features in total from our datasets, which are:

SL1: The number of reviews authored by the user.
SL2: The mean number of reviews authored by all users.
SL3: The standard deviation of the number of reviews authored by all users.
SL4: The number of reviews submitted for the hotel.
SL5: The mean number of reviews submitted for all hotels.
SL6: The standard deviation of the number of reviews submitted for all hotels.

The above features can be considered as a kind of "rich get richer" phenomenon where, for example, reviews authored by more experienced reviewers may have improved quality. It is uncertain if this concept of experience applies to hotels; however, our rationale for the latter three features is that when users write their own reviews they may, for example, respond to comments made in existing reviews submitted for a particular hotel, and thereby improve the quality of their own reviews.

3.1.3 Sentiment Features

Sentiment relates to how well users enjoyed their experience with a hotel. In this paper, we consider sentiment in terms of the score (expressed on a 5-star scale) that the user has assigned to a hotel. In addition, we consider the optional sub-scores that may be assigned by users (see Section 2.1). We extract the following features:

ST1: The score assigned by the user to the hotel.
ST2: The number of (optional) sub-scores assigned by the user.
ST3: The mean sub-score assigned by the user.
ST4: The standard deviation of the sub-scores assigned by the user.
ST5: The mean score over all reviews authored by the user.
ST6: The standard deviation of the scores over all reviews authored by the user.
ST7: The mean score assigned by the all users to the hotel.
ST8: The standard deviation of scores assigned by the all users to the hotel.

The analysis presented in Section 2.2 indicated that score was indeed an indicator of review helpfulness, where highly-scored reviews attracted the greatest number of positive helpfulness opinions. The importance of sentiment features from a classification perspective is examined in further detail in the evaluation section (Section 4).

3.1.4 Content Features

We consider several features in respect of review content:

C1: The number of terms in the review text.
C2: The ratio of uppercase and lowercase characters to other characters in the review text.
C3: The ratio of uppercase to lowercase characters in the review text.
C4: Review completeness (a) – an integer in the range [0,2] which captures whether the user has completed one, both or none of the optional *liked* and *disliked* parts of the review (see Section 2.1).
C5: Review completeness (b) – the number of optional personal and purpose of visit details that are provided by the user in the review (see Section 2.1).
C6: Review completeness (c) – the number of optional review-template questions that are answered in the review (see Section 2.1).

The first feature is designed to distinguish between reviews based on the length of the review-text. The second and third features are intended to capture whether or not the review text is well formed; for example, the absence of uppercase or punctuation characters is indicative of a poorly authored review, and such reviews are unlikely to be perceived favourably by users. The final three features provide a measure of review completeness, i.e. how much optional content has been included in reviews. We expect that more complete reviews are likely to be more helpful to users.

3.2 Recommendation via Classification

We can use our collection of review instances as supervised training data for a variety of standard classification algorithms. In this paper we consider the JRip, J48, and Naive Bayes classifiers [12]. Each technique produces a *classifier* from the training data which can be used to classify unseen instances (reviews) in the absence of helpfulness data. In addition, each classifier can return not just the predicted class (helpful vs. non-helpful), but also a *confidence* score for the associated prediction.

Prediction confidence can then be used to effectively translate review classification into review recommendation, by rank-ordering reviews classified as helpful according to their prediction confidence. Thus, given a set of reviews for a hotel, we can use a classifier to produce a ranked list of those reviews predicted to be helpful.

Other recommendation styles are also possible; for example, the Amazon approach of recommending the most-helpful highly-scored and poorly-scored product reviews to provide the user with contrasting reviews (Figure 3). All such approaches are, however, limited to those reviews that have attracted feedback on review helpfulness. The benefit of the approach described in this paper is that it can be used to recommend reviews that have not attracted any (or a critical mass of) feedback.

4 Evaluation

So far we have motivated the need for *review recommendation* as a complement to *product recommendation*. We have described how a classification approach can be adopted as a basis for recommendation. Ultimately, success will depend on classification accuracy and how this translates into useful recommendations. We now examine these issues in the context of a large-scale study using TripAdvisor data.

4.1 Datasets and Methodology

To provide training data for the classifiers, features were first computed over all review instances in the Chicago and Las Vegas datasets. To provide support when labeling reviews, we selected only those reviews with a minimum of $T = 5$ opinions as training data. In addition, we sampled from these reviews to produce balanced training data with a roughly equal representation of both *helpful* and *non-helpful* class instances. Table 2 shows statistics for the balanced datasets.

Following [4], we report *sensitivity* and *specificity*, which measure the proportion of helpful and non-helpful reviews that are correctly classified, respectively. In addition, we report *AUC* (area under ROC curve) which produces a value between 0 and 1; higher values indicate better classification performance. Further details on these metrics can be found in [3]. The relative performance of the JRip, J48, and Naive Bayes (NB) classification techniques are compared using Weka [12].

Table 2 Balanced dataset statistics

Dataset	# Users	# Hotels	# Reviews
Chicago	7,399	7,646	17,038
Las Vegas	18,849	10,782	35,802

4.2 Classification Results

Classification performance is measured using a standard 10-fold cross-validation technique. In the following sections we describe the classification results obtained across different groupings of features and feature types.

4.2.1 Classification using All Features

We begin by examining classification performance when all available features (that is, reputation, social, sentiment, content plus three generic features: *user-id*, *hotel-id* and *review date*) are considered. The sensitivity, specificity, and AUC results are presented in Figure 4, as the bars labeled 'A' for the Chicago and Las Vegas datasets. Overall, JRip was seen to out-perform J48 and NB for both datasets and across all evaluation metrics. In addition, J48 usually performed better than NB.

Reputation features include information about the helpfulness of other reviews authored by the review author, and for this reason they are likely to be influential. Thus we have also included results for training instances that include all features except reputation features, condition 'A\R' in Figure 4. As expected, we see a drop in classification performance across the datasets and algorithms suggesting that reputation features do in fact play an important role. We will return to this point in the next section, but for now we highlight that even in the absence of reputation features — and remember that these features are not available in all domains — classification performance remains high for both datasets with AUC scores > 0.72 for JRip.

4.2.2 Classification by Feature Category

The performance of classifiers trained using the reputation, social, sentiment, and content feature categories are also presented in Figure 4, as bars labeled 'R', 'SL', 'ST' and 'C', respectively. The results highlight the strong performance of the reputation features in particular. For example, the AUC metric clearly shows that reputation features provided the best performance, followed by sentiment features. In the case of the Las Vegas dataset, for example, the best performing classifier (J48) achieved an AUC of 0.82 and 0.73 using reputation and sentiment features, respectively. Both social and content feature sets were less successful, with J48 achieving an AUC of 0.60 and 0.61, respectively. Broadly similar trends were observed for the sensitivity and specificity metrics. In most cases, higher sensitivity rates were achieved, which indicates that more false positives were seen than false negatives.

Table 3 Features ranked by information gain (IG)

Rank	Chicago		Las Vegas	
	Feature ID	IG	Feature ID	IG
1	R1	0.085	R1	0.172
2	Hotel ID	0.077	ST1	0.095
3	SL4	0.052	ST3	0.079
4	SL1	0.051	ST5	0.057
5	ST1	0.047	R2	0.040
6	R2	0.045	Hotel ID	0.031
7	ST5	0.045	SL4	0.029
8	ST6	0.044	ST6	0.028
9	ST3	0.043	C1	0.023

4.2.3 Feature Selection

The analysis presented above examined the relative importance of the different feature categories. Such an analysis does not, however, consider the relative importance of individual features. Thus we show in Table 3 the top 9 features for both datasets, which are rank-ordered according to *information gain* (IG).

As expected, the reputation features proved to very significant; for example, the mean helpfulness of a user's reviews (**R1**) turned out to be the strongest single predictor of classification accuracy for both datasets. Overall, we find that 8 out of 9 features were common across both datasets, albeit with different rank orderings. More or less the same groupings of reputation, social and sentiment features were found, with social features proving to be more important (in terms of rank) than sentiment features in the Chicago dataset, and vice versa for Las Vegas.

In relation to social features, both the number of reviews submitted for the hotel (**SL4**) and the number of reviews written by the user (**SL1**) were among the top ranked features for the Chicago dataset, although only one (**SL4**) was ranked in the top 9 in the Las Vegas dataset. A total of 4 sentiment features (**ST1**, **ST3**, **ST5** and **ST6**) are ranked among the top features for both datasets (although in different order), reflecting the relatively good classification performance achieved by such features as shown in Figure 4. In particular, the importance of **ST1** (the score assigned by the user to the hotel) was previously discussed in Section 2.2. The power of this feature is further indicated in terms of information gain: for both datasets, **ST1** was the highest ranked sentiment feature, and was ranked 2nd and 5th for the Las Vegas and Chicago datasets, respectively.

Only a single content feature, the number of terms in the review text (**C1**), was located in the top features for one of the datasets (Las Vegas). None of the features relating to well-formed review text (**C2** and **C3**) were ranked highly. Further, none of the features that indicate review completeness (**C4**, **C5** and **C6**) were strong predictors of helpful reviews. It remains an open question as to why content features were not particularly useful predictors of review helpfulness. A more comprehensive analysis in respect of review content is certainly possible (see Section 5); we will consider content features afresh in future analysis.

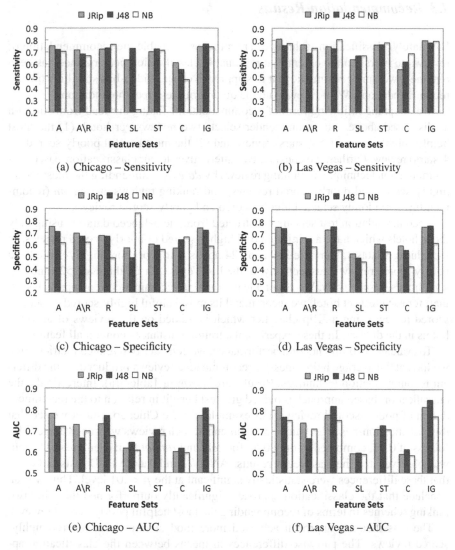

Fig. 4 Classification performance for the Chicago and Las Vegas datasets. Notation: A – all features, A\R – all excluding reputation features, R – reputation features, SL – social features, ST – sentiment features, C – content features and IG – top-9 features ranked by information gain

Finally, we examine classification performance when review instances were constructed using only the top 9 features as ranked by information gain. The results in Figure 4 show that best AUC performance was seen for both datasets using J48 with this approach. This finding suggests that the low information gain associated with the remaining features essentially introduced noise into the classification process and that their removal lead to an improvement in overall performance.

4.3 Recommendation Results

Ultimately, classification techniques are a means to enable the recommendation of reviews to users. To the extent that reasonable classification performance has been obtained, we can be optimistic that this approach can provide a basis for high quality recommendations. We now evaluate the quality of these recommendations.

We adopt the following form of recommendation. Taking our lead from Amazon as discussed above, our recommender selects two reviews per hotel: (1) the most helpful highly-scored ($\geq$ 4-stars) review and (2) the most helpful poorly-scored ($<$ 4-stars) review. Further, we consider two alternatives to our classification-based recommendation technique by ranking reviews by *date* (recommending the most recent highly-scored and poorly-scored reviews) and ranking reviews at *random* (recommending a randomly selected highly-scored and poorly-scored review).

Recommendation test sets are constructed from the balanced datasets using only those hotels which have a minimum of 5 highly-scored or poorly-scored reviews. In the Chicago dataset, there are 239 and 124 hotels with 5 or more highly-scored and poorly-scored reviews, respectively. In the Las Vegas dataset, there are 528 and 224 such hotels, respectively. We adopt a leave-one-out recommendation approach such that, for each test set hotel, we recommend its most helpful highly-scored or poorly-scored review using a JRip classifier which is trained on the reviews of all other hotels in the dataset. In these experiments, training instances contain all features.

To evaluate recommendation performance, we consider two related metrics. First we look at the average helpfulness of recommended reviews produced by the different recommendation techniques. Results are shown in Table 4(a). Interestingly, the classification-based approach provided greatest benefit in relation to the recommendation of poorly-scored reviews. For example, for the Chicago dataset we see that the classification-based technique recommended such reviews with an average helpfulness of 0.71, compared to only 0.58 for *date* and *random*; an even greater benefit was observed for the Las Vegas results. ANOVA and Tukey HSD tests indicated that these differences were statistically significant at the $p < .01$ level. Thus we can conclude that the classification approach significantly outperformed the other two ranking schemes in terms of recommending the most helpful poorly-scored reviews.

The classification approach achieved more modest improvements for highly-scored reviews. The pairwise differences in means between the classification approach and the two other strategies were statistically significant at the $p < .05$ and $p < .01$ levels, respectively, for the Chicago dataset. No significant differences between ranking schemes were found, however, for the Las Vegas dataset. This finding can be attributed to the high average review helpfulness that highly-scored reviews generally attracted (see Figure 2(b)), and thus the *date* and *random* ranking schemes were able to achieve comparable performance to the classification-based approach.

As a second evaluation metric, we consider how frequently our recommenders manage to select a review that is unambiguously helpful according to our definition given in Section 3; that is, a review that has received at least 75% positive opinions. The results are presented in Table 4(b). Overall, the trends are similar to those reported above, with the classification approach achieving the greatest im-

Table 4 Average recommendation performance over test set hotels. **a** average review helpfulness of recommended reviews. **b** percentage of helpful reviews in recommended reviews

(a)						(b)					
	Chicago			Las Vegas			Chicago			Las Vegas	
Score	Class.	Date	Rnd.	Class.	Date	Rnd.	Score	Class.	Date	Rnd.	Class.	Date	Rnd.
≥4-stars	0.83	0.79	0.75	0.82	0.81	0.81	≥4-stars	79	62	54	70	68	64
<4-stars	0.71	0.58	0.58	0.76	0.56	0.60	<4-stars	50	27	17	60	28	25

provements in the case of poorly-scored reviews. The results are also of interest, however, in relation to highly-scored reviews, since they indicate how even small changes in average review helpfulness translate into more significant recommendation improvements: many more unambiguously helpful reviews are recommended by the classification approach when compared to *date* and *random*. For example, in the case of the Chicago dataset, a percentage improvement of 5% in average review helpfulness from 0.79 (ranking by *date*) to 0.83 (ranking by classification) results in a relative improvement of 27% (from 62% to 79%) in the actual number of helpful reviews that are recommended. As expected, much smaller improvements were seen for the Las Vegas dataset, given that no statistically significant differences in average review helpfulness between ranking schemes were indicated for this dataset.

5 Discussion and Conclusions

The findings of Section 4 demonstrate that our approach achieved a high level of performance in terms of classifying and recommending the most helpful reviews. Greater performance was observed for poorly-scored reviews, which is significant given that these reviews were perceived on average as being less helpful by users, and hence the need for a scheme which can effectively rank such reviews. Overall, our findings are encouraging, taking into consideration that review helpfulness is a subjective notion and that many factors can influence user opinion in this regard.

There is rich scope for future work in this area and the following related work is of interest. In [7], a similar approach to review classification has been proposed, which considered feature sets relating to the structural, lexical, syntactic, semantic and some meta-data properties of reviews. Of these features, score, review length and unigram (term distribution) were among the most discriminating. (This work did not consider social or reputation features.) In [8], reviewer expertise was found to be a useful predictor of review helpfulness, capturing the intuition that people interested in a particular genre of movies are likely to author high quality reviews for movies within the same or related genres. Timeliness of reviews was also important, and it was shown that (movie) review helpfulness declined as time went by.

A classification approach was applied in [4] to distinguish between conversational and informational questions in social Q&A sites. In this work, features such as question category, text categorization and social network metrics were selected as the basis for classification and good performance was achieved. An analysis of credibility indicators in relation to topical blog post retrieval was presented in [11]. Some of the indicators considered were text length, the appropriate use of capitalisation and emoticons in the text, spelling errors, timeliness of posts and the regularity at which bloggers post. Work in relation to sentiment and opinion analysis is also of interest [9]; for example, the classification of TripAdvisor reviews for sentiment using content-based feature sets was considered in [1].

The framework introduced in this paper for the classification and recommendation of reviews is generalisable to other domains. In future work, we will apply our approach to review sites such as Amazon and Blippr; the classification of reviews from the latter site in particular pose new challenges, given that reviews in this domain are constrained to 160 characters in length. In addition, motivated by the above related work, we will explore the use of richer sets of review features in our analysis.

Acknowledgements This work is supported by Science Foundation Ireland under grant 07/CE/I1147.

References

1. Baccianella, S., Esuli, A., Sebastiani, F.: Multi-facet rating of product reviews. In: Advances in Information Retrieval, 31th European Conference on Information Retrieval Research (ECIR 2009), pp. 461 – 472. Springer, Toulouse, France (2009)
2. Bilgic, M., Mooney, R.J.: Explaining recommendations: Satisfaction vs. promotion. In: Beyond Personalization Workshop, held in conjunction with the 2005 International Conference on Intelligent User Interfaces. San Diego, CA, USA (2005)
3. Fawcett, T.: Roc graphs: Notes and practical considerations for researchers. In: Technical Report HPL-2003-4, HP Laboratories, CA, USA (2004)
4. Harper, F.M., Moy, D., Konstan, J.A.: Facts or friends? distinguishing informational and conversational questions in social q&a sites. In: Proceedings of the 27th International Conference on Human Factors in Computing Systems (CHI'09). Boston, MA, USA (2009)
5. Herlocker, J.L., Konstan, J.A., Riedl, J.: Explaining collaborative filtering recommendations. In: Proceeding on the ACM 2000 Conference on Computer Supported Cooperative Work, pp. 241–250. Philadelphia, PA, USA (2000)
6. http://www.pandora.com/
7. Kim, S.M., Pantel, P., Chklovski, T., , Pennacchiotti, M.: Automatically assessing review helpfulness. In: Proceedings of the Conference on Empirical Methods in Natural Language Processing (EMNLP 2006), pp. 423–430. Sydney, Australia (2006)
8. Liu, Y., Huang, X., An, A., Yu, X.: Modeling and predicting the helpfulness of online reviews. In: Proceedings of the 2008 Eighth IEEE International Conference on Data Mining (ICDM 2008), pp. 443–452. IEEE Computer Society, Pisa, Italy (2008)
9. Tang, H., Tan, S., Cheng, X.: A survey on sentiment detection of reviews. Expert Systems With Applications **36**(7), 10,760–10,773 (2009)
10. Tintarev, N., Masthoff, J.: The effectiveness of personalized movie explanations: An experiment using commercial meta-data. In: Proceedings of the 5th International Conference on Adaptive Hypermedia and Adaptive Web-Based Systems (AH 2008), pp. 204–213 (2008)
11. Weerkamp, W., de Rijke, M.: Credibility improves topical blog post retrieval. In: Proceedings of the Association for Computational Linguistics with the Human Language Technology Conference (ACL-08:HLT), pp. 923 – 931. Columbus, Ohio, USA (2008)
12. Witten, I.H., Frank, E.: Data Mining – Practical Machine Learning Tools and Techniques, 2nd Edition. Elsevier (2005)

Ontology-Driven Hypothesis Generation to Explain Anomalous Patient Responses to Treatment

Laura Moss, Derek Sleeman, Malcolm Sim, Malcolm Booth, Malcolm Daniel, Lyndsay Donaldson, Charlotte Gilhooly, Martin Hughes, John Kinsella

Abstract Within the medical domain there are clear expectations as to how a patient should respond to treatments administered. When these responses are not observed it can be challenging for clinicians to understand the anomalous responses. The work reported here describes a tool which can detect anomalous patient responses to treatment and further suggest hypotheses to explain the anomaly. In order to develop this tool, we have undertaken a study to determine how Intensive Care Unit (ICU) clinicians identify anomalous patient responses; we then asked further clinicians to provide potential explanations for such anomalies. The high level reasoning deployed by the clinicians has been captured and generalised to form the procedural component of the ontology-driven tool. An evaluation has shown that the tool successfully reproduced the clinician's hypotheses in the majority of cases. Finally, the paper concludes by describing planned extensions to this work.

1 Introduction

It is widely acknowledged that anomalous scenarios provide a key role in knowledge discovery; an anomaly can indicate to an expert that their understanding of a domain may require further refinement which in turn may lead to the discovery of new knowledge [6]. However, in a complex domain such as medicine, it can be difficult, especially for junior clinicians, to generate the required hypotheses to resolve such anomalies. The resolution of anomalies is important as it can enhance patient treatment.

Laura Moss, Derek Sleeman[1,2]
[1]Department of Computing Science, University of Aberdeen, Aberdeen, AB24 3UE

Malcolm Sim, Malcolm Booth, Malcolm Daniel, Lyndsay Donaldson, Charlotte Gilhooly, Martin Hughes, John Kinsella
[2]Section of Anaesthesia, Glasgow Royal Infirmary, University of Glasgow, Glasgow, G31 2ER

M. Bramer et al. (eds.), *Research and Development in Intelligent Systems XXVI*,
DOI 10.1007/978-1-84882-983-1_5, © Springer-Verlag London Limited 2010

The Intensive Care Unit (ICU) in a hospital provides treatment to patients who are often critically ill and possibly rapidly deteriorating. Such patients provide complex challenges for the attending clinician. To aid the clinician in monitoring and treating such patients, many modern ICUs are equipped with sophisticated patient management systems. These systems collect the patients' physiological measurements; record the infusions given to the patient, and note some interventions such as dialysis. The information recorded by the system is stored in a database and can be viewed at the patient's bedside or 'offline' at a later date. Access to the data stored in the patient management system at Glasgow Royal Infirmary's ICU has been provided for use in this study.

The focus of the work reported here is the development of a tool to assist clinicians in explaining why a patient has responded anomalously to treatment. To capture the process deployed by expert clinicians in such a scenario, detailed interviews were held with five ICU consultants from Glasgow Royal Infirmary (GRI) to identify anomalous patient responses based on their physiological data. Two further ICU clinicians from GRI were then asked to suggest potential explanations for the identified anomalies. Further, these interviews were examined by analysts to establish both how the hypotheses were generated and the types of hypotheses presented. The findings from this analysis form the basis of an ontology-driven hypothesis generation tool described below. A more detailed review of the interviews held with ICU clinicians can be found in Moss et al [13].

The rest of this paper is organized as follows: section 2 gives a brief literature review; section 3 discusses the interviews held with ICU clinicians; section 4 outlines the ontology-based tool, gives examples of use, and outlines an evaluation; section 5 discusses planned future work for this tool

2 Literature Review

Anomalous scenarios play a key role in knowledge discovery; Kuhn [6] defines an anomaly as a violation of the "paradigm-induced expectations that govern normal science". Such anomalies are of interest as they often point to the inadequacy of a currently held theory and require refinement of the related theory; consequently this can provide the impetus for the discovery of further domain knowledge. Analyses [16][12] have shown that the detection and explanation (using domain knowledge) of these anomalies force scientists to revise their knowledge in a number of ways; from a minor refinement of hypotheses to major changes of fundamental knowledge.

The generation of hypotheses as part of automated scientific discovery processes have been discussed widely in the literature [4][17][3], of most relevance to this work is Blum's work on the RX project which investigated the automatic generation and testing of hypotheses from a clinical database [14]. The work was successful in discovering a previously unknown correlation between prednisone and cholesterol when tested on a clinical database from rheumatology patients. However, it is not known whether this approach would be successful in other medical areas such as the

Intensive Care Unit (ICU) domain; much larger amounts of data can be retrieved in the ICU domain, and in particular the abstraction process that Blum deploys would have to become more sophisticated to handle temporal datasets.

Due to the complexity and amount of data in the ICU domain it is difficult for clinicians to be fully conversant with the data; further it is recognized that the ICU is a challenging domain in which to perform decision making [19]. Artificial Intelligence systems used in the ICU domain generally analyse real time data streams and provide sophisticated monitoring of the data streams, applying domain knowledge to assist in data interpretation. Some of these systems, such as those developed by the MIMIC II [1] project have been implemented 'live' in an ICU ward, whilst other systems use data 'offline'[7]. Despite the wide variety of decision-support systems developed for use in the ICU, such as RÉSUMÉ [20] and VIE-VENT [18], none have focused on providing support to clinicians when faced with anomalous patient behaviour.

3 Capturing the Identification & Explanation of Anomalous Responses to Treatment

Five ICU clinicians from Glasgow Royal Infirmary were presented with physiological data for 10 patients containing 1466 hourly sequences and asked to identify anomalous sequences in the data. Five of these patients had been previously identified as containing anomalous patient responses and five were randomly selected from the patient management system. A semi-structured interview was held with the clinicians and they were asked to 'talk-aloud' as they completed the task [10]. A grounded theory approach [8] was applied by the analyst (LM) to the protocols which resulted in the following coding categories (C to E describe anomalies):

A - Anticipated patient responses to treatment, possibly with minor relapses (default if clinician does not provide any other classification)
B - Anticipated patient responses to treatment, with significant relapses e.g., additional bouts of sepsis, cardiac or respiratory failure
C - Patient not responding as expected to treatment
D - Odd / unusual set of physiological parameters (or unusual rates of change)
E - Odd / unusual treatment

> "........ the thing that I am puzzled by in all this is the fact that the cardiac output went up when we increased their vasoconstrictor, I wouldn't necessarily expect that."
>
> **Taken from transcript of Clinician 4 discussing Patient 909**

Fig. 1 Anomalous Example

The coding categories were successfully verified by a second coder (DS)[1]. The clinicians identified a total of 65 anomalies. Figure 1 provides an example anomaly. The most interesting type of anomaly for the clinicians was category 'C', which describes scenarios where a patient is not responding as expected to treatment. It was decided that this category would be the focus of the second study.

The anomalies classified as 'C' (a total of 13) were used as the stimuli for a second set of interviews with two further ICU clinicians (not involved in the initial identification of anomalies). Separate interviews were held with these clinicians during which they were presented with a series of anomalies and given access to the patient data. The clinicians were asked if they could suggest potential explanations for the identified anomalies. An example of a hypothesis suggested for the anomaly shown in Figure 1 is given in Figure 2[2].

> "The patient is clearly deteriorating over the course of the day though, the urine volumes are decreasing, the oxygen requirement has gone up, probably this patient is just getting considerably sicker and they are just not responding to the noradrenaline."

Explanation provided by Clinician 6

Fig. 2 Hypothesis Example

Analysis [8] of the transcripts from these interviews led to the identification of a range of hypotheses which could be organised as the following categories: 1) clinical conditions, 2) hormone regulation, 3) progress of the patient's condition, 4) treatment, 5) functioning of the patient's organs and 6) errors in recordings.

The interviews were analysed further and a method of information selection and hypothesis generation used by the clinicians was identified. When generating a hypothesis each clinician began with an anomaly, for example the one shown in Figure 1, "*noradrenaline increased cardiac output and cardiac index*" [3], which can be broken down into the treatment, '*noradrenaline*' and the effect '*increase cardiac output and cardiac index*'. The clinician then proceeded to explain any combination of the treatment and anomalous effect. The clinicians appeared to use domain knowledge about treatment, medical conditions and the desired physiological state of the patient to suggest hypotheses that explain the treatment or effect. Further, the clinician appeared to use domain knowledge whilst examining the patient's data to determine facts; for example, the patient is suffering from a myocardial infarction. The patient's data can also be used to *eliminate* hypotheses. For example, one of the explanations for the anomaly detailed in Figure 1 was that the patient is getting worse, if the data does not show this, this hypothesis can be eliminated. The clinician repeated the process until they were satisfied that all viable hypotheses had been proposed.

---

[1] Further details on the analysis of protocols are provided in [13]

[2] Noradrenaline is considered as a vasoconstrictor

[3] Noradrenaline at low doses should not increase a patient's cardiac output and input, but at high doses this may be observed

4 Generating Hypotheses for Anomalous Responses to Treatment

A tool, named EIRA (Explaining, Inferring and Reasoning about Anomalies) has been developed based on the general model of hypothesis generation presented in Section 3. It is envisaged that EIRA will be used by clinicians as an 'offline' aid/tutoring tool when faced with an anomalous scenario. The work reported in this section describes the initial implementation of EIRA (planned further implementation of EIRA are discussed in Section 5). EIRA comprises: a knowledge base consisting of several OWL[4] ontologies and a Java based program implementing strategies extracted from domain experts' protocols.

4.1 Knowledge Base

As the analyst noted when analysing the interviews, the clinicians drew from a large knowledge base in order to create hypotheses. The knowledge base of EIRA comprises four ontologies which model the following sub-domains: the ICU domain, the patient data, human physiology, and time.

Although various ICU ontologies have been discussed in the literature, for example [15]), none were available to us at the time of development; further using a standard biomedical ontology (including [2, 11]) for this tool would not be appropriate, mainly due to their size. Instead we created our own (relatively small) ontologies for the task. These smaller ontologies, consisting solely of the knowledge required by the system provided many benefits when building and editing the ontologies with a standard ontology editor; inferencing using these ontologies is also quicker. We do, however, recognise that standardised biomedical ontologies have a role as an important reference point, particularly beneficial for interoperability, and should be used whenever possible. To support such usage, a simple alignment meta-ontology enables the definition of correspondences between concepts in our ontologies with concepts in these standard ontologies. We believe that the framework provided by these ontologies will enable their re-use in other medical domains.

The ICU domain ontology was developed in collaboration with an ICU clinician (MS) and it has been shown to be sufficient to support the clinical reasoning discussed in section 3. Four types of knowledge are described: disorders, treatments, disorder severity scores, and drugs.

The Drug class (a subclass of Treatment, visualised in figure 3) describes how drugs are used as treatments in the ICU domain. Features of a drug, such as activeDrugName, alternativeDrugNames, the anticipated length of time between the drug's administration to a patient and its effect being observed (the drug's timeToReact), and any contraindications of the drug (disorders or other treatments) have been modelled in the drug class; in addition, descriptions of a drug's effects, inter-

---

[4] http://www.w3.org/2004/OWL/

actions, and uses have been supported. Various types of drug effects are described: *expected* effects, *conditional* effects which occur under certain conditions, *rarely observed* effects which are rare but still theoretically possible, and (unwanted) *side* effects.

Drugs can interact with other drugs to produce anticipated and unanticipated physiological effects. For a particular drug, it is usually known which other drugs can interact with it and the associated effect. This is represented by the `Drug_Interaction` class (shown in figure 4). Each `Drug_Interaction` is associated with a drug (hasDrug), the interacting drug (interactsWith), and the physiological effects observed during the interaction (interactionEffect).

Various properties are used to represent different drug doses, as a particular drug may be given at different doses depending on the severity of the disorder for which the drug is being administered. Differences in how commonly (or not) a drug is used to treat particular disorders is also described.

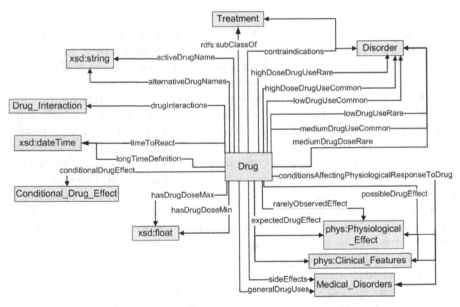

Fig. 3 Visualisation of the Drug Class from the ICU Ontology

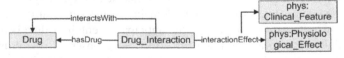

Fig. 4 Visualisation of the Drug_Interaction Class from the ICU Ontology

The Patient Data ontology has been designed to model the time series data which is typically collected in medical domains. The ontology defines a `Patient_Data` class, which represents the patient's `Sessions` and `Location`. The `Session` class models a treatment session, which in turn links a series of `Timepoints`; the later describe the `Readings` for a particular xsd:dateTime. Each `Reading` has a `Parameter` and value.

The `Human_Physiology` ontology models, at a high level, knowledge regarding organs and organ systems, clinical features, and physiological effects. The `Organ_System` and `Organ` classes are used to represent basic human physiology, with the hasOrgan property associating the organ system with its primary organ. The `Clinical_Feature` class provides a template for describing physiological states such as *low MAP* and *high temperature*. The `Physiological_Effect` class represents different types of effects that occur in the human body; two types of effects have been defined: parameter changes and symptoms.

4.2 Reasoning about Anomalies

Section 3 suggests an anomaly can be defined as a *treatment* and an anomalous *effect* and can be considered to take the form:

For an anomaly at Time (T) → Treatment $(TR)_{T-1}$, AND Anomalous Effect $(E)_T$

For example the anomalous statement shown in Figure 1 can be expanded to include relevant patient data as:

T = 12:00:00 Day 32 of Patient 583, TR = Noradrenaline, E = Increase Cardiac Output.

An anomaly is entered into EIRA in the format shown above (this is referred to as the 'original anomaly' in the rest of this document). EIRA then proceeds to determine if there are any other anomalous responses to treatment in addition to the original anomaly at this particular timepoint and then provides hypotheses for this set of anomalies.

4.2.1 Detecting Additional Anomalies

Anomalies, in addition to the anomaly identified by a clinician, can occur in a patient's dataset. EIRA can detect further anomalies at the anomaly time point(T). For example, in addition to the previous anomaly, the system may also detect that after administering noradrenaline, the patient's mean arterial pressure (MAP) reading is low. As discussed previously, an anomaly can be considered as a counterexample to domain knowledge. In this particular domain, this can be considered as:

Domain knowledge contains when *drug(D)* administered at T, *expected effect(E)* observed at *Time (T + 1)* AND patient data contains D at T AND *observed effect*, ¬ E at T + 1.

Additionally, when attempting to detect anomalies, EIRA identifies the drugs given to the patient at the anomaly time point[5] from the patient's data and retrieves the anticipated effects of administering each drug from the ICU ontology. When the anticipated response(s) have not occurred, the actual response observed in the data is noted. For example, the drug noradrenaline has been given to the patient at 12.00; further it is specified in the ICU ontology that noradrenaline is expected to increase systolic pressure, diastolic pressure, systemic vascular resistance (SVR) and MAP. These can be compared with the patient's readings and any discrepancies (for example, an observed decrease in MAP) are reported as additional anomalies.

4.2.2 Explaining Anomalous Responses to Treatment

To generate hypotheses for given anomalies, EIRA captures the various strategies (algorithms) and domain knowledge used by the two observed expert ICU clinicians and produce the types of hypotheses the clinicians proposed.

As identified in Section 3 the clinicians' hypothesis generation process focused on either providing an explanation for why the *treatment* in question did not work as anticipated, or concentrated on the reasons why the anomalous physiological *effect* might have occurred in the patient.

Although this system is implemented in the ICU domain, the algorithms listed below are believed to be generic and could be applied in other (medical) domains. Due to page limitations, we are unable to discuss each algorithm in detail, however, an example of the `Drug_ Interaction` algorithm is provided in Algorithm 1. The following is the `Drug_Interaction` algorithm expressed as a SWRL[6] rule to show how the concepts from the ontology are used:

$$Drug(?treatment) \land drugInteractions(?treatment, ?interaction) \land Drug\_Interaction(?interaction) \land$$
$$interactsWith(?interaction, ?otherDrug) \land Timepoint(?t) \land hasTime(?t, ?time) \land$$
$$hasReadings(?t, ?r) \land Reading(?r) \land readingParameter(?r, ?treatment)$$
$$\Rightarrow DrugInteractionHypothesis(?hyp) \land hasDrug(?hyp, ?treatment) \land$$
$$hasInteractingDrug(?hyp, otherDrug)$$

The algorithms are not dependent on each other, and all are executed in order to generate all possible hypotheses. Below we summarise the implemented algorithms:

1. `Conditional Drug Effects` - Under some known conditions a drug may have a different physiological effect on the patient than anticipated. For example, under high doses, noradrenaline may increase a patient's cardiac output, whereas at normal or low doses this would not be expected.
2. `Other Medical Conditions` - This method identifies whether the patient is suffering from another medical condition which has a symptom the same as the observed anomalous effect.

---

[5] Although the example given here concerns the anomaly time point, any time point in the data can be used to detect an additional anomaly

[6] http://www.w3.org/Submission/SWRL/

Algorithm 1 IdentifyDrugInteractions

1: **Response** - The anomalous response
2: **Treatment** - The anomalous treatment
3: **Time** - Time (T) in the patient's dataset at which the anomaly occurred
4: **InteractingDrugs** - Potential interacting drugs

5: Begin IdentifyDrugInteractions
6: Identify known drug interactions (DI) for *Treatment*
7: **for** Each DI **do**
8:    Identify the other drug (D_{int}) involved
9:    Determine if the patient was being given D_{int} at T
10:    **if** D_{int} was given at T **then**
11:      Add D_{int} to *InteractingDrugs*
12: **for** Each D_{int} in *InteractingDrugs* **do**
13:    **return** Hypothesis - Drug, D_{int}, may be interacting with *Treatment*

---

3. Other Medical Condition - Treatment - Identifies whether a treatment given to the patient for another medical condition is not working as anticipated and hence is responsible for the anomalous effect.
4. Drugs - Identifies whether another drug that the patient is receiving at the anomaly time could have the same effect (side effect or therapeutic effect) as the anomalous effect (and hence this further drug explains the observed anomaly).
5. Patient Improvement - An improvement in the patient may be the cause of the anomalous effect. This can be split into the following areas of improvement[7]:

   a. Overall Patient Improvement - Identifies whether the anomalous effect may be explained by a patient's *overall* clinical condition improving. For example, in the ICU a severity score is often associated with a patient's overall condition. This score can be calculated from the patient's physiological data. If the severity score has shown an improvement at the anomaly time point, then it can be concluded that generally the patient is improving.

   b. Improving Organ - Establishes whether one of the patient's organs could be spontaneously improving/recovering and hence could explain what otherwise would appear as an anomalous effect. For example, noradrenaline does not usually increase a patient's cardiac output, however, cardiac output is a measurement reflecting the condition of a patient's heart; if the majority of the other measurements of a patient's heart (e.g. heart rate) are also improving, it is possible that an improvement in a patient's cardiac performance may explain the anomalous effect (and not the noradrenaline).

   c. Specific Condition Improvement - Ascertains if a patient could be recovering from a *specific* previous clinical event and the anomalous effect can be explained as a consequence of this improvement. For example, an observed increase in cardiac output seen when noradrenaline is administered could be

---

[7] Improving Organ and Specific Condition Improvement can be considered as conceptually similar, however, they require distinct implementations and hence have been listed separately.

attributed to the patient recovering from sepsis. Unlike Improving Organ we cannot say that the heart has improved, only that one of the measurements of the heart has improved.

Complementary to the above analyses the following algorithms have been implemented to suggest hypotheses which may explain why the treatment has not worked as anticipated.

6. Conditions Affecting Treatment - Identifies whether the patient has a co-existing medical condition which can affect how well the treatment associated with the anomaly is working. For example, if a patient is an alcoholic, they can have a high cellular tolerance for the drug propofol i.e. they require a higher amount of the drug for an effect to be seen than with a non-alcoholic patient.
7. Drug Interactions - Establishes if the treatment associated with the anomalous effect has not worked as expected because of an interaction occurring with another treatment the patient is receiving. The secondary treatment may in some cases increase, decrease, or negate the expected effect of the primary treatment.
8. Low Dose of Treatment - Too low a dose of a drug may have been given to the patient and hence the intended effects have not been observed. This algorithm determines whether the dose of the drug associated with the anomalous effect is a 'low dose' (a low dose is taken to be the lower quartile (25%) of a drug's specified dose range).
9. Overall Condition Deterioration - Establishes if the patient's *overall* condition has deteriorated. If the patient's condition has deteriorated, the patient, in general, would require a higher dose of a drug for its intended effect to be observed. In some instances a patient can become too ill to respond to treatment. The overall condition of the patient is based on a severity score calculated from the patient's physiological data. If the severity score has worsened at the anomaly time point then it is inferred that the patient's overall condition has worsened.
10. Resistance to Treatment - Identifies if the patient could have become resistant to the treatment. When certain drugs are administered over a long period of time and/or at a high dose, a patient can become resistant to them and hence the drug has very little or no effect on the patient.

For each individual anomaly (from the set consisting of the original anomaly and any additionally identified anomalies), EIRA systematically works through each of the algorithms. At the end of the process the hypotheses for each anomaly are presented to the clinician. Figure 5 shows a segment of a sample output from EIRA. The numbers next to a hypothesis correspond to the numbered strategies above.

4.3 Evaluation

To evaluate the effectiveness of the hypothesis generation mechanisms, test cases were extracted from the interviews held with ICU clinicians. The test cases were

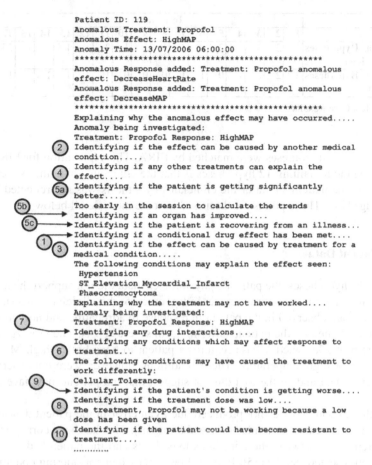

```
Patient ID: 119
Anomalous Treatment: Propofol
Anomalous Effect: HighMAP
Anomaly Time: 13/07/2006 06:00:00
**************************************************
Anomalous Response added: Treatment: Propofol anomalous
effect: DecreaseHeartRate
Anomalous Response added: Treatment: Propofol anomalous
effect: DecreaseMAP
**************************************************
Explaining why the anomalous effect may have occurred.....
Anomaly being investigated:
Treatment: Propofol Response: HighMAP
Identifying if the effect can be caused by another medical
condition.....
Identifying if any other treatments can explain the
effect....
Identifying if the patient is getting significantly
better.....
Too early in the session to calculate the trends
Identifying if an organ has improved....
Identifying if the patient is recovering from an illness...
Identifying if a conditional drug effect has been met....
Identifying if the effect can be caused by treatment for a
medical condition.....
The following conditions may explain the effect seen:
  Hypertension
  ST_Elevation_Myocardial_Infarct
  Phaeocromocytoma
Explaining why the treatment may not have worked....
Anomaly being investigated:
Treatment: Propofol Response: HighMAP
Identifying any drug interactions....
Identifying any conditions which may affect response to
treatment...
The following conditions may have caused the treatment to
work differently:
  Cellular_Tolerance
Identifying if the patient's condition is getting worse....
Identifying if the treatment dose was low....
The treatment, Propofol may not be working because a low
dose has been given
Identifying if the patient could have become resistant to
treatment....
.............
```

Fig. 5 Example Output

formed from the anomalies identified from the first group of interviews and the subsequent hypotheses provided by the clinicians in the second group of interviews (as detailed in section 3). In total, 15 test cases were selected with 25 hypotheses (in some test cases clinicians suggested multiple hypotheses). Each test case comprised: the time and date of the identified anomaly, details of the anomalous effect observed, the associated treatment, the hypotheses given by a clinician to explain this anomaly, and the patient's data for their complete stay (containing physiological readings e.g. Heart Rate and information about the drugs administered). During testing, each test case anomaly was entered into EIRA and we recorded whether the tool generated the same hypotheses as the ICU clinicians. A note was also made of whether the system detected the same additional anomalies that the ICU clinician had identified. Table 1 shows the comparison between the hypotheses suggest by the clinicians and by EIRA for the same anomaly.

	Test Cases															
	1	2	3	4	5	6	7	8	9	10	11	12	13	14	15	Total
No. of Hypotheses (Interview)	4	2	3	1	2	2	1	1	1	1	2	1	1	2	1	25
No. of Hypotheses (EIRA)	2	2	2	1	0	1	1	0	0	0	1	1	1	1	0	13

Table 1 Test Case Results

A total of 13 hypotheses were matched by EIRA. The explanation for EIRA not identifying the remaining 12 hypotheses is that the clinician's hypothesis were not captured in the patient's data or the clinician's hypothesis was not reflected in the knowledge base. These points are discussed in some more detail below:

4.3.1 Patient Data

For 8 of the hypotheses, the patient's physiological data did not support the hypothesis given by a clinician. For example, in test case 15, the clinician suggested that a low heart rate observed in the patient in response to adrenaline and noradrenaline could be explained by the patient suffering from severe sepsis. The *"severe sepsis"* condition in the knowledge base requires a patient to have both a high MAP and either a low or high temperature. These conditions, however, were *not* observed in the patient's data and so the tool did not suggest that the patient may have severe sepsis.

Another hypothesis was not produced due to an error in the patient dataset (noradrenaline was recorded in mls/hr instead of mg/hr). This has been corrected.

Discrepancies between the clinician's hypothesis and the patient's data are not entirely unexpected. Studies [5][9] have shown that when considering potential explanations for an anomaly the expert's domain knowledge can influence hypothesis testing when dealing with inconsistent evidence. Chinn & Brewer[5] found that when the subject's background knowledge was not consistent with the evidence (in this case the patient's data), subjects largely discount the data. It is possible that this phenomena is being observed in some of the situations here. Further, the expert may also be reporting patient states which are *partially* supported by the data.

4.3.2 Knowledge Base Content

For 3 hypotheses, the knowledge base did not have the required facts to create the same hypothesis as the clinician. For example, in test case 3, in response to noradrenaline given, the patient's systemic vascular resistance (SVR) decreased. The clinician suggested that sepsis may be responsible for the decrease in SVR. EIRA did not suggest sepsis because the knowledge base did not have a *decrease in SVR* identified as a symptom, however, it did contain a *low SVR* as a symptom of sepsis. It is suggested that in these cases, the knowledge base does not accurately reflect the clinicians' domain knowledge and clearly refinement of the knowledge base is required. This facility is suggested as an extension to EIRA in section 5.

Of the additional anomalies identified by the clinicians, 2 of the 3 were also identified by EIRA. The one case where the anomaly was not identified can be considered as a partial match; the clinician identified a *low* heart rate in response to the drug, propofol, as being anomalous whilst EIRA identified a *decrease* in heart rate as anomalous in response to propofol. EIRA did not use the term 'low heart rate' because the knowledge base only contained for that drug an 'increase in heart rate' as an expected effect relating to the patient's heart rate when administering propofol. If the knowledge base had also had a 'high heart rate' as an expected effect, EIRA would have identified the same anomaly as the clinician.

EIRA also produced a number of 'new' hypotheses for each test case (in addition to the hypotheses suggested by the clinician). These 'new' hypotheses haven't been evaluated but a planned future evaluation will involve an ICU clinician evaluating the 'new' hypotheses produced by EIRA for their clinical relevancy. In summary, the initial evaluation of EIRA is encouraging; in the majority of cases EIRA can adequately reproduce the precise hypotheses suggested by expert ICU clinicians.

5 Conclusions and Future Work

This paper outlines several interviews held with ICU clinicians to identify and provide hypotheses to explain anomalous patient responses to treatment. Further, a tool based on the processes captured from these interviews has been developed; additionally an evaluation of the system has produced promising results. Generally the hypotheses suggested by the clinicians are reproduced by the system; further the reasons why the remaining hypotheses were not reproduced have been adequately explained and will be addressed subsequently. Plans for future work include:

- **Further Evaluation** - The additional hypotheses produced by EIRA require evaluation by a domain expert for their clinical relevancy, further, upon completion of planned future stages of development, EIRA will be tested on a larger number of test cases.
- **Knowledge Base Refinement** - It would be beneficial to allow a clinician using EIRA to refine the domain ontologies. To enable this refinement, it is proposed that when a hypothesis is presented to the clinician, the clinician will be able to reject the hypothesis and provide a reason for its rejection. The relevant instances of the ontology will then be updated to reflect this 'feedback' from the clinician.
- **Inferring Information from the Knowledge Base** - As shown in the evaluation of the system, occasionally the domain knowledge has 'gaps' in it, which in some cases have prevented hypotheses from being suggested by the system. It would be useful to extend EIRA to make assumptions based on other instances in the ontology. For example, if property P has been observed for D_1 of drug class D then it is reasonable to infer that all sibling drugs of D_1 also have property P.

Acknowledgements Kathryn Henderson and Jennifer McCallum (CareVue Project) & the staff and patients of the ICU Unit, Glasgow Royal Infirmary. This work was an extension of the routine audit process in Glasgow Royal Infirmary's ICU; requirements for further Ethical Committee Approval have been waved. This work was supported under the EPSRC's grant number GR/N15764.

References

1. MIMIC II Project, Accessed August 2009. http://mimic.mit.edu/index.html.
2. Unified Medical Language System (UMLS), Accessed August 2009. http://www.nlm.nih.gov/pubs/factsheets/umls.html.
3. Blum, R L. Discovery, Confirmation, and Incorporation of Causal Relationships From a Large Time-Oriented Clinical Data Base: The RX Project. *COMP. AND BIOMED. RES.*, 15:164–187, 1982.
4. Bruce G. Buchanan and Edward A.Feigenbaum. Dendral and Meta-Dendral: Their Applications Dimension. *Artificial Intelligence*, 11:5–24, 1978.
5. Clark. A. Chinn, William F. Brewer. Factors that Influence How People Respond to Anomalies. In *Proc. of the Fifteenth Annual Conference of the Cognitive Science Society*, 1993.
6. D Kuhn. *The structure of scientific revolutions*. University of Chicago Press, 1962.
7. Jaap van den Heuvel, J. D. B. Stemerdink, Ad J. J. C. Bogers and David S. Bree. GUUS an expert system in the intensive care unit. *International Journal of Clinical Monitoring and Computing*, 7:171–175, 1990.
8. Juliet Corbin, Anselm Strauss. Grounded Theory Research: Procedures, Canons and Evaluative Criteria. *Qualitative Sociology*, 13:3–21.
9. K. Dunbar. Concept Discovery in a Scientific Domain. *Cognitive Science*, 17:397–434, 1993.
10. K.Anders Ericsson and Herbert A. Simon. *Protocol analysis: verbal reports as data.* MIT Press, 1993.
11. Kent A. Spackman, Keith E.Campbell. SNOMED RT:A Reference Terminology for Health Care.
12. L Darden. Strategies for Anomaly Resolution. *Cognitive Models of Science, Minnesota Studies in the Philosophy of Science*, :, 1992.
13. Laura Moss, Derek Sleeman, Malcolm Booth, Malcolm Daniel, Lyndsay Donaldson, Charlotte Gilhooly, Martin Hughes, Malcolm Sim and John Kinsella. Explaining Anomalous Responses to Treatment in the Intensive Care Unit. In *Proceedings of the 12th Conference on Artificial Intelligence in Medicine, AIME09*, 2009.
14. Michael G. Walker and Gio Wiederhold. Acquisition and Validation of Knowledge from Data. *Intelligent Systems*, :415–428, 1990.
15. N.F de Keizer, A.Abu-Hanna, R.Cornet, J.H.M. Zwetsloot-Schonk, C.P.Stoutenbeek. Analysis and Design of an Ontology for Intensive Care Diagnoses. *Methods of Information in Medicine*, 38:102–112, 1999.
16. Paul Thagard. *Conceptual Revolutions*. Princeton University Press, 1992.
17. P.Langley, G.L. Bradshaw, and H.A Simon. Rediscovering Chemistry With the Bacon System. *Machine Learning*, pages 307–329, 1983.
18. Silvia Miksch, Werner Horn, Chrisitan Popow, Franz Paky. VIE-VENT: knowledge-based monitoring and therapy planning of the artificial ventilation of newborn infants. *Artificial Intelligence in Medicine*, 10:218–229, 1993.
19. Vimla L. Patel, Jiajie Zhang, Nicole A. Yoskowitz, Robert Green, Osman R.Sayan. Translational cognition for decision support in critical care environments: A review. *Journal of Biomedical Informatics*, 41:413–431, 2008.
20. Yuval Shahar and Mark A. Musen. Knowledge-Based Temporal Abstraction in Clinical Domains. *Artificial Intelligence in Medicine*, 8:267–298, 1996.

REASONING

Dual Rationality and Deliberative Agents

John Debenham and Carles Sierra

Abstract Human agents deliberate using models based on reason for only a minute proportion of the decisions that they make. In stark contrast, the deliberation of artificial agents is heavily dominated by formal models based on reason such as game theory, decision theory and logic — despite that fact that formal reasoning will not necessarily lead to superior real-world decisions. Further the Nobel Laureate Friedrich Hayek warns us of the 'fatal conceit' in controlling deliberative systems using models based on reason as the particular model chosen will then shape the system's future and either impede, or eventually destroy, the subtle evolutionary processes that are an integral part of human systems and institutions, and are crucial to their evolution and long-term survival. We describe an architecture for artificial agents that is founded on Hayek's two rationalities and supports the two forms of deliberation used by mankind.

1 Introduction

This paper describes a form of agency that enables rational agents to move beyond the bounds of Cartesian rationalism. The work is founded on the two forms of rationality described by the two Nobel Laureates Friedrich Hayek [1] and Vernon Smith [2] as being within 'two worlds'. The work of Hayek and Smith is concerned with real systems and particularly with economic institutions. So the ideas here may not concern agents in closed systems such as computer games, but they do concern all real world agents and systems.

For computerised, intelligent agents the predominant logical distinction is between *deliberative* and *reactive* logic. Hayek and Smith's two rationalities relate

John Debenham
QCIS, FEIT, UTS, Sydney, Australia, e-mail: debenham@it.uts.edu.au and Carles Sierra
Institut d'Investigació en Intel·ligència Artificial - IIIA, Spanish Scientific Research Council, CSIC,08193 Bellaterra, Catalonia, Spain, e-mail: sierra@iiia.csic.es

M. Bramer et al. (eds.), *Research and Development in Intelligent Systems XXVI*,
DOI 10.1007/978-1-84882-983-1_6, © Springer-Verlag London Limited 2010

directly to two distinct forms of deliberation, and have little to do with autonomic reactivity that typically overrides other processes in both the human neuropsychological system and in intelligent agents.

Hayek and Smith identify; *constructivist rationality* that underpins rational predictive models of decision making; and, *ecological rationality* founded on the concept of "spontaneous order[1]" that refers to social institutions and practices that *emerge* from the history of an agent's interactions and are *not* pre-designed. For intelligent agency we interpret Hayek and Smith's two rationalities as:

- Constructivist. An agent's actions are determined by a theory that may be independent of the particular environment in which the agent is situated.
- Ecological. An agent's actions are the product of prior agents' actions only — this includes observations that an agent has made of its environment.

As the name suggests, ecological rationality is concerned with a richer form of bounded rationality than simplifying the calculation of a theoretically 'optimal' action by: rules for simplifying search, rules for terminating search or heuristic decision rules to select actions from an incomplete set of options. Ecological rationality is taken in the context of the Hayekian view [1] in which agents evolve themselves together with the norms of the systems they inhabit[2] whilst their environment changes. This all sounds rather Darwinian, but Hayek is careful to distinguish between genetic evolution and cultural evolution [op. cit. page 23].

Ecological rationality is deliberation that uses past experience and contextual triggers to build action sequences from experiential memory. Past experience is a precursor to ecological rationality. For example, as we have described them previously, trust and honour [4] and reputation [5], are purely ecological concepts. Building action sequences from experiential memory involves more than just retrieval. An agent has: to learn to imitate the actions that it believes that others do, to form expectations of the effect of actions, to select actions from a set of candidates, to adapt actions to suit the current norms and state of the environment, and when things don't work out to learn to experiment with untested actions.

Why would an agent be motivated to deliberate in a non-constructivist way? First, it may not be aware of a constructivist theory that addresses its goals[3]. Second, it may have difficulty articulating its needs and its context completely and accurately

---

[1] The term 'order' refers to: traditions, customs, norms, rules and guidelines. An agent may belong to a number of normative systems (or, electronic institutions [3]) whose norms may be shared with, or in conflict with, those of other systems. The 'extended order' includes the whole show. If a multiagent system interacts with human society then its norms will respect the rules and laws that apply to society as a whole.

[2] The evolution of individual agents and component systems are not considered in isolation — the whole ensemble evolves in response to itself and to the environment — they are *complex* systems. For example, in Hayek's extensive writing there is little mention of ethics as it too evolves.

[3] For example, the agent may desire to act so as to strengthen, or weaken, a relationship with a particular agent, perhaps to discharge or generate some social obligation, or it may desire to act so that it is seen to be behaving a particular way, perhaps by apparently behaving altruistically — there may not be a theory that satisfactorily balances these desires with more mundane desires concerning the effect of the actions that it can take.

Fig. 1 The agent framework.

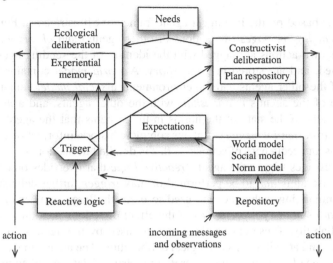

in the theory. Third, the data required by the theory to determine its actions may not be readily available. Fourth, it may not have sufficient time for all this to happen. Fifth, it may favour ecological deliberation simply because it leads to a superior outcome. For example, when selecting a bottle of wine, some human agents refer to books of ratings and prices and make a constructivist choice, whereas others rely on their merchant to make a choice for them — this choice is purely ecological, its 'rationality' is in the trust that has been built through repeated interaction.

This paper is related to the issue generally known as *bounded rationality* that dates back to David Hume and more recently to the early work of Herbert Simon. Bounded rationality refers to systems that are not founded on Cartesian rationalism; it has been widely addressed in economics [6], and is discussed in all good books on artificial intelligence, e.g. [7]. For over fifty years artificial intelligence research has spawned countless theories and systems that are *not* founded on Cartesian rationalism; one classic contribution being Rodney Brooks' work reported in his 'Computers and Thought' award-winning paper [8]. Despite these advances, work in multiagent systems has been heavily influenced by game theory, decision theory and logic [9]; this is in contrast to an original motivation for investigating 'distributed artificial intelligence' in the mid 1970s where intelligence *emerged* from the interactions between systems.

This paper is organised as follows. Various preliminaries are described in Section 2. Section 3 introduces the essential features of the agent architecture including the world model, and a 'social model' that is essential to ecological deliberation. Section 4 describes expectations of the effect of actions in the experiential memory— these expectations include measures of trust. Section 5 describes the ecological deliberative process, and Section 6 concludes.

2 Preliminaries

This work is based on the intelligent agent framework illustrated in Figure 1. An agent's *in-coming messages* (the actions of other agents) and *observations* of the effect of its own actions are tagged with the identity of the sending agent and the time received, and are stored in a *repository*. A *world model* contains beliefs of the state of the other agents and the environment, a *social model* contains beliefs of the state of the agent's *relationships* with the other agents, and a *norm model* contains beliefs of the state of the norms in the systems that the agent frequents. The agent's *experiential memory* contains complete historic information concerning prior actions and sequences of actions — this is detailed in Section 3.

Some messages trigger the agent's *reactive logic* that overrides other activities and may cause an *action* to be performed or may *trigger* further deliberative processes. Summarising techniques are used to distil the large number of incoming messages into summary *expectations* of the effect of actions including: trust, honour and reliability. These expectations may be used by the agent's constructivist deliberation, and are vital to its ecological deliberation. The agent aims to satisfy its *needs* using one of two forms of *deliberation*: *constructivist* (described in [10]) that is based on theories that call on *plans*, and *ecological* that uses past experience and contextual triggers to retrieve or build action sequences from experiential memory.

This paper draws from our work on information-based agency [11] that is well-suited to this purpose. It supports rich models of inter-agent relationships [12] that are a quintessential feature of emergent behaviour between agents, it supports rich models of trust, honour and reliability [4] that provide the rationale for ecologically rational behaviour, it includes a generate and test approach to planning [10], additionally it uses tools from information theory to manage uncertainty in a nice way. The main contribution of this paper is to describe a single agent that exhibits ecological deliberation, we show how it evolves as its experience grows.

We assume that a multiagent system $\{\alpha, \beta_1, \ldots, \beta_o, \xi, \theta_1, \ldots, \theta_t\}$, contains an agent α that interacts with negotiating agents, β_i, and information providing agents, θ_j. We assume that each dialogical interaction takes place within a particular institution that is represented by an *institutional agent*, ξ, [3]. Institutions, or normative systems, play a central role in this work. We will describe an *ontology* that will permit us both to structure the dialogues and to structure the processing of the information gathered by agents. Our agent α has two languages: $\mathcal{C}$ is an illocutionary-based language for communication, and $\mathcal{L}$ is a probabilistic first-order language for internal representation including the representation of its *world model* $\mathcal{M}^t$. $\mathcal{C}$ is described in [12].

We model ontologies following an algebraic approach [13]. An ontology is a tuple $\mathcal{O} = (C, R, \leq, \sigma)$ where:

1. C is a finite set of concept symbols (including basic data types);
2. R is a finite set of relation symbols;
3. $\leq$ is a reflexive, transitive and anti-symmetric relation on C (a partial order);
4. $\sigma : R \to C^+$ is the function assigning to each relation symbol its arity.

where $\leq$ is a traditional *is-a* hierarchy, and R contains relations between the concepts in the hierarchy.

The concepts within an ontology are closer, semantically speaking, depending on how far away are they in the structure defined by the $\leq$ relation. A measure [14] bases the *semantic similarity* between two concepts on the path length induced by $\leq$ (more distance in the $\leq$ graph means less semantic similarity), and the *depth* of the subsumer concept (common ancestor) in the shortest path between the two concepts (the deeper in the hierarchy, the closer the meaning of the concepts). Semantic similarity is then defined as:

$$\text{Sim}(c, c') = e^{-\kappa_1 l} \cdot \frac{e^{\kappa_2 h} - e^{-\kappa_2 h}}{e^{\kappa_2 h} + e^{-\kappa_2 h}}$$

where l is the length (i.e. number of hops) of the shortest path between the concepts, h is the depth of the deepest concept subsuming both concepts, and κ_1 and κ_2 are parameters scaling the contribution of shortest path length and depth respectively.

Given a formula $\varphi \in \mathscr{C}$ in the communication language we define the vocabulary or *ontological context* of the formula, $O(\varphi)$, as the set of concepts in the ontology used in it. Thus, we extend the previous definition of similarity to sets of concepts in the following way:

$$\text{Sim}(\varphi, \psi) = \max_{c_i \in O(\varphi)} \min_{c_j \in O(\psi)} \{\text{Sim}(c_i, c_j)\} \tag{1}$$

These definitions of semantic similarity are based only on the structure of the ontology, and are a first approximation to 'semantic distance' in a rich sense.

3 Agent Architecture

α acts by generating utterances, and observes by receiving them. α acts to satisfy a *need* that may be exogenous such as a need to trade profitably, triggered by another agent's actions, or endogenous such as α deciding that it owns more wine than it requires. Needs either trigger α's constructivist, goal/plan deliberative reasoning described in [10], or ecological deliberation described in Section 5.

Agent α receives all messages expressed in $\mathscr{C}$, they are time-stamped and sourced-stamped, qualified with a subjective belief function $\mathbb{R}^t(\alpha, \beta, \mu)$ that normally decays with time (see below), and are stored in a *repository* $\mathscr{Y}^t$ that contains information concerning every[4] action that α observes — presumably this will include all of those actions that α takes.

α's *experiential memory* contains a history of what happened when any goal-directed sequence of actions was triggered or when any individual action was observed. First an individual *action experience*, a, consists of:

---

[4] Practicality is not a concern here.

- the action, a_{act}, i.e. the utterance, the sending and receiving agents, and the time at which the action was taken,
- the trigger, or precondition, that signalled when the action was to be performed, a_{trig},
- any observed effect(s), a_{effect}[5], i.e. any identifiable responses that are an effect of a_{act} — see Section 4.

Then a *sequence experience*, s, consists of:

- the *goal* of the sequence, s_{goal}, that may have been to satisfy a need,
- a sequence of action experiences, $s_a = (a_i)_{i=1}^n$, where each action experience a_i is described as above,
- beliefs of the prevailing *environment*, s_{env}, that includes: the state of the agent's *norm model* (see Section 3.3), s_{norm}, the agents involved in the interaction, s_{agents}, and the state of the agent's *social model* (see Section 3.2) between the agents, s_{social}, i.e. $s_{env} = \{s_{norm}, s_{agents}, s_{social}\}$,
- a *rating*[6] of the outcome of the action sequence, s_{rate}, that enables an ecologically rational agent to develop its repertoire of actions.

α uses the contents of its experiential memory to: reuse successful action sequences, build new sequences from individual actions, and improve prior sequences by using its knowledge of individual action experiences.

The integrity of beliefs derived from observations decreases in time. α may have background knowledge concerning the expected integrity of a belief as $t \to \infty$. Such background knowledge is represented as a *decay limit distribution*. If the background knowledge is incomplete then one possibility is for α to assume that the decay limit distribution has maximum entropy whilst being consistent with the data. Given an uncertain belief represented as the distribution, $\mathbb{P}(X_i)$, and a decay limit distribution $\mathbb{D}(X_i)$, $\mathbb{P}(X_i)$ decays by:

$$\mathbb{P}^{t+1}(X_i) = \Delta_i(\mathbb{D}(X_i), \mathbb{P}^t(X_i)) \tag{2}$$

where Δ_i is the *decay function* for the X_i satisfying the property that $\lim_{t \to \infty} \mathbb{P}^t(X_i) = \mathbb{D}(X_i)$. For example, Δ_i could be linear: $\mathbb{P}^{t+1}(X_i) = (1 - \nu_i) \times \mathbb{D}(X_i) + \nu_i \times \mathbb{P}^t(X_i)$, where $\nu_i < 1$ is the decay rate for the i'th distribution. Either the decay function or the decay limit distribution could also be a function of time: Δ_i^t and $\mathbb{D}^t(X_i)$.

---

[5] These may be difficult to identify precisely, but recording effects is considerably more economical than recording posterior world states.

[6] This rating is not simply in terms of the extent to which the sequence outcome met the original need, but in a sense that includes the possibility that the other agents involved may have adapted their actions to take account of changes in circumstance that occur during the sequence itself, or even that they went "over the odds" and gave more than was expected of them in some sense. These ratings are on a fuzzy scale from -5 to $+5$ where 0 means "is perfectly acceptable", -5 means "ghastly, completely unacceptable" and $+5$ means "better than I could have dreamed of". Ratings are not a 'utility function' in any sense — they are a subjective, *ex post* assessment of outcomes that is totally dependent on the prevailing state of the environment.

3.1 World Model

In the absence of in-coming messages the integrity of $\mathcal{M}^t$ decays by Equation 2. The following procedure updates $\mathcal{M}^t$ for all utterances expressed in $\mathcal{C}$. Suppose that α receives a message μ from agent β at time t. Suppose that this message states that something is so with probability z, and suppose that α attaches an epistemic belief $\mathbb{R}^t(\alpha, \beta, \mu)$ to μ — this probability reflects α's level of personal *caution*. Each of α's active plans, s, contains constructors for a set of distributions $\{X_i\} \in \mathcal{M}^t$ together with associated *update functions*, $J_s(\cdot)$, such that $J_s^{X_i}(\mu)$ is a set of linear constraints on the posterior distribution for X_i. Examples of these update functions are given in Section 4.1. Denote the prior distribution $\mathbb{P}^t(X_i)$ by $\mathbf{p}$, and let $\mathbf{p}_{(\mu)}$ be the distribution with minimum relative entropy[7] with respect to $\mathbf{p}$: $\mathbf{p}_{(\mu)} = \arg\min_{\mathbf{r}} \sum_j r_j \log \frac{r_j}{p_j}$ that satisfies the constraints $J_s^{X_i}(\mu)$. Then let $\mathbf{q}_{(\mu)}$ be the distribution:

$$\mathbf{q}_{(\mu)} = \mathbb{R}^t(\alpha, \beta, \mu) \times \mathbf{p}_{(\mu)} + (1 - \mathbb{R}^t(\alpha, \beta, \mu)) \times \mathbf{p} \qquad (3)$$

and then let:

$$\mathbb{P}^t(X_{i(\mu)}) = \begin{cases} \mathbf{q}_{(\mu)} & \mathbf{q}_{(\mu)} \text{ is more interesting than } \mathbf{p} \\ \mathbf{p} & \text{otherwise} \end{cases} \qquad (4)$$

A general measure of whether $\mathbf{q}_{(\mu)}$ is 'more interesting than' $\mathbf{p}$ is: $\mathbb{K}(\mathbf{q}_{(\mu)} \| \mathbb{D}(X_i)) > \mathbb{K}(\mathbf{p} \| \mathbb{D}(X_i))$, where $\mathbb{K}(\mathbf{x} \| \mathbf{y}) = \sum_j x_j \ln \frac{x_j}{y_j}$ is the Kullback-Leibler distance between two probability distributions $\mathbf{x}$ and $\mathbf{y}$. Finally merging Equations 4 and 2 we obtain the method for updating a distribution X_i on receipt of a message μ:

$$\mathbb{P}^{t+1}(X_i) = \Delta_i(\mathbb{D}(X_i), \mathbb{P}^t(X_{i(\mu)})) \qquad (5)$$

This procedure deals with integrity decay, and with two probabilities: first, any probability z in the message μ, and second the belief $\mathbb{R}^t(\alpha, \beta, \mu)$ that α attached to μ.

$\mathbb{R}^t(\alpha, \beta, \mu)$ is estimated by measuring the 'difference' between μ and its subsequent verification. Suppose that μ is received from agent β at time u and is verified by ξ as μ' at some later time t. Denote the prior $\mathbb{P}^u(X_i)$ by $\mathbf{p}$. Let $\mathbf{p}_{(\mu)}$ be the posterior minimum relative entropy distribution subject to the constraints $J_s^{X_i}(\mu)$, and let $\mathbf{p}_{(\mu')}$ be that distribution subject to $J_s^{X_i}(\mu')$. We now estimate what $\mathbb{R}^u(\alpha, \beta, \mu)$ should have been in the light of knowing *now*, at time t, that μ should have been μ'.

The idea of Equation 3, is that $\mathbb{R}^t(\alpha, \beta, \mu)$ should be such that, *on average* across $\mathcal{M}^t$, $\mathbf{q}_{(\mu)}$ will predict $\mathbf{p}_{(\mu')}$. The *observed reliability* for μ and distribution X_i, $\mathbb{R}^t_{X_i}(\alpha, \beta, \mu) | \mu'$, is the value of k that:

$$\mathbb{R}^t_{X_i}(\alpha, \beta, \mu) | \mu' = \arg\min_k \mathbb{K}(k \cdot \mathbf{p}_{(\mu)} + (1 - k) \cdot \mathbf{p} \| \mathbf{p}_{(\mu')})$$

---

[7] Entropy-based inference is a form of Bayesian inference that is convenient when the data is sparse [15] and encapsulates common-sense reasoning [16].

3.2 Social Model

The *social model* contains beliefs of the state of α's relationships with other agents — it consists of two components. First, an *intimacy model* that for each agent β consists of α's model of β's private information, *and*, α's model of the private information that β has about α. Second, a *balance model* of the extent of reciprocity between pairs of agents. Private information is categorised first by the type of statement, using a set of illocutionary particles $\mathcal{F}$, and second by the contents of the statement, using the ontology $\mathcal{O}$. A categorising function $\kappa : U \to \mathcal{P}(\mathcal{F})$, where U is the set of utterances, allocates utterances to one or more illocutionary particle category.

$I^t_{\alpha/\beta}$ is α's model of β's private information; it is represented as real numeric values over $\mathcal{F} \times \mathcal{O}$. Suppose α receives utterance u from β and that category $f \in \kappa(u)$ then: $I^t_{\alpha/\beta(f,c)} = I^{t-1}_{\alpha/\beta(f,c)} + \lambda \times \mathbb{I}(u) \times \mathrm{Sim}(u,c)$ for any $c \in \mathcal{O}$, where λ is the learning rate, $I^t_{\alpha/\beta(f,c)}$ is the intimacy value in the (f,c) position in $\mathcal{F} \times \mathcal{O}$, $\mathbb{I}(u)$ is the Shannon information gain in $\mathcal{M}^t$ due to receiving u using Equation 5, and Sim is as in Equation 1. Additionally, the intimacy model decays in time in any case by $I^t_{\alpha/\beta} = \delta \times I^{t-1}_{\alpha/\beta}$ where $\delta < 1$ and very close to 1 is the decay rate.

$I^t_{\alpha\backslash\beta}$ is α's model of the private information that β has about α. Assuming that confidential information is treated in confidence α will know what β knows about α. This means that the same method can be used to model $I^t_{\alpha\backslash\beta}$ as $I^t_{\alpha/\beta}$ with the exception of estimating $\mathbb{I}(u)$ as it is most unlikely that α will know the precise state of β's world model — for this we resort to the assumption that β's world model mirrors α's and 'estimate' the information gain. Then the *intimacy model* is $I^t_{\alpha\beta} = (I^t_{\alpha/\beta}, I^t_{\alpha\backslash\beta})$. In [12] balance was defined as the element by element numeric difference of $I^t_{\alpha/\beta}$ and $I^t_{\alpha\backslash\beta}$. That definition is not suitable here.

$R^t_{\alpha/\beta}$ is a model of α's aggregated rating of β's actions in assisting α to achieve her goals and satisfy her needs. α will have a variety of goals that are categorised using a set of illocutionary particles $\mathcal{G}$ and the ontology $\mathcal{O}$. Suppose α triggers an action sequence s with goal $g = (k,d)$ when the state of the environment is e and on completion of the sequence rates the outcome as $\rho(\alpha, s, e)$ then:

$$R^t_{\alpha/\beta(k,c)} = R^{t-1}_{\alpha/\beta(k,c)} + \lambda \times \rho(\alpha, s, e) \times \mathrm{Sim}(d,c)$$

for any $c \in \mathcal{O}$, where $\rho(\alpha, s, e)$ is the fuzzy rating of the outcome of s as an integer in the range $[-5, +5]$, λ is the learning rate, $R^t_{\alpha/\beta(k,c)}$ is the aggregated rating in the (k,c) position in $\mathcal{G} \times \mathcal{O}$, and Sim is as in Equation 1. The model decays[8] in time in any case by $R^t_{\alpha/\beta} = \delta \times R^{t-1}_{\alpha/\beta}$ where $\delta < 1$ and very close to 1 is the decay rate. The *balance model* is the pair $R^t_{\alpha\beta} = (R^t_{\alpha/\beta}, R^t_{\alpha\backslash\beta})$.

---

[8] This form of decay means that in the limit all values in the model decay to 0 meaning "is perfectly acceptable". This may appear to be odd, but the model is used only to gauge divergence from the norm; it is *not* used to select a trading partner — that is a job for the trust model.

3.3 Norm Model

In Electronic Institutions [3], *norms* constrain the dialogues between agents particularly constraints that help to warrant the commitments between agents. [17] reviews various proposals for formalising norms including: conditional deontic logic, Z specification of norms, event calculus, hybrid metric interval temporal logic, social integrity constraints, and object constraint language. The formalism used is to some degree unimportant, and we do not favour any particular formalism in this paper. Our interest here is simply that each agent knows and models those norms that constrain its dialogical freedom, and more important any desire to negotiate with the other agents to modify those norms in some way.

4 Expectations

An ecologically rational agent's rationality lies only in its past experience. To behave rationally it will require some expectation, based on that experience, of what other agents will do. Experiential memory records each of the agent's individual experiences; it does not address expectation. We now derive expectations from this historic data. Expectations are considered for the two classes of experience in experiential memory. First, expectations concerning the effect of making a single action (i.e. utterance), second, expectations of the effect of triggering an action sequence.

4.1 Expected effect of a single action

We consider expectations concerning the effect of making a single action; that is, the expected a_{effect} given a_{act}. To make this problem tractable we consider only utterances for which a particular *form* of response is expected. For example, "what is the time?" or "send me a bottle of Protos[9]". For these utterances α utters u and expects to observe utterances, v, from a particular set of agents, Ω, and of a form from the set F. α's expectations are that:

$$\forall u \in U \cdot \text{Enact}^t_\alpha(u) \to \forall \beta \in \Omega \cdot \exists v \in U \cdot \exists w \in F$$
$$(\text{Observe}^{t_\beta}_\alpha(\text{Enact}_\beta(v)) \wedge \text{In}(v,w) \wedge \text{Form}(u,\beta,w))$$

(6)

where $\text{Form}(u,\beta,w)$ means that w is a form of response that α expects having uttered u, $\text{In}(v,w)$ means that v is an instantiation of w, and $t_\beta > t$. For example, u could be "what is the price of Protos", w could be "the price of Protos is x", and v could be "the price of Protos is €40".

---

[9] A fine wine from the 'Ribera del Duero' region, Spain.

For each agent $\beta \in \Omega$ we abbreviate the expectation of Equation 6 to $\mathbb{P}_{\beta}^{t}(v|u)$. In the absence of in-coming messages the conditional probabilities, $\mathbb{P}_{\beta}^{t}(v|u)$, should tend to ignorance as represented by the *decay limit distribution* and Equation 2. We now show how Equation 5 may be used to revise $\mathbb{P}^{t}(v|u)$ as observations are made. Let the set of possible utterances be $\Phi = \{v_1, v_2, \ldots, v_m\}$ with prior distribution $\mathbf{p} = \mathbb{P}_{\beta}^{t}(v|u)$. Suppose that message w is received, we estimate the posterior $\mathbf{p}_{(w)} = (p_{(w)i})_{i=1}^{m} = \mathbb{P}^{t+1}(v|u)$.

First, given the expectation $\mathbb{P}_{\beta}^{t}(v|u)$, if α observes that β utters v_k then α may use this observation to estimate $p_{(v_k)k}$ as some value d at time $t+1$. We estimate the distribution $\mathbf{p}_{(v_k)}$ by applying the principle of minimum relative entropy as in Equation 5 with prior $\mathbf{p}$, and the posterior $\mathbf{p}_{(v_k)} = (p_{(v_k)j})_{j=1}^{m}$ satisfying the single constraint: $J^{(v|u)}(v_k) = \{p_{(v_k)k} = d\}$.

Second, α may use the above observation to revise $\mathbb{P}_{\beta}^{t}(v'|u')$ when u and u' are semantically close in the sense of Equation 1. For example, u could be "please send me a chicken on Tuesday" and u' could be "please send me a duck on Thursday". Following the notation above this is achieved by: $J^{(v'|u')}(v_k) = \{p_{(v_k)k} = d \times g(\text{Sim}(u, u'))\}$ *provided that:* $d \times g(\text{Sim}(u, u')) > p_k$, where g is a function that moderates the values of the Sim function, and p_k is the prior value. Equation 4 will ensure that this update process only applies when $d \times g(\text{Sim}(u, u'))$ is sufficiently large to deliver positive information gain to $\mathbb{P}_{\beta}^{t+1}(v'|u')$.

The entropy $\mathbb{H}_{\beta}^{t}(v|u)$ estimates α's uncertainty in β's response given that α has uttered u. α may interact with more than one agent. Suppose that agent γ is an ideal agent who always responds impeccably then β's trust, honour or reliability is:

$$T_{\alpha}(\beta, \gamma, u) = 1 - \sum_{v} \mathbb{P}_{\gamma}^{t}(v|u) \log \frac{\mathbb{P}_{\gamma}^{t}(v|u)}{\mathbb{P}_{\beta}^{t}(v|u)}$$

measures the relative entropy between this ideal distribution, $\mathbb{P}_{\gamma}^{t}(v|u)$, and the distribution of β's expected actions, $\mathbb{P}_{\beta}^{t}(v|u)$, where the "1" is an arbitrarily chosen constant being the maximum value that this measure may have. This estimate is with respect to a single u. It makes sense to aggregate these values over a class of utterances, say over those u that are in the ontological context o, that is $u \leq o$:

$$T_{\alpha}(\beta, \gamma, o) = 1 - \frac{\sum_{u:u \leq o} \mathbb{P}_{\alpha}^{t}(u)\left[1 - M_{\alpha}(\beta, \gamma, u)\right]}{\sum_{u:u \leq o} \mathbb{P}_{\beta}^{t}(u)}$$

where $\mathbb{P}_{\alpha}^{t}(u)$ is a probability distribution over the space of utterances that α's next utterance to β is u.

4.2 Expected rating of an action sequence

We consider expectations concerning the effect of triggering an action sequence. Suppose that α triggers an action sequence, s with goal g where the state of the environment is e then we are interested in the rating of the outcome r. Given the rich meaning of the environment, as described in Section 3, it is reasonable to consider:

$$\mathbb{P}(\text{Observe}^{t'}(r) \mid \text{Enact}^t(s), e) \qquad (7)$$

If $\Omega \in e$ is the set of agents in e, then the aggregated rating[10] of their responsive actions leading to the sequence outcome is a subjective measure of their collective *trust, honour* or *reliability* — a fuller account of these estimates is given in [4].

We first consider a special case of the expected rating of a diminutive action sequence consisting of a single agent, $\Omega = \{\beta\}$, and a single action — as is observed in the case of "commitment followed by subsequent enactment". In this case if we use the method of Section 4.1 to estimate $\mathbb{P}^t_\beta(v|u)$ where u is the commitment and v the enactment then:

$$T_\alpha(\beta, u, e) = \sum_v \rho(\alpha, v, e) \times \mathbb{P}^t_\beta(v|u)$$

Then α's estimate of the *trust, honour* or *reliability* of β with respect to a class of utterances U will be:

$$T_\alpha(\beta, U, e) = \sum_{u \in U} T_\alpha(\beta, u, e) \times \mathbb{P}^t_\alpha(u)$$

where $\mathbb{P}^t_\alpha(u)$ is as above.

For action sequences in general we abbreviate the expectation of Equation 7 to $\mathbb{P}^t(r|s,e)$ that we may estimate directly using the same reasoning for estimating $\mathbb{P}^t_\beta(v|u)$ in Section 4.1 as r is over a discrete space. Then $T_\alpha(\Omega, s, e) = \mathbb{E}^t_\Omega(r|s, e)$ and $T_\alpha(\Omega, S, e) = \sum_{s \in S} T_\alpha(\Omega, s, e) \times \mathbb{P}^t_\alpha(s)$. $\mathbb{P}^t_\alpha(s)$ is discussed in Section 5.

We are also interested in forming a view on how effective various norms are. If an action sequence, s, takes place within a normative system, I, then it will be constrained by a well-defined set of norms, $N_s \subseteq I_{\text{norms}}$, from that system. Given a set of norms, N, let $S_N = \{s \mid N_s = N\}$ and $T_\alpha(N) = \sum_{s \in S_N} \mathbb{E}^t(r|s, e) \times \mathbb{P}^t_\alpha(s)$. An agent deliberates to satisfy its needs. Given a need, g, let S^t_g be the set of sequences that satisfy g to some degree, and $T_\alpha(g) = \sum_{s \in S^t_g} \mathbb{E}^t(r|s, e) \times \mathbb{P}^t_\alpha(s)$. For any $s \in S^t_g$, N_s will be its prevailing set of norms. Let $\mathbf{N}^t_g = \{N_s \mid s \in S^t_g\}$ we are interested in which norm set in $\mathbf{N}^t_g$ proves most reliable in the satisfaction of g, $T_\alpha(g \mid N \in \mathbf{N}^t_g) = \sum_{s \in S^t_g, N_s = N} \mathbb{E}^t(r|s, e) \times \mathbb{P}^t_\alpha(s)$.

---

[10] See Footnote 6.

5 Ecological deliberation

Human agents employ ecological deliberation for all but a very small proportion
of the decisions that they make. It appears that given a need, contextual triggers
somehow retrieve appropriate action sequences from experiential memory. The retrieval process does not require a complete match and operates tentatively when the
perceived environment is new, possibly by adapting the action sequence. This is
reminiscent of the work of Roger Schank on dynamic memory. α has the following
assets at its disposal to support ecological deliberation:

- an *experiential memory* — Section 3
- *expectations* — Section 4
- a *world model* — Section 3.1
- a *social model* — Section 3.2
- a *norm model* — Section 3.3

Together experiential memory and expectations make a potent pair. Experiential
memory contains details of action sequences, and expectations tell us what to expect
if those sequences are reused. The world, social and norm models describe the states
of affairs that α may desire to change.

An agent acts to satisfy its needs. An ecological agent's rationality lies in its
ability to predict how others will behave. This means that the actions that an ecological agent takes should attempt to shape its social model (i.e. *who* it interacts with),
its norm model (i.e. *how* it interacts) as well as its world model. An agent's social
relationships, and the structures of the institutions that it inhabits, are its means to
transcend its individual deliberative ability.

An agent will make an ecologically rational deliberative action by: reusing an
existing action sequence[11], improving an existing action sequence, adapting an existing action sequence, simplifying an existing action sequence, experimenting —
possibly by attempting to second-guess the rationale behind other agents' actions.
In the cases of improving, adapting or simplifying a sequence that is to be enacted
in a normative system this may involve prior negotiation of the norms when the
measures of effectiveness of norms in Section 4.2 will be useful.

Rather than give a tedious description of how each of the above operations may
be performed we simply assume that they all have been, and that we are confronted
with an enormous selection of previous, improved, adapted, simplified and created
action sequences.

Our problem then is: given a current need, the current norm state, and the current
states of the world, social and norm models, to select one sequence. We deal with
the complexity of matching the current goal and environment to those of previously
observed sequences with a 'super-Sim' function that moderates the expected rating
(Section 4.2) of each previously recorded sequence, s, to give expectations of the
rating, $r^t(s) \in [0,1]$, of how that sequence would perform if it was reused now in an
attempt to satisfy the current need.

---

[11] In case this appears to be a simple application of case-based-reasoning-style case retrieval, note
the complexity of the all important environment. The devil is in the environment.

Given that we now face the problem of devising a method that selects an action sequence it is worth considering first what we expect of that method. What it should *not* do is to say "That one is the best choice" that is pure constructivism. Worse still it would mean that by determining the agent's actions it would then pervert the agent's experiential memory for ever more.

What is needed is an evolutionary method of some sort — that may well be how humans operate. A problem with evolutionary methods is that we may not be prepared to accept poor performance while the method evolves, although permitting a method to explore and make mistakes may also enable it to discover. Given a need, g, and two sequences, s and s', that we expect to satisfy g to some degree, we estimate the two distributions, $\mathbb{P}^t(r^t(s)|s,e)$ and $\mathbb{P}^t(r^t(s')|s',e)$, and hence the probability that s will achieve a higher rating than s', $\mathbb{P}^t(r^t(s) > r^t(s')|s,s',e)$, and hence the probability that $s \in S_g^t$ is the best in S_g^t:

$$p_{g,s} = \mathbb{P}^t(r^t(s) > r^t(s')|s,s',e) \mid \forall s' \in S_g^t \; s' \neq s$$

then given need g, α selects $s \in S_g^t$ with probability $p_{g,s}$. This strategy favours sequences that perform well whilst re-visiting those who have performed poorly with a lower frequency.

5.1 Overall Strategy

Finally we consider how an agent combines constructivist and ecological deliberation. Ecological deliberation is by no means the poor relation of its Cartesian brother. Referring back to the 'wine merchant' example in Section 1, it may simply be that the recommendations of the wine merchant are better in all respects than those that the agent could derive from the data available. If this is so then a rational agent should surely prefer ecological deliberation. A rational agent builds an experiential memory and maintains an open mind on whether to choose constructivist or ecological deliberation. It reinforces the choices it makes by forming a view on which performs better by using its subjective ability to evaluate outcomes.

6 Discussion

The full realisation of the Hayekian vision of self-evolving agents situated in a world of self-evolving institutions is an extensive research agenda that is the subject of on-going research. For example, there is no clear means of achieving an orderly self-evolution of normative systems in a multi-system context. The contribution of this paper is to describe how a single agent can engage in ecological deliberation in addition to well-understood constructivist deliberation. This enables agents to evolve and adapt their deliberative processes as their environment and their fellow agents evolve. If the self-evolution of a single normative system, including its agents, can be achieved through ecological deliberation then we will be close to understanding self-evolving electronic institutions that will take multiagent systems technology to a new level.

References

1. F. A. Hayek, *The Fatal Conceit: The Errors of Socialism*, W. W. Bartley, Ed. University Of Chicago Press, 1991.
2. V. L. Smith, *Rationality in Economics: Constructivist and Ecological Forms.* Cambridge University Press, 2007.
3. J. L. Arcos, M. Esteva, P. Noriega, J. A. Rodríguez, and C. Sierra, "Environment engineering for multiagent systems," *Journal on Engineering Applications of Artificial Intelligence*, vol. 18, 2005.
4. C. Sierra and J. Debenham, "Trust and honour in information-based agency," in *Proceedings Fifth International Conference on Autonomous Agents and Multi Agent Systems AAMAS-2006*, P. Stone and G. Weiss, Eds. Hakodate, Japan: ACM Press, New York, May 2006, pp. 1225 – 1232.
5. ——, "Information-based reputation," in *First International Conference on Reputation: Theory and Technology (ICORE'09)*, M. Paolucci, Ed., Gargonza, Italy, 2009, pp. 5–19.
6. A. Rubinstein, *Modeling Bounded Rationality.* MIT Press, Cambridge, MA, 1998.
7. S. Russell and P. Norvig, *Artificial Intelligence: A Modern Approach*, 2nd ed. Prentice Hall, 2002.
8. R. A. Brooks, "Intelligence without reason," in *Proceedings of the 12th International Joint Conference on Artificial Intelligence*, R. Myopoulos and J. Reiter, Eds. Sydney, Australia: Morgan Kaufmann, August 1991, pp. 569–595.
9. S. Russell, "Rationality and intelligence," *Artificial Intelligence*, vol. 94, no. 1-2, pp. 57–77, July 1997.
10. C. Sierra and J. Debenham, "Information-based deliberation," in *Proceedings Seventh International Conference on Autonomous Agents and Multi Agent Systems AAMAS-2008*, L. Padgham, D. Parkes, J. Müller, and S. Parsons, Eds. Estoril, Portugal: ACM Press, New York, May 2008.
11. ——, "Information-based agency," in *Proceedings of Twentieth International Joint Conference on Artificial Intelligence IJCAI-07*, Hyderabad, India, January 2007, pp. 1513–1518.
12. ——, "The LOGIC Negotiation Model," in *Proceedings Sixth International Conference on Autonomous Agents and Multi Agent Systems AAMAS-2007*, Honolulu, Hawai'i, May 2007, pp. 1026–1033.
13. Y. Kalfoglou and M. Schorlemmer, "IF-Map: An ontology-mapping method based on information-flow theory," in *Journal on Data Semantics I*, ser. Lecture Notes in Computer Science, S. Spaccapietra, S. March, and K. Aberer, Eds. Springer-Verlag: Heidelberg, Germany, 2003, vol. 2800, pp. 98–127.
14. Y. Li, Z. A. Bandar, and D. McLean, "An approach for measuring semantic similarity between words using multiple information sources," *IEEE Transactions on Knowledge and Data Engineering*, vol. 15, no. 4, pp. 871 – 882, July / August 2003.
15. P. Cheeseman and J. Stutz, *Bayesian Inference and Maximum Entropy Methods in Science and Engineering.* Melville, NY, USA: American Institute of Physics, 2004, ch. On The Relationship between Bayesian and Maximum Entropy Inference, pp. 445 – 461.
16. J. Paris, "Common sense and maximum entropy," *Synthese*, vol. 117, no. 1, pp. 75 – 93, 1999.
17. A. García-Camino, J. A. Rodríguez-Aguilar, C. Sierra, and W. Vasconcelos, "Constraint rule-based programming of norms for electronic institutions," *Autonomous Agents and Multi-Agent Systems*, vol. 18, no. 1, pp. 186 – 217, February 2009.

Deriving Extensional Spatial Composition Tables

Baher El-Geresy, Alia I. Abdelmoty and Andrew J. Ware

Abstract Spatial composition tables are fundamental tools for the realisation of qualitative spatial reasoning techniques. Studying the properties of these tables in relation to the spatial calculi they are based on is essential for understanding the applicability of these calculi and how they can be extended and generalised. An extensional interpretation of a spatial composition table is an important property that has been studied in the literature and is used to determine the validity of the table for the models it is proposed for. It provides means for consistency checking of ground sets of relations and for addressing spatial constraint satisfaction problems. Furthermore, two general conditions that can be used to test for extensionality of spatial composition tables are proposed and applied to the RCC8 composition table to verify the allowable models in this calculus.

1 Introduction

Qualitative Spatial Reasoning (QSR) is concerned with the qualitative aspects of representing and reasoning about spatial entities. The challenge of QSR is to "provide calculi which allow a machine to represent and reason with spatial entities of higher dimension, without resorting to the traditional quantitative techniques prevalent in, for example, the computer graphics or computer vision communities" [3]. There are many possible applications of QSR, for examples, in Geographical Information Systems (GIS), spatial query languages, natural languages and many other fields.

Baher El-Geresy
University of Glamorgan, Wales, UK e-mail: bageresy@glam.ac.uk
Alia I. Abdelmoty
Cardiff University, Wales, UK e-mail: a.i.abdelmoty@cs.cf.ac.uk
Andrew Ware
University of Glamorgan, Wales, UK e-mail: jaware@glam.ac.uk

M. Bramer et al. (eds.), *Research and Development in Intelligent Systems XXVI*,
DOI 10.1007/978-1-84882-983-1_7, © Springer-Verlag London Limited 2010

One of the most widely referenced formalisms for QSR is the Region Connection Calculus (RCC), initially described in [11, 12] and intended to provide a logical framework for spatial reasoning.

Given a fixed vocabulary of relations, *Rels*, the composition table allows the answer of the following question by simple lookup: given two relational facts of the forms $R(a,b)$ and $S(b,c)$, what are the possible relations (from the set *Rels*) that can hold between a and c? Composition tables are essential tools for solving spatial constraint satisfaction problems, for example checking the integrity of a database of atomic assertions (involving relations in some set for which we have a composition table) by testing whether every three relations are consistent with the table [3].

An extensional interpretation of composition tables (CT) is a property that checks if the table is valid for the models it is associated with. The RCC theory allows regions in topological space as models with no restriction on their complexity. Previous research work have raised questions on the extensionality of the RCC CT and admitted that an extensional interpretation of the table is not compatible with the RCC theory [2, 1]. The question of when would a composition table have an extensional interpretation needs to be addressed. Answers to this question will allow for deeper understanding of current spatial calculi and their further development. The property of extensionality is a reverse interpretation of the property of composition. For example, one of the possible relations resulting from the composition $EC(touch)(a,b) \wedge EC(b,c)$ is the relation $EC(a,c)$. For extensionality to be achieved for any configuration of the relations $EC(a,c)$, there must exist a third object b such that both relations $EC(a,b)$ and $EC(b,c)$ exist.

In this paper, different type of regions that are possible models of the RCC theory are first identified and the extensionality problem is expressed in terms of the composition triads over the different combinations of those regions. Two general conditions are proposed that can be used to identify non-extensional cases in spatial composition. These are based on the property of connectivity of objects and space. The value of using these conditions are demonstrated through the application of a representation and reasoning approach that encapsulates the explicit representation of connection and hence always results in extensional compositions. Section 2 gives a brief survey of related work. In section 3, the extensionality problem is expressed. In section 4, the two general conditions for checking extensionality are proposed. Application of the proposed conditions is presented in section 6 on the defined extensionality problem. Summary and conclusions are given in section 6.

2 Related Work

RCC8 [3] is a topological constraint language based on eight atomic relations between extended regions of a topological space. Regions are regular subsets of a topological space, they can have holes and can consist of multiple disconnected pieces. The eight atomic relations DC (disconnected), EC (externally connected), PO (partial overlap), EQ (equal), TPP (tangential proper part),NTPP (non-tangential proper part) and their converse relations TPPi,NTPPi were originally defined in first-order logic. In this theory regular closed regions are considered, i.e., regions that are equivalent to the closure of their interior. The RCC8 theory does not distinguish between open, semi-open, and closed regions. Regions do not have to be internally connected, i.e. a regions may consist of different disconnected parts. It was shown by Duntsch [5, 4, 10, 8], that the composition of RCC8 is actually only a weak composition.

Weak composition ($\diamond$) of two relations S and T is defined as the strongest relation $R\varepsilon 2^A$ which contains the true composition SoT, or formally, $S \diamond T = R_i \varepsilon A | R_i \cap (SoT) \neq \phi$ [13].

Benett et al[1] call a weak composition table (entailed by Θ) extensional provided that the fact $CT(R,S) = \{T_1, \cdots, T_n\}$ always implies $\Theta \models \forall x \forall z [(T_1(x,z) \vee \cdots \vee T_n(x,z)) \leftrightarrow \exists y [R(x,y) \wedge S(y,z)]]$. Semantically speaking, this assures that , for any Θ model R and constants $a,c \in R$, the relational fact $T_i(a,c)$ also implies that there exists some constant $b \in R$ such that $R(a,b)$ and $S(b,c)$ holds, where T_i is a relation symbol taken from $CT(R,S)$. That is to say, Θ entails an extensional weak composition table if and only if each of its model is also an extensional model of this composition table.

Bennett [2] has pointed out that an extensional interpretation is not compatible with the RCC theory and had suggested the removal of the universal region u from the domain of possible referents of the region constants.

However, Li and Ying [9] proved that Bennett's conjecture is not valid and examined an RCC8 model comprising disks and regions with holes. They proved that no full extensional interpretation is possible. The extensionality of the table in the case of closed disks only has also been studied and proved [8]. Duntsch proposed RCC11 by considering the complement of a disk as a closed region (complemented closed disk algebra). Li and Ying [8] proved that the later algebra, whose domain contains only the closed disks and closures of their complements in the real plan is also an extensional model.

The above works so far have considered the extensionality of RCC8 for composition triads involving region with a hole. Because of the richness of the spatial domain, the results are not yet complete [10]. The approaches are based on visual reasoning with the triads and hence are not proven to be complete. They are also specific to the types of regions considered and could not therefore be generalized further to consider different models. Although exhaustive analysis was carried out for the cases considered, resulting in detailed labeling of the problem triads, explanations are lacking of when and under what conditions does the problem occur. The contribution of this work is two-fold. First, a method is proposed to identify conditions when extensionality is violated and secondly it is shown how extensional composition tables can derived by preserving the connectivity properties of space and its components.

3 Extensionality Problem of Composition Tables

Basic Notations:

For any $R, S, T \in R_8$, $\langle R, T, S \rangle$ denotes the fact that T is an entry in the cell specified by the ordered pair $\langle R, S \rangle$ in the RCC8 composition table, i.e. $T \in CT(R, S)$. As in [9] $\langle R, T, S \rangle$ is denoted a *composition triad*.

Our task is to verify, for each RCC model R and each triad $\langle R, T, S \rangle$ whether or not the following condition is true:

$$(\forall_{x,z} \in R)\left[\mathbf{T}_{x,z} \ \rightarrow \ (\exists y \in R)[\mathbf{R}(x,y) \wedge \mathbf{S}(y,z)]\right] \tag{1}$$

There are 178 possible triads in the RCC8 CT. If either R or S is the identity relation '=', then condition 1 is always true.

Regions in the RCC theory do not have to be open or closed or indeed internally connected and may consist of disconnected parts [3]. Three possible general configurations for regions can be distinguished in this theory, namely, closed disks (D), region with a hole (H) and a region with (at least two) disconnected parts (N), as shown in figure 1.

Fig. 1 Possible configurations of regions in topological space; closed disks, region with a hole and non-connected regions

Region triads are used to indicate the types of regions considered. Example of possible models include, $\langle D, H, N \rangle$, to indicate relations between a disk (D), region with a hole (H) and a region with non-connected parts (N), $\langle H, H, N \rangle$, $\langle N, N, N \rangle$, etc. In total, there are 16 possible triads.

The extensionality problem need to consider all possible permutations of the regions and hence verify condition 1 for all possible RCC models. The number of **composition triads** that needs to be considered is therefore 2848 (16 x 178).

Li and Ying [9] considered the region triads $\langle H, D, D \rangle$ (also equivalent to $\langle D, D, H \rangle$ as well as $\langle D, D, D \rangle$ in [10]. All possible relationships $T(x, z)$ satisfying these models were identified and then a visual search for region y was conducted to verify extensionality.

An annotated composition table is constructed where a superscript T^x is attached to each cell entry that leads to a non-extensional interpretation, as shown in table 1. All 178 cell entries were examined and the work concluded that an extensional model of the RCC8 composition table is only possible if the domain of possible regions is greatly restricted. In particular, regions with holes are disallowed. Also, that it would not be enough to "remove the universal region of the possible referents of the region constants" and suggested by Bennett [2]. The work also suggests by means of an example that "regions with two discrete components are possibly disallowed", but did not provide any evidence for it.

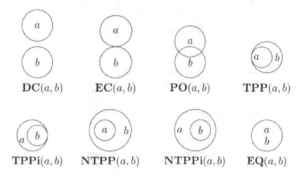

Fig. 2 Eight JEPD topological relations.

In what follows we use basic definitions for the interior, boundary and exterior of regions in a topological space. Let U be a topological space, $X \in U$ be a subset of U and $p \in U$ be a point in U.

- p is said to be an interior point of X if there is a neighborhood n of p contained in X. The set of all interior points of X is called the interior of X, denoted $i(X)$.
- p is said to be an exterior point of X if there is a neighborhood n of p that contains no point of X. The set of all exterior points of X is called the exterior of X, denoted $e(X)$.
- p is said to be a boundary point of X if every neighborhood n of p contains at least one point in X and one point not in X. The set of all boundary points of X is called the boundary of X, denoted $b(X)$.
- The closure of X, denoted $c(X)$, is the smallest closed set which contains X. The closure of a set is the union of its interior and its boundary.

Figure 3 shows the boundary, exterior and interior of the different regions considered in this work.

The question now is which of the 2484 triads imply non-extensional interpretation of the RCC8 CT.

∘	DC	EC	PO	TPP	NTPP	TPPi	NTPPi
DC	T	DC EC^x PO^x TPP^x NTPP	DC EC PO TPP NTPP	DC EC^x PO^x TPP NTPP	DC EC PO TPP NTPP	DC	DC
EC	DC EC^x PO^x TPPi^x NTPPi	DC EC^x PO^x= TPP TPPi	DC EC PO TPP NTPP	EC PO^x TPP^x NTPP	PO^x TPP^x NTPP	DC EC	DC
PO	DC EC PO TPPi NTPPi	DC EC PO TPPi NTPPi	T	PO TPP NTPP	PO TPP NTPP	DC EC PO TPPi NTPPi	DC EC PO TPPi NTPPi
TPP	DC	DC EC	DC EC PO TPP NTPP	TPP NTPP	NTPP	DC= EC^x PO^x TPP	DC EC^x PO^x TPPi^x NTPPi
NTPP	DC	DC EC	DC EC PO TPP NTPP	NTPP	NTPP	DC EC^x PO^x TPP^x NTPP	T
TPPi	DC EC^x PO^x TPPi^x	EC PO^x TPPi^x NTPPi	PO TPPi NTPPi	PO^x TPP TPPi= NTPP	PO^x TPP^x NTPP	TPPi	NTPPi
NTPPi	DC EC PO TPPi NTPPi	PO^x TPPi^x NTPPi	PO TPPi NTPPi	PO^x TPPi^x NTPPi	PO= TPP NTPP TPPi NTPPi	NTPPi	NTPPi

Table 1 Extensional Composition table for the RCC8 relations. R^x indicate composition results leading to non-extensional interpretation of the table .

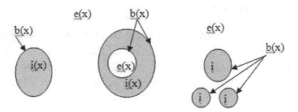

Fig. 3 Boundaries, interiors and exteriors of regions.

4 Connection and Extensionality

In any composition table involving three objects (x, y, z), for an entry in the table corresponding to objects x and z ($T(x, z)$) to be extensional requires the existence of another object y such that both relations $R(x, y)$ and $S(y, z)$ can be realised. If the resulting spatial configuration makes it impossible for a self-connected object to exist [1], then this entry is non-extensional.

---

[1] Recall that a region is called selfconnected if there is a path between any two points of the region that is completely contained in it.

In what follows, this connection property is used to study the extensionality properties of the RCC8 composition table and identify cases where extensionality is violated. If this property is explicitly modeled and considered in the reasoning formalism, the resulting composition table will always be extensional.

4.1 Extensionality of the Region Connection Calculus Composition Table

Three basic types of regions are normally considered in the literature, namely, a simple disk D, a region with a hole H and a disconnected region N. Sixteen possible region triads (D,H,N) need to be considered. One way to manage the study of the large number of possible relation triads in the composition table is to group them into two more general subsets; one with the set of containment relationship $(TPP,TPPi,NTPP,NTPPi)$, denoted (containment composition) and the other group with the rest of possible relationships (DC,EC,PO), denoted (non-containment composition). In what follows, conditions for an extensional interpretation of the triad of relations, $R(x,y)$, $S(y,z)$ and $T(x,z)$ are identified.

Non-Containment Composition Figure 4 shows possible scenarios in the case of simple regions for objects x and z and their relationships with a common object y, where $T(x,z) \in \{DC,EC,PO\}$.

The condition for an extensional interpretation of the relation triad (R,T,S) can be informally expressed as follows. A connected line must exist outside both object x and z which also intersects the boundaries of both objects. One possible such line is shown as a dashed line is shown in figure 4.

Let δx and δz represent the boundary components of both objects x and z respectively and $x°$ and $z°$ are the exterior components. Let l be line object. The extensionality condition can be stated as follows: $l \cap \delta x \neq \phi \wedge l \cap \delta z \neq phi \wedge l \cap \{x°,z°\} \neq \phi$

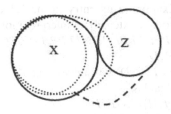

Fig. 4 x is touching, overlapping or disjoint from z. The connection constraint shown as a line joining the boundaries of the 2 objects.

Containment Composition A similar constraint can be defined for the case where $T(x,z) \in \{TPP, TPPi, NTPP, NTPPi\}$. The condition for an extensional interpretation of the relation triad (R, T, S) can be informally expressed as follows. A connected line must exist that joins the boundaries between both contained and container objects and this line must be completely embedded inside the container object. One possible such line is shown as a dashed line in figure 5.

This extensionality condition can be stated as follows: $l \cap \delta x \neq phi \wedge l \cap \delta z \neq \phi \wedge l \cap \{x^\circ, z^\circ\} \neq \phi$

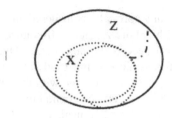

Fig. 5 x is contained in z. The connection constraint shown as a line embedded in z that joins the two boundaries of the 2 objects.

In what follows, we investigate the extensionality for the 16 possible combinations of region triads. We exclude the triad $\langle D, D, D \rangle$ which has already been proved.

Triads $\langle H, D, D \rangle$, $\langle D, N, H \rangle$, $\langle D, H, H \rangle$

This case has been studied in detail by Li [9] who enumerated all composition triads that will lead to non-extensional tables. 35 entries were identified, marked with a subscript (x) in table 1.

However, they failed to identify 4 possible triads based on the containment condition that will lead to non-extensionality condition. These triads are: $\langle DC, TPP, PO \rangle$, $\langle DC, TPPi, PO \rangle$, $\langle EC, TPP, PO \rangle$ and $\langle EC, TPPi, PO \rangle$.

Triads $\langle N, D, D \rangle$, $\langle D, H, N \rangle$

Figure 6(a) shows the relation $TPPi(N, D)$ that does not satisfy based on the containment condition. Examining its entry in the CT reveals that the following triads will therefore lead to non-extensional interpretations,

$\langle TPPi, TPPi, EC \rangle$, $\langle TPPi, TPPi, PO \rangle$, $\langle TPP, TPP, EC \rangle$, $\langle TPP, TPP, PO \rangle$.

Triads $\langle D, N, D \rangle$, $\langle D, H, D \rangle$

In this case, the relation $T(D, D)$ will always satisfy both conditions and so will always lead to extensional tables.

Triads $\langle H, N, N \rangle$, $\langle N, H, H \rangle$, $\langle N, D, H \rangle$

Figure 6(b) shows the relation $TPPi(H, N)$ that does not satisfy the containment condition. Examining its entry in the CT reveals that the following triads will therefore lead to non-extensional interpretations,

$\langle TPP, TPP, EC \rangle$, $\langle TPP!, TPP!, EC \rangle$, $\langle TPP, TPP, PO \rangle$, $\langle TPPi, TPPi, PO \rangle$.

Triad $\langle N, H, N \rangle$, $\langle N, D, N \rangle$

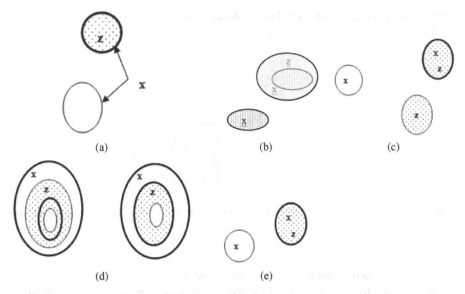

Fig. 6 Cases of relations failing the extensionality condition. (a) Relation $TPPi(N,D)$ between X and Z. (b) Relation $EC(H,N)$ between X and Z. X is a non-connected region that completely overlaps Z. (c) Relation $PO(N,N)$ between X and Z. (d) Relation $PO(H,H)$ and $EC(H,H)$ between X and Z. (e) Relation $TPP(D,N)$ between X and Z.

The relation PO(N,N), as shown in figure 6(c) leads to non-extensionality based on non-containment condition with the following triads: $\langle EC,PO,TPP \rangle$, $\langle PO,PO,TPP \rangle$ and $\langle TPP,PO,PO \rangle$

Triad $\langle H,N,H \rangle$ The composition table is extensional because the third object is not connected.

Triad $\langle H,D,H \rangle$

Here, the triads: $\langle EC,PO,EC \rangle$ and $\langle EC,EC,EC \rangle$ are problematic as shown in figure 6(d), due to violating the non-containment condition.

Triad $\langle D,N,N \rangle$

Here, the triads: $\langle TPP,TPP,EC \rangle$ and $\langle TPP,TPP,PO \rangle$ and $\langle PO,TPPi,EC \rangle \rangle$ are problematic as shown in figure 6(e), as the containment condition can not be satisfied.

5 Verifying the Extensionality of the Composition Table

Consider the region triad (D,D,H) and the relation triad (EC,EC,EC). This triad has been shown to be non-extensional in the case of the relation in figure 7(III). In this case, the disk x completely coincides with the hole in object z. This case is considered to be non-extensional as no object y can be found such that $EC(x,y)$ and $EC(y,z)$.

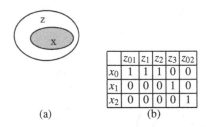

	z_{01}	z_1	z_2	z_3	z_{02}
x_0	1	1	1	0	0
x_1	0	0	0	1	0
x_2	0	0	0	0	1

(a)   (b)

Fig. 7 (a) $EC(x,z)$, where x is a disk and z is a region with a hole. (b) Corresponding intersection matrix.

Here, we examine this composition table entry more closely. We identify all possible scenarios for the composition and use a representation and reasoning approach that consider the connectivity of the space and its components to derive the resulting relationships between x and z. It is shown how the method results only in extensional relationships and hence demonstrates that the general treatment of objects as in the case of RCC8 is limited and that more specific representation of object complexity are needed.

In figure 8 the object and space components are labeled to indicate their different interior, boundaries and exteriors. In figure 9(III) a diagrammatical representation of the spatial relations for $R(x,y)$ and $S(y,z)$ are shown. Intersection matrices associated with the relationships are also shown to depict the intersection between their individual components. Three possible EC relationships can exist between y and z.

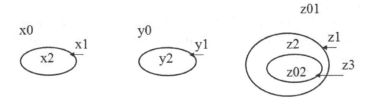

Fig. 8 Object and space components for regions x (disk), y (disk) and z (region with hole).

The non-extensional relationship between x and z is shown in figure 7 along with its corresponding intersection matrix.

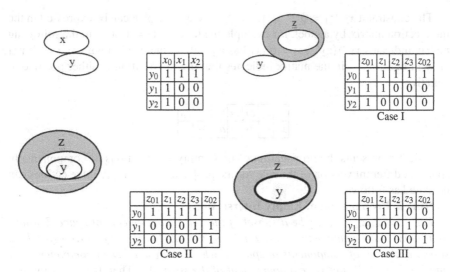

Fig. 9 $EC(x,y)$ and three different possible relationships $EC(y,z)$.

The composition $R(x,y) \circ S(y,z) \to T(x,z)$ is derived by composing their corresponding matrices and propagating the empty and non-empty intersections using the formalism defined in [7, 6]. Using the representation scheme of object and space as in figure 9, two reasoning rules are used to propagate empty and non-empty intersections between object components and the result is encoded in an intersection matrix. The rules are as follows.

Rule 1: Propagation of Non-Empty Intersections

Let $x' = \{x_1, x_2, \cdots, x_{m'}\}$ be a subset of the set of components of space X whose total number of components is m and $m' \leq m$; $x' \subseteq X$. Let $z' = \{z_1, z_2, \cdots, z_{n'}\}$ be a subset of the set of components of space Z whose total number of components is n and $n' \leq n$; $z' \subseteq Z$. If y_j is a component of space Y, the following is a governing rule of interaction for the three spaces X, Y and Z.

$$(x' \sqsupseteq y_j) \wedge (y_j \sqsubseteq z')$$
$$\to (x' \cap z' \neq \phi)$$
$$\equiv (x_1 \cap z_1 \neq \phi \vee \cdots \vee x_1 \cap z_{n'} \neq \phi)$$
$$\wedge (x_2 \cap z_1 \neq \phi \vee \cdots \vee x_2 \cap z_{n'} \neq \phi)$$
$$\wedge \cdots$$
$$\wedge (x_{m'} \cap z_1 \neq \phi \vee \cdots \vee x_{m'} \cap z_{n'} \neq \phi)$$

The above rule states that if the component y_j in space Y has a positive intersection with every component from the sets x' and z', then each component of the set x' must intersect with at least one component of the set z' and vice versa.

The constraint $x_i \cap z_1 \neq \phi \ \vee \ x_i \cap z_2 \neq \phi \cdots \ \vee \ x_i \cap z_{n'} \neq \phi$ can be expressed in the intersection matrix by a label, for example the label a_r ($r = 1$ or 2) in the following matrix indicates $x_1 \cap (z_2 \sqcup z_4) \neq \phi$ (x_1 has a positive intersection with z_2, or with z_4 or with both). A $-$ in the matrix indicates that the intersection is either positive or negative.

	z_1	z_2	z_3	z_4	$\cdots$	z_n
x_1	$-$	a_1	$-$	a_2	$-$	$-$

Rule 1 represents the propagation of non-empty intersections of components in space. A different version of the rule for the propagation of empty intersections can be stated as follows.

Rule 2: Propagation of Empty Intersections

Let $z' = \{z_1, z_2, \cdots, z_{n'}\}$ be a subset of the set of components of space Z whose total number of components is n and $n' < n$; $z' \subset Z$. Let $y' = \{y_1, y_2, \cdots, y_{l'}\}$ be a subset of the set of components of space Y whose total number of components is l and $l' < l$; $y' \subset Y$. Let x_i be a component of the space X. Then the following is a governing rule for the spaces X, Y and Z.

$$(x_i \sqsubseteq y') \ \wedge \ (y' \sqsubseteq z')$$
$$\rightarrow (x_i \cap (Z - z_1 - z_2 \cdots - z_{n'}) = \phi)$$

Remark: if $n' = n$, i.e. x_i may intersect with every element in Z, or if $m' = m$, i.e. z_k may intersect with every element in X, or if $l' = l$, i.e. x_i (or z_k) may intersect with every element in Y, then no empty intersections can be propagated for x_i or z_k. Rules 1 and 2 are the two general rules for propagating empty and non-empty intersections of components of spaces.

Note that in both rules the intermediate object (y) and its space components plays the main role in the propagation of intersections. The first rule is applied a number of times equal to the number of components of the space of the intermediate object. Hence, the composition of spatial relations becomes a tractable problem which can be performed in a defined limited number of steps.

The result intersection matrices for the three scenarios are shown below. In every case, the matrix is shown not to propagate the non-extensional matrix in figure 7.

Case I:

The result matrix for case I is as follows.

	z_{01}	z_1	z_2	z_3	z_{02}
x_0	1	b	?	?	?
x_1	a	a b	?	?	?
x_2	?	?	?	?	?

In the matrix above, ? is used to denote either 0 or 1. Letters are used to signify related constraints. So, entries labeled a denotes that at least one of the entries x_1, z_0 and x_1, z_1 should be 1.

As can be seen, the matrix above holds the constraint, $x_1 \cap (z_{01} \cup z_1) \neq \phi$. This constraint contradicts with the non-extensional matrix, where the constraint is

$x_1 \cap (z_{01} \cup z_1) = \phi$. Hence, the composition will not propagate the non-extensional relation.

Case II:

In a similar fashion to Case I, the result of composition for case II is as follows.

	z_{01}	z_1	z_2	z_3		z_{02}
x_0	?	?	?	b	?	1
x_1	?	?	?	a	b	a
x_2	?	?	?	?		?

Here, the contradictory constraint is $x_0 \cap z_{02} \neq \phi$ and hence, this composition will not propagate non-extensional relations.

Case III:

Similarly for case III, the result matrix is as follows.

	z_{01}	z_1	z_2	z_3	z_{02}
x_0	?	?	?	1	1
x_1	?	?	?	1	0
x_2	?	?	?	0	0

Here, the contradictory constraints are $x_0 \cap z_3 \neq \phi$ and $x_0 \cap z_{02} \neq \phi$.

It all three cases it was shown how the representation and reasoning methods result only in extensional relationships.

6 Conclusions

This paper addresses the question of extensionality of RCC8 composition table. Sixteen possible region triads have been identified that needs to be studied for this problem. Two of which have been addressed exhaustively in earlier works, but their methods could not be easily extended or generalized. We demonstrate the value of considering the connectivity of object and space components in deriving extensional composition tables. Two general conditions for extensionality are proposed and used to exhaustively test the exhaustively test the different types of regions in the RCC8 composition table. It is observed that the table will be extensional only in some cases ($\langle D,D,D \rangle$, $\langle D,H,D \rangle$, $\langle D,N,D \rangle$ and $\langle H,N,H \rangle$.). The result is important as ignoring the types of regions in the application of the spatial logics may lead to the propagation of non-valid reasoning results.

The results of this paper complements earlier work on regions with holes as well as clarifies the fact that extensional interpretation is not violated automatically by the existence of a non-disk object, but in fact will depend on the order in the composition triad. Further extension to this work is sought to investigate other existing composition tables and models of spatial calculi.

References

1. Bennett, B.: Logical representation for automated reasoning about spatial relationships. Ph.D. dissertation, University of Leeds (1998)
2. Bennett, B., Isli, A., Cohn, A.G.: When does a Composition Table provide a complete and tractable proof procedure for a relational constraint language? In: IJCAI-97 (1997)
3. Cohn, A., Bennett, B.: Qualitative Spatial Representation and Reasoning with the Region Connection Calculus. Geoinformatics 1, 275–316 (1997)
4. Duntsch, I., Wang, H., McCloskey, S.: Relational algebras in qualitative spatial reasoning. Fundamental Informaticae 39, 229–248 (1999)
5. Duntsch, I., Wang, H., McCloskey, S.: A Relation-algebraic approach to the Region Connection Calculus. Theoretical Computer Science 255, 63–83 (2001)
6. El-Geresy, B., Abdelmoty, A.: Towards a general theory for modelling qualitative space. International Journal on Artificial Intelligence Tools, IJAIT 11(3), 347–367 (2002)
7. El-Geresy, B., Abdelmoty, A.: Sparqs: a qualitative spatial reasoning engine. Journal of knowledge-based Systems 17(2-4), 89–102 (2004)
8. Li, S., Ying, M.: Extensionality of the RCC8 composition table. Fundamenta Informaticae 55, 363–385 (2003)
9. Li, S., Ying, M.: Region Connection Calculus: Its models and composition table. Artificial Intelligence 145, 121–146 (2003)
10. Li, S., Ying, M.: Relational reaosning in the Region Connection Calculus. Artificial Intelligence 160, 1–34 (2004)
11. Randell, D., Cohn, A., Cui, Z.: A Spatial Logic based on Regions and Connection. In: Proc. of third International Conference on Knowledge Representaiton and Reasoning, pp. 165–176 (1992)
12. Randell, D., Cohn, A., Cui, Z.: Computing Transitivity Tables: A Challenge for Automated Theorem Provers. In: CADE, Lecture Notes In Computer Science (1992)
13. Renz, J., Ligozat, G.: Weak composition for qualitative spatial and temporal reasoning. In: Proceedings of Principles and Practice of Constraint Programming, CP 2005, pp. 534–548 (2005)

A New Approach to Influence Diagrams Evaluation

Radu Marinescu

Abstract Influence diagrams are a widely used framework for decision making under uncertainty. The paper presents a new algorithm for maximizing the expected utility over a set of policies by traversing an AND/OR search space associated with an influence diagram. AND/OR search spaces accommodate advanced algorithmic schemes for graphical models which can exploit the structure of the problem. The algorithm also exploits the deterministic information encoded by the influence diagram and avoids redundant computations for infeasible decision choices. We demonstrate empirically the effectiveness of the AND/OR search approach on various benchmarks for influence diagrams.

1 Introduction

An influence diagram is a graphical model for decision making under uncertainty. It is composed by a directed acyclic graph where utility nodes are associated to profits and costs of actions, chance nodes represent uncertainties and dependencies in the domain and decision nodes represents actions to be taken. Given an influence diagram, a policy defines which decision to take at each node, given the information available at that moment. Each policy has a corresponding expected utility and the most common task is to find an optimal policy with maximum expected utility.

Over the past decades, several exact methods have been proposed to solve influence diagrams using local computations [13, 12, 5, 2]. These methods adapted classical *variable elimination* techniques, which compute a type of marginalization over a combination of local functions, in order to handle the multiple types of information (probabilities and utilities), marginalizations (sum and max) and combinations ($\times$ for probabilities, $+$ for utilities) involved in influence diagrams. Variable

Radu Marinescu
Cork Constraint Computation Centre, University College Cork, Ireland, e-mail: r.marinescu@4c.ucc.ie

M. Bramer et al. (eds.), *Research and Development in Intelligent Systems XXVI*,
DOI 10.1007/978-1-84882-983-1_8, © Springer-Verlag London Limited 2010

elimination based techniques are known to exploit the conditional independencies encoded by the influence diagram, however, they require time and space exponential in the *constrained induced-width* of the diagram.

An alternative approach for evaluating influence diagrams is based on *conditioning* (or *search*). These methods unfold the influence diagram into a *decision graph* (or *tree*) in such a way that an optimal solution graph corresponds to an optimal policy of the influence diagram. In this case, the problem of computing an optimal policy is reduced to searching for an optimal solution of the decision graph [4, 9, 11]. In contrast with variable elimination, search algorithms are not sensitive to the problem structure, use time exponential in the number of variables, but may operate in linear space.

This situation has changed in the past few years with the introduction of AND/OR search spaces for graphical models as a paradigm for search algorithms that exploit the problem structure [3]. In this paper, we specialize the AND/OR search space to influence diagrams and develop a depth-first search algorithm that explores a context-minimal AND/OR search graph for computing the optimal policy that maximizes the expected utility. Traversing the AND/OR graph allows search algorithms to achieve the same worst case time and space performance guarantees as variable elimination. It also allows a better exploitation of the deterministic information encoded by the influence diagram, thus avoiding redundant computations for impossible decision choices, as well as a better trade-off between time and space. Our experiments show that the new AND/OR search approach improves significantly over state-of-the-art algorithms, in some cases by several orders of magnitude of improved performance.

Following background on influence diagrams (Section 2), Section 3 presents the AND/OR search space for influence diagrams. In Section 4 we describe the AND/OR search algorithm for computing the optimal policy. Section 5 is dedicated to our empirical evaluation, while Section 6 concludes.

2 Background

2.1 Influence Diagrams

An *influence diagram* (ID) [4] is defined by $\mathcal{M} = \langle \mathbf{X}, \mathbf{D}, \mathbf{P}, \mathbf{R} \rangle$, where $\mathbf{X} = \{X_1, ..., X_n\}$ is a set of *chance* variables on multi-valued domains and $\mathbf{D} = \{D_1, ..., D_m\}$ (indices represent the order in which decisions are made) is a set of *decision* variables. The discrete domain of a decision variable denotes its possible set of actions. Every chance variable $X_i \in \mathbf{X}$ is associated with a conditional probability table (CPT), $P_i = P(X_i | pa(X_i))$, $pa(X_i) \subseteq \mathbf{X} \cup \mathbf{D} - \{X_i\}$. Each decision variable $D_i \in \mathbf{D}$ has a parent set $pa(D_i) \subseteq \mathbf{X} \cup \mathbf{D} - \{D_i\}$ denoting the set of variables that will be observed before decision D_i is made. The *reward* (or *utility*) functions $\mathbf{R} = \{r_1, ..., r_j\}$ are defined over subsets of variables $\mathbf{Q} = \{Q_1, ..., Q_j\}$, $Q_i \subseteq \mathbf{X} \cup \mathbf{D}$, called *scopes*. The

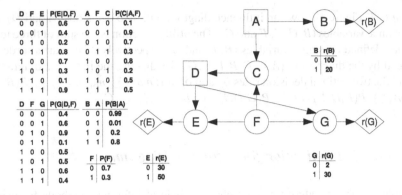

Fig. 1 A simple influence diagram.

directed acyclic graph of an ID contains nodes for the chance variables (depicted as circles) and decision variables (depicted as squares) as well as for the reward components (depicted as diamonds). For each chance or decision node there is an arc directed from each of its parent variables to it, and there is an arc directed from each variable in the scope of a reward component towards its reward node.

Given a temporal order of the decisions, an influence diagram induces a partial order $\prec$ on its variables. The set of chance variables observed before the first decision is denoted $\mathbf{I}_0$, the set of chance variables observed between decisions D_k and D_{k+1} is denoted $\mathbf{I}_k$, and the set of chance variables unobserved before the last decision is denoted $\mathbf{I}_m$. The partial order $\prec$ is: $\mathbf{I}_0 \prec D_1 \prec \mathbf{I}_1 \prec \ldots \prec D_m \prec \mathbf{I}_m$. An influence diagram that satisfies this condition is called *regular*.

A *decision rule* for a decision variable $D_i \in \mathbf{D}$ is a mapping: $\delta_i : \Omega_{pa(D_i)} \to \Omega_{D_i}$, where Ω_S is the cross product of the individual domains of the variables in $S \subseteq \mathbf{X} \cup \mathbf{D}$. A *policy* is a list of decision rules $\Delta = (\delta_1, \ldots, \delta_m)$ consisting of one rule for each decision variable. To *evaluate* an influence diagram is to find an *optimal policy* maximizing the expected utility. As shown in [5], this is equivalent to computing optimal decision rules for the quantity:

$$\sum_{\mathbf{I}_0} \max_{D_1} \ldots \sum_{\mathbf{I}_{m-1}} \max_{D_m} \sum_{\mathbf{I}_m} \left(\left(\prod_{P_i \in \mathbf{P}} P_i \right) \times \left(\sum_{r_i \in \mathbf{R}} r_i \right) \right) \qquad (1)$$

With every ID instance we can associate a *primal graph* which is obtained from the ID graph as follows. All the parents of chance variables are connected, all the parents of reward components are connected, and all the arrows are dropped. Reward nodes and their incident arcs are deleted.

In addition, IDs must be non forgetting in the sense that a decision node and its parents be parents to all subsequent decision nodes. The rational behind the no-forgetting constraint is that information available now should be available later if the decision-maker does not forget. In this paper we do not enforce this restriction.

Example 1. Figure 1 shows an influence diagram with two decisions (A and D) and five chance variables (B, C, E, F and G). The utility function is the sum of three local utilities defined on single variables (B, E and G, respectively). The partial order $\prec$ induced by the diagram is $\{A,C,D,B,E,F,G\}$. Evaluating the influence diagram is to find the two optimal decision rules δ_A^* and δ_D^* for: $max_A \sum_C max_D \sum_{B,E,F,G} P(B|A) \cdot P(C|A,F) \cdot P(E|D,F) \cdot P(F) \cdot P(G|D,F) \cdot (r(B)+r(E)+r(G))$.

2.2 Variable Elimination for Influence Diagrams

Variable elimination algorithms are characteristic of inference methods for evaluating influence diagrams. This approach reformulates Equation 1 using so-called *potentials* [5], in order to use one combination and one marginalization operator. A potential on a set of variables S is a pair $\Psi_S = (\lambda_S, \theta_S)$ of real-valued functions on Ω_S, where λ_S is non-negative. The initial conditional probability tables $P_i \in \mathbf{P}$ and utility functions $r_i \in \mathbf{R}$ are transformed into potentials $(P_i, 0)$ and $(1, r_i)$, respectively. A *combination* operator $\otimes$ and a *marginalization* (or *elimination*) operator $\downarrow$ are defined on these potentials, as follows:

(a) the **combination** of $\Psi_{S_1} = (\lambda_{S_1}, \theta_{S_1})$ and $\Psi_{S_2} = (\lambda_{S_2}, \theta_{S_2})$ is the potential on $S_1 \cup S_2$ given by $\Psi_{S_1} \otimes \Psi_{S_2} = (\lambda_{S_1} \cdot \lambda_{S_2}, \theta_{S_1} + \theta_{S_2})$;

(b) the **marginalization** of $\Psi_S = (\lambda_S, \theta_S)$ onto $S_1 \in \mathbf{X}$ is $\Psi_S^{\downarrow S_1} = (\sum_{S-S_1} \lambda_S, \frac{\sum_{S-S_1} \lambda_S \cdot \theta_S}{\sum_{S-S_1} \lambda_S})$

(assuming that $0/0 = 0$), whereas $\Psi_S^{\downarrow S_1} = (\lambda_S, max_{S_1} \theta_S)$ for $S_1 \subseteq \mathbf{D}$.

Evaluating an influence diagram is then equivalent to computing

$$Q = ((...((\Psi_{\mathbf{X} \cup \mathbf{D}}^{\downarrow \mathbf{I}_m})^{\downarrow D_m})^{\downarrow \mathbf{I}_{m-1}}...)^{\downarrow D_1})^{\downarrow \mathbf{I}_0}$$

where $\Psi_{\mathbf{X} \cup \mathbf{D}} = (\otimes_{P_i \in \mathbf{P}}(P_i, 0)) \otimes (\otimes_{r_i \in \mathbf{R}}(1, r_i))$ is the combination of the initial potentials, which can be done using usual variable elimination algorithms [5, 2]. Since the alternation of *sum* and *max* marginalizations does not commute in general, it prevents from eliminating variables in any order. Therefore, the computation of Q must be performed along *valid elimination orderings* that respect $\prec$, namely the reverse of the elimination order is some extension of $\prec$ to a total order [5]. The performance of variable elimination algorithms can be bounded as a function of the induced-width of the *induced graph* [2] that reflects the algorithm's execution. Given an influence diagram with primal graph G, variable elimination is time and space $O(N \cdot k^{w^*(o)})$, where $w^*(o)$ is the induced-width obtained along a valid elimination ordering o of G (also called *constrained induced-width*), k bounds the domain size and N is the total number of decision and chance variables [2].

3 AND/OR Search Spaces for Influence Diagrams

In this section we specialize the AND/OR search space for general graphical models to influence diagrams. AND/OR search spaces accommodate advanced algorithmic schemes for graphical models which can exploit the structure of the model [3]. Given an influence diagram with primal graph G, its AND/OR search space is based on a *pseudo tree* arrangement of G.

Definition 1 (pseudo tree). Let $G = (V, E)$ be the primal graph of an influence diagram $\mathcal{M}$ and let $\prec$ be the partial order induced on its variables. A directed rooted tree $\mathcal{T} = (V, E')$ is called *pseudo tree* if: (*i*) any arc of G which is not included in E' is a back-arc, namely it connects a node to an ancestor in $\mathcal{T}$; (*ii*) the ordering obtained from a depth-first traversal of $\mathcal{T}$ is an extension of $\prec$ to a total order.

3.1 AND/OR Search Tree

Given an influence diagram $\mathcal{M} = \langle \mathbf{X}, \mathbf{D}, \mathbf{P}, \mathbf{R} \rangle$, its primal graph G and a pseudo tree $\mathcal{T}$ of G, the associated AND/OR search tree, denoted $S_{\mathcal{T}}(\mathcal{M})$, has alternating levels of OR and AND nodes. The OR nodes are labeled X_i (resp. D_i) and correspond to the variables. The AND nodes are labeled $\langle X_i, x_i \rangle$ (resp. $\langle D_i, d_i \rangle$) and correspond to the values in the domains of the variables. The structure of the AND/OR search tree is based on the underlying pseudo tree $\mathcal{T}$. The root of $S_{\mathcal{T}}(\mathcal{M})$ is an OR node labeled with the root of $\mathcal{T}$. The children of an OR node X_i (resp. D_i) are AND nodes labeled with assignments $\langle X_i, x_i \rangle$ (resp. $\langle D_i, d_i \rangle$) that are consistent along the path from the root. The children of an AND node $\langle X_i, x_i \rangle$ (resp. $\langle D_i, d_i \rangle$) are OR nodes labeled with the children of variable X_i (resp. D_i) in the pseudo tree $\mathcal{T}$.

Based on earlier work [3], it can be shown that given an influence diagram and a pseudo tree $\mathcal{T}$ of depth h, the size of the AND/OR search tree based on $\mathcal{T}$ is $O(N \cdot k^h)$, where k bounds the domains of variables. Moreover, an ID instance having constrained induced-width w^* has a pseudo tree of depth at most $w^* \cdot \log N$, and therefore it has an AND/OR search tree of size $O(N \cdot k^{w^* \cdot \log N})$.

Example 2. Consider again the influence diagram from Figure 1. Figure 2(a) shows a pseudo tree of its primal graph, together with the back-arcs (dotted lines). Figure 2(b) shows a portion the AND/OR search tree based on the pseudo tree. Notice that a depth-first traversal of the pseudo tree yields an ordering that is consistent with the partial order of the diagram.

3.2 AND/OR Search Graph

Often different nodes in the AND/OR search tree root identical subtrees, and correspond to identical subproblems. Any two such nodes can be merged, reducing the

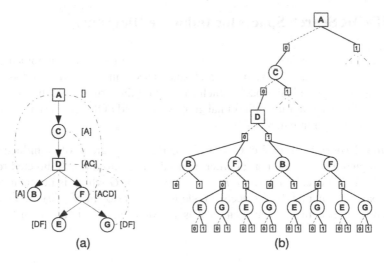

Fig. 2 AND/OR search tree for influence diagrams.

size of the search space and converting it into a graph. Some of these mergeable nodes can be identified based on *contexts* [3]. Given a pseudo tree $\mathscr{T}$, the context of an OR node labeled Y_i, where $Y_i \in \mathbf{X} \cup \mathbf{D}$, is defined as the set of ancestors of Y_i (in $\mathscr{T}$), ordered descendingly, that are connected (in the induced graph) to Y_i or to descendants of Y_i (in $\mathscr{T}$). It is easy to verify that $context(Y_i)$ separates in the primal graph (and also in the induced graph) the ancestors (in $\mathscr{T}$) of Y_i, from Y_i and its descendants (in $\mathscr{T}$). The *context-minimal AND/OR graph*, $C_{\mathscr{T}}(\mathscr{M})$, is obtained from the AND/OR search tree by merging all context mergeable OR nodes. Based on earlier work [3], it can be shown that given an ID instance $\mathscr{M}$ and a pseudo tree $\mathscr{T}$, the size of the context-minimal AND/OR graph relative to $\mathscr{T}$ is $O(N \cdot k^{w^*})$, where w^* is the constrained induced-width of $\mathscr{M}$ over a depth-first traversal of $\mathscr{T}$.

Example 3. Figure 3 shows the context-minimal AND/OR graph relative to the pseudo tree from Figure 2(a). The OR contexts of the variables are indicated in square brackets next to each node in the pseudo tree.

3.3 Arc Labeling

The arcs from Y_i to $\langle Y_i, y_i \rangle$, where $Y_i \in \mathbf{X} \cup \mathbf{D}$, are labeled with the appropriate combined values of the functions in $\mathbf{P} \cup \mathbf{R}$ that contain Y_i and have their scopes fully assigned. It is convenient to group the functions of the influence diagram into *buckets* relative to its pseudo tree, as follows. The bucket $B_{\mathscr{T}}(X_i)$ of a chance variable $X_i \in \mathbf{X}$ is the set of probability and reward functions (if X_i has no decision variables as descendants in $\mathscr{T}$) whose scopes contain X_i and are included in the path from root to X_i in $\mathscr{T}$. The bucket $B_{\mathscr{T}}(D_i)$ of a decision variable $D_i \in \mathbf{D}$ is the set of prob-

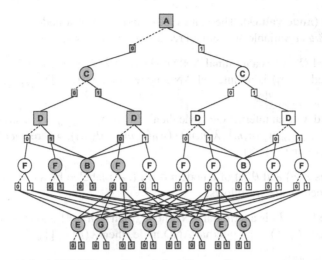

Fig. 3 Context-minimal AND/OR search graph for influence diagrams.

ability functions whose scopes contain D_i and are included in the path from root to D_i in $\mathscr{T}$. If D_i is the deepest decision variable in $\mathscr{T}$, then $B_{\mathscr{T}}(D_i)$ contains also the set of all remaining reward functions. In each bucket $B_{\mathscr{T}}(Y_i)$, where $Y_i \in \mathbf{X} \cup \mathbf{D}$, we denote the probabilistic and utility components by $B^\lambda_{\mathscr{T}}(Y_i)$ and $B^\theta_{\mathscr{T}}(Y_i)$, respectively.

Definition 2 (weights). Given an AND/OR search graph $C_{\mathscr{T}}(\mathscr{M})$ of an influence diagram $\mathscr{M}$, the *weight* of the arc (n,m), where Y_i labels n and $\langle Y_i, y_i \rangle$ labels m, is a pair (w_λ, w_θ) where w_λ (or $w_\lambda(n,m)$) is the *product* of all the probability functions in $B^\lambda_{\mathscr{T}}(Y_i)$ and w_θ (or $w_\theta(n,m)$) is the *sum* of all the utility functions in $B^\theta_{\mathscr{T}}(Y_i)$. Formally, $w_\lambda = \prod_{\lambda \in B^\lambda_{\mathscr{T}}(Y_i)} \lambda(asgn(\pi_m))$ and $w_\lambda = 1$ if $B^\lambda_{\mathscr{T}}(Y_i) = \emptyset$, while $w_\theta = \sum_{\theta \in B^\theta_{\mathscr{T}}(Y_i)} \theta(asgn(\pi_m))$ and $w_\theta = 0$ if $B^\theta_{\mathscr{T}}(Y_i) = \emptyset$, where $asgn(\pi_m)$ denotes the assignment along the path π_m from the root of $C_{\mathscr{T}}(\mathscr{M})$ to the AND node m.

Example 4. Consider again the influence diagram from Figure 1 with partial order (A,C,D,B,E,F,G). In this case, for example, the bucket of E contains the probability function $P(E|D,F)$ and the reward function $r(E)$. The weights (w_λ, w_θ) on the arcs from the OR node E to its AND children $\langle E, 0 \rangle$ and $\langle E, 1 \rangle$, along the path $\{A, \langle A, 0 \rangle, C, \langle C, 0 \rangle, D, \langle D, 0 \rangle, F, \langle F, 0 \rangle, E, \}$ are $(0.6, 30)$ and $(0.4, 50)$, respectively. Notice also that the buckets of variables A, C and D do not contain any functions and therefore the weights associated with the respective arcs are $(1, 0)$.

3.4 Value Function

With each node n in the weighted AND/OR graph $C_{\mathscr{T}}(\mathscr{M})$, we associate a *probability value* $\lambda(n)$ and a *utility value* $\theta(n)$ defined on the subspaces they root.

Definition 3 (node values). The values $\lambda(n)$ and $\theta(n)$ of a node $n \in C_{\mathscr{T}}(\mathscr{M})$ labeled by a *chance* variable are defined recursively as follows:

1 if n labeled $\langle X_i, x_i \rangle$ is a terminal AND node, then $\lambda(n) = 1$ and $\theta(n) = 0$;
2 if n labeled $\langle X_i, x_i \rangle$ is an internal AND node, then $\lambda(n) = \prod_{m \in succ(n)} \lambda(m)$ and
   $\theta(n) = \sum_{m \in succ(n)} \frac{\theta(m)}{\lambda(m)}$;
3 if n labeled X_i is an internal OR node then $\lambda(n) = \sum_{m \in succ(n)} w_\lambda(n,m) \cdot \lambda(m)$ and
   $\theta(n) = \sum_{m \in succ(n)} w_\lambda(n,m) \cdot \lambda(n,m) \cdot (w_\theta(n,m) + \theta(m))$, where $succ(n)$ are the
   children of n in $C_{\mathscr{T}}(\mathscr{M})$.

The values $\lambda(n)$ and $\theta(n)$ of a node $n \in C_{\mathscr{T}}(\mathscr{M})$ labeled by a *decision* variable are defined recursively, as follows:

1 if n labeled $\langle D_i, d_i \rangle$ is a terminal AND node, then $\lambda(n) = 1$ and $\theta(n) = 0$;
2 if n labeled $\langle D_i, d_i \rangle$ is an internal AND node, then $\lambda(n) = \prod_{m \in succ(n)} \lambda(m)$ and
   $\theta(n) = \sum_{m \in succ(n)} \frac{\theta(m)}{\lambda(m)}$;
3 if n labeled D_i is an internal OR node, then $\lambda(n) = max_{m \in succ(n)} w_\lambda(n,m) \cdot \lambda(m)$
   and $\theta(n) = max_{m \in succ(n)} w_\lambda(n,m) \cdot \lambda(n,m) \cdot (w_\theta(n,m) + \theta(m))$, where $succ(n)$
   are the children of n in $C_{\mathscr{T}}(\mathscr{M})$.

Clearly, the λ and θ-values of each node can be computed recursively, from leaves to root. If n is the root node of $C_{\mathscr{T}}(\mathscr{M})$, then $\theta(n)$ is the maximum expected utility of the initial problem. Alternatively, the value $\theta(n)$ can also be interpreted as the expected utility (for chance nodes) or maximum expected utility (for decision nodes) of the conditioned subproblem rooted at n.

3.5 Policy Graphs and Decision Rules

The context-minimal AND/OR graph $C_{\mathscr{T}}(\mathscr{M})$ of an influence diagram $\mathscr{M}$ contains the set of all policies for $\mathscr{M}$. A policy Δ is represented in $C_{\mathscr{T}}(\mathscr{M})$ by a *policy graph*, which is an AND/OR subgraph, denoted by $\mathscr{G}_\Delta(\mathscr{M})$, such that:

1 it contains the root s of $C_{\mathscr{T}}(\mathscr{M})$;
2 if a non-terminal OR node n, labeled by a *chance* variable, is in $\mathscr{G}_\Delta(\mathscr{M})$ then all
   of its children are in $\mathscr{G}_\Delta(\mathscr{M})$;
3 if a non-terminal OR node, labeled by a *decision* variable, is in $\mathscr{G}_\Delta(\mathscr{M})$ then
   exactly one of its children is in $\mathscr{G}_\Delta(\mathscr{M})$;
4 if a non-terminal AND node is in $\mathscr{G}_\Delta(\mathscr{M})$ then all its children are in $\mathscr{G}_\Delta(\mathscr{M})$.

Given a policy graph $\mathscr{G}_\Delta(\mathscr{M})$ with appropriate weights on its arcs, the value $\theta(s)$ of the root node s is the expected utility of the policy Δ. Therefore, the optimal policy for $\mathscr{M}$ corresponds to the policy graph with maximum expected utility. Moreover, it is easy to see that for any decision variable $D_i \in \mathbf{D}$ the variables in $context(D_i)$ are those that may affect directly the decision and therefore define the scope of the decision rule δ_i associated with D_i.

Algorithm 1: AO-ID($\mathcal{M}$): Depth-first AND/OR search.

---

1 if $\mathcal{M} = \emptyset$ then return $(1,0)$;
2 else
3   choose a variable $Y_i \in \mathbf{Y}$;
4   let n be an OR node labeled Y_i;
5       $\{\lambda(n), \theta(n)\} \leftarrow ReadCache(Y_i, context(Y_i))$;
6   if $\{\lambda(n), \theta(n)\} \neq NULL$ then return $\{\lambda(n), \theta(n)\}$;
7   else
8   if Y_i is a decision node then $\{\lambda(n), \theta(n)\} \leftarrow (-\infty, -\infty)$;
9   else if Y_i is a chance node then $\{\lambda(n), \theta(n)\} \leftarrow (1,0)$;
10   foreach $y_i \in Domain(Y_i)$ do
11   let m be an AND node labeled $\langle Y_i, y_i \rangle$;
12          $\{\lambda(m), \theta(m)\} \leftarrow (1,0)$;
13   foreach $k = 1..q$ do
14            $\{\lambda, \theta\} \leftarrow$ AO-ID($\mathcal{M}_k$);
15            $\lambda(m) \leftarrow \lambda(m) \cdot \lambda$;
16            $\theta(m) \leftarrow \theta(m) + \frac{\theta}{\lambda}$;
17   if Y_i is a decision node then
18            $\lambda(n) \leftarrow max(\lambda(n), w_\lambda(n,m) \cdot \lambda(m))$;
19            $\theta(n) \leftarrow max(\theta(n), w_\theta(n,m) \cdot \lambda(m) \cdot (w_\theta(n,m) + \theta(m)))$;
20   else if Y_i is a chance node then
21            $\lambda(n) += w_\lambda(n,m) \cdot \lambda(m)$;
22            $\theta(n) += w_\lambda(n,m) \cdot \lambda(m) \cdot (w_\theta(n,m) + \theta(m))$;
23      $WriteCache(Y_i, context(Y_i), \{\lambda(n), \theta(n)\})$;
24   return $\{\lambda(n), \theta(n)\}$

Example 5. For illustration, consider the policy graph highlighted in Figure 3. The two decision rules δ_A and δ_D can be read from the graph, as follows: δ_A: $A = 0$, δ_D: $D = 1$ if $(A = 0, C = 0)$ and $D = 0$ if $(A = 0, C = 1)$, respectively.

4 Depth-First AND/OR Graph Search

Search algorithms that traverse the AND/OR graph can be used to compute the optimal policy graph of an influence diagram as we will describe in this section.

A depth-first search algorithm, called AO-ID, that traverses the context-minimal AND/OR graph and computes the values of each node in the search space is described in Algorithm 1. The following notation is used: $\mathcal{M}$ is the problem with which the procedure is called and $\mathcal{T}$ is the pseudo tree that drives the AND/OR search graph. The algorithm assumes that variables are selected according to the pseudo tree arrangement. If $\mathcal{M}$ is empty, then the result is trivially computed (line 1). Else, AO-ID selects a variable Y_i (*i.e.*, expands the OR node n labeled Y_i) and iterates over its values (line 10) to compute the OR values $\{\lambda(n), \theta(n)\}$. The algorithm first attempts to retrieve the results cached at the OR nodes (line 5). If a valid cache entry is found for the current OR node n then the OR values $\{\lambda(n), \theta(n)\}$ are updated (line 6) and the search continues with the next variable. The context-based caching uses table representation. For each variable Y_i, a *cache table* is reserved in memory for each possible assignment to its context. During search, each table entry records the λ and θ-values below the corresponding OR node (for decision nodes, the table entry also records the argmax of the corresponding θ-value).

When AO-ID expands the AND node m labeled $\langle Y_i, y_i \rangle$ the problem is decomposed into a set of q independent subproblems ($\mathcal{M}_k$), one for each child Y_k of Y_i in $\mathcal{T}$. These subproblems are solved sequentially (lines 13-16) and the solutions accumulated by the AND values $\{\lambda(m), \theta(m)\}$ (lines 15-16). After trying all feasible values of Y_i, the solution to the subproblem below Y_i remains in $\{\lambda(n), \theta(n)\}$ which are first saved in cache (line 23) and then returned (line 24). Clearly, since AO-ID explores every node in the context-minimal graph just once, it is the case that:

Theorem 1 (complexity). *Given an ID with primal graph G and a pseudo tree $\mathcal{T}$ of G, algorithm AO-ID guided by $\mathcal{T}$ is sound and complete. Its time and space complexity is $O(N \cdot k^{w^*_{\mathcal{T}}(G)})$, where $w^*_{\mathcal{T}}(G)$ is the constrained induced-width.*

Extracting the Optimal Decision Rules

Once AO-ID terminates and returns the maximum expected utility $\mathscr{E}$, the optimal policy $\Delta^* = (\delta_1^*, ..., \delta_m^*)$ corresponding to $\mathscr{E}$ is obtained by processing the decision variables from first to last, as follows. Let D_i be the current decision variable. Its optimal decision rule, δ_i^*, is a function defined on $context(D_i)$ and maps every instantiation of $context(D_i)$ that is consistent with the previously computed optimal decision rules $(\delta_1^*, ..., \delta_{i-1}^*)$, to the corresponding cache entry recorded by AO-ID for D_i (*i.e.*, the optimal decision d_i for D_i).

Exploiting Determinism

Often the functions of an influence diagram may encode deterministic relationships (*i.e.*, hard constraints). Some of these constraints are represented by the zero-probability entries of the probability tables. In this case, it is beneficial to exploit the computational power of the constraints explicitly, via constraint propagation [3]. The approach we take for handling the determinism is based on the known technique of *unit resolution* for Boolean satisfiability (SAT) over a knowledge base (KB) in the form of propositional clauses (CNF) representing the constraints. One way for encoding constraints as a CNF formula is the *direct encoding* [14].

Algorithm 1 can then be modified as follows. Upon expanding an AND node, its corresponding SAT instantiation is asserted. If unit resolution leads to a contradiction, then the current AND node is marked as dead-end and the search continues by expanding the next node on the search stack. Whenever AO-ID backtracks to the previous level, it also retracts any SAT instantiation recorded by unit resolution. Notice that the algorithm is capable of pruning the domains of future variables in the current subproblem due to conflicts detected during unit propagation.

5 Experiments

In this section, we compare empirically the AND/OR search approach against state-of-the-art algorithms for exact evaluation of influence diagrams. We consider two AND/OR search algorithms that explore the context-minimal AND/OR graph and exploit the determinism that may be present in the influence diagram using constraint propagation. They are denoted by AO-ID+SAT and AO-ID+BCP, respectively. AO-ID+BCP is conservative and applies only unit resolution over the CNF that encodes the determinism, at each node in the search graph, whereas AO-ID+SAT is more aggressive and detects inconsistency by running a full SAT solver. We used the **minisat** solver (available online at *http://minisat.se/*) for both unit resolution as well as full satisfiability. For reference, we also ran the AND/OR graph search algorithm without constraint propagation, denoted by AO-ID. In all our experiments, the pseudo trees that guided the AND/OR search algorithms were generated using the *min-fill* heuristic [3].

The competing approaches are: (i) the bucket elimination (BE) algorithm [2] and (ii) a policy evaluation algorithm based on Cooper's algorithm [1] which is available from the Genie/Smile system (*http://genie.sis.pitt.edu*). The latter converts the influence diagram into a Bayesian network and finds the expected utilities of each of the decision alternatives by performing repeated exact inference in this network. We also note that the variable elimination algorithm by [5] which is available in the commercial Hugin shell (*www.hugin.com*) is equivalent with BE [2].

Random Influence Diagrams

We generated a set of 150 random influence diagrams based on the total number of nodes (N) and the number of decision nodes (d). The configurations chosen are shown in the first column of Table 1. We have from 40 to 160 nodes, 10 decision nodes and 5 utility functions (u), respectively. Each of the chance and decision variables had two parents chosen randomly, ensuring that the ID graph had no cycles and the decision nodes were connected by a directed path in the graph. The fraction of chance nodes that are assigned deterministic CPTs is a parameter, called the *deterministic ratio*. The CPTs for these nodes were randomly filled with 0 and 1; in the remaining nodes, the CPTs were randomly filled using a uniform distribution. Each utility function was defined over 3 randomly chosen variables (out of N), and its corresponding table was filled with integers drawn uniformly at random between 1 and 100, respectively. The domain size (k) of each variable is 2.

Each row in Table 1 contains the median CPU time in seconds, as well as the median induced width (w^*) and depth of the pseudo tree (h) obtained for 10 randomly generated diagrams with that configuration. A number in parenthesis (next to the CPU time) indicates only that many instances out of 10 were solved within the time or memory limit. Also, the table is organized into three horizontal blocks, each corresponding to a specific value of the deterministic ratio. Not surprisingly, BE and AO-ID were able to solve only the smallest instances and they ran out of memory

Random influence diagrams, deterministic ratio 0.50, 10 instances for each entry						
size (N,d,u,k)	(w*, h)	BE	Smile	AO-ID	AO-ID+SAT	AO-ID+BCP
(40,10,5,2)	(16, 26)	**1.12** (10)	24.32 (10)	12.65 (10)	30.47 (10)	7.88 (10)
(60,10,5,2)	(??, 34)	**57.68** (10)	86.35 (6)	542.09 (10)	250.53 (10)	182.64 (10)
(80,10,5,2)	(26, 43)	431.62 (5)	1295.51 (3)	3156.99 (6)	2294.49 (6)	**1312.71** (6)
(100,10,5,2)	(31, 48)	-	**7196.51** (1)	-	-	-
Random influence diagrams, deterministic ratio 0.75, 10 instances for each entry						
size (N,d,u,k)	(w*, h)	BE	Smile	AO-ID	AO-ID+SAT	AO-ID+BCP
(40,10,5,2)	(16, 26)	**0.61** (10)	1.89 (10)	2.08 (10)	1.19 (10)	0.87 (10)
(60,10,5,2)	(22, 34)	66.53 (10)	82.16 (8)	392.37 (10)	50.51 (10)	**23.66** (10)
(80,10,5,2)	(26, 43)	358.85 (5)	74.52 (4)	2448.75 (10)	**129.00** (10)	164.06 (10)
(100,10,5,2)	(31, 48)	-	88.57 (2)	-	1024.18 (10)	675.09 (10)
Random influence diagrams, deterministic ratio 0.90, 10 instances for each entry						
size (N,d,u,k)	(w*, h)	BE	Smile	AO-ID	AO-ID+SAT	AO-ID+BCP
(40,10,5,2)	(17, 27)	0.65 (10)	1.67 (10)	1.11 (10)	0.10 (10)	**0.03** (10)
(60,10,5,2)	(23, 34)	52.86 (10)	30.65 (9)	101.48 (10)	1.09 (10)	**0.37** (10)
(80,10,5,2)	(27, 42)	480.99 (4)	73.46 (6)	1711.81 (10)	3.06 (10)	**0.88** (10)
(100,10,5,2)	(31, 46)	516.59 (1)	26.03 (2)	-	9.12 (10)	**3.07** (10)
(120,10,5,2)	(36, 55)	-	-	-	23.92 (10)	**7.85** (10)
(140,10,5,2)	(39, 58)	-	30.98 (1)	-	97.46 (10)	**30.64** (10)
(160,10,5,2)	(43, 66)	-	-	-	140.26 (10)	**62.68** (10)

Table 1 Median CPU times in seconds for random influence diagrams of different sizes. Time limit 2 hours and 2GB of RAM. '-' stands for time-out or out-of-memory.

due to higher induced widths on larger problems. On the other hand, AO-ID+SAT and AO-ID+BCP, which exploit efficiently the determinism present in the diagrams, offer the overall best performance on this domain. Both methods scaled to much larger problem instances than their competitors, especially for the 0.90 deterministic ratio. For example, on the $(100,10,5,2)$ configuration with 0.90 deterministic ratio, BE solved one instance (in 516.59 sec), while Smile solved 2 out of 10 instances (in 26.03 sec). AO-ID+SAT and AO-ID+BCP solved all 10 instances of this problem class using 9.12 and 3.07 seconds, respectively. We also see that AO-ID+BCP was consistently faster than AO-ID+SAT. This was due to the lightweight constraint propagation scheme used by the former. Notice that Smile is competitive with AO-ID+BCP, however it solved about half as many instances as AO-ID+BCP.

Real-World Benchmarks

These influence diagrams are based on ground instances of real-world Bayesian networks from the UCI Graphical Models repository[1]. For our purpose, we converted each of these networks into an influence diagram by choosing at random d out of N variables to act as decisions and adding u ternary reward functions as in the case of random influence diagrams. Table 2 displays the results obtained on this dataset, where each row shows the median CPU time over 10 instances that were generated for each network by randomizing the choice of decision nodes. As before, the numbers in parenthesis (next to the CPU time) indicate how many instances out of 10 were solved. We also report the average induced-width (w^*) and depth (h) of the

---

[1] Available online at: http://graphmod.ics.uci.edu/group/Repository

Influence diagrams derived from real-world Bayesian networks, 10 instances for each entry.							
network	(N, d, u, k)	(w*, h)	BE	Smile	AO-ID	AO-ID+SAT	AO-ID+BCP
90-10-1	(90, 10, 5, 2)	(25, 48)	346.43 (8)	34.81 (10)	2262.48 (8)	20.75 (10)	**6.47** (10)
90-14-1	(186, 10, 5, 2)	(32, 73)	-	35.38 (7)	-	353.39 (10)	**100.84** (10)
90-16-1	(246, 10, 5, 2)	(32, 95)	-	1292.21(5)	-	3568.53 (5)	**674.89** (9)
blockmap_05_01	(690, 10, 5, 2)	(26, 89)	526.17 (10)	1223.95 (10)	2981.95 (4)	5.01 (10)	**0.69** (10)
blockmap_05_02	(845, 10, 5, 2)	(27, 85)	902.13 (2)	5111.03 (3)	-	20.93 (10)	**2.30** (10)
blockmap_05_03	(995, 10, 5, 2)	(28, 120)	892.21 (1)	4027.92 (2)	-	45.40 (10)	**3.35** (10)
hailfinder	(51, 5, 5, 11)	(10, 19)	**1.15** (10)	37.29 (10)	13.35 (10)	69.64 (8)	15.17 (10)
insurance	(22, 5, 5, 5)	(9, 17)	**0.45** (10)	6.56 (10)	9.68 (10)	32.09 (10)	8.51 (10)
mastermind_03_08_03	(1205, 15, 10, 2)	(25, 111)	440.22 (6)	6125.32 (1)	5233.73 (1)	967.17 (10)	**40.96** (10)
mastermind_04_08_03	(1408, 15, 10, 2)	(31, 124)	-	-	-	3833.30 (3)	**391.45** (8)
pathfinder	(106, 3, 5, 63)	(6, 15)	**0.14** (10)	1.72 (10)	1.60 (10)	1750.01 (10)	2.28 (10)
s386	(162, 10, 5, 2)	(21, 44)	34.70 (10)	4.27 (10)	21.02 (10)	26.82 (10)	**3.38** (10)
water	(29, 3, 5, 4)	(13, 22)	123.36 (9)	26.36 (10)	99.50 (10)	43.08 (10)	**11.13** (10)

Table 2 Median CPU times in seconds for influence diagrams derived from real-world Bayesian networks. Time limit 2 hours and 2GB of RAM. '-' stands for time-out or out-of-memory.

pseudo trees. We see that AO-ID+BCP is overall the best performing algorithm on this dataset, winning on 10 out of the 13 benchmarks tested and, in some cases, outperforming its competitors by almost two orders of magnitude (*e.g.*, *blockmap*). For example, on the *blockmap_05_02* benchmark, BE solved 2 out of 10 instances (in 902.13 sec), Smile solved 3 out of 10 instances (in 5111.03 sec), while AO-ID+SAT and AO-ID+BCP solved all 10 instances in 20.93 and 2.30 seconds, respectively. Notice again that BE and Smile are competitive with AO-ID+BCP only on the smallest problem instances (*e.g.*, *pathfinder*). The relatively worse performance of AO-ID+SAT/AO-ID+BCP can be explained by the computational overhead of constraint propagation which did not pay off in this case.

6 Conclusion

In this paper we extended the AND/OR search space for graphical models to influence diagrams and presented a depth-first AND/OR graph search algorithm for computing the optimal policy of an influence diagram. We also augmented the algorithm with constraint propagation in order to exploit the determinism that may be present in the diagram. The efficiency of our approach was demonstrated empirically on various benchmarks for influence diagrams containing a significant amount of determinism. Future work includes the extension of the AND/OR search algorithm into a Branch-and-Bound scheme in order to use domain-specific heuristic information [7]. We also plan to apply the AND/OR search approach to Limited Memory Influence Diagrams (LIMIDs) [6] as well as to the more general Plausibility-Feasibility-Utility (PFU) framework [10]. Finally, in order to alleviate the memory requirements of the algorithm, we can incorporate an adaptive caching mechanism, as suggested in [8].

Related work

Our approach is closely related to the decision graph search algorithms from [11]. A decision graph is a weighted AND/OR graph containing alternating levels of OR and AND nodes. OR nodes correspond to the decision variables whereas the AND nodes correspond to clusters of chance variables appearing between successive decision variables. Given an influence diagram, the size of its associated decision graph is exponential in the number of decision variables only. Unlike Qi and Poole's method, our approach requires the influence diagram to respect the regularity constraint only, does not require additional information wrt the decision alternatives (*i.e.*, framing functions [11]), it exploits the problem structure by using graph information only, it does not impose any restrictions on the utility functions and the arc weights of the context-minimal AND/OR search graph do not involve complex computation (*i.e.*, Bayesian inference) as they are derived solely from the influence diagram's input functions via simple arithmetic computations.

References

1. Cooper, G.: A method for using belief networks as influence diagrams. In: Uncertainty in Artificial Intelligence (UAI), pp. 55–63 (1988)
2. Dechter, R.: A new perspective on algorithms for optimizing policies under uncertainty. In: Artificial Intelligence Planning and Scheduling Systems (AIPS), pp. 72–81 (2000)
3. Dechter, R., Mateescu, R.: AND/OR search spaces for graphical models. Artificial Intelligence **171**(2-3), 73–106 (2007)
4. Howard, R.A., Matheson, J.E.: Influence diagrams. The principles and applications of Decision analyis. Menlo Park, CA, USA (1984)
5. Jensen, F., Jensen, F., Dittmer, S.: From influence diagrams to junction trees. In: Uncertainty in Artificial Intelligence (UAI), pp. 367–373 (1994)
6. Lauritzen, S., Nilsson, D.: Representing and solving decision problems with limited information. Mngmnt. Science **47**(9), 1235–1251 (2001)
7. Marinescu, R., Dechter, R.: AND/OR branch-and-bound for graphical models. In: International Joint Conference on Artificial Intelligence (IJCAI), pp. 224–229 (2005)
8. Mateescu, R., Dechter, R.: AND/OR cutset conditioning. In: International Joint Conference on Artificial Intelligence (IJCAI), pp. 230–235 (2005)
9. Pearl, J.: Probabilistic Reasoning in Intelligent Systems. Morgan Kaufmann (1988)
10. Pralet, C., Verfaillie, G., Schiex, T.: An algebraic graphical model for decision with uncertainties, feasibilities, and utilities. JAIR **29**(1), 421–489 (2007)
11. Qi, R., Poole, D.: A new method for influence diagram evaluation. Computational Intelligence **11**, 498–528 (1995)
12. Shenoy, P.: Valuation-based systems for Bayesian decision analysis. Operations Research **40**(3), 463–484 (1992)
13. Tatman, J., Shachter, R.: Dynamic programming and influence diagrams. IEEE Systems, Man, and Cybernetics (1990)
14. Walsh, T.: SAT vs CSP. In: Principles and Practice of Constraint Programming (CP), pp. 441–456 (2000)

Analogical proportions: another logical view

Henri Prade and Gilles Richard

Abstract This paper investigates the logical formalization of a restricted form of analogical reasoning based on analogical proportions, i.e. statements of the form *a is to b as c is to d*. Starting from a naive set theoretic interpretation, we highlight the existence of two noticeable companion proportions: one states that *a is to b the converse of what c is to d* (*reverse analogy*), while the other called *paralogical* proportion expresses that *what a and b have in common, c and d have it also*. We identify the characteristic postulates of the three types of proportions and examine their consequences from an abstract viewpoint. We further study the properties of the set theoretic interpretation and of the Boolean logic interpretation, and we provide another light on the understanding of the role of permutations in the modeling of the three types of proportions. Finally, we address the use of these proportions as a basis for inference in a propositional setting, and relate it to more general schemes of analogical reasoning. The differences between analogy, reverse-analogy, and paralogy is still emphasized in a three-valued setting, which is also briefly presented.

1 Introduction

Analogy appears in all domains of human activities, from day to day life to more intricate form of mathematics and scientific discoveries. Analogical reasoning plays an important role in human creativity and problem solving. This is probably why a large part of IQ tests try to monitor the individual ability to build up analogy. There is a long tradition in investigating analogy in philosophy, in human sciences (cognitive psychology, linguistics, anthropology,...). In Artificial Intelligence, the researches

Henri Prade
IRIT, Université Paul Sabatier, 31062 Toulouse Cedex 09, France e-mail: prade@irit.fr,

Gilles Richard
British Institute of Technology and E-commerce, Avicenna House 258-262 Romford Road London E7 9HZ, e-mail: grichard@bite.ac.uk

M. Bramer et al. (eds.), *Research and Development in Intelligent Systems XXVI*,
DOI 10.1007/978-1-84882-983-1_9, © Springer-Verlag London Limited 2010

date back to four decades. Diverse formalizations, e.g. [1, 2] and implementations of analogical reasoning [3, 4, 5] have been proposed (often in first order logic setting). See [6, 7] for overviews and discussions. However, it seems there is no commonly agreed formal theory describing analogical reasoning. Roughly speaking, analogy is understood as the possibility to transfer knowledge from a source s to a target t. Obviously, the models largely depend on the representation of s and t.

In this paper we focus on a form of analogical reasoning where the source and the target are pairs of items (a, b) and (c, d) building a so-called analogical proportion, usually denoted $a : b :: c : d$ and which can be read as a is to b as c is to d. For instance, "3 is to 4 as 15 is to 20" is an analogical proportion involving numbers and it holds because 3/4 = 15/20. Another example involving sequences of bits could be *01 is to 10 as 11 is to 00* just because 01 and 10 does not share any bit and this is the case with 11 and 00. In the same spirit, we could say *01 is to 11 as 10 is to 00* because they just share the second bit. In the following we propose a systematic analysis of analogical proportion in a propositional logic setting. The paper is organized as follows: the next section, starting from a well agreed interpretation of analogical proportion over sets, investigates other options and highlights the existence of two relations beside standard analogical proportion, namely *paralogical proportion* and *reverse analogical proportion*, exhibiting other kinds of relation between sets. In Section 3, using an abstract viewpoint leading to a first order definition of the three proportions, we study their general properties. Section 4 investigates their specific properties in a set theoretic interpretation framework, while Section 5 is devoted to the Boolean logic interpretation. In Section 6, we discuss the use of the proportions for inference purposes, and their relation with standard analogical reasoning. Section 7 outlines a tri-valued interpretation for the three types of proportion leading to a richer inferential setting. Finally we survey related works, and conclude.

2 Analogy revisited through set interpretation

Let us consider an analogical proportion involving 4 items a, b, c, d considered as subsets of a referential X. As usual, $\bar{a} = X \setminus a$ denotes the complement of a, i.e. the elements of X not in a. X may be for instance a set of properties. In this view, as suggested in [8], [9], a, b, c, d are in analogical proportion if a can be changed into b and c into d by adding and deleting the same elements. Using a formal counterpart of this idea [10], the analogical proportion $a : b :: c : d$ is specified by the constraints:

$$a \cap \bar{b} = c \cap \bar{d} \ \wedge \ \bar{a} \cap b = \bar{c} \cap d \quad (A_{set})$$

We immediately get the following known properties of an analogical proportion:

- $a : b :: a : b$ and $a : a :: b : b$ hold, but $a : b :: b : a$ will not hold in general;
- if $a : b :: c : d$ holds then $a : c :: b : d$ should hold (central permutation);
- if $a : b :: c : d$ holds then $c : d :: a : b$ should hold (symmetry).

As we can see, we characterize a pair of subsets (a, b) with the pair $(a \cap \bar{b}, \bar{a} \cap b)$. Analogy $a : b :: c : d$ is then interpreted as an equality between two pairs $(a \cap \bar{b}, \bar{a} \cap$

$b) = (c \cap \overline{d}, \overline{c} \cap d)$. Obviously, switching the second element of the pair to get the following equality $(a \cap \overline{b}, \overline{a} \cap b) = (\overline{c} \cap d, c \cap \overline{d})$, give rise to a new proportion that we call *reverse analogy* and denote with "!" defined as

$$a \cap \overline{b} = \overline{c} \cap d \ \wedge \ \overline{a} \cap b = c \cap \overline{d} \quad (R_{set})$$

This definition leads to the following expected properties:

- $a \, ! \, b \, !! \, b \, ! \, a$ (and $a \, ! \, a \, !! \, b \, ! \, b$) should hold (reverse reflexivity);
- if $a \, ! \, b \, !! \, c \, ! \, d$ holds then $c \, ! \, b \, !! \, a \, ! \, d$ should hold (odd permutation);
- if $a \, ! \, b \, !! \, c \, ! \, d$ holds then $c \, ! \, d \, !! \, a \, ! \, b$ should hold (symmetry).

But considering the potential meaningful combinations, we obviously have $a \cap b$ and $\overline{a} \cap \overline{b}$ which could be taken into account as well. It is easy to see that adding *one* of the two for defining analogy, e.g. $(a \cap \overline{b}, \overline{a} \cap b, a \cap b) = (c \cap \overline{d}, \overline{c} \cap d, c \cap d)$ leads to the *only* solution $a = c$ and $b = d$, which is definitely not interesting. So, we cannot enrich the first definition, but we can consider another viewpoint characterizing (a, b) using only $a \cap b$ and $\overline{a} \cap \overline{b}$ [1]. Then a new proportion between a, b, c, d could be defined via the constraints: $a \cap b = c \cap d \wedge \overline{a} \cap \overline{b} = \overline{c} \cap \overline{d}$. Since the use of $\overline{a} \cap \overline{b}$, may suggest that we refer to external elements not in a or b, thanks to the equality $\overline{a \cup b} = \overline{a} \cap \overline{b}$, an equivalent definition of this proportion (called here *paralogy*) is:

$$a \cap b = c \cap d \ \wedge \ a \cup b = c \cup d \quad (P_{set})$$

Due to the properties of $\cup$ and $\cap$, the new proportion, denoted with ";", satisfy:

- $a \, ; \, b \, ;; \, a \, ; \, b$ and $a \, ; \, b \, ;; \, b \, ; \, a$ always holds (bi-reflexivity);
- if $a \, ; \, b \, ;; \, c \, ; \, d$ holds $b \, ; \, a \, ;; \, c \, ; \, d$ should hold (even permutation);
- if $a \, ; \, b \, ;; \, c \, ; \, d$ holds then $c \, ; \, d \, ;; \, a \, ; \, b$ should hold (symmetry).

Leaving the set interpretation underlying A_{set}, R_{set} and P_{set}, we investigate a more abstract viewpoint in Section 3, by setting up first order postulates defining the three proportions and studying their consequences. The reader is referred to [11] for a more general introduction of the three proportions and a complementary study.

3 Abstract setting

Thanks to the previous analysis, we have established what should be the postulates defining analogy, reverse analogy and paralogy. Table 1 provides these postulates for the corresponding first order quaternary predicates denoted A, R and P involving 4 variables a, b, c, d (in order to simplify the notation, we omit the universal quantifiers in front of all the formulas). Following these postulates, it immediately comes:

Property 1 *If A is an analogy, then:*

- *the relation R defined as "$R(a, b, c, d)$ iff $A(a, b, d, c)$" is a reverse analogy.*
- *the relation P defined as "$P(a, b, c, d)$ iff $A(a, d, c, b)$" is a paralogy.*

---

[1] In fact, one might consider other relations, which would lead us outside analogy. For instance, $(a \cap b = c \cap d) \wedge (a \cap \overline{b} = c \cap \overline{d})$ is the equivalence between conditional objects $b|a$ and $d|c$, associated with the entailment $(a \cap b \subseteq c \cap d) \wedge (a \cap \overline{b} \supseteq c \cap \overline{d})$ at the root of nonmonotonic reasoning (where $b|a$ models a default rule 'if a then b'). See S. Benferhat, D. Dubois, H. Prade: Nonmonotonic reasoning, conditional objects and possibility theory. Artific. Intelligence, 92, 259-276, 1997.

Table 1 Postulates for Analogy, Reverse analogy and Paralogy

Analogy	Reverse analogy	Paralogy
$A(a,b,a,b)$ (or $A(a,a,b,b)$)	$R(a,b,b,a)$ (or $R(a,a,b,b)$)	$P(a,b,a,b)$ (or $P(a,b,b,a)$)
$A(a,b,c,d) \rightarrow A(a,c,b,d)$	$R(a,b,c,d) \rightarrow R(c,b,a,d)$	$P(a,b,c,d) \rightarrow P(b,a,c,d)$
$A(a,b,c,d) \rightarrow A(c,d,a,b)$	$R(a,b,c,d) \rightarrow R(c,d,a,b)$	$P(a,b,c,d) \rightarrow P(c,d,a,b)$

Proof. Let us consider P for instance. Since $A(a,d,c,b) \rightarrow A(a,c,d,b)$ holds, then its translation $P(a,b,c,d) \rightarrow P(a,b,d,c)$ holds, which is the characteristic postulate of paralogy (an equivalent form of it thanks to symmetry).

As we observe, each proportion is defined via 3 postulates and the first one, which is the constructive one, plays a specific role. Since the third postulate (symmetry) is satisfied by each of these relations, let us consider the 3 non equivalent forms of the first postulate for a given quaternary relation T satisfying the symmetry postulate:

- $T(a,b,a,b)$ (i - reflexivity)
- $T(a,b,b,a)$ (ii - reverse reflexivity)
- $T(a,a,b,b)$ (iii - identity)

Thanks to their second postulate, it appears that any of the relations P, A or R satisfies at least two forms of the first postulate: A satisfies (i) and (iii), R satisfies (ii) and (iii), and finally P satisfies (i) and (ii). It is obvious that the trivial relation T such that $\forall a, b, c, d, T(a,b,c,d)$ is simultaneously an analogy, a reverse-analogy and a paralogy, and thus satisfies (i), (ii) and (iii). But we have the following property:

Property 2 *If A is an analogy, then $\not\vdash A(a,b,b,a)$*
If R is a reverse-analogy, then $\not\vdash R(a,b,a,b)$
If P is a paralogy, then $\not\vdash P(a,a,b,b)$

Proof. a simple way to get the first result is to build up a model of analogical relation where $A(a,b,b,a)$ does not hold. The classical analogical proportion over the set of non null real numbers $\mathbb{R}^*$ where $a : b :: c : d$ iff $a * d = b * c$ is a model of analogical relation and does the job. Concerning the second property, we keep the same interpretation domain and we define $R(a,b,c,d)$ as $a * c = b * d$ which obviously defines a reverse-analogy: we do not have necessarily $aa = bb$. Same idea for paralogy. This completes the proof.

It is worth noticing that transitivity cannot be deduced from the postulates:

Property 3 *If T represents one of the 3 proportions, a transitivity-like property $T(a,b,c,d) \wedge T(c,d,e,f) \rightarrow T(a,b,e,f)$ is not deducible from postulates in Table 1*

Proof. Let us consider an analogy A. We have to build up a non transitive model of analogy. This can simply be done by considering a finite set U with exactly 6 distinct elements denoted $u_1, u_2, u_3, u_4, u_5, u_6$. Over U, we define a relation A such that $A(u,v,u,v)$ holds for every pair $(u,v) \in U \times U$, $A(u_1, u_2, u_3, u_4)$ holds as well as the 7 other analogies belonging to the class of (u_1, u_2, u_3, u_4). Idem for $A(u_3, u_4, u_5, u_6)$. It means we have only 16 ordered itemsets $(a,b,c,d) \in U^4$ s. t. $A(a,b,c,d)$ holds plus C_6^2 pairs (u,v) s. t. $A(u,v,u,v)$. Obviously A is an analogy: the 3 postulates hold by construction. Now, $A(u_1,u_2,u_3,u_4)$ and $A(u_3,u_4,u_5,u_6)$ hold by definition of A, but $A(u_1,u_2,u_5,u_6)$ does not hold because (u_1,u_2,u_5,u_6) is not a permutation of (u_1,u_2,u_3,u_4) or a permutation of (u_3,u_4,u_5,u_6). A similar construction does the job for reverse analogy and paralogy.

Basic properties of analogy can be deduced (with easy proofs) from the postulates:

Property 4 *If A is an analogical relation, then the 6 following properties hold:*
  $A(a,b,c,d) \rightarrow A(c,a,d,b)$ *(i) (by symmetry + central permutation)*
  $A(a,b,c,d) \rightarrow A(b,d,a,c)$ *(ii) (by central permutation + symmetry)*
  $A(a,b,c,d) \rightarrow A(b,a,d,c)$ *(iii) (by ii + central permutation)*
  $A(a,b,c,d) \rightarrow A(d,c,b,a)$ *(iv) (by iii + symmetry)*
  $A(a,b,c,d) \rightarrow A(d,b,c,a)$ *(v) (by iv + central permutation)*

Using Property 4, it is easy to see that if $A(a,b,c,d)$ holds then a total of 8 permutations (among 24) hold, including this one, its symmetric and all the six ones appearing in the above Property 4. This constitutes the first column of Table 2. As noticed in [8], the 16 remaining permutations are divided into two other classes of equivalent analogical proportions, corresponding to columns 2 and 3 of our table. Thus, given an analogical relation A, if one permutation of a column satisfies A,

Table 2 Analogy classes

a b c d	b a c d	c b a d
a c b d	b c a d	c a b d
d b c a	d a c b	d b a c
d c b a	d c a b	d a b c
c d a b	c d b a	a d c b
b d a c	a d b c	b d c a
c a d b	c b d a	a c d b
b a d c	a b d c	b c d a

all the remaining permutations of this column satisfy A also. It is also worth noticing that column 2 (or column 3) can be obtained from column 1 by application of Property 1: half of the permutations of a given column being obtained using reverse analogy and the other ones by paralogy. For instance, if (a,b,c,d) is an analogy, then (b,a,c,d) in column 2 is a reverse analogy and (c,b,a,d) in column 3 is a paralogy. But (b,c,a,d), also in column 2, is a paralogy, not a reverse analogy. It simply means that we cannot go from one column to the next one through a unique transformation. Similarly, using R instead of A as in Table 2, we can build a new, different partition with 3 equivalent classes, each one having 8 permutations, where permutations are equivalent under the postulates of reverse analogy. The same can still be done with paralogy P, leading again to a different partition. Back to the set interpretation, we now study the consequences of our definitions.

4 Set interpretation: more properties

Having in mind our set interpretation A_{set}, (resp R_{set} and P_{set}) for analogy (resp. reverse analogy and paralogy), let us examine what kind of properties can be inferred on top of the formal properties (which are valid for any interpretation). Most of the properties established here are quite new even in the case of analogy.

Analogy. Let us start with simple illustrative examples of the set interpretation of analogy, using definition (A_{set}) where $X = \{1,2,3,4,5,6,7\}$. For instance, we have $\{1,2,3,6\} : \{1,2,3,4\} :: \{1,2,5,6\} : \{1,2,4,5\}$ or $\{1,2,3,6\} : \{1,2,4,5,6\} :: \{1,2,3\} : \{1,2,4,5\}$. Note that the subsets may have different cardinalities. We restate below a list of properties already in [8] and we add some new properties.

Property 5 *The analogy relation defined with A_{set} satisfies:*

1. $a : b :: c : d \rightarrow b \cap c \subseteq a \subseteq b \cup c$
2. $a \cap b : b :: a : a \cup b$
3. For a,b,c,d finite, $a : b :: c : d \rightarrow |a| + |d| = |b| + |c|$
4. $(a : b :: c : d) \wedge (c : d :: e : f) \rightarrow (a : b :: e : f)$ (transitivity)
5. $a : b :: c : d \rightarrow a \cap e : b \cap e :: c \cap e : d \cap e$
6. $a : b :: c : d \rightarrow a \cup e : b \cup e :: c \cup e : d \cup e$

Proof. These properties easy follows from the definition (A_{set}). Here are some hints.

For (1), let be $x \in a$: if $x \notin b$ then $x \in a \setminus b = c \setminus d$ then $x \in c$, which proves $a \subseteq b \cup c$. Now if $x \in b \cap c$ and $x \notin a$ then $x \in b \setminus a = d \setminus c$ then $x \in d$: since $x \in c$ there is a contradiction: so $x \in a$ and $b \cap c \subseteq a$.

(2) is due to $(a \cap b) \setminus b = a \setminus (a \cup b) = \emptyset$ and $b \setminus (a \cap b) = b \setminus a = (a \cup b) \setminus a$.

(3): due to (A_{set}), since $|a| = |a \cap b| + |a \cap \bar{b}|$. We infer (4) from the transitivity of the equality. (5) and (6) directly follow from the previous characterization.

The first three statements have been given by [8]. However, this author never stated (A_{set}), the definition we start from. (4) expresses the transitivity of set-interpreted analogy. Formula (5) expresses a kind of stability of analogy with regard to conditioning (when the considered properties are restricted to the subset e). The result below is now easy and provides a simple characterization (A'_{set}) of analogy that does not use the complement operator any more:

Property 6 $a : b :: c : d$ *iff* (i) $a \cup d = b \cup c \wedge (ii)$ $a \cap d = b \cap c$ (A'_{set})

Proof. $\rightarrow$: follows immediately from Property 1 and P_{set}.

: if $x \in a \setminus b$, (i) implies $x \in c$ and (ii) implies $x \notin d$: then $a \setminus b \subseteq c \setminus d$. The remaining is similar using the absolute symmetry of the definitions.

[8] also only established that (A_{set}) entails (A'_{set}) while the equivalence holds. Since we have a complement operator $\bar{a} = X \setminus a$, we investigate how it behaves with analogy. The following is a direct consequence of the properties of $\setminus$ operator.

Property 7 $a:b::c:d \rightarrow \overline{b}:\overline{a}::c:d$

$a:b::c:d \rightarrow \overline{b}:c::\overline{a}:d;$ $a:b::c:d \rightarrow \overline{a}:d::\overline{b}:c$

$a:b::c:d \rightarrow \overline{a}:\overline{b}::d:c;$ $a:b::c:d \rightarrow \overline{a}:\overline{b}::\overline{c}:\overline{d}$

$a:b::\overline{b}:\overline{a}$ and $a:\overline{b}::b:\overline{a}$ hold

Note that $a:\overline{a}::b:\overline{b}$ does not hold in general. Indeed analogy is thought in terms of properties which are deleted or added between a pair of sets. When we go from the set a to the set $\overline{a}$ and from b to $\overline{b}$, obviously the properties which are kept deleted or added are not the same when a is distinct from b. For instance, $\{1,2,3\}:\{4,5,6,7\}::$ $\{1,2,3,4\}:\{5,6,7\}$ does not hold in the set interpretation since 4 is added when going from a to $\overline{a}$ while it is deleted when going from b to $\overline{b}$. However, one might have intuitively expected $a:\overline{a}::b:\overline{b}$ holds, due to a "meta-level" reading where the relation between a and $\overline{a}$ is the same as the one between b and $\overline{b}$, but this would suppose another abstract interpretation universe. It should not come as a surprise if we remember that analogy is only characterized by the 3 postulates of Section 3; but this does not constrain its behavior with respect to operators that are associated to a particular interpretative setting. Since reverse analogy is quite close to analogy, we omit its properties for the sake of brevity. We now briefly focus on paralogy.

Paralogy. Let us recall the set interpretation for paralogy:

$$a;b;;c;d \text{ iff } a \cap b = c \cap d \ \wedge \ a \cup b = c \cup d \ (P_{set})$$

Back to our illustrative example with $X = \{1,2,3,4,5,6,7\}$, an instance of paralogy is $\{1,2,3,6\};\{1,2,4,5\};;\{1,2,5,6\};\{1,2,3,4\}$. Paralogy is transitive (i.e. $(a;b;;c;d) \wedge (c;d;;e;f) \rightarrow a;b;;e;f))$; other properties can be easily established:

Property 8 $a;b;;c;d \rightarrow a \cup e;b \cup e;;c \cup e;d \cup e$

$a;b;;c;d \rightarrow a \cap e;b \cap e;;c \cap e;d \cap e$

$a;b;;c;d \rightarrow \overline{d};b;;c;\overline{a}$ and $a;b;;c;d \rightarrow \overline{a};\overline{b};;\overline{c};\overline{d}$

$a;\overline{a};;b;\overline{b}$ holds

Proof. The two first properties are obvious consequences of our definition. The two last ones follow the De Morgan's laws for sets.

Let us note that all our proportions are stable with the complement operator, i.e., $a \mid b \parallel c \mid d \rightarrow \overline{a} \mid \overline{b} \parallel \overline{c} \mid \overline{d}$ for $\mid \in \{:,;,!\}$. In the following section, we turn to the Boolean interpetation whose properties are easily derived from the naive set interpretation, since the powerset of a referential X is a Boolean algebra.

5 Boolean interpretation

Leaving the set interpretation, we can interpret our proportions over the Boolean lattice $\mathbb{B} = \{0,1\}$ with the standard operators $\vee, \wedge, \neg$. Let us start with analogy.

Analogy. We follow here the lines of [10]. We can use a direct translation of the set theoretic definitions where $\cup$ is replaced with $\vee$, $\cap$ with $\wedge$, complementarity with $\neg$. To simplify the notation, we write $u \equiv v$ to denote the formula $u \to v \wedge v \to u$. Of course, this logical notation underlies the equality of the truth values for u and v.

Definition 1 $a : b :: c : d$ *holds iff*

$$((a \wedge \neg b) \equiv (c \wedge \neg d)) \wedge ((\neg a \wedge b) \equiv (\neg c \wedge d)) = 1 \quad (A_{Bool})$$

This relation over $\mathbb{B}^4$ satisfies the properties of analogical proportion and several equivalent writings have been proposed in [10] e.g.

Definition 2 $(a : b :: c : d)$ *holds iff* $((a \to b) \equiv (c \to d)) \wedge ((b \to a) \equiv (d \to c)) = 1$.

Note that the above expression parallels the difference-based view of the analogical proportion. The results holding for the set theoretic interpretation are easy to restate: of course, there is no counterpart for the cardinality results but all the results below are straightforward translations of their set theoretic counterpart. Transitivity is satisfied, and e.g., the first proposition below is the counterpart of Property 6:

Property 9 $a : b :: c : d$ *holds iff* $((a \wedge d \equiv b \wedge c) \wedge (a \vee d \equiv b \vee c)) = 1$

Property 10 $\quad a : b :: c : d \to a \wedge e : b \wedge e :: c \wedge e : d \wedge e$
$a : b :: c : d \to a \vee e : b \vee e :: c \vee e : d \vee e$
$a : b :: c : d \to a \wedge e : b \wedge e :: c : d$ *when* $(e \vee c \equiv e \vee d) = 1$
$a : b :: c : d \to a \vee e : b \vee e :: c : d$ *when* $(e \wedge c \equiv e \wedge d) = 1$

Proof. The proof clones the one for sets using only the mutual distributivity of $\wedge$ and $\vee$. The two first implications are the translations of items 5 and 6 of Property 5.

As in the set theoretic setting, we have a negation operator: then the proposition below (whose proof is easy) is the Boolean counterpart of Property 7:

Property 11 $a : b :: c : d \to \neg b : \neg a :: c : d; \quad a : b :: c : d \to \neg b : c :: \neg a : d$
$a : b :: c : d \to \neg a : d :: \neg b : c; \quad a : b :: c : d \to \neg a : \neg b :: d : c$
$a : b :: c : d \to \neg a : \neg b :: \neg c : \neg d; \quad a : b :: \neg b : \neg a$ *hold.*

Paralogy. As for analogy, the Boolean interpretation of paralogy is a direct counterpart of the set interpretation:

Definition 3 $a; b; ; c; d \quad iff \quad ((a \wedge b \equiv c \wedge d) \wedge (a \vee b \equiv c \vee d)) = 1 \quad (P_{Bool})$

As for the analogy relation, it is straightforward to derive the properties of the Boolean interpretation of paralogy. We leave them to the interested reader, as well as the study of reverse analogy in the Boolean setting, due to the lack of space.

The most intuitive way to understand the Boolean interpretation is to consider our proportions as new Boolean operators and to examine their truth table below with the only values making the relations to hold (among 16 possibilities). Except for the first 2 lines, it appears that only 2 of our 3 relations can hold simultaneously.

Table 3 Proportion truth tables

Analogy				Reverse				Paralogy			
a	b	c	d	a	b	c	d	a	b	c	d
0	0	0	0	0	0	0	0	0	0	0	0
1	1	1	1	1	1	1	1	1	1	1	1
0	0	1	1	0	0	1	1	1	0	0	1
1	1	0	0	1	1	0	0	0	1	1	0
0	1	0	1	0	1	1	0	0	1	0	1
1	0	1	0	1	0	0	1	1	0	1	0

6 Inferences

When it comes to analogical reasoning, without any reference to the notion of proportion, it is simply viewed as a way to infer new conclusion starting from only one observation. Analogical reasoning has been mainly studied through the angle of first order logic [2, 6]. A basic first order formalization for analogical reasoning is to consider 2 terms s and t, to observe that they share a property P, and knowing the additional property Q for s, to infer $Q(t)$. This is known as the "analogical jump" and can be described as the following inference (simplified form):

$$\frac{P(s) \ \ P(t) \ \ Q(s)}{Q(t)} \quad (Basic \ pattern)$$

Obviously, this inference is not sound and a considerable amount of works has been done to identify the weakest external conditions making the inference scheme valid. More precisely, it is expected that a kind of connection between P and Q denoted $P \looparrowright Q$ will insure the inference below

$$\frac{P(s) \ \ \ P(t) \ \ \ Q(s) \ \ \ P \looparrowright Q}{Q(t)} \quad (Analogy)$$

to be sound. In the following, we focus on a propositional viewpoint, more suitable for immediate use in the context of classification for instance (see [12]).

Boolean case. Since our 3 proportions (analogy, reverse analogy and paralogy) are considered as Boolean formulas, it is natural to describe what can be inferred from a given situation with a set of valid inferences, involving these proportions in the premises of the inference schemes. Let us start from a simple example to understand our point. Suppose we observe $\neg a, b$ and $\neg c$ and we get a new d knowing only that d is in analogical proportion with the 3 previous values. We are faced to the problem of inferring the value of d. It is useful now to come to the clausal form of our proportions. The clausal form for analogical proportion is:

$$\{\neg a \lor b \lor c, \neg a \lor b \lor \neg d, a \lor \neg c \lor d, \neg b \lor \neg c \lor d,$$

$$a \lor \neg b \lor \neg c, a \lor \neg b \lor d, \neg a \lor c \lor \neg d, b \lor c \lor \neg d\}$$

and the clausal form for paralogy is:

$$\{\neg a \vee c \vee d, \neg a \vee \neg b \vee d, a \vee b \vee \neg c, b \vee \neg c \vee \neg d,$$

$$a \vee \neg c \vee \neg d, a \vee b \vee \neg d, \neg a \vee \neg b \vee c, \neg b \vee c \vee d\}.$$

Note that analogy and paralogy have exactly 8 clauses which cannot be reduced, and they do not share any clause. Each clause is falsified by a pattern of 3 literals for which there does not exist a fourth literal with which they form a proportion. Thus, the first clause $\neg a \vee b \vee c$ expresses syntactically that $a \ \neg b \ \neg c$ (i.e., 1 0 0 in semantical terms) cannot be analogically completed, while $a \vee \neg b \vee \neg c$ expresses the same w. r. t. $\neg a \ b \ c$ and 0 1 1. Similar observations would be also true for reverse analogy. Going back to our inference example, it is easy to check the pattern:

$$\frac{\neg a \quad b \quad \neg c \quad a : b :: c : d}{d}$$

by resolution using the 6th clause of the clausal form of $a : b :: c : d$. As expected, we have 6 valid inferences which are given in Table 4. We may notice that inferring the value of d starting from the values of a, b, c and the fact that $a : b :: c : d$ holds can be viewed as an equation solving problem: find d such that $a : b :: c : d$ holds knowing a, b, c. It works similarly for the two other proportions.

Table 4 Valid inferences with an analogical proportion

$\dfrac{a \ b \ c \ a{:}b{::}c{:}d}{d}$	$\dfrac{\neg a \ \neg b \ \neg c \ a{:}b{::}c{:}d}{\neg d}$	$\dfrac{\neg a \ \neg b \ c \ a{:}b{::}c{:}d}{d}$
$\dfrac{a \ \neg b \ c \ a{:}b{::}c{:}d}{\neg d}$	$\dfrac{\neg a \ b \ \neg c \ a{:}b{::}c{:}d}{d}$	$\dfrac{a \ b \ \neg c \ a{:}b{::}c{:}d}{\neg d}$

Boolean vector case. Now, let us consider the case where we deal with vectors $(a_1, \ldots, a_n)$ of Boolean values that encode the multiple binary features that describe a situation. Starting from a database of clean data, each piece of data being a row completely informed, we are faced with a learning-like task when we have to consider a new piece of data $d = (d_1, \ldots, d_n)$, partially informed, i.e. where only some features $k(d) = (d_1, \ldots, d_p), p < n$, are known, the values of the missing features $u(d) = (d_{p+1}, \ldots, d_n)$ having to be predicted. To perform our inductive step, we adopt the following general pattern (where $| \in \{:, ;, !\}$ denotes any kind of proportion):

$$\frac{\forall i \in [1, p], \ a_i | b_i || c_i | d_i}{\forall j \in [p+1, n], \ a_j | b_j || c_j | d_j}$$

It simply means that

if the known part $k(d)$ of d is componentwise in formal proportion (of type $|$) with $k(a), k(b)$ and $k(c)$ then it should be also true for the unknown part $u(d)$ of d for the same proportion $|$.

This is obviously a form of reasoning that is not sound, but which may be useful for trying to guess unknown values. As previously seen, we are in a position to safely infer d from $a : b :: c : d$ in the Boolean case, then we are done for the Boolean vector case where we work componentwise.

Let us consider an example where $m = 5$ and $a = (1,1,0,0,1)$, $b = (1,0,1,1,0)$, $c = (0,1,0,0,1)$. We have to predict the missing values for an item $d = (0,0,1,d_4,d_5)$ (here $p = 3$, $k(d) = (0,0,1), u(d) = (d_4,d_5)$). With our notation, we see that $k(a) : k(b) :: k(c) : k(d)$ holds for the first three features and we look for the pair of unknown attributes $u(d) = (d_4,d_5)$. Then we consider our previous inference scheme telling us that we should have: $0 : 1 :: 0 : d_4$ and $1 : 0 :: 1 : d_5$. Starting from the clausal definition of $a : b :: c : d$, we use the 6th clause $a_4 \vee \neg b_4 \vee d_4$ which allows to infer d_4, and the 2nd clause $\neg a_5 \vee b_5 \vee \neg d_5$ which allows to infer $\neg d_5$: it means $d_4 = 1$ and $d_5 = 0$ (that we could get from the truth table as well).

Basic pattern and analogical proportion. Reasoning with analogical proportions as above can be related to analogical reasoning, in the sense of the "Basic pattern" underlying analogy. Assume the source s is just a pair of items (a,b), the target t another pair (c,d), and the properties P and Q are conjunctions of relations:

$$P(a,b) = \bigwedge_{i \in [1,p]} P_i(a_i,b_i) \text{ and } Q(a,b) = \bigwedge_{i \in [p+1,n]} Q_i(a_i,b_i)$$

Since the pairs (a,b) and (c,d) share the property P, we say that the 4-uple a,b,c,d constitutes an analogical proportion, maybe in a generalized sense, still denoted $a : b :: c : d$. The inference becomes:

$$\frac{\bigwedge_{i \in [1,p]} P_i(a_i,b_i) \quad \bigwedge_{i \in [1,p]} P_i(c_i,d_i) \quad \bigwedge_{j \in [p+1,n]} Q_j(a_j,b_j)}{\bigwedge_{j \in [p+1,n]} Q_j(c_j,d_j)}$$

In the case where the Q_i's are functional relations (i.e., when $Q_i(x,y)$ holds then $y = f_i(x)$), we can deterministically compute the missing values of d due to the inferred property: $\forall i \in [p+1,n], d_i = f_i(c_i)$. A proper choice of the P_i's and Q_i's enables us to see the analogical proportion-based inference as a particular case of the above pattern. Namely, let P_i encode if the two binary feature values (a_i,b_i) (or (c_i,d_i)) are equal, or if the first is greater than the second one, or if the second is greater than the first one. Similarly Q_j stands for $=$, $>$, or $<$. Thus, the first predicate (i.e., $=$) covers the four patterns 1 1 1 1, 0 0 0 0, 1 1 0 0, 0 0 1 1, while the second (i.e., $>$) takes care of 1 0 1 0, and the third (i.e., $<$) one of 0 1 0 1.

7 Tri-valued interpretation

Of course, a strict Boolean interpretation does not give space for graded properties or features. Imagine for instance that we have to deal with properties whose satisfaction can be described in terms of three levels, say *low, medium or high*, (instead of the usual *yes* or *no*). Then we need the introduction of a 3rd value to take into account this fact. For the sake of simplicity, we focus now on the set $\mathbb{T} = \{-1,0,1\}$

where our items a, b, c and d can take their value[2]. In that case, the three relations may be defined via the algebraic operators + and -, as given in Table 5. It is quite

Table 5 3-valued models for analogy, reverse analogy and paralogy

Analogy	Reverse analogy	Paralogy
$a - b = c - d$	$a - b = d - c$	$a + b = c + d$

easy to prove that the previous definitions satisfy the required postulates for analogy, reverse analogy and paralogy over $\mathbb{T}$. Because of the third truth value, this interpretation is richer than the Boolean one. But the inference process can also be seen as an equation solving problem. In the tri-valued model, it appears, when the three equations are simultaneously solvable, that they can provide distinct solutions. However, it can be seen that any of these equations may fail to have a solution in $\mathbb{T}$.

To highlight the difference between our three relations, instead of following the lines of the previous section, we simply revisit the "parallelogram metaphor" often used when discussing analogical reasoning in a numerical setting. It amounts to consider a, b, c and d as elements on the real plan $\mathbb{R}^2$ and to interpret $a : b :: c : d$ as $\overrightarrow{ab} = \overrightarrow{cd}$. It simply means that the quadrilateral $abdc$ is a parallelogram. As in the case of set or Boolean interpretations, it is not true that we can simultaneously find a solution d to analogical, reverse analogical and paralogical equations whatever the values of a, b and c are in $\mathbb{T}^2$. Let us show an example where the three equations are solvable and where the three solutions denoted d_{ana}, d_{rev} and d_{para} (with obvious notations) are distinct, leading to three parallelograms (see Fig. 1).

8 Related works

The formal study of analogical proportions as an inferential tool has not been considered by many researchers. Klein [13] was apparently the first to do it, in a rather empirical manner, but his definition which amounts in propositional logic notation to write $(a : b :: c : d)$ holds iff $((a \equiv b) \equiv (c \equiv d)) = 1$ was not specific enough. More recently, Lepage [8] has provided a more formal analysis and discussion of analogical proportion. In his work, he ends up with 6 postulates. Our formal approach, based on 3 postulates only, is not limited to one type of proportion and allows to es-

---

[2] We can work equivalently with the scale $\{0, 1/2, 1\}$, or more generally with the unit interval scale as in fuzzy logic, and using multiple-valued logic operators, by writing counterparts of the constraints describing each type of proportion:

1. $max(0, a - b) = max(0, c - d)$ and $max(0, b - a) = max(0, d - c)$ for analogy. It can be equivalently written with Lukasiewicz implication, $min(1, 1 - a + b) = min(1, 1 - c + d)$ and $min(1, 1 - b - a) = min(1, 1 - d + c)$.
2. $max(0, a - b) = max(0, d - c)$ and $max(0, b - a) = max(0, c - d)$ for reverse analogy.
3. $max(0, a + b - 1) = max(0, c + d - 1)$ and $min(1, a + b) = min(1, c + d)$ for paralogy.

Other choices of multiple-valued logic operators naturally emerge: for instance, one may rather use Goguen implication $a \rightarrow b = ($ if $a > 0$ then $min(1, \frac{b}{a})$ else 1), leading to a model encoding arithmetic proportions. One may also consider another possible extension of (A), (R) and (P) converting $\cup$ to max-based disjunction and $\cap$ to min-based conjunction. The full study of the extension of our approach to fuzzy set connectives in the realm of appropriate algebras is left for further studies.

Fig. 1 We consider $a = (0, -1), b = (0,0), c = (+1,0)$ and it is easy to check that:
The unique d such that $a : b :: c : d$ is

$$d_{ana} = (+1, +1)$$

The unique d such that $a ! b !! c ! d$ is

$$d_{rev} = (+1, -1)$$

The unique d such that $a ; b ; ; c ; d$ is

$$d_{para} = (-1, -1)$$

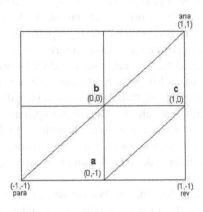

tablish a number of properties not previously discussed by Lepage. Miclet and Prade [10] have developed the Boolean logic interpretation for the analogical proportion, but they do not investigate the postulates and their consequences independently of any particular interpretation, nor consider the two other types of proportions introduced in this paper, nor discuss the relation of analogical proportion-based inference to more general forms of analogical reasoning, or the parallelogram metaphor.

Besides, beyond the set and Boolean logic interpretations, [14, 9, 15, 16] provide a large panel of algebraic models for analogical proportions, from semi-groups to lattices, through words over finite alphabets and finite trees. It would be interesting to investigate the use of reverse analogy and paralogy in such contexts of structures enriched by the existence of particular operators. Moreover, in [5], formal proportions of structured objects are investigated, going through second order logic substitutions: this approach allows its authors to capture high level mapping between highly structured universes. [9] might be viewed as a particular case of it. What paralogy and reverse analogy become in the higher order setting of [5] is a question worth raising. It would be also worth investigating how to interface, and maybe to hybridize, our postulate-based approach with [5] based on abstraction mapping.

Lastly, the use of analogy in cognition and especially in learning has been identified and discussed, e.g. [17]. Analogical proportions themselves have been recently used for machine learning purposes in [12], which focuses on classification problems, developing a kind of analogical version of the k-nearest neighbors algorithm by means of so-called "analogical dissimilarities", through a notion of distance coherent with an analogical proportion relation. It turns out that dissimilarity is maximal in some reverse analogy or paralogy situations. As in Lepage [8], [14] deeply investigates the use of analogical learning for natural language processing. The approach discussed in this paper may have some potential for learning. So, we may wonder if our different proportions may play specific roles in learning problems.

9 Conclusion

We have investigated the core properties of analogy-related proportions, starting from an axiomatic setting, free of any interpretation bias where two new kinds of proportion appear, namely paralogy and reverse analogy, close to analogy, but capturing intuitions other than the one underlying analogical proportion. While analogical and reverse analogical proportions focus on dissimilarities, paralogical proportions privilege a reading in terms of similarities. Then going to interpretations, we have unified former results and we have exhibited new properties within the set and Boolean logic interpretations, making clear the parallel between the two settings. Finally, our three-valued model highlights the fact that these three companion proportions which provide distinct options for a given problem, can be extended to more expressive representation settings. In that respect, the definitions given in Table 5 of Section 7 for the three proportions could be also generalized to any group operation (here denoted $+$), and the associated opposite operation (here denoted $-$).

Acknowledgments: We are very grateful to Laurent Miclet for his fruitful comments and for drawing our attention to the parallelogram metaphor.

References

1. Winston, P.H.: Learning and reasoning by analogy. Com. ACM, 23 (1980) 689–703
2. Davies, T.R., Russell, S.J.: A logical approach to reasoning by analogy. In: IJCAI-87, Morgan Kaufmann (1987) 264–270
3. Sowa, J.F., Majumdar, A.K.: Analogical reasoning. In: Proc. Inter. Conf. on Conceptual Structures. LNAI 2746, Dresden, Springer-Verlag (2003) 16–36
4. Gentner, D.: The Mechanisms of Analogical Learning. In: Similarity and Analogical Reasoning. Cambridge University Press (1989) 197–241
5. Schmid, U., Gust, H., Kühnberger, K., Burghardt, J.: An algebraic framework for solving proportional and predictive analogies. Eur. Conf. Cogn. Sci. 295-300 (2003)
6. Melis, E., Veloso, M.: Analogy in problem solving. In: Handbook of Practical Reasoning: Computational and Theoretical Aspects, Oxford University Press (1998)
7. Ippoliti, E.: Demonstrative and non-demonstrative reasoning by analogy. in: "Demonstrative and non-demonstrative reasoning in mathematics and natural science", C. Cellucci - P. Pecere (eds), Edizioni dell'Universia' di Cassino, 2006, 309-338 (arXiv:0810.5078) (2008) 24 p
8. Lepage, Y.: Analogy and formal languages. In: Proc. FG/MOL 2001. (2001) 373–378 (see also http://www.slt.atr.co.jp/ lepage/pdf/dhdryl.pdf.gz).
9. Stroppa, N., Yvon, F.: Analogical learning and formal proportions: Definitions and methodological issues. ENST Paris report (2005)
10. Miclet, L., Prade, H.: Handling analogical proportions in classical logic and fuzzy logics settings. In: Proc. 10th ECSQARU, Verona. Volume LNCS 5590., Springer (2009) 638–650
11. Prade, H., Richard, G.: Analogy, paralogy and reverse analogy: Postulates and inferences. In: Proc. 32nd Ann. Conf. on Artif. Intellig. (KI 2009), Paderborn, Sept. 15-18, Springer (2009)
12. Miclet, L., Bayoudh, S., Delhay, A.: Analogical dissimilarity: definition, algorithms and two experiments in machine learning. JAIR, 32 (2008) 793–824
13. Klein, S.: Culture, mysticism & social structure and the calculation of behavior. In: Proc. Europ. Conf. in AI (ECAI). (1982) 141–146
14. Stroppa, N., Yvon, F.: An analogical learner for morphological analysis. In: Proc. 9th Conf. Comput. Natural Language Learning (CoNLL-2005). (2005) 120–127
15. Miclet, L., Delhay, A.: Relation d'analogie et distance sur un alphabet defini par des traits. Technical Report 1632, IRISA (July 2004)
16. Barbot, N., Miclet, L.: La proportion analogique dans les groupes: applications aux permutations et aux matrices. Technical Report 1914, IRISA (July 2009)
17. Gentner, D., Holyoak, K.J., Kokinov, B.: (Eds.) The Analogical Mind: Perspectives from Cognitive Sciences. MIT Press (2001)

DATA MINING AND MACHINE LEARNING

Evaluating Clustering Algorithms for Genetic Regulatory Network Structural Inference

Christopher Fogelberg and Vasile Palade

Abstract Modern biological research increasingly recognises the importance of genome-wide gene regulatory network inference; however, a range of statistical, technological and biological factors make it a difficult and intractable problem. One approach that some research has used is to cluster the data and then infer a structural model of the clusters. When using this kind of approach it is very important to choose the clustering algorithm carefully. In this paper we explicitly analyse the attributes that make a clustering algorithm appropriate, and we also consider how to measure the quality of the identified clusters. Our analysis leads us to develop three novel cluster quality measures that are based on regulatory overlap. Using these measures we evaluate two modern candidate algorithms: FLAME, and KMART. Although FLAME was specifically developed for clustering gene expression profile data, we find that KMART is probably a better algorithm to use if the goal is to infer a structural model of the clusters.

1 Introduction

Genetic Regulatory Networks (GRNs) are directed graphical models of the causal relationships amongst genes [5]. For example, if the gene AAP1 in *S. cerevisiae* regulates ATP6 then there would be an edge AAP1 → ATP6 and the regulatory function f_{ATP6} that determines the expression level of ATP6 would depend on AAP1.

Genome-wide GRN inference is both difficult and important. It is difficult due to the noisy and incomplete data [2; 20], the size of the network and the fact that good inference algorithms are exponential in the number of genes. The statistical

Christopher Fogelberg
Oxford University Computing Laboratory, OX1-3QD, UK and the Oxford-Man Institute, OX1-4EH, UK, e-mail: christopher.fogelberg@comlab.ox.ac.uk

Vasile Palade
Oxford University Computing Laboratory, OX1-3QD, UK

M. Bramer et al. (eds.), *Research and Development in Intelligent Systems XXVI*,
DOI 10.1007/978-1-84882-983-1_10, © Springer-Verlag London Limited 2010

characteristics [3; 5; 15] of the network further amplify this. It is important as understanding an organism at a systemic level can guide and speed up pharmaceutical research, and it is essential to a full biological understanding. The biological and statistical features of GRN are described in more detail in [3; 5; 9].

One genome-wide technique is to cluster the data, but the resulting model does not specify regulatory relationships or functions. Another technique is to directly infer a structural model, but this is only tractable for small networks. One way of performing genome-wide structural inference is to cluster the data prior to further inference. In this paper we consider two key conceptual questions which arise when clustering for further inference, but which previous research has not considered:

1. What attributes make a clustering algorithm appropriate for further inference?
2. What makes one clustering of the data better for further inference than another?

Through this analysis, we develop three novel measures of cluster quality. Having identified FLAME [10] and KMART [17] as clustering algorithms with the right attributes, we use these novel measures to evaluate their suitability for further inference.

The paper is structured as follows. Section 2 describes clustering for GRN inference. Section 3.1 considers the first question, above, and Section 3.2 the second. Section 3.2 also describes the novel cluster quality measures. Section 4 summarises FLAME, KMART and the GreenSim [8] simulator. Section 5 compares FLAME and KMART, and Section 6 summarises our findings.

2 Previous Clustering Methods for GRNs

The value and importance of genome-wide GRN discovery and inference is increasingly recognised in modern research [12; 13; 21; 23; 24], and the genome-wide, clustering-only research described in Subsection 2.1 has led to some genome-wide structural inference techniques being developed. We summarise three of these in Subsection 2.2.

2.1 Clustering as Inference

Clustering has been applied to gene expression data sets for a decade or more in an attempt to reveal the underlying modular structure of GRN. Early work includes Eisen et al.'s [6] hierarchical clustering algorithm. More recently, Zhou et al. [32] used mutual information to measure gene similarity. Previous surveys of this research include [1; 15; 25; 26].

Fuzzy clustering algorithms are *soft clustering algorithms*. A soft clustering algorithm is one which allows a single gene to have partial membership in several clusters. This is relevant to GRN, where each gene may have multiple functional roles and different regulatory functions for each.

Biclustering algorithms simultaneously group a subset of the genes and a subset of the samples (e.g. time points). Madeira and Oliveira [19] survey biclustering for GRN, and biclustering has been used prior to further inference in [4] and [29]. Both of these examples are discussed in the next subsection. Because FLAME [10] and KMART [17] are detailed in Section 4 they have not been presented here.

2.2 Clustering for Further Inference

Bonneau et al. [4] uses cMonkey [22] to bicluster the data prior to inferring a differential equation model of the biclusters.

cMonkey is a biclustering algorithm that uses three data types simultaneously (gene *expression profiles* [9], promoter sequence motifs [7] and bicluster membership) to iteratively group the data into biclusters. Gene membership in clusters is assumed to be Poisson distributed with $\lambda = 2$, and this helps avoid excessive bicluster overlap [22, p. 18].

Given the Poisson assumption, the number of clusters is determined automatically. Although cMonkey could be generalised to use more or fewer (e.g. one) types of data, this does not appear to have been done yet, and the default use of multiple data types limits the range of situations the algorithm can be applied to.

Although it is not genome-wide, Yang et al.'s [29] work also considers further inference following a soft clustering. Note that the number of soft clusters must be fixed *a priori*. Using prior knowledge, 6 transcription factors ("module regulators") were selected and used to bicluster the genes and 6 different environmental conditions. From bicluster overlaps a simple directed regulatory model was inferred.

Horimoto and Toh's research ([14; 27]) is another example of genome-wide clustering and structural inference. In this research the Euclidean distance between the Pearson correlation of genes was used with a hard hierarchical clustering algorithm to group 2497 genes into clusters, and then a graphical Gaussian model of the clusters was inferred.

3 Selecting and Evaluating a Clustering Algorithm

Choosing a clustering algorithm to use prior to further structural inference is a two step process. In the first step (Subsection 3.1), a subset of all known clustering algorithms are selected as candidates based on their attributes (e.g. that they are soft). Each candidate algorithm can then be empirically evaluated against test data, and the results are compared to select one (Subsection 3.2).

3.1 What makes a clustering algorithm appropriate?

Almost any clustering algorithm can be used on expression profiles; however, when the algorithm is being used prior to further structural inference then it must also be:

- *Unsupervised*
- *Soft*
- *Robust*

These attributes are necessary for the following reasons. Because the number of true clusters of co-regulated genes is unknown *a priori*, the algorithm must be unsupervised and determine the number of clusters automatically. Similarly, an individual gene may be a member of several modules and have different regulatory relationships in each module. Thus, it is also important to use soft clustering. Finally, because microarray data often has missing data points, the clustering algorithm must be robust. One approach which addresses the problem of covered data is to estimate it, and [28] reports some success with this technique.

It may also be an advantage if the algorithm can identify non-ellipsoid clusters. This is because it is not clear what shape the (co-regulated) functional modules of genes will have in the expression data.

This attribute-based analysis was used to select KMART and FLAME as the best candidates from a range of algorithms before any experiments were carried out. The following section considers how the performance of two algorithms can be compared. Such an empirical comparison can be used to select an algorithm in the knowledge that all appropriate algorithms have been evaluated.

3.2 What makes a clustering algorithm good?

The goal of clustering for further inference is two-fold. Firstly, it should maximise the *regulatory overlap* of each cluster by *conservatively* clustering co-regulated genes together. Secondly and conversely, it should group genes into the smallest possible number of clusters.

For some problems we may have complete prior knowledge about which variables (e.g. genes) should be in which cluster, and this makes the clustering *fully supervised* and easy to evaluate. However, a GRN's true modular structure could not be known without perfect knowledge of the underlying network and extensive, complex mathematical analysis of the network's characteristics. For that reason it is not practical to consider fully supervised clustering of GRN.

Classic unsupervised cluster quality measures are based on the compactness of each cluster and the separation between them [15]. Because these measures are strongly correlated with the number of identified clusters (and are not always strongly correlated with the clusters' regulatory overlap) the cluster distance and separation are not the best quality measures to use when clustering for further inference. For that reason we have developed three novel cluster quality measures based on regulatory overlap.

3.2.1 Proposed Measures for Evaluating Clustering Algorithms

Although fully supervised clustering of GRN is not practical, it is possible to use information about the structure of the network to evaluate a clustering in a *partially supervised* fashion. In this subsection we present three novel cluster quality measures: the *Unique Regulator Count* (URC), the *Member Uniqueness* (MU) and the *Cluster Cohesion* (CC). These measures assume that the more regulatory overlap there is amongst the genes in a cluster the better.

In general, the smaller a cluster is the more regulatory overlap it will have. Because of this, the performance of two algorithms can only be directly compared by looking at their cluster quality when they identify a similar number of clusters. To evaluate them comprehensively, their performance should be compared over a range of situations and identified numbers of clusters.

Also, because smaller clusters usually have greater regulatory overlap, the optimal number of clusters depends on the data but is ideally something in the maximum range that further inference is tractable for, e.g., with Bayesian networks, 100–150.

The URC, MU and CC are calculated for single clusters and defined in equations 1–3. To calculate the quality of a clustering, the μ and σ of the CC, MU and URC of all of the clusters are calculated.

Let G be the set of genes and C be the set of clusters. Then $G_c = \{g \in G : g \in c, c \in C\}$ is the set of genes in cluster C. A gene's *regulatory profile* is the set of genes which regulate it. Let $r(g)$ denote the regulatory profile of g.

$$URC(c) = \left| \bigcup_{g \in G_c} r(g) \right| \quad (1) \qquad\qquad MU(c) = \frac{URC(c)}{\sum_{g \in G_c} |r(g)|} \quad (2)$$

$$CC(c) = \frac{\left(\sum_{g \in G_c} |r(g)| \right) / |G_c|}{URC(c)} \quad (3)$$

These measures can be understood as follows. The URC is the size of the union of a cluster's genes' regulatory profiles, and therefore is the number of unique regulators in a cluster. If genes in a cluster do not overlap much then the URC is larger, and if $\overline{URC_{\mathscr{A}}} > \overline{URC_{\mathscr{B}}}$ then algorithm $\mathscr{A}$ has probably clustered the genes less conservatively than $\mathscr{B}$.

The CC measures the regulatory overlap of each gene in a cluster c by dividing the mean number of regulators each gene has by $URC(c)$. A higher CC is better.

The MU is very similar to the CC, and also measures how much the regulatory profile of each gene overlaps with the regulatory profile of the others. A lower MU indicates a greater degree of overlap, and manual analysis of theoretical clusterings shows that MU correctly orders the clusters more often than CC does.

As the opposite extremes of one cluster per gene and one cluster for all genes are approached the behaviour of these measures change and they may not rank two clusterings accurately. However, we postpone detailed exposition of this as it is not relevant to the results in Section 5, and in any case such a clustering is not useful for further inference.

4 GreenSim, FLAME and KMART

This section summarises GreenSim, used to simulate realistic GRN, and two candidate clustering algorithms: FLAME [10] and KMART [17].

4.1 GreenSim

As classic compactness and separation measures are inappropriate, we proposed measures based on regulatory overlap (Subsection 3.2). However, this requires some knowledge of the underlying network. This can be achieved with a realistic simulator like GreenSim [8], and using a simulator also allows for a wide range of networks and time series to be simulated. This subsection summarises three key attributes of GreenSim.

Firstly, GreenSim generates networks with the same statistical characteristics as real biological networks. These include sub-graph structures, the exponential distribution over the regulatory in-degree and the Pareto distribution over the regulatory out-degree.

GreenSim also models gene expression levels in a continuous manner (using parameterisable and discrete time steps) and allows for full non-linear regulation. This is importantly different to other simulators (e.g. GeneSim [30; 31] and Kyoda et al.'s [18]).

Finally, GreenSim models both *biological noise* [20; 24] and *technical noise* [2; 16; 20; 24]. Biological noise is a consequence of the stochastic nature of gene transcription, and technical noise is due to biotechnological limitations.

4.2 FLAME and KMART

FLAME is a clustering algorithm developed especially to cluster gene expression profiles [10]. The algorithm is two-stage. In the first stage the similarity of each gene to the others is used to determine the number of cluster seeds. In the second stage cluster membership is iteratively updated till convergence.

FLAME is soft, and finds a dynamic number of clusters depending only on the data and the variable k, which specifies the size of a gene's local neighbourhood. To help conservatively cluster the genes, the results are post-processed and any gene-cluster membership < 0.05 is ignored.

KMART was developed for soft document clustering, but can also be used for clustering gene expression profile data. KMART adapts fuzzy ART [17] by continuing to search for sufficiently similar clusters even after the first is identified. We post-process KMART clusters in the same way as FLAME clusters.

5 FLAME versus KMART

This section compares FLAME and KMART. FLAME can use several different similarity measures, and data preprocessing may be useful for both algorithms. Subsections 5.1 and 5.2 consider these aspects first, then Subsection 5.3 analyses the performance of FLAME and KMART in a wide range of situations, and Subsection 5.4 considers their performance with noisy data. Due to space and because figures with the CC do not affect our conclusions in this case we do not include any. The results suggest how to best cluster biological data from unknown networks for further inference.

5.1 Similarity Measures for FLAME

Because FLAME can use a variety of similarity measures, exploratory clustering with 8 different measures was conducted:

- The Euclidean distance.
- The pair-wise Pearson correlation.
- The jackknife (arg-min leave-one-out resampling) Euclidean distance.
- The jackknife Pearson correlation.
- The Euclidean distance of the Pearson correlation ("Euc. Pearson").
- The jackknife Euclidean distance of the Pearson correlation.
- The Euclidean distance of the jackknife Pearson correlation.
- The jackknife Euclidean distance of the jackknife Pearson correlation.

Because KMART is built around the fuzzy ART [17] similarity measure it is not clear how it could use another. For that reason, this subsection only considers FLAME. The jackknife's advantage is that it can minimise the impact of an outlier. For this reason it may be a better distance measure in some situations. However, exploratory clusterings showed that Euclidean and Euc. Pearson were the only two which might be better than the others. For that reason this subsection only considers Euclidean and Euc. Pearson in more detail.

Using 5 GreenSim-simulated networks of 1000 genes and 3 different random seeds for each one, 15 time series gene expression data sets were simulated using

GreenSim. Values of k in the range 4–46 were used for FLAME with Euc. Pearson, and values of k in the range 5–70 were used for FLAME with the Euclidean distance.

5.1.1 Experimental Results and Analysis

These experiments showed that Euclidean and Euc. Pearson are very similar, but that Euclidean led to more conservative clusterings and is therefore slightly better. This can be seen in Figure 1, which shows that clusters found using Euclidean distance tend to be the same size, but have a lower URC.

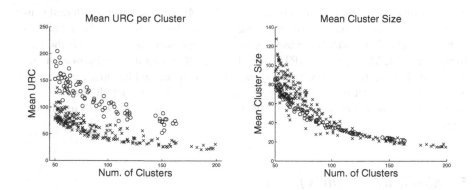

Fig. 1 The URC (LHS) and the mean cluster size (RHS). Error bars are not shown as they obscure too much detail. x's denote Euclidean results and o's denote Euc. Pearson results.

Figure 2 confirms this, but also shows how close the measures are: On average, the ratio of the URC to regulatory relations in a cluster is less when using the Euclidean distance, but Euc. Pearson clusters are slightly better when fewer than 75 are identified. This difference disappears as the number of clusters approaches the optimal number, 100–150.

5.2 Preprocessing for FLAME and KMART

Various forms of preprocessing were evaluated for FLAME and KMART. These included normalising the data so that it had mean 0 and variance 1, or taking $\log_2$ of the data. After preprocessing the data for KMART, it was linearly normalised so that it was in the range $[0, 1]$.

Preprocessing for clustering did not significantly improve the performance of FLAME or KMART in any of the considered cases, and [28, p. 521] reached the same conclusion with biological data. Note that the authors have found in current research that preprocessing the data after clustering and before inference is valuable.

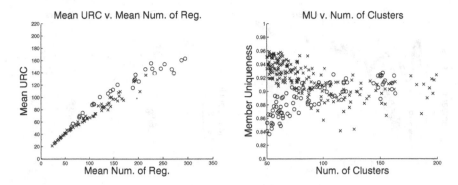

Fig. 2 The mean URC against $\sum_{g \in G_c} |r(g)|$ (LHS), and the MU (RHS). x's denote Euclidean results and o's denote Euc. Pearson results. For clarity, only a representative sub-sample of the results is display in the left-hand figure.

5.3 Comparing FLAME with KMART

This subsection compares the clustering performance of Euclidean distance FLAME to KMART for further inference. As before, 5 `GreenSim`-simulated networks with 1000 genes were used. For this experiment, time series using 10 different seeds were generated from each. The data was clustered using KMART with 19 vigilance values in the range 0.05–0.95 and using FLAME with 22 values of k in the range 5–68 (i.e. 2050 experiments in all).

5.3.1 Experimental Results and Analysis

As Figure 3 shows, KMART has a substantially better MU than FLAME. Further, the number of clusters identified for each parameter value of KMART are more tightly bunched than for FLAME. This suggests that it would be easier to guide KMART to identify the optimum number of clusters. Note that each cluster identified in each experiment was different from the other clusters identified in that experiment.

One concern is that the difference in the scores might be because either FLAME or KMART is at the theoretical limits of MU (one gene per cluster, or one cluster per gene). However, consider Figure 4. This shows that neither algorithm is at the limit.

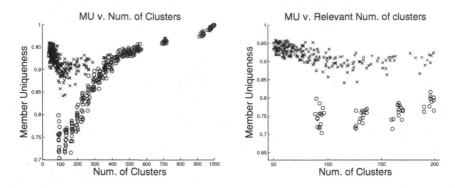

Fig. 3 The MU of FLAME and KMART over all clusters identified (LHS) and for the relevant/optimal number of clusters (RHS). x's denote FLAME results and o's denote KMART results. For clarity, only a representative sub-sample of the results is displayed, and error bars have been omitted.

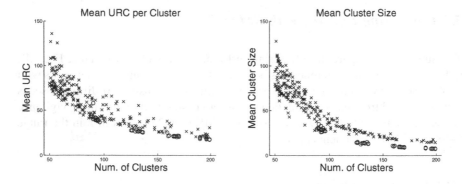

Fig. 4 Mean URC (LHS) and mean cluster size (RHS). x's denote FLAME results and o's denote KMART results. For clarity, only a representative sub-sample of the results is displayed and error bars have been omitted.

5.4 FLAME and KMART with Noisy Data

As in Subsection 5.1, we have used 5 networks with 1000 genes and 3 random seeds. The simulated noise was as follows:

- *Spot noise* with $p = 0.1$.
- *Span noise* with $p = 0.05$ and span size 3 ± 1.
- *Value noise* with $\sigma^2 = 0.1$.

These kinds of technical noise are detailed in [8], and the data corruption is comparable to or worse than in biological data. Futschik and Carlisle [11] used the *k*-nearest neighbours method [28] to estimate covered data before clustering with fuzzy c-means. This research adopted the same approach with $k = 15$ for both FLAME and KMART.

Although moderate random noise may affect the absolute quality of a clustering somewhat, the relative impact on FLAME and KMART should be minimal, and Figure 5 shows this. The MU of both algorithms is very similar with and without noise, and the mean URC of the clusters was also. This is as expected.

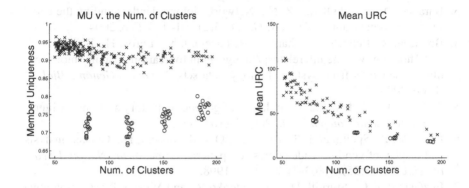

Fig. 5 The MU for KMART and FLAME with noise in the optimal range (LHS), and the number of unique regulators per cluster in the optimal range. x's denote noisy FLAME results and o's denote noisy KMART results. For clarity, only a representative sub-sample of the results have been displayed in the right hand figure and error bars have been omitted.

6 Conclusions and Future Work

This paper has made three key contributions to clustering for further inference of genome-wide GRN. Firstly, in Subsection 3.1, it has established the characteristics of an appropriate clustering algorithm, and in Subsection 3.2 it has presented three novel measures of cluster quality. In Section 5 it has compared two candidate algorithms, FLAME and KMART. Based on this analysis, KMART appears to be a better algorithm if clustering for further inference. Implementations of FLAME, KMART and GreenSim are available from the authors upon request.

One area of future research is membership-weighted or minimum-regulatory-strength versions of the MU and CC. For example, if gene i only regulates gene j very weakly then it is less important if other genes in j's clusters aren't regulated by i, and this should be considered when evaluating a cluster's regulatory overlap. Comparing KMART with other clustering algorithms could also be useful, and a more detailed exposition of the theoretical limits of MU and CC will be presented at a future date.

References

1. Azuaje, F.: Clustering-based approaches to discovering and visualing microar-ray data patterns. *Brief. in Bioinformatics*, 4(1):31–42, Mar. 2003.
2. Balagurunathan, Y., Naisyin, W., Dougherty, E. R., Danh, N., Bittner, M. L., Trent, J. and Carroll, R.: Noise factor analysis for cDNA microarrays. *J. of Biomed. Opt.*, 9(4):663–678, Jul./Aug. 2004.
3. Barabasi, A. L. and Oltvai., Z. N.: Network biology: Understanding the cell's functional organisation. *Nat. Rev. Genet.*, 5(2):101–113, Feb. 2004.
4. Bonneau, R., Reiss, D. J., Shannon, P., Facciotti, M., Leroy, H., Baliga, N. S. and Thorsson, V.: The inferelator: An algorithm for learning parsimonious reg-ulatory networks from systems-biology data sets *de novo. Genome Biol.*, 7 (R36), 2006.
5. de Jong, H.: Modeling and simulation of genetic regulatory systems: A litera-ture review. *J. of Comput. Biol.*, 9(1):67–103, 2002.
6. Eisen, M. B., Spellman, P. T., Brown, P. O. and Botstein, D.: Cluster analysis and display of genome-wide expression patterns. *Proc. of the National Acad. of Sci. USA*, 95(25):14863–14868, Dec. 1998.
7. FitzGerald, P. C., Sturgill, D., Shyakhtenko, A. and Vinson, B.: Comparative genomics of drosophila and human core promoters. *Genome Biol.*, 7:R53+, Jul. 2006.
8. Fogelberg, C. and Palade, V.: GreenSim: A genetic regulatory network simula-tor. Technical Report PRG-RR-08-07, Computing Laboratory, Oxford Univer-sity, Oxford, OX1-3QD, May 2008.
9. Fogelberg, C. and Palade, V.: *Foundations of Computational Intelligence*, chap-ter 1.1, Genetic Regulatory Networks: A Review and a Roadmap. Springer Verlag, 2008.
10. Fu, L. and Medico, E.: FLAME, a novel clustering method for the analysis of microarray data. *BMC Bioinformatics*, 8(3), Jan. 2007.
11. Futschik, M. E. and Carlisle, B.: Noise-robust soft clustering of gene expression time-course data. *J. of Bioinformatics and Comput. Biol.*, 3(4):965–988, 2005.
12. Gutenkunst, R. N., Waterfall, J. J., Casey, F. P., Brown, K. S., Myers, C. R. and Sethna., J. P.: Universally sloppy parameter sensitivities in systems biology models. *PLoS Comput. Biol.*, 3(10):e189, Oct. 2007.
13. Hayete, B., Gardner, T. S. and Collins, J. J.: Size matters: Network inference tackles the genome scale. *Mol. Syst. Biol.*, 3(77):1–3, Feb. 2007.
14. Horimoto, K. and Toh, H.: Statistical estimation of cluster boundaries in gene expression profile data. *Bioinformatics*, 17(12):1143–1151, 2001.
15. Jiang, D., Tang, D. and Zhang, A.: Cluster analysis for gene expression data: A survey. *IEEE Trans. on Knowl. and Data Eng.*, 16(11):1370–1386, 2004. ISSN 1041-4347.
16. Klebanov, L. and Yakovlev, A.: How high is the level of technical noise in microarray data? *Biol. Direct*, 2:9+, Apr. 2007. ISSN 1745-6150.
17. Kondadadi, R. and Kozma, R.: A modified fuzzy ART for soft document clus-tering. v. 3, pages 2545–2549, 2002. doi: 10.1109/IJCNN.2002.1007544.

18. Kyoda, K. M., Morohashi, M., Onami, S. and Kitano, H.: A gene network inference method from continuous-value gene expression data of wild-type and mutants. *Genome Informatics*, 11:196–204, 2000.
19. Madeira, S. C. and Oliveira, A. L.: Biclustering algorithms for biological data analysis: a survey. *IEEE/ACM Trans. on Comput. Biol. and Bioinformatics*, 1 (1):24–45, 2004. doi: 10.1109/TCBB.2004.2.
20. Nykter, M., Aho, T., Ahdesmäki, M., Ruusuvuori, P., Lehmussola, A., and Yli-Harja, O.: Simulation of microarray data with realistic characteristics. *Bioinformatics*, 7:349, Jul. 2006.
21. Pritsker, M., Liu, Y., Beer, M. A. and Tavazoie, S.: Whole-genome discovery of transcription factor binding sites by network-level conservation. *Genome Res.*, 14(1):99–108, Jan. 2004. doi: 10.1101/gr.1739204.
22. Reiss, D., Baliga, N. and Bonneau, R.: Integrated biclustering of heterogeneous genome-wide datasets for the inference of global regulatory networks. *BMC Bioinformatics*, 7(1):280, 2006. ISSN 1471-2105.
23. Schlitt, T. and Brazma, A.: Modelling gene networks at different organisational levels. *FEBS Lett.*, 579:1859–1866, Mar. 2005. ISSN 0014-5793.
24. Schlitt, T. and Brazma, A.: Current approaches to gene regulatory network modelling. *BMC Bioinformatics*, 8 Suppl 6, 2007. ISSN 1471-2105.
25. Shamir, R. and Sharan, R.: *Current Topics in Computational Biology*, chapter Algorithmic approaches to clustering gene expression data, pages 269–300. MIT press, Cambridge, Massachusetts, 2002. (T. Jiang, T. Smith, Y. Xu and M. Q. Zhang, eds).
26. Tibshirani, R., Hastie, T., Eisen, M., Ross, D., Botstein, D. and Brown, P.: Clustering methods for the analysis of DNA microarray data. Technical report, Stanford University, Oct. 1999.
27. Toh, H. and Horimoto, K.: Inference of a genetic network by a combined approach of cluster analysis and graphical Gaussian modeling. *Bioinformatics*, 18 (2):287–297, 2002.
28. Troyanskaya, O., Cantor, M., Sherlock, G., Brown, P., Hastie, T., Tibshirani, R., Botstein, D. and Altman, R. B.: Missing value estimation methods for DNA microarrays. *Bioinformatics*, 17(6):520–525, Jun. 2001. ISSN 1367-4803.
29. Yang, E., Foteinou, P. T., King, K. R., Yarmush, M. L. and Androulakis, I. P.: A novel non-overlapping bi-clustering algorithm for network generation using living cell array data. *Bioinformatics*, 23(17):2306–2313, 2007. doi: 10.1093/bioinformatics/btm335.
30. Yu, J., Smith, V. A., Wang, P. P., Hartemink, A. J. and Jarvis, E. D.: Using Bayesian network inference algorithms to recover molecular genetic regulatory networks. In *Int. Conf. on Syst. Biol. (ICSB02)*, Dec. 2002.
31. Yu, J., Smith, V. A., Wang, P. P., Hartemink, A. J. and Jarvis, E. D.: Advances to Bayesian network inference for generating causal networks from observational biological data. *Bioinformatics*, 20(18):3594–3603, 2004.
32. Zhou, X., Wang, X., Dougherty, E. R., Russ, D. and Suh, E.: Gene clustering based on clusterwide mutual information. *J. of Comput. Biol.*, 11(1):147–161, 2004.

Parallel Rule Induction with Information Theoretic Pre-Pruning

Frederic Stahl, Max Bramer and Mo Adda[1]

Abstract In a world where data is captured on a large scale the major challenge for data mining algorithms is to be able to scale up to large datasets. There are two main approaches to inducing classification rules, one is the *divide and conquer* approach, also known as the top down induction of decision trees; the other approach is called the *separate and conquer approach*. A considerable amount of work has been done on scaling up the divide and conquer approach. However, very little work has been conducted on scaling up the *separate and conquer approach*. In this work we describe a parallel framework that allows the parallelisation of a certain family of separate and conquer algorithms, the Prism family. Parallelisation helps the Prism family of algorithms to harvest additional computer resources in a network of computers in order to make the induction of classification rules scale better on large datasets. Our framework also incorporates a pre-pruning facility for parallel Prism algorithms.

1 Introduction

Induction of classification rules from data samples in order to predict previously unseen data can be traced back to the 1960s [1]. The two most popular approaches to classification rule induction are the *divide and conquer* approach and the *separate and conquer* approach. The *divide and conquer* approach induces classification rules by recursively breaking down the classification problem into sub-problems. The resulting rules are in the form of decision trees and thus *divide and conquer* is also known as the Top Down Induction of Decision Trees (TDIDT) [2]. TDIDT resulted in a wide range of classifiers such as the C4.5 and the C5.0 systems. The *separate and conquer* approach directly searches for a rule that explains a part of the training data, separates the part of the data that is covered by the rule and recursively searches for new rules on the remaining examples until there are no training instances left. *Separate and conquer* can be traced back to the 1960s to the AQ learning system [3]. Rule induction algorithms based on the *separate and conquer* approach often produce more general rules compared with decision trees on noisy training data. Notably the Prism algorithm [4] often produces qualitatively better rules than TDIDT especially on noisy data.

[1] School of Computing, University of Portsmouth, PO1 3HE, UK
{Frederic.Stahl; Max.Bramer; Mo.Adda}@port.ac.uk

M. Bramer et al. (eds.), *Research and Development in Intelligent Systems XXVI*,
DOI 10.1007/978-1-84882-983-1_11, © Springer-Verlag London Limited 2010

The fast development in processing power, storage and sensor technology, notably CCTV cameras leads to the generation and storage of larger datasets. However, researchers still wish to apply data mining algorithms such as classification rule induction algorithms to large datasets. There are two general approaches to scaling up classification rule induction algorithms; sampling and the development of parallel classification rule induction algorithms. Sampling the data before the classification rule induction algorithm is applied has been criticised by Catlett [5] who showed that the accuracy of an induced classifier increases with an increasing size of the training sample. However, Catlett conducted his research 18 years ago and datasets that were considered to be large in his work are commonplace today. In 1999 Frey and Fisher justified sampling by showing that the rate of increase of the accuracy of the classifier slows down with the rate of increase of the training data. However, applications that demand high classification accuracy and applications that are concerned with the discovery of new knowledge or where the data size is simply so large that even sampled versions are massive in size still desire scalable classification rule induction technology. The development of parallel classification rule induction algorithms has been concentrated on the TDIDT approach, notably by the SLIQ algorithm [6] and its successor SPRINT [7]. SPRINT claims to achieve a linear scale up with the increase of the training data; however Srivastava pointed out that the breath first search approach that SPRINT uses might result in workload balancing problems during its execution [8]. In general concerning the predictive accuracy, only parallel versions of decision tree induction algorithms showed an acceptable performance. The only attempt to parallelise algorithms of the *separate and conquer* approach to date is the Parallel Modular Classification Rule Induction (PMCRI) project [9]. The PMCRI framework has been constructed to parallelise algorithms of the Prism family. In this paper we present an implementation of PMCRI with the extension of a pre-pruning facility.

2 Modular Classification Rule Induction With Prism

The development of Prism is a result of the main criticism of TDIDT, which is the intermediate representation of classification rules in the form of a tree [4]. A tree representation of classification rules does not directly allow the induction of modular rules such as:

> IF a = 1 and b = 1 then class = A
> IF c = 1 and d = 1 then class = B

Such rules do not necessarily have common attributes in their rule terms unlike for the representation in tree format. Thus the induction of decision trees will produce unnecessarily large and confusing rule sets. Cendrowska's Prism algorithm induces modular rules. In subsequent studies Prism has also been shown to be less vulnerable to clashes. However, the Prism algorithm does not scale well on large datasets. A version of Prism that attempts to scale up Prism to larger datasets is the PrismTCS (**Prism** with **T**arget **C**lass, **S**mallest first) algorithm [10] which has been developed by one of the authors. PrismTCS has a comparable level of predictive accuracy to Prism. The only difference between the two algorithms is that whereas in Prism, the above described *separate-and-conquer* approach is applied for each class value in turn, in PrismTCS it is only applied once.

Our implementation of PrismTCS for continuous data only is summarised in the following pseudo code:

```
(a) working dataset W = restore Dataset;
    delete all records that match the rules
    that have been derived so far;
    target class i = class that covers the
    fewest instances in W;
(b) For each attribute A in W
    - sort the data according to A;
    - for each possible split value v of
      attribute A calculate the probability
      that the class is i for both subsets
      A < v and A ≥ v;
(c) Select the attribute that has the subset S
    with the overall highest probability;
(d) build a rule term describing S;
(e) W = S;
(f) Repeat b to e until the dataset contains
    only records of class i. The induced rule
    is then the conjunction of all the rule
    terms built at step d;
(g) restore Dataset = restore Dataset - W;
    Repeat a to f until W only contains
    instances of class i or is empty;
```

However there is a whole family of Prism algorithms besides Prism and PrismTCS. There is also PrismTC, which differs from PrismTCS in that it selects as target class the class that covers the most instances, rather than the least [11].

2.1 Pre-Pruning of Prism Classification Rules

Classifiers are usually pruned in order to reduce overfitting of classification rules. There are two general types of pruning, *post-pruning* and *pre-pruning*. Post-pruning methods are applied to the already trained classifier whereas pre-pruning is applied as the rules are being generated. Most parallel versions of TDIDT classifiers follow the post pruning approach with the reasoning that it takes only a small fraction of the overall induction time of the classifier [7, 8]. However, pre-pruning generally leads to slimmer classifiers and thus reduces the number of iterations of the algorithm and thus the classification rule induction time. A pre-pruning method introduced by Bramer [10] based on the J-measure of Smyth and Goodman [12] can be applied to both the TDIDT and the Prism family of algorithms and it shows on both families a good performance [10] with respect to predictive accuracy and the number of rule terms. Thus we will incorporate J-pruning in our PMCRI framework.

According to [12] a rule of the form *IF Y=y, THEN X=x* has the average information content of:

$$J(X;Y = y) = p(y) \cdot j(J;Y = y)$$

The J-measure is a product of two terms. The first term p(y) is the probability that the antecedent of the rule will occur. It is a measure of the *hypothesis simplicity*. The second term j(X;Y=y) is *the j-measure* or cross entropy. It is a measure of the *goodness-of-fit* of a rule and is defined by:

$$j(X;Y = y) = p(x \mid y).\log_2(\frac{p(x \mid y)}{p(x)}) + (1 - p(x \mid y)).\log_2(\frac{(1 - p(x \mid y))}{(1 - p(x))})$$

For further reading we refer to [12]. For J-pruning it is assumed that a rule having a high J-value will tend to have a high predictive accuracy. So the J-measure can be used to identify a point where a further specialisation of a rule is likely to become counter productive because of overfitting. In Prism J-pruning is performed by measuring the J-value of each rule after appending a rule term. If the J-value increases then the term is accepted otherwise the term is rejected and a clash handling procedure is invoked. If a rule is pruned Prism calculates the majority class in the subset. If it is not the target class then the entire rule is discarded and instances of the training subset that belong to the target class are deleted.

2.2 Scalability of Prism

We derived the theoretical complexity of Prism based on the number of calculations of the probability for a possible split value of an attribute contained in step *b* in the PrismTCS pseudo code above. We will call this number the number of cutpoints. In the best case scenario there would be only one attribute that determines the class of any data instance or all data instances would simply belong to the same class. It is difficult to describe an average case for the algorithm as the outcome is strongly dependent on the underlying pattern in the data. However, it is possible to describe the worse case. Let N be the number of data instances and M the number of attributes. A categorical attribute will at most occur once in a rule whereas a continuous one may occur twice, as with two rule terms it would be possible to describe any interval of values of a continuous attribute. Thus there will be a maximum number of $2M$ rule terms per rule. The maximum number of rules is $N-1$, meaning that each training instance except one is described by a separate rule. The *-1* is because if there is only one instance left in the training data we do not need to generate a further rule for it. The complexity of inducing the *kth* rule is $2M(N-k)$. For example if we induce the very first rule *(k=1)* we would have N instances available thus we would have $(N-1)$ cutpoint calculations per rule term. As there are a maximum of $2M$ rule terms there would be altogether $2M(N-1)$ cutpoint calculations. Summing this up for all possible rules leads to:

$$\sum_{k=1}^{N-1} (2M) \cdot (N-k) = 2M \cdot \frac{N \cdot (N-1)}{2} = O(N^2 M)$$

A complexity of $O(N^2 M)$ is very pessimistic and seems to be very unlikely to happen. In practice larger datasets may well contain fewer rule terms than smaller ones. Also J-pruning will reduce the number or rule terms induced as shown in [10].

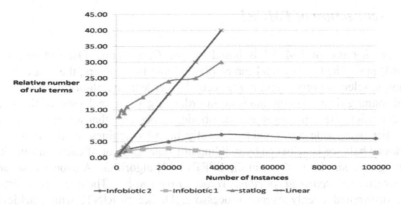

Fig. 1. Relative number of rule terms induced versus the size of the training data.

We ran PrismTCS with J-Pruning on several datasets. For each dataset we built samples of different sizes and measured the number of rule terms induced. We plotted the relative number of rule terms versus sample size in figure 1. The Statlog (Shuttle) dataset is from the UCI repository [13] and the infobiotics 1 and 2 datasets were retrieved from the infobiotics data repository which comprises large real world datasets for benchmark tests for machine learning tasks [14]. The Statlog dataset samples ranged from 1000 to 40000 instances and comprised 9 attributes and 5 classes; infobiotics 1 ranged from 1000 to 100000 instances comprising 20 attributes and 5 classes, infobiotics 2 also ranged from 1000 to 100000 instances but comprised 100 attributes and 5 classes. Figure 1 also contains the relative number and theoretical linear relative number of rule terms plotted versus the number of training instances and shows that there is no linear behaviour of the increase of the number of rule terms recognizable. The scaling results obtained in [9] strongly suggest a linear scaling behaviour of the Prism family with respect to the number of training instances while the number of rules and rule terms remains constant.

3 J-PMCRI: Parallel Modular Classification Rule Induction With J-Pruning

The basic idea is to distribute the workload of Prism over a network of computers by distributing the training data. Each computer in the network does its part in inducing the classifier. To realise such a loosely coupled system no special hardware is required. In PMCRI the classifier induced is exactly the same as would be induced from the serial version of the Prism algorithm.

3.1 Architecture of PMCRI

The architecture of PMCRI is based on the Cooperating Data Mining model (CDM) [15]. The CDM model can be divided into three layers; the first comprises a sample selection procedure; in the second layer learning algorithms work on the local training data and communicate in order to get a global view of the state of the classifier; the third layer is a combining procedure that assembles the final classifier using rule terms induced locally on all machines. In the first layer a workload balance is achieved by building attribute lists out of each attribute in the training data similar to those in the SPRINT [7] algorithm. Attribute Lists are of the structure <record id, attribute value, class value>. These attribute lists are then distributed evenly over n processors. Unlike SPRINT, which achieves a workload balance by splitting each attribute list into n chunks and distributes them evenly over n processors we distribute entire attribute lists evenly over n processors. Distributing parts of the attribute lists may achieve a better workload balance at the very beginning. However it is likely that it will result in a considerable workload imbalance later on in the algorithm as part attribute lists may not evenly decrease in size [8]. Distributing entire attribute lists may only impose a slight workload imbalance at the beginning of the algorithm in PMCRI. However the relative workload on each processor will approximately stay the same. Now having distributed the entire training data in the form of attribute lists, each processor will be able to induce a rule term, which is locally the best rule term for the attribute lists it holds in memory. Once each rule term is induced the participating machines need to exchange information in order to find out which one induced the globally best rule term. For this purpose we use a distributed blackboard architecture as in [16]. A blackboard architecture can be seen as a physical blackboard, that is observed and used by several experts with different knowledge domains that have a common problem to solve. Each expert will use its own knowledge plus information written on the blackboard by other experts in order to derive new information and in turn write it on the blackboard. As a software model this principle can be represented by a client server architecture. The basic architecture of PMCRI is shown in figure 2 [17]. The attribute lists are distributed over k machines in the network. The blackboard system is partitioned into two logical partitions, one for information about local rule terms on experts and one for global information.

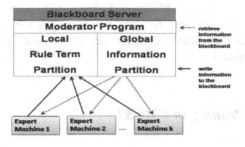

Fig. 2. The architecture of the PMCRI framework using a distributed blackboard architecture in order to parallelise any member of the Prism Family.

Every expert is hosted on a separate machine in the network and is able to induce the rule term that is locally the best one for the attribute lists it holds. It then writes information about the induced rule term on the local rule term information partition and awaits the global information it needs in order to induce the next rule term. The information submitted is basically the covering probability with which the induced rule term covers the target class on the local attribute list collection and the number of instances this rule term covers. If the local rule term information is submitted from all k expert machines the moderator program on the blackboard server will collect this information and use it in order to determine the globally best rule term. The moderator advertises the winning expert to all experts by writing the winning expert's name on the global information partition. The winning expert then will communicate the ids of the instances that are uncovered by this rule term to the other waiting experts using the blackboard system. Now the next rule term can be induced in the same way.

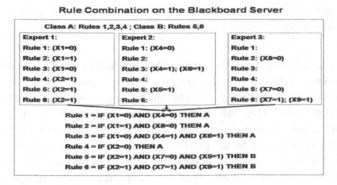

Fig. 3. Combining Procedure in PMCRI

At the end of the PMCRI execution each expert machine will hold a set of terms for each rule. The implementation of the combining procedure in layer three in the CDM model is realised by communicating all the rule terms locally stored at the expert machines to the blackboard. Each rule term is associated with information about the rule and the class for which the terms were induced. The moderator program then simply appends each rule term to its corresponding rule as illustrated in figure 3.

3.2 Parallel J-Pruning in PMCRI

The following steps listed below describe how PMCRI induces one rule [18] based on the Prism algorithm:

```
Step 1 Moderator (Prism) writes on "Global Information Partition" the
    command to induce locally best rule terms.
Step 2 All Experts induce the locally best rule term and write the
    rule terms plus its covering probability and the number of list
    records covered on the "local Rule Term Partition"
Step 3 Moderator (Prism) compares all rule terms written on the
    "Local Rule Term Partition"; adds best term to the current rule;
    writes the name of the Expert that induced the best rule term on
    the Global Information Partition
Step 4 Expert retrieves name of winning expert.
    IF Expert is winning expert {
        derive by last induced rule term uncovered ids and write
        them on the "Global Information Partition" and delete
        uncovered list records
    }
    ELSE IF Expert is not winning expert {
        wait for by best rule term uncovered ids being available
        on the "Global Information Partition", download them and
        delete list records matching the retrieved ids.
    }
```

In order to induce the next rule term, PMCRI would loop back to step one. For PMCRI to know when to stop the rule, it needs to know when the remaining list records on the expert machines are either empty or consist only of instances of the current target class. This information is communicated between the winning expert and the moderator program using the Global Information Partition.

J-pruning in Prism can be integrated in step 2 and 3 in the algorithm above and thus no further synchronisation is needed. That is because the attribute list from which the local rule term on an expert was induced contains enough information to calculate the J-value for the term concerned. The information needed to calculate the J-value is the count of how many data instances (list instances) the rule term covers, the count of how many instances covered by the rule term that are assigned with the target class, the total number of instances and the total number of instances covering the target class. Each expert calculates the J-value in step 2 and writes it on the blackboard. Then in step 3 of the moderator program the best rule term location can be determined by the following procedure if p is the covering probability, c the number of instances covered assigned with the target class, j being the rule terms J-value:

```
bestJ=0; bestProb=0; bestCov=0; ExpertInfo;
for each submitted rule term do{
   IF(t.p>bestProb OR (t.p==bestProb AND t.c>bestCov)){
       if(t.j>bestJ){
           ExpertInfo = "Best term induced on " t.ExpertName;}
       else{
           ExpertInfo = "prune rule";}
   }
}
```

The Moderator will write the content of "ExpertInfo" to the Global Information Partition on the blackboard. If the message contains the name of the winning expert the algorithm will continue with step 4, if it contains the info "prune rule" then each expert will invoke the clash resolution procedure outlined in section 2.1 and start the next rule.

4 Evaluation of the PMCRI Framework

In order to evaluate PMCRI we used the diabetes and yeast datasets from the UCI repository [13]. To create a larger and thus more challenging workload for PMCRI, we appended each dataset to itself in either a horizontal or a vertical direction. The base diabetes and yeast datasets each comprise roughly 100,000 data records and 48 attributes. Please note that in these experiments PMCRI's learning algorithm is based on PrismTCS and produces exactly the same rules as the serial version of PrismTCS would induce. Therefore there is no concern with issues relating to the comparative quality of rules generated by different algorithms. As all datasets were based on either the yeast or the diabetes dataset the induced classifiers were identical for all dataset sizes based on yeast and also for all datasets sizes based on diabetes. In particular the classifier induced on yeast produces 467 rules and the classifier on diabetes 110 rules. However, as all datasets comprised 48 attributes we will have imposed a slight workload imbalance for 10 processors as we only assign complete attribute lists to each processor. Thus, for the 10 expert configuration, two expert machines were holding 4 and eight experts were holding 5 attribute lists. The machines we used for all experiments in this section had a CPU speed of 2.8 GHz and a memory of 1 GB. The operating system used was XUbuntu. In general when we talk about processors in this section we in fact mean expert machines.

4.1 Size up And Capability Barriers of PMCRI

In size-up experiments a system's performance is examined on a fixed processor configuration on an increasing workload. In PMCRI the workload is equivalent to the number of data records that are used to train a Prism classifier. In general we hope to achieve a linear size-up meaning that the runtime is a linear function of the data set size.

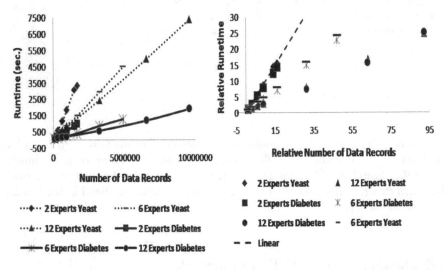

Fig. 4. Size up behaviour of PMCRI on portrait formatted yeast and diabetes dataset

The left hand side of figure 4 shows the runtimes plotted versus the number of yeast and diabetes dataset instances for PMCRI using different numbers of expert machines. In general we observe a linear behaviour for all configurations. What we can also read on the left hand side in figure 4 are the capability barriers of PMCRI. In a particular configuration of PMCRI the capability barrier is equivalent to the amount of data the framework can cope with. If we load too many attribute lists into the memory of the expert machines then the operating system on the expert machines will buffer parts of the lists to the swap memory on the hard drive in order to avoid a memory overflow. This buffering would cause a considerable overhead, thus a too large workload has to be avoided. We can see that the capability barrier of PrismTCS with PMCRI with 2 experts was reached after roughly 166000 data records and for PrismTCS with PMCRI with four machines after roughly 322000 data records. In PMCRI the capability barriers can be widened by adding more machines and thus more memory. Figure 6 shows that for PMCRI if the amount of memory is doubled the capability barriers will also double in size. We took a closer look into the size up behaviour of PMCRI. The right hand side of figure 4 represents the same data as the left hand side with the difference that both axes have been normalised. Now the ideal scaling behaviour for all processor configurations would be a straight line through the points (1,1), (2,2), (3,3) as displayed in figure 4. We can see that except for the serial version of PrismTCS all data points are below the ideal behaviour and thus indicate a slightly better behaviour than linear for PrismTCS parallelised using PMCRI. This can be explained by the fact that the communication does not increase linearly with the number of data records. There are two types of communication.

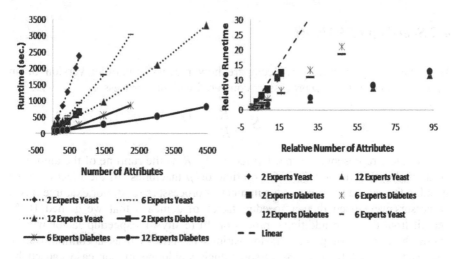

Fig. 5. Size up behaviour of PMCRI on landscape formatted yeast and diabetes dataset

The first type of communication are indices of list records that are covered or uncovered by the currently induced rule term, which increases linearly with the number of data records. However, for each rule term induced, PMCRI will broadcast information about the relevant rule term using the blackboard system. This second type of communication consists of only two values: the covering probability and the count with which the induced rule term covers the target class. This second type of communication is dependent on the total number of rule terms induced and not on the number of data records. As for all sizes of the diabetes dataset we induce the same amount of rule terms, this second type of communication stays constant and is the reason for a size-up being slightly better than linear. Figure 5 illustrates similar experiments as described above for figure 4. The difference is that this time 'landscape' versions of the yeast and diabetes datasets were taken into account. Again we observe a linear behaviour but this time for the runtimes of PMCRI with respect to the number of attributes rather than the number of data instances. We also observe the same behaviour for the capability barriers as for portrait data. We can see that the capability barrier of PrismTCS with PMCRI with 2 experts was reached after 768 attribute lists and for PrismTCS with PMCRI with four machines after roughly 1488 attribute lists. Again we took a closer look into the size-up behaviour of PMCRI. And again we normalised both the axes of the data of the left hand side of figure 5 and plotted them as shown on the right hand side of figure 5. Once more we observed a size up behaviour better than linear for the same reasons as stated above for the data in portrait format. This time even the first type of communication will stay constant as by adding more attributes the number of indices of list records that are covered or uncovered by the currently induced rule term stays constant as well.

4.2 Speed up of PMCRI

With the speed up factors we compare how much the parallel version of an algorithm is faster using p processors compared with one processor.

$$S_p = \frac{R_1}{R_p} \quad (1)$$

Formula 1 represents the speedup factors S_p. R_1 is the runtime of the algorithm on a single machine and R_p is the runtime on p machines. In the ideal case the speedup factors are the same as the number of processors used. For example if two processors were used then a speedup factor of 2 means that we gained 100% benefit from using an additional processor. In reality this speedup factor will be below the number of processors for various reasons such as a communication overhead imposed by each processor, which would be in our case caused by communication of information about rule terms and indices of list records. Then there is also the synchronization overhead. For example in the case of PMCRI if a processor has induced the locally best rule term it has to wait for the remaining machines to finish their rule term induction in order to receive or derive the indices that are covered from the globally best rule term. However, as stated in section 3 the relative workload of each processor stays constant thus a synchronisation overhead will not be overwhelming. Figure 6 shows the speed up factors of PrismTCS parallelised using PMCRI for different sizes of diabetes and yeast datasets. The left hand side of figure 6 shows the speedup factors for the data with different numbers of instances and the right hand side of figure 6 for the data with different numbers of attributes. We ran configurations of 2, 4, 6, 8, 10 and 12 processors against the serial version of PrismTCS. We can observe a general tendency that for a fixed dataset size with an increasing number of processors the speedup factors increase until they reach a maximum and then start to decrease again. We can also observe that the larger the dataset size the more processors are needed in order to reach the maximum speedup. Thus in general we can say the larger the amount of training data the more benefit we gain from using more expert machines.

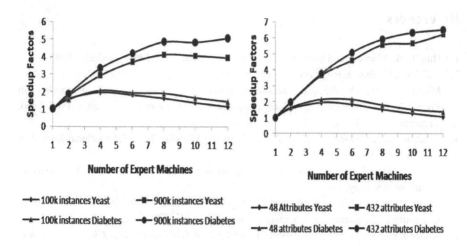

Fig. 6. Speedup behaviour of PMCRI.

5 Conclusions

We presented the work and results of the PMCRI framework, a Parallel Modular Classification Rule Induction framework. PMCRI harvests the computational power of a distributed network in order to make modular classification rule induction scale better on large datasets. We started the paper with a discussion of two general approaches to classification rule induction, the *divide and conquer* and *separate and conquer* approaches. There have been two general approaches to making the classification rule induction approach scale better on large datasets: sampling and parallelisation, but there has been no attempt to parallelise the *separate and conquer* approach. We continued the paper by discussing the Prism family of algorithms that follow the *separate and conquer* approach and discussed its quality and examined its scaling behaviour. We next discussed the suitability of Prism's pre-pruning method, J-pruning, for scaling up algorithms of the Prism family to large datasets. Next we presented the PMCRI framework with an integrated J-Pruning facility that helps to parallelise *separate and conquer* algorithms of the Prism family and similar ones. We evaluated PMCRI experimentally on a parallel implementation of PrismTCS. First we performed size-up experiments in order to determine PMCRI's scaling behaviour with respect to the number of data instances and attributes. In both cases we observed a size-up behaviour better than linear. Next we determined the speedup factors for several numbers of expert machines on several amounts of training data. We observed that the larger the amount of training data regarding the number of attributes and data instances the more processors are needed to achieve the maximum speedup.

References

1. Hunt E. B., Marin J., and Stone P. J., *Experiments in Induction*. 1966: Academic Press.
2. Quinlan J. R., *Induction of decision trees. Machine Learning*. Vol. 1. 1986. 81-106.
3. Michalski R.S., *On the quasi-minimal solution of the general covering problem*, in *Proceedings of the Fifth International Symposium on Information Processing*. 1969: Bled, Yugoslavia. p. 125-128.
4. Cendrowska J., *PRISM: an Algorithm for Inducing Modular Rules*. International Journal of Man-Machine Studies, 1987. 27: p. 349-370.
5. Catlett J., *Megainduction: Machine learning on very large databases*. 1991, University of Technology, Sydney.
6. Metha M., Agrawal R., and Rissanen J., *SLIQ: A Fast Scalable Classifier for Data Mining*. International Conference on Extending Database Technology EDBT'96), 1996.
7. Shafer J. C., Agrawal R., and Mehta M., *SPRINT: A Scalable Parallel Classifier for Data Mining*. Twenty-second International Conference on Very Large Data Bases, 1996.
8. Srivastava, A., et al., *Parallel Formulations of Decision-Tree Classification Algorithms*. Data Mining and Knowledge Discovery, 1999. 3(3): p. 237-263.
9. Stahl F., Bramer M., and A. M., *PMCRI: A Parallel Modular Classification Rule Induction Framework.*, in *Sixth International Conference on Machine Learning and Data Mining*. In Press, Springer: Leipzig.
10. Bramer M., *An Information-Theoretic Approach to the Pre-pruning of Classification Rules*. Proceedings of the IFIP Seventeenth World Computer Congress - TC12 Stream on Intelligent Information Processing. 2002: Kluwer, B.V. 201-212.
11. Bramer M., *Inducer: a public domain workbench for data mining*. International Journal of Systems Science, 2005. 36(14): p. 909-919.
12. Smyth, P. and R.M. Goodman, *An Information Theoretic Approach to Rule Induction from Databases*. IEEE Trans. on Knowledge and Data Eng, 1991. 4(4): p. 301-316.
13. Blake C. L. and Merz C. J, *UCI repository of machine learning databases*. 1998, University of California, Irvine, Department of Information and Computer Sciences.
14. Stout M., et al., *Prediction of recursive convex hull class assignments for protein residues*. Bioinformatics, 2008. 24(7): p. 916-923.
15. Provost F., *Distributed Data Mining: Scaling up and Beyond*, in *Advances in Distributed and Parallel Knowledge Discovery*, P.C. H. Kargupta, Editor. 2000, AAAI Press / The MIT Press.
16. Nolle L., Wong K. C. P., and Hopgood A., *DARBS: A Distributed Blackboard System*. Twenty-first SGES International Conference on Knowledge Based Systems, 2001.
17. Stahl F. and Bramer M., *P-Prism: A Computationally Efficient Approach to Scaling up Classification Rule Induction*, in *IFIP International Conference on Artificial Intelligence*. 2008, Springer: Milan.
18. Stahl F. and Bramer M., *Parallel Induction of Modular Classification Rules*, in *Twenty-eighth SGAI International Conference on Innovative Techniques and Applications of Artificial Intelligence*. 2008, Springer: Cambridge.

A kernel extension to handle missing data

Guillermo Nebot-Troyano and Lluís A. Belanche-Muñoz

Abstract An extension for univariate kernels that deals with missing values is proposed. These extended kernels are shown to be valid Mercer kernels and can adapt to many types of variables, such as categorical or continuous. The proposed kernels are tested against standard RBF kernels in a variety of benchmark problems showing different amounts of missing values and variable types. Our experimental results are very satisfactory, because they usually yield slight to much better improvements over those achieved with standard methods.

1 Introduction

In the last few years *kernel methods* have become a very popular topic of research. One of the most relevant problems in kernel-based learning machines, in terms of practical applications, is the *choice* of an appropriate kernel. This kernel should be a measure that adequately captures meaningful relations in the data. A proper kernel choice should result in more adequate learning machines, less likely to overfit and thus showing a better generalization ability.

Real-world data come from many different sources, described by mixtures of numeric and qualitative variables. These variables may require completely different treatments and are traditionally handled by *preparing* the data using a number of *coding methods*. These codings may entail an unknown change in input distribution or an increase in dimension, increasing the likelihood of overfitting and also the training or optimization time. Moreover, and most importantly, sometimes the data

Guillermo Nebot-Troyano
Faculty of Computer Science, Polytechnical University of Catalonia, Barcelona, Spain
e-mail: willynt@msn.com

Lluís A. Belanche-Muñoz (corresponding author)
Faculty of Computer Science, Polytechnical University of Catalonia, Barcelona, Spain
e-mail: belanche@lsi.upc.edu

M. Bramer et al. (eds.), *Research and Development in Intelligent Systems XXVI*,
DOI 10.1007/978-1-84882-983-1_12, © Springer-Verlag London Limited 2010

sets exhibit *missing values* by diverse causes. These missing values are always a serious problem because they require a preprocessing (either a coding or an imputation) of the dataset in order to be able to use a classical kernel.

In this work we present a method for dealing with missing values that rigorously extends *any* kernel to one that copes with missing information and without the need of any coding or imputation mechanism. The method can make use of distributional or probabilistic assumptions about the variables. In the often encountered situation that this knowledge is not available, we advocate for the use of *sample* statistics (very much like in Naïve Bayes methods), in the form of density estimation or frequentist probabilities; contrary to other methods, no parametric knowledge is required. In addition, the proposed kernels can accept mixed data types, a common situation in real-world data. We present successful experimental results against standard RBF kernels in a variety of benchmark problems showing different amounts of missing values and different variable types.

2 Preliminaries

The Support Vector Machine (SVM) was developed by Vapnik and his coworkers, initially for classification problems and has won great popularity as a tool for the identification of nonlinear systems [16]. A nice introduction to SVMs and kernel machines is [5]. A key idea in kernel machines is that of the *kernel*, but the SVM formulation does not include criteria to select a kernel function. A standard result for identifying such functions can be derived from Mercer's result [10]:

Theorem 1. *A continuous and symmetric function* $K : \mathcal{H} \times \mathcal{H} \rightarrow \mathbb{R}$ *is a kernel if it satisfies the condition:*

$$\int_{\mathcal{H} \times \mathcal{H}} K(x,y)g(x)g(y)dxdy \geq 0$$

for any function g such that $\int_{\mathcal{H}} (g(x))^2 dx < \infty$

If the function K gives rise to a positive integral operator, its evaluation can be expressed as an absolutely and uniformly convergent series (finite or infinite), almost everywhere [10]. Except for specific cases, it may not be easy to check whether this condition is satisfied. For this reason we show another, equivalent, definition:

Theorem 2. *The function* $K : \mathcal{H} \times \mathcal{H} \rightarrow \mathbb{R}$ *is a kernel if and only if for any finite subset* $\{x_1, x_2, ..., x_n\} \in \mathcal{H}$ *the associated kernel matrix* $K_{n \times n} = (k_{ij})$, *where* $k_{ij} = K(x_i, x_j)$ *is a symmetric positive semidefinite (PSD) matrix.*

This condition is in general easier to check than Mercer's condition. Among the most widely used and well-known kernels we find the Polynomial kernel $K(u,v) = (<u,v> +\gamma)^d$ with $\gamma \geq 0 \in \mathbb{R}$ and $d \in \mathbb{N}$ parameters (where $<,>$ denotes scalar product) and the Gaussian kernel, one of a number of kernels known as Radial Basis

Function (RBF) kernels, $K(u,v) = exp(-\frac{\|u-v\|^2}{2\sigma^2})$, with $\sigma \in \mathbb{R}$ a parameter. This one is by far the most popular choice of kernel in SVMs; it also includes the polynomial kernel as a limiting case.

Kernel functions can be conceptually regarded as similarity functions [14], although not all kernels fulfill all the properties for a similarity (e.g. boundedness). The work of Gower in general similarity measures [7] shows some partial coefficients of similarity for three different types of features: Dichotomous (Binary), Qualitative (Categoric) and Quantitative (Continuous and Discrete) features, that are shown to produce PSD matrices; these functions can hence be seen as kernels. For any two observations $x_i, x_j \in \mathcal{H}$ to be compared on the basis of a feature k a score s_{ijk} is built: first δ_{ijk} is defined as 0 when the comparison of x_i, x_j cannot be performed on the basis of feature k for some reason (e.g., by the presence of missing values); δ_{ijk} is 1 when such comparison is meaningful. The coefficient of similarity between x_i, x_j is defined as the average score over all the partial comparisons:

$$S_{ij} = \frac{\sum_{k=1}^{n} s_{ijk}\delta_{ijk}}{\sum_{k=1}^{n} \delta_{ijk}}. \tag{1}$$

The scores s_{ijk} are defined as follows [7]:

i) *For Dichotomous (binary) features*: The presence of the feature is denoted by $+$ and its absence by $-$; negative matches (i.e., absence - absence) are not considered meaningful. When there are no missing values for feature k,

	Values
observation x_i	$+$ $+$ $-$ $-$
observation x_j	$+$ $-$ $+$ $-$
s_{ijk}	1 0 0 0
δ_{ijk}	1 1 1 0

ii) *For Qualitative features*: Let $\mathbb{I}_{\{\cdot\}} = 1$ when the argument is true and 0 otherwise; then $s_{ijk} = \mathbb{I}_{\{x_{ik}=x_{jk}\}}$.

iii) *For Quantitative features*, $s_{ijk} = 1 - \frac{|x_{ik}-x_{jk}|}{R_k}$, where R_k is the *range* of feature k (the difference between the maximum and minimum attainable values).

Gower proves that, *if there are no missing values*, the matrix $S = (S_{ij})$ is PSD. This property may be lost when there are. An example will suffice: let $\mathcal{X}$ denote a missing value and consider three observations with four quantitative features in $[1,5]$ ($R_k = 4$), $x_1 = (1,2,3,1), x_2 = (1,3,3,\mathcal{X})$ and $x_3 = (1,3,3,5)$. In this case,

$$S = \begin{pmatrix} 1 & \frac{11}{12} & \frac{11}{16} \\ \frac{11}{12} & 1 & 1 \\ \frac{15}{16} & 1 & 1 \end{pmatrix}, \qquad \det(S) = -\frac{121}{2304} < 0$$

and therefore S is not PSD; but if we replace $\mathcal{X}$ by *any* precise value in $[1,5]$, then the matrix S is certainly PSD.

3 Main results

Missing information is an old issue in statistical analysis [9]. Missing values are very common in Medicine and Engineering, where many variables come from on-line sensors or device measurements, or are simply too costly to be measured at the same rate as other variables. In this section we present an approach that allows the *extension* of any kernel to one that is defined even in the presence of missing values. Moreover, the value returned by the kernels in this situation can be explained in meaningful terms. There are two basic ways of dealing with missing data, by *completing* the data description in a (hopefully) optimal way, or by *extending* the methods to work with incomplete descriptions. Our way to create kernels with missing values follows the latter idea and offers some important advantages:

1. Any kernel K can be extended to adapt to a dataset with missing values;
2. No preprocessing of the missing values is needed; we create kernels by calculating directly the values of $K(x, \mathscr{X})$ and $K(\mathscr{X}, \mathscr{X})$ where $\mathscr{X}$ represents a missing value –behaving as an *incomparable* element w.r.t. any ordering relation– without the need to estimate the value of $\mathscr{X}$;
3. There is no need of removing information because of the missing values; i.e., no information is lost;
4. Missing values are allowed both in training and *test* examples (which is quite difficult with traditional imputation methods).

Lemma 1. *Let $\mathscr{H}$ any set, $x_1, x_2, ..., x_n \in \mathscr{H}$ and let $f : \mathscr{H} \times \mathscr{H} \to \mathbb{R}$ a symmetrical function. Let $A \in \mathscr{M}_{n \times n}$ a PSD matrix where $A = [a_{ij}]$ with $a_{ij} = f(x_i, x_j)$. Let σ be any permutation of $x_1, ..., x_n$, i.e., $\sigma(x_1, ..., x_n) = (x_{\sigma(1)}, ..., x_{\sigma(n)})$; then the matrix $A^{\sigma} = [a_{ij}^{\sigma}]$ with $a_{ij}^{\sigma} = f(x_{\sigma(i)}, x_{\sigma(j)})$ is PSD.*

Proof. Let A and A^{σ} be the matrices of the lemma and let σ any permutation of $x_1, ..., x_n$, that is, $\sigma(x_1, ..., x_n) = (x_{\sigma(1)}, ..., x_{\sigma(n)})$. In order for A^{σ} to be PSD, we must prove that $\forall z \in \mathbb{R}^n$ $z^T A^{\sigma} z \geq 0$, provided $\forall y \in \mathbb{R}^n$ $y^T A y \geq 0$.

Then $0 \leq y^T A y = \sigma(y^T) \sigma(A) \sigma(y) = \sigma(y^T) A^{\sigma} \sigma(y)$, where $\sigma(y) = (y_{\sigma(1)}, ..., y_{\sigma(n)})$ and $\sigma(A) = [\sigma(a_{ij})]$, with $\sigma(a_{ij}) = f(x_{\sigma(i)}, x_{\sigma(j)}) = a_{ij}^{\sigma}$; i.e., $\sigma(A) = A^{\sigma}$. Now we know that $\forall y \in \mathbb{R}^n$, $\sigma(y^T) A^{\sigma} \sigma(y) \geq 0$, that is the same that $\forall z \in \mathbb{R}^n$ $z^T A z \geq 0$, because σ is a permutation function. $\square$

This result is important and useful because if we prove that one matrix, that depends on a symmetrical function, is PSD for an arrangement of the dataset, then the matrix is PSD for any rearrangement (reordering of the observations) of it.

Theorem 3. *Let K be a kernel in a set $\mathscr{H}$ (e.g. a similarity function) and P a probability density function in $\mathscr{H}$. Then the function*

$$\hat{K}(x, y) = \begin{cases} K(x, y), & \text{if } x, y \neq \mathscr{X}; \\ \int_{\mathscr{H}} P(y) K(x, y) dy, & \text{if } x \neq \mathscr{X} \text{ and } y = \mathscr{X}; \\ \int_{\mathscr{H}} P(x) K(x, y) dx, & \text{if } x = \mathscr{X} \text{ and } y \neq \mathscr{X}; \\ \int_{\mathscr{H}} P(x) \int_{\mathscr{H}} P(y) K(x, y) dy dx, & \text{if } x = y = \mathscr{X} \end{cases}$$

is a kernel in $\mathcal{H} \cup \{ \mathcal{X} \}$.

Proof. Developed in the Appendix, for clarity. □

Theorem 4. *Let K be a kernel in $\mathcal{H}$ (e.g. a similarity function) and P a probability mass function in $\mathcal{H}$. Then the function*

$$\hat{K}(x,y) = \begin{cases} K(x,y), & \text{if } x,y \neq \mathcal{X} \text{ ;} \\ \sum_{y \in \mathcal{H}} P(y)K(x,y), & \text{if } x \neq \mathcal{X} \text{ and } y = \mathcal{X}; \\ \sum_{x \in \mathcal{H}} P(x)K(x,y), & \text{if } x = \mathcal{X} \text{ and } y \neq \mathcal{X}; \\ \sum_{x \in \mathcal{H}} P(x) \sum_{y \in \mathcal{H}} P(y)K(x,y), & \text{if } x = y = \mathcal{X} \end{cases}$$

is a kernel in $\mathcal{H} \cup \{ \mathcal{X} \}$.

Proof. It is analogous to that of Theorem 3, changing the integrals by summations, since the summation has also the linearity property. □

3.1 Motivation of the extension

Given a two-place symmetric function $K : \mathcal{H} \times \mathcal{H} \to \mathbb{R}$, we aim to find that function κ that is the minimizer of

$$E[\kappa] = \int_{\mathcal{H}} \frac{1}{2} \int_{\mathcal{H}} (\kappa(z) - K(z,x))^2 p(z,x) \, dx \, dz$$

whose solution is $\kappa(z) = \int_{\mathcal{H}} K(z,x)p(x) \, dx$, by making use that, in the present situation, $p(z,x) = p(z)p(x)$. Therefore we define the kernel extension $\hat{K}(z, \mathcal{X}) = \kappa(z)$. The value of the kernel when *both* values are missing can be explained as follows. Focusing on one of the missing values, it certainly has to be one of the possible values, with some probability. Fixing it to, say, z, then the kernel has to be $K(z, \mathcal{X})$ by the previous result. The overall expression is therefore the *expectation* of $K(z, \mathcal{X})$ seen as a function of z.

3.2 Nonparametric Kernel Density estimation

If the densities or mass probability functions $f(x)$ are not known they can be estimated using the data set by applying non-parametric methods for estimation. One of these methods is the Parzen windows technique [11] or more generally *kernel density estimation* (KDE). A challenging task in the general case, in the univariate case the KDE approach is to consider $x_1, ..., x_n$ an i.i.d. sample of an absolutely continuous random variable X with unknown density $f(x)$, and define the empirical distribution function as $F_n(x) = n^{-1} \sum_{i=1}^{n} \mathbb{I}_{\{x_i \leq x\}}$, which is an estimator of the true (cumulative) distribution function $F(x)$ of X. Knowing that the density $f(x)$ is the derivative of the distribution function F we express $\hat{f}_h(x) = (2h)^{-1}[F_n(x+h) - F_n(x-h)]$, for a small $h > 0$. This is equivalent to the proportion of points in the interval $(x - h, x + h)$ divided by h. It is common that the amount of smoothing depends on the number of data points; then we have:

$$\hat{f}_h(x) = \frac{1}{n} \sum_{i=1}^{n} \frac{1}{h_n} \varphi\left(\frac{x - x_i}{h_n}\right) \tag{2}$$

A particular choice for the weight function (also called Parzen window or *uniform kernel*) is $\varphi(z) = \frac{1}{2}\mathbb{I}_{\{|z| \leq 1\}}$. Generally, φ and h must satisfy certain conditions of regularity, such that φ is bounded and absolutely integrable in $\mathbb{R}$ and integrates to 1 and $\lim_{n \to \infty} h_n = 0$. Usually, $\varphi(z) \geq 0$ and $\varphi(z) = \varphi(-z)$. Among the most widely used kernels we also find the Gaussian or the Epanechnikov kernels [6]. If the bandwidth h is very small then the estimation of the density function degenerates to a collection of n spikes centered at the data points. If h is too big then the estimation is oversmoothed and tends to the uniform distribution. A typical choice is $h = h_0 n^{-1/2}$, where h_0 is a free parameter to be determined. This estimation is consistent and asymptotically normal [13]. In this work we use the bandwidth selection method using pilot estimation of derivatives, described in [15].

3.3 Extended kernel using uniform KDE

We illustrate the previous ideas by coupling the extended version of the kernels developed in section 2 with KDE. Let $H \in \mathbb{R}$ be any bounded subset and denote $b = \sup_{x,y \in H} |x - y|$ and $a = \inf_{x,y \in H} |x - y|$. According to Theorem 3, for any finite subset $\{x_1, x_2, ..., x_n\} \in H$,

$$\hat{K}_1(x_i, x_j) = \begin{cases} 1 - \frac{|x_i - x_j|}{b-a}, & \text{if } x_i, x_j \neq \mathscr{X}; \\ g_1(x_i), & \text{if } x_i \neq \mathscr{X} \text{ and } x_j = \mathscr{X}; \\ g_1(x_j), & \text{if } x_i = \mathscr{X} \text{ and } x_j \neq \mathscr{X}; \\ G_1, & \text{if } x_i = x_j = \mathscr{X} \text{ and } i \neq j; \\ 1 & \text{if } x_i = x_j = \mathscr{X} \text{ and } i = j \end{cases}$$

is a valid PSD kernel, where

$$g_1(z) = \int_{-\infty}^{\infty} \hat{f}(x) \left(1 - \frac{|x - z|}{b-a}\right) dx = \int_{-\infty}^{\infty} \frac{1}{nh} \sum_{i=1}^{n} \varphi\left(\frac{x - x_i}{h}\right) \left(1 - \frac{|x - z|}{b-a}\right) dx$$

$$= \frac{1}{nh} \sum_{i=1}^{n} \int_{-\infty}^{\infty} \varphi\left(\frac{x - x_i}{h}\right) \left(1 - \frac{|x - z|}{b-a}\right) dx = \frac{1}{nh} \sum_{i=1}^{n} \frac{1}{2} \int_{x_i-h}^{x_i+h} \left(1 - \frac{|x - z|}{b-a}\right) dx$$

$$= \frac{1}{2nh} \sum_{i=1}^{n} \alpha_i(z), \qquad \text{with} \ \ \alpha_i(z) = \begin{cases} \frac{2h(b-z+x_i-a)}{b-a}, & \text{if } z > x_i + h; \\ \frac{2h(b-a)-(x_i-z)^2-h^2}{b-a}, & \text{if } x_i - h \leq z \leq x_i + h; \\ \frac{2h(b-x_i+z-a)}{b-a}, & \text{if } z < x_i - h \end{cases}$$

$$\text{and } G_1 = \int_{-\infty}^{\infty} \hat{f}(z) g_1(z) dz = \frac{1}{2nh} \sum_{i=1}^{n} \int_{-\infty}^{\infty} \frac{1}{nh} \sum_{j=1}^{n} \varphi\left(\frac{z-x_j}{h}\right) \alpha_i(z) dz =$$

$$= \left(\frac{1}{2nh}\right)^2 \sum_{i=1}^{n} \sum_{j=1}^{n} \int_{x_j-h}^{x_j+h} \alpha_i(z) dz = \left(\frac{1}{2nh}\right)^2 \sum_{i=1}^{n} \sum_{j=1}^{n} \beta_{ij}$$

with

$$\beta_{ij} = \begin{cases} \frac{4h^2(b-x_j+x_i-a)}{b-a}, & \text{if } x_i + h < x_j - h; \\ \frac{12(b-a)h^2-(x_i-x_j)^3-2h(4h^2+3(x_i-x_j)^2)}{3(b-a)}, & \text{if } x_j - h \leq x_i + h < x_j + h; \\ \frac{4h^2(3(b-a)-2h)}{3(b-a)}, & \text{if } x_j = x_i; \\ \frac{12(b-a)h^2+(x_i-x_j)^3-2h(4h^2+3(x_i-x_j)^2)}{3(b-a)}, & \text{if } x_j - h < x_i - h \leq x_j + h; \\ \frac{4h^2(b-x_i+x_j-a)}{b-a}, & \text{if } x_j + h < x_i - h \end{cases}$$

3.4 Extended kernel for categoric features

Consider now a categoric feature that takes values in the finite set $\mathcal{V} = \{v_1, ..., v_l\}$. An extended kernel can be built around Gower's result for qualitative features (section 2). The probability mass function f for this type of feature can be estimated in the usual way from the data set by the frequency of every modality among the values that are non-missing for this feature. Then, for all $v_i, v_j \in \mathcal{V}$,

$$K_2(v_i, v_j) = \begin{cases} \mathbb{I}_{\{v_i=v_j\}}, & \text{if } v_i, v_j \neq \mathcal{X}; \\ g_2(v_i), & \text{if } v_i \neq \mathcal{X} \text{ and } v_j = \mathcal{X}; \\ g_2(v_j), & \text{if } v_i = \mathcal{X} \text{ and } v_j \neq \mathcal{X}; \\ G_2, & \text{if } v_i = v_j = \mathcal{X} \text{ and } i \neq j; \\ 1 & \text{if } v_i = v_j = \mathcal{X} \text{ and } i = j \end{cases}$$

where $g_2(z) = \sum_{i=1}^{l} f(v_i) \mathbb{I}_{\{v_i=z\}} = f(z)$ and $G_2 = \sum_{i=1}^{l} f(v_i)^2$, is a PSD kernel in $\mathcal{V} \cup \{\mathcal{X}\}$.

3.5 Extended Heterogeneous Kernel

We show now how to create a full kernel in $\mathcal{H} = \mathcal{H}_1 \times ... \times \mathcal{H}_t$ from a collection of extended *partial* kernels K_i defined in the sets $\{\mathcal{H}_i\}_{i=1 \div t}$.

Theorem 5. *If* $\{K_i\}_{i=1 \div t}$ *are kernels defined in the sets* $\mathscr{H}_i$ *, the function:*

$$\mathscr{K}(x,y) = \frac{1}{t}\sum_{i=1}^{t} K_i(x_i, y_i) \tag{3}$$

is a kernel in the product space $\mathscr{H}$.

Proof. The sum of $t > 0$ PSD matrices is a PSD matrix; take any real $r > 0$ and a PSD matrix A, then rA is again PSD (in the present case, $r = 1/t$). $\square$

We will refer to (3) as an *Extended Heterogeneous Kernel* or EHK.

3.6 Adding flexibility to an EHK

Typically kernels have parameters that allow them to have a greater *flexibility*. In order to add this flexibility to an existing EHK, a non-linear *activation* function is needed, that depends on one parameter. Moreover, this activation function must preserve the PSD property.

Proposition 1. *Let K a Kernel in* $\mathscr{H}$ *and consider the function*

$$f_{act}(x) = \left(\frac{1}{1-\alpha x}\right)^{\frac{1}{\alpha}}$$

for any $\alpha \in (0,1)$. *Then* $f_{act}(K(x,y))$ *is a kernel in* $\mathscr{H}$.

Proof. Immediate using properties described in [4, 8]. $\square$

We will refer to $f_{act}(K(x,y))$ as an EHK with parameter α or EHK$_\alpha$.

4 Experimental work

Experimental work is now presented in different benchmarking data sets: a specially designed synthetic data set, several problems from the UCI repository [2] and a couple of our own. We perform a comparative study between SVMs using two variants of RBF kernels (see below) and SVMs using the two EHK kernels[1].

4.1 Synthetic data

Our first problem has been created artificially for illustrative purposes. It consists of 11 features generated from known distributions, as indicated in Table 1.

---

[1] We used the R language for statistical computing [1] extended with the *kernlab* package.

Table 1 Probability distributions[a] and their parameters for the artificially generated problem.

Feature	1	2	3	4	5	6	7	8	9	10
Distrib.	Gau	Poi	Gmt	Unf	Unf	Exp	Gau	Gau	Bin	Ber
Params.	μ, σ^2	λ	p	a, b	a, b	λ	μ, σ^2	μ, σ^2	n, p	p
Value	$\mu = 3$	$\lambda = 3$	$p = 0.6$	$a = -3$	$a = 100$	$\lambda = 4$	$\mu = 0$	$\mu = 0.5$	$n = 20$	$p = 0.28$
	$\sigma^2 = 0.5$			$b = 10$	$b = 200$		$\sigma^2 = 1$	$\sigma^2 = 2$	$p = 1/3$	

[a] Gau=Gaussian, Poi=Poisson, Gmt=Geometric, Unf=Uniform, Exp=Exponential, Bin=Binomial, Ber=Bernoulli.

The eleventh feature is categoric with four equally-probable modalities (say A, B, C and D). The rules that set the class feature are as follows. Let v a vector instance of the data set and v_i stand for the value of its i-th feature; then

- **if** $v_1 > 2 \wedge v_2 \geq 1 \wedge v_3 < 4 \wedge v_4 > -2.4 \wedge v_5 \geq 103 \wedge v_6 \leq 1 \wedge v_7 \geq -1.9 \wedge v_8 < 4 \wedge v_9 \geq 4 \wedge v_{10} = 0 \wedge (v_{11} = \text{``}B\text{''} \vee v_{11} = \text{``}C\text{''})$ **then** the class is 1;
- **if** $v_1 < 3.8 \wedge v_2 \leq 6 \wedge v_3 \leq 2 \wedge v_4 \leq 9.4 \wedge v_5 < 196 \wedge v_6 > 0.01 \wedge v_7 \leq 2 \wedge v_8 \geq -3 \wedge v_9 \leq 8 \wedge (v_{11} = \text{``}A\text{''} \vee v_{11} = \text{``}D\text{''})$ **then** the class is 1;
- **otherwise** the class is -1.

We created random samples 500 instances each, and then introduced 5%, 10%, ..., 85% of missing values, in steps of 5%. The aim is to ascertain how the methods can cope with the existence of an ever larger percentage of missing values. We use two methods to code missing values with the RBF kernel:

RBF1   missing values are imputed by mean or mode, depending on the feature being continuous or categoric.

RBF2   missing values are imputed by a zero and a new feature column is added with zeros; in the position of missing values, the zeros are replaced by ones.

In both methods, we code categorical attributes using a unary representation, a standard practice [12]. In Fig. 1 we see the results for the different methods. Each point is the mean of 50 different data sets. In each one, the methods were evaluated using 10 times of 10-fold cross-validation. EHK1 and EHKF1 represent the EHK and EHK_α kernels with the true density (or mass) function; EHK2 and EHKF2 represent the same kernels obtained using uniform KDE and frequentist probabilities.

We can see that the EHKF1 is the best method as could be expected, but EHKF2 is also quite good. For this reason, from here on, all the densities for numeric features are estimated using the kernel developed in section 3.3. Note also the drastic degradation of the RBF2 from 0% to 5%, probably due to the increment in input dimension (which only happens at this step). Also, at very high percentages (80% and more), all methods tend to perform as the baseline performance.

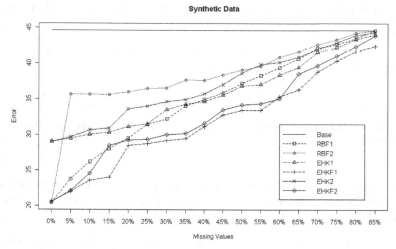

Fig. 1 Evolution of mean error (in %) in the synthetic problem for increasing percentages of missing values. The top horizontal line indicates the baseline performance using the majority class.

4.2 Real-world data sets

A description of the selected problems follows:

1. The CREDITCRX data set (from UCI) has 690 instances and 15 features of which 9 are categoric and 6 are numeric. It contains a 0.65% of missing values.
2. The HORSECOLIC data set (from UCI) has 366 instances and 22 features of which 12 are categoric, 7 are continuous and 3 are discrete. It contains a 23.75% of missing values. Note the original data set has 27 features; we have removed those numbered 3, 25, 26, 27 and 28 because they are declared as not relevant to the task. Further, two class features can be used: feature 23 (three possible cases: 'lived', 'died' and 'euthanized') and 24 (the horse had surgical lesion or not).
3. The FECALSOURCE data set has been donated by the Microbiology Department at the University of Barcelona. There are 144 instances with 10 dichotomous features, that are molecular tests signaling the presence of certain molecules in animal fecal samples. This dataset contains a 19.95% of missing values. The class feature has four possible cases: 'human', 'bovine', 'poultry' and 'porcine'.
4. The SERVO data set (from UCI) has 167 instances described by 4 many-valued categoric features. This data set does not contain missing values.
5. The WASTE WATER TREATMENT PLANT (WWTP) data set has been donated by the Chemical Engineering Department at the University of Girona [3]. There are 279 instances and 91 continuous features that represent lagged information of plant process output. This dataset contains a 32.83% of missing values.

In Table 2 we can see the results obtained with the different methods. These are the results of parameter optimization (C, σ for the two RBFs, C for EHK or C, α

for EHK$_\alpha$) using again the mean of 10 times of 10-fold cross-validation. The ε parameter was also optimized in the regression tasks (SERVO and WWTP).

Table 2 Detailed results. In case of classification tasks these are the error rates in % and the 'Base' results correspond to 100% minus the majority class; in regression tasks these are *normalized root mean square errors* (NRMSE) and the 'Base' results correspond to the best constant model[a].

Problem/Method	Base	RBF$_1$	RBF$_2$	EHK	EHK$_\alpha$
CREDITCRX	44.49	13.80	14.09	12.81	12.54
HORSECOLIC-23	38.53	29.23	29.90	29.14	27.54
HORSECOLIC-24	36.96	16.50	18.89	15.95	15.47
FECALSOURCE	65.54	31.37	29.32	25.21	23.87
SERVO	1.000	0.406	0.406[b]	0.541	0.321
WWTP	1.000	0.456	0.531	0.396	0.395

[a] This corresponds to a NRMSE of 1.

[b] In the SERVO problem there are no missing values, thus both RBF methods coincide.

The two RBF methods do not seem to yield significant differences in performance. Given that the parameters have been fully optimized in both cases, this may indicate a lower bound in performance that cannot be surpassed with such direct ways of missing value treatment. On the other hand, the two EHK kernels behave comparably well, delivering better mean results, sometimes substantially, as in the FECALSOURCE problem. This problem is notoriously difficult, having four classes with less than 150 observations in total. It also seems that, as expected, the more flexible kernel EHK$_\alpha$ is able to achieve general better results.

5 Conclusions

This paper has presented a rigorous extension for univariate kernels that is able to deal with missing values. We would like to emphasize that we have advocated for the use of *partial* (or univariate) kernels for every descriptive variable and the building of a final kernel as the composition or *aggregation* of these partial kernels, an idea that can be traced back to Vapnik [17]. From the obtained results it can be concluded that the derived kernels have yielded satisfactory results. In the first place, our extended kernels behave very well when using the true densities, which provides empirical support for the theoretically developed ideas. Second, the extended kernels using non-parametric density estimation behave reasonably well and markedly better than standard kernels. This can be specially realized in the experiments with synthetic data. This of course is no proof that they are always a better choice, but adds strong support to the motivations of the work and to the solutions envisaged.

A recognized drawback of the work is the computational time, which we expect to improve in the future, by making more extensive use of incremental computations. A clear avenue for future research is the extension of the method for other data types for the features; for example, bit strings, fuzzy features, ordinal features, etc, could be accommodated with ease. We also envisage the extension of other kernels for complex data types already present in the literature (e.g., for trees or text).

Acknowledgements. Authors wish to thank the Spanish CICyT Project CGL2007-65980-C02-01/HID and the anonymous reviewers for their helpful suggestions.

Appendix

Proof for Theorem 3. If $M = [m_{ij}]$ is a $m \times n$ matrix whose elements are continuous functions in an interval, then the integral of M is again a $m \times n$ matrix whose elements are the integrals of the elements of M, that is to say:

$$\int_a^b M = [\int_a^b m_{ij}] \quad \text{where } a, b \in \mathbb{R}.$$

Suppose we have a finite sample $x_1, \ldots, x_n \in \mathcal{H}$ of which k are non-missing values and $n - k$ are missing values. We order the sample so that the non-missing values go first and then come the missing ones, i.e., consider a permutation $\sigma(x_1, \ldots, x_n) = (x_{m_1}, x_{m_2} \ldots, x_{m_k}, x_{m_{k+1}}, x_{m_{k+2}}, \ldots, x_{m_n})$, with $x_{m_1}, \ldots, x_{m_k} \neq \mathcal{X}$ and $x_{m_{k+1}}, \ldots, x_{m_n} = \mathcal{X}$. Then define $\mathcal{K} = [k_{ij}]$ with $k_{ij} = \hat{K}(x_i, x_j)$, $A = [a_{ij}]$ with $a_{ij} = K(x_{m_i}, x_{m_j})$ and $A' = [a'_{ij}]$ with $a'_{ij} = \hat{K}(x_{m_i}, x_{m_j})$. Hence,

$$
A' = \left(
\begin{array}{ccc|ccc}
K(x_{m_1}, x_{m_1}) & \cdots & K(x_{m_1}, x_{m_k}) & \hat{K}(x_{m_1}, x_{m_{k+1}}) & \cdots & \hat{K}(x_{m_1}, x_{m_n}) \\
\vdots & \ddots & \vdots & \vdots & \cdots & \vdots \\
K(x_{m_k}, x_{m_1}) & \cdots & K(x_{m_k}, x_{m_k}) & \hat{K}(x_{m_k}, x_{m_{k+1}}) & \cdots & \hat{K}(x_{m_k}, x_{m_n}) \\
\hline
\hat{K}(x_{m_{k+1}}, x_{m_1}) & \cdots & \hat{K}(x_{m_{k+1}}, x_{m_k}) & \hat{K}(x_{m_{k+1}}, x_{m_{k+1}}) & \cdots & \hat{K}(x_{m_{k+1}}, x_{m_n}) \\
\vdots & \cdots & \vdots & \vdots & \ddots & \vdots \\
\hat{K}(x_{m_n}, x_{m_1}) & \cdots & \hat{K}(x_{m_n}, x_{m_k}) & \hat{K}(x_{m_n}, x_{m_{k+1}}) & \cdots & \hat{K}(x_{m_n}, x_{m_n})
\end{array}
\right)
$$

$$
= \left(\frac{A'_1 | A'_2}{A'_3 | A'_4} \right) \quad \text{where} \quad A'_1 = \left(
\begin{array}{ccc}
K(x_{m_1}, x_{m_1}) & \cdots & K(x_{m_1}, x_{m_k}) \\
\vdots & \ddots & \vdots \\
K(x_{m_k}, x_{m_1}) & \cdots & K(x_{m_k}, x_{m_k})
\end{array}
\right),
$$

$$
A'_2 = \left(
\begin{array}{ccc}
\int_{\mathcal{H}} P(x_{m_{k+1}}) K(x_{m_1}, x_{m_{k+1}}) dx_{m_{k+1}} & \cdots & \int_{\mathcal{H}} P(x_{m_n}) K(x_{m_1}, x_{m_n}) dx_{m_n} \\
\vdots & \cdots & \vdots \\
\int_{\mathcal{H}} P(x_{m_{k+1}}) K(x_{m_k}, x_{m_{k+1}}) dx_{m_{k+1}} & \cdots & \int_{\mathcal{H}} P(x_{m_n}) K(x_{m_k}, x_{m_n}) dx_{m_n}
\end{array}
\right),
$$

$A'_3 = (A'_2)^T$ and

$$A'_4 = \begin{pmatrix} \int_{\mathscr{H}} P(x_{m_{k+1}}) \int_{\mathscr{H}} P(x_{m_{k+1}}) K(x_{m_{k+1}}, x_{m_{k+1}}) dx_{m_{k+1}} dx_{m_{k+1}} & \cdots & \int_{\mathscr{H}} P(x_{m_n}) \int_{\mathscr{H}} P(x_{m_{k+1}}) K(x_{m_{k+1}}, x_{m_n}) dx_{m_{k+1}} dx_{m_n} \\ \vdots & \ddots & \vdots \\ \int_{\mathscr{H}} P(x_{m_{k+1}}) \int_{\mathscr{H}} P(x_{m_n}) K(x_{m_n}, x_{m_{k+1}}) dx_{m_n} dx_{m_{k+1}} & \cdots & \int_{\mathscr{H}} P(x_{m_n}) \int_{\mathscr{H}} P(x_{m_n}) K(x_{m_n}, x_{m_n}) dx_{m_n} dx_{m_n} \end{pmatrix}$$

An equivalent definition is $A' = \int_{\mathscr{H}} P(x_{m_n}) \ldots \int_{\mathscr{H}} P(x_{m_{k+1}}) A \, dx_{m_{k+1}} \ldots dx_{m_n}$, i.e.,

$$d'_{ij} = \int_{\mathscr{H}} P(x_{m_n}) \ldots \int_{\mathscr{H}} P(x_{m_{k+1}}) a_{ij} dx_{m_{k+1}} \ldots dx_{m_n} =$$

$$= \int_{\mathscr{H}} P(x_{m_n}) \ldots \int_{\mathscr{H}} P(x_{m_{k+1}}) K(x_{m_i}, x_{m_j}) dx_{m_{k+1}} \ldots dx_{m_n}$$

because, if:

i) $x_{m_i}, x_{m_j} \neq \mathscr{X}$, then

$$d'_{ij} = \int_{\mathscr{H}} P(x_{m_n}) \ldots \int_{\mathscr{H}} P(x_{m_{k+1}}) K(x_{m_i}, x_{m_j}) dx_{m_{k+1}} \ldots dx_{m_n} =$$

$$= K(x_{m_i}, x_{m_j}) \left(\int_{\mathscr{H}} P(x_{m_{k+1}}) dx_{m_{k+1}} \right) \ldots \left(\int_{\mathscr{H}} P(x_{m_n}) dx_{m_n} \right) = K(x_{m_i}, x_{m_j})$$

ii) $x_{m_i} \neq \mathscr{X}$ and $x_{m_j} = \mathscr{X}$ where $j = k+1, \ldots, n$, then

$$d'_{ij} = \int_{\mathscr{H}} P(x_{m_n}) \ldots \int_{\mathscr{H}} P(x_{m_{k+1}}) K(x_{m_i}, x_{m_j}) dx_{m_{k+1}} \ldots dx_{m_n} =$$

$$\left(\int_{\mathscr{H}} P(x_{m_{k+1}}) dx_{m_{k+1}} \right) \ldots \left(\int_{\mathscr{H}} P(x_{m_j}) K(x_{m_i}, x_{m_j}) dx_{m_j} \right) \ldots \left(\int_{\mathscr{H}} P(x_{m_n}) dx_{m_n} \right)$$

$$= \int_{\mathscr{H}} P(x_{m_j}) K(x_{m_i}, x_{m_j}) dx_{m_j}$$

iii) $x_{m_i} = x_{m_j} = \mathscr{X}$ where $i, j = k+1, \ldots n$, then

$$d'_{ij} = \int_{\mathscr{H}} P(x_{m_n}) \ldots \int_{\mathscr{H}} P(x_{m_{k+1}}) K(x_{m_i}, x_{m_j}) dx_{m_{k+1}} \ldots dx_{m_n} =$$

$$\left(\int_{\mathscr{H}} P(x_{m_{k+1}}) dx_{m_{k+1}} \right) \ldots \left(\int_{\mathscr{H}} P(x_{m_i}) \int_{\mathscr{H}} P(x_{m_j}) K(x_{m_i}, x_{m_j}) dx_{m_j} dx_{m_i} \right) \ldots \left(\int_{\mathscr{H}} P(x_{m_n}) dx_{m_n} \right)$$

$$= \int_{\mathscr{H}} P(x_{m_i}) \int_{\mathscr{H}} P(x_{m_j}) K(x_{m_i}, x_{m_j}) dx_{m_j} dx_{m_i}$$

Now we are going to prove that A' is PSD. Using the last expression for A':

$$y^T A' y = y^T \left(\int_{\mathscr{H}} P(x_{m_n}) \ldots \int_{\mathscr{H}} P(x_{m_{k+2}}) \int_{\mathscr{H}} P(x_{m_{k+1}}) A \, dx_{m_{k+1}} \ldots dx_{m_n} \right) y$$

which, by the linearity of the integral, is equal to

$$\int_{\mathscr{H}} P(x_{m_n}) \ldots \int_{\mathscr{H}} P(x_{m_{k+2}}) \int_{\mathscr{H}} P(x_{m_{k+1}}) (y^T A y) \, dx_{m_{k+1}} \ldots dx_{m_n} \qquad (4)$$

We know that $y^T A y \geq 0$ for all $y \in \mathbb{R}^n$, because K is a Kernel. The product of non-negative functions is non-negative and the definite integral of a non-negative function is non-negative. Therefore we have that $P(x_{m_{k+1}}) y^T A y$ is a non-negative function because $P(x) \in [0, 1]$ $\forall x \in \mathbb{R}$ and $y^T A y$ is a non-negative function. Then

$$\int_{\mathscr{H}} P(x_{m_n})(y^T A y) dx_{m_n} \geq 0$$

In general we will have that $\int_{\mathscr{H}} P(x_{m_{k+1}})(y^T A y) dx_{m_{k+1}}$ is a non-negative function and $P(x_{m_{k+2}}) \geq 0$. Therefore,

$$\int_{\mathscr{H}} \left(P(x_{m_{k+2}}) \int_{\mathscr{H}} P(x_{m_{k+1}}) y^T A y dx_{m_{k+1}} \right) dx_{m_{k+2}} \geq 0$$

Iterating this argument we conclude that (4) is a non-negative function for all $y \in \mathbb{R}^n$ and consequently A' is PSD. By Lemma 1 $\mathscr{K}$ is PSD, and so K is a Kernel. $\square$

References

1. R Development Core Team: R: A Language and Environment for Statistical Computing. R Foundation for Statistical Computing, Vienna, Austria. (2008)
2. Asuncion, A. and Newman, D.J. (2007). UCI Machine Learning Repository, http://www.ics.uci.edu/%7emlearn/MLRepository.html. Irvine, CA: University of California, School of Information and Computer Science.
3. Belanche, LL., Valdés, J.J., Comas, J., Roda, I. and Poch, M. (1999) Towards a Model of Input-Output Behavior of Wastewater Treatment Plants using Soft Computing Techniques. *Environmental Modeling & Software*, 14: 409-419. Elsevier, 1999.
4. Berg, C., Christensen, J.P.R. and Ressel, P. *Harmonic Analysis on Semigroups: Theory of Positive Definite and Related Functions*. Springer-Verlag, 1984.
5. Burges, J.C. A Tutorial on Support Vector Machines for Pattern Recognition. *Data Mining and Knowledge Discovery*, 2 (1998).
6. Duda, R. and Hart, P. *Pattern Classification and Scene Analysis*. Wiley (1973).
7. Gower, J.C. A general coefficient of similarity and some of its properties. *Biometrics*, 22, pp. 882-907 (1971).
8. Horn, R. and Johnson, C.R. *Matrix analysis*. Cambridge University Press, 1991.
9. Little, R.J.A. and Rubin, D.B. *Statistical analysis with missing data*. John Wiley, 1987.
10. Mercer, J. (1909). Functions of positive and negative type and their connection with the theory of integral equations. *Philos. Trans. Roy. Soc. London*, A 209: 415-446.
11. Parzen, E. On estimation of a probability density function and mode. *The Annals of Mathematical Statistics*, 33(3), pp. 1065-1076 (1962).
12. Prechelt, L. PROBEN1: A Set of Benchmarks and Benchmarking Rules for Neural Network Training Algorithms. Report 21/94. Fakultät für Informatik, Univ. Karlsruhe, 1994.
13. Rosenblatt, M. Remarks on Some Nonparametric Estimates of a Density Function. *The Annals of Mathematical Statistics*, 27(3), pp. 832-837 (1956).
14. Schölkopf, B. *Learning with kernels*. John Wiley, 2001.
15. Sheather, S. J. and Jones, M.C. A reliable data-based bandwidth selection method for kernel density estimation. *Journal of the Royal Statistical Society series* B, 53, 683690, 1991.
16. Vapnik, V. *The nature of Statical Learning Theory*. Springer-Verlag, New York, 1995.
17. Vapnik, V. The support vector method of function estimation. *Neural networks and machine learning*. C. Bishop (Ed.), NATO ASI Series F. Springer, 1998.

Template Learning using Wavelet Domain Statistical Models

Karthikeyan Natesan Ramamurthy, Jayaraman J. Thiagarajan and Andreas Spanias

Abstract Wavelets have been used with great success in applications such as signal denoising, compression, estimation and feature extraction. This is because of their ability to capture singularities in the signal with a few coefficients. Applications that consider the statistical dependencies of wavelet coefficients have been shown to perform better than those which assume the wavelet coefficients as independent. In this paper, a novel Gaussian mixture model, specifically suited for template learning is proposed for modeling the marginal statistics of the wavelet coefficients. A Bayesian approach for inferring a low dimensional statistical template with a set of training images, using the independent mixture and the hidden Markov tree models extended to the template learning case, is developed. Results obtained for template learning and pattern classification using the low dimensional templates are presented. For training with a large data set, statistical templates generated using the proposed Bayesian approach are more robust than those generated using an information-theoretic framework in the wavelet domain.

1 Introduction

Wavelet domain statistical models have found extensive applications in image denoising and coding. In this paper, the application of wavelet statistical models to the problem of template learning for generating a low dimensional statistical template in a Bayesian approach is addressed. There are two facets to this problem, one is to provide an appropriate statistical model for exploiting the wavelet coefficient dependencies, and the other is to use this statistical model for learning a low dimensional template in the wavelet domain for synthesis and classification. A specific type of Gaussian mixture modeling of the wavelet coefficients for a template learning ap-

Karthikeyan Natesan Ramamurthy, Jayaraman J. Thiagarajan, Andreas Spanias
School of Electrical, Computer and Energy Engineering, Arizona State University, USA.
e-mail: {knatesan,jjayaram,spanias}@asu.edu

M. Bramer et al. (eds.), *Research and Development in Intelligent Systems XXVI*,
DOI 10.1007/978-1-84882-983-1_13, © Springer-Verlag London Limited 2010

plication is described. The IM model proposed in [4] and wavelet HMT models proposed in [1] are extended to the case of multiple training images. The Viterbi algorithm for estimating the most likely states given a set of training images and the estimated parameters of the statistical model is derived. The problem of registering a set of training patterns to the template is also described in detail as a part of the template learning procedure. The proposed Bayesian approach for template learning is compared with the Template Learning from Atomic Representations (TEMPLAR), which is an information-theoretic framework and the advantages that our procedure has in terms of avoiding overfitting is demonstrated.

The relevant prior work on template learning and wavelet domain statistical models is presented in Section 2. Section 3 presents the wavelet domain statistical models developed for the purpose of template learning. The proposed approach for template learning, along with the Viterbi algorithm for estimating the states and a method for registration of training images with the template are presented in Section 4. Section 5 discusses the results for generating the low dimensional template with the training images and pattern classification using the generated template. The discussion concludes with comments in Section 6.

2 Prior Work

2.1 Template Learning

Template learning is the process of learning a representative pattern from the set of training patterns under consideration. The need to register the training images is inherent to the problem of template learning. Separation of background from the pattern of interest and modeling the local deformations are also key problems associated with template learning. An approach for template learning and classification in the wavelet domain, TEMPLAR, has been proposed in [2]. In this framework [2], the wavelet coefficients are assumed to follow a two-state Gaussian mixture distribution locally and an independence assumption is imposed on the coefficients. In general, edges represent the significant information in any pattern. Hence, TEMPLAR exploits the edge detection properties of the wavelet transform. The Minimum Description Length (MDL) principle, an information theoretic criterion, is used to select the significant coefficients that represent the edges in an image.

2.2 Wavelet Domain Statistical Models

Wavelet coefficients have been assumed to be statistically independent in many applications, because the wavelet transform approximately whitens a AR-1 process. However, they exhibit significant statistical dependencies within a particular

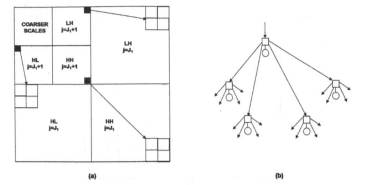

Fig. 1 (a) Parent-child relationship between wavelet coefficients across scale, (b) quad-tree structure of state connections between parents and children.

scale as well as across scales [3]. The marginal statistics of wavelet coefficients are highly non-Gaussian in nature [4] and therefore any wavelet statistical model should take the marginal statistics as well as the coefficient interdependencies into consideration. The Independent Mixture (IM) model captures the highly non-Gaussian marginal statistics of wavelet coefficients, using a two state Gaussian Mixture Model (GMM) and considers the coefficients to be independent [4]. An intuitive and effective Hidden Markov Tree (HMT) model builds on the IM model and captures the inter-scale dependencies between the coefficients [1], and this has been successfully used in denoising. The wavelet coefficients of an image form a natural quad-tree structure and a separate HMT model will be trained for the tree corresponding to each of the three subbands. The parent-child relationship and the quad-tree structure of the wavelet coefficients across scales are shown in Figure 1.

3 Wavelet Domain Statistical Models in Template Learning

Explicitly modeling the coefficient statistics when there are multiple training images, is a problem that has not been well addressed in the literature. Therefore, modeling the wavelet coefficient statistics is needed along with the statistical dependencies they exhibit with the other coefficients.

3.1 Proposed Gaussian Mixture Model

GMMs used for modeling wavelet coefficients have the form that assumes two zero mean Gaussians, one with a low variance and the other with a high variance [1]. For template learning, a different form of GMM needs to be used because the local statistics of wavelet coefficients need to be taken into consideration. The pattern

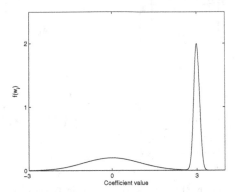

Fig. 2 Two state Gaussian mixture model for template learning. The low state (zero mean) models the background and smooth regions, whereas the high state (non-zero mean) corresponds to the pattern.

and background information need to be modeled efficiently, so that they can be clearly distinguished. The GMM proposed is a two state model and for the wavelet coefficient W_i, the density is given by,

$$f_{W_i}(w_i) = \sum_{m=1}^{M} p_{Q_i}(m) f_{W_i|Q_i}(w_i|Q_i = m). \tag{1}$$

The conditional density of the wavelet coefficients are given as $f_{W_i|Q_i}(w_i|Q_i = m) \sim \mathcal{N}(\mu_{i,m}, \sigma_{i,m}^2)$. The state $Q_i = 1$ represents a zero mean Gaussian and the state $Q_i = 2$ represents the Gaussian with non-zero mean.

Each wavelet coefficient W_i is assumed to have a separate $\mu_{i,2}$ and $\sigma_{i,2}^2$, whereas $\mu_{i,1} = 0$ and $\sigma_{i,1}^2$ is constrained to be the same for all the coefficients in a subband. An illustration of this mixture model is shown in Figure 2. The state $Q_i = 1$ models the background and smooth regions with a zero mean and common variance across the subband, whereas the state $Q_i = 2$ corresponds to the pattern. For convenience, $Q_i = 1$ will be referred to as the *low* state for the coefficient i and $Q_i = 2$ will be referred to as the *high* state. This model also agrees with the intuition that less parameters must be used to model the background and more parameters must be used for the actual pattern itself.

3.2 Extending the IM Model

The wavelet coefficients can be modeled as independent Gaussian mixtures using the prior density proposed in Section 3.1. It is assumed that there are T training images and the wavelet coefficient i of the training image t is given by w_i^t. w_i^t are assumed to be independent realizations of the random variable W_i that follows the GMM. $\mathbf{w}_i$ is a vector that has all the T realizations w_i^t of W_i. The EM algorithm is used to compute the parameters of the IM model given by $\Theta_{IM} = \{p_{Q_i}(1), \mu_{i,1}, \mu_{i,2}, \sigma_{i,1}^2, \sigma_{i,2}^2\}$, where $\mu_{i,1} = 0$ and $\sigma_{i,1}^2$ is constrained to be the same for all coefficients in a subband.

In the iteration l, the E-step computes the following conditional probability,

$$p(Q_i = m | w_i^t, \Theta_{IM}^{(l)}) = \frac{p(w_i^t | Q_i = m, \Theta_{IM}^{(l)}) p_{Q_i}(m)}{\sum_{m=1}^{M} p(w_i^t | Q_i = m, \Theta_{IM}^{(l)}) p_{Q_i}(m)}. \tag{2}$$

The M-Step estimates the parameters as,

$$p_{Q_i}(m) = \frac{1}{T} \sum_{t=1}^{T} p(Q_i = m | w_i^t, \Theta_{IM}^{(l)}), \tag{3}$$

$$\sigma_{i,1}^2 = \frac{\sum_{t=1}^{T} \sum_{k \in SB(i)} (w_k^t)^2 p(Q_k = 1 | w_k^t, \Theta_{IM}^{(l)})}{\sum_{t=1}^{T} \sum_{k \in SB(i)} p(Q_k = 1 | w_k^t, \Theta_{IM}^{(l)})}, \tag{4}$$

$$\mu_{i,2} = \sum_{t=1}^{T} w_i^t p(Q_i = 2 | w_i^t, \Theta_{IM}^{(l)}) / (T p_{Q_i}(2)), \tag{5}$$

$$\sigma_{i,2}^2 = \sum_{t=1}^{T} (w_i^t - \mu_{i,2})^2 p(Q_i = 2 | w_k^t, \Theta_{IM}^{(l)}) / (T p_{Q_i}(2)), \tag{6}$$

where $SB(i)$ returns the indices of all the coefficients in the subband corresponding to the coefficient i. The low state mean, $\mu_{i,1} = 0$ and the low state variance, $\sigma_{i,1}^2$ is the same for all coefficients in the subband.

3.3 Extending the HMT Model

The HMT model proposed in [1] will be extended to the case of multiple training images using the GMM proposed in the Section 3.1. Assuming that T is the number of training images and each image is decomposed into maximum possible scales, there are totally $3T$ independent wavelet trees. This is because of the assumption that each of the three quad-trees in the wavelet decomposition of an image will be considered independent of each other. In this discussion only one of the three trees per wavelet decomposition is considered, as the generalization to the case of multiple trees in an image is trivial.

The value of the wavelet coefficient at node i in a tree t is indicated by w_i^t. In the case of IM model, i indexes all the coefficients in the wavelet decomposition whereas in the HMT model, i indexes the coefficients in a tree correspond-ing to one of the subbands. The posterior probabilities $p(Q_i = m|\mathbf{w}^t, \Theta_{HMT}^{(l)})$ and $p(Q_i = m, Q_{\pi(i)} = n|\mathbf{w}^t, \Theta_{HMT}^{(l)})$ are computed using the relevant equations in [9]. The upward-downward step is equivalent to the E-step [9] and the parameter update is equivalent to the M-step. The parameters of the HMT model at iteration l are then computed using,

$$p_{Q_i}(m) = \frac{1}{T} \sum_{t=1}^{T} p(Q_i = m|\mathbf{w}^t, \Theta_{HMT}^{(l)}), \tag{7}$$

$$a_{i,\pi(i)}^{mn} = \sum_{t=1}^{T} p(Q_i = m, Q_{\pi(i)} = n|\mathbf{w}^t, \Theta_{HMT}^{(l)}) / (T p_{Q_{\pi(i)}}(n)), \tag{8}$$

$$\mu_{i,2} = \sum_{t=1}^{T} w_i^t p(Q_i = 2|\mathbf{w}^t, \Theta_{HMT}^{(l)}) / (T p_{Q_i}(2)), \tag{9}$$

$$\sigma_{i,1}^2 = \frac{\sum_{t=1}^{T} \sum_{k \in SB(i)} (w_k^t)^2 p(Q_k = 1|\mathbf{w}^t, \Theta_{HMT}^{(l)})}{\sum_{t=1}^{T} \sum_{k \in SB(i)} p(Q_k = 1|\mathbf{w}^t, \Theta_{HMT}^{(l)})}, \tag{10}$$

$$\sigma_{i,2}^2 = \sum_{t=1}^{T} (w_i^t - \mu_{i,2})^2 p(Q_i = 2|\mathbf{w}^t, \Theta_{HMT}^{(l)}) / (T p_{Q_i}(2)). \tag{11}$$

Note that $\sigma_{i,1}^2$ is common for all coefficients in the subband and $\mu_{i,1} = 0$ as in the case of IM model.

The EM procedure can be used to estimate the parameters of all the three quad-trees in the wavelet decomposition of an image. The final set of parameters for the three trees together is denoted by Θ_{HMT}^A and it can be used to estimate the low dimensional template Θ_{LD}.

4 Proposed Approach

The Bayesian approach for learning the parameters of a low dimensional template from a set of noisy observations using the IM and HMT wavelet domain statistical models is presented in this section. It essentially combines the three steps of parameter estimation using the IM or HMT models proposed in the previous section, state estimation using the Viterbi algorithm and registration of training images to the current estimate of the template.

4.1 Viterbi Algorithm for Estimating the Most Likely States

The Viterbi algorithm for a HMT model is presented in [5], where it is used for thresholding the wavelet coefficients of an image to denoise and enhance the edges. In this paper, we extend it to the case of multiple training images for the purpose of estimating a low dimensional template from a set of noisy, training images. The proposed Viterbi algorithm estimates the most likely states for the model using all the training images. This, in essence, fixes the state pointwise in the template so that conditional independence assumption can be imposed on the wavelet coefficients.

Given the observations of multiple trees of wavelet coefficients $\mathbf{w}^1, ..., \mathbf{w}^T$, the problem is to estimate the set of most likely states $\mathbf{q}$ and this can be expressed as,

$$\hat{\mathbf{q}} = \operatorname*{argmax}_{\mathbf{q}} p\left(\mathbf{q}|\mathbf{w}^1, ..., \mathbf{w}^T, \Theta_{HMT}\right). \tag{12}$$

Let $\mathscr{P}_i^t$ be the set of wavelet coefficients at the nodes in the shortest path on the tree t, between the root node and the node i, and $\mathscr{Q}_i$ be the states on the path. $\delta_i(q)$ is defined as the highest likelihood along a single path that ends at node i in state q and is calculated as,

$$\delta_i(q) = \max_{\mathscr{Q}_{\pi(i)}} f\left(\mathscr{P}_i^1, ..., \mathscr{P}_i^T, \mathscr{Q}_{\pi(i)}, Q_i = q|\Theta_{HMT}\right). \tag{13}$$

In order to find the best possible state sequence, the following steps are performed.

1. At the coarsest scale compute $\delta_1(q)$, for $q \in \mathscr{S}$, where $\mathscr{S} = \{1, 2\}$ is the set of possible states.

$$\delta_1(q) = p_{Q_1}(q) \prod_{t=1}^{T} g\left(w_1^t|\mu_{1,q}, \sigma_{1,q}^2\right) \tag{14}$$

2. Moving down the tree compute the following for each node in a subband

$$\delta_i(q) = \max_{z \in \mathscr{S}} \left(\delta_{\pi(i)} a_{i,\pi(i)}^{qz}\right) \prod_{t=1}^{T} g\left(w_i^t|\mu_{i,q}, \sigma_{i,q}^2\right) \tag{15}$$

$$\xi_{\pi(i)}(\mathscr{C}) = \operatorname*{argmax}_{z \in \mathscr{S}} \left(\delta_{\pi(i)} a_{i,\pi(i)}^{qz} a_{i,\pi(i)}^{sz} a_{i,\pi(i)}^{uz} a_{i,\pi(i)}^{vz}\right), \tag{16}$$

for $q \in \mathscr{S}$ and $\mathscr{C} = \{q, s, u, v\}$, where each quantity in $\mathscr{C}$, takes a value from the set $\mathscr{S}$. $\xi_{\pi(i)}(\mathscr{C})$ is the most likely state at node $\pi(i)$ to have the four children $\mathscr{C}$.

3. Compute the best possible state for each coefficient in the finest scale,

$$\hat{q}_i = \operatorname*{argmax}_{z \in \mathscr{S}} \left(\delta_i(z)\right). \tag{17}$$

4. Estimate $\hat{q}_i$ for the coefficients at node i, moving up the scale and backtracking the tree,

$$\hat{q}_i = \xi_i\left(\hat{q}_{c(i)}\right). \tag{18}$$

With the estimated state sequence $\hat{\mathbf{q}}$ for all the three trees, the nodes at which $\hat{q}_i = 1$, are called as *insignificant* and the nodes at which $\hat{q}_i = 2$ are called *significant*. For generating a low dimensional statistical template, the significant coefficients in a particular location across the training images are modeled individually with a non-zero mean Gaussian. All the insignificant coefficients in a subband across the training images are modeled together using a zero-mean Gaussian. The sets N_{ins} and N_{sig} contain the indices corresponding to the insignificant and significant coefficients respectively and $N = |N_{sig} \cup N_{ins}|$. The low dimensional template is parameterized by $\Theta_{LD} = \{\mu_i, \sigma_i^2\}_{i=1}^N$. If $i \in N_{sig}$, then Θ_{LD} is estimated as,

$$\mu_i = \frac{1}{T}\sum_{t=1}^T w_i^t \quad \text{and} \quad \sigma_i^2 = \frac{1}{T}\sum_{t=1}^T (w_i^t - \mu_i)^2. \tag{19}$$

If $i \in N_{ins}$, then the parameters are given by,

$$\mu_i = 0 \quad \text{and} \quad \sigma_i^2 = \frac{1}{T|N_{ins}|}\sum_{t=1}^T \sum_{k \in N_{ins}} (w_k^t)^2. \tag{20}$$

This low dimensional template estimated using the Viterbi can be compared with that of TEMPLAR. TEMPLAR uses an information-theoretic criterion to estimate the template, whereas a Bayesian approach is used here. For the IM case also, an algorithm similar to the Viterbi algorithm provided above can be used to infer the best possible states and (19) and (20) can be used to estimate Θ_{LD}.

4.2 Registration with the Low Dimensional Template

The problem of registering training observations to the template is a key step in template learning. From the parameters of the low dimensional template, Θ_{LD}, the equivalent spatial domain parameters, $\Theta_{LDS} = \{\mu, \Sigma\}$ can be computed using Gaussian algebra and the orthonormality of wavelet basis functions [10]. Registration of a training observation $\mathbf{u}$ can be performed using the Maximum Likelihood (ML) approach as,

$$\hat{\ell} = \arg\max_{\ell} \log p(\mathbf{D}\Gamma_\ell \mathbf{u}|\mu, \Sigma), \tag{21}$$

where $\mathbf{D}$ and Γ_ℓ are the Discrete Wavelet Transform (DWT) matrix and translation matrix respectively. This means that the estimation of the most likely transformation of the training observation to the template is done using a likelihood measure in the wavelet domain.

4.3 Learning the Template Parameters

Learning the parameters of the low dimensional template is done as an alternating maximization problem as done with TEMPLAR. The three steps of the iterative procedure for learning the template parameters with the HMT based algorithm are:

1. Parameter Estimation: The parameters of the HMT model, Θ_{HMT}^A, are estimated as per Section 3.3 using the wavelet coefficients of the registered images at the current iteration.
2. State Estimation: The most likely states, $\mathbf{q}$, of the nodes are computed using the Viterbi algorithm given in Section 4.1. The parameters of the low dimensional template Θ_{LD} are also estimated in this step using (19) to (20).
3. Registration: The registration of images to the low dimensional template in the wavelet domain, Θ_{LD}, is performed as per Section 4.2.

The three steps are repeated in sequence, till convergence is reached. The algorithm is said to have converged when the training images are perfectly aligned to the low dimensional template. Although a theoretical proof for convergence is not provided, in the experiments performed, convergence has always happened. Another important consideration is that, registration is performed using a robust and fast multiresolution approach from coarse to fine scale.

The complexity of parameter estimation using the HMT or IM algorithm for T training images of size N is order NT. State estimation using the Viterbi procedure and estimation of the low dimensional template, detailed in Section 4.1 are also of order NT complexity. The registration of training images to the low dimensional template is the most expensive procedure and for the set L of all possible transformations, the complexity is of order $|L|NT$. A low complexity procedure of order $|L|T \log N$ was developed for registering the training images to the template and reported in [10].

5 Results and Discussion

In this section, we provide the results for generating statistical low dimensional templates using the training data sets and pattern classification using the templates learned from the training sets.

5.1 Template Generation from the Training Sets

For the purpose of template generation three data sets are considered. The training data set A contains images from the MNIST database available online [6]. A total of 500 samples of each are chosen for training. Training data sets B and C are chosen

Fig. 3 Training data set B - First subject chosen from the Yale face database. 8 images are chosen from a set of 11 and they are cropped to remove most of the background.

Fig. 4 Training data set C - Fifteenth subject chosen from the Yale face database. The 8 images chosen are cropped to remove the background.

Fig. 5 Spatial mean of the template for training data set A with additive i.i.d. Gaussian noise (a) using IM based template learning, (b) using HMT based template learning, (c) using TEMPLAR.

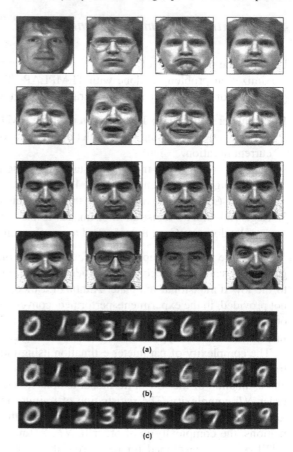

from the Yale face database available online [7] and are shown in Figures 3 and 4 respectively.

IM and wavelet HMT based template learning algorithms are used to infer the parameters of the low dimensional statistical template Θ_{LD}. The existing MATLAB implementation for the TEMPLAR algorithm was used to generate statistical templates using the same training data sets for comparison [8]. The images in all training sets are grayscale and have pixel values between 0 and 255. For the training data set A, the original digits of size 28×28 are scaled to 32×32 and i.i.d. Gaussian noise with standard deviation 25.5 is added. The training images are Haar wavelet transform is used for decomposing the images into maximum possible levels. All the 500 samples of each digits are used for training. The mean parameter of Θ_{LD} are transformed to the spatial domain and the mean templates for the digits are given in Figure 5.

The spatial mean of the templates under conditions of no noise show that the IM and HMT based template learning have performed automatic registration and the mean templates are comparable with that of TEMPLAR. The number of significant

Table 1 NUMBER OF SIGNIFICANT COEFFICIENTS ESTIMATED BY THE THREE ALGORITHMS FOR TRAINING DATA SET A

Digit	IM Based		HMT Based		TEMPLAR	
	With Noise	No Noise	With Noise	No Noise	With Noise	No Noise
0	588	499	492	688	696	882
1	328	281	280	520	385	860
2	518	483	464	584	627	880
3	524	477	468	632	648	884
4	467	454	426	594	616	882
5	475	466	443	663	624	880
6	495	462	427	574	562	869
7	436	381	340	557	555	844
8	574	512	469	589	572	879
9	459	453	424	615	589	848

coefficients chosen by each algorithm for a given digit are given in Table 1. TEMPLAR chooses the lowest number of significant states in each case and the IM based algorithm chooses the highest. From the table it can also be seen that, for some cases the number of significant states estimated by the HMT based algorithm is quite close to that of TEMPLAR. But the IM based algorithm always does a overestimate. HMT based significant state estimation is the framework proposed for template learning using Bayesian approach and it performs comparably with the information theoretic approach of TEMPLAR using MDL principle for state estimation, in certain cases.

The number of significant coefficients for the cases when the training set A is not corrupted with noise is given in Table 1. It can be seen that TEMPLAR severely overfits the data in every case because it estimates a large number of significant coefficients for all the templates. Large number of significant coefficients mean that most of the coefficients are treated as edges, whereas this is not the actual case. When overfitting happens, the generalization error increases and hence the template will not generalize well to the patterns outside the training set. IM and HMT based algorithms have much reduced overfitting when compared to TEMPLAR. When a large number of similar data are available, as in this case, a simple model such as TEMPLAR will overfit, whereas complex models such as IM and HMT will have a lesser chance of overfitting. This is because, complex models reliably estimate their parameters using the large training data set. In cases where the data set contains data with high similarity, additive noise tends to regularize and improves the generalization, as could be observed from the results of the previous experiment given in Table 1. Additive noise is also used to extend small training sets in order to prevent overfitting and improve generalization. This idea is used in the next experiment where the data sets B and C are extended by adding noise.

The templates generated for the training images of the data sets B and C are given in Figures 6 and 7 respectively. Each training data set is extended to 500 images and each image in the data set is scaled to 128×128 with i.i.d. Gaussian noise of standard deviation 25.5 added. For training set B, IM based algorithm estimates a total of 3776 significant states, HMT based algorithm estimates 2781 significant states and TEMPLAR estimates 3819 states. For the training data set C, 4124 significant

Fig. 6 Training data set B with additive i.i.d Gaussian noise: (a) and (b) State map and mean template using IM based template learning, (c) and (d) state map and mean template using HMT based template learning, (e) and (f) state map and mean template using TEMPLAR.

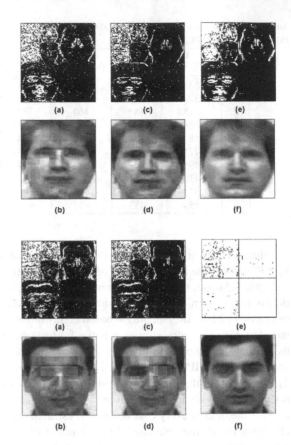

Fig. 7 Training data set C with additive i.i.d Gaussian noise: (a) and (b) State map and mean template using IM based template learning, (c) and (d) state map and mean template using HMT based template learning, (e) and (f) state map and mean template using TEMPLAR.

states are estimated by the IM based algorithm, 2993 by the HMT based algorithm and 15497 by TEMPLAR. It can be clearly seen that for the training data set C, TEMPLAR significantly overfits the data. However HMT and IM, being more complex models, do not overfit the data. Therefore, the proposed HMT and IM based models have a significant advantage over the existing TEMPLAR algorithm. Furthermore, the use of Viterbi state estimation to compute significant states and a low dimensional template guards against overfitting.

5.2 Pattern Classification using Learned Templates

The classification of test data using the generated templates is performed using an ML approach. The wavelet domain and its corresponding spatial domain template, denoted by Θ_{LD}^k and Θ_{LDS}^k respectively, are generated for each class k of the training data. Classification of the test data $\mathbf{u}$ is performed by registering the test data to each spatial domain class template Θ_{LDS}^k and finding the most likely class $\hat{k}$ using an ML

Fig. 8 (a) and (b) Original plane images, (c) and (d) spatial mean templates using IM based algorithm, (e) and (f) spatial mean templates using HMT based algorithm.

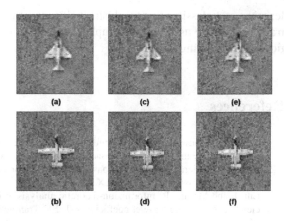

approach. The corresponding optimization problem can be posed as,

$$\hat{k} = \underset{k}{\operatorname{argmax}} \left[\max_{\ell^k} p(\mathbf{u}|\Theta^k_{LDS}, N^k_{sig}, -\ell^k) \right]. \tag{22}$$

The complexity of this step is linear with the number of transformations $|L|$. A low complexity version of this procedure is described in [10].

Two images of a plane [2] as given in Figures 8 (a) and (b) were used for classification. Each image was translated randomly to ± 3 pixels and corrupted with i.i.d. Gaussian noise of standard deviation 25.5. A total of 500 realizations of each image were used to form the template for each class using both the IM and the HMT based template learning algorithms. The templates generated with the IM based algorithm are given in Figures 8 (c) and (d) and with the HMT based algorithm are given in Figures 8 (e) and (f) respectively. Similarly, 500 realizations of each image were generated and were classified using the templates generated with no classification errors.

6 Conclusions

In this paper, we proposed a novel form of the Gaussian mixture model suited for the purpose of template learning. This was used along with the IM and HMT models, that were extended for the case of multiple training images. A Bayesian approach for learning a low dimensional template from a set of training observations using wavelet domain statistical models is the key contribution of this paper. Results show that models learned using the proposed approach are more robust when compared to models learned using an information theoretic framework, in cases of large training data sets. We can extend this framework to handle affine transformations of training images using our low-complexity framework for image registration [10]. Though this framework based on the wavelet transform provides good results in template learning and classification, sophisticated transforms such as the complex wavelet transform can be used to learn templates that are more robust to spatial transformations of the training images.

References

1. Crouse, M., Nowak, R. and Baraniuk, R.: Wavelet-based statistical signal processing using hidden markov models. IEEE Transactions on Signal Processing. **46**(4), 886–902 (1998).
2. Scott, C.: A hierarchical wavelet-based framework for pattern analysis and synthesis. M.S. thesis, Rice University, Houston, TX, USA (2000).
3. Liu, J. and Moulin, P.: Information-theoretic analysis of interscale and intrascale dependencies between image wavelet coefficients. IEEE Transactions on Image Processing. **10**(11), 1647–1658 (2001).
4. Chipman, H., Kolaczyk, E. and McCulloch, R.: Adaptive bayesian wavelet shrinkage. Journal of The American Statistical Association. **92**(440), 1413–1421 (1997).
5. Romberg, J.: A universal hidden markov tree image model. M.S. thesis, Rice University, Texas, USA (1999).
6. LeCun, Y., Bottou, L., Bengio, Y. and Haffner, P.: Gradient-based learning applied to document recognition. IEEE Transactions on Pattern Analysis and Machine Intelligence. **86**(11), 2278–2324 (1998).
7. Yale face database. Available online at http://cvc.yale.edu/projects/yalefaces/yalefaces.html.
8. Matlab code for wavelet-based template learning and pattern classification using TEMPLAR. Available online at http://dsp.rice.edu/software/templar.shtml.
9. Ramamurthy, K. N.: Template learning with wavelet domain statistical models for pattern synthesis and classification. M.S. thesis, Arizona State University, Tempe, AZ, USA (2008).
10. Ramamurthy, K. N., Thiagarajan, J. J. and Spanias, A.: Fast image registation with nonstationary Gauss-Markov random field templates. Accepted to the IEEE International Conference on Image Processing, Cairo, Egypt (2009).

OPTIMISATION AND PLANNING

Group Counseling Optimization: A Novel Approach

M.A.Eita[1] **and M.M.Fahmy**[2]

Abstract A new population-based search algorithm, which we call Group Counseling Optimizer (GCO), is presented. It mimics the group counseling behavior of humans in solving their problems. The algorithm is tested using seven known benchmark functions: Sphere, Rosenbrock, Griewank, Rastrigin, Ackley, Weierstrass, and Schwefel functions. A comparison is made with the recently published comprehensive learning particle swarm optimizer (CLPSO). The results demonstrate the efficiency and robustness of the proposed algorithm.

1 Introduction

One of the most fundamental principles in our world is the search for an optimal situation. Many scientific, engineering, and economic problems involve the optimization of particular objective functions. These problems include examples like minimizing the losses in a power grid by finding the optimal configuration of the components, or training a neural network to recognize images of people's faces. Numerous optimization algorithms have been proposed, with varying degrees of success.

Over the decades, traditional optimization techniques, such as linear programming and steepest-decent methods, are used. Because of certain drawbacks of these techniques and the increasing complexity of real-world optimization problems, there is an urgent need for better optimization algorithms. Many heuristic algorithms are therefore developed to solve various optimization problems. These algorithms combine rules and randomness to mimic natural phenomena. Examples are: the Genetic Algorithm [9,11], Evolution Strategies [18] such as Differential Evolution [22], Ant Colony Optimization [4], Particle

1 M.A.Eita, Faculty of Engineering, University of Tanta, EGYPT
e-mail: eta1232002@yahoo.com

2 M.M.Fahmy, Faculty of Engineering, University of Tanta, EGYPT
e-mail: mfn_288@hotmail.com

M. Bramer et al. (eds.), *Research and Development in Intelligent Systems XXVI*,
DOI 10.1007/978-1-84882-983-1_14, © Springer-Verlag London Limited 2010

Swarm Optimization [5,6,12], Bees Colony Optimization [17], Memetic Algorithms [16], and Cultural Algorithms [20].

The Genetic Algorithm mimics natural selection and genetic recombination. The algorithm works by choosing solutions from the current population and then applying genetic operators – referred to as mutation and crossover – to create a new population. Crossover is the partial swap between two parent strings to produce two offspring strings. Mutation is the occasional random inversion of bit values, generating non-recursive offspring.

The Evolution strategies are heuristics-based optimization techniques exploiting the ideas of adaptation and evolution. The essential idea behind Differential Evolution is the way the (ternary) recombination operator 'deRecombination' is defined for creating new solution candidates. The difference $x1-x2$ of two vectors $x1$ and $x2$ is weighted with a weighted and added to a third vector $x3$ in the population.

The Ant Colony Optimizer is based on the metaphor of ants seeking for food. It imitates the behavior of ants in laying a trail of pheromone to find the shortest path from the food source to their nest. Each ant that finds the food will excrete some pheromone on the path. By time, the pheromone density of the path will increase and more and more ants will follow it to the food and back to the nest. The higher the pheromone density, the more likely will an ant stay on a trail. The probability that a passing stray ant will follow this trail depends on the quantity of pheromone laid.

The Particle Swarm Optimizer emulates a biological social system like a flock of birds or a school of fish. When a swarm looks for food, its individuals will spread in the environment and when one of them finds food, it announces this to its neighbors. These neighbors can then approach the source of food, too.

The Bees Colony Optimization is inspired from the natural foraging behavior of honeybees to find the optimal solution in nectar collection [17]. The algorithm performs a kind of neighborhood search combined with random search.

The Memetic Algorithms are population-based approaches for heuristic search in optimization problems. They have been shown to be orders of magnitude faster than traditional genetic algorithms for some problem domains. Basically, they combine local search heuristics with crossover operators. For this reason, some researchers have viewed them as *hybrid* genetic algorithms.

The Cultural Algorithms are a branch of evolutionary computation where there is a knowledge component that is called the belief space in addition to the population component. In this sense, cultural algorithms can be seen as an extension to conventional genetic algorithms.

In this paper, we propose a new optimization approach that *emulates the human behavior in problem solving through counseling within a group*. The approach is called a *Group Counseling Optimizer* (GCO). The iterations involved in the solution algorithm are visualized as counseling sessions. Candidate solutions are progressively improved by either counseling with other members in the group or by self-counseling. This line of thinking, we believe, holds much promise since the human's behavior has, or should have, the highest quality when compared with the behavior of other (lower-class) creatures.

The remainder of the paper is organized as follows: Sect. 2 introduces counseling among humans as a problem-solving approach. In Sect. 3, the proposed algorithm, based on group counseling, is explained. In Sect. 4, the results of the experiments conducted on seven benchmark functions are given. The conclusions are finally discussed in Sect. 5.

2 Counseling as a Problem-Solving Approach

People with problems often seek out another person as a sounding board: someone with whom they can talk over their problems, experiment with various solutions and finally reach some resolution. Examples of this approach are seen when people have relationship difficulties or want to change jobs or places of residence. The person, for instance, who wants to change his or her job may be advised by another person who has experience of job opportunities that exist in related careers [2]. Hence, people start to seek help when they should make a decision or solve a problem.

Counseling can be thought of as a process of problem solving [3]. *Individual counseling* is an activity in which one person is helping (counselor) and one is receiving help (counselee) and in which the emphasis of that help is on enabling the other person to find solutions to problems [2].

However, individuals function most of their lives within groups. So, instead of the individual counseling there is another kind of counseling called *group counseling* that offers the unique advantages of providing group members with the opportunity to discover that their peers also have problems and to learn new ways of resolving problems by observing other members in the group deal with those problems. Unlike individual counseling relationships, a group provides each individual the opportunity to give as well as to receive help.

In the group, the members can discover that they are capable of understanding, accepting, and helping their peers, and that they can contribute to another person's life. Thus, members gradually begin to understand and accept themselves. The emerging trust in self and others facilitates the sharing of ideas and behaviors in a safe testing ground before applying those ideas and behaviors in relationships outside the group.

Group members come to function not merely as counselees, but they practically behave as counselees at certain times in the sessions and as counselors at other times. Unlike individual counseling, where information and care flow in a single direction, in a group, the flow of information and care is multi-directional, where each member participates in the giving and receiving of advice.

A list of rules exists for the group members [1]:

1. Let others know what your ideas are. What every member has to say is important. Sharing your thoughts and reactions with the group will stimulate other members and will help them to share what they are thinking.
2. Ask your questions. If you have a question or you want to know more about something, do not hesitate to ask.
3. Do not do all the talking. Others want to participate also, and they cannot if you take too long to express your ideas.
4. Help other members to participate. If someone looks as though he or she wants to say something but has not, encourage that person to do so.
5. Listen carefully to other members. Give a chance to the ideas of other persons, and try to understand what he or she is saying. Listen to other members in the way you would want them to listen to you.
6. Group members are here to help. Problems can be solved by working cooperatively together. In the process of helping others, you can help yourself. The information you have can be helpful to others. Suggesting alternatives or causes can help other members to make better decisions. This suggesting process of many alternatives is called *brainstorming*. In a brainstorming process, good ideas may be combined to form a new better idea [13].
7. Be willing to accept other viewpoints. Do not insist that you are right and everyone else is wrong. The other person just might be thinking the same thing. Try to help other members to understand rather than trying to *make* them understand.
8. Keep up with the discussion. If the discussion is confusing to you, say so.
9. In this group, to talk about your feelings and reactions is admissible.

In addition, individuals learn best when they become involved as participating and contributing members to the group. Each member needs to actively share in the group's decision making. Undoubtedly, group members will contribute to solving of the problem only by the best of their experiences.

Counseling can help some but not all people. Also, we should not assume that counseling can help in every situation [2].

In case when people depend on themselves in solving their problems, they exploit the best of their past experiences with some kind of *modification* seeking for a better, satisfactory solution.

The *group counseling optimization* approach developed here mimics the main ideas of human group counseling behavior illuminated above, without making use of all its details. This metaphor deserves utmost attention. The present paper, we hope, opens an avenue.

3 The proposed GCO Algorithm

The problem at hand is a single-objective, unconstrained, continuous optimization problem. Given a scalar function $f(X)$, where X denotes a set of D parameters x_d, $d=1,2,...D$, it is required to optimize $f(X)$ through appropriate values of x_d; optimization means either minimization or maximization.

The main idea of the proposed approach is as follows. Like other heuristics-based approaches, we begin with a certain number, m, of initial candidate solution vectors X^i in the D-dimensional search space, $X^i = (x_1^i, x_2^i, ... x_D^i); i = 1,2,..., m$. These solution vectors are then improved through successive iterations. We regard such m solution vectors in (each of) the different iterations as m members (persons) in a group. Member i is represented by the vector X^i, which in turn contains D components x_d^i, $d=1,2,...D$, designating what we consider the best experiences of the member. Note that the representation of a specific member generally varies from iteration to iteration. A new value of each component in a vector is produced by invoking the current values (experiences) of corresponding components in other vectors or by modifying the current value of the component itself. These are two strategies, each having distinct behavior properties as will be soon discussed. The situation is interestingly analogous to what happens in group counseling, where a person - in solving a problem - asks other people for help or, sometimes, depends on himself only.

Each iteration is visualized as a group counseling session, with m members. We obtain m candidate solutions X^i from each session (except the last one) which are improved successively in subsequent sessions. The final session is the *decision-making* session. It receives the eventual m candidate solutions and compares them with each other so that the best solution is determined, the solution X^* that optimizes the objective function $f(X)$.

The proposed group counseling optimizer (GCO) is a search algorithm inspired by the group counseling approach to solve problems. The algorithm requires a number of parameters to be set, namely: number of group members representing the population size (m), number of group members used as counselors (c), counseling probability (cp), maximum value of modification (mdf_max), and transition rate from exploration to exploitation (tr). The significance of these parameters will become apparent as we proceed.

The algorithm is executed through the following steps:

Step 1

The algorithm starts with m initial candidate solutions $X^i = (x_1^i, x_2^i, ...x_D^i); i=1,2,...m$, being placed randomly in the search space. We choose to locate the values of x_d^i in accordance with a beta distribution. As Fig. 1 shows, the beta probability density function $g(x)$, with its two parameters a and b being equal and less than unity, is of a symmetric U-shaped form. This implies that, most probably, the candidate solutions lie near the boundaries of the search space and that the global optimum is within this candidate solution set. For details of the beta distribution, see [8,10].

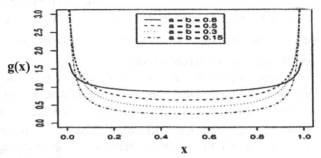

Fig. 1 U-shaped, symmetric beta probability density function

Step 2
The solution vectors X^i are substituted respectively into the objective function $f(X)$, yielding m values for $f(X^i)$, called fitness values.

Step 3
This is the first iterative step. For each solution X^i, we produce an alternative solution $X^{\prime i} = (x_1^{\prime i}, x_2^{\prime i}, \dots x_D^{\prime i})$. The production process is carried out *component-wise*. Each component $x_d^{\prime i}$ is obtained through one of two counseling strategies; namely,

    (a) *Other-members counseling*
    (b) *Self-counseling*

For each component $x_d^{\prime i}$, we start with generation of a random number, in the range [0,1], according to a uniform distribution. This number is here called a *counseling decisive coefficient* (*cdc*). If *cdc* is less than or equal to *cp* (set in the range [0,1]), we do other-members counseling; otherwise, we do self-counseling. In the following, we explain how to calculate $x_d^{\prime i}$ in each of these strategies.

Step 3a: Other-members counseling (*cdc ≤ cp*)
In this strategy, member i (X^i) is regarded as a counselee. It counsels c other members (counselors), chosen randomly out of the population, so that another (hopefully better) alternative component $x_d^{\prime i}$ is obtained. The value of $x_d^{\prime i}$ is calculated by summing *weighted* values of the corresponding components (best experiences) of the c counselors. These are the contributions of the relevant counselors, in a *brainstorming* process.

The weight, denoted by ω_k, of component d in counselor k ($k=1,2,\dots.c$) is a random number in the range [0, 1] with a uniform distribution,

$$\omega_k = rand\ (0,1) \tag{1}$$

Bear in mind that counselor k is some member i.

The c weights should sum to unity,

$$\sum_{k=1}^{c} \omega_k = 1 \tag{2}$$

The form of x'^{i}_{d} is expressed as

$$x'^{i}_{d} = \sum_{k=1}^{c} \omega_k * x_d^{rand\_int_k(1,m)} \tag{3}$$

where the superscript *rand_int(1,m)* is an *integer* random number in the range $[1,m]$ with a uniform distribution, and $x_d^{rand\_int_k(1,m)}$ is the value of component d of counselor k. Note particularly that set of c counselors in general varies from component to component (as d varies from 1 to D). It should also be clear that ω_k and *rand_int(1,m)* are both dependent on the values of i and d; these symbols are not superimposed on Eq.(3) for notational simplicity.

Step 3b: Self-counseling ($cdc > cp$)

In this strategy, an alternative component x''_d is obtained through modification of the current component x^{i}_{d}. This situation may be interpreted as follows. Member i, being involved in the counseling group, discovers that it is capable of suggesting a new component x''_d depending on its own best experience x^{i}_{d} with some specific modification. The value x^{i}_{d} is modified by adding a term $rand_d^{i}(-mdf, mdf)$. Here, *mdf* and *−mdf* are the greatest positive and negative values of modification, respectively. That is, the value of x^{i}_{d} will change in the range [-*mdf*,*mdf*]. The value of *mdf* plays a central role in whether the optimization algorithm performs 'exploration' or 'exploitation'. An equation which can be used to estimate *mdf* is

$$mdf = mdf\_max * (1 - \frac{itr}{itr\_max})^{tr} \tag{4}$$

where *mdf_max*, as stated previously, is a set value, *itr* is the iteration number, and *itr_max* is the total number of iterations. The exponent *tr* in Eq.(4) refers to a transition rate at which the search method changes from exploration to exploitation. Consequently, the form of x''_d is given by

$$x'^{i}_{d} = x_d^{i} + rand_d^{i}(-mdf, mdf) \tag{5}$$

As a further illustration, Fig. 2 shows the variation of *mdf* from *mdf_max* (at the very beginning of iterations) to zero (at *itr_max*) for different values of *tr*. It is evident that at a certain iteration, the value of *mdf* decreases as *tr* increases. In other words, as *tr* increases, exploration tends to exploitation in a smaller number of iterations. It is well known that all optimization algorithms have to compromise between exploration to exploitation so that the global optimum is eventually attained.

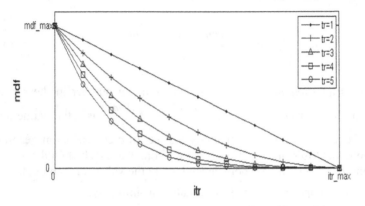

Fig. 2 Effect of transition rate (*tr*) on modification

The result of Step 3 is a set of m solution vectors X'^i. We emphasize the fact that, in general, some of the components x'^i_d of X'^i are produced by other-members counseling while the remaining components (of the same vector) are produced by self-counseling.

Step 4

Step 2 is repeated for X'^i (instead of X^i) and the fitness value, $f(X'^i)$, is evaluated. If $f(X'^i)$ is better than $f(X^i)$, then X'^i replaces X^i ($X^i \leftarrow X'^i$); otherwise, X'^i is ignored and X^i remains for possible subsequent improvement.

Repetition Steps (iterations)

Step 3 and 4 are repeated until a *stopping criterion* is met.

Final Step

This is a decision-making step. The *m* solutions, resulting from the last repetition step, are compared with each other based on the fitness values of the objective function. The best solution is taken as the optimum solution X^* (with acceptable error).

4 Experiments

The proposed GCO algorithm is tested in *minimization* problems using seven benchmark functions: two unimodal functions (Sphere and Rosenbrock) and five multimodal functions (Griewank, Rastrigin, Ackley, Weierstrass, and Schwefel) [7,14]. Also, it is compared with the comprehensive learning particle swarm optimizer (CLPSO) developed by Liang *et al.* [15].

4.1 Test Functions

The definitions of the benchmark functions used for testing are as follows:
  1) Sphere function

$$f_1(x) = \sum_{i=1}^{D} x_i^2$$

  2) Rosenbrock function

$$f_2(x) = \sum_{i=1}^{D-1} (100(x_i^2 - x_{i+1})^2 + (x_i - 1)^2)$$

  3) Ackley function

$$f_3(x) = 20 + e - 20 \cdot e^{-0.2 \cdot \sqrt{\frac{1}{D}\sum_{i=1}^{D} x_i^2}} - e^{\frac{1}{D}\sum_{i=1}^{D} \cos(2\pi x_i)}$$

  4) Griewanks function

$$f_4(x) = \sum_{i=1}^{D} \frac{x_i^2}{4000} - \prod_{i-1}^{D} \cos(\frac{x_i}{\sqrt{i}}) + 1$$

  5) Weierstrass function

$$f_5(x) = \sum_{i=1}^{D} (\sum_{k=0}^{k\,max} [a^k \cos(2\pi b^k (x_i + 0.5))]) - D \sum_{k=0}^{k\,max} [a^k \cos(2\pi b^k .0.5)],$$

$$a = 0.5, \quad b = 3, \quad k\,max = 20$$

6) Rastrigin function

$$f_6(x) = \sum_{i=1}^{D}(x_i^2 - 10 \cdot \cos(2\pi x_i) + 10)$$

7) Schwefel function

$$f_7(x) = 418.9829 \cdot D + \sum_{i=1}^{D} x_i \cdot \sin(\sqrt{|x_i|})$$

All the above functions are tested for dimension D=30. The global optima X^*, fitness values $f(X^*)$, and search ranges are given in Table 1.

Table 1. Global Optima and Search Ranges of Test Functions

f	X^*	$f(X^*)$	Search Range
f_1	[0,0,........,0]	0	$[-100,100]^D$
f_2	[1,1,........,1]	0	$[-2.048,2.048]^D$
f_3	[0,0,........,0]	0	$[-30,30]^D$
f_4	[0,0,........,0]	0	$[-600,600]^D$
f_5	[0,0,........,0]	0	$[-0.5,0.5]^D$
f_6	[0,0,........,0]	0	$[-5.12,5.12]^D$
f_7	[420,420,........,420]	0	$[-500,500]^D$

4.2 Parameter Settings

In conducting the experiments, we use the following parameter values for the GCO algorithm: number of group members m=40; parameters of beta distribution: a=b=0.25; number of counselors c=2; maximum number of fitness evaluations FEs=200,000. All experiments are run 30 times. The three parameters cp, tr, and mdf_max are set differently for the test functions, as indicated in Table 2. The parameters of the CLPSO algorithm are taken as specified in [15].

Table 2. Parameter settings for test functions

f	cp	tr	mdf_max
f_1	0.01	30.0	10.0
f_2	0.008	1.0	0.01
f_3	0.12	20.0	3.0
f_4	0.025	15.0	50.0
f_5	0.07	30.0	0.1
f_6	0.018	15.0	1.0
f_7	0.04	18.0	100.0

4.3 Results

Table 3 gives the mean values and standard deviations of the 30 runs of the test functions for the GCO algorithm, together with the CLPSO algorithm. Figure 3 illustrates the convergence characteristics, for the two algorithms, through the variation of the best function value as a function of FEs. The comparison demonstrates the success and effectiveness of the proposed GCO algorithm. Specifically, in the experiments conducted, the GCO outperforms the CLPSO for the first six benchmark functions and is well comparable to it for the seventh function (Schwefel).

Table 3. Mean and standard deviation of GCO and CLPSO algorithms

f	GCO	CLPSO
f_1	1.48881e-020 ± 8.05893e-020	2.3060e-019 ± 1.4236e-019
f_2	2.60961e-3 ± 3.20126e-3	19.0364 ± 3.2650
f_3	7.10543e-015 ± 0.0	1.367e-10 ± 5.389e-11
f_4	0.0 ± 0.0	7.785e-12 ± 3.076e-11
f_5	0.0 ± 0.0	5.095e-13 ± 2.176e-13
f_6	0.0 ± 0.0	2.823e-10 ± 3.513e-10
f_7	7.27596e-013 ± 9.06353e-013	1.819e-13 ± 5.55029e-13

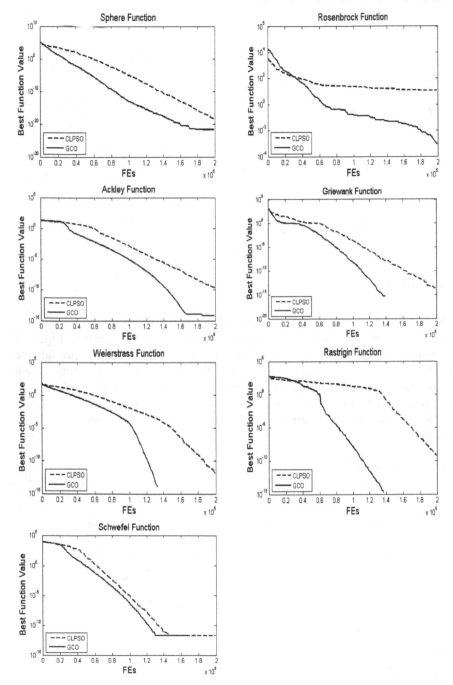

Fig. 3 Convergence characteristics of test functions

5 Conclusions

This paper introduces a novel heuristics-based, derivative-free optimization approach for single-objective functions, which we call a group counseling optimizer (GCO). Instead of mimicking the behavior of living organisms such as birds, fish, ants, and bees, we choose to emulate the behavior of the humans in solving their problems through group counseling. This is motivated by the fact that the human's thinking is, or should be, the most reasonable and influential, and group counseling is in essence a problem-solving technique.

The algorithmic iterations are visualized as counseling sessions, with counselees and counselors. Candidate solutions are progressively improved by means of one of two strategies: (a) other-members counseling or (b) self-counseling.

The approach is successfully applied to seven benchmark functions: two unimodal functions (Sphere and Rosenbrock) and five multimodal functions (Griewank, Rastrigin, Ackley, Weierstrass, and Schwefel). Global optima are reached without being trapped at local optima. Convergence characteristics are empirically studied in terms of the best function values *versus* fitness evaluations. Furthermore, a comparison is made with the comprehensive learning particle swarm optimizer (CLPSO). It is demonstrated that the GCO outperforms the CLPSO for six benchmark functions and is well comparable to it for the seventh function (Schwefel).

The proposed algorithm is seen to be interesting, promising, and readily applicable to many vital areas of optimization. We are currently investigating extension of the GCO to rotated benchmark functions [21] and multi-objective optimization problems [19].

Acknowledgements The authors would like to thank anonymous reviewers for helpful comments.

References

1. Berg, R.C., Landreth, G. L., Fall, K. A.: Group counseling: Concepts and procedures (4th ed.). Philadelphia (1998)
2. Burnard, P.: Practical counselling and helping. Routledge, London (1999)
3. Dixon, D.N., Glover, J.A.: Counseling: A problem-solving approach. Wiley, New York (1984)
4. Dorigo, M., Maniezzo, V., Colorni A.: The ant system: Optimization by a colony of cooperating agents. IEEE Trans. on Systems, Man, and Cybernetics Part B: Cybernetics, 26(1), 29–41 (1996)
5. Eberhart, R.C., Kennedy, J.: A new optimizer using particle swarm theory. In: Proc. of the Sixth International Symposium on Micro Machine and Human Science MHS'95, IEEE Press, 39–43, (1995)

6. Eberhart, R.C., Shi, Y., Kennedy, J.: Swarm Intelligence. Morgan Kaufmann, San Francisco, (2001)

7. Esquivel, S.C., Coello Coello, C. A.: On the use of particle swarm optimization with multimodal functions. In: Proc. Congr. Evol. Comput., vol. 2, Canberra, Australia, 1130–1136 (2003)

8. Gentle, J.E.: Random number generation and Monte Carlo methods — (Statistics and computing). Springer Science and Business Media, Inc. (2003)

9. Goldberg, D.E.: Genetic Algorithms in Search, Optimization and Machine Learning. Addison Wesley, Boston, MA (1989)

10. Gupta, A. K., Nadarajah, S.: Handbook of beta distribution and its applications, Marcel Dekker (2004)

11. Holland, J.H.: Adaptation in Natural and Artificial Systems. University of Michigan Press, Ann Arbor, MI (1975)

12. Kennedy, J., Eberhat, R.C.: Particle swarm optimization. In: Proc. of IEEE International Conference on Neural Networks, No. IV, IEEE Service Center, Piscataway, NJ, 1942–1948 (1995)

13. Kratcer, J., Leende, R.TH.A.J., van Engelen, J.M.L., Kunest, L.: InnovationNet: the Art of Creating and Benefiting from Innovation Networks. Van Gorcum (2007)

14. Lee, C.Y., Yao, X.: Evolutionary programming using mutations based on the levy probability distribution. IEEE Trans. Evol. Comput., vol. 8, 1–13 (2004)

15. Liang, J.J., Qin, A.K., Suganthan, P.N., Baskar, S.: Comprehensive learning particle swarm optimizer for global optimization of multimodal functions. IEEE Trans. Evolutionary Computation 10(3), 281-295 (2006)

16. Moscato, P.: On evolution, search, optimization, genetic algorithms and martial arts: towards memetic algorithms. Technical Report C3P 826, Caltech Concurrent Computation Program 158-79, California Institute of Technology, USA, Pasadena, CA (1989)

17. Pham, D.T., Ghanbarzadeh, A., Koc, E., Otri, S., Rahim, S., Zaidi, M.: The bees algorithm – a novel tool for complex optimization problems. In: Proc. of 2nd Virtual International Conference on Intelligent Production Machines and Systems IPROMS (2006)

18. Rechenberg, I.: Cybernetic Solution Path of an Experimental Problem. Royal Aircraft Establishment, Farnborough (1965)

19. Reyes-Sierra, M., Coello, C.A.C.: Multi-objective particle swarm optimizers: a survey of the state-of-the-art. International Journal of Computational Intelligence Research, 2(3), 287–308 (2006)

20. Reynolds, R.G.: An introduction to cultural algorithms. In: Proc. of the 3rd Annual Conference on Evolutionary Programming, World Scienfific Publishing, 131-139 (1994)

21. Salomon, R.: Reevaluating genetic algorithm performance under coordinate rotation of bencmark functions. BioSystems, vol. 39, 263–278 (1996)

22. Storn, R., Price, K.: Differential evolution – a simple and efficient adaptive scheme for global optimization over continuous spaces. Technical Report TR-95-012, International Computer Science Institute, Berkeley, CA (1995)

Firefly Algorithm, Lévy Flights and Global Optimization

Xin-She Yang

Abstract Nature-inspired algorithms such as Particle Swarm Optimization and Firefly Algorithm are among the most powerful algorithms for optimization. In this paper, we intend to formulate a new metaheuristic algorithm by combining Lévy flights with the search strategy via the Firefly Algorithm. Numerical studies and results suggest that the proposed Lévy-flight firefly algorithm is superior to existing metaheuristic algorithms. Finally implications for further research and wider applications will be discussed.

1 Introduction

Nature-inspired metaheuristic algorithms are becoming powerful in solving modern global optimization problems [2, 3, 5, 7, 9, 18, 17], especially for the NP-hard optimization such as the travelling salesman problem. For example, particle swarm optimization (PSO) was developed by Kennedy and Eberhart in 1995 [8, 9], based on the swarm behaviour such as fish and bird schooling in nature. It has now been applied to find solutions for many optimization applications. Another example is the Firefly Algorithm developed by the author [18] which has demonstrated promising superiority over many other algorithms. The search strategies in these multi-agent algorithms are controlled randomization, efficient local search and selection of the best solutions. However, the randomization typically uses uniform distribution or Gaussian distribution.

On the other hand, various studies have shown that flight behaviour of many animals and insects has demonstrated the typical characteristics of Lévy flights [4, 13, 11, 12]. A recent study by Reynolds and Frye shows that fruit flies or *Drosophila melanogaster*, explore their landscape using a series of straight flight

Department of Engineering, University of Cambridge,
Trumpington Street, Cambridge CB2 1PZ, UK
e-mail: xy227@cam.ac.uk

M. Bramer et al. (eds.), *Research and Development in Intelligent Systems XXVI*,
DOI 10.1007/978-1-84882-983-1_15, © Springer-Verlag London Limited 2010

paths punctuated by a sudden $90^{\varnothing}$ turn, leading to a Lévy-flight-style intermittent scale free search pattern. Studies on human behaviour such as the Ju/'hoansi hunter-gatherer foraging patterns also show the typical feature of Lévy flights. Even light can be related to Lévy flights [1]. Subsequently, such behaviour has been applied to optimization and optimal search, and preliminary results show its promising capability [11, 13, 15, 16].

This paper aims to formulate a new Lévy-flight Firefly Algorithm (LFA) and to provide the comparison study of the LFA with PSO and other relevant algorithms. We will first outline the firefly algorithms, then formulate the Lévy-flight FA and finally give the comparison about the performance of these algorithms. The LFA optimization seems more promising than particle swarm optimization in the sense that LFA converges more quickly and deals with global optimization more naturally. In addition, particle swarm optimization is just a special class of the LFA as we will demonstrate this in this paper.

2 Firefly Algorithm

2.1 Behaviour of Fireflies

The flashing light of fireflies is an amazing sight in the summer sky in the tropical and temperate regions. There are about two thousand firefly species, and most fireflies produce short and rhythmic flashes. The pattern of flashes is often unique for a particular species. The flashing light is produced by a process of bioluminescence, and the true functions of such signaling systems are still debating. However, two fundamental functions of such flashes are to attract mating partners (communication), and to attract potential prey. In addition, flashing may also serve as a protective warning mechanism. The rhythmic flash, the rate of flashing and the amount of time form part of the signal system that brings both sexes together. Females respond to a male's unique pattern of flashing in the same species, while in some species such as *photuris*, female fireflies can mimic the mating flashing pattern of other species so as to lure and eat the male fireflies who may mistake the flashes as a potential suitable mate.

The flashing light can be formulated in such a way that it is associated with the objective function to be optimized, which makes it possible to formulate new optimization algorithms. In the rest of this paper, we will first outline the basic formulation of the Firefly Algorithm (FA) and then discuss the implementation as well as analysis in detail.

2.2 Firefly Algorithm

Now we can idealize some of the flashing characteristics of fireflies so as to develop firefly-inspired algorithms. For simplicity in describing our Firefly Algorithm (FA), we now use the following three idealized rules: 1) all fireflies are unisex so that one firefly will be attracted to other fireflies regardless of their sex; 2) Attractiveness is proportional to their brightness, thus for any two flashing fireflies, the less brighter one will move towards the brighter one. The attractiveness is proportional to the brightness and they both decrease as their distance increases. If there is no brighter one than a particular firefly, it will move randomly; 3) The brightness of a firefly is affected or determined by the landscape of the objective function. For a maximization problem, the brightness can simply be proportional to the value of the objective function. Other forms of brightness can be defined in a similar way to the fitness function in genetic algorithms or the bacterial foraging algorithm (BFA) [6, 10].

In the firefly algorithm, there are two important issues: the variation of light intensity and formulation of the attractiveness. For simplicity, we can always assume that the attractiveness of a firefly is determined by its brightness which in turn is associated with the encoded objective function.

In the simplest case for maximum optimization problems, the brightness I of a firefly at a particular location $\mathbf{x}$ can be chosen as $I(\mathbf{x}) \propto f(\mathbf{x})$. However, the attractiveness β is relative, it should be seen in the eyes of the beholder or judged by the other fireflies. Thus, it will vary with the distance r_{ij} between firefly i and firefly j. In addition, light intensity decreases with the distance from its source, and light is also absorbed in the media, so we should allow the attractiveness to vary with the degree of absorption. In the simplest form, the light intensity $I(r)$ varies according to the inverse square law $I(r) = \frac{I_s}{r^2}$ where I_s is the intensity at the source. For a given medium with a fixed light absorption coefficient γ, the light intensity I varies with the distance r. That is

$$I = I_0 e^{-\gamma r}, \tag{1}$$

where I_0 is the original light intensity.

As a firefly's attractiveness is proportional to the light intensity seen by adjacent fireflies, we can now define the attractiveness β of a firefly by

$$\beta = \beta_0 e^{-\gamma r^2}, \tag{2}$$

where β_0 is the attractiveness at $r = 0$.

3 Lévy-Flight Firefly Algorithm

If we combine the three idealized rules with the characteristics of Lévy flights, we can formulate a new Lévy-flight Firefly Algorithm (LFA) which can be summarized as the pseudo code shown in Fig. 1.

Lévy-Flight Firefly Algorithm

```
begin
    Objective function f(x),     x = (x₁,...,x_d)^T
    Generate initial population of fireflies x_i (i = 1,2,...,n)
    Light intensity I_i at x_i is determined by f(x_i)
    Define light absorption coefficient γ
    while (t <MaxGeneration)
    for i = 1 : n all n fireflies
        for j = 1 : i all n fireflies
            if (I_j > I_i)
                Move firefly i towards j in d-dimension via Lévy flights
            end if
            Attractiveness varies with distance r via exp[−γr]
            Evaluate new solutions and update light intensity
        end for j
    end for i
    Rank the fireflies and find the current best
    end while
    Postprocess results and visualization
end
```

Fig. 1 Pseudo code of the Lévy-Flight Firefly Algorithm (LFA).

In the implementation, the actual form of attractiveness function $\beta(r)$ can be any monotonically decreasing functions such as the following generalized form

$$\beta(r) = \beta_0 e^{-\gamma r^m}, \qquad (m \geq 1). \tag{3}$$

For a fixed γ, the characteristic length becomes $\Gamma = \gamma^{-1/m} \to 1$ as $m \to \infty$. Conversely, for a given length scale Γ in an optimization problem, the parameter γ can be used as a typical initial value. That is $\gamma = \frac{1}{\Gamma^m}$.

The distance between any two fireflies i and j at x_i and x_j, respectively, is the Cartesian distance

$$r_{ij} = ||x_i - x_j|| = \sqrt{\sum_{k=1}^{d}(x_{i,k} - x_{j,k})^2}, \tag{4}$$

where $x_{i,k}$ is the kth component of the spatial coordinate x_i of ith firefly. For other applications such as scheduling, the distance can be time delay or any suitable forms.

The movement of a firefly i is attracted to another more attractive (brighter) firefly j is determined by

$$x_i = x_i + \beta_0 e^{-\gamma r_{ij}^2}(x_j - x_i) + \alpha \, \text{sign}[\text{rand} - \frac{1}{2}] \oplus \text{Lévy}, \tag{5}$$

where the second term is due to the attraction while the third term is randomization via Lévy flights with α being the randomization parameter. The product $\oplus$ means entrywise multiplications. The sign[rand-$\frac{1}{2}$] where rand $\in [0,1]$ essentially provides a random sign or direction while the random step length is drawn from a Lévy distribution

$$\text{Lévy} \sim u = t^{-\lambda}, \qquad (1 < \lambda \leq 3), \tag{6}$$

which has an infinite variance with an infinite mean. Here the steps of firefly motion is essentially a random walk process with a power-law step-length distribution with a heavy tail.

3.1 Choice of Parameters

For most cases in our implementation, we can take $\beta_0 = 1$, $\alpha \in [0,1]$, $\gamma = 1$, and $\lambda = 1.5$. In addition, if the scales vary significantly in different dimensions such as -10^5 to 10^5 in one dimension while, say, -0.001 to 0.01 along the other, it is a good idea to replace α by αS_k where the scaling parameters $S_k(k = 1, ..., d)$ in the d dimensions should be determined by the actual scales of the problem of interest.

The parameter γ now characterizes the variation of the attractiveness, and its value is crucially important in determining the speed of the convergence and how the FA algorithm behaves. In theory, $\gamma \in [0, \infty)$, but in practice, $\gamma = O(1)$ is determined by the characteristic length Γ of the system to be optimized. Thus, in most applications, it typically varies from 0.01 to 100.

3.2 Asymptotic Cases

There are two important limiting cases when $\gamma \to 0$ and $\gamma \to \infty$. For $\gamma \to 0$, the attractiveness is constant $\beta = \beta_0$ and $\Gamma \to \infty$, this is equivalent to say that the light intensity does not decrease in an idealized sky. Thus, a flashing firefly can be seen anywhere in the domain. Thus, a single (usually global) optimum can easily be reached. This corresponds to a special case of particle swarm optimization (PSO) discussed earlier. Subsequently, the efficiency of this special case is the same as that of PSO.

On the other hand, the limiting case $\gamma \to \infty$ leads to $\Gamma \to 0$ and $\beta(r) \to \delta(r)$ (the Dirac delta function), which means that the attractiveness is almost zero in the sight of other fireflies or the fireflies are short-sighted. This is equivalent to the case where the fireflies fly in a very foggy region randomly. No other fireflies can be seen, and each firefly roams in a completely random way. Therefore, this corresponds to the completely random search method.

As the Lévy-flight firefly algorithm is usually in somewhere between these two extremes, it is possible to adjust the parameters γ, λ and α so that it can outperform both the random search and PSO. In fact, LFA can find the global optima as well as all the local optima simultaneously in a very effective manner.

4 Simulations and Results

4.1 Validation

In order to validate the proposed algorithm, we have implemented it in Matlab. In our simulations, the values of the parameters are $\alpha = 0.2$, $\gamma = 1$, $\lambda = 1.5$, and $\beta_0 = 1$. As an example, we now use the LFA to find the global optimum of the

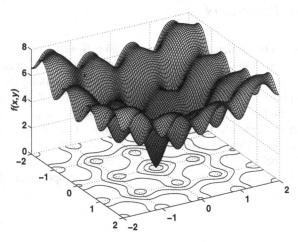

Fig. 2 Ackley function for two independent variables with a global minimum $f_* = 0$ at $(0,0)$.

Ackley function

$$f(\mathbf{x}) = -20\exp\left[-\frac{1}{5}\sqrt{\frac{1}{d}\sum_{i=1}^{d}x_i^2}\right] - \exp\left[\frac{1}{d}\sum_{i=1}^{d}\cos(2\pi x_i)\right] + 20 + e, \qquad (7)$$

which has a global minimum $f_* = 0$ at $(0,0,...,0)$. The 2D Ackley function is shown in Fig. 2, and this global minimum can be found after about 200 evaluations for 40 fireflies after 5 iterations as shown in Fig. 3.

Now let us use the LFA to find the optima of some tougher test functions. For example, the author introduced a forest function [19]

$$f(\mathbf{x}) = \left(\sum_{i=1}^{d}|x_i|\right)\exp\left[-\sum_{i=1}^{d}\sin(x_i^2)\right], \quad -2\pi \le x_i \le 2\pi, \qquad (8)$$

which has a global minimum $f_* = 0$ at $(0,0,...,0)$. The 2D Yang's forest function is shown in Fig. 4. However, an important feature of this test function is that it is non-smooth and its derivative is not well defined at the optima $(0, 0, ..., 0)$ as shown in Fig. 5.

4.2 Comparison of LFA with PSO and GA

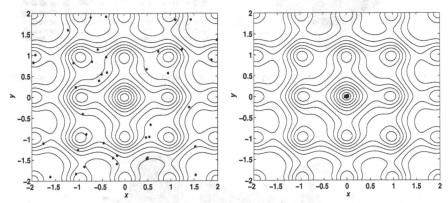

Fig. 3 The initial locations of the 40 fireflies (left) and their locations after 5 iterations (right).

Various studies show that PSO algorithms can outperform genetic algorithms (GA) [7] and other conventional algorithms for solving many optimization problems. This is partially due to that fact that the broadcasting ability of the current best estimates gives better and quicker convergence towards the optimality. A general framework for evaluating statistical performance of evolutionary algorithms has been discussed in detail by Shilane et al. [14]. Various test functions for optimization algorithms have been developed over many years, and a relatively comprehensive review of these test functions can be found in [2].

Now we will compare the LFA with PSO, and genetic algorithms for various standard test functions. We will use the same population size of $n = 40$ for all algorithms in all our simulations. The PSO used is the standard version without any inertia function, while the implemented genetic algorithm has a mutation probability of 0.05 and a crossover probability of 0.95 without use of elitism. After implementing these algorithms using Matlab, we have carried out extensive simulations and each algorithm has been run at least 100 times so as to carry out meaningful statistical analysis. The algorithms stop when the variations of function values are less than a given tolerance $\varepsilon \leq 10^{-5}$. The results are summarized in the following table (see Table 1) where the global optima are reached. The numbers are in the format: average number of evaluations (success rate), so $6922 \pm 537(98\%)$ means that the average number (mean) of function evaluations is 6922 with a standard deviation of 537. The success rate of finding the global optima for this algorithm is 98%.

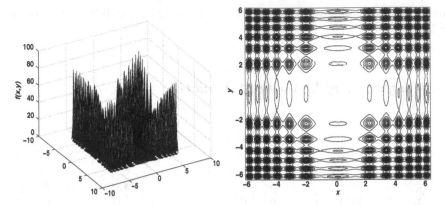

Fig. 4 Yang's forest function for two independent variables with a global minimum $f_* = 0$ at $(0,0)$.

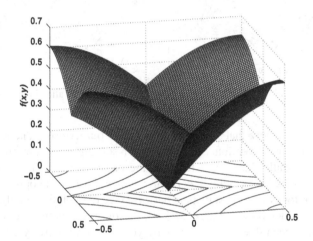

Fig. 5 Non-smoothness of Yang's forest function near the global minimum $(0,0)$.

We can see that the LFA is much more efficient in finding the global optima with higher success rates. Each function evaluation is virtually instantaneous on modern personal computer. For example, the computing time for 10,000 evaluations on a 3GHz desktop is about 5 seconds. Even with graphics for displaying the locations of the particles and fireflies, it usually takes less than a few minutes. Furthermore, we have used various values of the population size n or the number of fireflies. We found that for most problems $n = 15$ to 50 would be sufficient. For tougher problems, larger n can be used, though excessively large n should not be used unless there is no better alternative, as it is more computationally extensive.

Table 1 Comparison of algorithm performance

Functions/Algorithms	GA	PSO	LFA
Michalewicz ($d=16$)	$89325 \pm 7914(95\%)$	$6922 \pm 537(98\%)$	$2889 \pm 719(100\%)$
Rosenbrock ($d=16$)	$55723 \pm 8901(90\%)$	$32756 \pm 5325(98\%)$	$6040 \pm 535(100\%)$
De Jong ($d=256$)	$25412 \pm 1237(100\%)$	$17040 \pm 1123(100\%)$	$5657 \pm 730(100\%)$
Schwefel ($d=128$)	$227329 \pm 7572(95\%)$	$14522 \pm 1275(97\%)$	$7923 \pm 524(100\%)$
Ackley ($d=128$)	$32720 \pm 3327(90\%)$	$23407 \pm 4325(92\%)$	$4392 \pm 2710(100\%)$
Rastrigin	$110523 \pm 5199(77\%)$	$79491 \pm 3715(90\%)$	$12075 \pm 3750(100\%)$
Easom	$19239 \pm 3307(92\%)$	$17273 \pm 2929(90\%)$	$6082 \pm 1690(100\%)$
Griewank	$70925 \pm 7652(90\%)$	$55970 \pm 4223(92\%)$	$10790 \pm 2977(100\%)$
Yang	$37079 \pm 8920(88\%)$	$19725 \pm 3204(98\%)$	$5152 \pm 2493(100\%)$
Shubert (18 minima)	$54077 \pm 4997(89\%)$	$23992 \pm 3755(92\%)$	$9925 \pm 2504(100\%)$

5 Conclusions

In this paper, we have formulated a new Lévy-flight firefly algorithm and analysed its similarities and differences with particle swarm optimization. We then implemented and compared these algorithms. Our simulation results for finding the global optima of various test functions suggest that particle swarm often outperforms traditional algorithms such as genetic algorithms, while LFA is superior to both PSO and GA in terms of both efficiency and success rate. This implies that LFA is potentially more powerful in solving NP-hard problems which will be investigated further in future studies.

The basic Lévy-flight firefly algorithm is very efficient. A further improvement on the convergence of the algorithm is to carry out sensitivity studies by varying various parameters such as β_0, γ, α and more interestingly λ. These could form important topics for further research. In addition, further studies on the application of FLA in combination with other algorithms may form an exciting area for further research in optimization.

References

1. Barthelemy, P.: Bertolotti J., Wiersma D. S., A Lévy flight for light, *Nature*, **453**, 495-498 (2008).
2. Baeck, T., Fogel, D. B., Michalewicz, Z.: *Handbook of Evolutionary Computation*, Taylor & Francis, (1997).
3. Bonabeau, E., Dorigo, M., Theraulaz, G.: *Swarm Intelligence: From Natural to Artificial Systems*. Oxford University Press, (1999)
4. Brown, C., Liebovitch, L. S., Glendon, R.: Lévy flights in Dobe Ju/'hoansi foraging patterns, *Human Ecol.*, **35**, 129-138 (2007).
5. Deb, K., *Optimisation for Engineering Design*, Prentice-Hall, New Delhi, (1995).
6. Gazi, K., and Passino, K. M.: Stability analysis of social foraging swarms, *IEEE Trans. Sys. Man. Cyber. Part B - Cybernetics*, **34**, 539-557 (2004).
7. Goldberg, D. E.: *Genetic Algorithms in Search, Optimisation and Machine Learning*, Reading, Mass.: Addison Wesley (1989).

8. Kennedy, J. and Eberhart, R. C.: Particle swarm optimization. *Proc. of IEEE International Conference on Neural Networks*, Piscataway, NJ. pp. 1942-1948 (1995).

9. Kennedy J., Eberhart R., Shi Y: *Swarm intelligence*, Academic Press, (2001).

10. Passino, K. M.: *Biomimicrt of Bacterial Foraging for Distributed Optimization*, University Press, Princeton, New Jersey (2001).

11. Pavlyukevich, I.: Lévy flights, non-local search and simulated annealing, *J. Computational Physics*, **226**, 1830-1844 (2007).

12. Pavlyukevich, I.: Cooling down Lévy flights, *J. Phys. A:Math. Theor.*, **40**, 12299-12313 (2007).

13. Reynolds, A. M. and Frye, M. A.: Free-flight odor tracking in Drosophila is consistent with an optimal intermittent scale-free search, *PLoS One*, **2**, e354 (2007).

14. Shilane, D., Martikainen, J., Dudoit, S., Ovaska, S. J.: A general framework for statistical performance comparison of evolutionary computation algorithms, *Information Sciences: an Int. Journal*, **178**, 2870-2879 (2008).

15. Shlesinger, M. F., Zaslavsky, G. M. and Frisch, U. (Eds): *Lévy Flights and Related Topics in Phyics*, Springer, (1995).

16. Shlesinger, M. F.: Search research, *Nature*, **443**, 281-282 (2006).

17. Yang, X. S.: Biology-derived algorithms in engineering optimizaton (Chapter 32), in *Handbook of Bioinspired Algorithms and Applications* (eds Olarius & Zomaya), Chapman & Hall / CRC (2005).

18. Yang, X. S.: *Nature-Inspired Metaheuristic Algorithms*, Luniver Press, (2008).

19. Yang, X. S.: *Engineering Optimization: An Introduction with Metaheuristic Applications*, Wiley & Sons, New Jersey, (2010).

Improving Cooperative PSO using Fuzzy Logic

Zahra Afsahi[1], Mohammadreza Meybodi[2]

Abstract PSO is a population-based technique for optimization, which simulates the social behaviour of the fish schooling or bird flocking. Two significant weaknesses of this method are: first, falling into local optimum and second, the curse of dimensionality. In this work we present the FCPSO-H to overcome these weaknesses. Our approach was implemented in the cooperative PSO, which employs fuzzy logic to control the acceleration coefficients in velocity equation of each particle. The proposed approach is validated by function optimization problem form the standard literature simulation result indicates that the approach is highly competitive specifically in its better general convergence performance.

1 Introduction

Particle swarm optimization (PSO) was motivated from the simulation of simplified social behavior of animals (Kennedy and Eberhart 1995). It has already been applied successfully in many application areas where GA can be applied to (Eberhart and Shi 1998 b). However, the original PSO has difficulties in controlling the balance between exploration and exploitation where the environment itself is dynamically changed over the time. PSO cannot able to adapt dynamically to the changing environment and quickly converging toward an optimum in the first period of iteration. Another main drawback of the original PSO is that it may get stuck in a sub-optimal solution region and the problem usually gets harder for high-dimensional problems usually known as "curse of dimensionality". Hence, a new hybrid PSO algorithm is proposed in this paper. The proposed algorithm integrates both fuzzy logic and cooperative learning within a unified framework to further improve the performance. The use of fuzzy logic is suitable for dynamically tuning the programming coefficient C_1, C_2, since

[1] Zahra Afsahi

Systems & Quality V.P. MAPNA, Tehran, Iran, e-mail: afsahi_z@mapna.com.

Computer Engineering and Information Technology Department, Qazvin Azad University, Qazvin, Iran, e-mail: afsahi_ai@yahoo.com.

[2] Mohammad Reza Meybodi

Computer Engineering and Information Technology Department, Amirkabir University, Tehran, Iran, e-mail: mmeybodi@ce.aut.ac.ir.

M. Bramer et al. (eds.), *Research and Development in Intelligent Systems XXVI*,
DOI 10.1007/978-1-84882-983-1_16, © Springer-Verlag London Limited 2010

it starts a run with an initial value which is changed during the run. By using the fuzzy control approach, these parameters can be adaptively regulated according the problem environment and can balance the exploration and exploitation. The cooperative learning splits a composite high dimensional swarm into several smaller dimensional swarms, which cooperate with each other by exchanging information to determine composite fitness of the entire system. The rest of the paper is organized as follows. Section 2 describes the PSO algorithm. Section 3 motivates the cooperative learning in PSO algorithm. In section 4 we will introduce pervious works in hybrid models of fuzzy logic and PSO, briefly. Section 5 presents our hybrid fuzzy cooperative PSO algorithm. Performance evaluation of our approach is presented in detail in section 6. Conclusions are presented in section 7.

2 PSO algorithm

The particle swarm optimization (PSO) method is a member of the wide category of Swarm Intelligence methods (Kennedy et al., 2001) for global optimization problems. It was originally proposed by Kennedy as a simulation of social behavior, and it was initially introduced as an optimization method in 1995(Eberhart and Kennedy 1995, Eberhart et al., 1996). PSO is related with Artificial Life, and especially to Swarming theories. PSO is a population-based technique and each individual of the population has an adaptable velocity (position change), according to which it moves in the search space. Moreover, each individual has a memory, remembering the best position of the search space it has ever visited. Thus, its movement is an aggregated acceleration towards the best individual of a topological neighborhood. Suppose that the search space is D-dimensional, the ith particle of the swarm can be represented by a D-dimensional vector, $X_i = (x_{i1}, x_{i2}, ... x_{iD})$. The velocity (position change) of this particle, can be represented by another D-dimensional vector, $V_i = (v_{i1}, v_{i2}, ..., v_{iD})$. The personal best position associated with a particle i is the best position that particle has visited thus far, i.e. a position that yielded the highest fitness value for that particle. If f denotes the objective function, then the personal best of a particle at a time step is updated as:

$$y_i(t+1) = \begin{cases} y_i(t) & \text{if} \quad f(X_i(t+1)) \geq f(y_i(t)) \\ X_i(t+1) & \text{if} \quad f(X_i(t+1) < f(y_i(t)) \end{cases} \tag{1}$$

Depending on the social network structure of the swarm $l$best and $g$best experience of particles, exchange among them. For the $g$best model, the best particle is determined from the entire swarm. If the position of the best particle is denoted by the vector, then:

$$\hat{y}(t) \in \{y_0, y_1, \ldots, y_s \mid f(\hat{y}_j(t1))\} = \min\{f(y_0(t)), f(y_1(t)), \ldots, f(y_s(t))\} \tag{2}$$

For the *l*best model, a swarm divided into overlapping neighborhoods of particles. For each neighborhood N_j, a best particle is determined with position $\hat{y}_j$. The best particle is referred to as the neighborhood best particle, defined as:

$$\{\hat{y}_j(t+1) \in N_j \mid f(\hat{y}_j(t+1))\} = \min\{f(y_i)\} \quad \forall y_i \in N_j \tag{3}$$

Kennedy and Mendes recommended the Van-Neumann architecture (Kennedy and Mendes 2002), in which a particle's neighbors are above, below and on each side on a two dimensional lattice, to be the most promising one. For the each iteration of a gbest PSO algorithm, the j_{th} dimension of particle i_{th}'s velocity vector, and its position vector, X_i is updated as follows:

$$V_{i,j}(t+1) = w * V_{i,j}(t) + C_1 r_{1,j}(t)(y_{i,j}(t) - x_{i,j}(t)) + C_2 r_{2,j}(t)(\hat{y}_{i,j}(t) - x_{i,j}(t))$$
$$X_i(t+1) = X_i(t) + V_i(t+1) \tag{4}$$

Where C_1, C_2 are positive constants, called acceleration constant; r_1, r_2 are random numbers uniformly distributed in [0, 1]; and $n = 1,2,\ldots$ determines the iteration numbers. w is the first new parameter added into the original PSO algorithm, inertia weight (Shi and Eberhart 1998a, 1998b). The PSO algorithm performs repeated applications of the update equations until a specified number of iterations have been exceeded, or until a user-defined stopping criterion has been reached.

3 Cooperative learning in PSO

All the basic variants of PSO suffer from a common problem, which is quite apparent in several such stochastic optimization algorithms, curse of dimensionality. The original PSO uses a population of *d*-dimensional vectors. In cooperative learning (Bergh and Engelbercht 2004), instead of creating a composite swarm of *S* particles for a *d*-dimensional problem, we create *d* one-dimensional swarms, each comprising *S* particles. Each swarm attempts to optimize a single component of the solution vector, essentially a one-dimensional optimization problem. This decomposition used in the relaxation method (Southwell 1946). One complication is the fact that the function to be minimized, *f*, requires a *d*-dimensional vector as input. If each swarm represents only a single dimension of the search space, it is clearly not possible to directly compute the fitness of the individuals of a single population considered in isolation. Hence the fitness evaluation for a cooperative PSO is carried out by the introduction of a "context vector" (denote by b). For a d-dimensional problem, the context vector is also of d-dimensional size. Here when a given j_{th} swarm is active the "context vector" is formed by the gbest particles of the other (d-1) swarms, which are kept constant during the evaluation of the j_{th} swarm, and the j_{th} row of the "context vector" is filled with each particle of the j_{th} swarm one by one. Each such *context vector* formed is evaluated for its composite fitness. But note that, should some of the components in the vector be correlated, they should be grouped in the same swarm, since the independent changes made by the different swarms will have a detrimental effect on correlated variables (Friedman and Savage 1947). This results in some swarms having one-dimensional vectors and others having c-dimensional vector (c<d). In this paper we used the $CPSO - H_k$ algorithm, which combines $CPSO - S_k$ with PSO in an attempt to retain the best properties of both algorithms, and the mechanism for information exchange is to replace some of the particles in one half of the algorithm with the best solution discovered so far by the other half of the algorithm. Specially, after an iteration of the $CPSO - S_k$ half of the algorithm, the context vector $b(1, P_1.\hat{y})$ is used to overwrite a randomly chosen particle in the PSO half of the algorithm (the Q swarm). This is followed by an iteration of the Q swarm component of the algorithm, which yields a new global best particle, $Q.\hat{y}$. This vector is then split into sub-vectors of the right dimensions and used to overwrite the positions of randomly chosen particles in the P_j swarms.

During subsequent iterations more particles will be drawn to the global best particle, possibly discovring better solutions along the way, thus, the normal operation of the swarm is not disurbed.

4 Related works

Several algorithms have so far been proposed in literatures that have addressed the issue of using fuzzy logic in particle swarm optimization. Shi and Eberhart after introducing a linearly decreasing inertia weight to the PSO over the course of PSO, designed fuzzy systems to nonlinearly changing the inertia weight (Shi and Eberhart 2001a). This fuzzy system has some measurements of the PSO performance as the input and the new inertia weight as the output of the fuzzy systems. Kang, Wang, and Wu proposed a novel fuzzy adaptive optimization strategy for the PSO (Kang et al., 2006). In multi-optimum static programming mode (MSPPSO), the programming proportion factor of multi-optimum cannot be dynamically adjusted in the optimization process. On the basis of MSPPSO, a kind of fuzzy adaptive programming strategy based on double-variable and single-dimensional fuzzy control structure is proposed. Liu, Abraham and Zhang introduced the FATPSO algorithm. In this method, they proposed a fuzzy logic-based system to tune adaptively the velocity threshold (Liu et al., 2007). Niu, *et al.* employed T-S fuzzy model to represent a non-linear system. T-S fuzzy system is described by a set of fuzzy IF-THEN rules that represent local linear input-output relations of non-linear systems. The overall system is then an aggregation of all such local linear models (Niu et al., 2007). Noroozi and Meybodi combined fuzzy logics with PSO. In this method C_1, C_2 are controlled by 4 fuzzy rules. The result of this algorithm is affected directly by the way of choosing the fuzzy rules (Noroozi and Meybodi 2008a, 2008b). Zahiri and Seyedin introduced particle swarm classifier with the concept of intelligently controlling the search process of PSO to develop an efficient swarm intelligence based classifier. An intelligent fuzzy controller is designed to improve the performance and efficiently of the proposed classifier by adapting three important parameters of PSO, inertia weight, cognitive parameter and social parameter (Zahiri and Seyedin 2007). Abdelbar, Abdelshahid and Wunsch introduced fuzzy PSO, a generalization which differs from standard PSO, because of a new fuzzy variable, *charisma* (Abdelbar et al., 2005). In this method more than one particle in each neighbourhood can have a non-zero degree of charisma and consequently is allowed to influence others to a degree that depends on its charisma. Liu and Abraham proposed a hybrid meta-heuristic fuzzy scheme, called as variable neighbourhood fuzzy particle swarm algorithm, based on fuzzy particle swarm optimization and variable neighbourhood search to solve the QAP (Liu and Abraham 2007).

5 The Proposed System

5.1 Overview

The acceleration constants C_1, C_2 represent the weighting of the stochastic acceleration terms that pull each particle toward y and $\hat{y}$ positions. Low values allow particles to roam far from target regions before being tugged back, while high values result in abrupt movement toward target regions. Early experience with PSO (mostly trial and error) led us to set the acceleration constants C_1, C_2 equal to 2.0, but it is not a usual rule (Rantaweera et al., 2004). In the search process, sometimes social behaviour may be more important than cognitive behaviour and vice versa. Regarding some statistical parameters, which are calculated in the each iteration, it is possible to tune the cognitive parameter and social parameter adaptively to steer the whole swarm and each particle toward proper trajectory. For example, in the beginning of the search process, the global search is more important than local search. By tuning the cognitive parameter to a small value, the global search ability and maximal interaction in the swarm is achieved. Contrariwise, after enough iteration, when a good position is achieved, the cognitive parameter must be increased to emphasize local search ability. Part of search space explored by the particle should become smaller and smaller, when the fitness value of a particle becomes better and better. It means social interaction should be decreased. On the other hands, less improvement in the particle fitness causes a sociality search for the exploration. This means that the value of the cognitive parameter should be decreased and the value of the social parameter should be increased. The use of fuzzy logic would be suitable for dynamically tuning the cognitive parameter and social parameter, since it starts a run with an initial value which is change during the run. By using the fuzzy control approach, these parameters can be adaptively regulated according to the problem environment.

5.2 Fuzzy logic in $CPSO-H_k$

In this section we introduce our proposed algorithm, $FCPSO-H_k$. Fig. 1 illustrates the structure of our fuzzy system controller.

Fig. 1 The fuzzy system controller

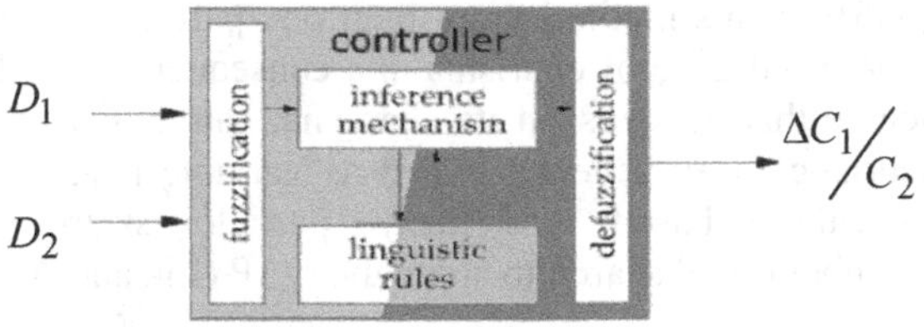

This system is composed of a knowledge base, that includes the information given by the expert in the form of linguistic control rules that include 25 rules which are shown in Table 1, a fuzzification and a defuzzification interface, two variables are selected as inputs to the fuzzy system: the distance between current position and its best position and the distance between current position and the best position of the whole swarm on each dimension and the output variable is the ratio between the programming coefficients, $\Delta C_1 / C_2$. For example when D_1 is "z" and D_2 is "HN", means that we are very close to local optimum and far away from global optimum by increasing C_2 and decreasing C_1, we can go far from local optimum and go toward global optimum, thus we set the fuzzy value of $\Delta C_1 / C_2$ to "LN". All the rules of Table 2 are based on this concept. The goal of these rules is controlling the balance between exploration and exploitation. There into, the value of the programming coefficients is obtained dynamically, because this value depends on the fuzzification of the D_1, D_2 and these parameters (D_1, D_2) change in each iteration.

Table 1 Fuzzy rule base for our system

D_1 / D_2	HN	LN	Z	LP	HP
HN	LP	MN	LN	LN	LP
LN	HP	Z	MN	Z	MP
Z	HP	MP	Z	MP	HP
LP	HP	Z	MN	LP	HP
HP	LP	LN	LN	LN	HP

It should be mentioned that different kinds of inputs, outputs, membership function shapes, membership function locations and fuzzy rules may be introduced and even these parameters can be optimized by another optimization algorithm. In this paper the membership function and its locations are selected and tuned manually. In the process of the fuzzification of input and output variables, we selected the same fuzzy sets. Fig. 2 shows the sketch map of memebership function.

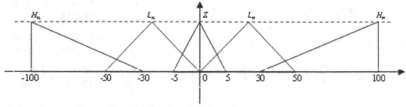

Fig. 2 sketch map of memebership function for fuzzy inputs

In $FCPSO\_H$ algorithm, the $CPSO - S_k$ algorithm executes for one iteration and follows by one iteration of the PSO algorithm and fuzzy rules are used in each iteration.

6 Experiments

In our experiments, the algorithms used for camparision were mainly PSO, $CPSO - H_k$, $FPSO$ and $FCPSO - H_k$. The four algorithms share many similarities, which are also ispired from the nature like the PSO. Each algorithm was tested with all the numerical functions shown in Table2. The first two functions, namely Sphere and Rosenbrock, have a single minimum, while the other functions are highly multimodal with multiple local minima. Some of the functions have the sum of their variables, some of them have the product, some of them have dimensional effect. We tested the algorithms on the different functions in 10, 30 and 100 dimensions. For each of these functions, the goal was to find the global minima. Each algorithm (for each benchmark) was repeated 50 times with different random population. Each trial used a fixed number of 35000 iterations.

Since the swarm size in all algorithms was 35 (The size of swarm were defined by users). The average fitness values of the best solutions throughout the optimization run were recorded and the averages and the standard deviations were calculated from 50 different trails. The standard deviation indicates the differences in the results during the 50 different trials.

Fig. 3–12 illustrate the mean best function values for the 5 functions with two different dimensions (i.e. 30 and 100-D) using the four algorithms. Each algorithm for different dimensions of the same objective function has similar performance. But in general, the higher the dimension is, the higher the fitness values are. It is observed that for PSO algorithm, the solutions get trapped in a local minimum within the first 2000 iterations both in low dimension and high dimension.

Table 2 Test functions, global optimum, search ranges and initialization ranges

Name	F	X^*	Search Range	Initiation Range
F1=Sphere	$f_1(x) = \sum_{i=1}^{D} x_i^2$	[0,0, ...,0]#	[-100, 100]D#	[-100, 50]D#
F2=Rosenbrock	$f_2(x) = \sum_{i=1}^{D-1}(100(x_i^2 - x_{i+1}^2)^2 + (x_i^2 - 1)^2)$	[1,1, ...,1]#	[-2.048, 2.048]D#	[-2.048, 2.048]D#
F3=Ackley	$f_3(x) = -20\exp\left(-0.2\sqrt{\frac{1}{D}\sum_{i=1}^{D}x_i^2}\right) - \exp\left(\frac{1}{D}\sum_{i=1}^{D}\cos(2\Pi x_i)\right) + 20 + e$	[0,0, ...0]#	[-32.76, 32.76]D#	[-32.768, 16]D#
F4=Greiwank	$f_4(x) = \sum_{i=1}^{D}\frac{x_i^2}{4000} - \prod_{i=1}^{D}\cos\left(\frac{x_i}{\sqrt{i}}\right) + 1$	[0,0 ...0]#	[-600, 600]D#	[-600, 200]D#
F5=Weierstrass	$f_5(x) = \sum_{i=1}^{D}\left(\sum_{k=0}^{kmax}\left[a^k \cos(2\pi b^k(x_i + 0.5))\right]\right) - D\sum_{k=0}^{kmax}\left[a^k \cos(2\pi b^k 0.5)\right] a = 0.5, b = 3, k\max = 20.$	[0,0, ...0]#	[-0.5, 0.5]D#	[-0.5, 0.2]D#
F6=Rastrigin	$f_6(x) = \sum_{i=1}^{D}\left(x_i^2 - 10\cos(2\pi x_i) + 10\right)$	[0,0, ...0]	[-5.12, 5.12]^D	[-5.12, 2]^D
F7=Non-continuous Rastrigin	$f_7(x) = \sum_{i=1}^{D}\left(y_i^2 - 10\cos(2\pi y_i) + 10\right)$ $y_i = \begin{cases} x_i & |x_i| < 1/2 \\ \frac{round(2x_i)}{2} & |x_i| >= 1/2 \end{cases}$ $for i = 1, 2, ..., D$	[0,0, ...0]	[-5.12, 5.12]^D	[-5.12, 2]^D
F8=Schwefel	$f_8(x) = 418.9829 * D - \sum_{i=1}^{D} x_i \sin\left(|x_i|^{\frac{1}{2}}\right)$	[420.96, ... 420.96]	[-500, 500]^D	[-500, 500]^D

$CPSO - H_k$, $FPSO$ has similar performance in some benchmark such as Griewank, Ackley and Sphere in low dimension, but in high dimensional (100D) problems the $CPSO - H_k$ algorithm has the better speed to convergence and in all benchmarks except Weiestrass and Schewel converged to a better solution.

$FCPSO - H_k$ as our proposed algorithm has the best performance in high dimension. It is interesting that even if other algorithms are very close to or better(Non-Continus Rastrigin) than $FCPSO - H_k$ in 10-D benchmarks, but a very large difference emerges in the case of 100-D benchmark problems. $FCPSO - H_k$ algorithm becomes much better than other algorithms in general besides for Schwefel. The average and the standard deviations for 50 trails are shown in Table 4 the larger the average are wider the standard deviations are usually. Reffering to the emprical results depicted in Table 4, for most of considered functions, $FCPSO - H_k$ demonstrated a consistent performance pattern among all the considered algorithms.

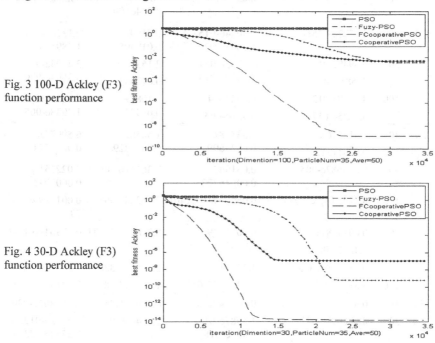

Fig. 3 100-D Ackley (F3) function performance

Fig. 4 30-D Ackley (F3) function performance

Table 3 Benchmark for simulation

Function	Fuzzy Variable	H_n	L_n	z	L_p	H_p
	$DI_{j,i}$	(-100,-50)	(-30,5)	(-5,5)	(-5,30)	(50, 100)
F1	$D2_{j,i}$	(-100,-50)	(-30,5)	(-5,5)	(-5,30)	(50, 100)
	$\Delta C_1 / C_2$	(-0.1,-0.04)	(-0.025, 0.005)	(-0.005, 0.005)	(-0.005 ,0.025)	(0.04, 0.1)

Table 4 comparing the results for the 10, 30 and 100-D function optimization problems

Function	D	Fuzzy Cooperative PSO	Cooperative PSO	PSO	Fuzzy PSO
F1	10	9.1231e-214±0	1.0872e-311±0	61.6±207.12	3.3297e-314±0
	30	3.0918e-077± 1.8117e-1134	4.7755e-033± 1.2981e-048	941.31±13119	1.1967e-040± 8.7323e-072
	100	7.7561e-021± 3.845e-026	0.024297± 0.13395	8598.2± 1.1316e+005	0.017353±15.814
F2	10	2.5446±1.2453	3.9871±2.8252	68.824±97.387	0.11752±1.2629
	30	14.574±21.26	23.7±6.7224	1610.6±7127.1	77.241±567.57
	100	152.46±1543.9	202.75±2090.5	18467± 2.344e+006	302.02±12146
F3	10	3.5527e-015±0	7.1054e-015± 5.9603e-029	0.7199± 0.019495	2.1316e-014± 1.7895e-028
	30	6.3949e-014± 2.5819e-028	7.676e-007± 4.5419e-014	2.1537± 0.012453	3.4204e-010± 3.3604e-020
	100	8.0149e-012± 3.4275e-017	0.0024424± 3.931e-005	3.1087± 0.0033343	0.0015692± 1.2933e-005
F4	10	0.012316± 0.00011212	0.23848± 0.0025699	1.5058± 0.0026229	0.59075± 0.0015774
	30	0±3.6682e-005	0.031942± 0.00046773	7.3611±0.30691	0.022151± 0.0007942
	100	4.329e-015± 2.033e-005	0.056724±0.01401	53.52±4.0891	0.0017299±0.05079
F5	10	0.0039687± 1.4817e-006	0.0021739± 0.078251	8.8185±0.39671	0.52964±0.13468
	30	0.031958±0.026626	1.4738±4.975	36.845±0.82859	1.2692±0.76157
	100	3.5173 ±1.3307	55.255±51.655	158.77±4.0891	39.213±168.38
F6	10	0±0	0±1.7744e-028	6.2292±1.2521	0±2.9801e-030
	30	0±5.6091e-031	1.5987e-014± 5.981e-018	109.4±40.833	6.2172e-012± 1.2733e-023
	100	2.8599e-013± 1.3782e-024	0.00024386± 0.0047854	720.05±569.89	0.0009424± 0.0433396
F7	10	1±0.44444	1±0.23333	34.066±15.034	8.8818e-015± 2.1778
	30	9±11.556	25±367.34	291.79±184.2	50±1154.2
	100	67±415.4	101±3534.8	1431.5±1718.3	424.25±6507.7
F8	10	4150.3±9.1909e-026	4150.4±2.6164e-017	4150.8± 0.001993	4151.1±0.011978
	30	12451±9.8048e-022	12451± 0.0010138	12456±0.21194	12454±0.13615
	100	41504±2.4793e-005	41538±210.68	41545±2.1434	41519±1.5792

7 Result

In this paper, we introduced the *FCPSO − H* as a solution to overcome the weakness of the PSO algorithm. The *FCPSO − H* algorithm uses the cooperative learning method to overcome the curse of dimensionality. We proposed a fuzzy logic-based system to tune adaptively the acceleration coefficient.

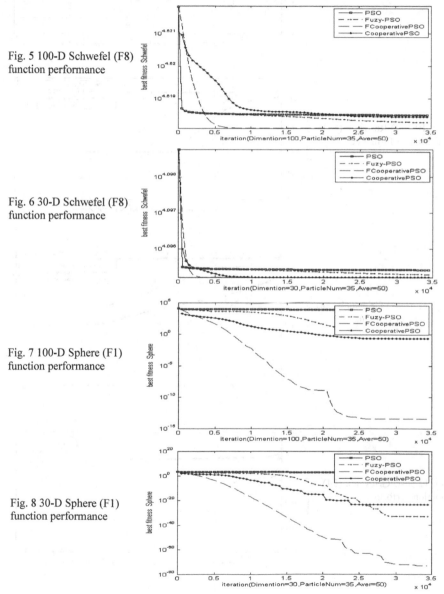

Fig. 5 100-D Schwefel (F8) function performance

Fig. 6 30-D Schwefel (F8) function performance

Fig. 7 100-D Sphere (F1) function performance

Fig. 8 30-D Sphere (F1) function performance

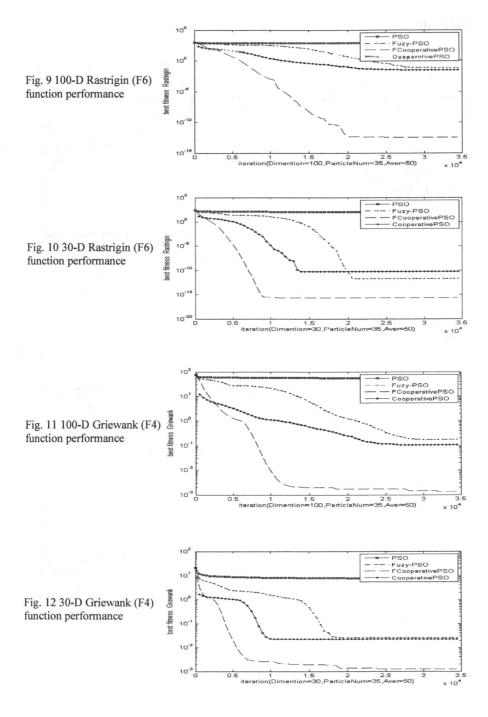

Fig. 9 100-D Rastrigin (F6)
function performance

Fig. 10 30-D Rastrigin (F6)
function performance

Fig. 11 100-D Griewank (F4)
function performance

Fig. 12 30-D Griewank (F4)
function performance

Tuning these coefficients adaptively can control balance between global search and local search. Moreover can make the particle continue moving and maintain the diversity of the population until the algorithm converges. Then we designed the fuzzy system with two variables as inputs and single-dimensional fuzzy control structure and validated the performance using eight benchmarks. The average results compared with other methods such as $CPSO - H_k$, $FPSO$ and PSO show that our proposed algorithm, $FCPSO - H$, has significant performance of convergence, especially for high dimensional functions. Further, in the view of us, the applications of fuzzy theory in PSO with intelligence characteristics can be discussed further in future and the convergence pattern can be improved to specific complex optimization functions.

References

1. Abdelbar, A.M., Adbelshahid, S., and Wunsch, D.C. (2005) 'Fuzzy PSO: A generalization of particle swarm optimization', *Proceedings of International Joint Conference on Neural Networks*, Montreal, Canada.
2. Bergh, V.B. and Engelbrecht, A.P. (2004) 'A cooperative approach to particle swarm optimization', *IEEE Transactions on Evolutionary Computation* (accepted for special issue on PSO).
3. Eberhart, R.C., Simpson, P.K, and Dobbins, R. (1996) 'Computational intelligence PC tools', *MA: Academic Press Professional*, Boston.
4. Eberhart, R.C. and Shi, Y. (1998b) 'Comparison between genetic algorithm and particle swarm optimization', In V. W.Porto, N. Saravanan, D. Waagen, and A. E. Eiben, Eds. Evolutionary Programming VII:Proc. *7th Ann. Conf. on Evolutionary Programming Conf,* San Diego, CA.Berlin: Springer-Verlag.
5. Friedman, M. and Savage, S.L. (1947) 'Planning experiments seeking minima', *In Selected Techniques of Statistical Analysis for Scientific and Industrial Research, and Production and Management Engineering*, C. Eisenhart, M. W. Hastay, and W. A. Wallis, Eds. New York: McGraw-Hill, pp. 363–372.
6. Kang, Q., Wang, L. and Wu, Q. (2006) 'Research on fuzzy adaptive optimization strategy of particle swarm algorithm', *International Journal of Information Technology*, Vol. 12, No.3.
7. Kennedy, J. and Eberhart, R.C. (1995) 'Particle swarm optimization', *Processing's of IEEE International Conference on Neural Networks (ICNN)*, Australia, pp. 1942-1948.
8. Kennedy, J., Eberhart, R.C. and Shi, Y. (2001) 'Swarm intelligence', Morgan Kaufmann.
9. Kennedy, J. and Mendes, R. (2002) 'Population structure and particle swarm performance', *Proceeding of the 2002 Congress on Evolutionary Computation*, Honolulu, Hawaii.
10. Liu, H., Abraham, A. and Zhang, W. (2007) 'Fuzzy adaptive turbulent particle swarm optimization', *Int. J. Innovative Computing and Application*, Vol. 1, No. 1.
11. Liu, H. and Abraham, A. (2007) 'A hybrid fuzzy variable neighbourhood particle swarm optimization algorithm for solving quadratic assignment problems', *Journal of Universal Computer Science*, Vol. 13, No. 7, pp. 1032-1054.
12. Niu, B., Zhu, Y., He, X., Shen, H. (2007) 'A multi-swarm optimizer based fuzzy modelling approach for dynamics systems', *Elsevier Science Publishers, ISSN*, Vol. 71, pp. 1436-1448.
13. Noroozibeyrami, M.H. and Meybodi, M.R. (2008a) 'Cooperative fuzzy particle swarm optimization', *Proceedings of the 2nd Joint Congress on Fuzzy and Intelligent Systems*, Malek Ashtar University of Technology, Tehran, Iran.

14. Noroozibeyrami, M.H. and Meybodi, M.R. (2008b) 'Improving particle swarm optimization using fuzzy logic', *Proceedings of the Second Iranian Data Mining Conference*, Amir Kabir University of Technology, Tehran, Iran.
15. Rantaweera, A., Halgamuge, S.K. and Watson, H.C. (2004) 'Self-organizing hierarchical particle swarm optimizer with time varying accelerating Coefficients', *IEEE Transactions on Evolutionary Computation* (accepted for special issue on PSO).
16. Shi, Y. and Eberhart, R.C. (1998a) 'Parameter selection in particle swarm optimization', *Proceedings of the 1998 Annual Conference on Evolutionary Computation*.
17. Shi, Y. and Eberhart, R.C. (1998b) 'A modified particle swarm optimizer', *Proceedings of the 1998 IEEE International Conference on Evolutionary Computation*, 69-73. Piscataway, NJ: IEEE Press.
18. Shi, Y. and Eberhart, R.C. (2001) 'Fuzzy adaptive particle swarm optimization', *Proceedings Congress on Evolutionary Computation 2001*, Seoul, Korea. Piscataway, NJ: IEEE Service Center.
19. Southwell, R.V. (1946) 'Relaxation methods in theoretical physics', *Oxford, U.K: Clarendon Press*.
20. Zahiri, S.H. and Seyedin, S.A. (2007) 'Swarm intelligence based classifiers', *Journal of the Franklin Institute 344*, pp. 362–376.

Context-sensitive Plan Execution Language for Adaptive Robot Behaviour

Herwig Moser, Toni Reichelt, Norbert Oswald and Stefan Förster

Abstract Faced with the growing complexity of application scenarios for autonomous robots, context-awareness and adaptivity are becoming more and more essential abilities to determine environmental circumstances and to adapt to them accordingly. While semantic technologies are widely used for the modelling of a robot's context, purposive robot behaviour is typically described using plan or plan execution languages which lack explicit semantics for context representations. Context-sensitive adaptive behaviour emerges from the whole transformation process though, from context-awareness to the subsequent execution of associated plans. This comprehensive view of adaptivity lacks sufficient treatment in the field of robotics. Addressing this issue, we have augmented the expressive plan execution language PLEXIL, allowing complex context expressions as Description Logic queries to form an integral part of constructs that define sophisticated behavioural reactions. To demonstrate the symbiosis of context-awareness and plan execution, the enhanced language PLEXIL-DL is employed in the avionics system for a reconnaissance mission of an Unmanned Air Vehicle.

1 Introduction

Robotics systems which operate in environments requiring a high degree of autonomy have to perpetually monitor their surroundings and adapt to situations which have an influence on their objectives and current or future tasks. The notion

Herwig Moser
University of Stuttgart, Germany, e-mail: herwig.moser@ipvs.uni-stuttgart.de

Toni Reichelt
Chemnitz University of Technology, Germany, e-mail: tonr@hrz.tu-chemnitz.de

Norbert Oswald, Stefan Förster
EADS Military Air Systems, Germany,
e-mail: {norbert.oswald, stefan.foerster}@eads.com

M. Bramer et al. (eds.), *Research and Development in Intelligent Systems XXVI*,
DOI 10.1007/978-1-84882-983-1_17, © Springer-Verlag London Limited 2010

of *context* is often used to describe the particular information that "characterises the situation of an entity" [6]. Conformant with other definitions of context (e.g., [11, 14, 5, 18, 25]), we will briefly define it here as the set of *relevant* information, necessary to gain an understanding of a situation. Having *Context-awareness* (*CA*) is a necessary prerequisite for deciding on the appropriate response to emerging situations.

The last decade has seen a surge in research in the area of CA, to a great extent coming from the mobile devices and ubiquitous computing sector (see [3, 12]). With the rise of Semantic Web technologies, ontologies in particular, *Description Logics* (*DLs*)-based knowledge representation got a boost from the research community [1]. DLs, with the standardised representation language *Web Ontology Language* (*OWL*) for some of its dialects, quickly got adopted by researchers in the context modelling field (e.g., [13, 24, 8]). Its power lies in the well developed subsumption reasoning which is exploited to perform inferences over collected context information, yielding a deeper understanding by discovery of implicit relations in instance data (often referred to as *higher level context*).

To be able to exploit context knowledge it is not sufficient to merely be "aware", but to actively translate awareness into action. In the field of robotics, action usually constitutes the execution of plans represented using plan or plan execution languages (e.g., [4]). While there exists work dealing with the integration of DLs into planning formalisms (see [10] and most notably [19]), the emphasis is on augmenting planning domain descriptions and associated planning algorithms for the benefit of higher expressiveness but not with context or CA in mind. The necessary focus from the CA perspective though lies on plan execution and monitoring. Existing *plan execution languages* [23] thus lack an explicit semantics for context representations.

Adaptive behaviour in the face of a dynamic environment though requires a context-sensitive plan execution, as adaptivity emerges from the entire transformation process: from attaining context-awareness through appropriate environment models to the subsequent execution of plans associated with particular situations. Such a comprehensive view of adaptivity, by exactly defining the association between context and plan, currently lacks sufficient treatment in the field of robotics.

We address this issue by augmenting the syntax and semantics of NASA's expressive *Plan Execution Interchange Language* (*PLEXIL*) such that CA, achieved through *DLs* context models, forms an *integral* part of the language. Based on the formal framework in [7], we integrated DL queries [21] into the language syntax and semantics and provide a software run-time capable of executing the extended language, called *PLEXIL-DL*. To demonstrate context-sensitive plan execution in practice, PLEXIL-DL is employed in the avionics system for a reconnaissance mission of an Unmanned Air Vehicle.

2 Description Logics

Description Logics denote a family of expressive knowledge representation formalisms. It has gained in attention in recent years, due to its use as the basis for the *Web Ontology Language (OWL)* [1] but also has found use in CA research as a way to represent context and exploit the power of DL subsumption reasoning [13].

The field of DLs offers an extensive body of research (see [1]), providing a thorough understanding of the complexity of reasoning and a wide range of tools for the processing of DLs-based representations. The design of DLs is such that the language constructs stay within a decidable fragment of *First-Order-Logic (FOL)*. *Conceptual Graphs (CG)* [20], which are often compared to DLs as an alternative FOL-based knowledge representation formalism, is undecidable for subsumption reasoning, the prime application of DLs inference. Less expressive fragments of CG have been developed, see [2], which do possess decidability but in turn can be mapped to fragments of DL offering the same expressiveness. With the availability of ontology modelling tools like Protégé[1], the intuitive graphical notation of CG also became available for DLs-based editors.

DLs describes domain knowledge in terms of a *Knowledge Base (KB)* K, which consists of a *TBox* T and an *ABox* A. While T describes general properties of domains, defining the relations between *concepts*, A contains statements about concrete instances of concepts, called *individuals*. Note that the assertions in A may change over time, reflecting newly gained knowledge. Example 1 presents a small KB, where I_K denotes the set of individuals present in K.

Example 1 (Knowledge Base). *Let* K *consist of the tuple* (T, A), *with*

$$T = \{Obstacle \equiv PhysicalObject \sqcap \exists crosses.Path\} \ and$$
$$A = \{PhysicalObject(o), Path(p), crosses(o, p)\}.$$

T *defines the* Obstacle *concept to be any* PhysicalObject *that crosses some* Path. A *asserts that the individual* o *is a* PhysicalObject *and that it crosses* p *which is a* Path. *Accordingly,* $I_K = \{o, p\}$.

We will briefly present the notion of *conjunctive ABox queries*, referred to as DLs queries in this paper, see [21] for details. A conjunctive ABox query Q consists of conjunctions of DL concept and role membership expressions, of the form $C(a)$ and $R(a, b)$, where a, b can either be individual names or existentially quantified variables. Query satisfaction by K is denoted as $K \models Q$. The expression $\langle x_1, \ldots, x_n \rangle \leftarrow Q$ denotes that the *distinguished* variables $x_1, \ldots, x_n$ occurring in Q must be bound to individual names, forming the query answer. The *answer set* of a query Q is the set of n-ary tuples such that $\{\langle a_1, \ldots, a_n \rangle \in I_K^n \mid K \models Q[x_1/a_1, \ldots, x_n/a_n]\}$, where $Q[x_i/a_i]$ represents the query Q, where every occurrence of distinguished variable x_i is substituted by the individual name a_i. We will denote the answer set of Q w.r.t. K as $\text{answer}_K(Q)$.

---

[1] http://protege.stanford.edu/

```
HandleObstacle:
{
  StartCondition: LookupOnChange(ObstacleSensor_obstacleInPath) == True;
  PreCondition: LookupNow(FuelGauge) - evasionCost > fuelThreshold,
  Command: evade();
}
```

Listing 1 Example of a PLEXIL node.

Example 2 (Query). *Let* K *be the KB of Example 1. Let* $Q = Obstacle(x)$ *be a query asking for Obstacles, where x is a distinguished variable such that* $\langle x \rangle \leftarrow Q$. *Then* $\mathsf{answer}_K(Q) = \{\langle o \rangle\}$ *because* $K \models Q[x/o]$.

3 PLEXIL

PLEXIL is a "high-level plan execution language" [7], where plans represent the output of an automated or mixed-initiative planning process [22]. The following will briefly introduce the main tenets of PLEXIL which are relevant for PLEXIL-DL, the full language specification can be found in [16].

PLEXIL plans are structured using so called *nodes*, each specifying exactly, using *node conditions*, what internal and external states must hold at the time of the first evaluation or at some point in the future for it to begin, repeat or finish execution. External conditions can be queried using so called *lookup* operations. Lookups in node conditions thus cause nodes to respond to environmental circumstances. PLEXIL differentiates between two kinds of basic lookup operations, `LookupNow` and `LookupOnChange`[2]. The former performs an immediate lookup, while the latter performs a `LookupNow` operation and if the returned value does not satisfy the overall condition, passively waits for an *event* before re-evaluating. An arbitrary number of changes may happen before an event occurs, triggered at the discretion of the plan execution software.

Besides conditions, nodes also possess a *body* which specifies the actual activity to perform when called into action. A node body may either constitute other (child) nodes, represent basic blocks of computation or invoke external functionality. The latter kind of node, called *command* node, is useful to make existing (legacy) code available to the plan.

Listing 1 shows a PLEXIL node which becomes active as soon as an obstacle is in the path, under the precondition that there is enough fuel to perform an evasive maneuver. Notice how the lookup opertion refers to symbolic names of external states, `ObstacleSensor_obstacleInPath` and `FuelGauge`.

---

[2] A third, `LookupWithFrequency`, is not considered as it is defined in terms of repeated `LookupNow` invocations.

3.1 Semantics

In this section we present an excerpt of a formal semantics of PLEXIL, described in [7], being relevant to our DL extension.

3.1.1 External World State

Let the external world state be represented by Σ, such that it contains a set of associations $\langle X = v \rangle$, where X is an external state variable name and v its value. A local copy of Σ, denoted Γ, is held by a plan and updated from Σ upon an external event and thus may not contain the same *values* as Σ in-between updates. Σ and Γ are termed *environments* and assumed to be functional, i.e., if $\langle X = v \rangle$ and $\langle X = w \rangle$ are both in one environment then $x = w$. A PLEXIL plan only has access to Γ when evaluating lookup operations. PLEXIL supports a limited number of possible value domains for external variables: integers, floats, ternary truth values and character strings [16].

3.1.2 Execution Semantics

A plan executes in discrete steps referred to as *macro steps*, which are triggered upon external events. Incoming events are processed in order of their reception and only one event is taken care of at a time. The processing of an event and *all its cascading effects* proceeds until *quiescence*, i.e., no more node state transitions are enabled [16]. This is referred to as *run-to-completion* semantics [7].

Macro steps are modelled using a so called *macro relation*. We present only that part of the macro relation definition which is relevant for our extension (cf. [7]). The occurrence of an external event is indicated by the abstract $\texttt{event}?(\Sigma_i, \Gamma, \pi)$ predicate, where π is the internal state of the PLEXIL plan and Σ_i the external environment before the i-th macro step iteration. In case of an event, the macro relation is defined to transfer the values of Σ_i to the local environment Γ, denoted Γ' after the update, and triggers a quiescence cycle. Equation (1) defines this transfer process.

$$\Gamma' = \begin{cases} \Sigma_i & \text{if } \texttt{event}?(\Sigma_i, \Gamma, \pi) \\ \Gamma & \text{otherwise} \end{cases} \tag{1}$$

4 PLEXIL-DL

We extend the PLEXIL syntax and semantics by allowing DLs queries to appear in lookup expressions, making node execution contingent on query results. The extensions of the environment Σ and its transfer to Γ forms the core of PLEXIL-DL semantics. Whereas in [7], Σ is defined as a set of native PLEXIL values and their associated identifier, we extend the set of identifiers to also represent DLs queries and the values to be corresponding query results. Since we preserve PLEXIL operator semantics, results of query expressions ultimately need to yield a value compatible with the PLEXIL type system.

4.1 Semantics

4.1.1 Extended External World State

Let Σ_Q represent that part of the external environment, such that for all associations $\langle \chi = v \rangle \in \Sigma_Q$, χ is interpreted as a DLs query and v its answer set, i.e., $v = \text{answer}_K(\chi)$ w.r.t. K (see Section 2). Revisions in K which affect $\text{answer}_K(\chi)$ are assumed to be directly reflected in Σ_Q. Our formalism does not rely on any concrete update mechanism but leaves it up to an implementation how these changes are propagated.

We define $\Sigma_{DL} = \Sigma \cup \Sigma_Q$ to represent the extended environment, thus including the native environment Σ. Figure 1 illustrates the extended environment Σ_{DL} and also shows the connection between the n-tuples of individuals in I_K, depicted using rectangles, grouped as a set of query results, depicted using circles, with the queries of Σ_Q.

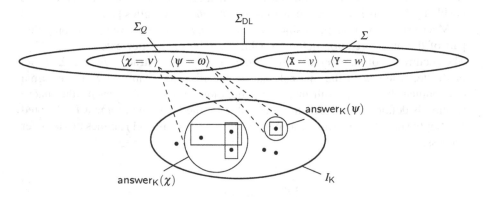

Fig. 1 Illustration of Σ_{DL} and the connection of query answers with Σ_Q.

4.1.2 Extended Execution Semantics

We have extended Equation (1), such that query results are projected to a value of one of the native PLEXIL type domains. The projection is performed by a function $\text{project}_\chi(v)$, which projects the query result v of query χ to a value of a native PLEXIL type. The definition of $\text{project}_\chi(v)$, for concrete χs, is to be done by plan creators. Equation (2) defines the replacement of Equation (1) extended by the projection of query results.

$$\Gamma' = \begin{cases} \Sigma_i \cup \{\langle \chi = \text{project}_\chi(v)\rangle | \langle \chi = v\rangle \in \Sigma_{Q_i}\} & \text{if event?}(\Sigma_{\text{DL}i}, \Gamma, \pi) \\ \Gamma & \text{otherwise} \end{cases} \quad (2)$$

5 Runtime

PLEXIL plans are executed by the so called *Universal Executive (UE)*[3]. We have developed a runtime which interfaces with the UE to facilitate execution of PLEXIL-DL plans. The runtime consists of a preprocessor, an execution layer and an auxiliary DL-based *Publish/Subscribe (P/S)* system called *Information Management System (IMS)* [15]. Internally, the IMS administrates a DL KB with integrated reasoner, such that incoming publications represent KB updates which cause subscriptions to be re-evaluated for potential matches. Subscriptions are formulated as DLs queries and any changes in the query answer is propagated to subscribers. Additionally, the IMS can be queried using a request/response protocol.

5.1 Extension of Lookup Operations

PLEXIL's syntactical means to define external state variable identifiers are insufficient to provide the expressiveness required by our extensions. We thus permit to specify an escaped expression using @[as opening and]@ as closing marker, in place of an identifier.

We represent queries using *Resource Description Framework (RDF)* triples and provide a predefined set of projection functions with reserved names, such as card, which returns the cardinality of the answer set.

Listing 2 shows the adapted PLEXIL node from Listing 1, having an extended LookupOnChange expression. The RDF expression corresponds to the DLs query from Example 2 and query results are projected using the previously mentioned card function, yielding the current number of obstacles and thus prompting an ac-

---

```
HandleObstacle:
{
  StartCondition: LookupOnChange(@[query = (?x, rdf:type, Obstacle),
                                   proj  = card]@) > 0;
  PreCondition: LookupNow(FuelGauge) - evasionCost > fuelThreshold;
  Command: evade();
}
```

Listing 2 Exemplary PLEXIL-DL node.

tion as soon as at least one obstacle exists. Given K of Example 1, the environment corresponds to $\Sigma_{DL} = \{\langle \texttt{FuelGauge} = v \rangle, \langle Obstacle(x) = \{\langle o \rangle\} \rangle\}$.

In order to be able to execute such a plan using the standard UE implementation, the query statement of the extended lookup needs to be transformed into a valid state variable identifier. Let $\texttt{stateVar}(\chi) = \delta$ be an *invertible* function, which maps a query χ to a valid PLEXIL state identifier δ, applied by the aforementioned preprocessor. Let $\texttt{stateVar}^{-1}(\delta) = \chi$ be the corresponding inverse function.

5.2 System Architecture

Based on Figure 2, which contains elements of the examples and code of previous sections, we now present the system architecture of the runtime. The topmost element on the left shows a PLEXIL-DL plan file, containing the query of Listing 2, abbreviated as `qryOb`, which references an OWL ontology, shown at the top right. Before being able to execute the plan, the preprocessor, shown underneath the plan file, transforms PLEXIL-DL queries into valid PLEXIL identifiers. The preprocessor keeps track of the original expressions, exporting mapping information used later on to evaluate queries and project their results.

The UE is now able to execute the plan, which has been reduced to the native PLEXIL format. Note that the PLEXIL-DL wrapper, shown in the middle, Registers the state variable it maintains at the UE. During execution, the UE invokes callbacks for each Lookup operation it encounters, requesting the associated value from state maintainers. By using $\texttt{stateVar}^{-1}$, the wrapper is able to retrieve the original query. Depending on whether the UE requests an immediate lookup or a later notification, the wrapper submits a Query to or Subscribes at the IMS. Any answer by the IMS, via an immediate Result or by Notifying the wrapper, is projected to the PLEXIL domain and propagated to the UE. In case of a subscription notification, an external Event is triggered by the wrapper. Additional external state lookups based on the original PLEXIL semantics remain unaffected by our Wrapper

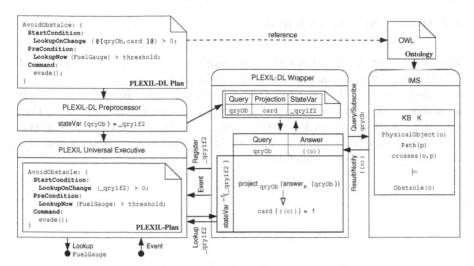

Fig. 2 Interplay of the components of the plan execution runtime.

6 Demonstration

PLEXIL-DL is being used in the mission system software of an *Unmanned Air Vehicle* (*UAV*). The runtime as presented in Section 5 forms the backbone of the avionics software by controlling all major operations. This section describes how PLEXIL-DL plans and the runtime fit into the *Service-oriented Architecture* (*SOA*) of which the mission system is built up from as well as demonstrating the context-sensitive behaviour of the UAV in a hostile environment.

6.1 Scenario Description

The UAV is sent on a reconnaissance mission to record images at certain locations. As a maintenance goal, it is to avoid hostile units which are not part of the reconnaissance task by circumventing their location. The UAV is given a preliminary flight plan as well as knowledge of known operating (hostile) units in the area. The UAV's sensors include a *Radar Warning Receiver* (*RWR*), which enable it to detect active radar emissions and the nature of the emitter.

The two core requirements, alongside other tasks, are reflected in the UAV's PLEXIL-DL plan. Specifically, there is an `TakeImage` and a `HandleObstacle` node, contingent on the UAV's reaching of certain waypoints respectively detection of obstacles in its path. The details of these nodes will be described below.

6.2 Mission System Architecture

The mission system is based on a SOA framework for unmanned systems (described in [17]). The idea being that *capabilities* of a UAV are modelled using service interfaces and implemented by respective components, transparently accessible through a suitable middleware. The components described in Section 5 and depicted in Figure 2 are actually represented as services in their own right. The UE and its proprietary Wrapper are contained in the *Mission Management System* (*MMS*) service, the IMS simply given a service interface.

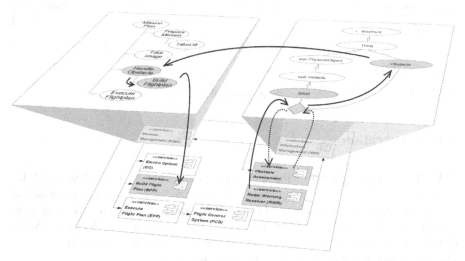

Fig. 3 The relationship between MMS, IMS and service architecture. Solid strong arrows represent the chain of causality for the "obstacle" situation.

To integrate service calls into PLEXIL-DL plans we have drawn an analogy between service methods and command nodes. Command names are interpreted as fully qualified service methods and attempted to be resolved and invoked by the PLEXIL-DL Wrapper. Figure 3 shows a snapshot of the conceptual causality relations between the various affected services for the "obstacle" situation. The lower level plane depicts the service interactions from the SOA perspective, arrows indicating control/data flow. The top level planes represent the inner workings of the MMS (left) and IMS (right) services. The curved strong arrows, originating from the RWR, follow the chain of causality from publication of a SAM site, its classification as an Obstacle with the help of the *Obstacle Assessor* (dotted arrows), the notification of the MMS to subsequent activation of the HandleObstacle node causing a replanning using the *Build Flight Plan* (*BFP*) service.

```
Class(Obstacle complete intersectionOf(
   PhysicalObject
   restriction(crosses someValuesFrom(Flightplan))))

ObjectProperty(crosses range(Flightplan))
```

Listing 3 Axioms defining an Obstaclein OWL Abstractct Syntax.

6.3 Mission Ontology

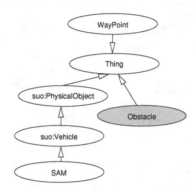

Fig. 4 An excerpt of the ontology hierarchy, with a focus on the concepts relevant for the demonstration.

The emphasis of the excerpt of the ontology shown in Figure 4 lies on the possibility to classify PhysicalObject instances as Obstacles if warranted. Specifically, the axioms in Listing 3 sufficiently define an Obstacle to be any PhysicalObject which also have some crosses restriction with some Flightplan. In that sense, an obstacle is specific to a certain flightplan which in turn may be flown by some certain air vehicle. For more details on the ontology design and its merits see [15].

6.4 Mission Execution

The code in Listing 4 is a simplified excerpt of the actual plan in use, showing how queries form a part of the conditions that enable the nodes introduced in Section 6.1. It serves to accompany the description of the various mission stages in the following table.

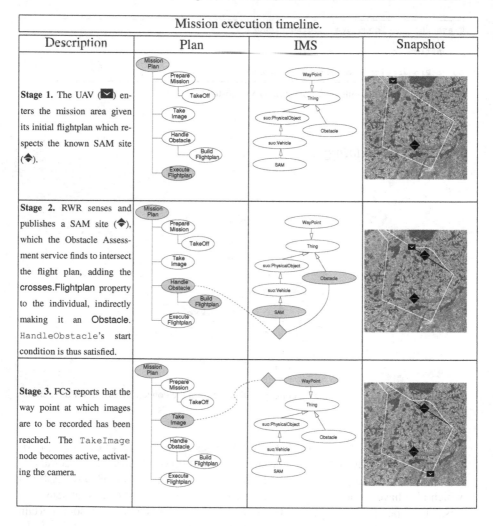

7 Conclusions and Future Work

Adaptive robot behaviour results from the synthesis of perception, comprehension, planning and execution processes. The notion of context-awareness plays a major role in this process, in that it is the prerequisite for deciding on the appropriate response to emerging situations. The presented technique in this paper constitutes a step towards realisation of such an adaptive behaviour in complex environments. Experiments deploying an unmanned aerial system within a reconnaissance mission simulation confirmed the fundamental adequacy of our approach for integrating context within plan execution.

```
ReccceMission:
{
  String flightPlanURI;
  Boolean newFlightPlan;

  TakeImage:
  {
    StartCondition: LookupOnChange(@[query = (?x, rdf:type, WayPoint) &&
                                             (?x, hasStatus, Reached),
                                      proj = exists]@) = True;
    Command: IElectroOptical.activateCamera(orientation);

  }

  HandleObstacle:
  {
    StartCondition: LookupOnChange(@[query = (?x, rdf:type, Obstacle),
                                      proj = card]@) > 0;
    EndCondition: isKnown(flightPlanURI);
    RepeatCondition: true;
    NodeList:
      BuildFlightPlan:
      {
        Command: flightPlanURI =
          IBuildFlighPlan.buildFlightPlan(
            LookupNow(@[query = (?x, rdf:type, Obstacle), proj = flatten]@);
      }
  }
}
```

Listing 4 PLEXIL-DL excerpt of UAV's mission plan.

Based on NASA's plan execution language PLEXIL to express a robot's plans, we make use of the Description Logic formalism to represent context models, exploiting DLs queries to retrieve the current context held in a DL Knowledge Base. Accordingly, we have extended the PLEXIL syntax and semantics by integrating DLs queries to form an integral part of those language features that express conditional actions, unifying context-awareness and sentient reactions to form adaptive robot behaviour.

Future work will deal with the update semantics of the backing KB and the implications for the PLEXIL-DL execution semantics. Especially the relationship between query results, i.e., the answer set, and the projection function warrant further investigation. For instance, the answer set may be interpreted to only contain the relevant KB changes instead of the set of all individuals satisfying the query. The advantages and disadvantages for either case depend on the purpose of the node but require further theoretical and practical treatment. Work in the area of believe revision for DL KBs, such as presented in [9], may need to be investigated.

References

1. Baader, F., Calvanese, D., McGuinness, D., Nardi, D., Patel-Schneider, P. (eds.): The Description Logic Handbook, 2nd edn. Cambridge University Press (2007)
2. Baader, F., Molitor, R., Tobies, S.: Tractable and decidable fragments of conceptual graphs. In: 7th International Conference on Conceptual Structures, pp. 480–493. Springer, London, UK (1999)
3. Baldauf, M., Dustdar, S., Rosenberg, F.: A survey on context-aware systems. Int. Journal of Ad Hoc and Ubiquitous Computing 2(4) (2007)
4. Beetz, M.: Plan-based Control of Robotic Agents, Lecture Notes in Artificial Intelligence, vol. LNAI 2554. Springer Publishers (2002)
5. Beigl, M., Krohn, A., Zimmer, T., Decker, C., Robinson, P.: Awarecon: Situation aware context communication. In: UbiComp 2003, pp. 132–139. Springer (2003)
6. Dey, A.K.: Understanding and using context. Personal and Ubiquitous Computing 5(1), 4–7 (2001)
7. Dowek, G., Muñoz, C., Pâsâreanu, C.S.: A formal analysis framework for plexil. In: 3rd Workshop on Planning and Plan Exec. for Real-World Sys. (2007)
8. Ejigu, D., Scuturici, M., Brunie, L.: An ontology-based approach to context modeling and reasoning in pervasive computing. In: Conference on Pervasive Computing and Communications Workshops. IEEE, IEEE (2007)
9. Flouris, G.: On belief change and ontology evolution. Ph.D. thesis, University Of Crete (2006)
10. Gil, Y.: Description logics and planning. AI Magazine 26(2) (2005)
11. Hong, C.S., Kim, H.S., Cho, J., Cho, H.K., Lee, H.C.: Context modeling and reasoning approach in context-aware middleware for urc system. Proc. of World Academy of Science, Engineering and Technology 26 (2007)
12. Kjær, K.E.: A survey of context-aware middleware. In: SE'07: Proc. of the 25th conference on IASTED Int. Multi-Conf. ACTA Press (2007)
13. Krummenacher, R., Strang, T.: Ontology-based context modeling. In: Proc. of the 3rd Workshop on Context Awareness for Proactive Systems (2007)
14. Meissen, U., Pfenningschmidt, S., Voisard, A., Wahnfried, T.: Context- and situation-awareness in information logistics. In: Workshop in Pervasive Information Management held in conjunction with EDBT (2004)
15. Moser, H., Reichelt, T., Oswald, N., Förster, S.: Information management for unmanned systems: Combining DL-reasoning with publish/subscribe. In: Proc. of SGAI 2008. Springer (2008)
16. NASA: PLEXIL Reference Manual. NASA (2008)
17. Oswald, N., Windisch, A., Förster, S., Moser, H., Reichelt, T.: A service-oriented framework for manned and unmanned systems to support network-centric operations. In: J. Zaytoon, J.L. Ferrier, J. Andrade-Cetto, J. Filipe (eds.) ICINCO-ICSO, pp. 284–291. INSTICC Press (2007)
18. Schmidt, A., Beigl, M., Gellersen, H.W.: There is more to context than location. Computers & Graphics Journal 23(6), 893–902 (1999)
19. Sirin, E.: Combining description logic reasoning with ai planning for composition of web services. Ph.D. thesis, University of Maryland (2006)
20. Sowa, J.F.: Conceptual Structures. Addison-Wesley (1984)
21. Tessaris, S.: Questions and answers: Reasoning and querying in description logic. Ph.D. thesis, Univ. of Manchester (2001)
22. Verma, V., Jónsson, A., Passareanu, C., Iatauro, M.: Universal executive and PLEXIL: Engine and language for robust spacecraft control and operations. In: Proc. of AIAA Space (2006)
23. Verma, V., Jónsson, A., Simmons, R., Estlin, T., Levinson, R.: Survey of command execution systems for nasa spacecraft and robots. In: Plan Execution: A Reality Check Workshop at ICAPS (2005)
24. Wang, X.H., Zhang, D.Q., Gu, T., Pung, H.K.: Ontology based context modeling and reasoning using owl. In: Pervasive Computing and Communications Workshops. IEEE (2004)
25. Yau, S.S., Liu, J.: Hierarchical situation modeling and reasoning for pervasive computing. In: SEUS-WCCIA, pp. 5–10. IEEE (2006)

KNOWLEDGE ACQUISITION AND EVOLUTIONARY COMPUTATION

Explaining How to Play Real-Time Strategy Games

Ronald Metoyer, Simone Stumpf, Christoph Neumann, Jonathan Dodge, Jill Cao, and Aaron Schnabel

Abstract Real-time strategy games share many aspects with real situations in domains such as battle planning, air traffic control, and emergency response team management which makes them appealing test-beds for Artificial Intelligence (AI) and machine learning. End user annotations could help to provide supplemental information for learning algorithms, especially when training data is sparse. This paper presents a formative study to uncover how experienced users explain game play in real-time strategy games. We report the results of our analysis of explanations and discuss their characteristics that could support the design of systems for use by experienced real-time strategy game users in specifying or annotating strategy-oriented behavior.

1 Introduction

Artificial Intelligence (AI) research has shifted focus in recent years from board games such as Chess or Go to real-time strategy (RTS) games, such as that shown in Figure 1, as test-beds for learning complex behavior. RTS games are typically carried out in a two-dimensional world in which multiple players concurrently compete for resources, build armies, and guide them into battle. Winning the game necessitates executing a strategy by placing game-playing units in a spatial environment and giving them tasks to do at the right time. RTS games are particularly appealing to AI because of the many levels of complexity involved in the game play, such

Ronald Metoyer, Simone Stumpf, Jonathan Dodge and Jill Cao
Oregon State University, Corvallis, OR 97331, metoyer|stumpf|dodge|caoch@eecs.oregonstate.edu

Christoph Neumann
Hewlett Packard, Corvallis, OR 97330, christoph.neumann@hp.com

Aaron Schnabel
9Wood, Inc., Springfield, OR 97477, schnabel@9wood.com

M. Bramer et al. (eds.), *Research and Development in Intelligent Systems XXVI*,
DOI 10.1007/978-1-84882-983-1_18, © Springer-Verlag London Limited 2010

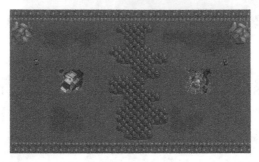

Fig. 1 Our customized version of the "Nowhere to Run, Nowhere to Hide" map for the real-time strategy game, Wargus.

as resource management, decision-making under uncertainty, spatial and temporal reasoning, adversarial reasoning, etc. [3]. Such challenges are also present in many other domains that require strategy execution, including air traffic control, emergency response management, and battle planning.

The typical approach has been to learn behavior from many instances of game play log data. However, this approach cannot be applied if there is sparse training data or if, in the extreme case, there is just a single game trace. This challenge could be overcome by allowing end users, not adept in machine learning, to inform learning algorithms about salient features and tasks by supplementing the game trace with explanatory annotations or demonstration. Facilitating additional user feedback to learning algorithms has been shown to produce improvement to learning in other domains [21].

Expert explanations could be used in a Natural Programming approach [14] as building blocks for the design of annotation or demonstration systems. While researchers have investigated expert game play in traditional games as well as more recent action games [17], to our knowledge, there has only been limited research that has investigated the explanations of experienced players for real-time strategy games.

By studying explanations of game play, we aim to uncover a user vocabulary that includes objects, spatial aspects, and temporal constraints. We also aim to help the design of annotation and demonstration tools for machine learning systems that operate on minimal user examples by trying to understand how behavior is enacted in game play. The contributions of our research are **1)** coding schemes useful for transcripts of real-time strategy game explanations **2)** identification of the content of game play explanations **3)** identification of the structure of game play explanations and **4)** a set of design implications for real-time strategy game annotations.

In this paper, we describe a formative user study designed to understand how experienced users explain strategies and game play. We begin by discussing the related literature and then describe our experimental design to capture explanations, including our methodology for coding the data. We present the results of our analysis and discuss the trends and characteristics of the explanations and how this information may be used to inform the design of end-user programming environments for agent behavior as well as for annotating strategy for machine learning systems.

2 Related Work

While the machine learning and AI communities have focused on real-time strategy games as a domain of interest for several years, to our knowledge, none of the research has attempted to understand how *people* describe their strategies. Instead, much of the literature in these areas is concerned with identifying a language for representing problems and solutions in complex learning and planning domains, such as *Wargus*[2]. Ponsen et al., for example, incorporate knowledge into their AI algorithms by hand coding domain knowledge for planning within the *Wargus* domain [15, 22]. Rather than finding a representation for *machines* to use for learning, we are interested in finding a language or representation for *people* to use for demonstrating or annotating behavior for a machine.

Notations for specifying behavior can be found in the end-user agent programming domain which has applications in many fields including robotics, video games, and education. Agent programming approaches generally fall under either *direct programming approaches* or *programming by demonstration*. In the direct programming case, some research has addressed the challenge of programming agent behavior by developing specialized APIs or code construction environments to support novice's use of a general purpose programming language. For example, the RoboCode project [12] allows a student to use and extend a Java API to define the behavior of a virtual tank within a 2D simulated environment. Alice [5] employs techniques such as drag-and-drop construction and live method execution to assist the user in programming agents with an object-oriented textual notation. In a similar fashion, Agentsheets [18] supports end-user programming of agents by using an object oriented notation that is augmented by fill-in forms and live execution within an environment that emphasizes the use of a 2D grid as a means to organize the simulation space [7]. Whereas these approaches focus on reducing fundamental challenges associated with general purpose programming languages, the focus of our experiment is to inform a notation which is grounded in the language of end users of a RTS game.

Programming by demonstration (PBD) systems have been shown to lower barriers to programming agents by allowing the user to simply demonstrate the proper behavior. Examples of such an approach are KidSim [20] and ToonTalk [8]. As noted by Modugno et al. [13] and Repenning [19], PBD still requires a notation to allow for editing and high-level specification and the form of that notation can affect the effectiveness of the PBD system.

3 Experiment Design

In order to explore how behavior is explained by users in real-time strategy games, our formative study followed a dialogue-based think-aloud design, in which we paired an experienced user with a novice to help elicit explanations of game play. The experienced user was asked to play the game while at the same time explaining what he was doing. The novice was able to observe the experienced user and ask for clarifications when necessary.

The dialogue-based think-aloud setup allows reasoning to be made explicit as explanations are given in a natural, interactive way through typical social communication with their partners. As an experienced user showed the novice how to play the game, he was able to draw attention to what mattered and to justify his actions in the context of situations as they arose. In response, novices were able to ask questions that clarified the experienced users' actions or explanations, drawing out additional details that may have otherwise been unclear.

We chose *Wargus* as the RTS environment for our study. *Wargus* [2], and its commercial equivalent *Warcraft II*, allows users to command orcs or humans in a medieval world that pits the player in battle against opposing factions. We used a contained battle scenario shown in Figure 1 where the computer controlled the opponent. In this simple map, the player starts off on one side of a barrier of trees that separates him or her from the enemy. There are a variety of ways that enable a player to play this scenario and overcome the enemy but the game is simple enough to be completed within a reasonable time.

Ten students participated in this study and were compensated for their time. Participants were assigned roles as experienced users and novices based on their experience with *Wargus* or *Warcraft II*. Participants with more than 20 hours of experience were considered experienced users, while novices had less than 2 hours of experience. Experienced users and novices were then randomly paired. Overall, the participants were made up of nine males and one female with an average age of 22.8 years. Experienced users consisted of five males, average age of 20.2 years, and novices were four males and one female, average age of 25.4 years.

The study session began after a brief paper tutorial, in which the participants were familiarized with units, resources, and basic game-playing instructions. The experienced users were asked to play the game while "thinking aloud" about what they were doing. The novices were instructed to ask the experienced users about any detail they did not understand. Each experiment session lasted approximately 35 minutes, during which two games were played by the experienced user. We used the *Morae* [1] system to record the screen as the game was played, and to record the interaction between experienced users and novices. All screen, video and audio data was automatically synchronized. After the session, we captured background and demographic information in the post-session questionnaire in addition to subjective evaluations and comments about game play during the study.

4 Methodology

In order to analyze the think-aloud data, we used content analysis to develop coding schemes for describing and understanding how game play is communicated [10]. We developed two sets of codes: the first set captures the *content* of explanations

Table 1 Content Coding Scheme

Code	Subcode	Description	Example
Object	Enemy Object	Important objects that are under the control of the opposing player	*"they* have no more *peons"*
	Fighting Object	Units that are used for fighting	"my *archers"*
	Production Object	Units that are involved in producing resources/are resources	"I'm building a *town hall"*
	Environmental Object	Object that is part of the game environment, not under the direct control of the game players	"I wanna not cut down those *trees*
	Unspecified Object	Player refers to an object indiscriminately.	"my *guys* here"
Action	Building / Producing	When the action described in the statement refers to building or producing things	"I'm going to build a farm"
	Fighting	When the action described in the sentence refers to fighting	"and you only attack one guy at a time"
Quantity	Unidentified Discrete	A reference to object quantity but vague amount	*"armies* of peasants are good"
	Identified Discrete	Reference to object quantity with a specific amount stated	"I want *a barracks"*
	Comparative	Reference to object quantity in comparison to an (sometimes unspecified) reference point	"we need *more* farms"
	Absolute	Reference to quantity extremes	"I went in and killed *all* their grunts"
Temporal	Ordering	Referring to the sequence in which things have to happen	"They'll tend to attack military units *before* peons"
	Timing	Referring to an absolute time	"Are those trees *now* wide enough to go through?"
	Speed	Referring to the speed at which things have to happen	"Be *really fast* in the early game"
	Repetition	how often things have to happen	"do that *again"*
Spatial	Distance	a relative distance between two objects (e.g. close to, away from)	"I'm trying to keep my archers *away* from fighting"
	Point	A specific place	"Is that a hole right *there"*
	Size	Absolute reference to an object's length or space	"Let's have them chop where the gap is *kind of big"*
	Arrangement	Specific spatial arrangement of objects	"and if you can get some archers *along the border* killing their peons"

(Table 1) while the second captures the *structure* of explanations (Table 2). We now describe our code development process in more detail.

In order to facilitate analysis, the audio of the experienced user and novice interactions was transcribed, and supplemented with time codes and information about game actions and gestures. Transcripts then were broken up into coding units. In

Table 2 Structure Coding Scheme

Code	Description	Example
Fact	A statement or opinion about how the world works, a current event, or a future outcome.	"farms supply food"
Depend	Language that reflects a dependency of one thing on another or a constraining fact. A statement that reflects a forced or enabled course of action due to a limiting or satisfied constraint.	"building archers requires wood"
Do	Prescriptive instructions on how to behave, in particular, talk about manipulating concrete things and taking concrete actions	"Build a farm"
Goal	A statement of intent or desired achievement that is non-specific about means or actions.	"Block them from reaching your ranged units"
History	A statement that describes an action or event that has already occurred in the past.	"They had ranged units and I didn't"
Mistake	A statement that negatively describes an action or event that has occurred in the past.	"It would have been good if I had gotten archers early on"
Question	A statement where further clarification is requested.	"Are those trees now wide enough to go through?"
UI	A statement that refers to software-specific features	"Control-1 just makes them group 1"

our approach, each sentence a participant uttered was segmented into one or more units. Sentences were broken up at coordinating conjunction (e.g. 'and', 'or') or subordinating conjunction (e.g. 'because', 'since'). Sentences were left intact if they contained correlative conjunctions (e.g. 'either…or', 'if…then').

Previous research has not provided any coding schemes applicable to our investigation. In order to develop coding schemes suitable to our aims, we employed an affinity diagramming approach to develop codes by examining random transcript sub-portions in a team setting [6]. After initial identification of candidate codes, we refined them iteratively and tested the reliability and coverage of coding application. In the refinement process, a candidate coding scheme included definitions of potential codes and corresponding examples from the transcripts. The candidate codes were applied independently by researchers to a randomly chosen transcript section and agreement measures were calculated. Any codes that proved difficult to apply were further refined and integrated into a revised candidate coding, which was in turn applied to a new random transcription section. Once sufficient agreement between the coders was reached, the remaining transcripts were coded by individual researchers.

Agreement measures are useful in developing codes that provide coverage of the area under investigation, and that can be consistently and reliably applied by different researchers [4, 16]. For the first coding scheme, the content codes, multiple codes could be applied to the same unit, making standard Kappa unsuitable as an agreement measure. We therefore calculated agreement between researchers using the Jaccard index, which is the intersection of two researchers' codes divided by the size of their union. We reached an overall code agreement of 80.12% for the content coding scheme.

For the second coding scheme, the structure codes, we used a slightly modified process to account for three raters using mutually exclusive codes. We calculated agreement in two different ways. We first calculated a simple agreement measure by using the proportion of actual agreements over possible agreements, applied pairwise between all three researchers; the average agreement over three researchers for the structure code set was 83.44%. We also calculated Fleiss' Kappa for this code set, which was 0.69 (agreement over 0.61 is usually considered substantial [11]).

5 Results and Discussion

One of our contributions is the development of two coding schemes that allow the structure and content of explanations to be explored within the realm of real-time strategy games (see Tables 1 and 2). These coding schemes could also be re-used or adapted for other domains that feature dynamically changing environments with spatial and temporal constraints.

5.1 *What Concepts are used in Explanations*

Understanding the content of user explanations can help in identifying concepts that an annotation language or demonstration system should cover. We analyzed the content codes (Figure 2) to understand what aspects were frequently mentioned in RTS explanations.

References to *Objects* (sometimes called entities) of the game environment occur most frequently (72.1%). Not surprisingly, participants talked most frequently about their own units (e.g. such as *Production* and *Fighting* units) but objects relating to

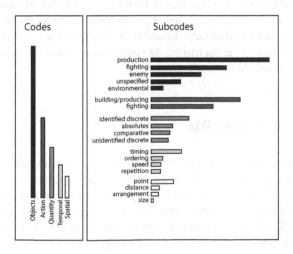

Fig. 2 Frequency of content code occurrences over all transcripts.

the *Enemy* are referenced very often (15%). This indicates that an important aspect of game play is monitoring the activity of one's opponent.

Spatial and temporal aspects of game play are important areas for learning. One challenge may be that explanations could be too vague or too infrequent to be able to generate good examples from which to learn. Surprisingly, we found that experienced players expressed *Spatial*, *Temporal*, and *Quantity* concepts frequently throughout the game, in 11.4%, 19.5%, and 28.9% of the coded units respectively. Participants were also very specific about these concepts. *Spatial* concepts occurred mostly in terms of *Point* specific locations (7.2%) such as "here" or "at the farm", *Temporal* concepts occurred most often as *Timing* statements (9.8%), such as "now" or "at the end" while participants often described a specific *Identified* discrete quantity (12.1%) or *Absolute* value (6.9%), such as "two units at a time" or "all". Even when they were not able to give a discrete quantity, they were able to give *Unidentified* values (5.5%), such as "little bit", or *Comparative* amounts (6.0%), such as "more footmen than archers". This indicates that experienced users tended to be very concrete in their explanations *while* playing the game. They were able to refer to particular numbers of objects, at particular locations, and indicated particular times at which events occurred.

Some concepts that were expressed are more abstract or complex, and may require specialized support. Some explanations referred to the spatial *arrangement* or *distance* of objects to each other in the game, while temporal constraints such as *ordering*, *speed*, or *repetition* were also mentioned.

Design implications: Users pay attention to aspects under their control as well as to aspects that are outside their realm of manipulation. Annotations need to account for monitoring of these outside factors, which may lead, in turn, to changes in future choices of actions. Any annotation or demonstration interface should account for and provide a means for specifying or choosing these specific concepts possibly through mouse pointing (point locations), time indicators for both discrete and comparative (now, early, as soon as, etc.), and a broad range of quantity selection mechanisms such as number entry for object quantities, object group selection, and selection/deselection of all objects. In addition, annotation and demonstration tools need to lend support to the user to easily specify more complex concepts that puts various objects in relation to each other.

5.2 Explaining How to Win

Choosing the right strategy and executing it correctly helps the user win the game. We investigated the structure of how experienced users explained the strategy and necessary actions. Figure 3 shows the set of structure codes and their distribution over all game transcripts. Participants mentioned *Goals* less frequently than expected (7.9%). While some participants used *Goal* codes more than others, it was surprising to us that experienced users did not provide high-level explanations of their strategy more frequently, especially considering that experienced users sum-

Fig. 3 Frequency of structure code occurrences over all transcripts. Fact occurs in 35% of the total transcript segments.

marized their strategies succinctly with general, high-level descriptions in the post-study questionnaire.

It appears that *Goal* as a high-level intent was only one way in which a strategy could be described by experienced users. In a *Do* code, an experienced player gave instructions on how to behave, focusing on specific actions in the pursuit of an intended strategy. In our study, experienced users employed *Do* more frequently than *Goals* (12.1%). Experienced users on the whole tended to explain their strategy during the interaction by using a finer granularity, in which they made detailed reference to what to do in the context of the game.

Do and *Goal* should be considered as a spectrum in which to explain strategy. While most experienced users preferred to explain strategy in terms of prescriptive instructions in pursuit of a higher level goal which is not necessarily verbalized, others tended to employ high-level descriptions of general intent instead. When these two codes (*Do* and *Goal*) are considered in combination, they made up a considerable amount of explaining of what to do to win the game (20%).

Understanding when strategy explanations occur is important in deciding when to make annotation or demonstration capabilities available. A reasonable but naive assumption would be that strategy is stated at the beginning and then enacted or decomposed into smaller tasks in the remainder of a game. In our study, strategy explanations in the form of *Do* or *Goal* were found interspersed throughout both games—even for the second game in a study session, in which participants could have omitted strategy explanations since they had already been covered previously.

Design implications: Our results show that experienced users provided many explanations of their intended behavior, but that they had a preference for choosing a certain level of granularity in which to express the strategy. Experienced users that chose high-level strategy explanations tended to provide fewer detailed, fine-grained strategies, and vice versa. The variance of users' preference for detail is an important factor to consider for notations in order to provide a match to the granularity of expression. Furthermore, notations for expressing strategy that are only available at the beginning of the game, and force decomposition in a top-down fashion, may run counter to how users prefer to explain strategy. In our study, strategy explanations were made in a situated way throughout, drawing on the surrounding context. Our findings imply that behavior annotation and/or demonstration could possibly benefit from environments that are tightly coupled to game play and that allow annotation and demonstration *within* the game context. In addition, annotation strategy behavior *within* the context of the environment should provide a means for detailed prescriptive instructions and the intent behind them while annotations outside of the environment may still benefit from a higher-level, general mechanism for specifying the strategy.

5.3 Explaining What to Notice

Actions in RTS games depend on the context in which they are enacted. What to do may draw on certain features of the situation, require constant monitoring, and may have to be adjusted based on unexpected outcomes. We were interested in how the context of game play is communicated in RTS games.

One problematic aspect of game play and the actions that a player could carry out is that there are potentially a myriad of features of the situation which could matter. How does an experienced player communicate which of these features to attend to? One such way is by statements that express *Facts*, which draw attention to certain features in the game that are important. In addition, *Depend* statements draw out constraints that need to be met in these particular features and situations.

Experienced players focused on highlighting the important features and constraints frequently. In our experiments, *Fact* and *Depend* structure codes combined occurred in 45% of the transcript (34.6% and 11.7%, respectively) (See Figure 3). We also found that *Fact* and *Depend* occurred constantly as the games proceeded.

Design implications: An interface for annotating or demonstrating strategy behavior should provide a simple and efficient means for describing the important current features in a situation. This allows a user to efficiently select important features that the behavior depends on. For demonstration or annotation for machine learning, for example, the context describes the important features that the system needs to take into consideration and feature selection is often a difficult problem in machine learning.

5.4 How Concepts Are Used in Strategy and Context

In order to complete the picture of game playing instructions, it it useful to consider what is explained and how it is explained at the same time. To do so, we computed the co-occurrence of structure codes with content codes.

To calculate co-occurrence, we counted, over all transcripts, the number of times a content code appeared in the same unit with a particular structure code. We computed the percentage of co-occurrence for each content/structure code pair by dividing the co-occurrences by the sum of the total number of times each of the two codes appeared in all transcripts. Figure 4 shows an example of the co-occurrence computation for *Enemy* and *Fact* over all transcripts.

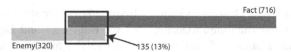

Fig. 4 Diagram demonstrating the co-occurrence calculation for *Enemy* and *Fact*.

The pattern of co-occurrence is complex but there are some patterns that occur across the codes (Figure 5). When giving explicit instructions (*Do* codes), participants talked mainly about *Production objects* and *Fighting Objects* and the act of *Producing/building* (12.6%, 9.3%, and 15.3% respectively). Addtionally, they tended to reference both *Unidentified discrete* and *Identified discrete* quantities and *Point* specific locations (8.5%, 10.5% and 9.0% respectively). This means that participants frequently gave specific instructions about 'where' to place 'how many' buildings and/or units for resource accumulation or battle. In contrast, *Goal* codes most frequently appeared with *Fighting*(9.2%), *building/producing*(6.5%), and the associated *Enemy*(6.7%) and *Fighting Objects*(6.3%). Additionally, they often mentioned *Goal* in concert with *Timing*(7.7%), *Arrangement*(6.7%), *Distance*(6.1%) codes. It appears that participants' specification of a higher-level strategy tended to be more concerned with laying out complex spatial concepts, coupled with specific temporal aspects.

Some patterns can also be discerned in explanations of what to notice. *Facts* frequently involve all *Objects* but in particular *Enemy objects*(13.0%) and *Fighting ob-*

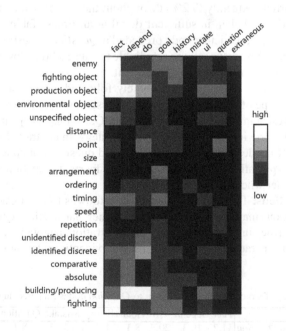

Fig. 5 The co-occurrences, over all transcripts, between structure codes and content subcodes.

jects(13.1%), whereas *Depend* codes most frequently co-occurred with *Production objects*(14.8%) and *Building/Producing*(15.3%). Both *Fact* and *Depend* also co-occur often with *Timing*(6.6% and 6.4% respectively) while *Depend* occurs more frequently with all kinds of *Quantity* references than does *Fact*. It seems that constraints on actions usually involve resource management but that constraints are not considered as much during monitoring opponents and battle planning. Additionally, constraints apparently are described in terms of the quantities necessary to achieve the strategy.

Design implications: In certain situations some aspects of the game play are more salient than others. In explaining strategy, specific instructions about what to do with objects may be easily given but more complex spatial concepts may need to be captured through annotations involving higher-level strategy. Similarly, constraints could be expressed easily for resources under one's own control but possibly are hard for complex battle situations involving opponent's resources.

5.5 When More Explanation Is Needed

Questions usually provide *explicit* requests for more information and are indications of information gaps [9]. Thus, we paid particular attention to questions that novices asked experienced users, since they indicate a breakdown in the novice's understanding.

Questions occurred frequently (9.2%) throughout the games, indicating that experienced users did not explain in sufficient detail at all times. Table 3 shows the percentage of times that a particular code preceded a *Question*. *Questions* occurred after every code, indicating that anything was liable to cause a breakdown. However, *Questions* after *Do* codes were especially frequent.

Table 3 also shows the code that immediately followed a question. This gives an indication of the type of answers that follow requests for more information. *Goal* and *Do* were not present in substantial numbers after *Questions*. It appears that experienced users did not provide answers in terms of strategy. In contrast, *Fact* (44.9%) and *Depend* (13.1%) codes most frequently followed questions. It appears that answers focused on explanations of what things were important (situation context) for the novice to consider when applying the strategy.

Design implications: The high incidence of breakdowns following actions (*Do*) indicates that notations may be useful to provide further clarification for these situations. Novel approaches in programming by demonstration, annotation, or machine learning could also generate questions that might help identify relevant information.

Table 3 The frequency of structure codes in relation to *Question* codes (in percentages)

	Fact	Depend	Do	Goal	History	Mistake	Question	UI
Code preceded *Question*	11.2	10.3	20.3	8.3	8.0	3.3	8.4	13.0
Code followed *Question*	44.9	13.1	6.5	1.9	4.2	0.5	8.4	14.0

Answers to these questions may be more likely to highlight which features to pay particular attention to.

5.6 Revisiting the Past

Some explanations do not occur concurrently with the execution. Experienced players sometimes referred to mistakes as well as present or past courses of action. Mistakes were pointed out rarely and randomly (1.9%). More frequent were references to what had gone on in the past, in the form of *History* codes (7.6%). The majority of these statements occurred at or towards the end of transcripts.

Design implications: Experienced users' mistakes and reflection on the past implies that a programming or annotating environment needs to give users the opportunity to connect observed behavior to causes of that behavior. This is in line with findings of Reeves et al. [17], who found that experts become better by reflection on their own play. It is therefore natural to assume that experienced users could explain their failures and successes by reflecting on their actions. Annotation tools should allow the user to pinpoint when the strategy started to go wrong or locate the turning point for success. In addition, an annotation or demonstration interface would possibly benefit from a means for 'recalling the context' for the user to properly annotate history.

6 Conclusion

We have presented a study aimed at understanding how and what experienced users explain in RTS games. Our first contribution is the development of two coding schemes that allow a structural, content, and combined investigation. Our second contribution is an analysis of the study data and the practical implications of our findings when designing an annotation or demonstration environment for specifying and coordinating complex behavior.

Gaining a rich understanding of how RTS game play is explained by users can lead to better annotation and demonstration tools for machine learning systems, and may also provide a first step annotation in other dynamic environments in which users must make real-time decisions within specific spatial and temporal constraints.

Acknowledgements The authors would like to thank the study participants and gratefully acknowledge support of the Defense Advanced Research Projects Agency under DARPA grant FA8650-06-C-7605. Views and conclusions contained in this document are those of the authors and do not necessarily represent the official opinion or policies, either expressed or implied of the US government or of DARPA.

References

1. Morae. TechSmith. Http://www.techsmith.com/morac.asp, Last accessed August 2009
2. Wargus. Http://wargus.sourceforge.net/, Last accessed August 2009
3. Buro, M.: Real-time strategy games: A new AI research challenge. In: IJCAI, pp. 1534–1535 (2003)
4. Carletta, J.: Assessing agreement on classification tasks: the kappa statistic. Comput. Linguist. **22**(2), 249–254 (1996)
5. Cooper, S., Dann, W., Pausch, R.: Alice: a 3-D tool for introductory programming concepts. In: Proceedings of the Fifth Annual CCSC Northeastern Conference on the Journal of Computing in Small Colleges, pp. 107–116. Consortium for Computing Sciences in Colleges (2000)
6. Holtzblatt, K., Beyer, H.: Making customer-centered design work for teams. Commun. ACM **36**(10), 92–103 (1993)
7. Howland, K., Good, J., Robertson, J.: Script cards: A visual programming language for games authoring by young people. In: IEEE Symposium on Visual Languages and Human-Centric Computing, 2006. VL/HCC 2006, pp. 181–186 (2006)
8. Kahn, K.: Toontalk–an animated programming environment for children. Journal of Visual Languages & Computing **7**(2), 197–217 (1996)
9. Kissinger, C., Burnett, M., Stumpf, S., Subrahmaniyan, N., Beckwith, L., Yang, S., Rosson, M.B.: Supporting end-user debugging: what do users want to know? In: AVI '06: Proceedings of the Working Conference on Advanced Visual Interfaces, pp. 135–142. ACM Press (2006)
10. Krippendorff, K.: Content Analysis: An Introduction to Its Methodology. Sage Publications, Inc (2003)
11. Landis, J., Koch, G.G.: The measurement of observer agreement for categorical data. Biometrics **33**(1), 159–174 (1977)
12. Li, S.: Rock 'em, sock 'em robocode! http://www-128.ibm.com/developerworks/java/library/j-robocode/ (2002)
13. Modugno, F., Corbett, A.T., Myers, B.A.: Graphical representation of programs in a demonstrational visual shell–an empirical evaluation. ACM Trans. Comput.-Hum. Interact. **4**(3), 276–308 (1997)
14. Myers, B.A., Pane, J.F., Ko, A.: Natural programming languages and environments. Commun. ACM **47**(9), 47–52 (2004)
15. Ponsen, M., Spronck, P.: Improving adaptive game AI with evolutionary learning. Master's thesis, Delft University of Technology (2004)
16. Raghoebar-Krieger, Sleijfer, Bender, Stewart, Popping: The reliability of logbook data of medical students: an estimation of interobserver agreement, sensitivity and specificity. Medical Education **35**(7), 624–631 (2001)
17. Reeves, S., Brown, B., Laurier, E.: Experts at play: Understanding and designing for expert skill (2007). In draft. http://www.digra.org/dl/db/07313.16293.pdf
18. Repenning, A.: Agentsheets: A tool for building domain-oriented dynamic, visual environments. Ph.D. thesis, University of Colorado at Boulder (1993)
19. Repenning, A.: Bending the rules: steps toward semantically enriched graphical rewrite rules. In: VL '95: Proceedings of the 11th International IEEE Symposium on Visual Languages, p. 226. Washington, DC, USA (1995)
20. Smith, D.C., Cypher, A., Spohrer, J.: Kidsim: programming agents without a programming language. Commun. ACM **37**(7), 54–67 (1994). DOI 10.1145/176789.176795
21. Stumpf, S., Sullivan, E., Fitzhenry, E., Oberst, I., Wong, W.K., Burnett, M.: Integrating rich user feedback into intelligent user interfaces. In: IUI '08: Proceedings of the 13th International Conference on Intelligent User Interfaces, pp. 50–59. ACM (2008)
22. W.Aha, D., Molineaux, M., Ponsen, M.: Learning to win: Case-based plan selection in a real-time strategy game. Case-Based Reasoning Research and Development pp. 5–20 (2005)

On the Structure of a Best Possible Crossover Selection Strategy in Genetic Algorithms

Jörg Lässig and Karl Heinz Hoffmann

Abstract The paper considers the problem of selecting individuals in the current population in genetic algorithms for crossover to find a solution with high fitness for a given optimization problem. Many different schemes have been described in the literature as possible strategies for this task but so far comparisons have been predominantly empirical. It is shown that if one wishes to maximize any linear function of the final state probabilities, e.g. the fitness of the best individual in the final population of the algorithm, then a best probability distribution for selecting an individual in each generation is a rectangular distribution over the individuals sorted in descending sequence by their fitness values. This means uniform probabilities have to be assigned to a group of the best individuals of the population but probabilities equal to zero to individuals with lower fitness, assuming that the probability distribution to choose individuals from the current population can be chosen independently for each iteration and each individual. This result is then generalized also to typical practically applied performance measures, such as maximizing the expected fitness value of the best individual seen in any generation.

1 Introduction

Designing a *Genetic Algorithm* (GA) for a certain given problem, there are many degrees of freedom to be fixed but often the choice of certain parameters or operators relies on experimental investigations and the experience of the programmer.

Such choices are e.g. the *representation of a solution* in the state space as an artificial genome, the choice of a *crossover operator* to form a new population in each iteration, the choice of a *mutation rate* or the choice of a *selection scheme*

Jörg Lässig
Technische Universität Chemnitz, Reichenhainer Str. 70, e-mail: joerg.laessig@cs.tu-chemnitz.de

Karl Heinz Hoffmann
Technische Universität Chemnitz, Reichenhainer Str. 70, e-mail: hoffmann@physik.tu-chemnitz.de

M. Bramer et al. (eds.), *Research and Development in Intelligent Systems XXVI*,
DOI 10.1007/978-1-84882-983-1_19, © Springer-Verlag London Limited 2010

for the individuals of a population for crossover. Today GAs are in broad practical application to problems in many different fields such as science, engineering or economics [2, 12, 14] and excellent experimental results have been obtained. But despite interesting theoretical progress in recent years [9, 10, 16], exact proves for optimal choices of design criteria are still missing.

This paper focuses on the last of the design criteria above, also called *parent selection*. In all variants of GAs some form of the selection operator must be present [3, 4]. The simplest approach is that the reproduction probability of an individual of the population is proportional directly to its fitness (*roulette-wheel selection*), but in most applications the fitness function is scaled first. In *windowing* the fitness of the worst individual is subtracted from each individual fitness before calculating the selection probabilities, i.e. $f'(\alpha) := f(\alpha) - f_w$ with $f(\alpha)$ as fitness function for individuals α in a state space Ω and f_w as minimum fitness value of an individual in the current population. According to *exponential reduction* a fitness function $f'(\alpha) := (c_0 f(\alpha) + c_1)^{c_2}$ is applied and *linear transformation* can be seen as a special case with $c_2 = 1$. In general c_0, c_1 and c_2 are positive constants. There are also approaches which consider only the fitness rank of the individuals $\alpha \in \Omega$, called *linear ranking selection*. Here we have a linear function $f'(\alpha) := c_0 r(\alpha) + c_1$ over a fitness ranking $r(\alpha)$ of the individuals in the current population. *Tournament selection* is a two phase process: first k individuals are selected with uniform probability in a preselection step (in most cases $k = 2$, called *binary tournament*) and then the individual with the best fitness value is considered for crossover.

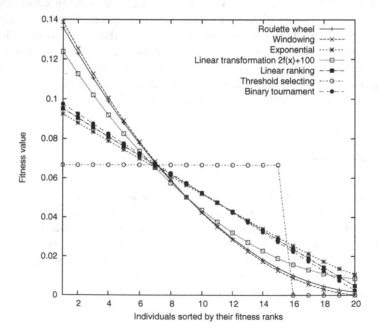

Fig. 1 Different selection strategies

In Fig. 1 the selection probabilities (y-axis) according to different strategies are visualized for each of 20 individuals in a hypothetical population (x-axis). Here the xth individual is assumed to have the artificially defined raw fitness value $f(x) = 2x^2 + x + 7$ as equivalent to an individual showing this fitness in a population of 20 individuals, which has been sorted by the fitness values of the individuals.

In the paper at hand we discuss how an optimal strategy may look like in general if the probability distribution can be chosen for each selection step independently. As introduced in [15], *threshold selecting* is a strategy which applies rectangular distributions with a certain cutoff rank v in each step for each choice of an individual for crossover, i.e. the selection is based over fitness ranks and the selection probability on the ranks is rectangular, cf. Fig. 1. These distributions include one or more individual(s) with the highest fitness value(s) with the same non-vanishing probability but all individuals with ranks v or higher are selected with probability zero. Note that there are many different strategies of this type because there are many choices of v. In this paper we show that one of these strategies must be optimal, not which one. Note that in difference to the strategy *truncation selection* [17], in *threshold selecting* different cutoff thresholds are allowed for different choices of individuals in the same iteration of the GA. In this sense *truncation selection* is a special case of *threshold selecting*.

Related work applying a proof technique as introduced below has been done by FRANZ *et al.* [8] to show for the acceptance rule in Monte Carlo methods, such as *simulated annealing* [13], *threshold accepting* [5] or TSALLIS *statistics* [6, 7], that threshold accepting is provably a best possible choice. Furthermore, the stochastic optimization algorithm *extremal optimization* [1] has been investigated [11].

2 Definitions

Consider combinatorial optimization problems with a finite state space Ω of states $\alpha \in \Omega$, which are possible solutions for the problem.

Definition 1 (State, fitness function).
A fitness function $f(\alpha)$ describes the quality of the solution α in a finite state space Ω and has to be maximized, i.e. states with a higher fitness are better.

Definition 2 (Generalized state and fitness).
If there are n states in a population of the GA, then each generation is equivalent to a tuple called generalized state $\boldsymbol{\alpha} := (\alpha_1, \alpha_2, \ldots, \alpha_n) \in \Omega^n = \boldsymbol{\Omega}$ with n finite. A generalized fitness function $f(\boldsymbol{\alpha})$ has to be defined as well, which is done here by

$$f(\boldsymbol{\alpha}) := \max\{f(\alpha_i) \mid i = 1, 2, \ldots, n\}. \tag{1}$$

To obtain good solutions, GAs proceed by randomly selecting a start population and then evolving it by selection and subsequent crossover operations. Mutations are also possible, but of no importance for our considerations, because the consecutive application of a crossover operator $\mathscr{C}$ with crossover probability p_c and a mutation operator $\mathscr{M}$ with mutation probability p_m can be considered as one application of an universal operator, i.e. $\alpha = \mathscr{M}[\mathscr{C}(\beta, p_c), p_m] = (\mathscr{M} \circ \mathscr{C})(\beta, p_m, p_c) =: \mathscr{U}(\beta)$.

The application of $\mathscr{U}$ instead of a pure crossover operator $\mathscr{C}$ does not change the reasoning applied later on. In both cases there is a rigorously defined probability to obtain a fixed state β from a given state α if the operator is applied (only the probability values change if mutation is integrated, which does not matter for the general setup). So be aware that despite our focus on crossover the following considerations include also operator applications with positive probabilities for mutations.

Definition 3 (Fitness ranking).
The individuals of a population can be ordered in a ranking which for all pairs (i, j) and $r(\alpha_i), r(\alpha_j) \in \mathbb{N}_n^+ = \{1, 2, \ldots, n\}$ satisfies: $r(\alpha_i) \leq r(\alpha_j) \Longleftrightarrow f(\alpha_i) \geq f(\alpha_j)$.

The individuals chosen for crossover are equivalent to tuples of fitness ranks, called *rank tuples*, which are the basis for the following crossover step:

Definition 4 (Rank tuple).
The possible rank tuples are described by vectors of chosen ranks $\mathbf{r} \in (\mathbb{N}_n^+)^m$, where $\mathbb{N}_n^+$ denotes the set $\{1, 2, \ldots, n\}$ of integers and m denotes the number of chosen ranks (equivalent to specific individuals) for the crossover step.

Technically, each of the individual members β_i of the current population β is assigned a rank $r(\beta_i)$, based on its fitness. For the choice of the m individuals in the tth crossover step of the GA, m time dependent probability distributions $d^{i,t}(r)$, $i = 1, 2, \ldots, m$ are defined over the ranks $r = 1, 2, \ldots, n$. For a given value r the value $d^{i,t}(r)$ is defined to be the probability to choose in the tth iteration of the algorithm rank r (equivalent to a specific individual) as ith rank in the rank tuple. Given this structure, a rank tuple of exactly m ranks $r = (r_1, r_2, \ldots, r_m)$ is chosen by the GA at time t and hence, m individuals from the current population.

Definition 5 (Feasible selection strategy).
The following assumptions are adopted:

(A1) Each step of the algorithm is independent of the former steps.
(A2) In each step t, $1 \geq d^{i,t}(1) \geq d^{i,t}(2) \geq \cdots \geq d^{i,t}(n) \geq 0$ holds for $i = 1, 2, \ldots, m$,
i.e. it is more probable to select individuals with lower rank (higher fitness) than individuals with a higher rank (lower fitness).
(A3) $\sum_{r=1}^n d^{i,t}(r) = 1$ for $i = 1, 2, \ldots m$, i.e. the distributions are normalized.

If all m distributions $\{d^{1,t}, d^{2,t}, \ldots, d^{m,t}\} =: \mathscr{D}_t$ applied in time step t of the algorithm fulfill (A1), (A2) and (A3) then, $\mathscr{D}_t$ is called feasible selection strategy.

Definition 6 (Threshold selecting strategy).
If $\mathscr{D}_t$ is a feasible selection strategy and if $\mathscr{D}_t$ consists only of distributions $d^{i,t} \in \mathscr{D}_t$ with $d^{i,t} \in \{\mathbf{v}_1, \mathbf{v}_2, \ldots, \mathbf{v}_n\} =: V$, $\mathbf{v}_1 = (1, 0, 0, \ldots, 0)^{\mathrm{tr}}$, $\mathbf{v}_2 = (1/2, 1/2, 0, 0, \ldots, 0)^{\mathrm{tr}}$, $\mathbf{v}_i = (1/i, 1/i, \ldots, 1/i, 0, 0, \ldots, 0)^{\mathrm{tr}}$, and $\mathbf{v}_n = (1/n, 1/n, \ldots, 1/n)^{\mathrm{tr}}$, then $\mathscr{D}_t$ is called threshold selecting strategy.

It is shown later on that it is optimal to apply a threshold selecting strategy in each iteration $t = 1, 2, \ldots, S$ of the optimization process but in general it is unknown which one. This means we just prove existence.

Due to the random nature of the selection process there is a transition probability to obtain individuals for crossover equivalent to a vector of chosen ranks $r = (r_1, r_2, \ldots, r_m)$ in time step $t = 1, 2, \ldots, S$:

$$\Lambda_r^{\text{Sel},t} = d^{1,t}(r_1) d^{2,t}(r_2) \cdots d^{m,t}(r_m). \tag{2}$$

In the crossover step an operator to produce new offspring is applied to the current population β. This operator may not be deterministic but determines the fixed probabilities $\Lambda_{\alpha r\beta}^{\text{Cro}}$ to obtain a new population $\alpha \in \Omega$ from $\beta \in \Omega$ and chosen ranks r. For each fixed pair r and β we have

$$\sum_{\alpha \in \Omega} \Lambda_{\alpha r\beta}^{\text{Cro}} = 1. \tag{3}$$

An exemplary procedure could work as follows: After getting m states from crossover, which are corresponding to the chosen ranks r of the old state β, m new states are created by recombining them. Including the current n states from β there are $n + m$ states available in this stage and n states are kept for the new generation α applying some standard procedure (e.g. keep the best n of all $n + m$ states). In the special case of generation replacement we have $n = m$ and β is replaced completely by the new states obtained from recombination.

Combining selection and crossover leads to a transition probability $\Gamma_{\alpha\beta}^t$ from one population β to the next population α. In summary, the dynamics of GAs can be described as a MARKOVian random walk in state space. For the development of the probability p_α^t to be in state α at iteration t (probability to have population α at time t) the master equation

$$p_\alpha^t = \sum_{\beta \in \Omega} \Gamma_{\alpha\beta}^t p_\beta^{t-1} \tag{4}$$

is applicable. Here $\Gamma_{\alpha\beta}^t$ is defined to be

$$\Gamma_{\alpha\beta}^t = \sum_{r \in (\mathbb{N}_n^+)^m} \Lambda_{\alpha r\beta}^{\text{Cro}} \Lambda_r^{\text{Sel},t} = \sum_{r \in (\mathbb{N}_n^+)^m} \Lambda_{\alpha r\beta}^{\text{Cro}} \prod_{i=1}^m d^{i,t}(r_i). \tag{5}$$

In the next step the dependence of the performance of the GA on the selection strategy, i.e. on the probability distributions $d^{1,t}, d^{2,t}, \ldots, d^{m,t}$ over the ranks in the population is investigated and we determine the structure of their optimal choice considering an optimization run with S steps ($t = 1, 2, \ldots, S$). Most commonly one of the following objectives is used to define optimality [8] (here slightly adapted in the notation for GAs):

Definition 7 (Optimization Objectives).

(O1) *The expected mean fitness of the best individual in the final population (after S steps) should be as large as possible.*

(O2) *The probability of having a final population containing a member of optimal fitness should be as large as possible.*

(O3) *The expected number of obtained populations during the execution of the algorithm which contain an individual of optimal fitness should be as large a possible.*

(O4) *The probability of obtaining a population which contains an individual of optimal fitness during the execution of the algorithm should be as large as possible.*

(O5) *The expected mean fitness $\langle f_{\mathrm{BSF}}^S \rangle$ of the best so far obtained individual during the algorithm execution in S iterations should be as large as possible, where the best so far fitness in step S is defined to be*

$$f_{\mathrm{BSF}}^S := \max\{f[\boldsymbol{\alpha}(t)] \mid t = 1, 2, \ldots, S\}. \tag{6}$$

We start with (O1) and (O2), which are somewhat simpler to treat. To optimize according to (O1) one chooses

$$g_1(\boldsymbol{\alpha}) := f(\boldsymbol{\alpha}) \overset{(1)}{=} \max\{f(\alpha_i) \mid i = 1, 2, \ldots, n\}, \tag{7}$$

which means essentially that the quality of a population is assumed to be equivalent to the quality of the best individual in the population, and to optimize according to (O2) one chooses

$$g_2(\boldsymbol{\alpha}) := \begin{cases} 1 \mid & \text{if } \boldsymbol{\alpha} \text{ contains a state with fitness } f_{\max} \\ 0 \mid & \text{otherwise}, \end{cases} \tag{8}$$

i.e. only states with fitness $f_{\max} := \max\{f(\alpha) \mid \alpha \in \Omega\}$ have objective values different from zero. The other objectives are described in Sect. 5. The objectives (O1) and (O2) are linear in the final state probabilities p_α^S, which is important for the proof. Note that also $\Gamma_{\alpha\beta}^t$ is linear in $d^{i,t}(r)$ for i fixed as can be seen from Eq. (5). The arguments below apply in general to any objective function which is linear in the final state probabilities p_α^S just as (O1) and (O2). The state probabilities at time t are considered as vector $\boldsymbol{p}^t$ and the linear objective function with values $g(\boldsymbol{\alpha})$ for each state $\boldsymbol{\alpha}$ as vector $\boldsymbol{g}$. If $(\cdot)^{\mathrm{tr}}$ denotes the transpose, the measure of performance is equivalent to

$$g(\boldsymbol{p}^S) = \boldsymbol{g}^{\mathrm{tr}} \cdot \boldsymbol{p}^S = \sum_{\alpha \in \Omega} g(\boldsymbol{\alpha}) p_\alpha^S \longrightarrow \max. \tag{9}$$

3 A Vector Space

In the following the distributions $d^{i,t}(r), r = 1, 2, \ldots, n$, are considered to be n dimensional vectors $\boldsymbol{d}^{i,t}$ with entries $d_r^{i,t} \in [0, 1]$. Now consider the case that $n - 1$ of these distributions $\boldsymbol{d}^{i,t}, i \in 1, 2, \ldots, n$, are fixed. Only one remaining distribution, denoted by $\boldsymbol{d}^{c_i,t}$, is open for optimization. The question is then how to choose $\boldsymbol{d}^{c_i,t}$ to maximize the objective function. As a consequence of the assumptions (A2) and

(A3) the region $\mathscr{F}$ of feasible vectors $\boldsymbol{d}^{c_t,t}$ is defined by the $n+1$ linear inequalities in (A2) and one linear equation in (A3), where the first inequality $1 \geq d_1^{c_t,t}$ follows from the others. Of the remaining n inequalities $n-1$ must be set to equations to find extreme points (vertices) in the region $\mathscr{F}$.

Letting V denote the set of extreme points of $\mathscr{F}$, the elements of V are exactly those vectors $\boldsymbol{d}^{c_t,t}$ which have the initial sequence of i entries equal to $1/i$ followed by a sequence of $n-i$ entries equal to zeros as introduced in Definition 6. Note that the elements of V are linearly independent. Then $\mathscr{F}$ is exactly the convex hull of V, which is a simplex, cf. Fig. 2.

Lemma 1. [8] *The convex hull of V and the region $\mathscr{F}$ defined by (A1) to (A3) are equivalent.*

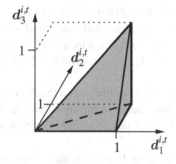

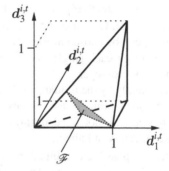

(a) Each possible distribution $\boldsymbol{d}^{i,t}$ is equivalent to a vector in a $\dim(\boldsymbol{d})$ dimensional space; the gray shaded region is equivalent to vectors which satisfy (A2)

(b) Condition (A3) constrains further to the small gray shaded region $\mathscr{F}$; only the vertices of this region can be equivalent to optimal distributions

Fig. 2 Visualization of the simplex $\mathscr{F}$ in three dimensions

4 Proving Optimality

Theorem 1 (Optimality of threshold selecting according to (O1) and (O2)). *Considering the randomized selection of individuals for crossover in iteration t of a genetic algorithm as defined above, a threshold selecting strategy gives the best implementation of this selection step in each generation, equivalent to the iterations $t = 1, 2, \ldots, S$ if the objective is linear in the state probabilities $\boldsymbol{p}^S$.*

Proof. First, the final step S of the optimization process is considered. The output of the last step is $\boldsymbol{p}^S$ and used to determine the value of the optimality criterion as in Eq. (9). In step S one has to solve the optimization problem in Eq. (9) for the given input $\boldsymbol{p}^{S-1}$. Using Eq. (4) one gets

$$g(\boldsymbol{p}^S) = \sum_{\alpha \in \Omega} g(\boldsymbol{\alpha}) p_{\boldsymbol{\alpha}}^S = \sum_{\alpha,\beta \in \Omega} g(\boldsymbol{\alpha}) \Gamma_{\alpha\beta}^S p_{\boldsymbol{\beta}}^{S-1} \longrightarrow \max \tag{10}$$

with $\Gamma_{\alpha\beta}^S$ given by Eq. (5). Note that in this stage $p_{\boldsymbol{\beta}}^{S-1}$ is fixed in any case to a value which has been determined by the first $S-1$ steps of the algorithm. Now the distributions in $\Gamma_{\alpha\beta}^S$, defined by

$$g(\boldsymbol{p}^S) \overset{(10)}{=} \sum_{\alpha,\beta \in \Omega} g(\boldsymbol{\alpha}) \Gamma_{\alpha\beta}^S p_{\boldsymbol{\beta}}^{S-1} \overset{(5)}{=} \sum_{\alpha,\beta \in \Omega} g(\boldsymbol{\alpha}) \left[\sum_{r \in (\mathbb{N}_n^+)^m} \Lambda_{\alpha r \beta}^{\mathrm{Cro}} \prod_{i=1}^{m} d^{i,S}(r_i) \right] p_{\boldsymbol{\beta}}^{S-1} \tag{11}$$

$$= \sum_{\alpha,\beta \in \Omega} g(\boldsymbol{\alpha}) d^{c_S,S} \cdot \boldsymbol{h}(\mathcal{D}_S^-) p_{\boldsymbol{\beta}}^{S-1} = d^{c_S,S} \cdot \sum_{\alpha,\beta \in \Omega} g(\boldsymbol{\alpha}) \boldsymbol{h}(\mathcal{D}_S^-) p_{\boldsymbol{\beta}}^{S-1} \longrightarrow \max$$

have to be optimized. Here $\mathcal{D}_S^-$ denotes the set of distributions $d^{1,S}, d^{2,S}, \ldots, d^{c_S-1,S}$, $d^{c_S+1,S}, \ldots, d^{m,S}$ and $\boldsymbol{h}(\mathcal{D}_S^-)$ is the vector which is obtained if $d^{c_S,S}, c_S \in \{1,2,\ldots,m\}$, gets factored out. Obviously this is possible for each distribution $d^{i,S}$ and hence the constant c_S can be chosen arbitrarily from $\{1,2,\ldots,m\}$. This means $g(\boldsymbol{p}^S)$ depends only linearly on each single distribution $d^{i,S}, i = 1,2,\ldots,m$, which selects the ith individual for crossover.

Consequently by the fundamental theorem of linear optimization the distributions can be chosen optimally as vertices $v \in V$. But, because the distributions of the previous steps are not fixed in the current stage of the proof, the optimal values $p_{\boldsymbol{\beta}}^{S-1}$ are currently unknown.

Hence, all possible combinations of vertices from V are considered for the distributions $d^{i,S}, i = 1,2,\ldots,m$. These are n^m possible choices. This finishes step S. Defining $g^{S-1}(\boldsymbol{\alpha}) = \sum_{\gamma \in \Omega} g(\boldsymbol{\gamma}) \Gamma_{\gamma\alpha}^S$ as new objective function (this has to be done in each of the n^m search branches independently) and considering now the step before, i.e. step $S-1$, one obtains

$$g^{\mathrm{tr}} \cdot \boldsymbol{p}^S = \sum_{\alpha,\beta \in \Omega} g^{S-1}(\boldsymbol{\alpha}) \Gamma_{\alpha\beta}^{S-1} p_{\boldsymbol{\beta}}^{S-2} \longrightarrow \max . \tag{12}$$

Obviously the same transformation as above can be applied to factor out $d^{c_{S-1},S-1}$, where $c_{S-1} \in \{1,2,\ldots,m\}$ and by the same arguments as above the optimal transition probabilities are found by taking $d^{c_{S-1},S-1}$ to be an element of V. Again this reasoning is valid for each distribution $d^{i,S-1}, i = 1,2,\ldots,m$. For all other steps $S-2, S-3, \ldots, 1$ the same argument holds as well, i.e. $d^{i,t}, i = 1,2,\ldots,m$ are all elements of the vertex set V. In the last step the search tree has $(n^m)^S$ branches and one of these branches is equivalent to the optimal choice of vertices of the complete iterative search process of the GA.

Hence, the proof shows that a rectangular distribution over the individuals with the lowest energy values in each generation in the iterations $t = 1,2,\ldots,S$ in GAs gives the best implementation of the selection step for each individual used for the crossover step in iteration t, i.e. a threshold selecting strategy is optimal.   □

5 Generalization

The arguments above are now generalized to cover besides (O1) and (O2) also the objectives (O3) to (O5). To obtain probability vectors $P_{\cup,F}^t$, representing for the different generalized states the probability of having obtained as least objective value F of an individual during the execution of t steps of the genetic algorithm, one has to introduce generalized transition probabilities

$$\hat{\Gamma}_{\alpha\beta,F}^t = \begin{cases} \delta(\alpha,\beta) \mid \text{if } f(\beta) \geq F \\ \Gamma_{\alpha\beta}^t \mid \text{otherwise ,} \end{cases} \tag{13}$$

where $\delta(\alpha,\beta)$ denotes the KRONECKER delta. These modified transition probabilities turn states with fitness at least F into absorbing states.

By construction, the probability to leave a generalized state with objective value at least F is zero. By Eq. (5), all values $\hat{\Gamma}_{\alpha\beta,F}^t$ are still linear in the selection probabilities of individuals.

It is now possible to specify a Master equation for the development of a probability distribution $p_{\alpha,F}^t$ to be in state α after t time steps:

$$p_{\alpha,F}^t = \sum_{\beta\in\Omega} \hat{\Gamma}_{\alpha\beta,F}^t\, p_{\beta,F}^{t-1} . \tag{14}$$

If α has an objective value $f(\alpha) \geq F$ then the random walk is trapped in this state but if $f(\alpha) < F$, no state with objective value F or better has been obtained so far. The accumulated probability to be in some generalized state with objective value at least F is given by

$$P_{\cup,F}^t = \sum_{\alpha\in\Omega, f(\alpha)\geq F} p_{\alpha,F}^t . \tag{15}$$

Because Ω is a finite state space, i.e. $|\Omega| < \infty$, there is only a finite set of possible objective values $f(\alpha)$. More specific, the number of different possible energy values is equivalent to the different values $f(\alpha_i)$ with $\alpha_i \in \Omega$, i.e. values $f(\alpha_i) \in \{F_1, F_2, \ldots, F_K\}$ with $F_1 < F_2 < \cdots < F_K$. Hence, for each possible value k the value $P_{\cup,F_k}^t$ is clearly defined. The probability that the highest so far obtained objective value is exactly given by F_k is given by

$$P_{\cap,F_k}^t = P_{\cup,F_k}^t - P_{\cup,F_{k+1}}^t , \tag{16}$$

where we introduced an objective value $F_{K+1} > F_K$ for the convenience of the notation. To address the objectives (O3) to (O5) it is not sufficient to multiply the final state probabilities with an objective vector g with $\dim(g) = |\Omega| =: L$. Instead a tuple $\mathcal{G} = (G^S, G^{S-1}, \ldots, G^1)$ of objective vectors for all time steps $t = 1, 2, \ldots, S$ with structure

$$G^t = [(g_{F_1}^t)^{\text{tr}}, (g_{F_2}^t)^{\text{tr}}, \ldots, (g_{F_{K+1}}^t)^{\text{tr}}]^{\text{tr}} \tag{17}$$

and with $\dim(G^t) = (K+1)L$ has to be defined to express a certain objective. First, Eq. (14) can be expressed in matrix notation equivalent to Eq. (9), integrating all modified transition probabilities $\hat{\Gamma}^t_{\alpha\beta,F}$ in matrices $\hat{\Gamma}^t_F$ and all probabilities $p^t_{\alpha,F}$ in vectors p^t_F with a development of probabilities according to $p^t_F = \hat{\Gamma}^t_F \cdot p^{t-1}_F$ and combining all possible objective values $F_1, F_2, \ldots, F_{K+1}$ in one equation by

$$
q^t = \begin{pmatrix} p^t_{F_1} \\ p^t_{F_2} \\ \vdots \\ p^t_{F_{K+1}} \end{pmatrix} = \begin{pmatrix} \hat{\Gamma}^{t-1}_{F_1} & 0 & \cdots & 0 \\ 0 & \hat{\Gamma}^{t-1}_{F_2} & \cdots & 0 \\ \vdots & \vdots & \ddots & \vdots \\ 0 & 0 & \cdots & \hat{\Gamma}^{t-1}_{F_{K+1}} \end{pmatrix} \cdot \begin{pmatrix} p^{t-1}_{F_1} \\ p^{t-1}_{F_2} \\ \vdots \\ p^{t-1}_{F_{K+1}} \end{pmatrix} = \hat{\Gamma}^t \cdot q^{t-1} . \tag{18}
$$

Assuming that the generalized states α are ordered according to some sorting in Ω and the number of a certain state $\alpha \in \Omega$ in this sorting is given by $s = s(\alpha)$, the following equivalence is given:

$$
q^t_{|\Omega|(k-1)+s(\alpha)} = q^t_{L(k-1)+s(\alpha)} = p^t_{\alpha,F_k} . \tag{19}
$$

Note that the unmodified chain is contained in this generalized chain at the positions $q^t_{LK+1}, q^t_{LK+2}, \ldots, q^t_{L(K+1)}$. Now it is possible to optimize for a given tuple of vectors

$$
\mathscr{Q} = (q^S, q^{S-1}, \ldots, q^1) \tag{20}
$$

according to arbitrary objective functions $\mathscr{G}(\mathscr{Q})$:

$$
\mathscr{G}(\mathscr{Q}) = \sum_{t=1}^{S} (G^t)^{\mathrm{tr}} \cdot q^t = \sum_{t=1}^{S} \sum_{i=1}^{L(K+1)} G^t_i q^t_i \longrightarrow \max . \tag{21}
$$

In this framework it is possible to optimize according to the objectives (O1) to (O5):

(O1) It is sufficient to choose $G^t = 0$ for time steps $t < S$ and $G^S = (0,0,\ldots,0,g_1)$.
(O2) The same holds if g_1 is replaced by g_2, i.e. $G^t = 0$ for time steps $t < S$ and $G^S = (0,0,\ldots,0,g_2)$.
(O3) The objective can be expressed by $G^t_i = 0$ unless $i > LK$, $\alpha_{(i \bmod L)} := s^{-1}(i \bmod L)$ and $f(\alpha_{(i \bmod L)}) = F_K$, in which case $G^t_i = 1$.
(O4) To express this objective it is sufficient to maximize $P^S_{\cap,F_K}$. This can be achieved by choosing $G^t = 0$ for time steps $t < S$ and $G^S_i = 0$ for $LK < i \le L(K+1)$, $\alpha_{(i \bmod L)} := s^{-1}(i \bmod L)$ unless $f(\alpha_{(i \bmod L)}) = F_K$, in which case $G^S_i = 1$.
(O5) Also this objective can be expressed within this framework, choosing
   (i) $G^t = 0$ for time steps $t < S$,
   (ii) $G^S_{L(k-1)+s(\alpha)} = 0$ for $k \in \{2,3,\ldots,K+1\}$ and $\alpha \in \Omega$ and $f(\alpha) < F_k$ and
   (iii) $G^S_{L(k-1)+s(\alpha)} = F_k - F_{k-1}$ for $k \in \{2,3,\ldots,K+1\}$ and $\alpha \in \Omega$ and $G^S_{s(\alpha)} = F_1$ for $\alpha \in \Omega$ for $k = 1$.

This can be obtained by expressing the *mean final best so far objective value* $\langle f_{\text{BSF}}^S \rangle$ using different values of $P_{\cap,F_k}^S$ and a number of given equivalences as described above to obtain Eq. (21), which finally has to be maximized:

$$\langle f_{\text{BSF}}^S \rangle \overset{(6)}{=} \sum_{k=1}^{K} P_{\cap,F_k}^S F_k \tag{22}$$

$$\overset{(16)}{=} \sum_{k=1}^{K} (P_{\cup,F_k}^S - P_{\cup,F_{k+1}}^S) F_k \overset{(15)}{=} \sum_{k=1}^{K} F_k \sum_{\substack{\alpha \in \Omega, \\ f(\alpha) \geq F_k}} p_{\alpha,F_k}^S - \sum_{k=1}^{K} F_k \sum_{\substack{\alpha \in \Omega, \\ f(\alpha) \geq F_{k+1}}} p_{\alpha,F_{k+1}}^S$$

$$\overset{(19)}{=} \sum_{k=1}^{K} F_k \sum_{\substack{\alpha \in \Omega, \\ f(\alpha) \geq F_k}} q_{L(k-1)+s(\alpha)}^S - \sum_{k=1}^{K} F_k \sum_{\substack{\alpha \in \Omega, \\ f(\alpha) \geq F_{k+1}}} q_{Lk+s(\alpha)}^S$$

$$= \sum_{k=1}^{K} F_k \sum_{\substack{\alpha \in \Omega, \\ f(\alpha) \geq F_k}} q_{L(k-1)+s(\alpha)}^S - \sum_{k=2}^{K+1} F_{k-1} \sum_{\substack{\alpha \in \Omega, \\ f(\alpha) \geq F_k}} q_{L(k-1)+s(\alpha)}^S$$

$$= \sum_{k=2}^{K+1} (F_k - F_{k-1}) \sum_{\substack{\alpha \in \Omega, \\ f(\alpha) \geq F_k}} q_{L(k-1)+s(\alpha)}^S + F_1 \sum_{\substack{\alpha \in \Omega, \\ f(\alpha) \geq F_1}} q_{s(\alpha)}^S$$

$$\overset{(iii)}{=} \sum_{k=2}^{K+1} \sum_{\substack{\alpha \in \Omega, \\ f(\alpha) \geq F_k}} G_{L(k-1)+s(\alpha)}^S q_{L(k-1)+s(\alpha)}^S + \sum_{\substack{\alpha \in \Omega, \\ f(\alpha) \geq F_1}} G_{s(\alpha)}^S q_{s(\alpha)}^S$$

$$= \sum_{k=1}^{K+1} \sum_{\substack{\alpha \in \Omega, \\ f(\alpha) \geq F_k}} G_{L(k-1)+s(\alpha)}^S q_{L(k-1)+s(\alpha)}^S \overset{(ii)}{=} \sum_{k=1}^{K+1} \sum_{\alpha \in \Omega} G_{L(k-1)+s(\alpha)}^S q_{L(k-1)+s(\alpha)}^S$$

$$= \sum_{i=1}^{L(K+1)} G_i^S q_i^S \overset{(i)}{=} \sum_{t=1}^{S} \sum_{i=1}^{L(K+1)} G_i^t q_i^t \overset{(21)}{=} \sum_{t=1}^{S} (G^t)^{\text{tr}} \cdot q^t = \mathcal{G}(\mathcal{Q}) \longrightarrow \max .$$

Note that the objectives (O1) to (O5) are linear functions of the probabilities q_i^t, $i \in \{1,2,\ldots,L(K+1)\}$, $t \in \{1,2,\ldots,S\}$. Now the following generalized theorem can be proven.

Theorem 2 (Optimality generalized according to (O1) to (O5)).
Considering the randomized selection of an individual for the crossover operator in iteration t of a genetic algorithm, a threshold selecting strategy gives the best implementation of this selection step in each generation, equivalent to the iterations $t = 1,2,\ldots,S$, if the objective is linear in the vector tuple $\mathcal{Q}$ as defined by Eq. (20).

Proof. Again, as in the proof for (O1) and (O2), the last step S has to be optimized first. The optimization problem as mentioned in Eq. (21) can be also expressed as

$$\mathcal{G}(\mathcal{Q}) = \sum_{t=1}^{S} (G^t)^{\text{tr}} \cdot q^t = \sum_{t=1}^{S} (G^t)^{\text{tr}} \cdot \hat{\Gamma}^t \cdot q^{t-1} = (G^S)^{\text{tr}} \cdot \hat{\Gamma}^S \cdot q^{S-1} + c \longrightarrow \max \tag{23}$$

by Eq. (18). We again focus on one arbitrary distribution $\boldsymbol{d}^{c_S,S}$, $c_S \in \{1,2,\ldots,m\}$, to be optimized. The values $\hat{\Gamma}^S_{\alpha\beta,E}$ as defined in Eq. (13) still depend only linearly on the probabilities $\Gamma^S_{\alpha\beta}$ and hence also only linearly on $\boldsymbol{d}^{c_S,S}$. The possible distributions according to (A2) and (A3) form a simplex just as argued already in the proof in Sect. 4 and hence, independently from the choice of the other distributions $\boldsymbol{d}^{i,S}$, $i \neq c_S$, an optimal value of $\mathscr{G}(\mathscr{Q})$ can be obtained for a vertex $\boldsymbol{v}^{c_S,S} := \boldsymbol{v}_i \in V$, which is a rectangular distribution as considered in the threshold selecting approach.

Because c_S has been chosen arbitrary from $\{1,2,\ldots,m\}$, this holds for all other values of c_S as well, i.e. in an optimal combination of distributions $\boldsymbol{d}^{1,S}, \boldsymbol{d}^{2,S}, \ldots, \boldsymbol{d}^{m,S}$, the distributions are equivalent to vertices $\boldsymbol{v}^{1,S}, \boldsymbol{v}^{2,S}, \ldots, \boldsymbol{v}^{m,S} \in V$. Which of these vertices are chosen depends only on the input vector $\boldsymbol{q}^{S-1}$ and this is determined by the pervious iterations of the algorithm. In this stage of the proof the vector is unknown because the distributions of the former steps still have to be fixed. Thus, we again have n^m possible combinations of the distributions $\boldsymbol{d}^{i,S}$, $i = 1,2,\ldots,m$, but at least one of them must be optimal. Now this construction can be continued in each of the n^m search branches with the step $S-1$, where the objective can be determined by considering the m probability distributions in time step S to be chosen. In step $S-1$ we have the maximization

$$
\begin{aligned}
\mathscr{G}(\mathscr{Q}) &= (\boldsymbol{G}^S)^{\mathrm{tr}} \cdot \hat{\boldsymbol{\Gamma}}^S(\boldsymbol{v}^{1,S}, \boldsymbol{v}^{2,S}, \ldots, \boldsymbol{v}^{m,S}) \cdot \hat{\boldsymbol{\Gamma}}^{S-1} \cdot \boldsymbol{q}^{S-2} + (\boldsymbol{G}^{S-1})^{\mathrm{tr}} \cdot \hat{\boldsymbol{\Gamma}}^{S-1} \cdot \boldsymbol{q}^{S-2} + c' \\
&= [(\boldsymbol{G}^S)^{\mathrm{tr}} \cdot \hat{\boldsymbol{\Gamma}}^S(\mathscr{V}^S) + (\boldsymbol{G}^{S-1})^{\mathrm{tr}}] \cdot \hat{\boldsymbol{\Gamma}}^{S-1} \cdot \boldsymbol{q}^{S-2} + c' \\
&= (\tilde{\boldsymbol{G}}^{S-1})^{\mathrm{tr}} \cdot \hat{\boldsymbol{\Gamma}}^{S-1} \cdot \boldsymbol{q}^{S-2} + c' \longrightarrow \max .
\end{aligned}
\tag{24}
$$

Here $\mathscr{V}^S$ denotes a threshold selecting strategy, i.e. the set $\boldsymbol{v}^{1,S}, \boldsymbol{v}^{2,S}, \ldots, \boldsymbol{v}^{m,S}$ of vertices, and $(\tilde{\boldsymbol{G}}^{S-1})^{\mathrm{tr}}$ is the implicitly defined objective function for step $S-1$. Also in this step the dependence on each single chosen distribution $\boldsymbol{d}^{i,S-1}$, $i = 1,2,\ldots,m$, is only linear and with the same argument as above there is an optimal combination $\boldsymbol{d}^{1,S-1}, \boldsymbol{d}^{2,S-1}, \ldots, \boldsymbol{d}^{m,S-1}$ of distributions, equivalent to vertices $\boldsymbol{v}^{1,S-1}, \boldsymbol{v}^{2,S-1}, \ldots, \boldsymbol{v}^{m,S-1} \in V$. These chosen vertices depend only on the input $\boldsymbol{q}^{S-2}$.

The remaining steps $S-2, S-3, \ldots, 1$ can be processed in a similar way and in each step distributions equivalent to vertices from V are obtained as optimal solutions. This completes the proof. Hence, threshold selecting is also for all objectives (O1) to (O5) an optimal strategy. □

6 Intuitive Understanding

How can the optimality of a *threshold selecting strategy* be interpreted and understood intuitively? First, obviously not all individuals can be chosen for crossover in a certain generation and hence, a selection step is inevitable for evolutionary progress. But, the major point is that it is in general clearly defined whether it is good or bad to consider a certain individual for crossover in a given population and the algorithm should consider it either always or never. Additionally, between individuals which should be considered for crossover there is no qualitative difference concerning the final result. In nature, genes with favorable phenotypes are more likely to survive and reproduce than those with less favorable phenotypes. Consequently modeled, in GAs artificial genes with higher fitness values are more likely to survive and reproduce than those with lower fitness values. But as demonstrated, ideally only genes from an elitist group of the v best ones should survive. This fact is intuitively applied by animal breeders, who influence the reproduction process actively instead of letting nature play dice.

7 Conclusion

In this paper the problem of selecting individuals from the population of a GA for crossover based on a fitness function has been considered. The master equation was the tool to describe the corresponding dynamics of the optimization process as random walk in a state space and some basic assumptions on the probability distributions for selecting the individuals in a certain generation have been formulated.

The goal was to find transition probabilities assuring the optimal control of the evolutionary development in the GA. Rectangular distributions of selection probabilities over the fitness ranks of the individuals are provably optimal, provided the performance is measured by a linear function in modified state probabilities, which includes many reasonable choices as for instance maximizing the mean fitness of the best individual in the final population or the maximization of the mean final best so far fitness of an individual obtained during the optimization process.

The proof above is based on the fundamental theorem of linear programming, which states that a linear function defined on a simplex reaches its maximum at a vertex. The proof does not state that all optimal crossover selection strategies in GAs are rectangular, i.e. we did not rule out that other strategies may perform equally well, but we proved that they do not perform better.

As presented, the proof can be applied for most practically implemented crossover procedures in GAs with independent probability distributions for the selection of the crossover individuals and both for the *generation replacement model*, where the mating pool has size n for populations of size n, and also for the *steady-state replacement model*, where only some individuals are replaced [18].

Currently, the knowledge that best performance can be achieved using *threshold selecting* is only of limited use in practice, since the cutoff ranks v to be used are not known in advance. Hence, it would be interesting to find arguments how to choose from all possible threshold selecting strategies the best or at least a competitive one in each iteration of the algorithm. The insights for the practitioner are also restricted by the permission of different probability distributions for the choice of the individuals in the same iteration of the GA as used in the proof above. It would be interesting to investigate the case where the selection of the different individuals for crossover in one iteration has to take place according to the same distribution.

References

1. S. Boettcher and A. G. Percus. Extremal Optimization: Methods derived from Co-Evolution. In *GECCO-99, Proceedings of the Genetic and Evolutionary Computation Conference*, pages 825–832, Orlando, Florida, July 1999.
2. P. G. Busacca, M. Marseguerra, and E. Zio. Multiobjective Optimization by Genetic Algorithms: Application to Safety Systems. *Reliability Engineering & System Safety*, 72(1):59–74, April 2001.
3. M. Chakraborty and U. K. Chakraborty. An Analysis of Linear Ranking and Binary Tournament Selection in Genetic Algorithms. In *Proceedings of the International Conference on Information, Communications and Signal Processing*, pages 407–411, Singapore, September 1997.
4. U. K. Chakraborty, K. Deb, and M. Chakraborty. Analysis of Selection Algorithms: A Markov Chain Approach. *Evolutionary Computation*, 4(2):133–167, 1997.
5. G. Dueck and T. Scheuer. Threshold Accepting: A General Purpose Optimization Algorithm Appearing Superior to Simulated Annealing. *Journal of Computational Physics*, 90:161–175, 1990.
6. A. Franz and K. H. Hoffmann. Optimal Annealing Schedules for a Modified Tsallis Statistics. *Jounal of Computational Physics*, 176(1):196–204, February 2002.
7. A. Franz and K. H. Hoffmann. Threshold Accepting as Limit Case for a Modified Tsallis Statistics. *Applied Mathematics Letters*, 16(1):27–31, January 2003.
8. A. Franz, K. H. Hoffmann, and P. Salamon. Best Possible Strategy for Finding Ground States. *Physical Review Letters*, 86(23):5219–5222, June 2001.
9. T. Friedrich, P. S. Oliveto, D. Sudholt, and C. Witt. Theoretical Analysis of Diversity Mechanisms for Global Exploration. In *Interational Genetic and Evolutionary Computation Conference 2008*, pages 945–952, Atlanta, Georgia, July 2008. ACM Press.
10. E. Happ, D. Johannsen, C. Klein, and F. Neumann. Rigorous Analyses of Fitness-Proportional Selection for Optimizing Linear Functions. In *Interational Genetic and Evolutionary Computation Conference 2008*, pages 953–960, Atlanta, Georgia, July 2008. ACM Press.
11. K. H. Hoffmann, F. Heilmann, and P. Salamon. Fitness Threshold Accepting over Extremal Optimization Ranks. *Physical Review E*, 70(4):046704, October 2004.
12. S. Kikuchi, D. Tominaga, M. Arita, K. Takahashi, and M. Tomita. Dynamic Modeling of Genetic Networks Using Genetic Algorithm and S-System. *Bioinformatics*, 19(5):643–650, 2003.
13. S. Kirkpatrick, C. Galatt, and M. Vecchi. Optimization by simulated annealing. *Science*, 4598:671–680, 1983.
14. A. Kolen. A Genetic Algorithm for the Partial Binary Constraint Satisfaction Problem: an Application to a Frequency Assignment Problem. *Statistica Neerlandica*, 61(1):4–15, February 2007.
15. J. Lässig, K. H. Hoffmann, and M. Enăchescu. Threshold Selecting: Best Possible Probability Distribution for Crossover Selection in Genetic Algorithms. In *Interational Genetic and Evolutionary Computation Conference 2008*, pages 2181–2185, Atlanta, Georgia, July 2008. ACM Press.
16. A. Moraglio and R. Poli. Inbreeding Properties of Geometric Crossover and Non-geometric Recombinations. In C. R. Stephens, M. Toussaint, D. Whitley, and P. F. Stadler, editors, *Foundations of Genetic Algorithms: 9th International Workshop*, pages 1–14, Mexico City, Mexico, June 2007. Springer Berlin.
17. H. Mühlenbein and D. Schlierkamp-Voosen. Predictive Models for the Breeder Genetic Algorithm. *Evolutionary Computation*, 1(1):25–49, 1993.
18. D. Srinivasan and L. Rachmawati. An Efficient Multi-objective Evolutionary Algorithm with Steady-State Replacement Model. In *Proceedings of the 8th annual conference on Genetic and evolutionary computation*, pages 715–722, Seattle, Washington, USA, July 2006.

Chunking Natural Language Texts using Evolutionary Methods*

John Atkinson and Juan Matamala

Abstract This paper describes a new approach to natural-language chunking using genetic algorithms. This uses previously captured training information to guide the evolution of the model. In addition, a multi-objective optimization strategy is used to produce unique quality values for objective functions involving the internal and the external quality of chunking. Experiments and the main results obtained using the model and state-of-the-art approaches are discussed.

1 Motivation

Traditional full natural language parsing aims to provide as detailed as possible analysis of the sentence structure. Full parsing is a challenging task involving the development of the full grammar for the language as well as the computational challenges involved in identifying the most plausible parse of a given sentence. However many natural-language processing (NLP) applications do not necessarily require a complete syntactic analysis. On the other hand, parsers can usually generate multiple syntax trees for the same input text leading to ambiguity and efficiency problems. Many of the these tasks can adequately be performed by identifying the noun phrases (NP), verb phrases (VP), etc and the relationships between these entities. Shallow (or partial) parsing can be used to recover some limited syntactic infor-

John Atkinson

Department of Computer Sciences, Universidad de Concepcion, Chile, e-mail: atkinson@inf.udec.cl

Juan Matamala

Department of Computer Sciences, Universidad de Concepcion, Chile, e-mail: jmatam@udec.cl

* This research is partially sponsored by the National Council for Scientific and Technological Research (FONDECYT, Chile) under grant number 1070714 *"An Interactive Natural-Language Dialogue Model for Intelligent Filtering based on Patterns Discovered from Text Documents"*

M. Bramer et al. (eds.), *Research and Development in Intelligent Systems XXVI*,
DOI 10.1007/978-1-84882-983-1_20, © Springer-Verlag London Limited 2010

mation from natural language sentences [10]. This often involves *chunking* which refers to the process of unnested grouping the words into chunks given their morphosyntactical tags [1, 10]. On the other hand, there are distributional and variation problems related to the target language, a lack of lexical and syntactical electronic resources for languages and finally the lack of huge training corpus required for specific domains.

This work proposes a new approach to chunking which makes good use of the search capabilities of a *Genetic Algorithm* (GA) and previous training data obtained from annotated corpus. We hypothesize that an evolutionary model for chunking can produce competitive results when comparing with other state-of-the-art techniques.

The remain of this article is organized as follows: section 2 discusses the main state-of-the-art approaches to chunk parsing, in section 3 an evolutionary model for chunking natural-language texts is proposed, section 4 highlights the main experiments and results using our model, and the main conclusions are discussed in section 5.

2 Related Work

Natural-language parsing involves the procedure of bringing basic morphosyntactic categories into high-level syntactic relationships with each other. This is probably the most commonly encountered form of corpus annotation after *Part-of-Speech* (POS) tagging (aka. lexical tagging). Usually a parser looks for valid tree parses for an input natural-language sentence. Since this must recursively find different structures, techniques usually have serious efficiency problems in analyzing massive amounts of texts.

To reduce the search space and resolve ambiguity issues, partial (or shallow) analysis for some specific syntactical groups of the input sentence can be carried out. The most popular shallow parsing strategy is known as *Chunking* [1] which identifies the non-recursive cores of various phrase types in text, possibly as a precursor to full parsing or information extraction. The paradigmatic shallow parsing problem is NP chunking, which finds the non-recursive cores of Noun Phrases.

Computationally, text chunking consists of dividing a text in syntactically correlated parts of words. For example, the sentence *"He reckons the current account deficit will narrow to only 1.8 billion in September."* can be divided into chunks as follows:

```
[NP He] [VP reckons] [NP the current account deficit]
[VP will narrow] [PP to] [NP only 1.8 billion] [PP in]
[NP September] .
```

State-of-the-art chunking techniques can be divided into two types: those based on grammar rules and those using supervised machine-learning techniques [1, 3, 10]. Methods using explicit rules for chunking are not accurate when dealing with huge amounts of texts. Furthermore, this is an extremely time-consuming task as these rules are usually manually built. An early significant improvement to chunking was achieved by using *Memory-based Learning* (MBL) in which the parser automatically learns the classification rules based on previously annotated examples [3]. One of the problems with this approach is the availability and preparation of examples which is an intensive task. On the other hand, the search algorithm used for finding chunks is based on similarity measures which restrict the type of chunk pattern to be looked for in the training corpus. A more flexible and adaptive rule-based technique for chunking is based on *Transformation-based Learning* (TBL). This was originally applied to lexical, syntactical and semantic tagging but further adapted to shallow analysis. Initially, TBL hypothesizes a set of very simple learning rules. The technique then iteratively looks for rules that better correct the errors made by the previously proposed rules. Despite its high computational cost to validate the rules in each iteration, variations of the strategy have incorporated restrictions on the search space for each iteration to improve the chunker performance [9]. Statistical-based methods such as *Maximum Entropy* parsers (*MaxEnt*) have also been used to address these issues [8]. A related method which uses probabilities for prediction and classification producing better performance by reducing the number of required training data is based on *Hidden Markov Models* (HMM) in which hidden states of the model keep likely chunk tags and visible states contain the part-of-speech (POS) or lexical tags [11]. An important drawback is that as the number of hidden states grows the method becomes less effective in exploring the search space than other techniques such as Support Vector Machines (SVM) [9, 12].

Mixture of methods using assemble of classifiers has also been exploited for chunk classification [13, 10]. However, experiments have shown that this synergy does not always guarantee the best results. Furthermore, the size of the training corpus has showed to significantly affect the performance of these methods. A promising strategy to explore and modify huge amounts of hypothesis in parallel involves using evolutionary computation methods, in particular, Genetic Algorithms (GA). Recent results in POS tagging and text mining show that the technique is worth exploiting for NLP purposes. An early GA-based lexical tagger [2] evolves a population of candidate sequences of lexical tags (chromosomes) corresponding to the words of an input text by selecting the best sequence of tags or modifying these in case they have not been obtained yet. Each hypothesis is then assessed in terms of its fitness which considers the context of a word (i.e., left and right tags) and the number of words in a sentence [2].

3 A New Approach to Natural Language Chunking based on Genetic Algorithms

This work proposes a new approach to natural-language chunking using evolutionary computation techniques (i.e., *Genetic Algorithms* which have demonstrated substantial improvement over a variety of random and local search methods [6]. This is accomplished by their ability to exploit accumulating information about an initially unknown search space in order to bias subsequent search into promising subspaces. Compared with classical search and optimization algorithms, GAs are much less susceptible to getting stuck to local suboptimal regions of the search space as they perform global search by exploring solutions in parallel. GAs are robust and able to cope with noisy and missing data, they can search spaces of hypotheses containing complex interacting parts, where the impact of each part on overall hypothesis fitness may be difficult to model.

Our GA-based chunking model receives a natural-language text and assigns the corresponding syntactical chunks for each sentence based on previously computed training information from annotated corpus. The model can be divided into two phases: training and chunking.

From a set of natural-language scientific texts (training texts), the training task computes probabilities of POS tags and chunks based on a n-gram language model [7]. The model is then capable of receiving new natural-language documents and have them chunked. Specifically, the training phase extracts two kinds of underlying information from the annotated texts:

1. *Associations between lexical and chunk tags:* based on Bayesian models, information regarding the likely associations between POS tags and chunks is captured.
2. *Sequencing data:* based on a statistical language model, sequences of n-grams are obtained using Hidden Markov Models.

Resulting training information is further used to guide the GA that automatically assigns chunks to new natural-language texts. The initial population for the GA is generated by randomly combining candidate chunks.

In order to assess the quality of the generated hypotheses, a multi-objective optimization was applied to determine how good a sequence of chunks is for a sentence based on intra-chunk and inter-chunk associations. This is carried out using structural and lexical information obtained from an annotated corpus.

3.1 Training

In order to carry out the chunk parsing, an annotated corpus of natural-language texts was used. This contains sentences annotated with standard POS and chunk tags. For capturing training data, statistical language models were applied to extract knowledge which will guide the GA. In particular, n-gram language models were adapted and used [7].

A n-gram model predicts the occurrence of a symbol in a sequence based on the $n - 1$ previous contexts, in words, this makes explicit the structure of the symbols. For our approach, a 2-gram (aka. bi-gram) language model was applied to the training corpus with the symbols being the chunk tags. An example of applying this model to text's sentences can be seen in table 1. The benefit of bi-gram modeling is based on the assumption that there is a relevant connection between contiguous chunks in a sentence.

Chunk 1	Chunk 2	Chunk 3	Chunk 4
NP_1	NP_2	VP_3	PP_4

$\Rightarrow$

Previous Chunk	Next Chunk
NP_1	NP_2
NP_2	VP_3
VP_3	PP_4

Table 1 Representation for a Sentence (left) and Bi-Grams (right)

The bi-gram model computes the probability of a sequence of chunks c based on the previous context: $P(c) = P(c_1) \prod_{i=2}^{n} P(c_i \mid c_{i-1})$. Therefore, the probability of assigning a chunk c_i (of a sentence) given a previous chunk c_{i-1} is computed as: $P(c_i \mid c_{i-1}) = \frac{N(c_{i-1}, c_i)}{N(c_{i-1})}$, where $N(c_{i-1}, c_i)$ is the number of occurrences of sequence of chunks (c_{i-1}, c_i) within the training corpus, and $N(c_{i-1})$ is the number of occurrences of chunk c_{i-1} within the same corpus.

3.2 Evolutionary Chunking

In our evolutionary approach, chunk classification can be seen as an optimization problem in which the best chunk tags should be assigned to the words of a sentence. For this, the GA requires new representation schema, genetic operators and evaluation metrics for the hypotheses.

The GA procedure is based on the Darwinian principle of survival of the fittest. An initial population is created containing a predefined number of individuals (or solutions), each represented by a genetic string (incorporating the variable information). Each individual has an associated fitness measure, typically representing an objective value. The concept that fittest (or best) individuals in a population will produce fitter offspring is then implemented in order to reproduce the next population. Selected individuals are chosen for reproduction (or crossover) at each generation, with an appropriate mutation factor to randomly modify the genes of an individual, in order to develop the new population. The result is another set of individuals based on the original subjects leading to subsequent populations with better (min. or max.) individual fitness. Therefore, the algorithm identifies the individuals with the optimising fitness values, and those with lower fitness will naturally get discarded from the population.

3.2.1 Hypothesis Representation

In order to code each chromosome representing a sequence of chunks, a three-dimensional structure is used. This contains the words of a sentence, their POS tags and their automatically assigned chunks. Note that as the GA goes on, the words and POS tags remain unchanged for a chromosome. An example of the representation of the hypothesis for the sentence below can be seen in figure 1:

```
He reckons the Current account deficit will narrow to
only #1.8 billion in September
```

where the chromosome shows the 3-dimension structure containing components extracted from a standard *Wall Street Journal* (*WSJ*) corpus (an empty gene shows that the previous chunk is kept).

He	reckons	the	Current	account	deficit	Will	narrow	
PRP	VBZ	DT	JJ	NN	NN	MD	VB	
NP	VP	NP	NP	NP	NP	VP	VP	·········

Fig. 1 Example of a Multi-dimensional Representation for a Chromosome

At the beginning, a sequence of words of a sentence is assigned a random chunk. As the GA goes on, the size of this chunk becomes bigger or smaller based on the quality of the assigned chunk. Genetic operators can modify the content or the size of the chunk hence its structure may vary accordingly. However, the size of the chromosome is fixed as a word must always be tagged with a chunk.

An initial population of hypotheses for the GA is created from a set of randomly generated combinations of chunks for each word of an input sentence. Overall, chunks can be assigned from a set of 36 types of chunks extracted from the standard *Penn Treebank II tagset*[2]. Note that dimensions 1 and 2 remain unchanged whereas the dimension representing the chunk depends on the assigned chunks. Each chunk covers segments of the input sentences from 1 (one word) to the length of the sentence.

3.2.2 Fitness Evaluation

In order to automatically assess the quality of the chunks generated for each individual, a fitness function is proposed. For our model, the evaluation considers two objective functions:

1. *Quality of the sequence of chunks (aka. inter-chunk objective):* assesses the structure of the sequence of chunks for a sentence based on the frequencies of chunks obtained from training data.

---

[2] http://www.cis.upenn.edu/ treebank/

2. *Quality of an individual chunk (aka. intra-chunk objective):* assesses the sequence of POS tags for each individual chunk of a sentence based on the frequencies of lexical tags assigned to chunks in the training data.

Both objectives are computed by using data generated from a training annotated corpus. In order to compute the intra-chunk measure (F_{intra}), sequences of n-grams are obtained using HMM [7]. This considers probabilities of POS tags associated to chunks. This is, the probability that a POS tag is associated to a chunk is computed for all the POS tags of a sentence. The rationale for this is that some POS tags are assumed to be more likely to occur within a chunk than other. For each gene, the metrics calculates $P(POS_i/Chunk_j)$ which represents the conditional probability that POS_i tag occurs given that the current chunk is $Chunk_j$. Next, the resulting intra-chunk measure considers how likely the sequence of pairs (POS tags and Chunks) is for the sentence of $n-1$ words as: $F_{intra} = \prod_{j=1}^{N_c} \sum_{i=0}^{L(j)-1} P(POS_i/Chunk_j)$, where N_c is the number of chunks of a sentence and $L(j)$ is the length of the chunk j.

0	1	2	3	4	5	6	7	8	9	10	11	12	13	14
He	reckons	the	current	Account	deficit	Will	narrow	to	only	#	1.8	billion	in	September
PRP	VBZ	DT	JJ	NN	NN	MD	VB	TO	RB	#	CD	CD	IN	NNP
NP	VP	NP				VP		PP	NP				PP	NP

Fig. 2 A Sample Hypothesis

Computating the objective value of the example is as follows: for the inter-chunk measure (F_{inter}), the objective value is obtained by computing the probability of the sequence of chunks for the input sentence and having then multiplied so to obtain an objective function value. For example, assume the following sequence of chunks in a sentence: *"NP | VP | NP | VP | PP | NP | PP | NP"*. For the first chunk (*NP*), the probability of this being the start of the sentence is first computed. Next, the probability that the second chunk being *VP* giving that the previous one was *NP*, and so on. The product of these values represents the inter-chunk fitness for a sequence of chunks as follows:

$$F_{inter} = \frac{P(NP \mid START) * P(VP \mid NP) * P(NP \mid VP) * P(VP \mid NP) *}{P(PP \mid VP) * P(NP \mid PP) * P(PP \mid NP) * P(NP \mid PP)} \quad (1)$$

Note that in order to avoid zero values when this objective function is applied to a sequence which does not appear in the training set, a default low value is assumed for the probabilities. In order to compute a unique fitness value, several evolutionary multi-objective optimization techniques including aggregation (i.e., weighted sum of the objective functions), SPEA-II (the improved *Strength Pareto Evolutionary Algorithm*) and the *Non-Dominated Sorting Genetic Algorithm* (NSGA-II) were assessed [5]. However, the *Precision* and *Recall* values of the model using NSGA-II were observed to outperform the other methods hence it was used for the current experiments.

Here, the final fitness value for each hypothesis is based on the number of individuals being dominated by each individual. For this, the objective vector becomes the pair (F_{intra}, F_{inter}).

Hypothesis	F_{intra}	F_{inter}	Fitness
1	1	2	-3
2	2	3	1
3	4	4	2
4	5	5	3

Table 2 Objective and fitness values for sampled hypotheses

The resulting fitness for four chromosomes can be seen at table 2. For hypothesis 1, its objective vector $(1,2)$ is dominated by the rest of the individuals (3) so this gets a fitness which is the negative number of the individuals that dominate this hypothesis. Hypothesis 2 dominates hypothesis 1 so this gets the fitness value of 1, hypothesis 3 dominates individuals 1 and 2 so this gets a fitness value of 2 and hypothesis 4 dominates individuals 1,2 and 3 so this gets a value of 3, hence individual 4 is the fittest individual and so this is closer to the Pareto front than other hypotheses.

The overall fitness of an individual which considers the objective functions above is computed by a multi-objective optimization strategy based on the *NSGA-II* algorithm [5]. This uses a ranking method that emphasizes on the good solution points and tries to maintain a population of such points throughout the procedure. NSGA-II maintains diversity in its population by a crowding method, which eliminates focusing on certain regions of the solution space, and explores different regions in the Pareto front. The concept of non-dominated sorting is underlined by the ranking selection method which keeps track of the good solution points, and the niche method which maintains stable subpopulations of these solutions [5].

3.2.3 Genetic Operators

In order to modify and improve the individuals of the population, genetic operators have been designed including selection, crossover, and mutation.

- **Selection**
  A selection operator picks up the best hypotheses to be reproduced based on the fitness values. For this model, a binary tournament selection strategy was applied [6]. This randomly selects pairs of individuals from the whole population and those having highest fitness values are considered for reproduction.
- **Crossover**
  A new constrained crossover operator was designed to exchange chunks from two different hypotheses of the population. For this, two random individuals

are randomly selected, a single crossing point is chosen and the chunks are exchanged. The single-point crossover exchanges chunks from two selected individuals at a ramdonly selected point and generates two new offspring according to a crossover probability P_c. Since that only valid hypotheses must be generated, if the crossing point falls within a chunk's segment, the operator automatically corrects the resulting crossover so to obtain valid chromosomes. Consequently, the size of the chunk may vary as a result of a new change in a word's assigned chunk. For example, figure 3(a) shows individuals selected for crossover, and the crossing points being position 9 for hypotheses 1 and 4, and position 2 for hypotheses 2 and 3.

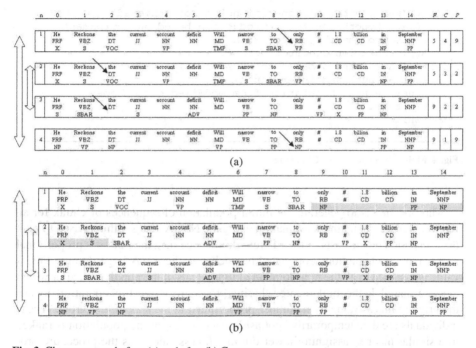

Fig. 3 Chromosomes before (a) and after (b) Crossover

The new offspring after applying the operator can be seen in figure 3(b). The dark dimension highlights the segment on which the exchange was performed. Crossover between individual 1 and 4 does not produce any problem at all as for both cases the crossing point is at the beginning of a chunk. However, exchanging chromosomes 2 and 3 produces a broken chunk which must be corrected scanning from left to right until the invalid segment is found. The chunk which is in the crossing point is then identified and the gene representing the chunk is copied several times into the offspring until the chunk becomes valid.

- **Mutation**

For the mutation operator, a random modification of each chunk is made for a sequence of words with a mutation probability (P_m) using a pool of available chunks.

The overall structure of the GA for evolutionary chunking using these new operators can be seen at figure 4.

```
Generate an initial population from random sequences of chunks
Evaluate fitness    based on NSGA-II using objective values
                (intra-chunk and inter-chunk)
t=0
While (max. number of generations is not achieved)
    Select hypotheses for reproduction based on tournament
    Apply Crossover operator with Pc
    Apply Mutation operator with Pm
    Evaluate fitness based on NSGA-II using objective values
    (intra-chunk and inter-chunk)
    Generate next population from modified chromosomes
    t = t + 1
End-While
```

Fig. 4 Multi-Objective GA for Chunking

The first step is to generate the initial population of sequences of chunk for an input sentence. Next, fitness evaluation using the NSGA-II algorithm is used to rank the population on the basis of their Pareto dominance (i.e., the fitness is proportional to the number of solutions dominated by each hypothesis). A large dummy fitness value is assigned to all the non-dominated individuals of the population, after which they are shared. In the implemented sharing procedure, a selection operation divides the original fitness value by a number proportional to the size of that group. These individuals are then temporarily kept aside, and the rest of the population is ranked in a similar manner, assigning lower dummy fitness values, as the procedure proceeds. This dummy fitness value plays an important part in the reproduction of the next generation, and intuitively, individuals with larger fitness values produce more offspring than the rest of the population. Once the population has been evaluated, the best hypotheses are selected for reproduction based on a binary tournament as previously explained. Next, crossover and mutation operations are applied to the selected chromosomes. Finally, the new offspring replaces the previous individuals to generate the next set of hypotheses.

4 Experiments and Results

In order to assess the effectiveness of the proposed evolutionary model for chunking, a series of experiments was carried out. A first part aimed to tune the different parameters of the GA and a second part assessed how accurate the model was compared to other state-of-the-art approaches.

The different experiments were based on the standard annotated corpus *Wall Street Journal* (WSJ) from which chapters 15 to 18 were used for training (200.000 words) and chapter 20 was used for testing (50.000 words). This corpus contains English sentences annotated with POS tags which were generated using the Brill's tagger [4]. These sentences also contain their corresponding chunks which are later removed for testing purposes. Approximate chunk distribution for the *WSJ* corpus is as follows: 51% for *Noun Phrase* (NP), 20% for *Verb Phrase* (VP), 20% for *Prepositional Phrase* (PP), 4% for *Adverb Phrase* (ADVP), and minor proportions for the other syntactical groups. For evaluation and comparison purposes, the methods only use the *NP* chunk as this becomes one of the most frequent, useful and popular chunks for several current chunkers.

4.1 Tuning the Model

In order to adjust the evolutionary model, different configurations for the GA were evaluated using the training data from WSJ. These considered experiments aiming at analyzing the robustness of the method under different settings such as the population size (*PopSize*), the number of generations (*NumGen*), and the probabilities of crossover (P_c) and mutation (P_m), respectively. Tests are carried out by considering the best of six runs of the GA for every setting. The best configurations were determined by using standard performance metrics of *Precision* (P), *Recall* (R) and the $F - score$. Final experiments suggested that best performance ($F - score > 0.92$) is achieved for $PopSize = 800$, $NumGen = 800$, $P_m = 0.01$ and $P_c = 1.0$.

Individual objective functions measuring the quality of the generated chunks can also be seen at figure 5 for intra-chunk evaluations. For visualization purposes, objective values are drawn using different scales for 800 generations. Nevertheless, objective values for the best solutions remain unchanged roughly after generation 400. Furthermore, a graphic showing the scaled Euclidean distance between the best objective values and the target for two multi-objective optimization strategies (SPEA and NSGA-II) can be seen in figure 6 (for visualization purposes, only the first 100 generations are shown).

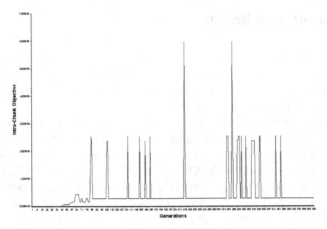

Fig. 5 Evolution of Intra-chunk Objective Values versus *NumGen*

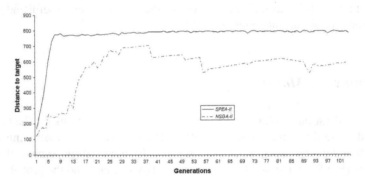

Fig. 6 Evolution of the distance to target using two multi-objective methods: SPEA-II and NSGA-II

4.2 Effectiveness of the Model

In order to assess the relative effectiveness of our evolutionary model for chunking, the results obtained for the different real experiments were compared with those of the best competitive state-of-the-art chunking techniques using chapter 20 of WSJ as test data. The main results of the NP chunkers can be seen in table 3.

The results of our evolutionary model for NP chunking can be seen in table 4 using different population sizes. Parameters of the GA considered $P_c = 1.0, P_m = 0.01$ on the *WSJ* corpus and produced a *Precision* of 92.5% and a *Recall* of 93.1% ($F - score = 92.7\%$). This shows the promise of the method when comparing with current methods. Note that most of the current methods requires a significant training corpus to produce these results. However, the table suggests that the effectiveness of our model might not be significantly affected when reducing the size of the training corpus.

Technique	Precision	Recall	F-score
Memory-based Learning	94.04%	91.00%	92.50%
Support Vector Machine	93.89%	93.92%	93.91%
Hidden Markov Model	92.30%	92.68%	92.49%
Transformation-based Learning	91.80%	92.30%	92.05%

Table 3 Performance for some state-of-the-art NP chunking approaches

Num	PopSize	Precision	Recall	F-score
1	400	89.3%	87.2%	88.2%
2	820	92.3%	89.1%	90.6%
3	850	92.5%	93.1%	92.7%

Table 4 Performance of our Model for NP chunking

In order to investigate the robustness of model on different sizes of training corpus, further experiments were carried out. The rationale for this is that creating training corpus for chunking is an extremely costly task. In addition, current techniques strongly depend on this corpus to produce better results. Hence methods which are less dependent on the size of the training data are preferred.

The model was trained by using the whole training data as used by other chunking techniques (table 3) and the results are shown in figure 7 in terms of the $F-score$ metrics. The GA considered the parameters $PopSize = 800$, $NumGen = 800$, $P_c = 1.0$, $P_m = 0.01$.

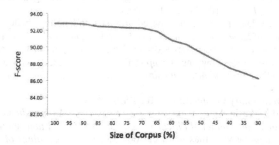

Fig. 7 Performance versus size of training data

The graphic shows that as the size of the training corpus slightly decreases, the effectiveness does not show a significant drop for $F-score$. Significant decreases are not observed until reducing 70% of the training corpus. This suggests that the model is not highly dependent of the size of the corpus so in terms of used resources this may be even more efficient than some of the state-of-the-art chunking methods.

Despite outperforming some of the current techniques, the lower effectiveness when compared with the best of table 3 may be due to the distribution of the tags in the training corpus. This may not directly affect the generation of hypotheses, but the way the fitness evaluation is computed.

5 Conclusions

In this work, a new evolutionary model for natural language chunking was proposed. The model uses Genetic Algorithms and multi-objective optimization techniques in order to assess candidate solutions in terms of quality metrics involving intra-chunk and inter-chunk probabilistic associations. A training corpus of annotated sentences with lexical and syntactical tags is used to capture training information that guides the GA toward the best solutions.

Experiments for NLP chunking, show the promise of the GA-based model for chunking syntactical groups such as noun phrases from a corpus of unseen natural-language texts. Compared with state-of-the-art chunking techniques, the performance of the model makes it very competitive. In addition, settings involving reductions on the amount of required training corpus also show that the model's performance does not significantly drop when reducing the size of the training data. That is, the method may require less training corpus to achieve the previous results which is a practical advantage as annotating training corpus for text analysis purposes is an extremely demanding task.

References

1. S. Abney. Parsing by chunks. In R. Berwick, S. Abney, and C. Tenny, editors, *Principle-Based Parsing: Computation and Psycholinguistics*, pages 57–278. Kluwer Academic Publishers, Boston, 1991.
2. E. Alba, G. Luque, and L. Araujo. Natural language tagging with genetic algorithms. *Information Processing Letters*, 100(5):173–182, 2006.
3. S. Argamon and I. Dagan. A memory-based approach to learning shallow natural language patterns. *Journal of Experimental and Theorethical Artificial Intelligence*, 10:1–22, 1999.
4. Eric Brill. Transformation-based error-driven learning and natural language processing: A case study in part-of-speech tagging. *Computational Linguistics*, 21(4):543–565, 1995.
5. K. Deb. *Multi-Objective Optimization using Evolutionary Algorithms*. John Wiley and Sons, 2001.
6. K. DeJong. *Evolutionary Computation*. MIT Press, 2004.
7. D. Jurafsky and J. Martin. *Speech and Language Processing: An Introduction to Natural Language Processing, Computational Linguistic, and Speech Recognition*. Prentice Hall, 2000.
8. R. Keoling. Chunking with maximum entropy models. *Proceedings of the Internacional Conference on Natural Language Leraning, CoNLL-200 pages 139-141, Portugal*, 2000.
9. T. Kudo and Y. Matsumoto. Chunking with support vector machines. *Proc. of NAACL 01*, 2001.
10. X. Li and D. Roth. Exploring evidence for shallow parsing. *Proc. of the Annual Conference on Computational Natural Language Learning, Toulouse, France*, pages 1–7, 2001.
11. A. Molina and F. Pla. Shallow parsing using specialized HMM. *The Journal of Machine Learning Research*, 20(2):595–613, 2002.
12. H. Takamura and Y. Matsumoto. Feature space restructuring for SVMs with application to text categorization. In Lillian Lee and Donna Harman, editors, *Proceedings of EMNLP-01, 6th Conference on Empirical Methods in Natural Language Processing*, pages 51–57. Association for Computational Linguistics, Morristown, US, 2001.
13. E. Tjong and K. Sang. Memory-based shallow parsing. *The Journal of Machine Learning Research*, 20(2):559–594, 2002.

SHORT PAPERS

Multi-Agent Reinforcement Learning - An Exploration Using Q-Learning

Caoimhín Graham, David Bell, Zhihui Luo[1]

Abstract It is possible to exploit automated learning from sensed data for practical applications - in essence facilitating reasoning about particular problem domains based on a combination of environmental awareness and insights elicited from past decisions. We explore some enhanced Reinforcement Learning (RL) methods used for achieving such machine learning using software agents in order to address two questions. Can RL implementations/methods be accelerated by using a Multi-Agent approach? Can an agent learn composite skills in single-pass?

1 Introduction

Reinforcement learning in its most basic sense is the ability to map situations to actions; in the world of machine learning it provides us a mechanism by which a software agent can act autonomously based on inputs, and perform a sequence of steps in order to fulfil a goal, selecting steps which maximise long-term reward [SUBA98]. It is often the case that the goal is not known by the agent in advance; rather the agent receives 'rewards' for interacting with other objects in the environment in particular ways so that there is a direct correlation between encouraged action and positive reward. Reinforcement learning can be modeled as a Markov Decision Process, MDP [PUT05], composed by four tuple $< S, A, P, R >$; i.e. State set S - a finite set of states S_i in an environment; Action A - a set of actions A_i that can be execute by the agent; Transition probability P - the probability of transition from a current state to its successor state; Reward R – the probability of gaining a reinforcement value from environment. So S is composed of n sub-state spaces S_i , each representing a different environment state. If we assume that an agent can learn for each sub-state independently, without interference from other sub-states - then this can be regarded as skill training [LBM08]. Thus each skill $Skill_i$ for use within the environment is dependent only on the originating sub-state S_i and its associated action A_i. Using the above approach it has been shown [LBM08] that forming composite agent skills using data obtained from individual skill-sets that are determined using a Q-Learning [QL92] approach can result in a dramatic improvement in the learning curves for particular tasks. In this paper we will present a preliminary, exploratory study of the performance bottlenecks associated with such learning agents and how these can be overcome to yield increases in

---

[1] School of Electronics, Electrical Engineering and Computer Science
Queen's University Belfast, e-mail: {cgraham26,da.bell,zluo02}@qub.ac.uk

M. Bramer et al. (eds.), *Research and Development in Intelligent Systems XXVI*,
DOI 10.1007/978-1-84882-983-1_21, © Springer-Verlag London Limited 2010

both efficiency and accuracy. In order to achieve such skill learning the Q-Learning algorithm, see [QL92] for details, was implemented using a co-operational concurrent approach whereby two software agents would explore an environment and share information about their findings. In essence both agents share a central Q-Learning table which they both update. Skill learning can be regarded here as an autonomous software agent taking a number of actions to reach a goal. A skill is the subset of actions that an agent can use to achieve this goal within an environment [LBM08].

2 Impact of various factors on an Agent's Performance

A key factor in the Q-Learning [QL92] method is the learning rate. The learning rate for the Q-Learning algorithm can be set between zero and one, and it is important to decide upon an optimal setting which respects the necessity both to exploit existing knowledge and to explore the environment to maximize the long term reward. We investigated this first, as it is needed for the subsequent studies.

If we assume that given prior knowledge (skills) a task is easier to perform, it is important to determine the time it takes to acquire that 'knowledge'. If we can reduce the time it takes to learn a skill, then we cause an increase in performance and efficiency. This allows us to explore the possibility of improving the learning curve by reducing the time it takes to learn a skill. In this investigation the possibility of accelerating the learning process by introducing the notion of two co-operating agents in a problem domain where a single skill is to be learned was explored.

We are interested in how negative and positive reinforcement learning methods can be used together to form a learning strategy for a composite skill set. For the initial study the agents seek out a goal state in a grid whilst trying to avoid obstacles within the environment which result in a negative reward value. We would like to know whether this learning method can be accelerated using co-operating agents. We also want to determine how scalable the learning approach using co-operating agents is, and to identify whether the bottleneck in learning an optimal policy is directly dependent on the number of agents exploring an environment or the effect of changing the environment itself. *Ab Initio* the time performance of each of a pair of co-operating agents was expected to show an increase over that of a single agent. The performance of two co-operating agents was expected to show a similar increase in performance to that of a single agent when acquiring a composite skill. Furthermore, the environment was expected to be a major performance bottleneck in determining an agent's performance - i.e. agents should perform better in an environment where available reward is effectively doubled, and worse when it is halved. The present study is not be to seen as a comprehensive scientific investigation, but rather as a project to provide initial evidence to support or refute our conjectures, with a view to designing controlled experiments. A secondary objective was to develop a visual teaching aid for reinforcement learning in a configurable environment.

3 The Investigation

For the purposes of this investigation the Q-Learning [QL92] algorithm used in paper [LBM08] was utilized. For ease of representation and explanation the agents in this test environment were represented as mice, the goal as cheese and obstacles as mouse traps. Co-operating agents share a centralized memory space or 'Q-Table' [QL92] which can be accessed and updated by each agent independently. The communication pattern which allows co-operating agents to share information can be seen in figure 1 below. A single agent on the other hand lacks the ability to collaborate and update the same shared memory space - any output from the process of learning is re-usable only by it (figure 2).

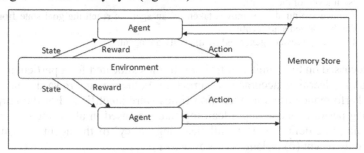

Figure 1. Multiple Agent Environment Interaction Diagram

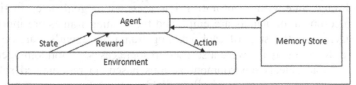

Figure 2. Single Agent Environment Interaction Diagram

The long-term aim of this research is to identify performance bottlenecks that exist within an agent's operating environment and how the software agent can adapt its learning strategy in becoming more adept at acquiring particular skills. Previous research has identified the idea of 'agent based skill learning' [GT95] and noted the learning proficiency with which agents reason about the past decisions they have made whilst defining their own unsupervised learning policy. The experiments described in the following sections use a combination of negative and positive reinforcement learning methods for multi-technique learning and to prove whether combining the learning stages of two separate techniques or sub-skills in forming a generalised composite skill can give an overall performance increase for the agent and reduce the learning space. Positive and negative triggers in the environment can be likened to the various techniques that the agents must learn to perform - we use attraction and avoidance here for this. To further accelerate the learning process it is believed that when sharing a common memory space, agents can learn with greater proficiency – our main goal in this study.

4 Experiments

The main goal of these experiments was to determine the extent to which performance of the Q-Learning [QL92] algorithm can be accelerated by using co-
operating software agents to explore an environment and the extent to which this
can directly accelerate the learning of composite skill-sets.

In order to measure the performance the following outputs were collected:

1. The execution time of the algorithm.
2. The number of training frames in a given test scenario (this can be regarded as the
   level of refinement of the knowledge mined or in more abstract terms, the current
   'skill level' of the agent).
3. The average number of moves taken by an agent to reach the goal state from a randomly selected start location.
4. The average reward generated by the software agent.

We focussed on the number of training frames allocated for a particular test and
the resulting learning accuracy in terms of both average reward and average
moves. Performance traits in execution times were identified. For the purpose of
measuring performance a single learning rate was used in all of the experiments;
the learning rate defines the overall 'learning-policy' of the agent i.e. whether it
favours only recent (0) or long-term reward (1).

A single training frame is defined as the time from when an agent starts to
navigate through an environment until it intersects with a goal state. In situations
where two co-operating agents are employed the training frames are independent
between agents. At the start of each training frame the agent's start position is
randomised. Random agents were also used in some cases. A random agent is defined as one that selects environment actions based on randomised selections.
Learning means obtaining a list of all available actions for an environment state
and selecting the action that has the highest associated action value. At the start of
an agent simulation all action values are set equal - in such situations the learning
agent obtains a list of all available actions and selects one at random. Positive reinforcement learning dictates that an agent receives a reward when performing a
desired action and in all other situations it receives a small negative reward.
Negative reinforcement learning provides a large negative reward value when the
agent performs an undesired action. We used both methods together within the
same environment and explored the possibility of acquiring composite skills in
this case. A software workbench was developed to conduct the experimental investigations. This workbench allows a researcher to define a customised environment and agent parameters either by using a bespoke user interface or by
scripting their execution. The workbench also outputs the results of the simulation
in real time to give the user a visual representation of the test in progress. This
user interface shows the following: The Environment; Movement of the agent (s)
throughout the environment; Up-to-date results for each training frame.

The following experiments were conducted during the course of this
investigation:

- **Experiment 1:** Determine an optimal learning rate for the Q-Learning [QL92] algorithm given a basic agent environment i.e. a single goal.
- **Experiment 2:** Assess the performance impact on the learning space when using co-operating agents to explore an environment whilst acquiring a single skill.
- **Experiment 3:** Determine whether an agent can form a learning policy which allows it to acquire a composite skill-set in the process of exploring its environment using a combination of positive and negative reinforcement learning methods.
- **Experiment 4:** Determine whether co-operating agents can form a learning policy which improves the acquiring of a composite skill, in turn accelerating the learning process.
- **Experiment 5:** Determine whether the performance benefits gained through the use of co-operating agents scale to different environment types where the expected convergence value is either doubled or halved for a single learning agent.

A learning rate of 0.7 was found to be best for our studies – it gave a consistently accurate learning policy that was, on average superior to the other learning rates that were tested. During the initial stages of learning, using co-operating agents gives better performance than using a single agent, but over the course of execution both ultimately reach the same convergence point and performance will be identical between agents. Over time the performance benefit of using co-operating agents lessens. Co-operating agents, however, clearly reach higher performance levels much earlier in the course of execution. It is also interesting to note that at the same stage in learning co-operating agents have executed twice as many training frames as single agents. At the same point in learning, i.e. when both co-operating and single agents have completed the same number of training frames, performance is approximately equal.

The conclusion is that co-operating agents can learn a skill to a greater accuracy than that of single agents in a reduced time space. Ultimately however given enough training frames a single agent can become as accurate as a co-operating agent as both reach the optimal convergence point. Using a combination of negative and positive reinforcement learning methods it is possible to learn a composite skill in a single pass. To identify potential performance bottlenecks in an agent's performance two different test scenarios were devised: placing obstacles within the environment in a pre-defined manner as to lessen the routes agents can select which lead to the goal state; placing obstacles randomly within the environment. The difference in the growth of both the average number of moves and average reward generated can be summarised by 2 key points: The agent will strive to find the most efficient route to the goal state from its current location and produce an average number of moves to indicate this; The agent will strive to find the most rewarding route to the goal state from its current location and produce an average reward to indicate this.

In the restricted environment execution times required for both single and co-operating agents are approximately equal. This is because the environment is sufficiently complex that, irrespective of agent's start position, the task is difficult to fulfil. In other words all agents in the restricted environment are constrained not by their own efficiency but rather the design of the environment itself. In an unrestricted environment co-operating agents gradually take less time to complete execution than single agents. This is due to the way the agents share information. As both agents share a centralised memory, during the early stages of learning all of the obstacles within the environment are identified allowing the agents to route around the obstacles and intersect with the goal state. The same is true for single agents in that they identify obstacles within the environment, but 2 agents sharing information can be > 50% more efficient than 1 agent. A situation where this trait was recorded occurred in experiment 4 when comparing the execution times of single and co-operating agents within an unrestricted environment. The test framework has proved that performance is scalable for different environment conditions and that an agent's behaviour and performance is directly related to its environment. In situations where the available reward was informally doubled, an increase in the agent's performance was noted, and when reward was halved a performance decrease was recorded. This is consistent with what was expected.

5 Discussion and Conclusion

A future goal is to explore the possibility of allowing the user to create and test locally designed environments by ways of an inbuilt 'scenario designer' within the software workbench. For the purposes of this study the solution developed was adequate but for further investigations the inclusion of such a feature would be of benefit. Moreover, full 'agent co-operation' was not achieved; as a simple expedient a centralised Q-Learning memory store was utilised. In complex situations using many agents a more efficient mechanism would need to be used i.e. QUCRL *[QQL08]*. In some cases, actual performance was lower than expected and this was due to the overheads involved in implementing the communication between co-operating agents, or the Q-Learning features. The number of training frames executed is the key performance bottleneck. At the same stage of execution we witness approximately equal performance levels. It was shown that composite skills can be learned by using a combination of positive / negative reinforcement learning methods and that this learning can be further accelerated by using co-operating agents. It has been demonstrated that environmental factors are the main performance bottleneck. Further investigation would require only minor adaption of the existing workbench and test suite.

References

1. [PUT05] Puterman,M.L., Markov Decision Processes: Discrete Stochastic Dynamic Programming. 2005: Wiley-Interscience
2. [SUBA98] Sutton,R. & Barto,A., Reinforcement Learning: An Introduction. 1998: MIT Press
3. [QL92] Watkins,C. & Dayan,P., Q-Learning. Machine Learning, 8(3-4):279--292, 1992, 1992
4. [LBM08] Bell, Luo & McCollum, Skill Combination in Reinforcement Learning, 2008
5. [GT95] Tesauro,G. Temporal Difference Learning & TD-Gammon, 1995
6. [QQL08] Agogino,A. & Tumer,K, Quicker Q-Learning in Multi-Agent Systems, 2008

Leveraging Sub-class Partition Information in Binary Classification and Its Application

Baoli Li and Carl Vogel[1]

Abstract Sub-class partition information within positive and negative classes is often ignored by a binary classifier, even when these detailed background information is available at hand. It is expected that this kind of additional information can help to improve the differentiating capacity of a binary classifier. In this paper, a binary classification strategy via multi-class categorization is proposed to leverage sub-class partition information when they are available. Empirical studies on the 20 newsgroups dataset demonstrate the benefits of this strategy. Furthermore, a preliminary application of this binary classification strategy for multi-label classification problem is given with promising results.

1 Introduction

Binary classification, which aims at classifying an item positively or negatively with respect to a class, is important. On one hand, it can be directly applied to solve some practical problems, e.g. spam filtering. On the other hand, binary classifiers can be assembled to solve multi-class classification problems [1] and multi-label classification problems [4].

In multi-class classification, an item belongs to only one of a set of predefined classes. Error Correcting Output Codes (ECOC) provides a general framework to transform a multi-class problem into a set of binary classification problems [2]. In this framework, each class is assigned a unique codeword, which is a binary string of length N. With each bit i of these codewords, the original multi-class dataset is split into two mixed classes: one contains all samples of the classes that have value 1 at bit i of their codewords, and the other has all the remaining samples. The N binary classifiers corresponding to each bit are therefore learned for classifying a new sample and producing a codeword for it. The predicted class is the one whose codeword is closest to the codeword produced by the N binary classifiers.

---

[1] Trinity College Dublin, Dublin 2, Ireland, email: {baoli.li ,vogel}@cs.tcd.ie

This research is supported by the Science Foundation Ireland (Grant 07/CE/I1142) as part of the Centre for Next Generation Localisation (www.cngl.ie) at Trinity College Dublin.

M. Bramer et al. (eds.), *Research and Development in Intelligent Systems XXVI*,
DOI 10.1007/978-1-84882-983-1_22, © Springer-Verlag London Limited 2010

In multi-label classification, an item may be assigned to more than one class. A commonly used approach to address multi-label problem is the so-called one-vs-rest (a.k.a. one-vs-all) strategy, in which each potential class is examined by a binary classifier. To train a binary classifier for a class, the samples of this class in the training set are used as positive samples, where the rest samples from all other classes form the negative class.

As shown in the above situations, when we build a binary classifier for solving a complex problem, positive and/or negative classes may be derived by artificially or randomly combining several sub-classes, and the sub-class partition information is available at hand. Unfortunately, the current binary classification methods never take into account this kind of information. Intuitively, this additional information could help improve the performance of a binary classifier.

In this research, we propose a simple strategy to improve binary classification via multi-class categorization for applications where sub-class partition information within positive and/or negative classes is available. Based on sub-class partition information, a multi-class classifier is built and a new item is labeled according to its prediction. As multi-class categorization may implicitly capture the interactions between sub-classes, we expect that fine sub-classes will help differentiate the coarse positive and negative classes with high accuracy.

In the following sections, we explain our proposed strategy and empirically investigate whether this binary classification strategy with sub-class information is better than the traditional binary classification strategy. Experiments on the 20 newsgroups dataset demonstrate that this intuitive strategy can lead to better performance on average, especially the macro-averaging scores. Then, in section 4, we further explore to apply this strategy in solving a multi-label classification problem. Section 5 concludes the paper with planned future work.

2 Binary Classification via Multi-class Categorization

Our proposed strategy targets at solving a special kind of binary classification, where positive and/or negative classes artificially consist of several sub-classes. Suppose that the positive and negative classes in a binary classification problem contain $|P|$ and $|N|$ sub-classes, respectively, where $P=\{p_1, p_2, ..., p_{|P|}\}$ and $N=\{n_1, n_2, ..., n_{|N|}\}$. Our strategy then works as follows:

a). Build a multi-class classifier C_m, which considers $|P|+|N|$ sub-classes.

b). Classify a new item α with the above learned classifier C_m and suppose its prediction is c.

c). If $c \in P$, α is labeled as positive; otherwise, α belongs to negative class.

If the multi-class classifier C_m supports probability output, the probability sums of sub-classes within P and N will be used for final decision. This binary classification strategy is expected to work with any multi-class categorization algorithm.

3 Experiments and Discussions

3.1 Dataset and Experimental Design

To show the effectiveness of the proposed strategy, we experiment with the 20 Newsgroups dataset. The dataset is nearly evenly partitioned across 20 different newsgroups, each corresponding to a different topic. Among the different versions of this dataset, we use the so called bydate version[2] which is sorted by date and divided into a training set (60%) and a test set (40%), without cross-posts (duplicates or multi-labeled documents) and newsgroup-identifying headers. The total number of newsgroup documents in the "bydate" version is 18,846, with 11,314 for training and 7,532 for testing. We choose this dataset for experiments because it is almost balanced and without multi-label cases. We hope to remove the effects caused by these two factors.

To get binary datasets, we randomly choose one or more original classes and combine them together as a positive class and take the rest to form its complementary negative class. This way is similar to what we do when we use binary classification to solve a complex problem, e.g. multi-class classification with ECOC.

With the 20 newsgroups dataset, we have totally 616,665 ($=C_{20}^1+C_{20}^2+...+C_{20}^{10}$) possible separations, which can be classified into ten types: 1vs19 (1 class as positive and the rest 19 classes as negative), 2vs18, 3vs17, ..., and 10vs10. As the number of possible separations is so huge, to make our experiments tractable, we randomly choose at most 100 separations from different types. Obviously, we only have 20 different separations of type 1vs19, and so we totally experiment with 920 different separations[3]. Separations from the same type roughly have the same class distribution. For example, in the separations of type 1vs19, the ratio of positive documents to negative documents is around 1 to 19.

We compare our proposed strategy with the traditional binary classification strategy that doesn't take into account sub-class information even though it is available. We label the traditional strategy as BIN, and ours as 2vM.

We experiment with a widely used text categorization algorithm: Naïve Bayes with multinomial model [3]. At the preprocessing stage, we remove stop words, but without stemming. Words appearing only in one document are ignored. After these processing, we get totally 49,790 words as features. The two common metrics, Micro-F1 and Macro-F1 measures, are used to evaluate performance.

---

[2] http://www.ai.mit.edu/~jrennie/20Newsgroups/.
[3] The 920 binary separations of the 20 newsgroup dataset are available at http://www.cs.tcd.ie/Baoli.Li/BTCvM/.

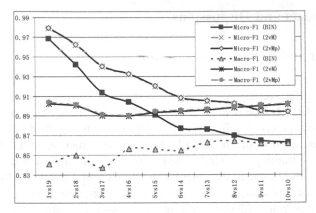

Figure 1. F-1 measures of the two strategies on the 20 newsgroups dataset.

3.2 Results and Discussions

Figure 1 shows the performance of the two binary text classification strategies (BIN and 2vM). The values are the averages of all separations of the same type. Figure 1 also shows the performance of a variant of 2vM (labeled as 2vMp), which uses the probability output for decision. 2vMp and 2vM have very close performance, although the former is statistically significantly better than the latter.

The figure does demonstrate the effectiveness of the simple strategy, i.e. binary classification with sub-class information. As the dataset becomes more balanced, the difference of Mic-F1 between BIN and 2vM grows larger, where that of Mac-F1 gets smaller. With the extremely imbalanced separation (1vs19), the Mic-F1 of the 2vM strategy is just a little higher than that of the traditional BIN strategy (0.9789 vs 0.9683). Comparatively speaking, the performance of 2vM is more stable than that of BIN. In the 920 runs, 2vM beats BIN 901 times on Mic-F1 with average gain 0.02863 and 805 times on Mac-F1 with average gain 0.04857, where BIN beats 2vM 19 times on Mic-F1 with average gain 0.00376 and 115 times on Mac-F1 with average gain 0.01729.

As the dataset changes from imbalanced to balanced, Mic-F1 is getting worse, while Mac-F1 is steadily becoming better. For example, in figure 1, the Mic-F1 of BIN drops 10.87% from 0.9683 to 0.8630, while that of 2vM goes down 8.75% from 0.9789 to 0.8933. At the same time, the Mac-F1 of BIN increases 2.42% from 0.8413 to 0.8617, and that of 2vM drops a little bit from 0.9025 to 0.9013.

The trend of Mic-F1 conforms to our intuition, as we can easily get higher accuracy with an extremely imbalanced dataset by simply outputting the major one of the two classes. If the two classes within a dataset have more equal size, the problem will become harder because the uncertainty of such a dataset becomes higher. As Mac-F1 score is more influenced by the performance on rare classes, the overall average scores are poor on imbalanced datasets because classifiers often perform poorly on rare classes.

The imbalance of datasets also contributes to the following phenomenon: the deviation between Mic-F1 and Mac-F1 is larger for imbalanced separations than for balanced separations. When dataset is getting balanced, Mic-F1 and Mac-F1 will become very close.

We need to point out that the above analyses are based on the overall tendency, as the values are averages of many runs. The performance difference between 2vM and BIN is statistically significant (P values of t-test for Mic-F1 and Mac-F1 are 4.3E-269 and 8.2E-116, respectively), but it doesn't mean that 2vM can beat BIN on every possible separation. With 2vM, we are more likely to get better results. It is therefore sensible to choose 2vM strategy if we are not allowed to compare these two strategies offline.

Actually, we also tested the proposed strategy with another dataset (Reuters-21578-SL-8Class, also available at http://www.cs.tcd.ie/Baoli.Li/BTCvM/) and other two categorization algorithms: SVM and kNN. We obtained similar conclusions. Due to space limit, we have to omit all these results in this paper.

4 Application: Multi-label Classification

Empirical study shows that 2vM is a good substitute for BIN when sub-class partition information is available. We then explore to apply this 2vM strategy to solve some practical problems. In a preliminary application, we considered a multi-label text classification problem.

As we mentioned earlier, one-vs-rest is a widely used strategy for multi-label classification [4]. It trains a set of binary classifiers, each of which corresponds to a class. When classifying a new document, these binary classifiers are applied in turn and decide whether the new document could be classified into each class. The most possible class will be given to those documents that are not assigned any class label by those binary classifiers.

We experiment with the two binary classification strategy (BIN and 2vM) and Naïve Bayes algorithm on the Reuters-21578 dataset (Apte' Split[4]) with 91 classes (90 classes with an unknown class). The widely used metrics for multi-label classification, Hamming Loss [4] and Micro-Averaging F1, are used for measuring performance. Hamming Loss captures the differences between a system's output and the golden answer. The less the hamming loss is, the better the system's performance is. To build the multi-class classifier required by the 2vM strategy, we take each existing label combination as a new class and thus transform a multi-lable problem into a multi-class single-label problem.

---

[4] http://kdd.ics.uci.edu/databases/reuters21578/reuters21578.html.

Table 1 gives the experimental results. With the 2vM strategy, we get better results. The Hamming Loss value drops 35.87% from 0.009323 to 0.005979, where Mic-F1 increases 8.48% from 0.703087 to 0.762723. The probablity variant 2vMp can boost the results a little bit.

Table 1. Results of BIN and 2vM for multi-label classification.

Strategy	BIN	2vM	2vMp
Hamming Loss	0.009323	0.005979	0.005959
Micro-Avg. F-1	0.703087	0.762723	0.763454

5 Conclusion and Future Work

In this paper, we empirically demonstrate the effectiveness of a simple strategy for improving binary classification via multi-class categorization when sub-class information is available. On average, the proposed 2vM strategy brings better results over the traditional binary classification strategy (BIN), especially for macro-averaging scores and on imbalanced datasets. In a preliminary application, we employed the proposed strategy to solve a multi-label classification problem and got promising results. In the future, we are planning to experiment with more datasets. We assume the proposed strategy could be applicable to not only text data but also other classification data. We also expect to use this strategy to enhance those multi-class categorization algorithms based on binary classification, e.g. error correcting output codes.

References

1. Erin L. Allwein et. al. 2000. Reducing Multiclass to Binary: A Unifying Approach for Margin Classifiers. Journal of Machine Learning Research, 1: 113-141.
2. Rayid Ghani. 2000. Using Error-Correcting Codes for Text Classification. In Proceedings of ICML-2000.
3. Andrew Mccallum and Kamal Nigam. 1998. A Comparison of Event Models for Naive Bayes Text Classification. In Proceedings of AAAI/ICML-98 Workshop on Learning for Text Categorization.
4. Grigorios Tsoumakas and Ioannis Katakis. 2007. Multi-Label Classification: An Overview. Journal of Data Warehousing and Mining, 3(3):1-13.

A Linguistic Truth-Valued Temporal Reasoning Formalism and Its Implementation

Zhirui Lu, Jun Liu, Juan C. Augusto, and Hui Wang*

Abstract Temporality and uncertainty are important features of many real world systems. Solving problems in such systems requires the use of formal mechanism such as logic systems, statistical methods or other reasoning and decision-making methods. In this paper, we propose a linguistic truth-valued temporal reasoning formalism to enable the management of both features concurrently using a linguistic truth valued logic and a temporal logic. We also provide a backward reasoning algorithm which allows the answering of user queries. A simple but realistic scenario in a smart home application is used to illustrate our work.

1 Introduction

One of the common problems in decision making is how to make the best possible decision based on uncertain information in dynamic environments, which exists in many applications, e.g., smart homes, risk management, disaster monitoring and management, weather forecast, and stock market analysis, etc. Combining logic system into decision support system is one of feasible methodologies to handle these complex problems, and such logic systems are usually merged by many-valued/fuzzy logic and temporal logic. The reason using such combined system is that the complex problems can be separated into two major parts to handle, *uncertainty* and *temporality*. To handle uncertainty through logic approaches, many works have been done, e.g., [1-3]; for handling the temporality through logic approaches, see [4-6]. However, in the real application, the uncertainty and temporality may exist at the same time. Accordingly, some combined logic systems have been introduced, e.g., [7-11]. As a continuous work of [11] which combined reasoning scheme using multi-valued logic system and linear temporal logic system [12], in this paper, a linguistic truth-valued temporal reasoning framework is outlined. Then the main focus is given on the backward reasoning algorithm, in which the supporting tree structure is used to make the whole

* School of Computing and Mathematics, Faculty of Computing and Engineering, University of Ulster at Jordanstown, Newtownabbey, BT37 0QB, Northern Ireland, UK
Lu-Z1@email.ulster.ac.uk, {j.liu, jc.augusto, h.wang}@ulster.ac.uk

M. Bramer et al. (eds.), *Research and Development in Intelligent Systems XXVI*,
DOI 10.1007/978-1-84882-983-1_23, © Springer-Verlag London Limited 2010

process of the backward algorithm more efficient and clear. And a simple but realistic scenario is provided for illustration.

1.1 Problem Description: a Realistic Scenario

There are numerous applications with the need of reasoning about both time and uncertainty. For example, Smart Home systems [13], which rely on data gathered by sensors, have to deal with the storage, retrieval, and processing of uncertain and time constrained data. Consider a scenario where the task is to model a kitchen monitored by sensors in a Smart Home system. Assume the cooker is on (*cookerOn*, a sensor detecting cooker being activated), but the motion sensor is not activated (*-atKitchen*, *atKitchen* is a sensor detecting location of the house occupant is in the kitchen). If no motion is detected after more than three units of time (*umt3u*), then we consider the cooker is unattended (*cu*). In this case, at the next unit of time, the alarm will be on (*alarmOn*) to notify the occupant that the cooker has been left unattended. Here the cooker and the occupant are both monitored by sensors, but there may be a problem with these sensors which may not return accurate information about the status of cooker or position of the occupant, and some causal relationships may not be always certain. The proposed reasoning framework can be used to analyse such uncertain and time constrained situations to make rational decisions.

1.2 Basic Definitions

In order to manage the uncertainty, we assume that a state is not just true or false, but certain to some degree, and the certainty degree is taken from a linguistic term set which is an ordered structure uniformly distributed on a scale. We apply the linguistic computational symbolic approach, acts by direct computation on linguistic values. This method seems natural because the linguistic evaluations are just approximations which are given and handled when it is impossible or unnecessary to obtain more accurate values. Let $L = \{v_i\}$, $i=0,\ldots, m-1$, be a finite and totally ordered linguistic term set. Any label, v_i, represents a possible value for a linguistic variable. Moreover, L must have the characteristics below: 1) The set is ordered: $v_i \leq v_j$ if $i \leq j$; 2) There is a negation operator: $(v_i)' = v_j$ such that $j = m - I$; 3) There is a maximization operator: $\text{Max}(v_i, v_j) = v_j$ if $v_i \leq v_j$; 4) There is a minimization operator: $\text{Min}(v_i, v_j) = v_i$ if $v_i \leq v_j$; 5) There is an implication operator, $\rightarrow$: $V \times V \rightarrow V$ defined by $v_i \rightarrow v_j = v_{m+j-i}$ $(i, j \in \{0,\ldots, m\})$; 6) There is a product operator (called Łukasiewicz product): $\otimes$: $V \times V \rightarrow V$ defined by $v_i \otimes v_j = v_{\max(0, i+j-m)}$. $(L, \leq, \rightarrow, ')$, in short L, forms an algebra called as Łukasiewicz linguistic truth-valued implication algebra [14]. Łukasiewicz logic has been studied in numerous papers on fuzzy and many-valued logic. Pavelka showed in [1] that the only natural way of formalizing fuzzy logic for truth values in a finite chain or the unit interval $[0, 1]$ is by using the Łukasiewicz implication operator or some isomorphic forms of it.

2 Algorithm to Implement the Backward Reasoning Strategy

This section explains the process followed to answer queries posted to our system. This section offers a Backward Reasoning algorithm in which query is taken as a starting point and then reason backwards in time from the goal to the facts that sustain a conclusion. The advantage of this strategy is that focused by a goal (a specific query) it only explores part of the Knowledge Base that is necessary to answer the query. The search process is then more focused and efficient than in the forward reasoning mode. We provide next an informal explanation of the strategy. In describing the implementation we will resort to two concepts, supporting tree and the list of activation times [12-13].

Notation: suppose that we want to judge whether $Query([-]s, t, v_\alpha)$ is true or not (i.e., whether $([-]s, t, v_\beta)$: $v_\beta \geq v_\alpha$ or not). Here we use '$[-]s$' as an abbreviation for 's or $-s$'. We represent with λ to be $v_i \in L$, one of many possible linguistic values which is considered the minimum level of credibility for a proposition (a "credibility threshold"). For a tree to be activated each rule $(s_1 \wedge s_2 \wedge \ldots \wedge s_n \rightarrow s, v_\tau)$ or $(s_1 \wedge s_2 \wedge \ldots \wedge s_n \rightarrow Os, v_\delta)$ in the tree should be such that for all s_i: (s_i, t, v_{β_i}), $v_{\beta_i} \in L$, $v_\theta = \mathrm{Min}_i(v_{\beta_i}) \geq v_{m+\alpha-\tau} \geq \lambda$ or $v_\theta = \mathrm{Min}_i(v_{\beta_i}) \geq v_{m+\alpha-\delta} \geq \lambda$ respectively, $i=1,\ldots, n$ (in fact assume $v_\theta = \mathrm{Min}_i(v_{\beta_i})$), to find the suitable v_θ supporting a given state s such that $Query([-]s, t, v_\alpha)$ is true, it requires $v_\alpha \geq v_\theta \otimes v_\tau$ following the MTMP rule [11], it leads to the condition that is $v_\theta \geq v_{m+\alpha-\tau}$. Actually this can be called a backward search strategy. The algorithm is given further down.

In step (1) "Obtain list AcTimes of Activation Times" means AcTimes is the decreasing order list that is obtained from merging the decreasing ordered lists of activation times for STT_s and STT_{-s}.

In step (2) "t becomes the next available time closest to *time* in AcTimes" means t is made max(AcTimes) and that time is extracted from the AcTimes list. If $Query([-]s, t, v_\alpha)$ with $0 \leq t <$ time then s is assumed to hold at *time* by persistency because should its truth value have changed in between t and *time* then a tree to support $Query(s', t', v_{\beta'})$ with s' the opposite of $[-]s$, $v_{\beta'} \geq v_\alpha$, and $t < t' \leq$ *time* should have been found at an earlier step.

Notice that same-time rules are requested to be cycle free and "stratified" [12]. Each cycle generated by a query at time t will have a finite number of iterations until they are evaluated at 0.

Input:
- the sets of independent and dependent states: S_I, S_D
- a set of non-cyclic Same-Time Rules, R_s
- a set of Next-Time Rules, R_n

- a set of facts *called* initial conditions (I_c) which provide the truth values of states in $S_I \cup S_D$ at time 0
- a set of known events, E, describing state ingressions
- a credibility threshold λ
- $Query([-]s, t, v_\alpha)$

Output: whether $Query([-]s, t, v_\alpha)$ is true or not (i.e., whether $([-]s, t, v_\beta): v_\beta \geq v_\alpha$
or not) and an explanation for the answer

IF $holds([-]s, time, v_\beta) \in I_c$ or $occurs(ingr([-]s),(time-1)^*, v_\beta) \in E$ with $v_\beta \geq v_\alpha$
  THEN answer "true" ["false"] and give fact as explanation
  ELSE $(Query([-]s, t, v_\alpha)$ must be inferred by deduction, possibly by persistence)
    obtain the sets of trees STT_s and $STT_{\neg s}$
    1) Obtain list AcTimes of Activation Times
    2) t becomes the next available time closest to *time* in AcTimes
    3) REPEAT
      a) find a tree in STT_s, $STT_{\neg s}$ with main rule
      (a1) $r: (s_1 \wedge s_2 \wedge \ldots \wedge s_n \rightarrow [-]s, v_\tau) \in R_s$ activated at t such that $v_\tau \geq v_\alpha$, and
        *) for each $s_i \in S_I$: $holds(s_i, t, v_{\beta_i})$ with $v_\theta = Min_i(v_{\beta_i})$ such that

$$v_\theta = Min_i(v_{\beta_i}) \geq v_{m+\alpha-\tau} \geq \lambda.$$

        **) for each $s_d \in S_D$: $holds(s_d, t, v_{\beta_d})$ with $v_{\beta_d} \geq \lambda$, or

      (a2) $r: (s_1 \wedge s_2 \wedge \ldots \wedge s_n \rightarrow Os, v_\delta) \in R_n$ activated at t such that $v_\delta \geq v_\alpha$,
        *) for each $s_i \in S_I$: $holds(s_i, t-1, v_{\beta_i})$ with $v_\theta = Min_i(v_{\beta_i})$ such that

$$v_\theta = Min_i(v_{\beta_i}) \geq v_{m+\alpha-\delta} \geq \lambda.$$

        **) for each $s_d \in S_D$: $holds(s_d, t-1, v_{\beta_d})$ with $v_{\beta_d} \geq \lambda$

      b) IF $[-]s$ can be proved true from a tree
        THEN answer "true" ["false"] and use the tree as the explanation
        ELSE t becomes the next available time closest to *time* in AcTimes
    UNTIL $(([-]s, t, v_\alpha)$ can be proved true from a tree).

Notice than whilst in (a1-*) finding out whether $holds(s_i, t, v_{\beta_i})$ with $v_\theta = Min_i(v_{\beta_i}) \geq v_{m+\alpha-\tau} \geq \lambda$ only requires checking whether $occurs(ingr([-]s),(time-1)^*, v_\beta) \in E$ with $v_\beta \geq v_\alpha$ or not; in (a1-**) checking that for each $s_d \in S_D$: $holds(s_d, t, v_{\beta_d})$ with $v_{\beta_d} \geq \lambda$ means using this algorithm through a separate recursive call with $Query(s_d, t, v_{\beta_d})$ for each one of those s_d.

3 Reasoning under Uncertainty in a Smart Home

According to Section 1.1, we assume a 7-level uncertainty degree classification for such information: $L_7 = \{v_0 = false, v_1 = very\ low, v_2 = low, v_3 = medium, v_4 = high, v_5 = very\ high, v_6 = true\}$, and we need to decide after a sequence of events with various levels of uncertainty associated if the alarm should be turned on in such circumstances.

Independent atomic states: *cookerOn*, ±*atKitchen*, *umt3u*.

Dependent atomic states: ±*cu*, ±*hazzard*, ±*alarmOn*, −*umt3u*, −*cookerOn*.

Same-time rules:

Stage 1:   *R1.* −*atKitchen* ∧ *cookerOn* ∧*umt3u* → *cu* ,
         R2. −*cookerOn* → −*alarmOn* , *R3.* −*cookerOn* → −*hazzard* ,
         R4. −*cookerOn* → −*umt3u* , *R5.* −*cookerOn* → −*cu*

Stage 2:   *R6.* *cu* → *alarmOn* , *R7.* *cu* → *hazzard*

Next-time rule: *R8.* *alarmOn* → O (−*cookerOn*)

All rules except *R6*, *R7* and *R8* are concerned with the cooker, so we set the certainty degree of these rules to be true (v_6). But because *R1* also involves more sensors, to detect presence at kitchen and sensing absence of movement (another sensor involved) then we can bring its confidence down another level, so we have: $R1(v_4)$, $R2(v_5)$, $R3(v_5)$, $R4(v_5)$, $R5(v_5)$, $R6(v_6)$, $R7(v_6)$, $R8(v_6)$. We define the trigger level of all rules to be v_3 and provide the events as follows:

Occurs(*ingr*(*atKitchen*), 0*, v_5), *Occurs*(*ingr*(*cookerOn*), 0*, v_5),
Occurs(*ingr*(−*atKitchen*), 1*, v_5), *Occurs*(*ingr*(*umt3u*), 4*, v_5).

Table 1 shows the final result of the query through the backward reasoning algorithm, and we can see that, the algorithm does not search all the states in every time slot, it only focuses on the relate states, ignore those unrelated ones (blank cells in Table 1).

Table 1. The states explored by the Backward Reasoning algorithm as a consequence of "Query(alarmOn, 5, v_3)?"

State \ Time	5	4	3	2	1	0
alarmOn	v_3					
Cu	v_3					
umt3u	v_5					
atKitchen	v_1	v_1	v_1	v_1		
cookerOn	v_5	v_5	v_5	v_5	v_5	

4 Conclusions

This paper provided a linguistic truth-valued temporal reasoning framework which can be applied to handle the decision-making problems with uncertainty in dynamic systems. A backward reasoning algorithm was also provided, which complemented a previous forward reasoning algorithm and is more focused and suitable for efficient query answering. The scenario used to exemplify how the algorithm works shown that the system is usable. We are currently analyzing the extension to consider time interval representation and handling.

References

1. Pavelka, J.: On fuzzy logic I: multiple-valued rules of inference, II: enriched residuated lattices and semantics of propositional calculi, III: semantical completeness of some multiple-valued propositional calculi. Zeitschr. F. Math. Logik und Grundlagend. Math., Vol. 25, pp. 45-52, 119-134, 447-464 (1979).
2. Gottwald, S.: A Treatise on Many-Valued Logics, Studies in Logic and Computation, vol. 9, Research Studies Press Ltd., Baldock (2001).
3. Xu, Y., Ruan, D., Qin, K., Liu, J.: Lattice-valued Logic: An Alternative Approach to Treat Fuzziness and Incomparability. Springer-Verlag (2003).
4. Galton, A.: Temporal Logics and Their Applications, Academic Press, London (1987).
5. Augusto, J.: A General framework for Reasoning about Change. New Generation Computing, Vol. 21, pp. 209-247, Ohmsha, Ltd and Springer Verlag (2003).
6. Kröger, F., Merz, S.: Temporal Logic and State Systems, Springer (2008).
7. Dubois, D., HadjAli, A., Prade. H.: Fuzziness and uncertainty in temporal reasoning. JUCS, Vol.9, pp.1168-1195 (2003).
8. Escalada-Imaz, G.: A temporal many-valued logic for real time control systems. In: Proceeding of the 9th International Conference on Artificial Intelligence: Methodology, Systems, and Applications, pp. 91-100 (2000).
9. Mucientes, M., Iglesias, R., Regueiro, C., Bugarin, A., Barro. S.: A fuzzy temporal rule-based velocity controller for mobile robotics. Fuzzy Sets and System, Vol. 134, pp. 83-99 (2003).
10. Schockaert, S., Cock, M.: Temporal reasoning about fuzzy intervals. Artificial Intelligence, vol. 172, pp. 1158-1193 (2008).
11. Lu, Z., Liu, J., Augusto J., Wang H.: Multi-valued temporal reasoning framework for decision-making. In: Proceeding of the 8th International FLINS Conference, pp. 301-306 (2008).
12. Galton, A., Augusto, J.: Stratified causal theories for reasoning about deterministic devices and protocols. In: Proceedings of 9th International Symposium on Temporal Representation and Reasoning, pp.52-54 (2002)
13. Augusto, J., McCullagh, P., Croft V., Walkden. J.: Enhanced healthcare provision through assisted decision-making in a smart home environment. Proceedings of 2nd Workshop on Artificial Intelligence Techniques for Ambient Intelligence (AITAmI07), pp.27-32 (2007).
14. Liu, J., Martinez, L., Xu, Y., Lu, Z.: Automated Reasoning Algorithm for Linguistic Valued Lukasiewicz Propositional Logic. In: Proceedings of the 37th International Symposium on Multiple-Valued Logic (ISMVL'07), pp.29 (2007).

Extending arc-consistency algorithms for Non-Normalized CSPs

Marlene Arangu and Miguel A. Salido and Federico Barber

Abstract Arc-consistency algorithms are widely used to prune the search space of CSPs. Two of the most well-known and frequently used arc-consistency algorithms for filtering CSPs are AC3 and AC4. These algorithms repeatedly carry out revisions and they require support checks for identifying and deleting all unsupported values from the domains. Nevertheless, many revisions are ineffective, that is, they cannot delete any value and they consume a lot of checks and time. In this paper, we present AC4-OP and AC3-NN, two extended versions of AC4 and AC3 respectively, for dealing with non-normalized CSPs. Furthermore AC4-OP is an optimized version of AC4 that manages the binary and non-normalized constraints in only one direction, storing for their later evaluation the inverse supports that are found. The use of AC4-OP reduces number of constraint checks by 50%. Also, the average of propagations is reduced by at least 15% while pruning the same search space as AC4.

1 Introduction

Arc-consistency is the basic propagation mechanism that is probably used in all CSP solvers [3]. Proposing efficient algorithms for enforcing arc-consistency has always been considered as a central question in the constraint reasoning community. However, the main arc-consistency techniques are focused on normalized CSPs, that is, CSPs where any pair of variables can be restricted to no more than one constraint. Nevertheless, many real problems are modeled with constraints that involve the same set of variables (non-normalized CSPs), so it is necessary to develop filtering techniques to manage these resultant CSPs.

The main reason for studying AC3[5] and AC4[6] are the following: (1) they are one of the widely and frequently used algorithms for maintaining arc-consistency

Marlene Arangu, Miguel A. Salido, Federico Barber
Instituto de Automática e Informática Industrial, Universidad Politcnica de Valencia, Camino de Vera, s/n, Valencia, Spain. e-mail: {marangu,msalido,fbarber}@dsic.upv.es

M. Bramer et al. (eds.), *Research and Development in Intelligent Systems XXVI*,
DOI 10.1007/978-1-84882-983-1_24, © Springer-Verlag London Limited 2010

[2]; (2) the ideas about arc consistency algorithms always allow extensions to non-normalized binary CSPs [3]; and, (3) we can add the bidirectionality for AC4 in order to reduce its cost.

By following standard notations and definitions in the literature [3, 1, 4], we summarize the basic definitions and notations used in this paper:

Constraint Satisfaction Problem, CSP is a triple $P = \langle X, D, R \rangle$, where X is the finite set of variables $\{X_1, X_2, ..., X_n\}$. D is a set of domains $D = \{D_1, D_2, ..., D_n\}$ such that, for each variable $X_i \in X$, there is a finite set of values that each variable can take. R is a finite set of constraints $R = \{R_1, R_2, ..., R_m\}$ which restrict the values that the variables can simultaneously take.

Support value: Given $a \in D_i$, $b \in D_j$. If $\langle X_i, a \rangle$ and $\langle X_j, b \rangle$ satisfy the constraint R_{ij}, then b supports a. **Symmetry of the constraint:** If the value $b \in D_j$ supports a value $a \in D_i$, then a supports b as well.

Arc-consistency: A *value $a \in D_i$ is arc-consistent* relative to X_j, iff there exists a value $b \in D_j$ such that $\langle X_i, a \rangle$ and $\langle X_j, b \rangle$ satisfy the constraint R_{ij}. A *variable X_i is arc-consistent* relative to X_j iff all values in D_i are arc-consistent. A *CSP is arc-consistent* iff all the variables are arc-consistent.

In this paper, we limit our attention to binary and non-normalized CSPs (**binary**: all constraints in R involve two variables; **non-normalized**: different constraints may involve exactly the same variables). We denote: R_{ij} as the direct constraint defined over the variables X_i and X_j (given by the user). R'_{ji} as the same constraint in the inverse direction over the variables X_i and X_j (inverse constraint)[1].

2 AC4-OP algorithm

The main AC4 [6] algorithm has two phases: initialization of the data structures and propagation. These initializations are used: to remember pairs of consistent values of variables (matrix S); to count "supporting" values from the domain of the variable (matrix *Counter*); to remove those values that do not have any support and to remember them (matrix M and queue Q). In order to manage non-normalized instances, the matrix *Counter* of Initialization phase of AC4 must be increased with the variable *total* (*Counter = Counter + total* instead of *Counter = total*). We denote AC4-NN as the AC4 algorithm with this change.

We propose the AC4-OP algorithm(see Algorithms 1 and 2). It uses the same structures than AC4, but it adds a new array, named *suppInv*, to store the supports of each value of a variable. Thus, the size of *suppInv* is the maximum size of all domains (*maxD*). Thus, after the revision of the values $a \in D_i$ are updated (*Counter*$[X_i, a, X_j]$), we can prune $b \in D_j$ whose *suppInv*$[b] = 0$ (if any). Thus, we do not need to evaluate the inverse constraint R'_{ji}.

Due to the fact that the same pair of variables X_i, X_j may be involved in more than one constraint R_{ij} (non-normalized CSPs), the counters of supports may have

---

[1] in [3] inverse constraint is named transposition.

Algorithm 1: Procedure InitializeAC4OP

Data: $P = \langle X, D, R \rangle$ /*R involves direct constraints*/
Result: initial=**true** and P', Q, S, M, *Counter* or initial=**false** and P' (which is arc-inconsistent).
begin

```
1      Q ← {}
2      S[X_j, b] ← {}  / * ∀X_j ∈ X ∧ ∀b ∈ D_j * /
3      M[X_i, a] = 1  / * ∀X_i ∈ X ∧ ∀a ∈ D_i * /
4      Counter[X_i, a, X_j] = 0  / * ∀X_i, X_j ∈ X ∧ ∀a ∈ D_i * /
5      suppInv[b] = 0  / * ∀b ∈ [1, maxD] * /
6      for every arc R_ij ∈ R do
7          for each a ∈ D_i do
8              total = 0
9              for each b ∈ D_j do
10                 if (⟨X_i, a⟩, ⟨X_j, b⟩) ∈ R_ij then
11                     total = total + 1
12                     Append(S[X_j, b], ⟨X_i, a⟩)
13                     Counter[X_j, b, X_i] = Counter[X_j, b, X_i] + 1
14                     suppInv[b] = suppInv[b] + 1
15                     Append(S[X_i, a], ⟨X_j, b⟩)

16             if total = 0 then
17                 remove a from D_i
18                 if D_i = φ then
                       return initial = false
19                 else
                       if S[X_i, a] ≠ {} then
20                         Q ← Q ∪ ⟨X_i, a⟩

21                 M[X_i, a] = 0
22             else
23                 Counter[X_i, a, X_j] = Counter[X_i, a, X_j] + total

24         for each b ∈ D_j do
25             if suppInv[b] = 0 then
26                 remove b from D_j
27                 if D_j = φ then
28                     return initial = false
29                 else
                       if S[X_j, b] ≠ {} then
30                         Q ← Q ∪ ⟨X_j, b⟩

31                 M[X_j, b] = 0
32             else
                   suppInv[b] = 0

33     return initial = true and Q, M, S, Counter
   end
```

---

previous stored values before constraint sharing the same variables. Pruning is carried out according to the counters in each constraint. The counter of supports of variable X_i (*total*) is initialized to 0 for each value $a \in D_i$. However, the counter of supports of variable X_j (inverse supports) must be split in two different counters: $Counter[X_j, b, X_i]$ and $suppInv[b]$. The array $suppInv$ stores the number of supports for each value of X_j. This array is initialized to zero (see Algorithm 1, step 5). When the value $b \in D_j$ supports the value $a \in D_i$, $suppInv[b]$ will be increased (see Algorithm 1, step 14). During the loop of steps 9-15, the array is updated in order to be analyzed in step 25. Upon completion of processing all values of D_i, if a value b of

---

Algorithm 2: Procedure AC4-OP

Data: A CSP, $P = \langle X, D, R \rangle$
Result: true and P' (which is arc-consistent) or **false** and P' (which is arc-inconsistent)
begin
1   InitilizeAC4OP(P)
2   **if** $initial = true$ **then**
3   **while** $Q \neq \phi$ **do**
4   select and delete $\langle X_j, b \rangle$ from queue Q
5   **for** *each* $\langle X_i, a \rangle \in S[X_j, b]$ **do**
6              $Counter[X_i, a, X_j] = Counter[X_i, a, X_j] - 1$
7   **if** $Counter[X_i, a, X_j] = 0 \wedge M[X_i, a] = 1$ **then**
8   remove a from D_i
9   **if** $D_i = \phi$ **then**
                    return false
10   **else**
11   **if** $S[X_i, a] \neq \{\}$ **then**
12                     $Q \leftarrow Q \cup \langle X_i, a \rangle$
13              $M[X_i, a] = 0$

14   **return** true
15   **else**
        return false
end

D_j has not any support ($suppInv[b] = 0$), then this value is pruned from the domain D_j. If $suppInv[b] > 0$ then b is supported and it is initialized to 0 (see Algorithm 1, step 32) for further use of this array.

Furthermore, AC4-OP only propagates those tuples that are supported by another tuple. (See steps 20, 30 of Algorithm 1, and step 12 of Algorithm 2). Thus, AC4-OP avoids inefficient propagations of tuples for Q, and it avoids inefficient constraint checking of those tuples.

3 AC3-NN

AC3[5] algorithm was originally designed for directed graphs (it only process R_{ij} and it does not process R_{ji}). Subsequent references of AC3 found in literature [1, 3, 4] assume that the constraints should be assessed in both directions: direct constraint R_{ij} and inverse constraint R_{ji}. Furthermore, many authors assume that CSPs are binary and there exist only one constraint between each pair of variables (normalized). However, a CSP can be non-normalized, that is, there exist some constraints between two variables ($R_{ij}, R'_{ij}, R''_{ij}$, etc).

We propose the AC3NN algorithm (see Algorithm 3) for deal with non-normalized CSP. In order to distinguish the constraints that involve the same pair of variables, we denote each constraint R_{ij} by a pair $C :< C.id, C.R >$ such as $C.id$ is a label (integer number) and $C.R$ is the own constraint. Thus if C represents a direct constraint R_{ij}, then C' represents the inverse constraint R_{ji}.

Algorithm 3: Procedure AC3NN

Data: A CSP, $P = \langle X, D, R \rangle$
Result: **true** and P' (which is arc consistent) or **false** and P' (which is arc inconsistent because some domain remains empty)

begin

```
 1      Cm = ∅
 2      n = 0
 3      for every constraint Rij ∈ R do
 4          New (C)
 5          Assign C.id = n and C.R = Rij
 6          Append (Cm, (C))
 7          n++
 8          New (C')
 9          Assign C'.id = n and C'.R = Rji
10          Append (Cm, (C'))
11          n++
12      for every constraint C do
13          Append (Q, (C))
14      while Q ≠ ∅ do
15          select and delete Cp from queue Q
16          Rij = Cp.R
17          if Revise(Rij) = true then
18              if Di ≠ ∅ then
19                  Append (Q, (Ck)) with (Ck.id ≠ Cp.id) and (Ck.R = Rki); ∀ Ck ∈ Cm
20              else
21                  return false /*empty domain*/
22      return true
```

end

---

4 Experimental Results

In this section, we present some results to empirically demonstrate the practical efficiency of AC4-OP and AC3-NN. To this end, we compare the behavior of AC4-NN (non-normalized version of AC4), AC4-OP and AC3-NN in non-normalized CSPs. The experiments were performed on random problems. A random CSP instance was characterized by the 4-tuple $< n, d, m, b >$, where n was the number of variables; d the domain size; m the number of binary constraints; and b the number of non-normalized constraint. All the variables maintained the same size domain. We evaluated 50 test cases for each type of problem. The experiments were conducted on a PC Intel Core 2 Q9550 (2.83 GHz processor and 3 GB RAM).

Table 1 shows the number of Cc and running time in arc-consistent instances: $< n, 100, 800, 2 >$. The results show that the number of Cc and running time were lower in AC4-OP than AC4-NN in all cases with an average of 50% and 30%, respectively. Furthermore, Cc and time were lower in both AC4-NN and AC4-OP than in AC3-NN in all cases. This is due to the fact that AC4-NN and AC4-OP looked for all supports and AC3-NN looked for only one support.

Table 2 shows the number of Cc in arc-consistent instances $< 50, 100, m, 2 >$. The results were similar concerning the number of Cc was also reduced by AC4-OP in all cases by more than 50%. Also, the running time was reduced by AC4-OP in all cases by more than 8% in relation to AC4-NN.

Table 1 Running time (ms) and Number of constraint checks by using AC4NN, AC4-OP and AC3NN in arc-consistent and non-normalized instances $< n, 100, 800, 2 >$.

n	pruning	AC4-NN		AC4-OP		AC3-NN	
		(Time)	(Cc)	(Time)	(Cc)	(Time)	(Cc)
50	50	2095	16009901	1794	8005001	39	2145001
70	70	2201	16013901	1851	8007001	47	2147001
90	90	2286	16017901	1884	8009001	46	2149001
110	110	2338	16021901	1862	8011001	32	2150001
130	130	2514	16025901	1878	8013001	31	2151001
150	150	2548	16029901	1831	8015001	31	2153001

Table 2 Running time and number of constraint checks (Cc) using AC4 and AC4-OP in arc-consistent and non-normalized instances $< 50, 100, m, 2 >$.

m	pruning	AC4-NN		AC4-OP		AC3-NN	
		(Time)	(Cc)	(Time)	(Cc)	(Time)	(Cc)
100	50	406	2009889	391	1004995	1	272495
200	50	624	4009901	589	2005001	1	540001
300	50	832	6009901	774	3005001	16	807501
400	50	1047	8009901	965	4005001	16	1075001
500	50	1243	10009901	1146	5005001	16	1342501
600	50	1447	12009901	1343	6005001	31	1610001
700	50	1635	14009901	1510	7005001	31	1877501

5 Conclusions

Filtering techniques are widely used to prune the search space of CSPs. In this paper, we present two versions of AC3 and AC4 for binary non-normalized CSPs, called AC3-NN and AC4-OP, respectively. AC4-OP algorithm prunes the same search space as AC4, but its efficiency is provided by both the initialization strategy and the propagation strategy. In the evaluation section, it can be observed that the number of constraint checks and running time were reduced by AC3-NN and AC4-OP.

References

1. R. Barták. Theory and practice of constraint propagation. In J. Figwer, editor, *Proceedings of the 3rd Workshop on Constraint Programming in Decision and Control*, 2001.
2. R. Barták. Constraint propagation and backtracking-based search. In *Lecture Notes. First international summer school on CP*, 2005.
3. C. Bessiere. Constraint propagation. Technical report, CNRS/University of Montpellier, 2006.
4. R. Dechter. *Constraint Processing*. Morgan Kaufmann, 2003.
5. A. K. Mackworth. Consistency in networks of relations. *AI*, 8:99–118, 1977.
6. R. Mohr and T.C. Henderson. Arc and path consistency revised. *AI*, 28:225–233, 1986.

Remainder Subset Awareness for Feature Subset Selection

Gabriel Prat-Masramon and Lluís A. Belanche-Muñoz

Abstract Feature subset selection has become more and more a common topic of research. This popularity is partly due to the growth in the number of features and application domains. It is of the greatest importance to take the most of every evaluation of the inducer, which is normally the more costly part. In this paper, a technique is proposed that takes into account the inducer evaluation both in the current subset and in the remainder subset (its complementary set) and is applicable to any sequential subset selection algorithm at a reasonable overhead in cost. Its feasibility is demonstrated on a series of benchmark data sets.

1 Introduction

In the last few years *feature selection* has become a more and more common topic of research, a fact probably due to the growth of the number of features involved. These problems are very common in medicine and biology; e.g. molecule classification, gene selection or medical diagnostics.

This work addresses the problem of *selecting a subset of features* from a given set by introducing a general-purpose modification for feature subset selection algorithms which iteratively select and discard features. The idea is to use the evaluation of the inducer in the so-called *remainder set* (the set complementary to the subset of selected features) as an additional source of information.

Gabriel Prat-Masramon
Faculty of Computer Science
Polytechnical University of Catalonia
Barcelona, Spain e-mail: grat@lsi.upc.edu

Lluís A. Belanche-Muñoz
Faculty of Computer Science
Polytechnical University of Catalonia
Barcelona, Spain e-mail: belanche@lsi.upc.edu

M. Bramer et al. (eds.), *Research and Development in Intelligent Systems XXVI*,
DOI 10.1007/978-1-84882-983-1_25, © Springer-Verlag London Limited 2010

2 The Remainder Set of Features

It is common to see feature subset selection in a set Y of size n as an *optimization problem* where the search space is $\mathscr{P}(Y)$ [5]. In this setting, the *feature selection problem* is to find an optimal subset $X^* \in \mathscr{P}(Y)$ which maximizes a given evaluation criterion $J : \mathscr{P}(Y) \rightarrow [0,1]$ (filter or wrapper). We will refer to $J(X)$ as the *usefulness* of feature subset X [1].

When the goal is to find an optimal subset X^*, it seems plausible to choose an X_k in a stepwise and greedy way (1). That is what the well known sequential forward generation (SFG) and sequential backward generation (SBG) algorithms do [8, 6].

$$X_k = \arg\max_{X \in \mathbf{S}_k} J(X), \qquad k = 1, \ldots, n \qquad (1)$$

In real problems features are far from independent, thus not always the best subset in every iteration has to point to the best overall solution. Quite possibly there is some combination of features that *would* lead to a final better solution if chosen now. By considering the current set of features X_k another set is implicitly created, the set of *remaining* features or *remainder set* $Y_k = Y \setminus X_k$. This set can also give information about the new feature to be added or removed at every step. We claim that, in many cases, a way to improve the detection of *feature interactions* is to assess how the addition/removal of a feature to/from X_k (a removal/addition, from the point of view of Y_k) affects the *usefulness* of Y_k.

2.1 Theoretical analysis and examples

The intuitive explanation for using the remainder set is that the optimal set X^* that the algorithm is trying to find could be either in X_k, in Y_k or split among the two. J should give higher values to a set containing X^* and its value should diminish when removing a feature from X^*. Then one should add the best feature to X_k, and whose removal is worse for Y_k, i.e. to maximize $J(X_k)$ and minimize $J(Y_k)$. The general idea is called *Remainder Subset Awareness* (RSA) for obvious reasons. This RSA idea tries to alleviate some of the weaknesses of SFG and SBG:

1. SFG (specially at its first steps) evaluates the features on their own, not taking into account the relationships between them [3]; thus two features that are very good when used together but that are not that good individually may not be selected. Note these two features would *both* belong to the remainder set, that should be then affected by the removal of either.
2. SBG (specially at its first steps) evaluates each feature with all the irrelevant and redundant features that there may be in Y; this may discard a relevant feature early on, due to the disturbing effects of the irrelevant ones over J.

---

[1] It is very convenient to include resampling in the evaluation criterion; e.g. J could be a cross-validated value.

More formally, by definition of $X^* \equiv \arg\max_{X \in \mathscr{P}(Y)} J(X)$ we have that $J(X^*) > J(X^* \setminus \{x\}), \forall x \in X^*$. But on the other hand, it is not true that $J(X_k \setminus \{z\}) > J(X_k \setminus \{x\}), \forall X_k \supset X^*, \forall x \in X^*, \forall z \notin X^*$. This inequality states that removing a feature in X^* from any set X_k that contains X^* is always more harmful than removing a feature not in X^* from this same set. If this was always true, then SBG would always find X^*, as it would remove one feature not in X^* at each step, until X^* was found. It would be always true only if the J criterion was not affected by the addition of irrelevant of redundant features. It will certainly not be true if the features in $X_k \setminus X^*$ affect the results of J. As stated in the introduction, irrelevant or redundant features often lead classifiers to find false regularities (specially in small sample situations) instead of learning from the features that really determine the target.

Two artificial problems have been chosen to illustrate the potential benefits of the RSA idea. The choice has been made due to their special characteristics that make either SFG or SBG fail to find the best solution. As the structure and best solution to these problems is known the benefits can be clearly explained.

- The CORRAL data set has two classes and six boolean features (A_0; A_1; B_0; B_1; I; C). Feature I is irrelevant, feature C is correlated to the class label 75% of the time, but the other four features can be combined to fully predict the class value. SFG will choose C first as it is the best feature when taken all alone [4]. The hypothesis is that the *usefulness* of the remainder set would be so high if C was chosen that SFG enhanced with the RSA idea would not choose it.
- The ANTICORRAL data set has been generated *ad hoc* for this paper. It is a three class problem with 11 continuous features ($I_1, I_2, \ldots, I_9, C_1, C_2$). Features I_1 to I_9 follow a normal distribution with mean equal to the class of the example and a standard deviation of 1. Feature C_1 is generated as $C_{1i} = \mathcal{N}(\mu = Y_i, \sigma^2 = 0.5)$, while feature C_2 is generated by the formula: $C_{2i} = C_{1i} - Y_i + \mathcal{N}(\mu = 1, \sigma^2 = 0.2)$. The class can be predicted using C_1 and C_2. The hypothesis is that SBG will readily discard C_2 in the *firsts* steps, due to the influence of the I_j features; while RSA will detect the harm to Y_0 when discarding C_2 and find the best solution.

The two hypothesis were confirmed by the results of the experiments run using the algorithms and the experimental setup explained in the following sections. Table 1 shows mean *error rates* and the p-value of the Wilcoxon-Mann-Whitney (WMW) test, indicating that the difference is statistically significant at the 95% level. The table also shows the median number of selected features and its absolute deviation.

Table 1 Results for SFG on CORRAL and SBG on ANTICORRAL. SFG$^+$ and SBG$^+$ are SFG, SBG enhanced with the RSA idea; F, F^+ stand for the final number of features.

Problem	SFG/SBG	SFG$^+$/SBG$^+$	p-value	F	F^+
CORRAL	0.077	0.009	**0.002**	5.0±0.0	4.0±0.0
ANTICORRAL	0.132	0.023	**0.007**	7.0±2.2	2.0±0.0

2.2 Combination function

With the above formulation we have a multi-objective problem, since not always the subset with maximum $J(X_k)$ will be the same as the subset with minimum $J(Y_k)$. Therefore, a trade-off has to be found that partly optimizes both. A reasonable alternative is to choose the subset which maximizes some predefined function f of the two criteria among the two candidate subsets:

$$\arg\max_{X \in S_k} f[J(X), J(Y \setminus X)], \qquad k = 1, \dots, n \tag{2}$$

The function $f : (0,1)^2 \to (0,1)$ is chosen to be *continuous* in both arguments, *increasing* in the first and *decreasing* in the second. It also should allow control on the relative importance of the two arguments (thus it is non-symmetric). A sequential algorithm can then be modified by *replacing* the function to maximize at each step from the one in (1) to the one in (2).

Various functions that satisfied the previous conditions have been tested. We choose the best function based on our experiments which was one of the simplest:

$$f(x,y) = \frac{x \cdot w_x - y \cdot w_y + 1}{2}, \quad w_x, w_y \in (0,1). \tag{3}$$

These weights have to be selected taking into account the weaknesses of SFG and SBG presented above. We take the weights to be proportional to the *usefulness* of the set we are about to modify: $w_x = J(X_{k-1})$ and $w_y = J(Y \setminus X_{k-1})$. Thus giving more importance to more useful sets: when X_k is better than Y_k, the features that make it even better are preferred; when Y_k is better than X_k (e.g. at the first steps of SFG) those that harm Y_k the most are preferred over others that helped X_k more.

3 Experimental work

Experimental work is now presented in order to assess the described modifications using SFG and SBG and their RSA counterparts SFG$^+$ and SBG$^+$. The algorithms were implemented using the R language [7]. We used well-known datasets from the UCI repository [1], as well as *microarray* gene expression problems, with scarce data and high dimensionality, all of them listed in Table 2. Each experiment consists of an *outer* loop of 5x2-fold feature selection [2]. It keeps half of the examples out of the feature selection process and uses them as a test set to evaluate the quality of the selected features. For every step of the outer loop, two feature selection processes are conducted with the same examples, one with the original algorithm and one with the RSA version. The selected objective function is the 1-nearest neighbor (1NN) learner, since arguably 1NN is one of the inducers that suffers the most in presence of redundant or irrelevant features. However, the modifications do not depend on this choice and others could be possible. This evaluation is resampled in another (*inner*)

Table 2 Used datasets. Left: UCI data sets descriptions. Right: Microarray data sets descriptions

Problem	features	classes	examples
IONOSPHERE	34	2	351
IRIS	4	3	50
MAMMOGRAM	65	2	86
MUSK	166	2	476
SONAR	60	2	208
SPECT	22	2	267
SPECTF	44	2	267
WAVEFORM	21	3	5,000
WDBC	10	2	699

Problem	features	classes	examples
BREAST CANCER	24,481	2	97
COLON TUMOR	2,000	2	62
GCM	16,063	14	190
LEUKEMIA	7,129	2	72
LUNG CANCER	12,533	2	181
PROSTATE CANCER	12,600	2	136

5x2-fold cross-validation loop for a more informed estimation of subset usefulness. Forward methods run until all the features are selected and backward ones until all have been removed. Then the *best* of the obtained sequence of subsets is returned. This subset is evaluated in the corresponding test set using the same 1NN inducer. Finally a WMW test is conducted on the sets of classification errors from each algorithm to determine whether the difference is statistically significant.

The results are displayed in Table 3. The table also shows the median of the size of the final selected subsets and its absolute deviation. Few results are signaled as

Table 3 Detailed results. Figures in boldface correspond to statistically significant improvements.

Problem	SFG	SFG$^+$	F	F^+	SBG	SBG$^+$	F	F^+
IONOSPHERE	0.133	0.122	5±3.0	5.5±1.5	0.144	0.128	10.50±5.9	6.5±1.5
IRIS	0.075	0.072	2±1.5	2±1.5	0.080	0.070	2±1.5	1±0.0
MAMMOGRAM	0.291	0.286	9±5.9	11.5±3.7	0.302	0.265	14±11.9	11.50±3.0
MUSK	0.133	0.140	50±11.1	47.5±7.4	0.161	0.157	31.5±17.0	49.5±18.5
SONAR	0.214	**0.183**	21.5±10.4	23±8.15	0.190	0.180	17±4.5	27±4.5
SPECT	0.227	0.211	11±3.0	8±3.0	0.240	0.230	4.5±2.2	7±4.5
SPECTF	0.263	0.255	10.5±5.2	7.5±5.2	0.277	0.270	16±5.9	11±7.4
WAVEFORM	0.223	**0.216**	15±3.0	16.5±3.0	0.224	**0.215**	16±1.5	17.00±3.0
WDBC	0.086	0.085	19±5.9	18±4.5	0.083	0.085	17.5±8.2	15±8.9
BREAST CANCER	0.289	0.286	29±15.6	49±22.2	0.328	0.315	23±16.3	21±17.0
COLON TUMOR	0.258	0.252	20±14.8	11.5±11.9	0.219	0.216	30±34.8	25±30.4
GCM	0.501	0.491	45±22.2	44±27.4	0.561	**0.503**	34±25.2	60.5±29.7
LEUKEMIA	0.094	0.092	2.5±0.7	2±2.2	0.092	0.089	8.5±3.7	3±1.48
LUNG CANCER	0.031	0.028	2±0.0	7.5±3.0	0.045	0.032	9±5.2	3.5±2.2
PROSTATE CANCER	0.103	0.134	12±5.19	14.5±5.2	0.132	0.157	29±20.8	19.5±15.6

statistically significant according to the WMW test at the 95% level (*p*-value lower than 0.05). Two of them when comparing SFG to SFG$^+$ and another two when comparing SBG to SBG$^+$. In all these cases the statistically significant differences signal the RSA enhancement as better than the original SFG or SBG algorithms. The RSA versions of the algorithms outperformed the conventional versions in the 78.5% of the experiments. It is seen that for SFG performance is in general increased while keeping the number of selected features roughly equal. Only a 28.5% of the results had more features using the modified versions. Thus, whenever the algorithms are in ties or very close to, the modified versions offer a solution with lower number of features, which is attractive from the point of view of feature selection.

4 Conclusions

Our results indicate a general *improvement* in performance while keeping the size of the final subset roughly equal or lower. The fact that the modified version does not always improve on the results should not be a surprise. According to the *No free lunch* theorems, if an algorithm achieves superior results on some problems, it must pay with inferiority on other problems. However, it is possible to modify a search algorithm to obtain a version that is generally superior in performance to the original version [9]. In the present situation this fact can be explained by the way the modified version selects subsets of features. Consider two features: one that makes a significant reduction in performance at the remainder set and not a big change in the performance of the current set; and one that increases the performance of the selected set a bit more than the first feature but does not make a big change on the remainder set. A conventional algorithm would always select the latter while the modified version would likely select the former. That could lead the modified version to avoid local extrema and ultimately end in a better subset; however, when a set close to the optimal subset has been selected, the modification may cause the algorithm to loose precision in choosing the last features. For future work we plan to fine-tune the proposed combination function in order to avoid this weakness.

References

1. Blake, Merz, C.J.: UCI repository of machine learning databases (1998)
2. Dietterich, T.G.: Approximate statistical tests for comparing supervised classification learning algorithms. Neural Computation **10**, 1895–1923 (1998)
3. Guyon, I., Elisseeff, A.: An introduction to variable and feature selection. J. Mach. Learn. Res. **3**, 1157–1182 (2003)
4. John, G.H., Kohavi, R., Pfleger, K.: Irrelevant features and the subset selection problem. In: Proc. of the 11th ICML, pp. 121–129. Morgan Kaufmann, New Brunswick, NJ, USA (1994)
5. Langley, P.: Selection of relevant features in machine learning. In: Proceedings of the AAAI Fall Symposium on Relevance, pp. 140–144. AAAI Press, New Orleans, LA, USA (1994)
6. Pudil, P., Novovicová, J., Kittler, J.: Floating search methods in feature selection. Pattern Recognition Letters **15**(11), 1119–1125 (1994)
7. R Development Core Team: R: A Language and Environment for Statistical Computing. R Foundation for Statistical Computing, Vienna, Austria (2008)
8. Whitney, A.W.: A direct method of nonparametric measurement selection. IEEE Trans. Comput. **20**(9), 1100–1103 (1971)
9. Wolpert, D., Macready, W.G.: No free lunch theorems for optimization. IEEE Trans. Evolutionary Computation **1**(1), 67–82 (1997)

An e-Manufacturing environment for Open Manufacturing Systems

Adriana Giret and Vicente Botti

Abstract In this paper an agent-supported infrastructure for e-Manufacturing is proposed as the enabling tool for implementing virtual collaborative manufacturing environments. In such an environment an Open Manufacturing process is seeing as a virtual scenario in which different manufacturing services are choreographed and orchestrated in order to get a product by different autonomous entities from different manufacturing systems.

1 Introduction

Innovation and utilization of advanced information and communication technologies are becoming more and more important to an enterprise. New technologies are revolutionizing the way manufacturing and supply chain management are implemented. The convergence of Internet and manufacturing systems provides the basis for the creation of a new generation of computing solutions that can dramatically improve the responsiveness of organizations to better communicate with their customer and suppliers. Moreover, this new situation makes possible the rapid and easy on-demand creation of virtual manufacturing enterprises (open manufacturing systems) made up of different manufacturing partners that collaborate in order to fulfil the customer needs. Collaborative manufacturing environments demonstrate considerable potential in responding to this need. A collaborative environment integrating diverse information systems can enable the creation of "virtual" enterprises with competencies to effectively and efficiently share their knowledge and collaborate with each other in order to compete in a global market. To do so, it is crucial to collaborate "electronically" via Internet Web-based technologies. In order to coordinate multiple manufacturing activities from different companies in an open manufactur-

Adriana Giret and Vicente Botti
Departamento de Sistemas Informaticos y Computacion,
Universidad Politecnica de Valencia, e-mail: {agiret,vbotti}@dsic.upv.es

M. Bramer et al. (eds.), *Research and Development in Intelligent Systems XXVI*,
DOI 10.1007/978-1-84882-983-1_26, © Springer-Verlag London Limited 2010

ing process and to guarantee the integration of different engineering tools, it is very important to have an efficient collaborative e-Manufacturing environment.

Multi-agent system (MAS) represents one of the most promising technological paradigms for the development of open, distributed, cooperative, and intelligent software systems. Moreover, the areas of Service Oriented Computing and Multi-agent Systems are getting closer and closer. Both trying to deal with the same kind of environments formed by loose-coupled, flexible, persistent and distributed tasks [3]. An example of this fact is the new approach of Service Oriented Multi-agent Systems (SOMAS). In this work we present an agent-supported infrastructure for e-Manufacturing collaborative environments. In this approach virtual on-demand enterprises are created and executed as Open Manufacturing Systems, in wich PROSA types of agents support the cooperation scenarios to enable the production of products by manufacturing entities from different manufacturing companies.

2 ASeM: an Agent Supported e-Manufacturing environment

An open virtual enterprise can be viewed as a temporary alliance between various partners and services to support certain activity or a set of activities [4]. In ASeM we look into open agent-based technology to support Web-based collaboration between organizations within open virtual enterprises.

In our approach we focus on service-oriented MAS [3] view of collaboration that is compatible with Web service standards [8] based on XML, SOAP, and WSDL. We define a Web-based MAS collaboration system for e-Manufacturing which could be used to support small to large-scale businesses that wish to collaborate in an open virtual enterprise through services available on their respective online manufacturing systems.

The system architecture (Figure 1) we propose is designed to be hosted on a server or servers managed and owned by an organization of e-Manufacturing supported agents (eMSA) which are the providers of collaboration services and security issues but not members of any of the open virtual enterprises that might use the environment. Apart from this group of supported agents, the system architecture provides a group of configurable agents, called collaboration-specific agents (CSA), which can be used by the enterprise virtual partners as mediator and facilitator agents in the collaborative scenarios. When instantiated, every CSA represents a capability enabler agent of a given virtual partner in the e-Manufacturing environment. This second group of agents are PROSA [7] types of agents that can be used to configure any kind of open manufacturing process. In this way, we have four types of agents: product, resource, work-order, and staff. A product agent stores the process and product knowledge needed to insure the correct manufacture of the product. It acts as an information server for the other agents in the collaborative environment. A resource agent offers production capacity and functionality to the other agents. A work order agent represents a task in a manufacturing system. It is responsible for doing the work assigned on time and in the right way. It manages the products

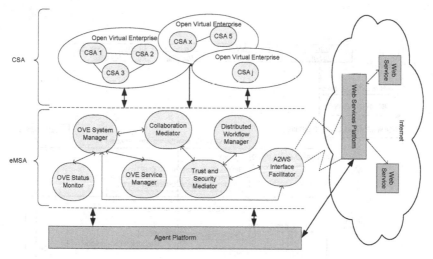

Fig. 1 ASeM Architecture

that are being produced, the product status models, and all the logistic processing information related to the task. A staff agent can assist the other types of agents with expert knowledge. Each of the CSAs is responsible for one of the following manufacturing controlling aspects: internal logistic, manufacturing planning, and resource management.

ASeM has two main components: a) support for the creation and management of collaborative business activities (to mediate services) in an open virtual enterprise, and; b) the use of teams of user configured agents that collaborate through service-oriented computing. The first is provided by the group of eMSA, depicted in Figure 1. While the second components, made up by groups of interacting CSAs, are created on-demand whenever a new open virtual enterprise is required. Moreover, the e-Manufacturing environment will provide collaboration scenario patterns for CSAs that can be easily configured in order to setup a new virtual enterprise venture.

When a manufacturing company registers to use the e-Manufacturing environment the user fills in a series of Web-based forms to enter data which is stored in the customer description associated with its *Customer Mediator* agent. This is only subsequently accessible by the company who created it or agents in the system under certain rules. At the same time collaboration related data is maintained by the *Customer Mediator* such as the set of services the customer wish to offer and the various partners it has made virtual enterprise agreement with. A company registered in ASeM has many options to execute via the Web-based interface. It may configure CSA type of agents in order to define or update PROSA agents and its services. It may order its *Customer Mediator* agent to search for interesting virtual enterprise ventures to joint to. It may get information on the status of the different collaboration scenarios in which it is a partner. It may query the different agree-

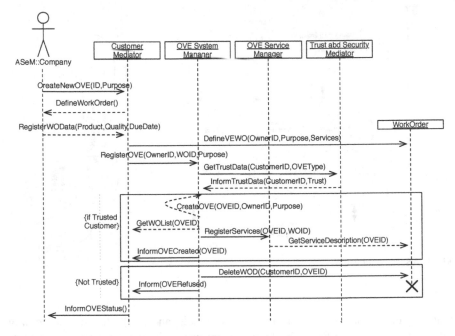

Fig. 2 Cooperation diagram for the creation of an open virtual enterprise

ments it has made using ASeM. It can get the different work-orders it has to execute in its factory floor. Finally, it can decide to exit a given virtual enterprise.

Figure 2 depicts the cooperation diagram for a virtual enterprise creation interaction. A registered manufacturing company starts the cooperation scenario defining the virtual enterprise features interacting with its *Customer Mediator* agent (using the Web-based interface). In this definition process, the virtual enterprise purpose is stated and the required *Work Order Agents* are defined. This data is used by the *Customer Mediator* agent in order to request the creation of the virtual enterprise to the *OVE System Manager*. When receiving such a request the *OVE System Manager* queries the *Trust and Security Mediator* in order to get trust data associated with the customer for the type of virtual enterprise that is being requested. Depending on the trust data, the *OVE System Manager* decides to create or not the virtual enterprise. In the first case the virtual enterprise is accepted and registered in the system, together with the list of *Work Order Agents* associated. In this process the services defined for the virtual enterprise are also registered by the *OVE Service Manager*. Finally the customer is informed on the creation of the virtual enterprise. When the virtual enterprise is refused, due to trust data, the *Work Order Agents* are deleted from the system and the customer is informed as well.

A manufacturing company can order its *Customer Mediator* agent to search for possibilities to joint a virtual enterprise. In this case the *Customer Mediator* agent starts a cooperation scenario with the *Collaboration Mediator* agent in order to keep updated information on the virtual enterprises that are advertizing collaboration opportunities. When a collaboration opportunity is found the *Collaboration Mediator* facilitates all the data to the *Customer Mediator* who estimates the advantages to collaborate in. In case the *Customer Mediator* decides to collaborate, the *Collaboration Mediator* puts in contact the *Customer Mediator* with the *Production Mediator* agent and the *Customer Mediator* of the given virtual enterprise. All this process is supervised by the *Trust and Security Mediator* agent.

The manufacturing company is kept informed on the status of the different collaborations scenarios in which it is participating in thanks to the *Distributed Workflow Manager*, the *OVE Status Monitor* and its *Customer Mediator* agent. Moreover, the updated list of the work orders the manufacturing company has agreed to execute in its factory floor can be obtained.

3 Discussion and Final Remarks

An ongoing research topic has been the technology and modules needed [4, 9, 1] to support virtual enterprise processes which are based on interaction between services implemented by different organizations in the virtual enterprise. Camarinha-Matos *et al.* proposed an open PRODNET architecture [2] to support industrial virtual enterprises with special focus on the needs of small and medium-sized enterprises. The architecture supports different enterprise behaviours through the internal module and the cooperation layer. Sandakly *et al.* [5] proposed an approach to build a virtual enterprise software infrastructure that offers persistence, concurrent access, coherence, and security on distributed data-store based on distributed shared memory paradigm. A platform, Persistence Distributed Store (PerDiS), was developed in this research. Tang *et al.* developed a Web-based platform called E-DREAM [6] to support the distributed information management and role management in an agile virtual enterprise. Yoo and Kim [10] developed a Web-based knowledge management system for facilitating seamless sharing of product data among application systems in virtual enterprises.

ASeM is a step ahead to the new trends in today's e-Manufacturing, the Open Manufacturing System approach. In this type of manufacturing systems any manufacturing capability (represented by an agent) from any manufacturing company can enter or exit the manufacturing system implemented as a virtual enterprise. ASeM provides the executing elements to implement such a system in an easy, flexible and secure way. Moreover, the technological advances in Internet Computing that facilitates the execution of this kind of systems are included in ASeM. It provides the required supported agents and a group of user-configurable agents to implement open virtual enterprises in an easy, flexible and secure way. ASeM has two main components: a) support for the creation and management of collaborative business activities (to mediate services) in an open virtual enterprise, and; b) the use of teams of user configured agents that collaborate through service-oriented computing. In this way, ASeM integrates Multi-agent System technology and Service Oriented

Computing in order to define the e-Manufacturing environment. ASeM provides to e-Manufacturing the flexibility and scalability of the agent approach and the interoperability of Web services.

We are working on defining new collaboration scenarios patterns that can be configured on-demand by the users, in order to facilitate the creation of different types of virtual enterprises. At the same time, we are working to fully integrate ASeM with the factory floor of any manufacturing system. In this way, the e-Manufacturing environment could directly control the factory.

4 Acknowledgments

This paper was partially funded by the Consolider programme of the Spanish Ministry of Science and Innovation through project AT (CSD2007-0022, INGENIO 2010).

References

1. Bright, D., Quirchmayr, G.: Supporting web-based collaboration between Virtual Enterprise partners. In: Proceedings of the 15th International Workshop on Database and Expert System Applications (DEXA'04). IEEE Press (2004)
2. Camarinha-Matos, L., Afsarmanesh, H., Osorio, A.: Flexibility and safety in a Web-based infraestructure for virtual enterprises. International Journal of Computer Integrated Manufacturing **14**, 66–82 (2001)
3. Huhns, M., Singh, M.: Reseach directions for service-oriented multiagent systems. IEEE Internet Computing **Service-Oriented Computing Track. 9**(1) (2005)
4. Petrie, C., Bussler, C.: Service Agent and Virtual Enterprises: A survey. IEEE Internet Computing **July-Agost 2003**, 1–12 (2003)
5. Sandakly, F., Garcia, J., Ferreira, P., Poyet, P.: Distributed shared memory infrastructure for virtual enterprise in building and construction. Journal of Intelligent Manufacturing **12**, 199–212 (2001)
6. Tang, D., Zheng, L., Chin, K., Li, Z., Liang, Y., Jiang, X., Hu, C.: E-DREAM: A Web-based platform for virtual agile manufacturing. Concurrent Engineering: Research and Applications **10**, 165–183 (2002)
7. Van Brussel, H., Wyns, J., Valckenaers, P., Bongaerts, L., Peeters, P.: Reference Architecture for Holonic Manufacturing Systems: PROSA. Computers In Industry **37**, 255–274 (1998)
8. W3C: http://www.w3c.org. Accessed October (2008)
9. Wynen, F., Perrin, O., Bitcheva, J., Godart, C.: A model support collaborative work in virtual enterprises. In: Proceedings BPM'2003, vol. Lecture Notes in Computer Science, 2678, pp. 104–119. Springer-Verlag, Eidhoven, Holland (2003)
10. Yoo, S., Kim, Y.: Web-based knowledge management for sharing product data in virtual enterprises. International Journal of Production Economics **75**, 173–183 (2002)

Applications and Innovations in Intelligent Systems XVII

BEST APPLICATION PAPER

Corpus Callosum MR Image Classification

A. Elsayed, F. Coenen, C. Jiang, M. García-Fiñana, and V. Sluming

Abstract An approach to classifying Magnetic Resonance (MR) image data is described. The specific application is the classification of MRI scan data according to the nature of the corpus callosum, however the approach has more general applicability. A variation of the "spectral segmentation with multi-scale graph decomposition" mechanism is introduced. The result of the segmentation is stored in a quad-tree data structure to which a weighted variation (also developed by the authors) of the gSpan algorithm is applied to identify frequent sub-trees. As a result the images are expressed as a set frequent sub-trees. There may be a great many of these and thus a decision tree based feature reduction technique is applied before classification takes place. The results show that the proposed approach performs both efficiently and effectively, obtaining a classification accuracy of over 95% in the case of the given application.

1 Introduction

The application of data mining techniques to image data involves a number of challenges relating to the representation of images into an appropriate format that permits the application of data mining techniques. This pre-processing typically involves some form of image segmentation to identify image features/objects; followed by the recasting of the image set into some appropriate format.

This paper is focused on a particular application domain, the classification of Magnetic Resonance (MR) image data, more specifically the classification of MR image data according to the nature of the *corpus callosum*. The corpus callosum

Ashraf Elsayed , Frans Coenen, Chuntao Jiang: Department of Computer Science
Marta García-Fiñana: Centre for Medical Statistics and Health Evaluation
Vanessa Sluming: School of Health Sciences
The University of Liverpool, UK
e-mail: {a.el-sayed,coenen,c.jiang,m.garciafinana,vanessa.sluming}@liv.ac.uk

M. Bramer et al. (eds.), *Research and Development in Intelligent Systems XXVI*,
DOI 10.1007/978-1-84882-983-1_27, © Springer-Verlag London Limited 2010

is a highly visible structure in MR images whose function is to connect the left hemisphere of the brain to the right hemisphere, and be responsible for communication between these two hemispheres. The specific application used to illustrate the described classification process is the categorisation of MR images into one of two classes: (i) musicians and (ii) non-musicians. However, the process has more general applicability.

The classification process commences with the segmentation of the input images. With respect to the specific application reported here this is to identify the corpus callosum. For this purpose a variation of a standard image segmentation technique, *spectral segmentation*, is introduced. A registration process is then applied, so that each identified corpus callosum is founded upon the same origin. The pixel representations, for each corpus callosum, is then tessellated and stored in a quad-tree data structure, one tree per image. The advantage offered by the quad tree representation, unlike some other representations, is that information about the spatial relationships between individual pixels is maintained. These trees are then processed to identify frequent sub-trees that occur across the input image set. For this purpose a weighted graph mining algorithm was developed to take into consideration that greater significance should be assigned to quad-tree nodes closer to the root than nodes further away. The identified sub-trees then formed the fundamental elements of the feature space. Each image was then represented in terms of this feature space using individual feature vectors.

From experimentation it was discovered that the number of features (frequent sub-trees) could be substantial and that many features seemed to play no part in the resulting classification. To reduce the number of features to a more manageable number a feature selection mechanism was applied using a decision tree algorithm; features that did not appear in the decision tree were removed from the input set. A second application of the decision tree algorithm then yielded the final classifier (although any other appropriate classifier generator could have been used). The results, in terms of the specific application under investigation, were found to be very good.

This paper makes a number of contributions:

- A new approach to image pre-processing (for image mining) founded on weighted frequent sub-graph mining, is described; an approach that has much broader potential application.
- An interesting image mining application which offers clear medical benefits with respect to medical diagnosis (e.g. neurological disorders) is described. To the best knowledge of the authors there are no corpus callosum studies that take the "shape" of the callosum into consideration (most studies reported in the literature concentrate of the size of the callosum).
- A new variation, founded on an intensity threshold, of the established spectral segmentation with multi-scale graph decomposition approach.

The rest of this paper is organised as follows. The application domain is described in Section 2 and some relevant previous work in Section 3. The proposed classification process is described in Section 4. The various steps in the process:

segmentation, registration and tessellation, weighted graph mining, feature selection and image classification are described in Sections 5, 6, 7, 8 and 9 respectively. An evaluation of the approach is reported in Section 10, followed by some conclusions in Section 11.

2 The Application Domain

The focus of the work described here is brain MR images, and in particular a specific structure in these images called the corpus callosum. An example image is given in Figure 1. The corpus callosum is located in the centre of the image, the fornix is a related structure which often "blurs" into the corpus callosum and presents a particular challenge in the context of segmentation. The corpus callosum is of interest to medical researchers for a number of reasons. The size and shape of the corpus callosum have been shown to be correlated to sex, age, neurodegenerative diseases (such as epilepsy) and various lateralized behaviour in people. It is conjectured that the size and shape of the corpus callosum reflects certain human characteristics (such as a mathematical or musical ability). It is a very distinctive feature in MRI brain scans.

Several medical studies indicate that the size and shape of the corpus callosum, in humans, are correlated to sex [1, 6, 19], age [19, 21], brain growth and degeneration [9, 14], handedness [5] and various types of brain dysfunction [7, 11]. In order to find such correlations in living brains, Magnetic Resonance (MR) is regarded as the best method to obtain cross-sectional area (and shape) information of the corpus callosum. Since manual tracing of the corpus callosum in MRI scans is time consuming, operator dependent, and does not directly give quantitative measures of shape; there is a need for automated and robust methods for localization, delineation and shape description of the corpus callosum. This is then the motivation for the work described here.

3 Previous Work

Image classification systems tend to rely on a pre-processing step, specific to an application, to extract a (reduced) set of "interesting" features from the image data. This set is then used as the input to a classification algorithms. There is a significant body of literature covering the domain of image mining and image classification with application in many areas.

There is also a substantial body of work directed at the mining of MR images. For example Chen and Herskovits [2] present a Bayesian-network for joint classification founded on voxelwise MR image analysis. This work considers associations between cerebral morphology of all brain voxels and age or sex. The approach includes an embedded feature selection phase in classifier learning. Ruan et

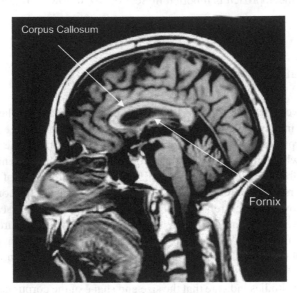

Fig. 1 corpus callosum in a midsagittal brain MR image.

al. [18] present a fully automatic three-dimensional classification of brain tissues for MR images into three types of main tissues: Gray Matter, White Matter, and Cerebrospinal fluid and mixtures of these brain tissues. Chun and Greenshields [3] describe a three dimensional image classification technique, founded on the Markov and Gibbs Random Field models. A Bayesian context decision rule is adopted and an MRF-GRF stochastic model is used for the classification of Multi-Echo MR images. This work, and similar work, is directed at the classification of MR images in their entirety; the work described here concentrates on regions of interest within MR images.

To the best knowledge of the authors there has been little work on the application of data mining techniques to study the corpus callosum. Two studies of note are that of Herskovits and Gerring [10] and that of Machado et al. [15]. Herskovits and Gerring describe a Bayesian network approach to Lesion-Deficit Analysis (LDA) that identifies associations between elements of the brain including the corpus callosum. Machado et. al apply a visual data mining method MRI scan data to reveal differences in the callosal morphology between male and female samples.

4 Methodology

In this section an overview of the proposed MR image classification process is presented, further detail is given in the following sections. A block diagram outlining the process is given in Figure 2 (the directed arcs indicate data flow). The process commences with image segmentation to extract the objects (regions) of interest, in the case of the application under consideration here this is the corpus callosum midsagittal slice of a 3D brain MR image. The next step is to represent the pixel defined corpus callosum segments as quad-trees (one quad-tree per image), using a predefined level of decomposition. For this representation to be effective a registration process must first be applied to the corpus callosum segments. The third step is to apply a weighted graph mining technique to identify frequently occurring sub-trees within the quad-tree data set. The identified sub-graphs are then the attributes/features used to define each corpus callosum in terms of a *feature vector*. As there may be a great many of these, and it is conjectured that some may be redundant or superfluous, the fourth step is to apply a feature selection technique (to reduce the number of attributes by removing *irrelevant* features from the features vector). In the final step, the reduced data set is submitted to the classifier generator (A decision tree algorithm in Figure 2).

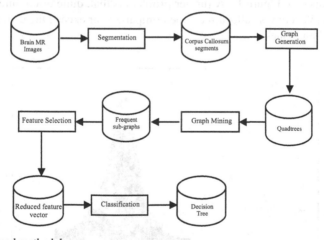

Fig. 2 Proposed methodology

5 Image Segmentation

The objective of image segmentation is to partition images into meaningful regions. For the work described here a variation of the *multi-scale spectral image segmentation* algorithm by Cour and Shi (2005) was used [4]. Cour and Shi's algorithm works on multiple scales of the image in parallel, without iteration, to capture both coarse and fine level details, using the Normalized Cuts partitioning framework for each image segmentation [20]. The algorithm has been shown to work well in many studies; however it was found that, in the context of the corpus callosum, the algorithm did not work as well as expected. This was because of various reasons: firstly medical MR images have a lot of noises, secondly in MR images the intensity-level distributions between different soft tissues are not widely distributed and moreover the complexity of tissue boundaries cause many pixels to contain mixtures of tissues. For this reason, we need to enhance the contrast of the MR images. A variation of Cour and Shi's algorithm was therefore developed that applied a threshold interval to extract objects with the same intensity values (such as the corpus callosum) during the application of the segmentation. This was found to give a much improved result.

Our proposed variation of Cour and Shi's algorithm is founded on the observation that the corpus callosum, which is located at the centre of the brain, comprises *white matter tissue* (i.e. the pixel represented corpus callosum has high intensity values). Although one can visually recognize the outline of the corpus callosum (Figure 1), portions of its boundary are indistinct, which can make it difficult to apply segmentation algorithms based on edge information alone. This is particularly the case at the top portion of the corpus callosum, and between the corpus callosum and the Fornix (see Figure 1). A further problem is that, quite often, intensity variations within the corpus callosum can be comparable or exceed the difference with the surrounding tissues.

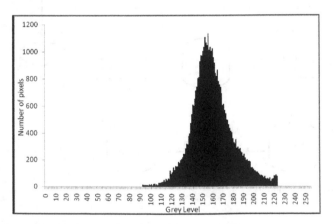

Fig. 3 Histogram of the pixel grayscale values of the corpus callosum.

Figure 3 shows a pixel intensity value histogram of the corpus callosum derived from 30 selected MR images (256 gray levels were used) where the corpus callosum was very well defined and easy to detect using Cour and Shi's algorithm. From the figure it can be seen that:

• The corpus callosum tends to have relatively high intensity values, and

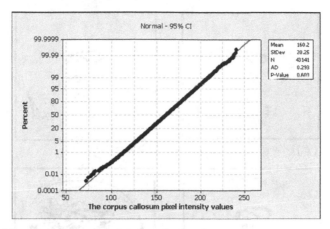

Fig. 4 Probability plot of the corpus callosum pixel values.

• The distribution of intensity values seems to follow the normal distribution.

The latter is demonstrated in Figure 4 which shows that the corpus callosum pixel values follow the normal distribution with mean $\bar{X} = 160$ and standard deviation $S = 20$. Figure 5a shows that with a threshold interval of $\bar{X} \pm S$, the corpus callosum can barely be recognized. With a threshold interval $\bar{X} \pm 2S$ a relatively distinct callosum shape is evident with a few other non-adjacent structures visible as shown in Figure 5b. With the threshold interval set at $\bar{X} \pm 3S$, the corpus callosum is clearly defined, although additional non-adjacent structures are also visible (Figure 5c). In Figure 5d, the corpus callosum starts to "blur" into the surrounding tissues using a threshold interval wider than $\bar{X} \pm 3S$. The significance here is that although the threshold values may differ depending on individual images, the high intensity property of the corpus callosum can be exploited to yield a segmentation algorithm that is both effective and efficient across the input image set. Therefore the interval $\bar{X} \pm 3S$ was chosen, so as to exclude intensity values outside the interval. This strategy was incorporated into Cour and Shi's algorithm and used to successfully extract the corpus callosum (and other incidental objects with the same intensity values).

6 Registration and Tessellation

After segmentation a registration process was applied to the pixel represented images which were then tessellated and stored in a quad-tree representation. Prior to the registration process some *data cleaning* was also undertaken to remove the "incidental objects" discovered during segmentation. The heuristic used was that the object representing the corpus callosum can be identified using statistical measures (it is the largest object and is locate in roughly the centre of the brain). Having identi-

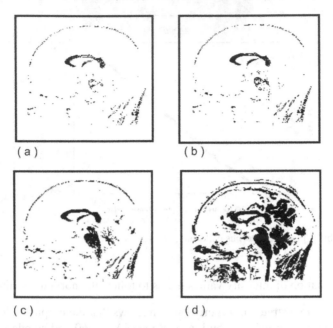

Fig. 5 Thresholding with various threshold intervals.

fied the corpus callosum object any other high intensity objects were not considered to be part of the corpus callosum and were removed.

On completion of data cleaning the registration process was undertaken by fitting each identified corpus callosum into a Minimum Bounding Rectangle (MBR). The tessellation process then comprised recursively decomposing the given MBR space into quadrants. Each quadrant was represented by a node in the quad-tree (with colour black or white), with the root of the quad-tree represented the entire MBR space. The tessellation process continued with each of the quadrants "sofar" being again partitioned into sub-quadrants, and so on. The process was terminated when a predefined level of granularity was reached, or a particular sub-quadrant was sufficiently homogeneous (95% black or white).

The advantage of the quad-tree representation was that it maintained information about the relative location and size of groups of pixels (i.e. the shape of the corpus callosum). Nodes nearer the root of the tree represented a larger group of pixels than nodes further away from the root. The use of the quad-tree data structure was considered to be of particular relevance in the context of the corpus callosum as medical opinion suggested that the shape and size of the corpus callosum is of interest [1, 6, 19, 21].

The next stage was to process the quad-tree represented images to identify significant features that occur across the image set (i.e. the set of quad- trees). This was achieved using a bespoke frequent sub-graph mining technique described in the following section.

7 Weighted Graph Mining

There are various forms of graph/tree mining. In the context of this paper the form of graph mining of interest is transaction graph mining, where the images are represented as a collection of small graphs or trees. Graph mining is broadly concerned with the discovery of interesting patterns in graph or tree data, the interesting patterns are typically frequent sub-graphs. and thus the phrase "frequent sub-graph mining" is often used. The challenge of frequent sub-graph mining is that it necessitates the repeated generation and comparison of candidate sub-graphs, the so called graph isomorphism checking problem. The basic approach is to "grow" candidate sub-graph that occur frequently in the graph set, however this is a computationally expensive process.

Given the quad-tree representation advocated in this paper, nodes nearer the root node are considered to be more significant than others. A weighted frequent sub-graph mining algorithm was therefore developed. The weightings were calculated according to the proximity of individual nodes to the root node in each tree. This weighting concept was built into a variation of the well known gSpan algorithm [22]. The algorithm operates in a depth first search manner, level by level, following a "generate, calculate support, prune" loop. Candidate sub-graphs are pruned if their *support* (frequency with which they occur across the graph set) is below a user defined "support threshold". Note that a lower threshold will identify a greater number of frequent sub graphs. Space restrictions preclude further detailed discussion of this algorithm here, however, interested readers are referred to Jiang and Coenen (2008) [12].

Application of the Weighted gSpan algorithm allowed for the identification of frequent sub-graphs (trees), within the quad-tree represented corpus callosum segments, representing common substructures (features) within the data set. Experimentation indicated that, to capture the necessary level of detail, a low support threshold was required. However this produced a large number of frequent sub-graphs many of which were redundant. A feature selection operation (discussed in the following section) was thus applied to the identified frequent sub-graphs.

8 Feature Selection

Feature selection is a well understood process used in Data Mining for removing irrelevant features from the feature space so as to enhance computational efficiency. Feature selection has attracted a great deal of attention within the data mining community, especially in the context of classification and prediction where the aim is to identify features that are "strong discriminators". Classic feature selection methods select individual features whose distribution has a strong correlation with individual class labels. Reported methods [23] include: frequency thresholding, information gain, mutual information, Pearson Correlation, and the χ^2 statistic. An acknowledged shortcoming of these methods is that redundant features may be selected due to ignorance of the dependency between features. In order to overcome this "wrapper methods" have been proposed that adopt a classifier model to rate the feature subsets and determine highly discriminative features [13]. However, such wrapper methods can be computational expensive. A straightforward wrapper method is to apply a decision tree generator to the features [8]. In this context decision tree algorithms offer the advantage that they inherently estimate the suitability of features for separation of objects representing different classes. Features that are included as "choice points" in the decision tree are thus selected, while all remaining features are discarded.

For the work described here, the well established C4.5 algorithm [17] was used. The objective was to select a sub-set of features (frequent sub-graphs) with strong discriminative power. The results presented in Section 10 below indicate that this strategy was particularly effective.

9 Classifier Generation

The final stage in the process was to build the desired classifier using the identified set of discriminating features. Any appropriate classifier generator can be used for this purpose, however in the reported experiments (Section 10) Quinlan's C4.5 algorithm was used. The reasons for selecting a decision-tree algorithm were that they are: (i) a very popular and effective data-mining technique, (ii) non-parametric and (iii) computationally fast[17].

10 Experimentation and Evaluation

A number of experiments were undertaken to analyse the performance of the proposed method in terms of classification accuracy. The experiments described here used an MR image set comprising 106 brain images divided equally into two categories (53 images per category): musician and non-musician. It is acknowledged that, in data mining terms, a data set of 106 records is small. One of the challenges of the work described here is the limited amount of raw data available for experimentation. This is because of a number of difficulties that are presented when collecting MR image data, namely: (i) they are extremely expensive to produce, and (ii) the time consuming nature of MRI scanning. Consequently the MR image data sets available for research are relatively small, compared to the usual data sets used for the evaluation of data mining techniques.

As noted above each pixel represented corpus callosum segment is translated, using the described process, into a quad-tree representation. The maximum number of leaf nodes in any quad-tree is given by 4^N where N is the quad-tree level. The quad-tree levels applied in the experiments were 4, 5, 6 and 7 (equating to a maximum number of nodes of 256, 1024, 4096 and 16384 respectively). Note that the level of detail increases with the number of quad-tree levels.

Table 1 shows the classification results obtained using Ten Cross Validation (TCV) with a quad-tree level of 4. The *F-before* and *F-after* columns indicate the number of features before and after the application of feature selection. The *C-before* and *C-after* columns give the classification accuracy before and after feature selection. The support threshold is the minimum frequency with which a sub-graph must occur across the data set for the sub-graph to be considered "frequent".

Table 1 Classification accuracy for corpus callosum segments represented as 4-Level Quad-trees (maximum of 256 tree nodes)

Levels	Support	F-before	C-before	F-after	C-after
4	20	24549	46.23	15	70.75
4	30	4264	46.23	16	69.81
4	40	1193	50.94	18	68.87
4	50	639	50.94	19	71.7
4	60	262	54.72	16	68.87
4	70	151	50.94	21	61.32
4	80	86	51.89	16	52.83
4	90	54	52.83	17	50.94

Table 2 Classification accuracy for corpus callosum segments represented as 5-Level Quad-trees (maximum of 1024 tree nodes)

Levels	Support	F-before	C-before	F-after	C-after
5	20	16094	56.6	12	90.57
5	30	4630	51.89	12	83.96
5	40	2100	48.11	10	80.19
5	50	1155	53.77	13	85.85
5	60	637	65.09	14	80.19
5	70	405	55.66	14	81.13
5	80	252	55.66	18	80.19
5	90	130	54.72	17	70.75

Tables 2, 3 and 4 show the classification obtained using TCV with quad-tree levels of 5, 6 and 7 respectively. The column headings should be interpreted in the same way as for Table 1.

Inspection of Tables 1, 2, 3 and 4 demonstrate that the overall classification accuracy improves after the application of the feature selection strategy. The best classification accuracy of 95.28% (19 correct classifications per 20 images) was obtained using a quad-tree level of 6 coupled with a 30% support threshold. Regardless of the quad-tree level, the trend of the classification accuracy improved as the threshold support decreased. This is because more frequent sub-graphs are identified as can be seen from the *F-before* columns. It is likely that as the support threshold increases, significant sub-graphs are not discovered by the graph mining algorithm.

Table 3 Classification accuracy for corpus callosum segments represented as 6-Level Quad-trees (maximum of 4096 tree nodes)

Levels	Support	F-before	C-before	F-after	C-after
6	20	35223	60.38	11	85.85
6	30	9461	66.98	10	95.28
6	40	4059	67.92	12	84.91
6	50	2260	50.00	11	83.96
6	60	1171	60.38	11	90.57
6	70	741	53.77	13	83.96
6	80	433	54.72	13	77.36
6	90	232	43.40	14	75.47

Table 4 Classification accuracy for corpus callosum segments represented as 7-Level Quad-trees (maximum of 16384 tree nodes)

Levels	Support	F-before	C-before	F-after	C-after
7	20	448683	48.00	13	83.80
7	30	34440	50.00	12	85.85
7	40	11998	45.28	11	89.62
7	50	6402	50.94	10	86.79
7	60	3317	60.38	13	87.74
7	70	2032	53.77	13	75.47
7	80	1117	50.94	13	76.42
7	90	476	52.83	12	78.30

From the tables it can also be observed that accuracy increases as the quad-tree levels are increased, up to level 6, and then begins to fall of. It is conjectured that this is because "over fitting" starts to take place as the quad-tree representation starts to get too detailed.

The results presented in Tables 1, 2, 3 and 4 are summarised by the graph presented in Figure 6, which plots classification accuracy (Y axis) against support threshold (X axis) for the sequence of quad-tree levels featured in the experiments.

Image segmentation and graph mining are both computationally expensive processes. The time complexity for the image segmentation was about 2 minutes per image. For the given data set the graph mining algorithm took some 2 minutes to process and identify several thousand frequent sub-graphs. The graph mining algorithm took significantly longer to identify much larger numbers of frequent sub-graphs. The worst case was the 448,683 frequent sub-graphs found when the quad-tree level was set to 7 and the support threshold to 20%. Typically the entire classification process took several minutes to process the 106 image test set.

11 Conclusions

In this paper an approach to MR image classification based on graph-mining has been described. The work was directed at a particular MR image classification ap-

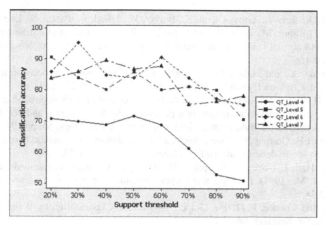

Fig. 6 Classification accuracy for brain MRI images represented in different Quad-tree levels.

plication, the classification of MR images according to the nature of the corpus callosum featured within these images. However, the approach has more general applicability. Of particular note is the use of feature vectors constructed from frequent sub-graphs identified using a weighted variation of gSpan. The results obtained are extremely encouraging and clearly demonstrate the utility of the approach. Future work will include the application of the process to other brain MR image applications, for example to the automated identification of disorders such as Epilepsy. The research team are also interested in alternative methods of pre-processing MR image data, and mechanism for post-processing of results. In the context of the latter the generation of explanations to support classification of new data is considered to be significant (i.e. the retracing of a classification result to the features in the input image that caused the classification).

References

1. Allen, L., Richey, M., Chain, Y. and Gorski, R. (1991). Sex differences in the corpus callosum of the living human being. *Journal of Neuroscience*, 11, pp 933-942.
2. Chen, R. and Herskovits, E.H. (2005). A Bayesian Network Classifier with Inverse Tree Structure for Voxelwise Magnetic Resonance Image Analysis. Proc ACM SIGKDD 2005, pp 4-12.
3. Chun, J. and Greenshields, R. (1995). Classification algorithm for Multi-Echo Magnetic Resonance Image using Gibbs distributions Proc 3rd Int. Conf. on Image Analysis Applications and Computer Graphics, Spinger LNCS, pp 419-426.
4. Cour, T., Benezit, F. and Shi, J. (2005). Spectral Segmentation with Multiscale Graph Decomposition. In Proceedings of the 2005 IEEE Computer Society Conference on Computer Vision and Pattern Recognition (Cvpr'05), 2, pp 1124-1131.
5. Cowell, P., Kertesz, A. and Denenberg, V. (1993). Multiple dimensions of handedness and the human corpus callosum. *Neurology*, 43, pp 2353-2357.
6. Davatzikos, C., Vaillant, M., Resnick, S.,Prince, J., S. Letovsky, S. and Bryan, R. (1996). A computerized approach for morphological analysis of the corpus callosum. *Journal of Computer Assisted Tomography*, 20, pp 88-97.

7. Duara, R., Kushch, A., Gross-Glenn, K., Barker, W., Jallad, B., Pascal, S., Loewenstein, D., Sheldon, J., Rabin, M., Levin B. and Lubs, H. (1991). Neuroanatomic differences between dyslexic and normal readers on magnetic resonance imaging scans. *Archives of Neurology*, 48, pp 410-416.

8. Grabczewski, K. and Jankowski, N. (2005). Feature selection with decision tree criterion. Proc 5th Int. Conf. on Hybrid Intelligent Systems (HIS'05), pp 212-217.

9. Hampel, H., Teipel, S., Alexander, G.,Horwitz, B., Teichberg, D., Schapiro, M. and Rapoport, S. (1998). corpus callosum atrophy is a possible indicator of region and cell type-specific neuronal degeneration in Alzheimer disease. *Archives of Neurology*, 55, pp 193-198.

10. Herskovits EH, Gerring JP. (2003). Application of a data-mining method based on Bayesian networks to lesion-deficit analysis. Proc, Neuroimage. pp 1664-73.

11. Hynd, G., Hall, J., Novey, E., Eliopulos, D., Black, K., Gonzalez J., Edmonds, J., Riccio, C. and Cohen, M. (1995). Dyslexia and corpus callosum morphology. *Archives of Neurology*, 52, pp 32-38.

12. Jiang, C. and Coenen, F. (2008). Graph-based Image Classification by Weighting Scheme. Proc. AI'2008, Springer, pp 63-76.

13. Kohavi, R. and John, G. (1997). Wrappers for feature subset selection. Artificial Intelligence, 97(1-2), pp 273-324.

14. Lyoo, I., Satlin, A., C. K. Lee, C. and Renshaw, P. (1997). Regional atrophy of the corpus callosum in subjects with Alzheimer's disease and multi-infarct dementia. *Psychiatry Research*, 74, pp 63-72.

15. Machado, A., Gee, J., Campos, M., (2004). Visual data mining for modeling prior distributions in morphometry Signal Processing Magazine, IEEE Volume 21, Issue 3, May 2004 pp 20-27.

16. Magoulas, G. and Prentza, A. (1999). Machine learning in Medical Applications, Workshop on Machine Learning in Medical Applications (ACAI-99), pp 53-58.

17. Quinlan R. (1993). C4.5: A program for machine learning, Morgan Kaufmann.

18. Ruan, S., Jaggi, C., Xue, J., Fadili, J. and Bloyet, D. (2000). Brain Tissue Classification of Magnetic Resonance Images Using Partial Volume Modeling. IEEE Transactions on Medical Imaging, 19(12), pp 1179-1187

19. Salat, D., Ward, A., Kaye, J. and Janowsky, J. (1997). Sex differences in the corpus callosum with aging. *Journal of Neurobiology of Aging*, 18, pp 191-197.

20. Shi, J. and Malik, J. (2000). Normalized Cuts and Image Segmentation, IEEE Transactions on Pattern Analysis and Machine Intelligence (PAMI).

21. Weis, S., Kimbacher, M.,Wenger, E. and Neuhold, A. (1993). Morphometric analysis of the corpus callosum using MRI: Correlation of measurements with aging in healthy individuals. *American Journal of Neuroradiology*, 14, pp 637-645.

22. Yan, X. and Han, J. (2002). gspan: Graph-based substructure pattern mining. In ICDM'02: 2nd IEEE Conf. Data Mining, pp 721-724.

23. Yang, Y. and Pedersen, J. (1997). A comparative study on feature selection in text categorization. In D. H. Fisher, editor, Proceedings of ICML-97, 14th International Conference on Machine Learning, Nashville, US, 1997. Morgan Kaufmann Publishers, San Francisco, US, pp 412-420.

AI AND DESIGN

Architectures by Design: The Iterative Development of an Integrated Intelligent Agent

Nick Hawes

Abstract In this paper we demonstrate how a design-based methodology can be used to iteratively produce designs for an information-processing architecture that integrates various intelligent capabilities. This methodology allows us to explain system performance in terms of changes to an existing architecture design, with the explanations being supported by performance data from an implementation of the design. We present an instance of this design methodology applied to the development of an architecture that integrates anytime deliberative capabilities with reactive behaviours and goal management. Iterations of the design are implemented and evaluated in the computer game *Unreal Tournament*.

1 Introduction

This paper presents an example of the use of a *design-based methodology* applied to the design of an intelligent agent. This example demonstrates how the empirical evaluation of an implementation of an intelligent system can help refine a set of requirements for the system and the derived designs. This development approach allows agent designers to account for and explain the eventual behaviour of systems by reference to these requirements and designs, and the informed changes made to them based on experimental results.

Nick Hawes
Intelligent Robotics Lab, School of Computer Science, University of Birmingham, UK e-mail: n.a.hawes@cs.bham.ac.uk

M. Bramer et al. (eds.), *Research and Development in Intelligent Systems XXVI*,
DOI 10.1007/978-1-84882-983-1_28, © Springer-Verlag London Limited 2010

2 Design-Based Methodology

It is an agent's information-processing architecture that is key to its ability to integrate various intelligent capabilities. It is therefore crucial that such architectures can be evaluated in a way that is objective and that allows comparisons with similar architectures. In the past, information-processing architectures have been developed in various ways. Some have been the modelled directly on biological systems, some have been designed to explicitly produce certain phenomena, and some have emerged directly from the need to place certain components in a single system.

When examining this previous work, objective evaluation and comparison of architectures is not always possible because researchers do not regularly reference design-neutral requirements for their architectures, or the trade-offs inherent in making design decisions. It is our belief that these parts of the design process should be made explicit in order to contribute knowledge to the science of constructing integrated cognitive systems. To support this, we follow a design-based methodology when developing information-processing architectures. This is an approach to explaining how systems (biological, non-biological, existing, hypothetical etc.) work, based on how they are designed. The term was introduced in [16] where the approach was used to analyse familiar concepts, such as emotion. This design-based methodology can be considered as directly related to Dennett's design stance [3].

Although most AI researchers would argue that they work from a design stance, as they produce abstract representations of their systems, many do not consider the *design space* in which their single design is located. It is only by comparing designs to other designs that occupy neighbouring design space that we can develop an understanding of particular design features (e.g. when comparing the trade-offs between two designs that differ on one feature) [17].

The methodology we follow is based on the following steps:

1. Determine the requirements of the system you are trying to design. These should be based on the required functionality of the final system. Requirements determine the *niche* or role that the proposed design is intended to occupy (for discussions of the relationship between design space and niche space see [17]).
2. Produce designs which satisfy these requirements. When developing agents, the proposed designs will be agent architectures (which could include detailed specifications of representations, processing styles, information exchange strategies etc.).
3. Implement the design or designs. Whilst the main purpose of implementation is to produce a working system, this step may also lead to a better understanding of how parts of the design interact, and provide a deeper understanding of the requirements of the design.
4. Evaluate how well the implementation reflects the design, and to what degree this design meets the requirements specified in Step 1. This evaluation can done by experimental or analytical means.

5. Examine the design space surrounding the implemented design to study how changes to it could provide additional functionality that may or may not allow it to better meet the specified requirements.

Although the steps are discretised here to allow clearer explanation, they can overlap or be performed in parallel. When this is the case, later steps can feed back into earlier steps, modifying the overall direction of the research.

The following sections summarise four iterations of the above methodology applied to the task of developing an intelligent agent for a computer game. Due to space constraints we mostly focus on how the evaluation of an implementation (Step 4) supports the exploration of design space (Step 5).

3 Background & Assumptions

The initial motivation behind the work presented here was to design an intelligent agent for use in action-orientated computer games. To challenge the state-of-the-art (both in terms of the games industry and AI research on games), we decided to investigate methods of integrating deliberative planning with reactive behaviours in a hybrid agent architecture. We decided to take this approach because we view the behaviour generated by an agent following a deliberative plan as more goal-orientated than the behaviour generated by an agent just reacting to its world. We also assume that agent behaviour that is more goal-oriented appears more intelligent to observers (e.g. humans playing a game against the agent), and therefore prefer agent designs which provide better support for this. Although this is quite a limited characterisation of the space of possible approaches to generating intelligent behaviour, we use it as one of the key requirements for the subsequent design work.

By choosing to design an agent for a game world we already face a set of general requirements for the system: it must be able to cope with a world that is *interactive*, *real-time* and *complex*. This means that the agent must deal with a world that changes through the actions of both it and others, at a rate that is out of its control, and the choice of potential actions available is not trivial. Reasoning about future actions in such a world challenges a number of assumptions that have been made by many planning approaches in the past [15]. Rather than build mechanisms to tackle such problems into a planning algorithm, we view it as the task of the whole agent architecture to support intelligent behaviour in such worlds in an integrated fashion. We have chosen to design the architecture from scratch (rather than adopt an existing solution) to ensure that the planner's functionality is fully integrated with the functionality of other components within the architecture.

4 Scenario

The design and implementation of the agent is based around a scenario called *Capture The Flag* (CTF), which is a type of game found in many multi-player computer games. It is a game played between two or more opposing teams, where each team is made up of one or more players. The aim of the game is to score a set number of points, or to have the most points when the game ends (after a fixed amount of time). Each team has a base, on which a flag rests. To score a point, a player must take the opposing team's flag from their base and then get it back to their own base. This action will score a point only if the team's own flag is at their base when the player returns with the opposition's flag.

Agents in our CTF scenario can only perform a small number of actions. These are limited to running, jumping, picking up and putting down objects, and using weapons (this is typical for many computer games). In the CTF scenario, typical behaviours for agents include guarding their team's flag, attempting to steal the opposition's flag, trying to prevent the opposition from scoring, and assisting a team mate that has captured the opposition's flag.

One of the principal motivations for the selection of this scenario was the desire to evaluate our designs in a real game environment. Only very few games provide the kinds of interfaces necessary to support the addition of an AI character written from scratch, and most of these are first-person shooters. The CTF game type is prevalent in these types of games, whilst providing a level of complexity above that of the typical "kill one another until the time runs out" scenarios found in many other games types.

Even with these advantages, there are reasons why the CTF domain is flawed as a testing ground for AI techniques. First, although it is more complex than many other game types (and hence more challenging for the applied techniques), it falls short of the level of complexity represented by many existing AI testbeds. As such, it provides a less than adequate test of the agent's problem solving abilities. A second reason the domain is flawed is that success in CTF is usually determined by 'physical' skills such as aiming ability and reaction times, rather than cognitive abilities (cf. [2]). Because of this, a purely reactive, rather than hybrid or deliberative, agent would generally perform better at most aspects of the CTF scenario.

The agent implementations discussed in the following sections were produced using Pop11 with the SimAgent toolkit [19]. They play Capture The Flag in the game *Unreal Tournament* [4] via the Gamebots interface [8].

5 Iteration One: The Basic Agent

The architecture for our initial attempt at designing an agent for the CTF scenario can be seen in Figure 1. It is based around the CogAff architecture schema [18], with the thick lines representing segments of the schema that are being utilised. The overall design was informed by previous work within our research group, and by the constraints of the scenario. The following paragraphs discuss the design and implementation of the components within the architecture. This is followed by an evaluation of the implementation. For more detailed descriptions of all the components see [7].

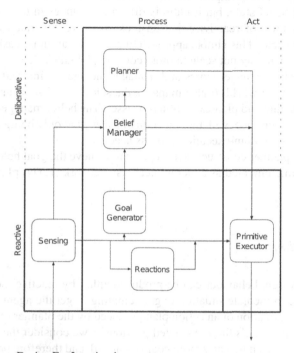

Fig. 1 Architecture Design For Iteration 1.

Sensing: The sensing component translates events from the external world (i.e. the Gamebots interface to *Unreal Tournament*) into representations that the agent can process.

Execution: The primitive executor takes action commands (e.g. move to the opponent's base, turn to face opponent etc.) from other components and produces the appropriate actions in the world. This component is implemented as a set of Teleo-Reactive Programs [13]. The primitive executor is essential in the architecture as it separates the mostly continuous, regularly changing, detailed knowledge about the external world (which it operates on to perform actions), from the more discrete, static knowledge useful for reasoning about it (which it receives as commands). Without this component the agent's deliberative components would have to deal with "real-world" type knowledge (such as coordinates) and also run the risk that this information may become out of date as it processes it.

Reactions: The reaction component monitors incoming sense data and quickly generates appropriate action responses to the current situation (e.g. it attempts to move the agent to safety when it is being attacked). These actions are send to the primitive executor. The reactions are implemented as a set of condition-action rules.

Goal Generation: The goal generator also monitors incoming sense data. Its task is to generate new goals based on this information. It can generate six different goals, each of which has a fixed importance value. The goal-generator has no access to the agent's current belief state, but is entirely driven by changes in the external world. This enables a level of reactivity that ensures goals are generated quickly when relevant events occur. This simple approach to goal generation is feasible in limited game scenarios, but may not scale to more complex domains.

Beliefs: The belief manager stores and manages the agent's internal state, including beliefs about the world. It also manages the selection of goals and handles the subsequent planning and plan-execution processes. The belief manager selects goals based on their importance, with the selection of a new goal only being allowed when neither a planning or plan-execution process is active.

Planning: The planner constructs action plans to achieve the goal held by the belief manager. It is implemented as a hierarchical task network (HTN) planner based on UMCP [5].

5.1 Evaluation

In this agent design, behaviour can be produced either by reactive mechanisms responding to the immediate situation (e.g. attempting to get the agent out of harm's way), or by the execution of an action plan produced by the planner (e.g. attempting to capture the opponent's flag). As stated previously, we consider the latter of these types of behaviour as inherently more goal-orientated, and therefore prefer our agent to spend more time acting in this way. This requirement has led us to select particular metrics by which we can measure the performance of the implementations of our designs. The metrics we use are:

- **Planning time**: The amount of time an agent spends planning during a single game.
- **Wasted planning time**: The amount of time an agent spends planning for a goal after the goal is no longer valid.
- **Execution time**: The amount of time an agent spends executing plans during a single game.
- **Wasted execution time**: The amount of time an agent spends executing plans to achieve a goal after the goal is no longer valid.
- **Percentage of goals selected**: The percentage of proposed goals that an agent selects and starts planning for.

Wasted time is bad because it is time that should be used for a more important process, and as such represents a measure of latency between the events in the world and the agent's behaviour. The notion of "waste" is judged by examining the importance of the current planning or execution goal, and comparing it to the importance

Iteration	1	2	3	4
Avg. Planning Time	138 secs	209 secs	186 secs	157 secs
Avg. Wasted Planning Time	37 secs	27 secs	0 secs	0 secs
Avg. Execution Time	153 secs	93 secs	105 secs	135 secs
Avg. Wasted Execution Time	95 secs	0 secs	0 secs	0 secs
Avg. Percentage of Goals Selected	24%	22%	26%	32%

Table 1 Results from the four iterations of the design process.

of goals that are being generated in the meantime. If a more important goal is generated, then all subsequent effort is considered wasted, because it could be spent pursuing the new goal. Goal *achievement* is not used as a metric because it proved very hard to reliably attribute the achievement of a particular goal to the actions of a single agent in our scenario.

Four instantiations of the previously described architecture were used to create two teams of two agents to compete across ten CTF games in *Unreal Tournament*. The values for the evaluation metrics were averaged across these forty separate agent instantiations, and are presented in column 1 of Table 1.

From examining these results, along with the basic agent design, it can be seen that the fact that the agent continues to execute plans once its goals are no longer valid appears to be the biggest source of wasted time. As this is the first iteration of the design process, we have nothing to compare the average percentage of goals selected against. Without a suitable comparison, it is hard to know how this value reflects the performance of the agent. The need for comparison is not as important when analysing the amount of time wasted though, as any amount of wasted time reflects a drop in the agent's real-time performance.

6 Iteration Two: Execution Interrupts

The previous analysis led to the identification of periods during which the agent is executing a plan when it should really be pursuing a different goal. To attempt to eliminate these periods, we must alter the previously presented agent design. Rather than discuss the design of the whole architecture, we will only focus on the changes made to the previous design. The new design can be seen in Figure 2.

It is the belief manager that holds the key to reducing the amount of time wasted during plan execution. In the basic design, when the goal generator proposes a goal that is more important than the one currently being pursued, the belief manager simply stores this goal. Then, when the agent finishes what it is currently doing (either planning or executing) the goal is selected. To reduce the amount of execution time wasted by the agent, we need to redesign the belief manager to immediately halt the execution of a plan if it is discovered that this plan's goal is no longer the agent's current goal (i.e. a more important goal has been proposed). But, rather than alter the behaviour of the belief manager too drastically, we can make a small alteration

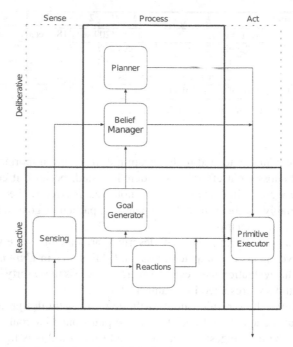

Fig. 2 Architecture Designs For Iterations 2 & 3 (the dotted line indicates the additional connection for Iteration 3).

to it, and add a new component to the architecture to handle the rest of the necessary behaviour. The small alteration to be made to the belief manager is to allow it to immediately select a proposed goal to be the current goal if the proposed goal is more important than the current goal. The new component to be added to the agent architecture is the *interrupt manager*.

The interrupt manager's role within the agent architecture is to monitor the goal held by the belief manager and ensure that the primitive executor is not executing a plan for any other goal. It takes input from the belief manager about the current goal, and from the primitive executor about the current action goal. If the goal supplied by the belief manager differs from the one supplied by the primitive executor (which would happen if a more important goal has been proposed), the interrupt manager generates an interrupt event. This should cause plan execution to stop and allows the belief manager to start a planning process for the new goal.

Given the ability to interrupt plan execution, it is desirable to see what other conditions might warrant an interrupt being generated. Game worlds can change quickly and unexpectedly, and this can lead to situations where the agent is executing a plan for a goal that is no longer valid, but no new goal of higher importance has been proposed (e.g. when an agent is attempting to score a point but another agent has possession of the flag). If this happens then the agent should adopt another goal, but if this new goal is of a lower importance, then it won't generate an interrupt based on importance. To overcome this we must give the interrupt manager the ability to generate interrupts when a plan is being executed, but the associated goal is no longer valid. To do this, not only must the interrupt manager cause execution to be halted, but it must cause the belief manager to deselect the current goal. This is necessary because a valid new goal with lower importance cannot be selected whilst the belief manager holds a goal of higher importance. The interrupt manager plays a similar role in the agent architecture as the environment monitors do in the CPEF continual planning system [11].

The interrupt manager is implemented as a set of reactive rules for comparing the current execution goal to the goal held by the primitive executor, and for evaluating whether the current execution goal is valid given the agent's beliefs about the world. This latter process could be implemented deliberatively (e.g. by comparing the preconditions for actions in the current plan against the state of the world), but a reactive implementation was chosen for speed and efficiency. This is feasible in this case because the number of beliefs that can affect a plan's validity are quite limited.

6.1 Evaluation

Experimental results for this iteration of the design process can be seen in column 2 of Table 1. They show that the agent no longer wastes any time executing plans when the associated goals are no longer appropriate. As a result of this, the overall amount of time the agent spends executing plans has decreased, and consequently it has more time to spend planning. Although the amount of time the agent spends planning has increased, the results demonstrate a decrease in the amount of planning time that is wasted by the agent. It is likely that this change isn't connected to the alterations made to the agent's design, because none of the interfaces to the planner were modified. Along with this unexpected positive change, the results show an unexpected negative change. The percentage of goals selected has dropped below its value in the first iteration. With less time spent executing plans, it should be expected that this value would rise as the agent is able to complete more plan-act cycles and therefore present the belief manager with more opportunities to select goals.

Although the design proposed in this second iteration improves upon the previous design in most respects, there still appears to be a significant amount of time being wasted by the agent during planning processes. This time wasting behaviour is not strictly due to the speed of the planner (although a faster planner would waste less time), but is due to the fact that unlike the execution process, the planner is not interruptible in this design. The next iteration of the design process will address this.

7 Iteration Three: Simple Planner Interrupts

In this iteration of the design process, the changes made previously to allow execution processes to be interrupted are extended to apply to planning processes too. Only two changes are made to the design and implementation of the agent in this iteration. The interrupt manager in connected to the planner, and the implementation of the planner is altered to allow interrupts to occur. This can be seen in Figure 2.

7.1 Evaluation

The results in column 3 of Table 1 show that altering the design to allow planning to be interrupted as well has had positive effects. The agent now wastes no planning or execution time, and the average amount of time an agent spends planning has dropped by a similar amount to the amount of time it was previously wasting during the planning process. The average amount of time the agent spends executing has also risen due to the reduction in planning time. The complete eradication of wasted time during planning and execution has led to an increase in the percentage of goals that the agent can select, as the new design provides a greater number of opportunities for the agent to adopt a new goal.

8 Iteration Four: Anytime Planning

Now that the amount of time wasted by the agent has been reduced to zero, we can look for other, less obvious flaws in the agent design. The results from the third iteration of the design process show that the agent still spends a great deal of time planning. Although none of this time is "wasted" using our (admittedly limited) metrics, it is still possible to argue that the agent is wasting time during both planning and execution. If a planning or execution process is interrupted and halted, then the time spent on that process is effectively wasted as the agent has not gained any benefit from the process (except possible inadvertent gains), and the partial results of the process are discarded.

If the agent could anticipate when interrupts to a process are likely to occur, and make use of the results of the incomplete process before this, then the deleterious effect of interrupts could be overcome. Although this is an interesting design choice, it is not possible to apply this to plan execution processes. Despite the fact that execution processes can be interrupted at any time, at no point is there anything concrete that can be retrieved from this process to use at a later date. Any gains made from partially enacted execution processes will be the results of actions taken during execution (e.g. gaining a favourable world position or observing an interesting event), not as the result of anything returned or stored by the execution process.

For the agent's planning process, this idea of using partial results is much more viable. Any processing effort expended during planning a process results in the space of possible plans being pruned of invalid plans, so that the planning agent gains a better understanding of what a likely solution will be. If the planning process can be halted in sufficient time before an anticipated interruption, then this partial result can be used to guide subsequent execution. This approach will allow the agent to achieve its selected goals before they become invalid (i.e. before an interruption should occur) and reduce the amount of time spent on planning processes that are eventually discarded. This fourth iteration of the design process will investigate the design changes necessary to support this behaviour. The resulting design can be seen in Figure 3.

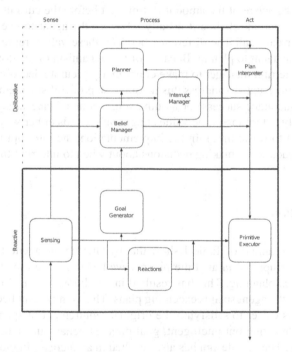

Fig. 3 Architecture Design For Iteration 4.

To support the use of partial results, the planner must be redesigned as an *anytime planner*. For this we use the approach described [7]. The result is an anytime extension of the UMCP planner which produces plans that increase in quality monotonically with respect to time. This enables rational judgements to be made about interrupt times.

The anytime planner produces partially complete HTN plans in the UMCP formalism. The plans are complete in that they contain specifications of actions for the entire plan, but they are incomplete because some of the steps are represented at an abstract level (i.e. they are not suitable as input for the primitive executor). To enable the agent to act out these plans, they must first be translated into primitives. This is the task of the *plan interpreter*. The plan interpreter must be implemented in a way that ensures that the minimum of time is wasted after an interrupt has occurred. Therefore we implemented it as a cut-down reactive planner with fixed plans for each possible abstract action. Given a plan containing abstract actions, it quickly produces a plan that is completely primitive, but that is not always correct. This is typical of the trade-offs that must be made when using an anytime algorithm.

In this iteration, the interrupt manager must be able to spot situations in which, in order for the agent to avoid wasting planning time and to maximise its ability to achieve goals, it is necessary for the agent to interrupt its planner and use the partial results to guide execution. Rather than being based on importance-based comparisons, this new type of interrupt is heavily reliant on time. Typically the interrupt manager must be aware of the amount of time left before the current goal becomes invalid and the amount of time it usually takes for the agent to execute a plan to achieve the current goal. The difference between these values represents the time available for the agent to plan in. Because of the dynamism of the domain, it is difficult for the interrupt manager to make consistently accurate decisions about when to generate an interrupt. To address this it could use probabilistic methods (although this may not guarantee success) or assume some value of inaccuracy when examining previously determined time values (e.g. five seconds either way, but this may cause the agent to waste time). In the implementation, the interrupt manager takes the latter approach when making decisions about when to interrupt the planner.

8.1 Evaluation

The results in column 4 of Table 1 show that by altering the agent design to allow preemptive interrupts of an anytime planner we have reduced the amount of time the agent spends planning. This has resulted in an almost identical increase in the amount of time the agent spends executing plans. This is important because it means that the agent is closer to satisfying the original requirement of spending as much time as possible acting out intelligent, goal-directed behaviour, rather than relying on its reactions. The new design has also resulted in an increase in the percentage of suggested goals that the agent selects. This is because the design changes effectively speed up the time the agent takes to run through a plan-act cycle, giving it more opportunities to select proposed goals.

9 Related Work

The agent architecture produced as a result of our design-based methodology is similar to many other hybrid architectures in the literature. Many architectures for intelligent agents combine deliberation with reactive plan execution, e.g. [20, 1], but do not take the additional step of using an anytime planner. The SOMASS system [10] employs HTN planning and reactive action interpretation as our final agent design does, but also does not have the additional mechanisms for anytime behaviour. The Excalibur project [12] employs an anytime planner for controlling computer game agents, but does not integrate it into an architecture containing the reactive control mechanisms necessary to cope with dynamic game worlds. Many other agents have been developed for game worlds (e.g. [9, 6]), but they tend to be variations on purely reactive systems.

In terms of the metholdology we employed to create our architecture, there are not many similar processes documented in the AI literature. The most prominent alternative approach is Bryson's Behaviour-Oriented Design (BOD), which has also been applied to the development of an Unreal Tournament bot [14]. Although BOD is also an interative methodology targeted at system behaviour, it is intended only for behaviour-based systems, and as such is much more limited in scope than the design-based methodology followed here. That said, its limited scope allows it to specify a much more precise (and therefore informative) set of steps which any designer much work though.

10 Conclusion

In this paper we demonstrated how a design-based methodology can be used to produce new iterations of an agent design based on the analysis of implementations of preceding designs. This method provides a framework for demonstrating how changes in a design affect how the design satisfies a particular set of requirements. In this instance we used a small set of empirical metrics to evaluate the designs with regard to the original requirements. The ultimate result of this is that the design process produces agent designs that are a demonstrably better fit for their intended niche than other designs that are nearby in design space. Empirical evaluation demonstrates this, with instantiations of the agents produced in the fourth iteration of the design process winning 70% of 3 vs. 3 games, and 90% of 2 vs. 2 games against instantiations of agents from the first iteration [7].

References

1. Bonasso, R.P., Firby, R.J., Gat, E., Kortenkamp, D., Miller, D.P., Slack, M.G.: Experiences with an architecture for intelligent, reactive agents. J. Exp. Theor. Artif. Intell. 9(2-3), 237–256 (1997)
2. Cavazza, M.: Merging planning and path planning: On agent's behaviours in situated virtual worlds. In: Proceedings of the AISB'00 Symposium on AI Planning and Intelligent Agents, pp. 17–24. Birmingham, UK (2000)
3. Dennett, D.C.: Brainstorms: Philosophical Essays on Mind and Psychology. MIT Press, Cambridge, MA (1978)
4. Epic Mega Games: Unreal Tournament. GT Interactive (1999)

5. Erol, K.: Hierarchical task network planning: Formalization, analysis, and implementation. Ph.D. thesis, Department of Computer Science, The University of Maryland (1995)
6. Gordon, E., Logan, B.: Game over: You have been beaten by a GRUE. In: D. Fu, S. Henke, J. Orkin (eds.) Challenges in Game Artificial Intelligence: Papers from the 2004 AAAI Workshop, pp. 16–21. AAAI Press (2004)
7. Hawes, N.: Anytime deliberation for computer game agents. Ph.D. thesis, School of Computer Science, University of Birmingham (2004)
8. Kaminka, G.A., Veloso, M.M., Schaffer, S., Sollitto, C., Adobbati, R., Marshall, A.N., Scholer, A., Tejada, S.: Gamebots: A flexible test bed for multiagent team research. Communications of the ACM **45**(1), 43–45 (2002)
9. Laird, J.E., Duchi, J.C.: Creating human-like synthetic characters with multiple skill levels: A case study using the soar quakebot. In: Papers from the 2001 AAAI Spring Symposium on Artificial Intelligence and Computer Games, pp. 54–58 (2001)
10. Malcolm, C.: A hybrid behavioural/knowledge-based approach to robotic assembly. In: Evolutionary Robotics: From Intelligent Robots to Artificial Life (ER'97), pp. 221–256. AAI Books, Tokyo, Japan (1997)
11. Myers, K.L.: Cpef: A continuous planning and execution framework. AI Magazine **20**(4), 63–70 (1999)
12. Nareyek, A.: Intelligent agents for computer games. In: Computers and Games, Second International Conference (CG 2000), *Lecture Notes in Computer Science*, vol. 2063, pp. 414–422. Springer (2002)
13. Nilsson, N.J.: Teleo-reactive programs for agent control. Journal of Artificial Intelligence Research **1**, 139–158 (1994)
14. Partington, S.J., Bryson, J.J.: The Behavior Oriented Design of an Unreal Tournament character. In: T. Panayiotopoulos, J. Gratch, R. Aylett, D. Ballin, P. Olivier, T. Rist (eds.) The Fifth International Working Conference on Intelligent Virtual Agents, pp. 466–477. Springer, Kos, Greece (2005)
15. Pollack, M.E., Horty, J.F.: There's more to life than making plans. AI Magazine **20**(4), 71–83 (1999)
16. Sloman, A.: Prolegomena to a theory of communication and affect. In: A. Ortony, J. Slack, O. Stock (eds.) Communication from an Artificial Intelligence Perspective: Theoretical and Applied Issues, pp. 229–260. Springer, Berlin, Heidelberg (1992)
17. Sloman, A.: The "semantics" of evolution: Trajectories and trade-offs in design space and niche space. In: H. Coelho (ed.) Progress in Artificial Intelligence, 6th Iberoamerican Conference on AI (IBERAMIA), pp. 27–38. Springer, Lecture Notes in Artificial Intelligence, Lisbon (1998)
18. Sloman, A.: Varieties of affect and the cogaff architecture schema. In: Proceedings of the AISB'01 Symposium on Emotion, Cognition and Affective Computing, pp. 1–10 (2001)
19. Sloman, A., Logan, B.: Building cognitively rich agents using the sim_agent toolkit. Communications of the ACM **43**(2), 71–77 (1999)
20. Wilkins, D.E., Myers, K.L., Lowrance, J.D., Wesley, L.P.: Planning and reacting in uncertain and dynamic environments. Journal of Experimental and Theoretical AI **6**, 197–227 (1994)

From Source Code to Runtime Behaviour: Software Metrics Help to Select the Computer Architecture.

Frank Eichinger, David Kramer, Klemens Böhm and Wolfgang Karl

Abstract The decision which hardware platform to use for a certain application is an important problem in computer architecture. This paper reports on a study where a data-mining approach is used for this decision. It relies purely on source-code characteristics, to avoid potentially expensive program executions. One challenge in this context is that one cannot infer how often functions that are part of the application are typically executed. The main insight of this study is twofold: (a) Source-code characteristics are sufficient nevertheless. (b) Linking individual functions with the runtime behaviour of the program as a whole yields good predictions. In other words, while individual data objects from the training set may be quite inaccurate, the resulting model is not.

1 Introduction

The question which computer architecture is best suited for a certain application is of outstanding importance in the computer industry. With the continuous refining of computer architectures, this problem becomes even more challenging. Think of the high degree and various forms of parallelism (multicores), heterogeneity due to application-specific accelerators, interconnection technology on the chip, or the memory hierarchy. The design space is huge and leads to a broad variety of processor architectures. It is not at all obvious which architecture is best suited for a specific application. For example, due to the branch-prediction unit, an application with predictable branches benefits from a long pipeline, while a shorter pipeline is bet-

Frank Eichinger, Klemens Böhm
Institute for Program Structures and Data Organisation (IPD)
Universität Karlsruhe (TH), Germany, e-mail: {eichinger,boehm}@ipd.uka.de

David Kramer, Wolfgang Karl
Institute for Computer Science and Engineering (ITEC)
Universität Karlsruhe (TH), Germany, e-mail: {kramer,karl}@ira.uka.de

M. Bramer et al. (eds.), *Research and Development in Intelligent Systems XXVI*,
DOI 10.1007/978-1-84882-983-1_29, © Springer-Verlag London Limited 2010

ter for unpredictable branch behaviour. The question which architecture yields the best performance is particularly important for high-performance computing where an expensive system is purchased for a few or even only one application.

Traditional approaches use experimental executions, simulations or analytical models to identify the best computer architecture for a given application. For instance, when a computing centre plans to procure a new cluster for a specific application, one way to do so is to compare the runtime behaviour of this application on different platforms. This obviously is time-consuming and expensive, and the platforms in question must be available in the first place. Similar arguments apply to state-of-the-art simulation approaches: In-depth simulation is time-consuming, in particular with machine models that are sophisticated. Finally, due to the increasing complexity of computer systems, establishing analytical models of the computer architectures in question is extremely hard. This may lead to a relatively poor reliability of these models, compared to experimental executions and simulations. In consequence, techniques are sought which help to decide between several platforms for a specific application. Ideally, such techniques should not require any execution or simulation and should be based on an analysis of the application in question. Some approaches exist which can make a decision between several platforms [5, 8]. They rely on the assumption that similar programs perform alike when executed on the same machine. However, in addition to measures deduced from the source code, these approaches make use of runtime-related characteristics, such as branch probabilities or instruction counts. To generate these characteristics, simulations or program runs on real hardware are necessary.

This article reports on the results of a study that investigates another method to determine the best computer architecture for a given application. The method likewise assumes that similar applications have similar execution behaviour. But in contrast to the previous work, we have consciously decided not to take any runtime-related information of the application in question into account. In this current study we characterise the application entirely by means of measures gained from the source code. In other words, we hypothesise that there is a strong correlation between program properties encoded in the source code and the execution behaviour, and that this correlation can be exploited. This hypothesis may appear to be unsettling – taking only source-code characteristics into account obviously is much less informative than runtime behaviour! In particular, it is difficult to impossible to infer how often a certain function is typically executed. Another issue is that source-code metrics, i.e., existing measures that quantify characteristics of the source code, typically are defined on the function level rather than on the level of entire programs, while we are interested in predictions for programs as a whole. Having said this, the method examined here is a data-mining approach with the following distinctive feature: It links individual functions with the runtime behaviour of the program as a whole. Even though this approach clearly is simplistic, i.e., the characterisation of individual functions may be *very* inaccurate, it yields a prediction accuracy for entire programs which is surprisingly high. In retrospect, our explanation is as follows: Since applications typically consist of a large number of functions, there is a lot of training data which, on average, compensates for that simplification. I.e., we provide evidence that source-code characteristics alone are indeed helpful to predict a good computer architecture. More specifically, our contributions are as follows:

Software Metrics. The software-engineering community has proposed a number of software metrics in order to represent source-code characteristics and properties. Originally, these metrics have been cast as quality measures rather than as performance indicators. Preliminary investigations of ours have revealed that measures based on the control flow of functions are particularly promising to predict runtime behaviour. Consequently, we define and derive a number of metrics, such as graph invariants, based on the control-flow graphs (CFGs) [1] of the functions. We use these metrics in addition to more common ones.

Classification Framework. We propose a classification setting for our specific context and evaluate it. This setting is not obvious: While most metrics are available at the function level, we want to choose the best architecture for a program as a whole. Instead of potentially lossy aggregation approaches, we propose a framework where we first learn at the function level before deploying classifier-fusion techniques to come up with predictions at the program level.

Evaluation. Our case study features an evaluation using five systems from the online database of the SPEC CPU 2000 and 2006 benchmark suites. The results are that, for 'relatively similar' computer architectures to choose from, and with the runtime behaviour of only few programs used as training data, our approach achieves an average prediction accuracy of 78% when choosing between two systems.

Correlation of Software Metrics and Runtime Behaviour. Our main concern, from a 'research' perspective, has been to confirm (and to exploit) the relationship between source-code properties and runtime behaviour, on different platforms. Besides the fact that the approach investigated here does indeed yield a statement regarding the computer architecture best suited, our evaluation shows that the correlation between source-code properties and runtime behaviour is remarkably strong.

Paper outline: Section 2 presents related work, Section 3 describes the process of acquiring software metrics, before we describe the data-mining process in Section 4. Section 5 presents our results, which are discussed in Section 6. Section 7 concludes.

2 Related Work

In the past, various approaches to predict the runtime or the runtime behaviour of given applications have been proposed. Newer approaches propose the use of machine-learning approaches for this prediction.

In [2, 16] the authors use multilayer neural networks to predict the performance of the multigrid solver SMG 2000 on a BlueGene/L cluster. The parameter space includes the cluster configuration as well as the size of the grid used. The training set used consists of performance results on an actual platform using a collection of random points from the parameter space. In contrast to our approach, these approaches can only be used to predict the performance of a parametrised application on a cluster with different configurations. In addition, they require time-consuming training-data generation.

Another possible use of neural networks is described in [6]. Here, İpek et al. use neural networks to predict the performance of points in the design space. Neural networks are used to approximate the design space and to create a model of it. The model built predicts the performance of points with high accuracy and has been applied to memory hierarchy and chip-multiprocessor design spaces.

To ease the generation of analytical models of complex high-performance systems, Kühnemann et al. have developed a compiler tool for automated runtime prediction of parallel MPI programs [9]. The tool analyses the source code of MPI programs to create an appropriate runtime-function model for the communication overhead and for the computation. Properties of the underlying machine are needed for proper prediction of the computation effort.

Another method for performance prediction is [8] from Joshi et al. They use inherent program characteristics to measure the similarity between programs. Instead of using microarchitecture-dependent measures for characterisation, such as cycles per instruction, cache-miss rate or runtimes, they use microarchitecture-independent ones. These measures include the instruction mix, the size of the working set and branch probabilities. To generate the measures, either simulation or execution of the application is necessary. Based on [8], the authors exploit the similarity between programs for performance prediction of applications in the SPEC CPU 2000 benchmark suite [5]. They use microarchitecture-independent characteristics and performance numbers from an application to build a so-called benchmark space. To predict the performance of an application, the developer has to compute a point in the benchmark space using the same characteristics. Comparing our approach to [5] reveals that both approaches can predict the runtime-behaviour of an application in question on given platforms and have advantages and disadvantages. [5] uses runtime-related microarchitecture-independent characteristics in the prediction process. The advantage is that predictions are likely to be more precise. A drawback is that the execution of the application on an existing platform or a detailed simulation is necessary. Saveedra and Smith [14] use a similar approach as proposed in [5], but they use program and machine characteristics to estimate the performance of a given Fortran program on an arbitrary machine. A drawback of all these approaches is the usage of architecture-dependent characteristics which are time-consuming to create. Our approach in turn does not require such characteristics.

Finally, [3] studies the same problem as this current paper, but with a different approach based on graph mining and control-flow graphs. The technique described here yields better results.

3 Software-Metric Data

In this study we try to predict the best-performing platform by means of standard data-mining techniques. More precisely, we only use software characteristics derived from the source code, but no runtime or platform-related information. In order to use source-code metrics as input for data-mining algorithms, we describe the software entities with feature vectors of software-metrics values. The software-engineering community has been very active in defining metrics based on source code [7]. These metrics are primarily used to quantify the quality and the maintainability of applications and have not been intended to characterise runtime behaviour. However, we deploy a number of these metrics as well as some metrics defined by ourselves exactly to this end. Source-code metrics cover various aspects of software, e.g., statements used, source-code quality, complexity and understandability. We decided not to use any of the numerous metrics dealing with source-code size and understandability, such as the various lines of code (LOC) measures or any measure concerned with comments. These metrics strongly depend on the coding scheme used and do not have any impact on the program complexity and therefore on the runtime behaviour. Besides these measures, we do not exclude any other metric a priori. This is because we are not aware of any previous experience in predicting runtime behaviour based on source-code metrics. Even if some metrics such as McCabe's cyclomatic complexity [11] are debatable [15], we leave it to the data-mining algorithm to decide which metrics are useful for our purpose.

CPU 2000			**CPU 2006**		
177.mesa	176.gcc	255.vortex	400.perlbench	436.cactus-ADM	464.h264ref
179.art	181.mcf	256.bzip2	401.bzip2	445.gobmk	470.lbm
183.equake	186.crafty	300.twolf	403.gcc	454.calculix	481.wrf
188.ammp	197.parser		429.mcf	456.hmmer	482.sphinx3
164.gzip	253.perlbmk		433.milc	458.sjeng	
175.vpr	254.gap		435.gromacs	462.lib-quantum	

Table 1 SPEC benchmark programs used.

In order to derive source-code metrics from the benchmark programs, we employ a standard tool from software engineering: RSM from M Squared Technologies LLC. We derive the metrics and characteristics for every function in every program from the SPEC CPU 2000 and 2006 benchmark suites. As these benchmarks have been assembled with the intention to cover a broad variety of different domains, they are a good basis for the classification of new programs. – The RSM tool does not provide any metrics from Fortran source code. We therefore limit our experiments to the C and C++ benchmark programs. Table 1 lists all 31 programs we use for our experiments.

RSM delivers a huge variety of metrics, in particular *counts*, *quality measures* and *complexity measures*.[1] The ones we use for our purpose are listed in Table 2. *Counts* refer to simple counts of statements and syntactical elements such as braces and brackets. The *quality measures* refer to counts of certain kinds of program quality, which could also have an impact on execution behaviour. For example, one of

---

[1] See the RSM documentation for details on specific metrics:
http://msquaredtechnologies.com/m2rsm/docs/rsm_metrics.htm

368   Frank Eichinger, David Kramer, Klemens Böhm and Wolfgang Karl

these counts is increased whenever a variable is assigned to a literal value. Finally, the *complexity measures* describe the complexity of the function interface and the cyclomatic complexity [11] of the underlying control-flow graph [1].

Counts	memory_free_count	notice_50_count	freq_sdev
abort_count	open_brace_count	notice_50_percent	freq_sum
break_count	open_bracket_count	notice_50_type	loop_depth_max
case_count	open_paren_count	notice_119_count	loop_depth_mean
class_count	return_count	notice_119_percent	loop_depth_sdev
close_brace_count	switch_count	notice_119_type	loop_depth_sum
close_bracket_count	typedef_count	notice_all_count	loops_max
close_paren_count	union_count		loops_mean
const_count	while_count	**Complexity Measures**	loops_sdev
default_count		cyclomatic_complexity	loops_sum
define_count	**Quality Measures**	interface_complexity	nodes
do_count	notice_22_count	interface_params	num_pred_max
else_count	notice_22_percent	interface_returns	num_pred_mean
enum_count	notice_22_type	total_complexity	num_pred_sdev
exit_count	notice_27_count		num_pred_sum
for_count	notice_27_percent	**CFG Measures**	num_succ_max
goto_count	notice_27_type	back_edges_max	num_succ_mean
if_count	notice_28_count	back_edges_mean	num_succ_sdev
include_count	notice_28_percent	back_edges_sdev	num_succ_sum
inline_function_count	notice_28_type	back_edges_sum	record_count
literal_strings_count	notice_44_count	edges	registers
macros_count	notice_44_percent	freq_max	
memory_alloc_count	notice_44_type	freq_mean	

Table 2 Source code and control-flow-graph (CFG) measures used.

    The set of metrics from RSM includes only a few measures regarding the structure and the complexity of the application. As observed in preliminary experiments, measures based on the control flow of functions might be important when predicting runtime behaviour. Therefore, we have decided to use more metrics than those provided by RSM and to derive measures from control-flow graphs [1]. Such graphs are widely used in software engineering and are a common way of representing code in compilers internally. Basic blocks of code without any jump statements are the nodes, and the control dependencies between these blocks are the edges. We use the front-end of the GNU Compiler Collection (gcc) to derive control-flow graphs of all functions. From these graphs, we calculate some graph invariants, *CFG Measures* (cf. Table 2), such as the number of nodes and edges of a control-flow graph, the number of loops and the aggregated in- and out-degrees of the nodes of the graph. We use these measures as further metrics generated purely from the source code.

    The metrics used (cf. Table 2) are certainly not an exhaustive set of metrics defined by the software-engineering community. For example, we do not take object-oriented metrics for the C++ programs into account. (Most of our programs are C programs.) However, our goal rather is to demonstrate and to make use of the correlation of source-code properties and runtime behaviour and not to investigate the usefulness of any metric possible. In Section 5 we will demonstrate that the metrics used are well suited, and that the results are useful.

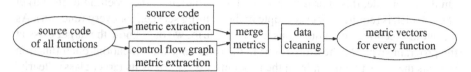

Fig. 1 Metric-generation workflow.

Before actually using the data we do some data cleaning in order to ease the data-mining process. We do this by eliminating measures containing null values in more than 95% of all functions as well as measures displaying always the same value. We deem these attributes irrelevant as they do not influence the quality predictions but increase runtime. Figure 1 summarises the metric-generation process.

4 Data-Mining Process

A naïve way to predict the runtime behaviour of a given program is to describe every program using a set of metrics and to train a machine-learning algorithm on it. This approach is not practical. One reason is that most source-code metrics are defined on the function level rather than on the program level (cf. Section 3). The definition of program-level metrics would certainly be possible, but would require new tools, and – more important – such metrics would represent a very coarse view on the application. As an example, a count of if-statements for an entire program would rather be a statement on the total size of the program than on the complexity of its functions. Another possibility would be aggregating function-level measures to the program level. Such an approach, e.g., the arithmetic mean of *counts* of possibly thousands of functions belonging to one program, would lead to imprecise predictions due to the loss of potentially important fine-grained information. Another reason which opposes direct learning on program level is that suitable runtime information is usually only available for a relatively small number of programs. Learning with such small datasets typically is not feasible. This is because it is hard to generalise from tens of programs in order to learn a hopefully universal prediction model. The limited number of programs available is due to the huge costs of executing, say, hundreds of programs on a number of different platforms. We for our part use 31 benchmark programs (listed in Table 1) where the runtime information is available (cf. Section 5). In the following we develop an approach which works well with a number of programs of this magnitude. Note that we only make use of execution times (and no further runtime-related measures) of the benchmark programs in our learning dataset. To classify a program, no execution of the program is necessary – measures are only derived from the source code.

To address the problems discussed when learning on the program level, we have decided to perform machine learning on the function level. On the one side, this approach is feasible since the software metrics are available at this level of detail. On the other side, this approach leads to a new challenge: the labelling of the target class, which is required for every tuple in the training set (i.e., for every function). As we avoid executions or simulations in our scenario, we only know the target class at the program level. We therefore resort to the following simplification: Each function inherits the fastest platform from the program it is part of as its target class. Clearly, this approach ignores the characteristics of the different functions. But nevertheless, we hypothesise that it yields predictions of acceptable quality. The hope is that there are not too many functions that are untypical for the performance of the program, and a large number of functions in the training set will compensate those functions.

Program/Function	$Metric_1$	$Metric_2$	$\cdots$	$Metric_n$	Platform
$Program_A/function_1$	3	7	$\cdots$	34	System 5
$Program_A/function_2$	2	7	$\cdots$	45	System 5
$\cdots$	$\cdots$	$\cdots$	$\cdots$	$\cdots$	System 5
$Program_A/function_{|A|}$	3	7	$\cdots$	24	System 5
$Program_B/function_1$	3	4	$\cdots$	42	System 2
$Program_B/function_2$	6	4	$\cdots$	61	System 2
$\cdots$	$\cdots$	$\cdots$	$\cdots$	$\cdots$	System 2
$Program_B/function_{|B|}$	1	4	$\cdots$	23	System 2
$\cdots$	$\cdots$	$\cdots$	$\cdots$	$\cdots$	$\cdots$

Table 3 Example learning dataset.

Table 3 is an example of the datasets used. The rows correspond to each function ($function_i$) of every benchmark program ($Program_A, Program_B, ...$). For our experiments we use the benchmark programs listed in Table 1. The columns correspond to the source-code metrics, which we compute for every function ($Metric_1$, ..., $Metric_n$). The column $Platform$ contains the target class, which is the same for all functions of a program. In the experiments we use all metrics enumerated in Table 2. The example dataset in Table 3 contains $System\ 2$ and $System\ 5$ as examples of two possible target platforms.

Using a dataset as in Table 3, we learn a prediction model to classify data without class information ($Platform$). In other words, such a model can make predictions for each function in isolation. To obtain a prediction for a program as a whole, which consists of a number of functions, these predictions need to be integrated. We for our part use the majority-vote technique, a standard scheme to combine multiple classifications [10]. Experiments with other combination techniques such as the usage of weights have lead to results which, on average, are not better than majority vote in our specific context.

In summary, our prediction approach consists of two steps. In the first step we learn a classification model (Figure 2). This is based on a training dataset as shown in Table 3, consisting of source-code metrics at the function level (cf. Section 3) and target systems derived from the execution times at the program level.

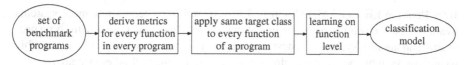

Fig. 2 Learning workflow.

In the second step we predict the platform best suited for applications with unknown runtime behaviour (Figure 3). This prediction at the function level is based on the same metrics as used for learning. Afterwards, we merge these results into one overall prediction at the program level.

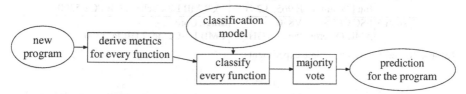

Fig. 3 Prediction workflow.

Besides the selection problem studied here using classification and classifier fusion techniques, the direct prediction of the runtime on a certain machine is a related, but different problem. At first sight, this could be done similarly using regression techniques. However, the runtime not only depends on the program given, but also on the parameters used and the data processed. Such information is available for certain configurations of, say, benchmark-program runs, but not for new programs in general. Hence, we limit our study to that selection problem.

5 Experiments

In order to demonstrate the usefulness of our approach and to show the correlations between properties observed in the source code and the runtime behaviour on different platforms, we perform a case study utilising the SPEC CPU benchmark programs as described in Section 3. As the SPEC CPU benchmarks are broad, i.e., cover many application domains, we have purposefully decided to deploy this benchmark, as opposed to any other set of training examples, e.g., home-grown programs.

The runtimes of the programs are published on the SPEC homepage[2], and we make use of this data. We decided to use a subset of the systems available, listed in Table 4. For these systems, runtime data is available for both, the CPU 2000 and the CPU 2006 benchmark. The systems cover single-, dual- and quadcore architectures as well as different memory hierarchies and processors: Intel Xeon, Intel Pentium 4,

---

[2] http://www.spec.org/benchmarks.html

Intel Pentium EE and AMD Opteron. There would have been a few more systems available. As we want to run experiments where one system is fastest with some programs and another system is fastest with other programs, it would not be reasonable to include systems performing (almost) always better than all other systems.

System	Vendor & Processor	Processor-Type & Memory
System 1	Bull SAS NovaScale B280 Intel Xeon E5335, 2.0 GHz	QuadCore 2 x 4 MB L2-Cache, 8 GB PC2-5300
System 2	Dell Precision 380 Intel Pentium 4 670, 3.8 GHz	SingleCore 2 MB L2-Cache, 2 GB PC2-4200
System 3	HP Proliant BL465c AMD Opteron 2220, 2.8 GHz	DualCore 2 x 1 MB L2-Cache, 16 GB PC2-5300
System 4	Intel D975XBX motherboard Intel Pentium EE 965, 3.7 GHz	DualCore, HT 2 x 2 MB L2-Cache, 4 GB PC2-5300
System 5	FSC CELSIUS V830 AMD Opteron 256, 3.0 GHz	SingleCore 1 MB L2-Cache, 2 GB PC3200

Table 4 Systems used for runtime experiments.

Based on the systems considered, we set up a number of experiments. We evaluate the performance of our approach by predicting the fastest platform for a benchmark program. In each experiment, we take care that different processor models are used, and that all systems are best suited for a significant number of programs. More specifically, in order to ease data mining and the comparison of the results, the experiments feature situations where the distribution of the systems being fastest is as balanced as possible. Table 5 lists the experiments with the systems compared.

Experiment	Platforms	Processors
Experiment 1	System 5 vs. System 2	Opteron vs. Pentium 4
Experiment 2	System 3 vs. System 4	Opteron vs. Pentium EE
Experiment 3	System 3 vs. System 1	Opteron vs. Xeon
Experiment 4	System 3 vs. System 1 vs. System 4	Opteron vs. Xeon vs. Pentium EE

Table 5 Experiments.

Experiments 1, 2 and 3 are binary prediction problems where the task is to chose one out of two platforms, Experiment 4 is a three-class prediction problem. We limit ourselves to these experiments and do not run experiments where to choose between all systems. This is because the training data from the 31 programs available would not provide enough learning examples to choose from more than three systems. In the following, we show that predictions with two or three target systems are possible. We do not expect any difficulties when choosing from more systems when more training examples are available.

We evaluate our approach using different learning algorithms such as neural networks, support vector machines and decision trees. As we have achieved the best results using the C5.0 decision-tree algorithm (a variant of the well known C4.5 algorithm [13]) implemented in the SPSS Clementine data-mining suite, we will focus on the C5.0 classifier in the following. However, the results with other classifiers are not significantly different.

We conduct all experiments using stratified 2-fold-cross-validation: We use half of the programs for learning and the other half for testing, in two iterations. We deem this evaluation scheme adequate for our dataset consisting of 31 programs for learning and classification. We then derive the *accuracy*, i.e., the percentage of programs with correct prediction, as well as the *speedup*. Here, the *speedup* is the improvement in execution time over the average execution time on all systems in the experiment. Averaging the execution time of the systems is a fair baseline, as it mimics random selection of the underlying system. The *speedup* can be compared to the highest possible speedup, $speedup_{max}$. This is the improvement in execution time when selecting the fastest platform for each benchmark program. In our scenario, the *speedup* measure is more significant than *accuracy*. To illustrate, predicting a system slightly worse than the best one would decrease *accuracy* but would affect the *speedup* only slightly. This is consistent with our goal to select fast architectures. We have consciously decided not to consider any error or confidence level information in our evaluation. This is because some decisions made by our majority-vote scheme might be tight. This is natural in our setting where some individual functions might be misclassified. We expect the large number of data tuples to compensate this effect, as discussed before. Table 6 contains our experimental results.

Experiment	accuracy	speedup	$speedup_{max}$
Experiment 1	74.19%	1.08	1.13
Experiment 2	77.42%	1.05	1.11
Experiment 3	83.87%	1.11	1.12
Experiment 4	67.74%	1.10	1.19

Table 6 Experimental results.

Experiment	accuracy	speedup	$speedup_{max}$
Experiment 1a	64.52%	1.05	1.13
Experiment 2a	67.74%	1.03	1.11
Experiment 3a	83.87%	1.11	1.12
Experiment 4a	64.52%	1.10	1.19

Table 7 Results without *quality measures*.

There is a high accuracy in the range from 74% to 84% for binary classifications (78% on average) and 68% for the three class case. This is signifficantly higher than the a priori probability for selecting the larger class (55% for Experiments 1 and 2, 58% for Experiment 3 and 42% for Experiment 4). More important, the predictions actually improve the total execution time. On average, 63% of the highest speedup possible is reached with the predictions of our approach. These results not only are of practical relevance, i.e., the prediction of the system best suited. They also confirm the hypothesis that there is a strong relationship between source-code characteristics and runtime behaviour.

Looking at Experiments 1, 2 and 3, we investigate the impact of the individual metrics used. Our motivation is not to learn more about individual metrics, but to see if there are important categories (cf. Table 2) and less important ones. The C5.0 implementation used can assess which attributes occur most frequently close to the root of the decision tree. Such an analysis of all trees generated reveals that the following five attributes are the most important ones, in decreasing order: *exit_count*, *notice_22_type*, *freq_sum*, *edges* and *notice_27_percent*. Therefore, attributes from all categories in Table 2 turn out to be important to predict runtime behaviour. As we did not expect a high impact of the *quality measures* (i.e., *notice_22_type* and *notice_27_percent*), we run our experiments again, but without using the *quality measures*. Table 7 contains the results.

The experiments show that the *quality measures* have an influence in Experiments 1, 2 and 4 where the accuracy decreases, but are not relevant in Experiment 3 where the same results are obtained. This behaviour can be explained as follows: *Quality measures* are rarely used in the decision trees in Experiment 3, and other metrics are more significant in this experiment. As one example of the *quality measures*, the metric *notice_27_percent* indicates a high number of function-return points (`return`-statements). Even if intended as a code-quality measure, this measure also quantifies the complexity of a function. This explains why this metric indeed contributes to the classification results.

6 Discussion

The approach investigated here has turned out to be useful for a fast identification of the best-suited architecture for a given application, in terms of runtime. Even for an expert it would be difficult to impossible to determine a good architecture by only looking at the source code. Up to now, traditional approaches such as benchmarking are used to this end. But compared to our approach, benchmarking has two disadvantages: First, it requires access to the systems in question, to actually run the benchmark programs. Our approach in turn only requires execution times (and no further runtime characteristics) for the benchmark programs used for learning – but not for the program for which the best architecture shall be predicted. Further, as long as one relies on standard benchmarks such as the SPEC benchmark used here, the runtimes on various systems are available 'for free', e.g., in an online database. This information can therefore be used to build the classification model. When applying the model, no runtime-related information is needed. Second, benchmarking requires time, ranging from a few minutes up to several hours. Our approach, in contrast, requires only a few seconds to determine the architecture best suited.

Since we have used only programs from the SPEC benchmark suites, our prediction accuracy is actually better than it looks at first sight, as we now explain. Applications can be roughly categorised into three classes: I/O-intensive, memory-intensive, and compute-intensive. Most of the SPEC CPU benchmark programs used here are compute-intensive, and none of the SPEC CPU 2006 programs used (cf. Table 1) shows any significant I/O-activity [17]. Each benchmark program has a memory footprint of less than 1 GB [4], which is smaller than the main memory of the systems we used. In addition, the platforms used for our experiments are relatively similar. Each of them uses the same x86 instruction-set architecture and only differs in the implementation, e.g., the pipeline of the Pentium 4 670 in System 2 is longer than the one in the AMD Opteron 256 of System 5. So we expect the prediction accuracy to increase when not only compute-intensive benchmarks are used, but also I/O-intensive or memory-intensive ones. It is also likely that our prediction accuracy increases when using a broader variety of systems, e.g., systems with a different instruction-set architecture like Itanium or PowerPC processors.

One potential way of improving our results further would probably be to make use of the different degrees of importance of functions. A rule of thumb says that 10% of all functions are responsible for 90% of the workload. As we have explicitly decided not to consider any runtime information in this study, our approach gives the same importance to every function, even to functions which are never called during an actual execution. In our current research – and in contrast to the main hypothesis of this current study – we investigate whether (and by how much) the utilisation of function-call frequencies can improve prediction quality.

7 Conclusions and Outlook

The question which platform yields the best performance for a certain application is a fundamental issue in the computer industry. Traditional approaches to deal with this issue make use of simulations, analytical models or experimental executions. This means that either a simulation model, an analytical model or an existing system must be available. Furthermore, these approaches are rather time-consuming. The approach studied in this current paper in turn deploys data-mining methods in order to do the prediction as follows: We generate metrics by analysing the source code of the application in question. We use off-the-shelf benchmarks to generate training data for a classifier, i.e., we extract those metrics for the benchmark programs. A classifier then determines the best suited computer architecture based on a given set of characteristics. A distinctive feature of our classification approach is that it works with fine-grained software metrics on the function level, while it derives predictions for entire programs. Its classification accuracy in our experiments has been 78% on average. The approach can predict the runtime behaviour of benchmark programs with previously unknown runtime behaviour on the target platforms, allowing to choose the best platform.

The work described here is part of a larger effort aiming at the deployment of data-mining techniques for system design and computer-architecture problems. On one hand, we are currently trying to increase the classification accuracy further. For example, we are currently investigating the usage of program-dependence-graph [12] metrics. Such graphs can be derived from static source code and include data dependencies, in addition to control dependencies as in control-flow graphs. We reckon that such dependencies are relevant for execution performance, as data dependencies affect pipelining and register usage, and the metrics used so far might not sufficiently cover these aspects. Further, we are examining the impact of function-call frequencies on prediction quality, as described in Section 6. On the other hand, future investigations will try to reveal dependencies between source-code properties and computer-architecture characteristics with our approach. Up to now, our objective has been to predict the fastest platform for a given application. We plan to investigate how to correlate the source-code related metrics with micro-architectural details, e.g., the cache architecture, and how to generate respective predictions. From a computer-architecture point of view, this would be of enormous help when designing processors for specific applications.

Acknowledgements

We are indebted to Nikolay Iakovlev, Markus Korte and Stephan Schosser for their valuable contributions, suggestions and discussions.

References

1. Allen, F.E.: Control Flow Analysis. In: Proc. of a Symposium on Compiler Optimization, SIGPLAN Notices, pp. 1–19 (1970)
2. Castillo, P.A., Mora, A.M., Guervós, J.J.M., Laredo, J.L.J., Moretó, M., Cazorla, F.J., Valero, M., McKee, S.A.: Architecture Performance Prediction Using Evolutionary Artificial Neural Networks. In: Proc. of the European Workshop on Bio-Inspired Heuristics for Design Automation (EvoHOT) (2008)
3. Eichinger, F., Böhm, K.: Selecting Computer Architectures by Means of Control-Flow-Graph Mining. In: Proc. of the Int. Symposium on Intelligent Data Analysis (IDA) (2009)
4. Henning, J.L.: SPEC CPU 2006 Memory Footprint. SIGARCH Comput. Archit. News 35(1), 84–89 (2007)
5. Hoste, K., Phansalkar, A., Eeckhout, L., Georges, A., John, L.K., Bosschere, K.D.: Performance Prediction Based on Inherent Program Similarity. In: Proc. of the Int. Conf. on Parallel Architectures and Compilation Techniques (PACT) (2006)
6. İpek, E., McKee, S.A., Singh, K., Caruana, R., de Supinski, B.R., Schulz, M.: Efficient Architectural Design Space Exploration via Predictive Modeling. ACM Trans. Archit. Code Optim. 4(4), 1–34 (2008)
7. Jones, C.: Applied Software Measurement. McGraw-Hill (2008)
8. Joshi, A., Phansalkar, A., Eeckhout, L., John, L.: Measuring Benchmark Similarity Using Inherent Program Characteristics. IEEE Trans. Computers 55(6), 769–782 (2006)
9. Kühnemann, M., Rauber, T., Runger, G.: A Source Code Analyzer for Performance Prediction. In: Proc. of the Int. Parallel and Distributed Processing Symposium (IPDPS) (2004)
10. Kuncheva, L.I.: Combining Pattern Classifiers: Methods and Algorithms. Wiley (2004)
11. McCabe, T.: A Complexity Measure. IEEE Trans. Software Eng. 2(4), 308–320 (1976)
12. Ottenstein, K.J., Ottenstein, L.M.: The Program Dependence Graph in a Software Development Environment. SIGSOFT Softw. Eng. Notes 9(3), 177–184 (1984)
13. Quinlan, J.R.: C4.5: Programs for Machine Learning. Morgan Kaufmann (1993)
14. Saavedra, R.H., Smith, A.J.: Analysis of Benchmark Characteristics and Benchmark Performance Prediction. ACM Trans. Comput. Syst. 14(4), 344–384 (1996)
15. Shepperd, M.: A Critique of Cyclomatic Complexity as a Software Metric. Software Engineering Journal 3(2), 30–36 (1988)
16. Singh, K., İpek, E., McKee, S.A., de Supinski, B.R., Schulz, M., Caruana, R.: Predicting Parallel Application Performance via Machine Learning Approaches. Concurrency and Computation: Practice and Experience 19(17), 2219–2235 (2007)
17. Ye, D., Ray, J., Kaeli, D.: Characterization of File I/O Activity for SPEC CPU 2006. SIGARCH Comput. Archit. News 35(1), 112–117 (2007)

Learning to Improve E-mail Classification with numéro interactive

Dean M. Jones

Abstract This paper describes some of the ways in which we use artificial intelligence technologies in *numéro interactive*, a Customer Interaction Management system. In particular, we focus on the classification of e-mail messages into one of multiple business categories. We describe different features that are extracted from e-mail messages to help in this classification, and the improvement in the overall classification accuracy that results from the use of each kind of feature.

1 Introduction

The traditional call centre, where agents employed by a business or other organisation respond to customers on the phone, is evolving into a multi-channel *contact centre*. Many organisations now allow people to contact them using a variety of different channels. Although telephony has long been the dominant channel, over the last few years many organisations have opened up other channels. E-mail and web site forms are already widely available, and SMS and Instant Messaging are increasingly being utilised.

The increase in the number of available channels is beneficial for customers as it allows them to choose their preferred channel, possibly switching channels depending on their circumstances. They can choose the most convenient channel depending on the time (for example, at night only a limited number of options may be available), location (do they have access to a computer or only a telephone?), or the type of contact required (it may be possible to satisfy a simple information requirement from an organisation's website, whereas a more complex request will require a detailed conversation).

Dean M. Jones
numéro software, Douro House, 11-13 Wellington Road South, Stockport, SK4 1AA; e-mail: dean.jones@thisisnumero.co.uk

M. Bramer et al. (eds.), *Research and Development in Intelligent Systems XXVI*,
DOI 10.1007/978-1-84882-983-1_30, © Springer-Verlag London Limited 2010

From the organisation's perspective, the increase in the number of available channels creates the challenge of trying to handle customer contacts across all of these channels as efficiently as possible while maximising customer satisfaction. There are a number of options available for improving the efficiency of contact centres. Firstly, an organisation can use customer self-service to reduce the need for customers to contact them. This involves providing the means for customers to satisfy their own requirements (a strategy known as *deflection*). Secondly, an organisation can try to reduce the time required by agents to process the messages that they do receive. Thirdly, messages can be processed completely automatically without human intervention. This latter option can be seen as the limiting case of reducing the handle time, where the handle time is zero, but we view it as separate because it requires a different technological approach.

A number of technology-based solutions are available for implementing deflection. One widely deployed example is the provision of a "Frequently-asked Questions" section on a website where customers can search for the information they require. Another example is the use of a secure area on a website where customers can perform their own account management tasks, such as changing their contact details. Other channels can also be used to implement customer self-service, for example telephony self-service is normally implemented using a combination of IVR and speech recognition technology.

With regard to reducing the average handle-time, software can help in a variety of ways. Some examples are:

1. in many organisations, different agents are responsible for handling different types of messages. This is often based on the skills or responsibilities of the individual agents. For example, one team of agents may be responsible for handling enquiries about orders while another team is responsible for handling enquiries about product availability. Additionally, where messages may be received in a variety of languages, they should be routed to agents who can understand the relevant language;
2. an organisation may define different service-level agreements for different types of message. For example, an organisation may wish to handle complaints from customers about the quality of service they have experienced relatively quickly. Correct identification of the content of messages allows an organisation to ensure that they are handling messages with the appropriate priority;
3. if an identifier such as an order number or account number can be extracted from a message, the corresponding data can be retrieved from a back-office system and presented to the agent alongside the message, providing important context to help the agent resolve the enquiry. Furthermore, if the system can determine that the message belongs to an ongoing thread of conversation, the history of that conversation can also presented to the agent alongside with the message;
4. if the category of the message can be identified, the user interface that is presented to the agent who handles the message can be tailored to that category. For example, where the system presents an agent with predefined content to use in a response, this content can be filtered and ordered according to the type of mes-

sage. The controls and options available on an agent's user interface can also be varied according to the category of the message.

Automated handling of some types of messages is possible if the system can correctly identify the type of message with a high degree of confidence. Examples of the kinds of messages that can be handled automatically include:

1. a business process may require that a customer provide some particular piece of information in their request. For example, an e-mail enquiry about the status of an order will need the corresponding order number. If an analysis of the content of a message reveals that the required information is not included, an automated request for further information can be sent to the customer, ensuring that the request is only presented to an agent when all of the necessary information has been submitted;
2. some types of message can be responded to automatically using an appropriate standard response. For example, if a message has been automatically identified with sufficient confidence as an enquiry about job vacancies, a pre-defined response can be sent which redirects the sender to the relevant section of the organisation's website.

Unfortunately, due to the variety and complexity of customer requests, it is not possible to generate automated responses for all types of message using current technology, but often a few kinds of message can be identified with sufficient accuracy. The question of what level of accuracy is required for a category before automated responses are enabled for that category is a decision for the relevant organisation; we typically find that around 95% accuracy for a category is required before an organisation is willing to allow automated responses to be enabled for that category.

Software which attempts to perform these tasks automatically must analyse the content of a message in detail. The extent to which artificial intelligence technology, especially natural-language processing (NLP) technology, can be used to reduce the average handle time per message and to enable automated responses is the subject of this paper. In particular, we focus on the problem of how to accurately classify e-mail messages into one of multiple business categories.

Although text categorisation in general is a well-studied area (see [10] for a summary of approaches to this problem), relatively little research has been reported on the specific problem of classifying e-mail into multiple business categories. Much of the existing literature on e-mail classification focusses on the more straightforward binary classification problem of spam detection. There has been some work in the closely-related field of *e-mail foldering*, which addresses the problem of automatically organising personal e-mail into multiple folders. The MailCat system [11] uses a modified version of AIM [1], a TF-IDF based classifier [9], to predict the correct folder for an e-mail with roughly 80% to 90% accuracy. The RIPPER rule-induction classifier has been shown [4] to have superior performance to a TF-IDF classifier, performing well on e-mail foldering even when only a small number of training samples are available.

One of the main problems when comparing the results reported for different classifiers on e-mail foldering is that different e-mail corpora are used for the evaluations. For example, both [11] and [4] report results using the authors' personal e-mail. The availability of the Enron corpus [5] should help address this issue. This corpus consists of a large number of e-mails which were subpoenaed from the Enron Corporation and subsequently made publicly available. E-mail foldering experiments have been performed using the Enron corpus [2], demonstrating that a classifier based on the simple Winnow algorithm [6] performs as well as (and in some cases better than) the more complex Support Vector Machine and Maximum Entropy methods.

The main issues which distinguish both e-mail foldering and the problem we address from binary text categorisation are:

1. multi-class classification is more difficult than binary classification. When attempting to choose a single category from many, there is simply more scope for error than when there are only 2 categories. Also, many e-mails can legitimately belong to multiple categories. This can be a consequence of the content of the message (as customers often include multiple queries within a single e-mail) or a lack of distinction in the categories; some categories are based on the topic of the message whereas other categories are based on the attitude of the customer. For example, if we allow the two categories *orders* and *complaints* then a complaint about an order belongs to both of these categories.
2. compared to the types of documents that are often used in text categorisation research, such as scientific papers or patent applications, e-mails are relatively short. In the corpus we use for the tests described later in Sect. 5, the average length of a message is around 200 tokens (about 1200 characters). A classifier therefore has less data available with which it can make a decision;
3. even with the small amount of data that is typically available, much of it is not relevant to the decision about the category that the message belongs to. For example, it is not unusual for a legal disclaimer that is appended to the end of a message to be longer than the actual content of the message itself. Also, e-mails are often sent as a reply to a previous message; in this case, e-mail clients typically append the previous message to the bottom of the new message. The new message may belong to a different category than previous messages in the conversation. Consequently the text contained in the old part of the message is not relevant to the correct classification of the new message. In our test corpus, the average length of the main text is approximately 80 tokens (about 480 characters), which is less than half the total length of the average message;
4. typically, the number of example documents that are available for training is relatively low. The training data must be manually curated, which is a time-consuming and therefore expensive process. Often, an organisation will accept the initial reduced accuracy that results from this, as long as the system improves over time as it learns from manual classifications made by agents.

Rather than focus on the algorithmic aspect of this task, our experiments focus on *feature generation*, which is the problem of generating features from input data for a machine-learning algorithm to analyse. Feature generation utilises information that is generated during the analysis of the content of messages as they proceed through

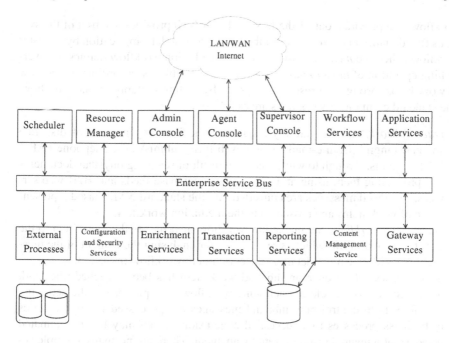

Fig. 1 *numéro interactive* Service-oriented Architecture

numéro interactive. The next section contains a high-level overview of this system, and we then describe the process of message *enrichment*, during which the detailed content analysis is performed, in more detail.

2 numéro interactive

numéro interactive is a multi-channel Customer Interaction Management system that is deployed in contact centres to manage customer enquiries and to automate the associated business processes. It combines natural-language processing, content management, workflow, a declarative rule engine, workforce management, and business intelligence technologies.

numéro interactive is based on a service-oriented architecture as shown in Fig. 1. It consists of a large set of individual services which act as components that can be combined into a single application using customisable workflows. The components services are exposed as SOAP endpoints and the workflow definitions adhere to the standard BPEL workflow language. The workflow definitions are enacted by the workflow engine which orchestrates the flow of messages (referred to as *work items* once they have entered *numéro interactive*) through the system. The workflows can be tailored to match specific requirements and business processes. A set of standard workflows are provided out-of-the-box, each of which provides a subset of the system's functionality and which are combined into a complete application by a master workflow called the *mediation* workflow. The mediation workflow defines the overarching operation of *numéro interactive*. It is responsible for co-ordinating the flow of work items through the rest of the system by calling the appropriate workflow. The standard component workflows are as follows:

- *gateway workflow*: the gateway acquires work from any number of disparate sources, ranging from e-mail servers, web form submissions, telephone PABX / IVR systems, through to white-mail (the result of scanning physical documents and processing them using an OCR system), database feeds and B2B web services. Retrieved messages are converted into the standard XML-based representation of work items and passed on to the mediation workflow.
- *enrichment workflow*: the mediation workflow next passes the work item to the enrichment workflow, which is responsible for analysing the content of the message. We will give more detail on the enrichment workflow in Sect. 3.
- *actioning workflow*: once an inbound work item has been enriched, the work item is routed to the relevant actioning workflow. The purpose of the actioning workflow is to control how inbound messages are processed through a series of business processes to a successful conclusion, which may be an automated response or a manual response sent by an agent. There are normally multiple actioning workflows available; the particular actioning workflow to use for a given message is selected based on properties of the message, such as the category it was allocated to, the channel from which it entered the system, and so on. This allows different types of message to be processed according to different business processes.
- *outbound workflow*: outbound work items may be generated either automatically or manually by an agent. The outbound workflow is responsible for quality assurance of outbound work items (for example, checking that they do not contain inappropriate language) and then formatting and sending the final message.

There are a number of additional services provided that are not included as components of workflows. Notably, the Content Management Service provides a repository for reusable content which is available to agents when composing outbound messages. It is also used as a repository for knowledge-base articles that provide agents with guidance and it supplies content to a suite of components that can be inserted into a web site as part of a deflection strategy. For example, it can be used as a repository of frequently-asked questions which can be made available on a web site.

3 Work Item Enrichment

As noted in the previous section, the analysis of the content of work items is performed by the services that collectively form the enrichment workflow. The main services that are called during this workflow are:

- *main-text identification*: this service is responsible for identifying the *main text* of the message, which is that portion of the body of the message which contains the text relevant to the purpose of the message;
- *form extraction*: work items that come from some channels (such as web forms) often have a structured body. The form extraction service is responsible for identifying and extracting the various elements of such structured messages;
- *language identification*: identifies the natural language of the message;
- *named-entity extraction*: identifies entities such as names, addresses, order numbers, account numbers, etc;
- *customer and case identification*: determines whether the work item is from a known customer and, if so, whether it belongs to an ongoing conversation;
- *rule-based classification*: assigns a category to a message using declarative rules. It employs a general-purpose rule engine which allows rules to be written against properties of a work item;
- *statistical classification*: if the rule-based classifier was not able to allocate the work item to a category, this service performs a statistical analysis of the main text of the work item in order to allocate it to a category. This service is the main focus of this rest of this paper and it is described in more detail in the next section.

4 E-mail Classification

Earlier versions of *numéro interactive* provided a rule-based mechanism for classification of work items. Some types of work item are particularly amenable to classification using rules, such as those that conform to one of a small set of pre-defined formats. For example, there are a relatively small number of standard "out-of-office" response templates that are used by many users. These can be identified using simple rules, such as regular expressions. This kind of simple filtering allows many messages to be accurately classified with a high degree of confidence.

Although it is possible to achieve high levels of precision using a rule-based approach, changes to the product requirements made the addition of a machine-learning approach to classification very compelling. Firstly, we wanted to introduce support for multiple languages. Previously, the product was English-only, but (as noted in Sect. 3) the current version of *numéro interactive* can identify the language of the message. Classification of work items in multiple languages using a rule-based approach would multiply the overhead of rule creation and maintenance, as we would need additional rules for each language.

Secondly, we wanted to reduce the cost of installation and maintenance of the product. Configuring the rules for each new deployment of the system can be very labour-intensive. There is also the additional ongoing cost involved in maintaining the rules. With rule-based systems, it is reasonably straight-forward to create a classifier with high-precision and low-recall using a small number of rules. Increases in this level of recall can be achieved at the expense of some precision by increasing the number of rules. However, as the number of rules increases, it becomes difficult to manage the interaction between them, making it difficult for the system administrator to fully predict the impact of any changes to the rules.

As well as satisfying these requirements, there are additional benefits associated with the machine-learning approach. For example, it is very useful if a classifier can associate a confidence measure with the decisions that it makes. This measure can then be taken into account when deciding whether an automated response should be sent. With a rules-based approach, confidence values are somewhat *ad hoc*, whereas many machine-learning algorithms offer confidence measures based on a principled probabilistic framework.

Although *numéro interactive* now incorporates a statistical classifier, a rule-based classifier is still available. Not only can some kinds of message be handled very accurately using a few rules, but this has a beneficial effect on the accuracy of statistical classification. In general, the accuracy of statistical classification decreases as we increase the number of categories it must identify. By handing responsibility for the identification of some categories to the rule-based classifier, we can reduce the number of categories that the statistical category allocation is responsible for.

There are now three different statistical classifiers available in *numéro interactive*: a Naïve Bayes classifier, a classifier based on the Winnow algorithm [6], and a Maximum Entropy classifier [3] which utilises an implementation of the L-BFGS quasi-Newton optimisation algorithm [7]. The experiments we describe here use the Winnow classifier. Although the Naïve Bayes classifier performs well on the language classification problem (the current language classifier service uses the Naïve Bayes classifier), it has not proved adequate when trying to identify the semantic category of work items. The Maximum Entropy classifier provides very good accuracy on most classification tasks, but an exposition of the algorithm would require more space than we have available.

The Winnow learner generates a statistical (but not probabilistic) classifier using an on-line training algorithm which updates the classifier only when a mistake is made. It is similar to the well-known Perceptron algorithm [8], the main difference being that updates are multiplicative rather than additive. It maintains a vector of weights $w^c = \{w_1^c, \ldots, w_n^c\}$ for each category c where each entry in a vector corresponds to a weight for a particular feature (the entries in vectors are initialised to 1) and n is the number of the features that occur in at least one work item in the training set. A work item that is to be classified is first converted into a vector $x = \{x_1, \ldots, x_n\}$ of feature values; in this description, we consider only binary features, so each feature value is either 0 or 1. The classifier generates a score Ω^c for each category by summing the weights for each feature in the work item:

$$\Omega^c = \sum_{i=1}^{n} w_i^c x_i$$

The score is then compared to some threshold θ to determine whether the work item is a member of the category or not. The classifier can be seen as implementing the following function:

$$f(w^c, x) = \begin{cases} 0 \text{ if } \Omega < \theta; \\ 1 \text{ if } \Omega \geq \theta. \end{cases}$$

During the training phase, the classifier is shown the training data one work item at a time. When the classifier makes a mistake on a work item, the corresponding vector is updated. If the error was a false negative, the weights for the features in the training instance are increased by multiplying them by a *promotion factor* α, where $\alpha > 1$. If the error was a false positive, the weights for all features in the training instance are multiplied by a *demotion factor* β, where $\beta < 1$. Although Winnow as originally described is an on-line algorithm, we train it in batch mode by repeatedly running the training algorithm over the training data until no mistakes are made (or some threshold for the number of iterations is reached).

In some versions of Winnow, θ is simply the number of features in a work item: $\theta = \sum_{i=1}^{n} x_i$. As described by [12], we find that a more accurate classifier is generated if we define a *thick threshold* $[\theta^-, \theta^+]$ where $\theta^- < \theta < \theta^+$. For positive training instances, a mistake is deemed to have been made if the score lies within the range $[\theta, \theta^+]$, and for negative instances, if the score lies within $[\theta^-, \theta]$. In the experiments described later, we use a fixed-width threshold of 0.5.

Note that at classification time, we simply choose the category with the highest score for a work item.

4.1 Feature Generation

As noted above, before the text in a work item can be used to train a classifier, it must be converted to a representation that the training algorithm can understand. This process is known as *feature generation*. We provide a number of options in *numéro interactive* for generating features. Some of these are:

- *tokens*: the individual tokens in the text of a work item are taken as the basic set of features. These are binary features which indicate only the presence or absence of a word. For example, we take all of the tokens in the subject and body of an e-mail as the basic set of features for that message;
- *form extraction and main-text identification*: as noted earlier, not all of the text in the body of a message is relevant to the classification of that message. In training a classifier, we can take into account the results of the form extraction and main-text identifier services in order to strip out irrelevant parts of the message;
- *stemming*: in text categorisation, the number of dimensions for a learner (*i.e.* the number of features in the training corpus) is typically quite high. *Dimensionality reduction* covers a number of techniques that are used to reduce the size of the feature set for the learner. *Stemming*, which involves reducing words to a common morphological root, is a simple technique for performing dimensionality reduction on word token features;
- *orthogonal sparse bigrams*: orthogonal sparse bigrams (OSBs) [12] are token-pairs which span some defined window of text. For example, from the text "I

would like to order" with a window size of 4, the following token-pairs would be generated:

```
I would
I * like
I * * to
would like
would * to
would * * order
like to
like * order
to order
```

(the asterisks represent skipped words);

- *named entities*: the results of the named-entity extraction process can provide useful information to improve the accuracy of classification. Intuitively, the fact that a message contains an address, for example, increases the probability that the message is a change-of-address request; knowing that a message contains an order number makes it more likely that it is an order enquiry, and so on.

One additional refinement is that we allow a hierarchy of categories to be defined. We have found that one of the main sources of classification errors is due to confusion between similar categories. For example, suppose an organisation specifies that work items should be classified into the categories *Order Delivery Enquiries*, which should include only questions about when an order will be delivered, and *Order Return Enquiries*, which should include only questions about how to return a previously-received order. There will be a lot of shared vocabulary across these two categories and messages of both kinds are likely to include order-number named entities. It is reasonable to assume (and our experience has shown this to be the case) that there will be more misclassifications between these two categories than between two less similar categories.

The next section describes the effects on the accuracy of classification that results from using the different methods of feature generation and from organising categories into a small hierarchy.

5 Results

In order to demonstrate the use and effectiveness of the feature generators listed in the previous section, we present the results of a number of tests using the Winnow classifier. Due to the lack of publicly-available e-mail corpora which match the specific problem we address, we have used a proprietary corpus of e-mails that has been provided by one of our customers. This manually-curated corpus consists of 700 e-mails and web form submissions, each allocated to one of 14 business categories and evenly distributed across these categories (instead of the names of the

	A	B	C	D	E	F	G	H	I	J	K	L	M	N	Mean
TOK	60	80	44	56	98	96	86	78	60	54	70	46	72	62	68.71
FEMTI	54	84	84	74	100	100	96	88	82	68	64	66	84	66	79.28
STEM	62	84	46	60	94	98	90	96	52	54	60	48	76	62	70.14
TOK+OSB3	56	82	54	56	98	100	86	80	70	40	72	52	76	68	70.71
TOK+NE	60	88	56	56	98	98	94	90	56	62	62	44	78	70	72.29
ALL	80	84	82	72	100	100	88	94	88	58	70	84	86	66	82.29

Table 1 Classification results using different feature generators

original business categories, we use the letters A-N). Of the scenarios that we encounter with customers, this corpus is representative of the simpler end of the scale in terms of the number of categories and availability of training data. As the e-mails in the corpus have been processed by *numéro interactive*, the classifier has access to the results of the various services, including form extraction, main text identification and named-entity extraction.

The results of the first test are shown in Table 1. As with subsequent tests, these results were generated using a single k-fold cross-validation with k=5, holding out 10 work items per category per fold. In the first test, we initially use only the raw tokens in the subject and body of the work items as the base set of features (this classifier is labelled TOK). We then modify or supplement this base set in four different ways: restricting the tokens to the main text of a work item, based on the results of form extraction and main text identification (FEMTI), applying stemming to the tokens (STEM), supplementing the tokens with OSBs using a window size of 3 (TOK+OSB3), and supplementing the tokens with named entities (TOK+NE) such as names, telephone numbers, postal addresses, orders numbers, account numbers, etc. Finally, we give the results of applying all of these *i.e.* stemming the tokens in the main text of a message and supplementing these with OSBs and named-entities. The table contains a column giving the accuracy for each category and a column for the mean of these results. In these tests, the classifier was configured to always make a decision about the category that a work item belongs to and values given are for recall (*i.e.* the number of true positives divided by the sum of the true positives and false negatives for a category) as this is how we report accuracy to our customers.

The second set of tests demonstrate the effect of grouping semantically-similar categories together. Based on their semantic similarity, categories A and B have been grouped, as have C and N, and I and J. We trained a first-level classifier by combining half of the training data from the grouped categories *e.g.* we combined half of the training data for category A with half of the training data for category B and used this as the training data for the category AB (we use half the training data from the combined categories in order to maintain a balance with the amount of training data available for the non-combined categories). We then train a second-level classifier for each of these groups which can distinguish between the combined categories; all work items that are allocated to the category AB by the first-level classifier are passed to the second-level classifier that can distinguish between categories A and B. The results generated by the first-level classifier are shown in Table 2. Results

AB	CN	D	E	F	G	H	IJ	K	L	M	Mean
90	84	76	100	100	94	94	86	64	82	86	86.91

Table 2 Results with grouped categories

are shown for the second-level classifiers in Table 3. Table 4 shows the overall results achieved from the combination of these classifiers. This is the most important result as it documents the overall accuracy of the system and best illustrates the performance of the system as experienced by users.

6 Discussion

Of the different modifications to feature generation that are shown in Table 1, focussing the classifier on the results of the form extraction and main text identification services demonstrates by far the largest performance gain. It is often the case that messages which belong to the same conversation should be classified under different categories. Stripping away the history from the message allows the classifier to focus only on the categorisation of the most recent message. This can make the difference between being able to automate the handling of messages allocated to a category or not. As shown in Table 1, the accuracy of category G improves from 86% with the TOK classifier, to 96% with the FEMTI classifier (and 94% in the final results in Table 4), which is in the region where an organisation may allow automated responses to be sent (as mentioned earlier, in our experience organisations typically require accuracy around 95% before allowing automated responses to be enabled).

Considering the combination of all feature generation improvements (the ALL row in Table 1), the improvements from each change are not cumulative as we cannot simply add all of the improvements from the individual changes to give the accuracy of the ALL classifier. However, the additional correct decisions made by the FEMTI classifier do not subsume the additional corrections made by the other improved classifiers, as these other classifiers show better scores on some categories than the FEMTI classifier. For example, the TOK+NE classifier is capable of correctly classifying work items that the FEMTI classifier cannot, and *vice versa*. Each of the modifications to feature generation potentially provides useful and unique information to the learning algorithm.

In our experience, the use of stemming consistently improves the accuracy of our classifiers. We believe that the reason for this is related to the relatively small amount of training data that we typically have access to. Dimensionality reduction is especially effective when there is limited training data available, as it allows the training algorithm to learn using a reduced set of features.

The use of hierarchical categories not only improves the overall accuracy of classification, but has a significant impact on the ability to allow the use of automated responses to messages. As demonstrated by the results in this paper, the accuracy of

AB-classifier			CN-classifier			IJ-classifier		
A	B	Mean	C	N	Mean	I	J	Mean
92	90	91	90	92	91	92	84	88

Table 3 Results for the second-level classifiers

A	B	C	D	E	F	G	H	I	J	K	L	M	N	Mean
82.8	81	75.6	76	100	100	94	94	79.12	72.24	64	82	86	77.28	83.15

Table 4 Classification results using hierarchical categories

second-level classifiers is typically quite high. These classifiers are similar to e-mail spam filters in that they often only have to make binary classification decisions, and they share with spam filters the ability to make classification decisions with sufficient accuracy that their decisions can form the basis for automated handling of messages. We must however add the caveat that automation is only possible where the decisions made by the first-level classifier do not result in too many work items being incorrectly sent to the second-level classifier.

7 Conclusions

We have described some of the ways in which we use AI technology in *numéro interactive*. In particular, we have shown how natural language processing and machine learning technology has been used to improve the efficiency of handling messages sent to a customer contact centre. In the final results shown in Table 4 there are four categories (E, F, G and H) which are candidates for automation. If we assume an even distribution of received messages across the categories, this could represent over 25% of messages being handled automatically.

We believe that the results shown here illustrate an important point in the practical application of machine learning. Often, the focus is on the algorithms involved, and indeed this is often very beneficial. For example, we found that the Winnow and Maximum Entropy classifiers provide much better performance than the Naïve Bayes classifier. However, we also found that data-oriented methods significantly improved the accuracy of our e-mail classification. Firstly, knowledge of the structure of typical e-mails allows us to focus the efforts of the classifier on the main text of messages, with the increase in accuracy demonstrated by the FEMTI classifier. Secondly, understanding the application domain and the relationships between categories allowed us to group some of the categories together in the first-level classifier and then distinguish between them using a second tier of classifiers; this approach delivered a further improvement in accuracy. In summary, we believe that this demonstrates how the application of machine learning technology can benefit from an in-depth understanding of the application domain and the data involved.

Acknowledgements I am grateful to all of my colleagues at numéro, many of whom have contributed to this work. In particular, I would like to thank Chris Downes-Ward, Lawrence Harding and Ciaran Jessup, who provided very useful comments on an earlier version of the paper.

References

1. Barrett, R., Selker, T.: AIM: A new approach for meeting information needs. Tech. rep., IBM Research (1995)
2. Bekkerman, R., McCallum, A., Huang, G.: Automatic categorization of email into folders: Benchmark experiments on Enron and SRI corpora. Tech. Rep. IR-418, Center of Intelligent Information Retrieval, UMass Amherst (2004)
3. Berger, A.L., Della Pietra, S.A., Della Pietra, V.J.: A maximum entropy approach to natural language processing. Computational Linguistics **22**(1), 39–71 (1996)
4. Cohen, W.W.: Learning rules that classify e-mail. In: Papers from the AAAI Spring Symposium on Machine Learning in Information Access, pp. 18–25. AAAI Press (1996)
5. Klimt, B., Yang, Y.: The Enron corpus: A new dataset for email classification research. In: Proceedings of ECML-2004, 15th European Conference on Machine Learning, pp. 217–226. Springer Verlag (2004)
6. Littlestone, N.: Learning quickly when irrelevant attributes abound: A new linear-threshold algorithm. Machine Learning **2**(4), 285–318 (1988)
7. Nocedal, J.: Updating quasi-newton matrices with limited storage. Mathematics of Computation **35**, 773–782 (1980)
8. Rosenblatt, F.: The perceptron: A probabilistic model for information storage and organization in the brain. Psychological Review **65**(6), 386–408 (1958)
9. Salton, G., McGill, M.J.: Introduction to Modern Information Retrieval. McGraw-Hill, New York, NY, USA (1983)
10. Sebastiani, F.: Machine learning in automated text categorization. ACM Computing Surveys **34**(1), 1–47 (2002)
11. Segal, R.B., Kephart, J.O.: Mailcat: an intelligent assistant for organizing e-mail. In: AGENTS '99: Proceedings of the third annual conference on Autonomous Agents, pp. 276–282. ACM, New York, NY, USA (1999)
12. Siefkes, C., Assis, F., Chhabra, S., Yerazunis, W.S.: Combining winnow and orthogonal sparse bigrams for incremental spam filtering. In: Proceedings of ECML-2004, 15th European Conference on Machine Learning, pp. 410–421. Springer Verlag (2004)

COMMERCIAL APPLICATIONS OF AI

An AI-Based System for Pricing Diverse Products and Services

S. Shakya, C. M. Chin and G. Owusu[1]

Abstract This paper describes an applied research work that looks at different ways to effectively manage resources. Particularly, it describes how revenue management techniques can be used to balance demand against capacity, and describes a system that uses different OR and AI techniques to intelligently price diverse products and services. This system can produce pricing policies for wide range of products and services regardless of the model of demand used. The system incorporates a model specification layer, which provides flexibility in defining the demand model for different products. It also incorporates an optimisation layer, which takes the specified model as an input and produces the pricing and production guidelines for the product. The system can be either used as a stand alone system or can be incorporated as a generic modelling and optimisation component within a larger revenue management system.

1 Introduction

Pricing is one of the key decisions that a firm needs to make in order to survive in a competitive marketplace. If done carefully, it can be a valuable tool to achieve number of different business goals, such as profit maximisation, demand management, value creation, etc.

Traditionally, pricing policies were made according to one of the following three criteria [14].

1. Cost-plus pricing – is based on the cost of production, where a profit margin is added on top of total cost.
2. Market-based pricing – tries to beat the price of the competitors.
3. Value-based pricing – is based on how much value consumers puts on the product.

---

1 Intelligent Systems Research Centre, BT Innovate and Design, Ipswich, IP5 3RE, UK
{sid.shakya, eric.chin,gilbert.owusu}@bt.com

M. Bramer et al. (eds.), *Research and Development in Intelligent Systems XXVI*,
DOI 10.1007/978-1-84882-983-1_31, © Springer-Verlag London Limited 2010

Each of these strategies has its downside. For example, cost-plus pricing ignores competition and customer values, market-based pricing ignores cost and customers value, and value-based pricing ignores cost and the competition. A better way of pricing would be to consider, for each combination of these three criteria, a customised pricing to suit that particular combination. For example, depending upon the combination of cost, value and market, price for a train ticket from London to Reading could be £40 if the standard class ticket was purchased by a business commuter through the ticket counter, and £35 if it was purchased online. The price could be 15% less if the same ticket was purchased by a student or a senior citizen, and even less if it was purchased in advance of two weeks. The key idea here is to charge the right price, to the right customer, at the right time, such that the revenue is maximised and number of unused seats is minimised. This is the scenario where the revenue management techniques [19] [11] can be useful.

Revenue management is a well known technique in Operation Research (OR) that helps firm to make scientifically sound pricing (and production) decisions for their products (and services) in order to extract maximum value from them. They are sometimes referred to as yield management [12] or pricing and revenue optimisation [14]. The field of revenue management emerged in the late 1970s, mainly, due to the advancement in information technology, which allowed airline companies to build the electronic booking systems, enabling them to efficiently access large amount of customer data. This data was then used to effectively segment price-sensitive leisure customers from non price-sensitive business customers and to offer different prices to each of these segments. This resulted in increased profit from sales of seats which would otherwise be left unused. The success of revenue management in airline industry was soon followed by other industries such as car rentals, hotels and cruse liners. More recently, revenue management is being increasingly applied in other industries, such as retail [8][2][1], wholesale [14] and auctions [16], mainly, to apply different prices for their product in different demand periods, to increase revenue by applying markdown and/or promotional pricing, and to efficiently manage resource by controlling the demand.

For a global firm with a large number of diverse products and services, a significant effort is required for pricing their products. Pricings, in many cases, involve manual input from skilled staffs and experts. Furthermore, in many products and services, there can be a necessity to manage customer demand effectively to better utilise resources. In other words, there can be a necessity to shift the demand for the product (or service) from a higher demand period, where available resources are not enough to fulfil the demand, to a lower demand period, where resources are left unused. One of the key tools in OR, for balancing demand and managing resources, is the pricing policy. It has been shown that by pricing high during high demand period, a significant shift in demand to lower demand period, with lower price, can be achieved. With this in view, revenue management techniques could be the key to resolving both the pricing and demand management issues that exists within a large firm's diverse products and services. There is however a further obstacle to this - the cost. Even if the firm seeks to follow a revenue management avenue, the current trend in this area involves building a highly customised system for each specific product. Following this path would not be a cost effective solution, requiring the firm to build individual pricing system for each of their products and services.

In this paper, we present an applied research work to develop a generic revenue management system for pricing diverse products and services. The system provides a generic platform for modelling wide range of products and services, and combines it together with a powerful optimisation engine based on different AI techniques. The system can be either used as a stand alone system or can be incorporated as a generic modelling and optimisation component within a larger revenue management system.

The paper is structured as follows. Section 2 describes the pricing problem faced by large firms and also describes the motivation behind this work. Section 3 presents the built system as a solution to this problem. It also describes the architecture of the proposed system and the AI techniques used in it. Section 4 highlights some of the key benefits of this system. Section 5 outlines key contribution of this work and conclude the paper.

2 Problem Description and Motivation

A typical revenue management system can be seen as a combination of two key components, (Figure 1).

1. Estimation/forecasting component
2. Optimisation component

The estimation/forecasting component takes customer purchase history as input and uses this data to find how various different factors affect the demand for that product. These factors themselves, as well as the effect of these factors on demand, can be significantly different from product to product. For example, demand for an engineer to fix the phone line on any given day may depend on the price charged for the engineer on that day, the number of big business in that geographical region, the time of the day or week, and so on; where as demand for a broadband product, apart from its current price, may also depend on the competitor's prices, the advertising campaign, promotional offers and so on. These interactions are captured within a model, also known as demand model [19], or price-response model [14]. The key task of the estimation/forecasting component is to estimate the parameters of the demand model and also forecast the demand for the future periods.

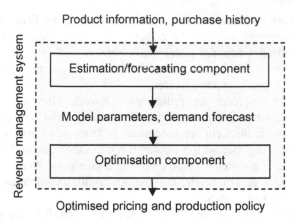

Figure 1 Two key components of a revenue management system

The parameters estimated by the estimation/forecasting component are then passed to the optimisation component, which then uses it to produce revenue-maximising pricing and production policies. Typically, both of these components are highly customised depending upon the demand model used, i.e., they are customised for each individual products.

2.1 Scenarios

Let us review a few scenarios where a firm has large number of different products and services to price. For instance, let us take the scenario of a large nation-wide transport company, where pricing may have to be done across its different transport wings (bus or train), and can possibly have hundreds of different fare classes. A large media house, such as TV channels or satellite/cable networks, can also have a large number of diverse products and services which have to be correctly priced. For example media contents such as films and documentaries can be priced differently for sport content. Peak time advertising slots have to be priced differently to off peak slots. Also, different user subscriptions to different services have to be priced differently.

Another very good example of the firm with diverse range of products and services are the large supermarket chains, where they sell wide variety of products, ranging from food and groceries to electronic appliances and clothing. In most cases, they tend to go for cost-plus pricing or market based pricing. The following list shows some of the typical products and services within a supermarket chain.

    a.   Food product, such as milk and sugar
    b.   Optional luxury items such as wines and flowers
    c.   Seasonal and festive items such as Christmas products and barbeque items.
    d.   Home electronic items such as digital cordless phones or widescreen TVs.
    e.   Essential clothing items such as children's trousers

As stated earlier, demand for each of these different products can depend on various different factors, which could result in very different demand models. For example, demand for a red wine may depend on its price, as well as on the time of the week and the weather. Whereas, demand for a widescreen TV may depend on its price, the competitor's price, the upcoming sporting events and so on. In order to optimise prices and maximise the revenue from such a diverse range of products and services, the firm would require implementing customised revenue management system for each of these different models. This would result in more lengthy and costly solution to revenue management.

In next section we give a more formal description to the pricing problem.

2.2 Problem Description

We define revenue management as a task to find a set of optimal prices that maximise the revenue from a product (or a set of related products) (1).

$$\max_{p_{ij}, \forall i=1..m, j=1..n} R = \sum_{i=1}^{m} \sum_{j=1}^{n} d_{ij}(p_{ij} - c_{ij}) \qquad (1)$$

Here, R is the total revenue, m and n are the total products and total periods in the planning horizon respectively, p_{ij} is the price of ith product in j^{th} period, d_{ij} is the total demand (or sale) of ith product in j^{th} period, and c_{ij} is the cost associated with i^{th} product in j^{th} period. The task is to find prices, p_{ij}, for all products in all periods such that the total revenue is maximised.

The objective function (1) can be further constrained with different price and production rules associated with the product. For example, each price and sale can be constrained with some lower and upper bound, and can be written as,

$$\underline{p}_{ij} \leq p_{ij} \leq \overline{p}_{ij}, \qquad \text{For all } i=1...m \text{ and } j=1...n \qquad (2)$$

$$\underline{d}_{ij} \leq d_{ij} \leq \overline{d}_{ij}, \qquad \text{For all } i=1...m \text{ and } j=1...n \qquad (3)$$

where $\underline{p}_{ij}$ and $\overline{p}_{ij}$ are the lower and upper bound for price p_{ij}, and $\underline{d}_{ij}$ and $\overline{d}_{ij}$ are the lower and upper bound for total sale d_{ij}. Usually upper bound to the price is imposed in order to satisfy some business rules, for example, to compete with the price of the rival products, and lower bound to the price is imposed in order to not let the value of the product decrease in the market place. Similarly, upper and lower bound (also known as capacity constraint) is imposed on the sale in order to, for example, not have the sale more than the total available capacity, or to not allow this value to go negative.

Also, instead of imposing capacity constraint on each individual product in each individual periods, it can also be imposed on the aggregated sale over the products (4), or over the periods (5), or over both products and periods (6).

$$\underline{d}_j \le \sum_{i=1}^{m} d_{ij} \le \overline{d}_j, \quad \text{For all } j = 1...n \tag{4}$$

$$\underline{d}_i \le \sum_{j=1}^{n} d_{ij} \le \overline{d}_i, \quad \text{For all } i = 1...m \tag{5}$$

$$\underline{d} \le \sum_{i=1}^{m} \sum_{j=1}^{n} d_{ij} \le \overline{d} \tag{6}$$

Furthermore, demand for a product i in a period j, d_{ij}, depends on the price for that product in that period, p_{ij}, and also on other various factors specific to that product and its surrounding environment. These dependencies are encapsulated by the demand model, which can be written as

$$d_{ij} = f(p_{ij}, F) \tag{7}$$

where, $f(.)$ is the demand function, $F = \{F_1, F_2,...,F_k\}$ is a vector of factors influencing demand. For example, these factors may involve: prices for the same product on other periods, prices for the other product in the same period, price for the other products in other periods, time of the year, competitor's information, special events, and so on. In order to estimate the demand accurately, it is essential to incorporate these factors in the demand model.

Depending upon the pattern observed in the historical demand data for the product, the demand model, $f(.)$, could have different mathematical form, such as linear, sigmoid, convex, nonlinear, multi-pick, and so on, and can also incorporate various degree of uncertainty making them stochastic or deterministic. Demand model capturing these factors, together with other constraints and uncertainties, can vary widely depending upon the types of product and/or services, and their surrounding environment. Consequently, optimisation algorithms to solve these models may require a significant product specific customisation.

Let us give a simple example of the typical demand model and the typical model solving optimisation algorithms. In its simplistic form, demand for a product, d_{ij}, depends only on its price, p_{ij}. Assuming the linear relationship between price and demand, such a demand model can be written as (8).

$$d_{ij} = D_{ij} + a_{ij}p_{ij} \qquad (8)$$

Here, D_{ij} is the total market size for the product i in period j, i.e. the total number of potential customer, and a_{ij} is the slope of demand, i.e. the sensitivity parameter modelling the effect of p_{ij} on d_{ij}.

However, assuming the sigmoid relationship between price and demand, the demand model can be written as (9).

$$d_{ij} = K_{ij} \frac{1}{1 + e^{b_{ij} + c_{ji}P_{ji}}} \qquad (9)$$

Here, K_{ij} represents the market size for the product i in period j, and b_{ij} and d_{ij} c_{ij} are the parameter modelling the effect of p_{ij} on d_{ij}.

Even for these two versions of simple demand model, solving the pricing problem defined in (1) with traditional mathematical programming may involve implementing two different algorithms, for example, linear programming for (8) and nonlinear programming for (9). Furthermore, demand for a product in a period, in general, not only depends on its own price but also on the prices of other products in other periods, and also on other various different factors. Due to the complex relationship between these different factors, the developed model may not be easily quantifiable in a closed mathematical form, and could only be captured in a qualitative form. This significantly limits the use of mathematical programming techniques which are traditionally used for revenue management.

3 Solution

From previous two sub-sections, it is clear that there are two key limitations to the current revenue management approaches. They require the model to be mathematically well defined, limiting the accuracy and expressiveness of the model. Also, they are not generic enough to be able to produce pricing for different products with different demand models. Having a large number of different products and services, these limitations can pose a serious obstacle to a large firm that wish to implement a cost effective revenue management system.

In order to overcome these limitations, a flexible demand modelling and revenue optimisation system is built. This system provides a framework that allows both quantitative and qualitative information to be incorporated in the model. The specified model is then automatically used to produce revenue maximising price and production guidelines. The architecture of the presented system together with underlying AI techniques is described next. Since this is an application oriented paper, we do not go into detail on the technical implementation of these techniques.

3.1 Inputs and Outputs

The input to the system is the specification of the demand model for a product and the output of the system is the recommendations on revenue optimising price and production. Figure 2 gives an example of the input and output of the system. Here the input is a simple linear demand model $d_{ij} = D_{ij} + a_{ij}p_{ij}$ and its parameters – the base demand D_{ij}, the slopes a_{ij}, costs c_{ij}, and the price and capacity constraints $\underline{p}_{ij}, \overline{p}_{ij}, \underline{d}_{ij}, \overline{d}_{ij}$. These inputs are then used to formulate the pricing problem, as shown in (1). The solution to this problem, i.e., the optimum prices and corresponding demands[2] with such prices, p_{ij}, d_{ij}, for each products in each periods during the planning horizon, is returned as the output of the system.

$$d_{ij} = D_{ij} + a_{ij}p_{ij}$$

$$D_{ij}, a_{ij}, c_{ij}, \underline{p}_{ij}, \overline{p}_{ij}, \underline{d}_{ij}, \overline{d}_{ij}$$

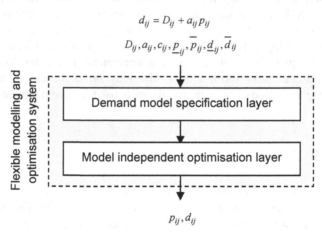

$$p_{ij}, d_{ij}$$

Figure 2 Example input and output

Also shown in Figure 2 is the two layered architecture of the system.

1. Demand model specification layer
2. Revenue optimisation layer

---

[2] Demand can be thought of as the indicator of how much to produce or how much can be sold.

3.2 Demand Model Specification Layer

Demand model specification layer provides an interface that is designed to help users of the system to specify their product specific demand model. This also makes sure that the specified model complies with the format required by the revenue optimisation layer. It provides a template that can be easily altered by the user to define the complex relationship between various factors in the model. As shown in Figure 3, it consists of a generic demand model interface that can be extended to define different types of generic, or product specific, demand models. The layer does not put restrictions on the type of demand model that the user can define, and allows definitions from very simple "if-then" models to very complex expert systems.

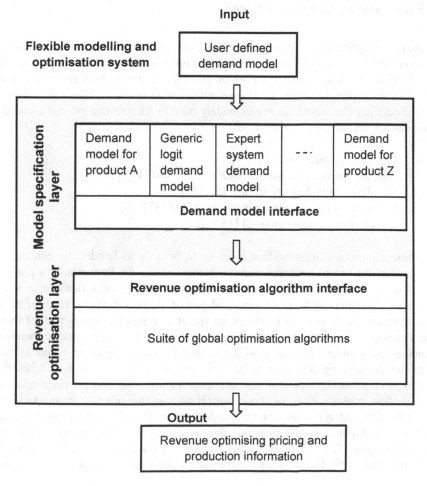

Figure 3 Architecture of the system

This interface then passes the model to the revenue optimisation layer for optimisation. Appendix A shows a simplified object relationship between the components of the model specification layer and its connection to revenue optimisation layer.

On a more practical side, the demand model specification layer also provides a facility to automatically create the instance of the demand model interface given the user choices. Furthermore, it includes some of the generic demand models, such as linear, logit or constant elasticity models, taking into consideration some of the common influencing factors. These models can be readily used, as required, by the user without having to build their own models.

3.3 Revenue Optimization Layer

Revenue optimisation layer forms the core of the system and implements different AI techniques to solve the revenue optimisation problem as defined in (1). Particularly, it consists of a suite of different global optimisation algorithm, specifically adapted to solve the revenue optimisation problem. This suite consists of different popular search heuristics widely used in AI community, and currently includes several different versions[3] of

1. Genetic algorithms (GA) [3][9]
2. Particle swarm optimisation algorithms (PSO) [4][5]
3. Simulated annealing algorithms (SA) [6]
4. Estimation of distribution algorithms (EDA) [7][10]
5. Hill climbing heuristics (HC) [15]

These algorithms are modified in order to be able to handle the constraints involved in the revenue management problems (eq. 2 - 6). Particularly, a penalty for violation of constraints is introduced to the original objective function in order for these algorithms to focus on the valid part of the search space. Each of these algorithm consist of number of algorithm specific operators, however all of them are developed in such the way that they support a single generic revenue management problem interface, which is specifically designed to communicate with the demand specification layer. This generic problem interface takes the unique demand model from the demand specification layer and provides it to the optimisation process. Each of these algorithms can individually understand and optimise different types of demand models given that the model specification follows the demand model interface defined in model specification layer. As shown in Figure 3, the demand model interface in model specification layer can communicate with the revenue optimisation algorithm interface in revenue

---

[3] such as binary and real valued versions

optimisation layer and pass on the problem specific demand model to the optimisation algorithm. The optimisation algorithm then optimises the price for that product, taking into account the specific demand model. Simplified object relationship between different components of the revenue optimisation layer and how they interact with model specification layer is shown in appendix A.

The heuristic based optimisation algorithms, used in the system, are developed within AI community and are widely used to solve different real world optimisation problems. Some of them, such as GA and EDA fall in the category of evolutionary algorithms, PSO fall in the category of swarm intelligence algorithm and simulated annealing and HC falls in the category of local search algorithms. For the purpose of this paper, we do not go into detail on the technical aspects of these algorithms. Interested readers are suggested to see corresponding literatures. Some technical detail on how these algorithms are customised to incorporate constrains, appearing in revenue management problems, is described in [17] [18].

On a more practical aspect, the revenue optimisation layer, on top of generic global optimisation algorithms, also incorporates some customised mathematical programming algorithms under the single umbrella of revenue optimisation algorithm interface. Users, if required, can use these customised algorithms for solving specific types of problems that satisfies the demand model requirements of these algorithms. By default, the system runs over the set of all algorithms and outputs the best result found by them. It also allows user to choose any specific (set of) algorithm from the suite. The system can be used as a stand alone revenue optimisation system or can be incorporated as a generic revenue optimisation component within a larger revenue management system.

4 Benefits

In contrast to mathematical programming algorithms, typically implemented in the traditional revenue management systems, the presented system implements a suite of heuristic based optimisation algorithms that does not require gradient information about the model and thus does not depend on the functional form of the demand model. In other words, the presented system does not put restriction on the form of the problem being optimised and therefore allows the system to be extremely flexible in defining the demand model. For example, the system allows solving revenue management problems using any of (8) and (9) without needing to implement two different mathematical programming algorithms. In fact, the system goes far beyond this, allowing demand function to be of any form, i.e. it does not care about the form of right-hand-side term in the equation (7). This allows greater flexibility in defining the demand function, $f(p_i, F)$.

Just to give an example, apart from (8) and (9), the system also allows $f(p_i, F)$ to be an if-then-else condition as shown in (10),

$$d_{ij} = \begin{cases} x & \text{if } p_{ij} \geq k \text{ and } F_i \leq l \\ y & \text{if } p_{ij} < k \text{ and } F_i > l \\ z & \text{Otherwise} \end{cases} \qquad (10)$$

where, x, y, z, k and l can be some constants or functions. Furthermore, $f(p_i, F)$ can be modelled as an expert system (or any black box system) with no specific mathematical form, as shown in (11), that would take p_{ij} and F as an input and produce the demand, d_{ij}, as an output.

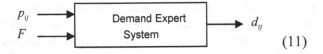

$$(11)$$

Such flexibility in the system further allows different types of loops and conditions to be included in the demand model and could increase the expressiveness and accuracy of the model. Another benefit of the system is that it allows user to focus their time on modelling the problem and produce more realistic and effective demand models rather than worrying about the implementation of customised optimisation algorithm. This is particularly important in the larger organisation with diverse range of products and services.

5 Conclusion

In this paper, we have described an AI-based system for revenue management within the scenario of large firms. The system allows flexibility in defining demand models for a range of different products and services, and can optimise price and production policy independent of the form of the demand model. The two key advantages of the system that resulted from its use of AI techniques are

    a.   Significant reduction in cost for implementing revenue management system, since the user only need to build the model and do not need to build a customised algorithm to solve it

    b.   Increased expressiveness of the revenue management model, since demand model is no longer restricted to satisfy some specific mathematical property.

Furthermore, the described system provides various extensions in the form of wizards and templates, in order to further ease the model description and optimisation process. The system is currently at its prototype stage and the instance of it is planned to be incorporated to the wider resource management toolkit, known as Field Optimisation Suite (FOS) [13]. FOS consists of number of other resource management tools, such as planning and scheduling tools, demand forecasting tools, capacity reservation tools and people management tools. The addition of revenue management tool would give this toolkit an extra dimension, and would allow resource managers to effectively use price as a tool to manage resources, whilst maximising the revenue at the same time.

References

1. Baker, W., Marn, M.V., Zawada, C.: Price smarter on the net. Harvard Business Review **79** (2001)
2. Ferdows, K., Lewis, M.A., Machura, J.A.M.: Rapid-fire fulfilment. Harvard Business Review **82**, 104–110 (2004)
3. Goldberg, D.: Genetic Algorithms in Search, Optimization, and Machine Learning. Addison-Wesley (1989)
4. Kennedy, J., and Eberhart, R.C.: Particle swarm optimization. In: Proceedings of the IEEE International Conference on Neural Networks, vol. IV, pp. 1942–1948. IEEE Press, Piscataway, NJ (1995)
5. Kennedy, J., Eberhart, R.C.: A discrete binary version of the particle swarm algorithm. In: Proceedings of the Conference on Systems, Man, and Cybernetics, pp. 4104–4109. IEEE Press, Piscataway, NJ (1997)
6. Kirkpatrick, S., Gelatt, C.D., Vecchi, M.P.: Optimization by simulated annealing. Science, Number 4598, 13 May 1983 **220, 4598**, 671–680 (1983).
7. Larrañaga, P., Lozano, J.A.: Estimation of Distribution Algorithms: A New Tool for Evolutionary Computation. Kluwer Academic Publishers (2002)
8. McWilliams, G.: Lean machine: How dell fine-tunes its pc pricing to gain edge in slow market. Wall Street Journal (June 8, 2001)
9. Mitchell,M.: An Introduction To Genetic Algorithms. MIT Press, Cambridge, MA (1997)
10. Mühlenbein, H., Paaß, G.: From recombination of genes to the estimation of distributions: I. binary parameters. In: H.M. Voigt, W. Ebeling, I. Rechenberg, H.P. Schwefel (eds.) Parallel Problem Solving from Nature – PPSN IV, pp. 178–187. Springer, Berlin (1996).
11. Narahari, Y., Raju, C.V., Ravikumar, K., Shah, S.: Dynamic pricing models for electronic business. Sadhana **30**(part 2,3), 231–256 (April/June 2005)
12. Netessine, S., Shumsky, R.: Introduction to the theory and practice of yield management. INFORMS Transactions on Education 3(1) (2002)
13. Owusu, G., Voudouris, C., Kern, M., Garyfalos, A., Anim-Ansah, G., Virginas, B.: On Optimising Resource Planning in BT with FOS. In: Proceedings International Conference on Service Systems and Service Management , pp. 541–546, (2006)
14. Phillips, R.: Pricing and revenue optimization. Stanford University Press (2005)
15. Russell, S.J., Norvig, P.: Artificial Intelligence: A Modern Approach. Pearson Education (2003)
16. Sahay, A.: How to reap higher profits with dynamic pricing. MIT Sloan management review **48**, 53–60 (2007)
17. Shakya, S., Oliveira, F., Owusu, G.: An application of GA and EDA to Dynamic Pricing. In: proceedings of Genetic and Evolutionary Computation COnference (GECCO2007), pp. 585–592. ACM, London, UK (2007)
18. Shakya, S., Oliveira, F., Owusu, G.: Analysing the effect of demand uncertainty in dynamic pricing with eas. In: M. Bramer, F. Coenen, M. Petridis (eds.) Research and Development in Intelligent Systems XXV: Proceedings of AI-2008, The Twenty-eighth SGAI International Conference on Innovative Techniques and Applications of Artificial Intelligence, pp. 77–90. Springer-Verlag London, Cambridge, UK (2008)
19. Talluri, K., van Ryzin, G.: The Theory and Practice of Revenue Management. Springer, Berlin Heidelberg, New York (2004)

Appendix A: Object relationship between different components of the system

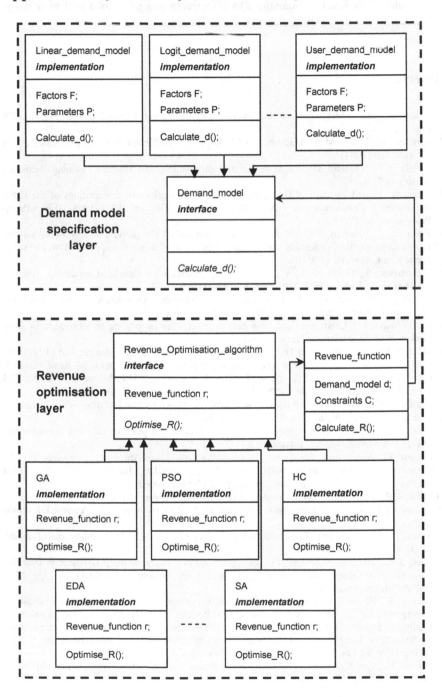

An Interval Type-2 Fuzzy Multiple Echelon Supply Chain Model

Simon Miller and Robert John

Abstract Planning resources for a supply chain is a major factor determining its success or failure. In this paper we build on previous work introducing an **Interval Type-2 Fuzzy Logic model** of a multiple echelon supply chain. It is believed that the additional degree of uncertainty provided by Interval Type-2 Fuzzy Logic will allow for better representation of the uncertainty and vagueness present in resource planning models. First, the subject of **Supply Chain Management** is introduced, then some background is given on related work using Type-1 Fuzzy Logic. A description of the Interval Type-2 Fuzzy model is given, and a test scenario detailed. A **Genetic Algorithm** uses the model to search for a near-optimal plan for the scenario. A discussion of the results follows, along with conclusions and details of intended further work.

1 Introduction

There are a number of definitions of Supply Chain Management (SCM), each having minor variances but describing the same core idea. SCM is the management of material flow in and between facilities including vendors, manufacturing/assembly plants and distribution centres [19]. Planning the allocation of resources within a Supply Chain (SC) has been critical to the success of manufacturers, warehouses and retailers for many years. Mastering the flow of materials from their creation to the point of sale offers considerable advantages to those within a well managed SC.

Simon Miller
Centre for Computational Intelligence, De Montfort University, Leicester, UK e-mail: smiller@dmu.ac.uk

Robert John
Centre for Computational Intelligence, De Montfort University, Leicester, UK e-mail: rij@dmu.ac.uk

M. Bramer et al. (eds.), *Research and Development in Intelligent Systems XXVI*,
DOI 10.1007/978-1-84882-983-1_32, © Springer-Verlag London Limited 2010

Poorly managed resources result in two main problems: stock outs (a shortage of stock) and surplus stock.

The consequence of stock outs is lost sales, and potentially lost customers. Surplus stock causes additional holding cost and the possibility of stock losing value as it becomes obsolete. Holding some surplus stock is advantageous however; safety stock can be used in the event of an unexpected increase in demand or to cover lost productivity.

The problem has been addressed numerous times in the literature using different approaches. An overview of traditional and Computational Intelligence approaches to supply-chain resource planning can be found in [14]. In this paper we present a novel approach to modelling the supply chain using Type-2 Fuzzy Logic (T2FL)[12] that is optimised by means of a Genetic Algorithm (GA)[6].

This research is part of a project on demand forecasting and resource planning (Data Storage, Management, Retrieval and Analysis: Improving Customer Demand and Cost Forecasting Methods, funded by the Technology Strategy Board in the UK). The project aims to: (1) improve the forecasting of demand by using a variety of disparate sources of data and statistical and Machine Learning (ML) methods for analysis; (2) improve the allocation of resources in which the generated forecast is used as an input, the output being is a (long- or short-term) plan of raw materials and resources within the supply chain required in order to meet such demand. The research presented here is intended to address the second aim. Various degrees of uncertainty are present in the different data sources used. This uncertainty is further amplified in the generated forecast by applying methods of analysis with (again) varying degrees of inherent uncertainty. Furthermore, other data that is often used in resource planning such as transportation and other costs, customer satisfaction information, etc. is also uncertain. Therefore, FL and especially T2FL are particularly appropriate for this problem. While Type-1 FL (T1FL) has successfully been used many times for modelling SC operation (see Section 2), T2FL has been shown to offer a better representation of uncertainty on a number of problems (e.g., [5] and [8]). In [15] the authors applied Interval Type-2 Fuzzy Logic (IT2FL) to a 2 tier distribution resource model and it was shown to work well. This paper presents an IT2FL model of a multiple echelon SC problem which is optimised by a GA to find a near-optimal configuration. The term 'echelon' (or 'tier') is used to describe a group of nodes that operate at the same stage in a supply chain, e.g., retailers. A multiple echelon supply chain is one that incorporates many stages, e.g., suppliers, manufacturers, warehouses and retailers.

The paper is organised as follows: Section 2 discusses Fuzzy Logic and its application to SCM. Section 3 introduces the model and the test case used for evaluation. The results from the experiments on the test case are presented in Section 4. Section 5 concludes the paper with a summary and future research directions.

2 Fuzzy Logic for Supply Chain Management

FL and GAs have been successfully used for supply chain modelling [14] and are particularly appropriate for this problem due to their capacity to tackle the inherent vagueness, uncertainty and incompleteness of the data used. A GA [6] is a heuristic search technique inspired by evolutionary biology. Selection, crossover and mutation are applied to a population of individuals representing solutions in order to find a near-optimal solution. FL is based on fuzzy set theory and provides methods for modelling and reasoning under uncertainty, a characteristic present in many problems, which makes FL a valuable approach. It allows data to be represented in intuitive linguistic categories instead of using precise (crisp) numbers which might not be known, necessary, or may in general be too restrictive. For example, statements such as *'the cost is about n'*, *'the speed is high'* and *'the book is very old'* can be described. These categories are represented by means of a membership function which defines the degree to which a crisp number belongs to the category. In this research the aim is to allow linguistic terms to be used by Supply Chain Managers when describing their operation. For example, instead of asking for crisp numbers to describe the current stock level of a product, we may allow them to make statements like 'Warehouse A has *About 500* of product 1' or even more abstract 'Warehouse A's stock level of product 1 is *low'*. By removing the need for exact information it is possible to produce a system that is much more usable when the information available is vague, uncertain or incomplete. T1FL has been applied to SC modelling numerous times with good results. Some of the research that is considered most relevant for this paper is discussed in the following paragraphs.

Petrovic et al. [16] use fuzzy sets to model vagueness and imprecision in customer demand, external supplier reliability and supply within a multiple echelon single product supply chain. The system demonstrates the effect of differing conditions and strategies on fill rate and holding costs of a SC. The results of the evaluation show that there is a slight improvement in the performance of the SC when the inventories are partially co-ordinated. In [17] Petrovic et al. employ two-level fuzzy optimisation to find ideal order-up-to quantities in a one warehouse-multiple retailer SC. The problem is decomposed for individual control of the warehouse and retailers; a co-ordination mechanism provides overall control of the SC. Customer demand, inventory levels, holding cost, and shortage cost are represented by fuzzy sets. A measure of satisfaction is derived from the cost incurred at each element. The solution produced by the system is the best compromise between members, though not necessarily the cheapest.

In [1] a fuzzy system is used with a GA to model a 3 tier SC. The model uses a global policy of management with emphasis on integrating the production and distribution models. The GA searches for a near-optimal configuration; fuzzy sets are used to describe costs, returns, production capacities, storage capacities and forecasts. The proposed fuzzy method, a crisp method and a non-integrated method are compared. The crisp system is unable to produce a feasible configuration if actual demand is lower than the forecast. In contrast, the fuzzy model presented is robust and able to cope with fluctuation in demand and production capacity with little impact on profitability. The non-integrated model performed significantly worse than the fuzzy integrated model.

A similar approach is presented by Wang and Shu [20] in their multiple echelon SC model. FL is used to represent customer demand, processing time and delivery reliability; a GA finds order-up-to levels. The system attempts to find the configuration that incurs the minimum cost. An optimism-pessimism index is set by the user and passed to the system. When optimistic, the model assumes the best case scenario for material response time. A pessimistic attitude produces the opposite effect. The results show that more pessimistic strategies increase the fill rate, reducing the sales lost through stock outs, and incur higher inventory cost as more stock is kept. More optimistic strategies result in a drop in fill rate and an increase in sales loss, though inventory cost is also reduced.

In these examples we have seen how T1FL has been used to tackle the resource planning problem. However type-1 fuzzy sets represent the fuzziness of the particular problem using a 'non-fuzzy' (or crisp) representation - a number in $[0, 1]$. Dubois and Prade[3] when discussing this issue say:

> To take into account the imprecision of membership functions, we may think of using type-2 fuzzy sets...

As Klir & Folger [10] point out:

> ..it may seem problematical, if not paradoxical, that a representation of fuzziness is made using membership grades that are themselves precise real numbers.

This paradox leads us to consider the role of type-2 fuzzy sets as an alternative to the type-1 paradigm. Type-2 fuzzy sets [12] are where the membership grades are not numbers in $[0, 1]$ but are type-1 fuzzy sets. They can be thought of as 'fuzzy fuzzy'. Type-2 fuzzy sets have been widely used in a number of applications (see [7] and [11] for examples) and on a number of problems, T2FL has been shown to outperform T1FL (e.g., [5] and [8]). In previous work [15] the authors have shown that Interval Type-2 Fuzzy Logic (IT2FL) [13] is an appropriate method of modelling a 2 tier distribution network. IT2FL has been used because it is computationally cheaper than general T2FL as it restricts the additional dimension, referred to as secondary membership function, to only take the values 0 or 1. We believe that the extra degree of freedom will allow a better representation of the uncertain and vague nature of data used in SCM. In this paper we propose an IT2FL model of a multiple echelon SC. Further extensions to the model since previous work published by the authors[15] include a measure of customer service level and maximum capacity that nodes can supply. By adding the notion of customer service level to our model we allow the user to trade-off between customer service level and cost. For example, the user may want to see the effect on the operating cost of a supply chain of altering the acceptable service level from 96% to 95%. It may prove that a small change in service level effects a large change in cost, making it attractive for the supply chain manager. By adding finite capacity to the model we enable users to specify limits on how much stock can pass through nodes. This forces the GA to find solutions that take into account these limits (by spreading supply across nodes or periods) instead of assuming that infinite amounts of stock can be handled.

Section 3 describes the created model in detail, as well as the test case used for evaluation.

3 Model

The proposed model represents the interaction of nodes within a multi-echelon supply chain. In each echelon there are one or more nodes that supply the subsequent echelon with one or more products, and receive stock from the preceding echelon. The first echelon receives goods from an external supplier which is assumed to have infinite capacity, the final echelon supplies the customer. Below the first echelon, capacity is limited by product.

Customer demand is provided by a fuzzy forecast which is given to the model at run-time. This forecast represents the demand placed upon the final echelon in the SC. Echelons above this can see their own demand by looking at the suggested inventory levels at the succeeding echelon, as they will be required to supply these items.

In order to use the model the following information must be provided:

- Number of echelons (not including the end customer)
- Number of nodes in each echelon
- Number of end customers
- Number of products
- Number of periods
- Service level required (as a percentage of orders filled completely)
- Capacities for each product (amount that can be produced at one node in one period)
- Distance matrix containing distances between nodes in successive echelons
- Forecast of customer demand
- Suggested inventory levels
- Costs including:

  - Batch cost
  - Production cost
  - Transport cost
  - Holding cost (as a percentage of purchase price)
  - Purchase price

Using this information the model will calculate the cost of the given resource plan. The total cost of a plan is made up of the following:

Batch cost The cost of setting up an order is called the batch cost. This represents the cost of administration, setting up any machines that are required, and picking the items for dispatch. There is a flat fee for each batch which is charged once at each warehouse for the production of a particular item for a particular customer.

Production cost Each product is assigned an individual production cost. The total production cost for each batch is calculated by multiplying the number of items by their production cost.

Transport cost The cost of transporting goods is produced using a matrix of distances between warehouses and customers, and a list of transport costs per km/mile. The product of the relevant cost and mileage gives the overall transport cost for a batch of product.

Holding cost A holding cost is charged if a product is kept at a node for more than one period. The cost is calculated by taking a specified percentage of the purchase price of the goods held, for items carried over from one period to the next. The purpose of the charge is to represent the cost of storing items, the depreciating value of stock and the losses incurred by tying up capital in unsold stock.

Stock out cost Stock out is the shortfall of a product in a particular period. In this model we make the assumption that the end customer is always provided with an item. If it is not in the warehouse, it is purchased at purchase price from a competitor. The stock out cost is the sum of the value of items that had to be purchased in this period. Stock out cost is applied to all but the final echelon that supplies the end customer. In the final echelon service level is used to determine how good a solution is. To apply a stock out penalty as well would be to penalise a solution twice for the same shortfall, leading to the GA being pressured to find solutions that satisfy 100% of customer demand, regardless of the service level required by the user.

Echelon cost The echelon cost is the sum of the batch, production, transport, holding and stock out costs for an echelon.

Service penalty To discourage solutions that do not meet service level requirements, a service penalty is added to the cost of poor solutions in proportion to a solution's distance from the target service level. Service level is calculated by taking the percentage of customer demand that is satisfied. To measure satisfaction the fuzzy sets for the current stock level and the forecast are compared. An agreement index is calculated by looking at where the sets intersect, or is set to 1 if the inventory level exceeds the forecast. As stated before, stock out penalities are not applied here. It may appear that a more satisfactory solution would be to simply measure service level throughout the chain and not use stock out penalties. However in practice applying service level throughout the model resulted in the GA finding solutions in which the nodes within the chain placed little or no orders on each other, enabling solutions to achieve a good service level without meeting a significant amount of end customer demand. Stock outs need to be charged within the chain however, else the GA finds solutions in which only the final echelon before the customer supplies any product.

3.1 Interval Type-2 Fuzzy Logic

IT2FL[13] has been used to represent some of the values within the model. Other than the authors' previous work, examples in the literature (as discussed in Section 2) have focused on the use of T1FL; we believe there exists an opportunity to exploit the extra degree of uncertainty provided by IT2FL in a model of this type.

As the model operates on IT2 fuzzy numbers, fuzzy arithmetic is used to calculate costs. This involves taking fuzzy sets, discretising them, performing the arithmetic operation, and then reconstructing the fuzzy set. In this model, fuzzy sets are represented using a series of α-cuts. Each set is an array of pairs of intervals. Each pair shows the area of values covered at a particular value of μ, the first interval is the left hand side of the set, and the second the right. Storing the sets in this way removes the need to discretise before fuzzy arithmetic is performed, and then reconstruct the result. Operations on the IT2 fuzzy sets are performed at interval level, corresponding intervals (at the same μ) are taken from two sets, the operation performed and the result stored in a third fuzzy set.

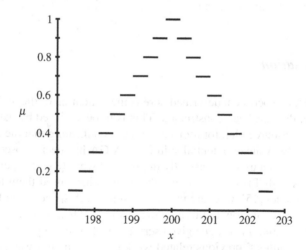

Fig. 1 Interval representation of IT2 fuzzy set *'about 200'*

The following values are represented by IT2 fuzzy numbers: forecast demand, inventory level, transportation distances, transportation cost, stock out level, stock out cost, carry over and holding cost. For each of these values we can use the linguistic term *'about n'*, e.g., forecast demand of product 1 for customer 1 in period 1 may be *'about 200'*. Figure 1 shows how the set *'about 200'* may look with the α-cut representation used, where x is the scale of values being represented. The set is described using a collection of pairs of intervals. Each pairing represents the left and right hand intervals of the set for a given value of μ. As stated before, representing the set in this way considerably simplifies the arithmetic operators that are applied as simple interval arithmetic is used throughout, without discretisation or reconstruction.

3.2 Defuzzification

We have seen that values in the resource planning model are represented using IT2FL. Within the model this is useful as we can describe the uncertainty present in the supply chain. For the user however it is not explicit enough to state 'This resource plan will have a total cost of *about £1,000,000*' or 'Warehouse A should stock *about 300* of Product 1'. In order to produce an output that can be applied to a real-world supply chain, some of the IT2 fuzzy numbers need to be defuzzified. Defuzzification is the process of taking a fuzzy set (in this instance an IT2 fuzzy set) and deriving a single crisp value from it. To do this, the method proposed by Karnik and Mendel [9] is used. This is a widely used method that finds an interval representing the centroid of a type-2 fuzzy set. The interval can then be used to obtain a crisp number by finding its mean.

3.3 Optimisation

The focus of the experiment described here is the validation of the multiple echelon IT2FL model that has been constructed. This is to be achieved by using the model to find a good resource plan for a given forecast, confirming that the model can be used to precisely evaluate potential solutions. A GA has been chosen for this purpose. GAs have been used successfully in previous work (e.g., [18] and [4]) to find good solutions with T1FL models, and the authors have used them to good effect on an IT2FL model [15]. GAs are useful when a search space is too large to allow evaluation of every solution. In this case the GA is used to search for a resource plan that incurs the minimum cost at a given service level. The setup of the GA has been taken from the authors' previous related work [15] in which it was shown to work well. The GA has a population of 250 individuals and is executed for 500 generations, in all 125,000 solutions are evaluated out of a total possible search space of 1.1318×10^{112} solutions. New generations consist of: 1% individuals produced with elitism, 20% copied individuals, 20% individuals created with single point crossover and 59% of individuals created using mutation. A description of the chromosome, operators and processes employed follows.

Chromosome The chromosome used to describe potential solutions is a 5 dimensional matrix of inventory levels. The dimensions are ordered as follows:

1. Echelon
2. Period
3. Source

4. Destination
5. Product

Each element of the matrix contains a value representing the number of items held in an echelon, in a time period, by a source node, for a destination node of a particular product.

Initial population The initial population is randomly generated. Each element of the resource plan matrix can be one of 6 values between 0 and the capacity limit for a particular product. This has been done to reflect the fact that in industry, products are usually manufactured in round quantities. If the model suggests that a warehouse should make 102 of product 1, this could lead to difficulties and extra expense. Limiting the valid inventory numbers also has the side effect of reducing the search space. In this case 6 values works well with a capacity of 500 as it can be used to represent the values 0 to 500 in steps of 100. If this method of dividing the possible values proves to be inappropriate for a given problem, the discretisation can be altered.

Fitness evaluation Fitness is evaluated using the IT2FL model described. Candidate solutions are given to the model which evaluates them, and returns the cost. The cheaper a solution is, the fitter it is judged to be. In reality, cost may not be the only factor in deciding how much of a product to stock at each warehouse. Other criteria such as customer service level can also be used to prevent the system from choosing solutions that do not meet service requirements. To this end, the service level of each solution is calculated as discussed in Section 3 and a penalty added to solutions with a customer service level that does not meet the specified target.

Selection Selection is performed using a fitness ranking proportionate method similar to *roulette wheel selection*. First, all solutions in the population are ranked by fitness. They are then given a number of elements of an array in proportion to their fitness ranking. For example, if we have a population of 250 the fittest individual would be allocated 250 elements in the array, the second fittest 249 and so on. An element of the array is then selected at random, and the identification number of the individual it contains is used to retrieve a parent. This tombola style approach ensures that it is possible for any individual to be selected, while weighting in favour of those with greater fitness.

Crossover Crossover is achieved with a single point crossover. Two parents are selected using the method of selection described. Then, a new individual is created with the first half of the first parent and the second half of the second parent. Resource plans have 5 dimensions: echelon, period, source node, destination node and product. For crossover, parents are divided by product. If we have 4 products the first 2 products of the first parent and the final 2 of the second parent will be used to create a new individual. This spans throughout all dimensions, so for each echelon, period, source and destination the first 2 products would be taken from the first parent and the second 2 from the second.

Mutation To create a mutated individual, a parent is selected, then one of the elements of its resource plan is randomly replaced with another valid value to create a new child.

3.4 Test Scenario

To test the model a scenario has been created. Table 1 shows the configuration of the supply chain. Each customer requires 200 items of each product, and each node can handle a maximum of 500 items in a period. Table 2 gives the operating costs of the supply chain. To calculate transport costs, the model needs to know the distance between nodes. Table 3 shows the distances between nodes in successive echelons.

Table 1 Test case supply chain

Echelons	4
Nodes	2 per echelon
Products	2
Periods	6
Service level required	95%

Table 2 Supply chain costs

	Product	
	1	2
Batch cost	£100	
Production cost	£30	£40
Transport cost	£2	£3
Purchase value	£50	£70
Holding cost	£5	£7

To find a good cost for comparison, a resource plan was created that matched demand in each period, using nodes that are closest to one another. When put into the model, a cost of £529,287.31 was produced. It should be noted that this plan will satisfy 100% of customer orders, the test scenario will allow solutions that satisfy 95% of orders and as such may be cheaper.

Table 3 Supply chain distances

	Dest. node	
Src. node	1	2
Echelon 1		
Node 1	100	200
Node 2	200	100
Echelon 2		
Node 1	200	100
Node 2	100	200
Echelon 3		
Node 1	100	200
Node 2	200	100

4 Results

To test whether the model could be used to find good resource plans the model was used with the GA described in Section 3.3. The GA was executed 40 times with differing random seeds. Table 4 shows the cost of the best solutions found in each of the first 10 runs along with its service level and time. Table 5 shows the mean cost, time and service level of the best solutions in all 40 tests, and the standard deviation in the costs. The results show that using the model, the GA is able to consistently find solutions that are cheaper than the benchmark solution. All of the solutions found achieve a service level close to the target set, this shows that the penalties imposed by the model encourage discovery of solutions that match the requirements of the user.

Table 4 Results of first 10 test runs

Seed	Cost	Service level	Time
0	£502,496.75	95.83%	2000s
1	£511,470.63	95.83%	2080s
2	£511,552.31	95.83%	2018s
3	£520,084.69	95.83%	2049s
4	£500,498.69	95.83%	1996s
5	£510,751.56	95.83%	2061s
6	£505,909.00	95.83%	2021s
7	£502,990.06	95.83%	2001s
8	£505,564.56	95.83%	2017s
9	£522,328.06	95.83%	2052s

An extra test was conducted to see how the quality of solutions would be affected by specifying a customer service level of 100%. This would also allow a comparison between the solution found and the ideal solution described earlier. The ideal solution is the perfect solution for a 100% service level costing £529,287.31. In the experiment (with one run only) the GA was able to find a solution that satisfied all

Table 5 Overall results of test runs

Mean Cost	Std. Dev. of Cost	Mean Service Level	Mean Time
£508,043.22	6093.19	95.83%	2499.68s

end customer demand costing £535,195.75 in 500 generations, just 1.1% more than
the ideal solution. The generation limit is applied to constrain the amount time it
takes for the GA to run. Previous work by the authors [15] has shown that if the GA
is left to run, it will find the optimal solution to a similar problem.

We can use the results as an indicator of the validity of the multiple echelon
model presented. The GA is guided purely by fitness and is blind to the practicalities
of the solutions that it finds. Figure 2 shows the progress of one of the test runs. The
fact that it evolved toward cost-effective sensible plans shows that the model is able
to differentiate between good and bad solutions to a high level of detail. If this were
not the case the GA may find solutions that are cheap but non-sensical, or could
result in a situation where the GA is unable to find good resource plans at all.

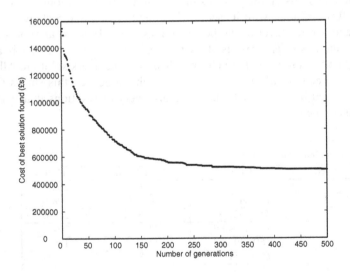

Fig. 2 Evolution of cost of best solution found

5 Conclusion

In this paper we have presented an IT2FL multiple echelon supply chain model.
Using IT2FL allows us to model the fuzziness present in supply chain operation,

allowing the user to input data that is uncertain. IT2FL has been chosen as it is believed that the extra level of uncertainty over T1FL offered will benefit a model of this type, while avoiding the computational complexity of a general T2FL model.

The model builds on previous work by the authors [15] by representing multiple echelon supply chains, customer service level and finite capacity. Using the model, it was shown that a GA was able to find good multiple echelon resource plans that were both cost-effective and sensible. In this case the GA is solely guided by cost and service level, it is essentially 'blind' to the practicality of the solutions it finds. That it was able to find good solutions is taken as indication of the model's validity.

Work is ongoing. Future work will include testing the model on more complex problems that have been solved by other methods to allow comparison, and applying the model to real world scenarios. Extensions of the model will include looking at how alternative methods of representing type-2 fuzzy sets (e.g. geometric [2]) could be used to improve the model's description of the uncertainty in the supply chain.

Acknowledgements The research reported here has been funded by the Technology Strategy Board (Grant No. H0254E).

References

1. R.A. Aliev, B. Fazlollahi, B.G. Guirimov, and R. R. Aliev. Fuzzy-genetic approach to aggregate production-distribution planning in supply chain management. *Information Sciences*, 177:4241–4255, 2007.
2. S. Coupland and R. I. John. Geometric type-1 and type-2 fuzzy logic systems. *IEEE Transactions on Fuzzy Systems*, 15(1):3 – 15, February 2007.
3. D. Dubois and H. Prade. *Fuzzy Sets and Systems: Theory and Applications*. Academic Press, 1980.
4. C. Fayad and S. Petrovic. A fuzzy genetic algorithm for real-world job shop scheduling. In *Proceedings of the 18th international conference on Innovations in Applied Artificial Intelligence. Bari, Italy.*, pages 524–533, 2005.
5. H.A. Hagras. A hierarchical type-2 fuzzy logic control architecture for autonomous mobile robots. *IEEE Transactions on Fuzzy Systems*, 12(4):524–539, August 2004.
6. J.H. Holland. *Adaptation in natural and artificial systems: an introductory analysis with applications to biology, control, and artificial intelligence*. Ann Arbor: University of Michigan, 1975.
7. R.I. John and S. Coupland. Type-2 fuzzy logic a historical view. *IEEE Computational Intelligence Magazine*, 2(1):57–62, February 2007.
8. N. Karnik and J. Mendel. Applications of type-2 fuzzy logic systems to forecasting of timeseries. *Information Sciences*, 120:89–111, 1999.
9. N. Karnik and J. Mendel. Centroid of a type-2 fuzzy set. *Information Sciences*, 132:195–220, 2001.
10. G.J. Klir and T.A. Folger. *Fuzzy Sets, Uncertainty and Information*. Prentice Hall, 1988.
11. J. M. Mendel. Advances in type-2 fuzzy sets and systems. *Information Sciences*, 177(1):84–110, January 2007.
12. J.M. Mendel and R.I. John. Type-2 fuzzy sets made simple. *IEEE Transactions on Fuzzy Systems*, 10(2):117–127, April 2002.
13. J.M. Mendel, R.I. John, and F. Liu. Interval type-2 fuzzy logic systems made simple. *IEEE Transactions on Fuzzy Systems*, 14(6):808–821, December 2006.

14. S.M. Miller, V. Popova, R. John, and M. Gongora.   Improving resource planning with soft computing techniques.   In *Proceedings of UKCI 2008, De Montfort University, Leicester, UK.*, pages 37–42, September 2008.   available at: http://www.cci.dmu.ac.uk/preprintPDF/SimonUKCI(2).pdf.
15. S.M. Miller, V. Popova, R. John, and M. Gongora. An interval type-2 fuzzy distribution network. In *Proceedings of 2009 IFSA World Congress/EUSFLAT Conference*, pages 697–702, Lisbon, Portugal, July 2009.
16. D. Petrovic, R. Roy, and R. Petrovic. Supply chain modelling using fuzzy sets. *International Journal of Production Economics*, 59:443–453, 1999.
17. D. Petrovic, Y. Xie, K. Burnham, and R. Petrovic. Coordinated control of distribution supply chains in the presence of fuzzy customer demand. *European Journal of Operational Research*, 185:146–158, 2008.
18. M. Sakawa and T. Mori. An efficient genetic algorithm for job-shop scheduling problems with fuzzy processing time and fuzzy duedate. *Computers & Industrial Engineering*, 36:325–341, 1999.
19. D.J. Thomas and P.M. Griffin. Coordinated supply chain management. *European Journal of Operational Research*, 94(1):1–15, October 1996.
20. J. Wang and Y-F. Shu. Fuzzy decision modelling for supply chain management. *Fuzzy Sets and Systems*, 150(1):107–127, 2005.

Allocating Railway Platforms Using A Genetic Algorithm

M. Clarke, C. J. Hinde, M. S. Withall, T. W. Jackson, I. W. Phillips, S. Brown, and R. Watson

Abstract This paper describes an approach to automating railway station platform allocation. The system uses a Genetic Algorithm (GA) to find how a station's resources should be allocated. Real data is used which needs to be transformed to be suitable for the automated system. Successful or 'fit' allocations provide a solution that meets the needs of the station schedule including platform re-occupation and various other constraints. The system associates the train data to derive the station requirements. The Genetic Algorithm is used to derive platform allocations. Finally, the system may be extended to take into account how further parameters that are external to the station have an effect on how an allocation should be applied. The system successfully allocates around 1000 trains to platforms in around 30 seconds requiring a genome of around 1000 genes to achieve this.

1 Introduction

A typical British railway station has several platforms each servicing rail-lines to and from the station. A station's main purpose is to allow a train to arrive, stop and depart to a predetermined schedule, ensuring that the train is able to continue its journey on time. To effectively accommodate every train's timetabling needs

M. Clarke, C. J. Hinde, M. S. Withall,I. W. Phillips
Department of Computer Science, Loughborough University
e-mail: M.Clarke-05@student.lboro.ac.uk
e-mail: {c.j.hinde,m.s.withall,t.w.jackson,i.w.phillips}@lboro.ac.uk

T. W. Jackson
Department of Information Science, Loughborough University

S. Brown, R. Watson
RWA Rail, Epinal Way, Loughborough
e-mail: {steve.brown,robert.watson}@rwa-rail.co.uk

M. Bramer et al. (eds.), *Research and Development in Intelligent Systems XXVI*,
DOI 10.1007/978-1-84882-983-1_33, © Springer-Verlag London Limited 2010

many factors have to be considered, whilst adhering to very strict time and location constraints.

The purpose of this system is to create an application that can be used to carry out the task of platform allocation for a railway station timetable using industry standard data. A secondary purpose is to create a system that can be extended to employ extra constraints as they arise and also to integrate smoothly with a train timetable application reported elsewhere, and a resource allocation system yet to be fully researched.

The authors include professional train planners and the project's aim is to enable them to perform train planning more efficiently and effectively. The authors admit that human skills are necessary to arrive at a satisfactory solution and the evolved solutions may be examined and edited by the human train planners.

1.1 Background

Research work has been under way for some years to develop and implement software that can provide much greater support and, gradually, should enable better schedules (both in terms of robustness and efficient use of resources) to be produced in less time. [2, 3, 10, 12] provide useful summaries of these developments up to the late 1990s, covering timetable planning, crew and rolling stock scheduling, freight car routing, yard models, car management (all focused on a freight-dominated North American/Australian-style freight railway operation).

Work focused on generating timetables was limited until the last few years, and, as Carey (1994) highlighted (and this has not changed materially since), what there was tended to focus on single track railways (see [1, 14, 22, 27], appropriate for North America and Australia, but of very limited relevance for typical European railways or complex Mass Transit networks, with short headways, trains every few minutes and diverging routes or connections to be maintained.

Of relevance is work looking to construct timetables so as to achieve an overall customer benefit, such as minimising passenger waiting time (see [11]), or a combination of this and operating cost (see [9, 23]). Whilst this is focused on the passenger, it does not fit very well with the developing European railway industry structure, where railway infrastructure providers need to focus on the requirements of their customers, the train operators, more than the ultimate customer, the passenger or the freight shipper.

Carey worked for some years on the generation of timetables for complex European railway networks. In [4, 8, 5, 6, 7], he describes and extends the discussion on algorithms to generate timetables, highlighting along the way the particular problem of station infrastructure complexity and considering whether this should be treated as a separate computing task. Comparable work has also been undertaken in the Netherlands. [19, 24] providing early papers setting out work to develop algorithms for generating railway timetables; this has culminated in the development and implementation of the 'DONS' software package for Railned, the Netherlands state-owned railway infrastructure provider [16].

More recently work on timetable generation has continued to emerge from Dutch universities, but focused typically on generating a 'standard hour' timetable [25, 20]) rather than the less regular type of timetable often found in the UK. The number of papers, and the complexity of the timetabling problem being investigated, have increased in the last few years, with [21, 17, 26, 28]) describing research underway seeking to generate feasible timetables for complex European railways. The European Commission now provides a web site for researchers to share information on research under way in this area.

Also of interest is the approach adopted by London Underground through until 2008, which was the subject of a paper presented by [29], although 'metro' operations have rather simpler timetabling challenges than 'main line' railways.

Platform allocation is currently done manually in the UK. For many locations train planners use spreadsheets or even graph paper and then transfer the solution into the train planning systems. Some software (e.g. RailSys) has the functionality to 'drag and drop' trains between platforms and highlights conflicts. In all cases the train planner in not given any support in terms of which platforms to use for particular trains to get an acceptable solution.

2 Problem Analysis

Allocation of station platform time to any participating train requires all the information related to the station to be known. For a traditional 'stopping' train information concerning its anticipated arrival time at the station, how long it requires platform time for and when it departs must be established before the allocation of a platform can take place. This must be obtained from the available industry data that are used to record and distribute train route information to all those parties that need it.

A single train route details the stations that a train will either stop at, or pass through but the data do not provide the inverse relation, to answer 'what trains are stopping at, or passing through, station X?'. To obtain these data preprocessing must be performed providing a relation between stations and trains.

Pre-processing of the data is necessary before the allocation of platforms can take place. Analysing train data may be divided into two parts, with a further third part necessary to do the actually platform allocation. Each part acts as a pre-requisite to the next, leading to a final integrated system.

2.1 Part one: Linking trains to stations

A Common Interface Format file (CIF) [18], holds route data from the Network Rail Train Services Database (TSDB) in an electronic format. The data only provide details of a train's route data, and do not directly provide anticipated station use. This information must be deduced from the data supplied.

RWA have to resolve which trains are scheduled to arrive at which stations from the CIF files. From using arrival and departure information it is possible to deduce all the trains that will stop at a specific station. Until all the anticipated trains that use a station are known, it is difficult to accurately allocate suitable platform time to all those on the timetable without any clashes.

To provide a solution to this the system must be able to process CIF data and associate every route with the stations that it is anticipated to stop at, or pass through. Once associated it is be necessary to convey this information to the user, giving them access to a station's basic timetable so that it may be viewed before any platform allocation is performed.

2.2 Part two: Platform Allocation (Internal)

Once all trains have been linked to their stations, they need to be given an appropriate platform allocation. A station is likely to have many platforms, varying from station to station, and has to accommodate trains that arrive or depart within minutes of one another.

By using the earlier calculations the system has the timings for every train at a station, what time a train arrives, how long it is stationary for, and when it is scheduled to depart. From this calculated information it is possible to see where train routes interfere or 'clash' with one another.

The suitability of an allocation can be judged upon the number of these clashes, where a timetable allocation with fewest clashes is best.

There are potentially further considerations than the timing constraints of a route, with the possibility of commercial and service line requirements that need to be adhered to. A train is often able to arrive only via a certain set of lines, dictated by where it has come from, and may only leave on a limited set thus restricting the platforms it may choose [7].

A particular rail company may want all their trains to use the same platform on a particular route, due to commercial considerations. The system needs to be able to accommodate such requirements where possible, whilst ensuring minimum disruption of train routes.

2.3 Part three: Extended Platform Allocation (External)

Further constraints on a railway station and its environment can directly or indirectly affect a train's route to and from a station.

This increases the complexity of the system and the processes that manage the data associated with performing platform allocation. There are other problems that need to be considered, such as two trains scheduled to depart on different lines but where the lines cross at a nearby junction.

Train characteristics can also dictate where a train should be given platform time, as different trains could potentially have differing travel speeds that again could potentially lead to trains 'catching' each other up and cause disruption between trains external to the station. Potential clashes need to be resolved with minimal interference to either train, this is known as 'headway'.

Introducing tighter constraints on how a train is to be allocated platform time allows the system to be able to accurately perform the allocation for the station's timetable using complete data. Many new constraints may arise as train policy changes and the system must be capable of dealing with these.

3 Documentation analysis

There are several pieces of documentation that are currently used for the platform allocation.

3.1 Common Interface File (CIF) Document

The CIF file holds the data on the schedule for a train and all the necessary route information in a standardised format (Figure 1). The CIF file is a sequential text file consisting of fixed length records of 80 characters.

It contains various record types that are denoted by a 'record identity', the first two characters of the record. The record type determines the structure of the record.

The CIF is the main source of train information that will be required when carrying out platform allocation. Associating all the train data requires the processing of the majority of the data held in this file. The development will be primarily concerned with train data for the Glasgow area. In particular the main station that will be the focus of development and testing is Glasgow Central and the results presented in this paper use these data.

All necessary train information must be extracted from the CIF, and to assist in this process is the aid of a CIF End User Specification document[18] that details all the possible CIF data.

3.2 End User Specification Document

A typical train route will be structured with 5 forms of record type.

BS   Basic Schedule Record

BSNG41032060612061208111111100 P002A09   123579003 DMUS   075   S
BX   SRY
LOAYRR   1810 18104   TB
LIDLRYMPL   1814H00000000
LIMAYBOLE 1821 1821H   18211821   T
LIKKERRAN   1826H00000000   2
LTGIRVAN 1837 1837UL   TF

Fig. 1 A collection of CIF records concerning a single train route within the Glasgow area

- Details the main characteristics of the train route
- Identifies a unique Train UID code to determine the route
- Information on header ID (the train header unit)
- Details on operational days, train speed and further characteristics

BX   Basic Schedule Extra Record

- Is an extra record for the BS with a few fields to detail Continental Europe trains

The next three records of LO, LI and LT are all concerned with the stations that the train will interact with.

LO   Origin Location Record

- Always used to denote the initiation of a train route, the station at which the route commences.

LI   Intermediate Location Record

- Details on whether the train is stopping or passing and its requirements at a station during the route.

LT   Terminating Location Record

- Concerned with the final station that the route will terminate at.

LO, LI and LT records hold the majority of information on train arrival and depart times. As such they are essential to performing the initial train association.

Focusing in on a single LO record (Figure 1), the majority of information regarding the departing train can be derived based upon the record descriptions given the End User Specification document (Table 1).

This extract is taken from a CIF file detailing the train routes for the Glasgow area on a single day (Wednesday 11th October 2006). This file has nearly 39000 records, illustrating the quantity of data that currently has to be processed just to satisfy a single day's worth of timetabling for a city area.

Table 1 Breakdown description of a single LO CIF record fields

Value	Field Name	Size	Format	Comment
LO	Record Identity	2	A	origin Location Record
AYRR	Location	8	A	TIPLOC- unique station code
1810	Scheduled Arrival	5	A	24-hour format
1810	Public Departure	4	N	24-hour format(unpopulated)
4	Platform	3	A	Platform intended to be used
TB	Activity	12	A	'TB' (Train Begins- mandatory value)

3.3 Docking Movement File

A final document is a spreadsheet detailing the train movements for a day at a single station. Movements of trains, or header movement, occur typically at a station where a terminating train is then used to form the train for a later originating route. The file is a listing of all the movements at a station whilst detailing the expected station use of any arriving train such as what line and platform the train should be using.

Also data on the process of station switching is detailed where a train may need to move from one platform to another in order to continue on its route, as it may now need to switch lines in order to reach its next destination.

Information regarding this needs to be used to handle constraints concerning external requirements for a station's platform allocation. For it to be useful the information concerning trains needs to be linked in some form to the already existing data extracted from the CIF file.

4 System Specification and Design

Section 2 discussed the need to associate the train data and establish the quantity and type of data that needs to be included, thus allowing platform time to be distributed more precisely.

The high-level design illustrates the need for a separate association module that allows all the necessary pre-processing to be performed before a Genetic Algorithm [15] is implemented. Two input files will be required to implement a train association function, the CIF file containing the train data and a configuration file.

4.1 Specification

4.1.1 Linking trains to stations

This creates a data structure of station timetables all correctly associated with their entire train schedule for the day. Records are read in from the CIF sequentially, establishing the train information from the BS record that precedes the stop information of a train route. Each stop record is then processed establishing the station, stop timings and any further details. These are then added to the relevant station schedule, its insertion position determined by its time value. Having the final station schedule in an already sorted order allows easier execution of the Genetic Algorithm and fitness calculation for platform allocations. Once all CIF records have been processed every stop record should be associated to a station schedule, giving all station timetables that can now be in the position to perform platform allocation.

4.1.2 Genetic Algorithm

The appropriate station timetable is selected for allocation.

Specifying the Genetic Algorithm parameters state the structure of execution for the algorithm, whilst the input of a Docking Movement File, Section 3.3, will give details of any external considerations that the allocation module will have to consider.

An initial population of candidates is generated at random adhering to the chromosome structure that is to be operated upon. Each initial candidate in the population has a fitness value assigned to determine its suitability as a plausible solution [13]. Breeding phases are then executed round by round, generating new candidates through the use of pre-determined operators. At each round the population fitness for every member is recalculated and the process of selection is started again for the next generation. This continues until either a fit solution is achieved or the round limit has been reached.

As with associated train data, a single station timetable can be stored for intended future use. Past single station timetables can also be restored when wanting to just perform an allocation on a known station. Once achieved with the use of the Genetic Algorithm the solution can be stored permanently on the file system. Likewise previously generated allocations can be restored through the system.

There is the ability to amend already processed schedules by allocation that allows a single train record platform allocation to be altered individually. The fitness can then be recalculated to evaluate the suitability of this amended candidate.

4.2 Store and Loading Data File Design

In addition to being able to perform the necessary processing of train data and achieving platform allocation solutions, there will be the need to have functionality that will allow the permanent storage and retrieval of outputted data.

Associated data, a single station timetable schedule and single allocation candidates have all been identified as those data structures that a user of the system may wish to store digitally. Likewise a facility then must be in place to make use of previously saved data that may need further processing by a user.

These files that are formed from storing the data must be designed to a particular format so that the system is able to distinguish them apart from one another when coming to restoring them back to the system.

5 Genetic Algorithm Design

There are to be several determining factors that have to be processed by the allocation algorithm when implementing the Genetic Algorithm.

5.1 Timings

Arrival and depart times at the station is the primary factor to distributing a station platform to a train record.

These times are used to ensure that when trains arrive, are stationary and depart a station at their scheduled platform, no other trains will clash with them.

A clash can occur between two trains A and B when

- Train A does not depart from a station platform before a later train B arrives at the same platform.
- Train A does not depart from a station platform before a later train B requires the same platform to depart from (when train B is the commencement of a train route).

Using this as the main factor for deriving the suitability of a candidate for platform allocation, an initial Genetic Algorithm structure can be devised along with the required chromosome composition.

5.2 Genetic Algorithm Structure

To form the basis of the Genetic Algorithm, the process to schedule platforms for trains that are to arrive at a single station using a simplified platform structure will follow:

- Each candidate solution comprises of a timetable schedule established by associating all train data.
- The population is formed from many of these timetables with their allocations.
- Each timetable lists the unique trainUID (acting as the identifier for that train route) and the platform that it has been allocated. (Table 2)
- A train record holds the necessary information on the train, and its parameters used to decide on the fitness of the proposed allocation. (Table 2)

- The fitness function is applied to each genome initially to test for the number of clashes that occur across the platforms allocations applied.
- The higher the number of clashes the more unfit the solution and thus will be less likely to be included in the next generation of candidates.
- A candidate that has a smaller number of clashes will have a stronger fitness and be more likely to be selected for the next population for breeding.
- The size of the chromosome is determined by the number of train routes that are to be scheduled at the station in question.
- If there are 20 trains to be allocated then each chromosome will comprise of separate 20 genes (train records).

5.3 Chromosome Structure

Table 2 Primary Genetic Algorithm Chromosome Structure

Candidate A						
	Arrival Time	Depart Time	Platform		Clash?	
Train A	1102	1105	1		Y	
Train B	1104	1107	1		Y	B with A
Train C	1108	1115	3		Y	
Train D	1109	1110	2		N	
Train E	1110	1112	3		Y	E with C
Train F	1115	1116	2		N	
Train G	1115	1117	1		N	
Train H	1119	1121	4		Y	
Train I	1120	1120	4		Y	I with H
Train J	1126	1128	4		N	
Platforms	1,2,3,4			Fitness		3

The chromosome used is the Platform number.

5.4 Genetic Algorithm Parameters

Initiation of the algorithm requires several predefined parameters that distinguish the behaviour of the search.

Population Size: the number of potential candidates that must exist before any genetic operations can be applied.

Tournaments: the number of breeding phases that the algorithm is limited to perform until a fit solution is achieved.

Fitness Target: the target for the algorithm, should a candidate achieve this value the current round should finish execution and the algorithm should stop. A zero (0) target is generally expected but others may be defined.

Reproduction Rate: the proportion of candidates generated through reproduction in the breeding phase as a percentage of the total population.

Crossover Rate: similar to the Reproduction Rate, but denotes the proportion of candidates generated for the population via the Crossover operator.[1]

Mutation Rate: A percentage value of the possibility of mutation occurring, usually small.

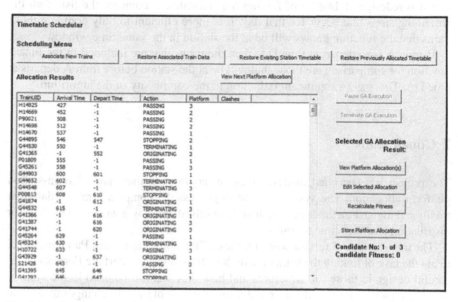

Fig. 2 Interface for Allocation Results Viewing and Processing

6 System Output

The system has a GUI that enables the user to view the results, for example Train to Station linking, GA Execution Output, Platform Allocation Results (Figure 2).

The system interface is very flexible. For example, if there is more than one candidate solution then the user can step through them, which allows the train planners to explore possibilities.

---

[1] Reproduction Rate and Crossover Rate are required to sum to 100% so to generate the necessary population value.

6.1 Fitness Function

The fitness is simply the number of clashes in the schedule. However, some stations have hundreds of trains on their schedule for a single day, calculating a fitness of a candidate needs to be efficient.

For the originally designed fitness function design, if a station had 1000 trains to allocate, then an algorithm comparing station and timing constraints for every train with every other train a population of 100 would require between 50 million and a billion comparisons to establish the fitness of the entire population.

To reduce the execution time and complexity of the algorithm, the fitness function was redesigned. Instead of forcing the algorithm to compare the list of all the remaining stops that occur for that day, it is more efficient to only compare those trains that the function knows will be at the station in the same time window.

If train A is to depart at time DA, then the trains that are included in the fitness function for comparison are those that will be at the station before train A departs at time DA. This gave a significant reduction in the complexity of the algorithm.

7 Conclusions

The project has succeded in developing an application that can aid train-station platform allocation. The system is able to process the complex array of data that traditional manual methods have to handle, whilst delivering a workable method for distributing platform time to trains.

The introduction of further working files, CIF Configuration and Parameter File, to aid the task of linking the train data in the CIF (Common Interface Format) led to careful design in those file structures and how they were to be used in the system. They give more control to the user and if the structure of the CIF changes then these files can be modified to allow the system to process later versions.

The association of data puts the timetable allocator in a position of having all the station timetables at their disposal with accurate information on those schedules.

The Genetic Algorithm to allocate platform time at a station can quickly achieve an allocation with minimal clashing between scheduled trains. The system gives feedback to the user so if it appears that an allocation will not be achieved, the parameters of the algorithm can be easily changed.

The system allows the manual alteration of allocations if a maximally fit solution is unavailable. A user can accurately specify a platform allocation that the system has failed to find. Providing the ability to automatically and manually specify platform allocation is more likely to lead a fit allocation being achieved.

The Docking Movement File has not been considered at this stage as most stations do not require this, so this system has addressed a large part of the problem.

This project met and addressed the requirements of the first two problems outlined in the analysis. It has successfully used a Genetic Algorithm to perform platform allocation for a station in a generalised manner. The genome used is very large compared to other problems tackled using a genetic algorithms, however the large search space is populated very heavily with possible solutions. One requirement of train planners is for a variety of solutions to choose from. This system delivers that.

References

1. Brannlund, U., Lingberg, P., Nou, A., J.E., N.: Railway timetabling using lagrangian relaxation. Transportation Science **32**, 358–369 (1998)
2. Bussieck, M., Kreuzer, P., Zimmermann, U.: Discrete optimisation in public rail transport. Mathematical Programming **79**, 415–444 (1997)
3. Caprara, A., Fischetti, M., Toth, P., Vigo, D., Guida, P.: Algorithms for railway crew management. Mathematical Programming **79**, 123–141 (1997)
4. Carey, M.: A model and strategy for train pathing with choice of lines, platforms and routes. Transportation Research Part B **28**, 333–353 (1994)
5. Carey, M., Carville, S.: Testing schedule performance and reliability for train stations. Journal of the Operational Research Society **511**, 666–682 (2000)
6. Carey, M., Carville, S.: Scheduling and platforming trains at busy complex stations. Transportation Research Part A **37**, 195–224 (2003)
7. Carey, M., Crawford, I.: Scheduling trains on a network of busy complex stations. Transportation Research Part B **41**, 159–178 (2007)
8. Carey, M., Lockwood, D.: A model, algorithms and strategy for train pathing. Journal of the Operational Research Society **46**, 988–1005 (1995)
9. Chang, Y., Yeh, C., Shen, C.: A multiobjective model for passenger train services planning: application to Taiwans high-speed line. Transportation Research Part B **34**, 91–106 (2000)
10. Cordeau, J.F., Toth, P., Vigo, D.: A survey of optimization models for train routing and scheduling. Transportation Science **32**, 380–404 (1998)
11. Daduna, J., Voss, S.: Practical experiences in schedule synchronisation. In: J. Daduna, I. Branco, J. Pinto Paixao (eds.) Computer-Aided Transit Scheduling, pp. 39–55. Berlin (1995)
12. Ferreira, L.: Planning australian freight rail operations: an overview. Transportation Research Part A **31**, 335–348 (1997)
13. Floreano, D., Mattiussi, C.: Bio-Inspired Artificial Intelligence Theories, Methods, And Technologies. MIT Press (2008)
14. Higgins, A., Kozan, E., Ferreira, L.: Optimal scheduling of trains on a single line track. Transportation Research Part B **30**, 147–161 (1996)
15. Holland, J.: Adaption in Natural and Artificial Systems. The University of Michigan Press (1975)
16. Hooghiemstra, J., Kroon, L., Odijk, M., Salomon, M., Zwaneveld, P.: Decision support systems support the search for win-win solutions in railway network design. Interfaces **29**(2), 15–32 (1999)
17. Ingolotti, L., Barber, F., Tormos P.and Lova, A., Salido, M., Abril, M.: A scheduling order-based method to solve timetabling problems. Current Topics in Artificial Intelligence. Lecture Notes in Artificial Intelligence **4177**, 52–61 (2006)
18. Kitchin, S.: Common Interface File — End User Specification. Network Rail, 23 edn. (2005)
19. Kroon, L., Romeijn, H., Zwaneveld, P.: Routing trains through railway stations: complexity issues. European Journal of Operational Research **98**, 485–498 (1997)
20. Liebchen, C.: Symmetry for periodic railway timetables. Electronic Notes in Theoretical Computer Science **92**(1) (2003)
21. Liebchen, C.: The 2005 timetable of berlin underground - the first mathematically optimized service concept for railways in practice. In: Proceedings of the 2nd International Seminar on Railway Operations Modelling and Analysis. Hannover, Germany (2007)

22. Mees, A.: Railway scheduling by network optimisation. Mathematical and Computer Modelling **15**(1), 33–42 (1995)
23. Nachtigall, K., Voget, S.: Minimising waiting times in integrated fixed interval timetables by upgrading railway tracks. European Journal of Operational Research **103**, 610–627 (1997)
24. Odijk, M.: A constraint generation algorithm for construction of periodic railway timetables. Transportation Research Part B **30**, 455–464 (1996)
25. Peeters, L., Kroon, L.: A cycle based optimization model for the cyclic railway timetabling problem. In: S. Voss, J. Daduna (eds.) Computer-Aided Scheduling of Public Transport. Springer, Berlin (2000)
26. Rodriguez, J.: A study of the use of state resources in a constraint-based model for routing and scheduling trains. In: Proceedings of the 2nd International Seminar on Railway Operations Modelling and Analysis. Hannover, Germany (2007)
27. Salim, V., Cai, X.: A genetic algorithm for railway scheduling with environmental considerations. Environmental modelling and software **12**, 301–309 (1997)
28. Tormos, P., Lova, A., Barber, F., Ingolotti L. Abril, M., Salido, M.: A genetic algorithm for railway scheduling problems. In: Metaheuristics for Scheduling In Industrial and Manufacturing Applications. Springer (2007). URL http://arrival.cti.gr/index.php/Documents/0081
29. Wallace, R.: Train scheduling - migration from manual methods to scalable computer platforms. In: J. Daduna, I. Branco, J. Pinto Paixao (eds.) Computer-Aided Transit Scheduling, pp. 321–333. Springer, Berlin (1995)

FURTHER AI APPLICATIONS

An Optimal Dynamic Threat Evaluation and Weapon Scheduling Technique

H.Naeem[1] and A.Masood[2]

Abstract   Real time scheduling problems demand high level of flexibility and robustness under complex dynamic scenarios. Threat Evaluation (TE) and Weapon Assignment (WA), together TEWA is one such complex dynamic system having optimal or near optimal utilization of scarce defensive resources of supreme priority. Several static solutions of TEWA have been proposed. This paper discusses an optimal dynamic multi-air threat evaluation and weapon allocation algorithm using a variant of Stable Marriage Algorithm (SMA). WA uses a new dynamic weapon scheduling algorithm, allowing multiple engagements using shoot-look-shoot strategy, to compute near-optimal solution. Testing part of this paper shows feasibility of this approach for a range of scenarios.

1 Introduction

The tools and doctrines of war fighting keep evolving with the technology. In this Information age, we see new and more powerful war fighting tools (both offensive and defensive). Countries are digitizing their Surveillance Control and Reporting (SCR) system. Threat Evaluation and Weapons Assignment (TEWA), a process which sits at the heart of SCR system, comprises a number of critical operations that must be performed under time and resource constraints. For an efficient TEWA system there is a need to create a balance between effectiveness and efficiency of weapon systems [1], [2]. Manual TEWA systems can't provide optimality because of inadequate awareness due to limited error-prone and uncertain information available, human limitations like operator's observation, vision range constraint, personal knowledge base in terms of experience, perception and understanding of the situation along with physical and mental health conditions. Most semi-automated TEWA systems usually use some type of greedy algorithm thus affecting the optimality of the solution and failing in multi-target scenario [3].

1 National University of Science and Technology, Rawalpindi, Pakistan
jinnny@gmail.com

2 National University of Science and Technology, Rawalpindi, Pakistan
amasood@mcs.edu.pk

M. Bramer et al. (eds.), *Research and Development in Intelligent Systems XXVI*,
DOI 10.1007/978-1-84882-983-1_34, © Springer-Verlag London Limited 2010

Several static solutions of TEWA have been proposed. This paper discusses an optimal dynamic multi-air threat evaluation and weapon allocation algorithm using a variant of Stable Marriage Algorithm (SMA). WA is based on a new flexible dynamic weapon scheduling algorithm, allowing multiple engagements using shoot-look-shoot strategy, to compute near-optimal solution. Testing part of this paper shows the feasibility of this approach for a range of scenarios.

Section 2 of this paper presents an overview of TE, WA, Stable Marriage Algorithm (SMA), dynamic closed loop weapon allocation and defense strategies. Section 3 covers our approach to TEWA. The performance of proposed model is discussed and compared with an alternative greedy algorithm in section 4. Section 5 finally concludes this paper.

2 TEWA and Solution Approches

TEWA is a two phased complex dynamic system having an ever-changing complex environment. First phase consists of evaluation and ranking of targets according to the degree of threat they impose to a defended asset (DA), while the reactive assignment of weapon systems (WSs) to these threats is done in second phase. When number of attacking threats "n" is small, TEWA is simple. If n=1, threat neutralization is straight forward. In a multi-target scenario (n>1), with an increasing n, TEWA becomes more and more complex, as more feasible choices are to be made for threat ranking and neutralization. Threat ranking is crucial because for an optimal solution, we need to decide which of several threats represent highest danger and thus be neutralized as early as possible. Threats can be ranked on the basis of expected degree of harm they can impose to a DA also known as "Threat Index" [5]. Suppose we have "n" number of threats represented by T_i, i=1, 2, 3… n. The outcome of TE phase will be a ranked ordered list T= $\{T_1, T_2, T_3… T_n\}$ such that Threat Index $I_1 > I_2 > I_3 > … > I_n$.

Typically two models are used for TE namely capability based TE Model and Intent based TE model. First model ranks targets according to their capability index, ability of the target to inflict damage to a DA whereas, the formal one estimates intent (will of a target to inflict damage to a DA) of a target to calculate threat index [5]. To estimate intent and capability of a threat, different parameters can be used for example target type, speed, direction and heading, weapon envelope and lethality etcetera (for capability index)and heading (bearing and course), velocity, altitude and speed etcetera(for intent Index calculation) [5]. But, capability and intent both have their own significance. Best model for TE can be obtained by combining capability and index – i.e. Opportunity based TE model.

After the calculation of these parameters, there is a need to calculate final Threat Index of each identified threat. Literature survey shows Bayesian networks and fuzzy logic rules can be used to solve this problem. Fredrik and Falkman, compared these two approaches, presents their pros and cons in [4]. Bayesian networks have sound mathematical foundation within probability theory and thus handle missing evidence more easily. Bayesian networks calculate threat values well-separated but they demand more development time than the fuzzy inference system. In fuzzy logic system, uncertain evidence can not be handled explicitly. Thus according to Fredrik and Falkman, a mixture of these two approaches can be used for an optimal solution [4].

Once, threats have been ranked we need to neutralize them by assigning each threat to the best available WS. This assignment is done in WA phase. Output of TE phase affects decisions regarding weapon allocation to a specific target in WA. However, this data alone is not enough for making such a decision. WA is a complex phase; we also need to know other parameters related to DA and WSs.

WA corresponds to the selection of the best available weapon system for threat neutralization i.e. selecting which WSs to be used to neutralize a particular target in near optimal way. [6] – [12] provide a good literature on WA problem. TEWA, being a real time system is subject to uncertainties and hard set of external constraints. Due to dynamic ever-changing environment, assignment problems might need to be re-solved, this makes scheduling problem even more complex to design and implement [5]. If a system has M number of Weapon systems (WSs) of different types having their own lethality index, priority, rate of fire, field of fire, elevation angle etcetera. Based on these parametric values, WSs are assigned to each threat.

WA can be seen as a special case of job shop scheduling problem where threats are jobs and WSs are machines and we want to schedule n jobs on m machines under a certain set of constraints. The efficiency of this assignment/scheduling depends on the type and significance of parameters used in Threat index calculation. Tin G. and P. Cutler classified parameters related to TEWA into critical and sorting parameters [4]. We amended this classification a little in our previous paper on TEWA [13] to divide these parameters into three overlapping categories i.e. (1) Triggering Parameters- Different thresholds used in to initiate a certain function. For example initial threat index is used to trigger TEWA process, status of a WS to be allotted (like Free to Fire, On Hold and Tight), (2) - Sorting Parameters- Parameters used to rank main entities of the system i.e. threats, DAs and WSs for example, threat priority, threat index, opportunity index, intent index, capability index, lethality Index, condition (Up, Down, Destroyed), status of a WS and time to WS. (3) -Scheduling Parameters -Parameters used in assignment decision for example, weight of WS-Target pair (parametric equation using lethality index of a WS in combination with Time to WS and load on WS), Maximum elevation of a WS, Stabilization time and Rate of Fire (ROF) of a WS.

Objective of WA depends upon defense strategy set by the commander. A commander may want to maximize the total expected value of the DAs that survive after all attacks and allocations (maximization function), or the defense may want to minimize the total expected survival value of the survived targets (minimization function). The first approach is known as preferential defense strategy and the model used is known as DA based WA model while the later one is called subtractive defense strategy and the model is called, target based WA model [14]. For preferential strategy to be successful, the defense must, with high probability, destroy all of the targets aimed for DAs, attacking each aimed target with enough ammunition so as to make its survival and thus expected damage value minimum. This sounds infeasible from ammunition point of view; hence, defense is often required to choose which of the DAs should actually be defended and assign all its WSs to the defense of these DA. When number of threats per DA is small, subtractive defense strategy changes to preferential defense strategy. The efficiency of preferential strategy depends on the accuracy of information available on the other hand; success of subtractive strategy is inversely proportional to number of threats directed to each DA [13]. Most DA based solutions assume no coordination/synchronization between targets, Das and WSs. As stated earlier, TEWA is both subject to uncertainties and unpredictable scenarios. Thus, hard selection of defense strategy cannot give optimal solution. There is a need to use semi-automated hybrid defense strategy.

Execution model of WA can either be static or dynamic. Dynamic execution model take notion of time into account whereas static models use processes defined over a single time horizon [15]. Dynamic models are though tough to design and implement but enable us to make multiple engagements in stages by observing the outcomes of previous engagement before making any further engagements (information feedback) [16].

Threat weapon pairing can be done using some matching algorithm like Stable Marriage Algorithm (SMA), that finds a matching between men and women, considering preference lists in which each person expresses his/her preference over the members of the opposite gender. The output matching must be stable; means there is pair having an incentive to differ [17]. Two relaxations can be considered in SMA, namely, incomplete lists and ties in lists. In incomplete list, a person can exclude some members whom he/she does not want to be matched with. The hospitals/residents problem (HR) is a many-to-one extension of SMA. Student-project allocation problem (SPA) is a variant of HR, in which students are assigned to projects based on his/her preferences over projects. Many-to-many stable marriage algorithm, is a more general variant of SMA than HR, it allows both men and women have quota [17]. Applying SMA on TEWA, we model threats as men and WSs as women. Realistically speaking, one threat may be required to be traced by multiple WSs, and a WS may trace multiple threats. Hence many-to-many SMA seems to be suitable for this kind of system.

To further enhance the optimality of solution TEWA is decision support oriented having heir its own set of threat and weapon libraries. To avoid the selection of un-optimal and inappropriate WS, these libraries should be correlated [13]. The information about the kill probabilities and lethality index for each weapon-target pair can be obtained from correlated libraries.

3 Our Approach

Our solution to TEWA is a two phase process, where in first phase, threats are evaluated, threat index is calculated using opportunity based TE approach, threats are ranked according to this index and finally threats and DAs are paired using a variant of many-to-many SMA. In second phase, for each DA-threat pair, WA is performed using dynamic weapon scheduling algorithm that allows multiple engagements using shoot-look-shoot strategy to compute near optimal engagement solution.

Let defense has I number of DAs, each having its own set of WS, vulnerability index, priority and status (Free to Fire, On Hold, Tight). Let total number of WSs is J. Each DA can be attacked by ay number of threats of any type and lethality, suppose total number of threats be represented by K. The main objective of TEWA is to neutralize each target as optimally as possible, reducing the amount of expected damage to DAs and ammunition used.

Before we go into the details of our approach, let's look at the set of assumptions we are making.

- TEWA application receives track position (latitude, longitude and altitude), IFF, threat type and speed of each track as input parameter. System consists of three main modules i.e. Simulator, Communicator and TEWA application. Simulator has a Global Information System (GIS) application. It acts like a RDX – Radar data Extractor. It sends track positions according to one set scan rate. TEWA application contains its own GIS application, capable of deploying DAs and WSs.

- We will assume that each WS is coupled with one and only one DA, the one it is responsible to guard against potential threats and can't be use to defend some other DA unless explicitly mentioned.

- Before applying TEWA, DA and WS deployment is saved and an initial kill capability of each DA against every possible type of threat is calculated. This capability defines an initial probability with which a DA can neutralizer a particular target.

- Communicator is responsible for all communication between other two modules; Simulator and TEWA application are invisible to each other.

- Apart from preferential and subtractive strategies we introduce another hybrid defense strategy using parametric equations. User can save deployment and simulator scenarios to perform same simulation using different defense strategy or using different parameter values

- We will assume that impact of a target on DA is dependent of other targets assigned to it but independent of other DAs

3.1 Threat Evaluation Phase

Main aim of TE is to evaluate the threats on the basis of their intent and capability parameters and assign each threat to a DA that has maximum potential in terms of WS (capacity, power, load etc) to neutralize this target. Mathematically this problem can be seen as a constrained matching where, we match the elements of D with elements of T where

$$D = \{DA_1, DA_2, DA_3, DA_4, \dots DA_I\} \, where \, I = total \, number \, of \, DAs \qquad (1)$$

and

$$T = \{T_1, T_2, T_3, T_4, \dots T_K\} \, where \, K = total \, number \, of \, Threats \qquad (2)$$

This pairing is subject to following constraint:

$$\sum_{x=1}^{I}(Assigned_{x,y}) = 1 \, where \, y \in k \, for \, k = \{1,2,3, \dots , K\} \qquad (3)$$

Means, there exists synchronization among DAs - a particular target is assigned to one and only one DA. As soon as it is out of the scope of assigned DA, it is assigned to next most suitable DA it is heading towards. For this section and WA description following notations will be used:

$D = \{DA_1, DA_2, DA_3, DA_4, \dots DA_I\} \, set \, of \, DAs$

$W = \{W_1, W_2, W_3, W_4, \dots W_J\} \, set \, of \, WSs$

$T = \{T_1, T_2, T_3, T_4, \dots T_K\} \, set \, of \, identified \, threats$

$I \overset{def}{=} \, Count \, of \, DAs$

$J \overset{def}{=} \, Count \, of \, WSs$

$K \overset{def}{=} \, Total \, number \, of \, Targets$

$\alpha = Weight \, Assigned \, to \, Intent \, parameters$

$\beta = $ Weight Assigned to Capability parameters

$\gamma = $ Weight Assigned to Opportunity parameters

$\delta = weight \, paramneter \, for \, Load$

$\varphi_k = Intent \, index \, of \, K^{th} \, threat$

$\varphi'_k = Capability \, index \, of \, K^{th} \, threat$

$\varphi''_k = Opportunity \, index \, of \, K^{th} \, threat$

$T_i = set \, of \, threats \, heading \, towards \, DA_i$

$N_i = Number \, of \, threats \, heading \, towards \, DA_i$

$V_i = Vulnerability \, Index \, of \, DA_i$

$V_i = Vulnerability\ Index\ of\ DA_i$

DT= Threshold on difference between different terms

TT= Triggering threshold for TEWA

LT= Lethality Threshold

LdT= threshold related to load parameter

Lethal = Lethality Index of a WS

To start TEWA Boolean variable S is checked

$$S=\begin{cases} 1 & if\ initial\ threat\ index\ of\ threat\ k \geq TT \\ 0 & Otherwise \end{cases} \tag{4}$$

For each threat satisfying start condition, intent and capability index are calculated as follows:

IntentIndex={ $\alpha * (\ F(Speed), +F(heading) + F(course\ variation) + F(Altitude)$ }

Where,

$$F(Speed)=\begin{cases} 1 & if\ |current\ speed\ of\ T_i - Attack\ Speed\ of T_i| \leq DT \\ 0 & Otherwise \end{cases} \tag{5}$$

i.e. if current speed of threat T_i is close to attack speed of threat T_i, it shows intent of T_i to inflict injury similarly,

$$F(Altitude)=\begin{cases} 1 & if\ |current\ Altitude\ of\ T_i - Attack\ Altitude\ of T_i| \leq DT \\ 0 & Otherwise \end{cases} \tag{6}$$

$$F(Course\ Variation)=\begin{cases} 1 & if\ Threat\ T_i\ manuevers \\ 0 & Otherwise \end{cases} \tag{7}$$

To calculate course variation, previous heading is compared with current heading of Ti. Mathematical calculation of heading is as follows:

If a DA is represented with circle and threat with a point at different time stamps, considering two points at time instance t0 and t1, we get a line. Using circle line intercept we calculate the points where threat velocity vector will intercept with DA circumference.
Equation of DA (8) and extension of velocity vector (9) would be

$$(x - x_0)^2 + (y - y_0)^2 = r^2 \tag{8}$$

$$y = mx + c \tag{9}$$

Expanding (8) and putting 9 in it we have

$$x^2 + x_o^2 - 2xx_0 + (mx + c)^2 + y_o^2 - 2(mx + c)y_0 = r^2 \tag{10}$$

Solving (10) we have

$$x^2(1 + m^2) + x\big(2(mc - x_0 - y_0)\big) + (x_o^2 + y_o^2 - r^2 + c^2 - 2y_0c) = 0 \tag{11}$$

We can solve (11) using quadratic equation as shown below

$$\frac{-b \pm \sqrt{b^2 - 4ac}}{2a} \tag{12}$$

Where,

$$a = (1 + m^2)$$

$$b = 2(mc - x_0 - y_0)$$

$$c = x_o^2 + y_o^2 + c^2 - r^2 - 2y_0c$$

The roots of this solution will give us entry and exit points of threat for a particular DA. By comparing these points with current location, we can estimate heading of a threat, whether it is moving towards or away from the DA. Our approach to matching first makes pseudo pairs between threats and DAs. For each threat-DA pseudo pair, if roots of (12) exist, we calculate other parameters like Distance from DA, time to DA (Arrival time AT) as given by (13).

$$AT_{i,k} = \frac{\sqrt{\Sigma_{i=1}^{I}(POI_{i,k} - Position_k)^2}}{V_k} \tag{13}$$

The numerator shows Distance from DA, and denominator shows target's speed. The pseudo pair that has lesser $AT_{i,k}$ and is headed towards that DAi will have higher intent value for DAi as compared to a threat Tm that has almost same parameter set but a greater $AT_{i,k}$ at the same time stamp t0. Threats are ranked according to their final threat index.

Our approach takes into account the probabilities of success to make our solution more robust. When a battlefield scenario (DA and weapon deployment) is created, an initial kill probability (KP) of each DA is calculated for all possible type of threats present in threat library. KP shows probability of success, as it shows the probability that a given threat will be neutralized if assigned to this particular DA. This probability decreases as the load on DA increases. So it is rapidly changing.

$$K.P_{i,k} = \prod_{k=1}^{K}\left(\prod_{j=1}^{J}\left(1 - \big((\alpha\varphi_k + \beta\varphi'_k - \delta \, \text{Load}_j) * \text{Candidte}_{j,k}\big)^{\text{Belong}_{i,j}}\right)\right) \tag{14}$$

Where

$$\text{Candidte}_{j,k} = \begin{cases} 1 & if \; \text{Lethal}_j \geq LT \\ 0 & Otherwise \end{cases} \tag{15}$$

$\text{Belong}_{i,j} = 1$, when WS_j belongs to DA_i.

Based on these parameters, capability and intent parameters of threat (collectively called opportunity parameters), a weight is calculated for each DA-threat pseudo pair. $K.P_{i,k}$ is given more weight in normal settings, based on defense strategy weight values for different parameters are changed. As the load increases on a DAi, $K.P_{i,k}$ decreases by a factor specified by δ. Due to this load balancing, and pair feasibility analysis, chances of proposal rejection minimize. Finally a proposal is sent for DA-threat pseudo pair that has maximum pseudo proposal weight.

3.2 Weapon Allocation Phase

Mathematically this problem can also be seen as a constrained matching where, we match the elements of W with elements of T where

$$W = \{WS_1, WS_2, WS_3, , \dots WS_J\} where \; J = total \; number \; of \; WSs \qquad (16)$$

and

$$T = \{T_1, T_2, T_3, T_4, \dots T_K\} where \; K = total \; number \; of \; Threats \qquad (17)$$

This module uses somewhat similar approach. This pairing is subject to following constraint:

$$\sum_{z=1}^{J}\left(Assigned_{y,z}\right) = 1 \; where \; y \in k \; \text{for k} = \{1,2,3, \dots , K\} \qquad (18)$$

Means, there exists synchronization among WSs - At one time a particular target can be engaged by one and only one WS. Though if a user wants he can enable threat queuing. If a target engagement fails, it is assigned to another suitable WS. If user wants he can enable multiple engagements, allowing one threat to be traced by multiple WSs at a time, to stay on the safe end, if one WS misses the target, other is ready to neutralize it. This multiple engagement can be enabled when number of threats per DA is less than a specific threshold. Figure 1 shows flow diagram of WA phase.

For multiple engagements, a new constraint is added. A DA can allow multiple engagements if load on DA is less than a certain threshold LdT. Even then, locking will be done for one and only one threat i.e. for any $WS_j \in W$

$$MultipleEng_i = \begin{cases} 1 & if \; \text{Load}_i \leq LdT \\ 0 & Otherwise \end{cases} \qquad (19)$$

$$\sum_{k=1}^{K} Locked_{j,k} = 1 \qquad (20)$$

And also for any threat $k \in K$

$$\sum_{j=1}^{J} Locked_{j,k} = 1 \qquad (21)$$

Threat-Weapon pairing is dependent of other threats scheduled on that particular WS and other WSs. This constraint introduces load balancing. Two other important constraints added in this section are scheduling constraint and allocation constraint as stated below:

$$
ValidAssign_{j,k} = \begin{cases} 1 & \text{if Maximum Elevation of WS}_j \leq \text{Required Elevation for } T_k \\ 0 & \text{Otherwise} \end{cases} \tag{22}
$$

While allowing multiple targets to be traced by a WS_j, we introduce a scheduling constraint that says, two targets T_x and T_y can be traced by a single $WS_j \in W$, if and only if

$$
|AT_{j,x} - AT_{j,y}| \geq Stabilization\_Time_{\ j} + TimeToFireOneRound_j \tag{23}
$$

and

$$
ValidAssign_{j,k} = \begin{cases} 1 & \text{if Maximum Elevation of WS}_j \leq \text{Required Elevation for } T_k \\ 0 & \text{Otherwise} \end{cases} \tag{24}
$$

To schedule a threat on WS_j, it is necessary that a proposal be accepted by WS_j.

$$
Scheduled_{j,k} = \begin{cases} 1 & \text{if } j \in W \text{ and proposal}_{i,k} = 1 \text{ and Porposal}_{j,k} = 1 \\ 0 & \text{Otherwise} \end{cases} \tag{25}
$$

Where,

$$
proposal_{j,k} = \begin{cases} 1 & \text{if } j \in WS_i \text{ Porposal}_{i,k} \text{ is accepted} \\ 0 & \text{Otherwise (no proposal is sent)} \end{cases} \tag{26}
$$

For every WS we calculate four points. Entry point- Point from where threat will approach, exit point- point from where target is expected to leave if left unhandled, and two launch points for entry and exit points. Launch point calculation is crucial as weapons in general don't follow a straight path to the point of intercept. Hence, an accurate description of the flight path is mandatory for an accurate hit. Gravitational force and other physical phenomena known as ballistics make a curved weapon trajectory – projectile motion. Moreover, we need to consider relative motion of target during the time of weapon flight for a successful hit. To hit a target, we aim a WS at some point in space displaced from target current position. This displacement is known as lead. For lead calculation we use relative velocity of a target and weapon time of flight of a WS (time of travel of a Weapon) from launch point to target.

4 Testing and Analysis

To test our approach we implemented three modules as stated earlier. Scenarios were generated using our own designed GIS based component named simulator, which allows threat scenarios to be saved and loaded as and when required. Proposed algorithm was tested and analyzed for a range of scenarios. We generated different scenarios to test optimality of implemented system, ranging

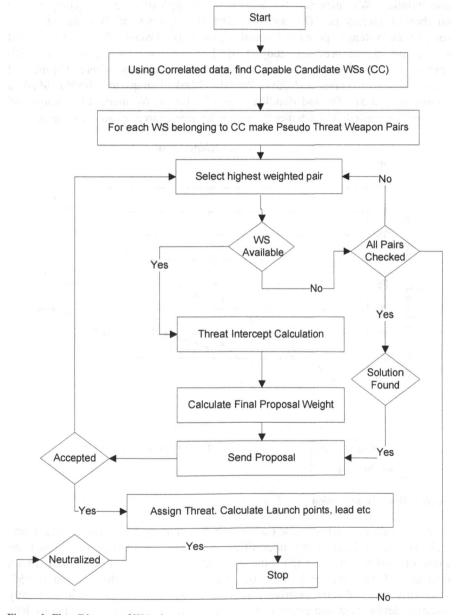

Figure 1: Flow Diagram of WA phase

from simple relaxed scenarios to complex critical ones. The greedy algorithm used for comparison, looks for minimum arrival time without looking at the capability and intent values. It always operates under subtractive defense strategy objective. We tested out system for different type of attack patterns, maneuvering and uncertainties. We increased the amount of complexities by directing greater number of threats per DA and reducing the number of WS per DA. We categorized system response as Unmasked, Partially Masked, Masked and Catered as we did in our previous study, [13]. Likewise, we took average of each simulation and divided the response into four classes where Un-masked corresponds to a value of 1-25%, Partially Masked maps to 26-50%, Masked corresponds to 51-75% and Handled shows 76-100%. We marked the amount of ammunition wasted in an attempt to over-neutralize a threat as ammunition loss.

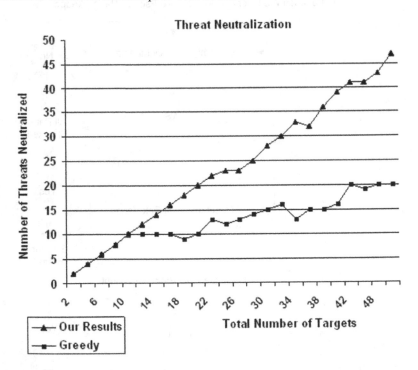

Graph 1: Threat Neutralization

We calculated asset loss for each threat that managed to cross a DA; it was assigned to, without being neutralized. Damage calculation was based on capability index of a threat times the vulnerability index of a DA combined with number of WSs deployed in that DA. With I=5, J=30 and threat count K =50, asset loss was ~5% for relatively relaxed threat distribution, with a slightly complex deployment and threat distribution it turned out to be ~9%. Up to 40% maneuvering was tested and found to be catered by the system, where greedy failed badly. Due to the lack of synchronization between WSs; greedy algorithm often results in over-neutralization whereas, proposed algorithm makes sure that at a time one and only one WS neutralizes a particular target at any given time. Graph 1 and 2 compares threat neutralization and ammunition usage pattern of our algorithm with that of greedy

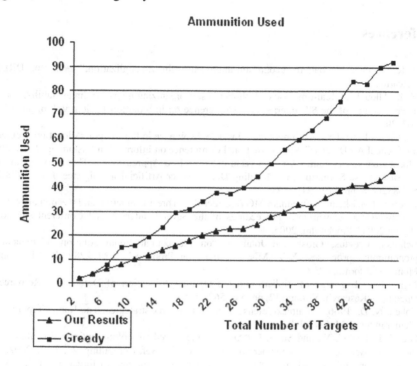

Graph 2: Ammunition Used

Our optimization algorithm maximizes total number of neutralized threats using minimum possible ammunition. On the other hand, greedy algorithm works the opposite way, i.e. as number of threats increase, number of neutralized threats decreases and amount of ammunition used increases manifolds.

5 Conclusions

Threat Evaluation (TE) and Weapon Assignment (WA), together TEWA is a real time scheduling problem demining high level of flexibility and robustness under complex dynamic scenarios. This paper discussed an optimal dynamic multi-air threat evaluation and weapon allocation algorithm using a variant of Stable Marriage Algorithm. WA phase used a new dynamic weapon scheduling algorithm, allowing multiple engagements using shoot-look-shoot strategy, to compute near-optimal solution. Although this algorithm is computation intensive but, even under stressful conditions, it comes up with near optimal solution where greedy fails.

References

1. M. K. Allouche, "A pattern recognition approach to threat stabilization," tech. rep., DRDC Valcartier. 2006.
2. M. K. Allouche, "Real-time use of Kohonen's self-organizing maps for threat stabilization, " in Proceedings of the 8th International Conference on Information Fusion, vol. 6, pp. 153–163, 2005.
3. Tin G. and P. Cutler, "Accomodating Obstacle Avoidance in the weapon Allocation Problem for Tactical Air Defense", 9th International Conference on Information Fusion, pp. 1-8, 2006.
4. F.Johansson, G.Falkman, "A Comparison between Two Approaches to Threat Evaluation in an Air Defense Scenario" , in Modeling Decisions for Artificial Intelligence, ISBN: 978-3-540-88268-8, pp. 110-121, 2008.
5. Paradis S, Benaskeur A, Oxenham MG & Cutler P, , "Threat evaluation and weapon allocation in network-centric warfare", Proceedings of the Seventh International Conference Fusion, "Usion 2004", Stockholm, 2005.
6. Bellman, Dreyfus, Gross and Johnson, "on the computational solution of dynamics programming processes: XIV: Missile Allocation Problems", RM 2282, RAND, Santa Monica California, 1959.
7. Pugh, G. E, Lagrange Multipliers and the Optimal Allocation of Defense   Resources, Operations Research, Volume 12, pp. 543-567, 1964 .
8. Cohen, N. D., 1966, An attack-defense game with matrix strategies, The Rand Corporation, Memorandum RM-4274-1-PR.
9. Lee, Z. J., Lee, C. Y., and Su, S. F. "An immunity based ant colony optimization algorithm for solving weapon-target assignment problem". Applied Soft Computing, 2, 39-47, 2002.
10. F. Johansson and G. Falkman,. "A Bayesian network approach to threat evaluation with application to an air defense scenario", in Proceedings of 11th International Conference on Information Fusion, pp. 1-7.10, 2008.
11. Soneji H. Deepak, "A comparison of Agent based Optimization approaches applied to the Weapon to targets Assignment Problem", 2006.
12. Lee, Z. J., Su, S. F., and Lee, C. Y. A Genetic Algorithm with Domain Knowledge for Weapon-Target Assignment Problems. Journal of the Chinese Institute of Engineers, 25, 3, 287-295, 2002.
13. H.Naeem, A.Masood, M.Hussain. K.Shoab "A Novel Two-Staged Decision Support based Threat Evaluation and Weapon Assignment Algorithm", IJCSIS, 2009.
14. Hossein, P.A., Athans, M.: Preferential Defense Strategies. Part 1: The Static Case, 1990.
15. J. Berger and D.Leong, 1994, "The resolution of an Open Loop Resource Allocation Problem using a Neural Network Approach", 27th Annual Simulation Symposium, pp. 51-58.
16. Patrik A. Hosein, James T. Walton and M. Athans, 1988, "Dynamic Weapon Target Assignment Problem with Vulnerable C2 Nodes", by Massachusetts Inst. of Tech. Cambridge Lab for Information and Decision Systems.
17. K. Iwama, "A Survey of the Stable Marriage Problem and Its Variants", in the proceedings of International Conference on Informatics Education and Research for Knowledge-Circulating Society, 2008.

On Assisting a Visual-Facial Affect Recognition System with Keyboard-Stroke Pattern Information

I.-O. Stathopoulou, E. Alepis, G.A. Tsihrintzis, and M. Virvou

Abstract Towards realizing a multimodal affect recognition system, we are considering the advantages of assisting a visual-facial expression recognition system with keyboard-stroke pattern information. Our work is based on the assumption that the visual-facial and keyboard modalities are complementary to each other and that their combination can significantly improve the accuracy in affective user models. Specifically, we present and discuss the development and evaluation process of two corresponding affect recognition subsystems, with emphasis on the recognition of 6 basic emotional states, namely happiness, sadness, surprise, anger and disgust as well as the emotion-less state which we refer to as neutral. We find that emotion recognition by the visual-facial modality can be aided greatly by keyboard-stroke pattern information and the combination of the two modalities can lead to better results towards building a multimodal affect recognition system.

1 Introduction

Recently, the recognition of emotions of users while they interact with software applications has been acknowledged as an important research topic. How people feel may play an important role on their cognitive processes as well [12]. Thus the whole issue of human-computer interaction has to take into account users' feelings. Picard [22] points out that one of the major challenges in affective computing is to try to improve the accuracy of recognizing people's emotions. Improving the accuracy of emotion recognition may imply the combination of many modalities in user interfaces. Indeed, human emotions are usually expressed in many ways. For example, as we articulate speech we usually move the head and exhibit various facial emotions [13].

I.-O. Stathopoulou, E. Alepis, G.A. Tsihrintzis, and M. Virvou
Department of Informatics, University of Piraeus, Piraeus 185 34, Greece e-mail: {iostath,talepis,geoatsi,mvirvou}@unipi.gr

M. Bramer et al. (eds.), *Research and Development in Intelligent Systems XXVI*,
DOI 10.1007/978-1-84882-983-1_35, © Springer-Verlag London Limited 2010

There is an increasing interest within the human-computer interaction (HCI) community in designing affective engagement with interfaces [15]. This is especially the case of computer-based educational applications that are targeted to students who are in the process of learning. Learning is a complex cognitive process and it is argued that how people feel may play an important role on their cognitive processes as well [12]. A way of improving interaction and, thus, learning is recognizing the users' emotions by observing them during their engagement with the educational application and then adapting its interaction to their emotional state. Indeed, research in psychology and neurology shows that both body and mind are involved in emotional experiences [7, 8, 10] and emotions influence people's bodily movements [9]. Therefore, observing users may provide a system with adequate information for recognizing users' emotions. Picard [22], on the other hand, argues that people's expression of emotion is so idiosyncratic and variable, that there is little hope of accurately recognizing an individual's emotional state from the available data. Therefore, many researchers have pointed out that there is a need for combining evidence from many modes of interaction so that a computer system can generate as valid hypotheses as possible about users' emotions (e.g. [18, 20]).

Towards this task, a shortage of empirical studies have appeared in the literature. Indeed, after an extensive search of the literature, we found that there is a shortage of empirical evidence concerning the strengths and weaknesses of these modalities. The most relevant research work is that of De Silva et al. [11] who performed an empirical study and reported results on human subjects' ability to recognize emotions. However, De Silva et al. focus on the audio signals of voice concentrating on the pitch and volume of voice rather than lingual keywords that convey affective information. On the other hand, in our research we have included the lingual aspect of users' spoken words on top of the pitch and volume of voice and have compared the keyboard-stroke patterns results with the results from the other two modes so that we can see which modality conveys more information for human observers.

Ideally evidence from many modes of interaction should be combined by a computer system so that it can generate as valid hypotheses as possible about users' emotions. This view has been supported by many researchers in the field of human computer interaction [5, 21, 22]. However, progress in emotion recognition based on multiple modalities has been quite slow. Although several approaches have been proposed to recognize human emotions based on facial expressions or speech, relatively limited work has been done to fuse these two and other modalities to improve the accuracy and robustness of the emotion recognition system [3]. Specifically, in the area of unimodal emotion recognition, there have been many studies using different, but single, modalities. Facial expressions [19, 24], vocal features [6, 25], body movements and postures [4, 2], physiological signals [23] have been used as inputs during these attempts, while multimodal emotion recognition is currently gaining ground [21, 3].

Nevertheless, most of the works consider the integration of information from facial expressions and speech and there are only a few attempts to combine information from body movement and gestures in a multimodal framework. Gunes and Piccardi [14], for example, fused at different levels facial expressions and body gestures information for bimodal emotion recognition. Further, el Kaliouby and Robinson [16] proposed a vision-based computational model to infer acted mental states from head movements and facial expressions. So far the problem of emotion recognition through multiple modalities in human-computer interaction has been approached by other mathematical methods. A lot of them have been described in a comprehensive review of the field made in [17]. Such methods include rule-based systems, discriminate analysis, fuzzy rules, case-based and instance-based learning, linear and nonlinear regression, neural networks, Bayesian learning, Hidden Markov Models, Bayesian networks etc. However, multi-criteria decision making methods have not been used yet in the problem of affect recognition through multiple modalities.

In view of the above, it is our aim to improve the accuracy of visual-facial emotion recognition by assisting it with information from other modalities. In this paper, we are considering assisting the visual-facial modality with keyboard-stroke pattern information. Currently, a system that combines two modalities, namely keyboard-stroke pattern information and audio-lingual information, has been already constructed and is described briefly in [1]. Towards combining keyboard-stroke patterns and the visual-facial modality, we had to determine the extent to which these two different modalities can provide emotion recognition independently. Moreover, we had to specify the strengths and weaknesses of each modality. In this way, we could determine the weights of the criteria that correspond to the respective modalities from the perspective of a human observer. In previous work of ours, we conducted empirical studies involving human subjects and human observers concerning the recognition of emotions from keyboard-stroke patterns and visual-facial modalities and presented the results from their combination [35]. In this paper, we present the results from combining the visual-facial modality with keyboard-stroke pattern information and discuss the advantages that derive from their combination. Specifically, in Section 2, we briefly present our facial expression recognition system, which constitutes the visual-facial modality and present evaluation results regarding its recognition accuracy. In Section 3, we present our keyboard-stroke pattern information-based emotion recognition system and evaluate its performance. In Section 4, we combine the two emotion recognition modalities. Finally we draw conclusions and point to future work, in Section 5.

2 Visual - Facial Affect Recognition Modality

2.1 Facial Expression Database

Since our search in the literature and World Wide Web didn't result to a complete facial expression database we built our own facial expression database. The process of acquiring image data and building this database is described extensively in [32]. The final dataset consisted of 250 different persons, each forming the seven expressions: "neutral", "happy", "sad", "surprised", "angry"', "disgusted" and "bored-sleepy".

2.2 Feature Description

¿From the collected dataset, we identified differences between the "neutral" expression of a model and its deformation into other expressions. This led us to the identification of the some important facial features [32], that can represent these changes in mathematical terms, so as to form the feature vector. These facial points are widely used in facial processing systems and they can help us in the in the computation of the facial features which will be used as an input to the classifiers. The aim of feature extraction process is to convert pixel data into a higher-level representation of shape, motion, color, texture and spatial configuration of the face and its components. Specifically, we locate and extract the corner points of specific regions of the face, such as the eyes, the mouth and the eyebrows, and compute variations in size or orientation from the "neutral" expression to another one. Also, we extract specific regions of the face, such us the forehead or the region between the eyebrows, so as to compute variations in texture. Namely, the extracted features are:

- Mouth Ratio
- Left Eye Ratio
- Right Eye Ratio
- Head ratio
- Texture of the chin: Measurement of the changes of the texture of the chin compared to 'neutral' expression
- Texture of the region between the eyebrows: Measurement of the changes of the texture f the region between the eyebrows compared to 'neutral' expression
- Texture of the left cheek: Measurement of the changes of the texture of the left cheek compared to 'neutral' expression
- Texture of the right cheek: Measurement of the changes of the texture of the right cheek compared to 'neutral' expression
- Texture of the forehead: Measurement of the changes of the texture of the forehead compared to 'neutral' expression
- Mouth Orientation: Measurement of the changes of the orientation of the mouth compared to 'neutral' expression
- Left Brow Orientation: Measurement of the changes of the orientation of the left brow compared to 'neutral' expression
- Right Brow Orientation: Measurement of the changes of the orientation of the right brow compared to 'neutral' expression

The above features form the resulting feature vector which is fed to the classifiers for training and testing as we describe in the next Section. The feature extraction process and systems results are analyzed and presented for various stages of the development of our system in [26], [27], [30], [29], [28], [31], [33].

2.3 Neural Network Architecture

In order to classify facial expressions, we developed a two layer artificial neural network which is fed with the input data: (1) mouth dimension ratio, (2) mouth orientation, (3) left eye dimension ratio, (4) right eye dimension ratio, (5) measurement of the texture of the left cheek, (6) measurement of the texture of the right cheek, (7) left eye brow direction, (8) right eye brow direction, (9) face dimension ratio, (10) measurement of the texture of the forehead, (11) measurement of the texture of the region between the brows, and, (12) measurement of the texture of the chin. The network produces a 7-dimensional output vector which can be regarded as the degree of membership of the face image in each of the 'neutral', 'happiness', 'surprise', 'anger', 'disgust-disapproval', 'sadness' and 'boredom-sleepiness' classes. An illustration of the network architecture can be seen in Figure 1. The neural network based facial expression recognition system, is called **NEU-FACES** [31, 33, 34].

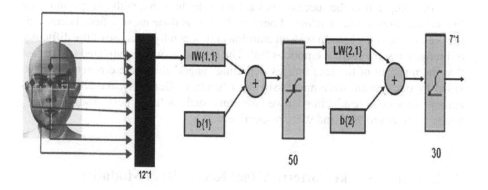

Fig. 1 The Facial Expression Neural Network Classifier

2.4 Classification Performance Assessment

The System managed to classify the emotion's based on a person's face quite satisfactory. The neural network was trained with a dataset of 230 subjects forming the 7 emotion classes, in total of 1610 face images. We tested the classifier with the rest 20 subjects forming the 7 facial expressions corresponding to 7 equivalent emotions, which formed a total of 140 images. The results are summarized in Table 1. In the three first columns we show the results from our empirical studies to humans, specifically the first part of the questionnaire in the first column, the second part in the second column and the mean success rate in the third. In the fourth column we depict the success rate of our neural network based facial expression recognition system for the corresponding emotion.

Table 1 Results of the Facial Expression Classification System Compared to Human Classifiers

Emotions	Questionaire results	NEU-FACES System Results
Neutral	61,74%	100%
Happiness	82,57%	90%
Sadness	58,33%	60%
Disgust	16,19%	65%
Boredom-Sleepiness	64,39%	75%
Anger	72,92%	55%
Surprise	92,61%	95%

As we can observe, the NEU-FACES achieved higher success rates in most of the emotion compared to the success rates achieved by humans, with exception to the 'anger' emotion, where it achieved only 55%. This is done mostly, first, because of the pretence we may have in such an emotion and, secondly, because of the difficulty of humans to show such an emotions full. The second is further validated by the fact that the majority of the face images depicting 'anger' that were erroneously classified by our system, were misclassified as 'neutral'. Generally, the NEU-FACES achieve very good results in positive emotions, such as 'happiness' and 'surprise', where he achieved 90% and 95%, respectively.

3 Keyboard-Stroke Pattern Affect Recognition Modality

3.1 Overview of the System

In this section, the overall functionality and emotion recognition features of our system, Edu-Affe-Mikey is described. The architecture of Edu-Affe-Mikey consists of the main educational application with the presentation of theory and tests, a programmable human-like animated agent, a monitoring user modeling component and a database. While using the educational application from a desktop computer, students are being taught a particular medical course. The information is given in text form while at the same time the animated agent reads it out loud using a speech engine. The student can choose a specific part of the human body and all the available information is retrieved from the systems' database. In particular, the main application is installed either on a public computer where all students have access, or alternatively each student may have a copy on his/her own personal computer. An example of using the main application is illustrated in Figure 2. The animated agent is present in these modes to make the interaction more human-like.

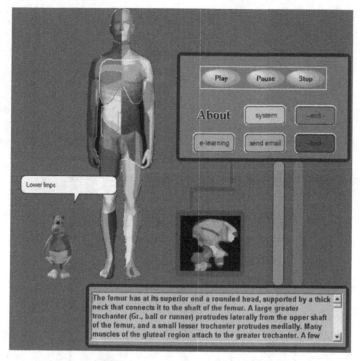

Fig. 2 A screen-shot of theory presentation in Edu-Affe-Mikey educational application

While the users interact with the main educational application and for the needs of emotion recognition a monitoring component records the actions of users from the keyboard and the microphone. These actions are then processed in conjunction with the multi-criteria model and interpreted in terms of emotions. The basic function of the monitoring component is to capture all the data inserted by the user either orally or by using the keyboard and the mouse of the computer. The data is recorded to a database and the results are returned to the basic application the user interacts with. Figure 3 illustrates the "monitoring" component that records the user's input and the exact time of each event.

Instructors have also the ability to manipulate the agents' behaviour with regard to the agents' on screen movements and gestures, as well as speech attributes such as speed, volume and pitch. Instructors may programmatically interfere to the agent's behaviour and the agent's reactions regarding the agents' approval or disapproval of a user's specific actions. This adaptation aims at enhancing the "affectiveness" of the whole interaction. Therefore, the system is enriched with an agent capable to express emotions and, as a result, enforces the user's temper to interact with more noticeable evidence in his/her behaviour.

Figure 4 illustrates a form where an instructor may change speech attributes. Within this context the instructor may create and store for future use many kinds of voice tones such as happy tone, angry tone, whisper and many others depending on

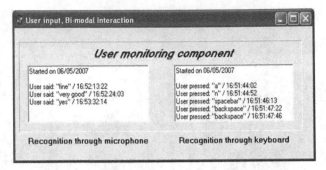

Fig. 3 Snapshot of operation of the user modeling component

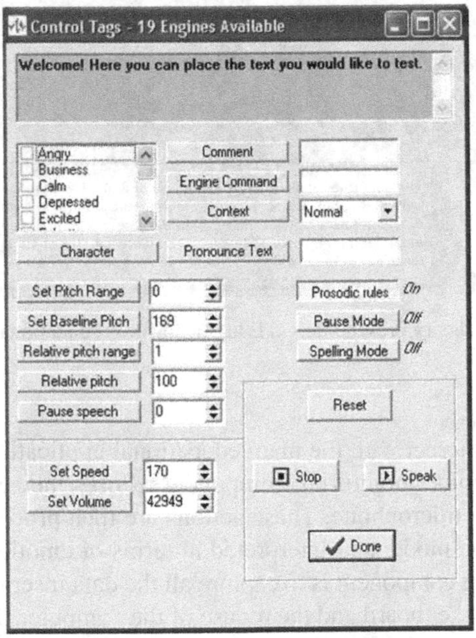

Fig. 4 Setting parameters for the voice of the tutoring character

the need of a specific affective agent-user interaction. In some cases a user's actions may be rewarded with a positive message by the agent accompanied by a smile and a happy tone in the agent's voice, while in other cases a more austere behaviour may be desirable for educational needs. Figure 5 illustrates how an instructor may set possible actions for the agent in specific interactive situations while a user takes a test.

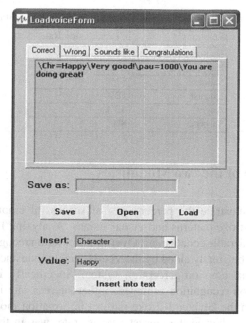

Fig. 5 Programming the behaviour of animated agents depending on particular students' actions

3.2 Evaluation of the System

In this section we present and compare results of successful emotion recognition in audio mode, keyboard mode and the two modes combined. For the purposes of our study the whole interaction of all users with the educational application was video recorded. Then the videos collected were presented to the users that participated to the experiment in order to perform emotion recognition for themselves with regard to the six emotional states, namely happiness, sadness, surprise, anger, disgust and the neutral emotional state. The participants as observers were asked to justify the recognition of an emotion by indicating the criteria that s/he had used in terms of the audio mode and keyboard actions. Whenever a participant recognized an emotional state, the emotion was marked and stored as data in the system's database. Finally, after the completion of the empirical study, the data were compared with the systems' corresponding hypothesis in each case an emotion was detected. Table 2 illustrates the percentages of successful emotion recognition of each mode after the incorporation of modes' weights and the combination through the proposed multi-criteria approach.

Table 2 Results of the Keyboard-stroke patterns mode for emotion recognition

Emotions	Classification Rate
Neutral	32%
Happiness	39%
Sadness	34%
Disgust	12%
Anger	42%
Surprise	8%

4 Combination of the two Modalities

In Figure 6, we illustrate the percentages of successful emotional recognition through keyboard-stroke patterns and visual means. Analyzing Figure 6, we may come up with considerable conclusions. Overall the emotion recognition by keyboard-stroke patterns can be greatly aided by the visual-facial mode and lead to the development of a bimodal emotion perception system. Specifically, in most cases, the visual-facial emotion recognition achieved higher success rate in recognizing the emotion rather than the keyboard-stroke pattern information mode. The only case that the two modes achieved the closest success rate, was in the presence of the emotion of 'anger'. In this case, their combination can lead to better results. The two modes are complementary in a high degree while in other cases where both have high or low percentages of successful emotion recognition we still have gaining since we improve the probability of emotion recognition by adding emotion recognition data from the two modalities.

Overall, based on these results, when combining the outputs from each modality, a greater degree of confidence should be given to the recognition rate by the visual-facial modality rather than the keyboard-stroke patterns modality, in the occurrence of the majority of emotions. An exemption to this case may be occurred in the presence of the emotion of 'anger', where the output of the two modalities should be handled in equal terms.

5 Conclusions - Future Work

In this paper we have described and discussed the results of two systems that concern the keyboard-stroke patterns and the visual-facial recognition of human users' emotions. These two systems can be combined towards the development of a bi-modal affective computer system that can perform affect recognition taking into account the strengths and weaknesses of each modality. ¿From the results of the modes, we found that the keyboard-stroke patterns emotion recognition modality can be greatly aided by the visual-facial modality. emotion states, usually the states that contain 'negative' emotions, , such as 'anger', 'sadness' and 'disgust', are equally recognized from the two modes. On the other hand, positive emotion states, such as

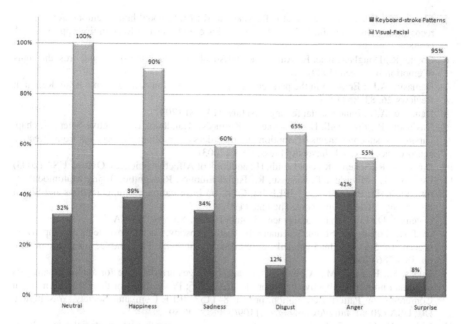

Fig. 6 Combining the two modalities

the 'happiness' and the 'surprise', are better recognized by the visual-facial mode. There is ongoing research of construction of an affective user interface that will use the different modalities as criteria for recognition of emotions and will use the results of performances for each modality as the basis for the specification of weights. This and other related work is going to be presented in a future publication.

References

1. Alepis, E., Virvou, M., Kabassi, K.: Affective student modeling based on microphone and keyboard user actions. In: ICALT '06: Proceedings of the Sixth IEEE International Conference on Advanced Learning Technologies, pp. 139–141. IEEE Computer Society, Washington, DC, USA (2006)
2. Berthouze, B.N., Kleinsmith, A.: A categorical approach to affective gesture recognition. Connection Science **15**(4), 259–269 (2003). http://eprints.ucl.ac.uk/3368/
3. Busso, C., Deng, Z., Yildirim, S., Bulut, M., Lee, C.M., Kazemzadeh, A., Lee, S., Neumann, U., Narayanan, S.: Analysis of emotion recognition using facial expressions, speech and multimodal information. In: ICMI '04: Proceedings of the 6th international conference on Multimodal interfaces, pp. 205–211. ACM, New York, NY, USA (2004). http://doi.acm.org/10.1145/1027933.1027968
4. Camurri, A., Lagerlöf, I., Volpe, G.: Recognizing emotion from dance movement: comparison of spectator recognition and automated techniques. Int. J. Hum.-Comput. Stud. **59**(1-2), 213–225 (2003). http://dx.doi.org/10.1016/S1071-5819(03)00050-8

5. Chen, L.S., Huang, T.S., Miyasato, T., Nakatsu, R.: Multimodal human emotion/expression recognition. In: Proc. Int'l Conf. Automatic Face and Gesture Recognition, pp. 366–371 (1998)

6. Cowie, R., Douglas-cowie, E.: Automatic statistical analysis of the signal and prosodic signs of emotion in speech (1989)

7. Damasio, A.R.: Emotion in the perspective of an integrated nervous system. Brain Research Reviews **26**, 83–86 (1998)

8. Damasio, A.R.: Fundamental feelings. Nature **413**, 781 (2001)

9. Davidson, R., Pizzagalli, D., Nitschke, J., Kalin, N.: Handbook of Affective Sciences, chap. Parsing the subcomponents of emotion and disorders of emotion: perspectives from affective neuroscience. Oxford University Press, USA (2003)

10. Davidson, R., Scherer, K., Goldsmith, H.: andbook of Affective Sciences. Oxford, USA (2003)

11. De Silva, L., Miyasato, T., Nakatsu, R.: Facial Emotion Recognition Using Multimodal Information. In: Proceedings of IEEE Int. Conf. on Information, Communications and Signal Processing - ICICS. Singapore, Thailand (1997)

12. Goleman, D.: Emotional Intelligence. Bantam Books, New York, USA

13. Graf, H., Cosatto, E., Strom, V., Huang, F.: Visual prosody: Facial movements accompanying speech. In: 5th IEEE International Conference on Automatic Face and Gesture Recognition, pp. 381–386 (2002)

14. Gunes, H., Piccardi, M.: A bimodal face and body gesture database for automatic analysis of human nonverbal affective behavior. In: ICPR '06: Proceedings of the 18th International Conference on Pattern Recognition, pp. 1148–1153. IEEE Computer Society, Washington, DC, USA (2006). http://dx.doi.org/10.1109/ICPR.2006.39

15. Isbister, K., Hook, K.: Evaluating affective interactions (introduction to special issue). International journal of human-computer studies **65**(4), 273–274 (2007)

16. Kaliouby, R., Robinson, P.: Generalization of a vision-based computational model of mind-reading. pp. 582–589 (2005). 10.1007/11573548_75. http://dx.doi.org/10.1007/11573548_75

17. Liao, W., Zhang, W., Zhu, Z., Ji, Q., Gray, W.D.: Toward a decision-theoretic framework for affect recognition and user assistance. Int. J. Hum.-Comput. Stud. **64**(9), 847–873 (2006). http://dx.doi.org/10.1016/j.ijhcs.2006.04.001

18. Oviatt, S.: User-centered modeling and evaluation of multimodal interfaces. IEEE Proceedings **91**(B), 1457–1468 (2003)

19. Pantic, M., Rothkrantz, L.J.M.: Automatic analysis of facial expressions: the state of the art. IEEE Transactions on Pattern Analysis and Machine Intelligence **22**, 1424–1445 (2000)

20. Pantic, M., Rothkrantz, L.J.M.: Toward an affect-sensitive multimodal human-computer interaction. In: Proceedings of the IEEE, pp. 1370–1390 (2003)

21. Pantic, M., Rothkrantz, L.J.M.: Toward an affect-sensitive multimodal human-computer interaction. Proceedings of the IEEE **91**(9), 1370–1390 (2003). 10.1109/JPROC.2003.817122

22. Picard, R.: Affective computing: challenges. Internationa Journal of Human-Computer Studies **59**(1-2), 55–64 (2003). 10.1016/S1071-5819(03)00052-1

23. Picard, R.W., Vyzas, E., Healey, J.: Toward machine emotional intelligence: Analysis of affective physiological state. IEEE Transactions on Pattern Analysis and Machine Intelligence **23**, 1175–1191 (2001)

24. Pierrakos, D., Papatheodorou, G.P.C., Spyropoulos, C.: Web usage mining as a tool for personalization: A survey. User Modeling and User Adapted Interaction **13**(4), 311–372 (2003)

25. Scherer, K.R.: Adding the affective dimension: A new look in speech analysis and synthesis. pp. 1808–1811 (1996)

26. Stathopoulou, I.O., Tsihrintzis, G.: A neural network-based facial analysis system. In: Proceedings of the 5th International Workshop on Image Analysis for Multimedia Interactive Services. Lisboa, Portugal (2004)

27. Stathopoulou, I.O., Tsihrintzis, G.: An Improved Neural Network-Based Face Detection and Facial Expression Classification System. In: IEEE International Conference on Systems, Man, and Cybernetics. The Hague, Netherlands (2004)

28. Stathopoulou, I.O., Tsihrintzis, G.: Detection and Expression Classification Systems for Face Images (FADECS). In: Proceedings of the IEEE Workshop on Signal Processing Systems (SiPS05). Athens, Greece (2005)
29. Stathopoulou, I.O., Tsihrintzis, G.: Evaluation of the Discrimination Power of Features Extracted from 2-D and 3-D Facial Images for Facial Expression Analysis. In: Proceedings of the 13th European Signal Processing Conference. Antalya, Turkey (2005)
30. Stathopoulou, I.O., Tsihrintzis, G.: Pre-processing and expression classification in low quality face images. In: Proceedings of 5th EURASIP Conference on Speech and Image Processing, Multimedia Communications and Services (2005)
31. Stathopoulou, I.O., Tsihrintzis, G.: An Accurate Method for eye detection and feature extraction in face color images. In: Proceedings of the 13th International Conference on Signals, Systems, and Image Processing. Budapest, Hungary (2006)
32. Stathopoulou, I.O., Tsihrintzis, G.: Facial Expression Classification: Specifying Requirements for an Automated System. In: Proceedings of the 10th International Conference on Knowledge-Based Intelligent Information Engineering Systems, LNAI: Vol. 4252, pp. 1128–1135. Springer-Verlag, Berlin, Heidelberg (2006). http://dx.doi.org/10.1007/11893004
33. Stathopoulou, I.O., Tsihrintzis, G.A.: Neu-faces: A neural network-based face image analysis system. In: ICANNGA '07: Proceedings of the 8th international conference on Adaptive and Natural Computing Algorithms, Part II, LNCS: Vol. 4432, pp. 449–456. Springer-Verlag, Berlin, Heidelberg (2007). http://dx.doi.org/10.1007/978-3-540-71629-7₅1
34. Stathopoulou, I.O., Tsihrintzis, G.A.: Comparative performance evaluation of artificial neural network-based vs. human facial expression classifiers for facial expression recognition. In: KES-IMSS 2008: 1st International Symposium on Intelligent Interactive Multimedia Systems and Services, SCI: Vol. 142, pp. 55–65. Springer-Verlag, Berlin, Heidelberg (2008). http://dx.doi.org/10.1007/978-3-540-68127-4
35. Virvou, M., Tsihrintzis, G.A., Alepis, E., Stathopoulou, I.O., Kabassi, K.: Combining empirical studies of audio-lingual and visual-facial modalities for emotion recognition. In: KES '07: Knowledge-Based Intelligent Information and Engineering Systems and the XVII Italian Workshop on Neural Networks on Proceedings of the 11th International Conference, LNAI: Vol. 4693, pp. 1130–1137. Springer-Verlag, Berlin, Heidelberg (2007). http://dx.doi.org/10.1007/978-3-540-74827-4₁41

Feature Selection for Wheat Yield Prediction

Georg Ruß, Rudolf Kruse

Abstract Carrying out effective and sustainable agriculture has become an important issue in recent years. Agricultural production has to keep up with an ever-increasing population by taking advantage of a field's heterogeneity. Nowadays, modern technology such as the global positioning system (GPS) and a multitude of developed sensors enable farmers to better measure their fields' heterogeneities. For this small-scale, precise treatment the term *precision agriculture* has been coined. However, the large amounts of data that are (literally) harvested during the growing season have to be analysed. In particular, the farmer is interested in knowing whether a newly developed heterogeneity sensor is potentially advantageous or not. Since the sensor data are readily available, this issue should be seen from an artificial intelligence perspective. There it can be treated as a *feature selection* problem. The additional task of yield prediction can be treated as a multi-dimensional regression problem. This article aims to present an approach towards solving these two practically important problems using artificial intelligence and data mining ideas and methodologies.

1 Introduction

In the recent past, it has become obvious that agriculture is playing a crucial role for sustaining the economy and population growth. In industrialised as well as in developing countries, improvements can be made by introducing modern GPS and advanced sensor technology to make use of a field's heterogeneity. Since this heterogeneity implies a small-scale, precise crop treatment, the term *precision agriculture* has been introduced. According to [34], precision agriculture is the sampling,

Georg Ruß, Rudolf Kruse
Otto-von-Guericke-Univ. Magdeburg, Germany e-mail: {russ,kruse}@iws.cs.uni-magdeburg.de

M. Bramer et al. (eds.), *Research and Development in Intelligent Systems XXVI*,
DOI 10.1007/978-1-84882-983-1_36, © Springer-Verlag London Limited 2010

mapping, analysis and management of production areas that recognises the spatial variability of the cropland.

In artificial intelligence terms, the area of precision agriculture (PA) is quite an interesting one as it involves methods and algorithms from numerous areas that the artificial intelligence community has been dealing with extensively. When analysing the data flow that results from using PA, one is quickly reminded of *data mining*: an agriculturist collects data from his cropland (e.g., when fertilising or harvesting) and would like to extract information from those data and use this information to his (economic) advantage. Obviously, he is also interested in knowing whether a particular sensor which has been introduced will eventually be of use to him in terms of predicting current year's yield precisely.

Two major parts emerge from the above issue: deciding whether a sensor is useful for yield prediction is actually a feature selection task; and the necessary yield prediction turns out to be a multi-dimensional regression problem. Both parts have been studied extensively in AI and numerous approaches exist.

1.1 Research Target and Article Structure

With this contribution we aim at developing a suitable approach to evaluate sensor data. We are interested in identifying those sensors which are most applicable for measuring a field's heterogeneity. Here, a *good* sensor is supposed to improve the precision of yield prediction. Eventually, a feature selection approach shall be developed. Since existing work has mainly been devoted to using feature selection with a classification task, but not a regression task, this work is aimed at evaluating regression approaches. Furthermore, some more research will be devoted to finding a generally applicable regression model which is to be used in the feature selection approach.

In two ways, the feature selection approach taken here is novel: first, the application area of precision agriculture data is certainly a new one. Second, feature selection has mainly been used for classification tasks instead of regression tasks.

Our previous work in this area has been focused on either evaluating regression models ([26], [27], [29]) or visualising the existing agriculture data [28]. Results from these articles will be incorporated into our feature selection approach where appropriate.

After a brief overview of the available data in Section 2, our feature selection approach will be presented in Section 3. The experimental layout and the results are presented in Section 4. In the end, a conclusion is given and future work is pointed out.

2 Data Description

The data available in this work have been obtained in the years 2003–2006 on three fields near Köthen, north of Halle, Germany[1]. All information available for these 65-, 72- and 32-hectare fields[2] was interpolated using kriging [32] to a grid with 10 by 10 meters grid cell sizes. Each grid cell represents a record with all available information. During the growing season of 2006, the latter field was subdivided into different strips, where various fertilization strategies were carried out. For an example of various managing strategies, see e.g. [30], which also shows the economic potential of PA technologies quite clearly. The field grew winter wheat, where nitrogen fertilizer was distributed over three application times during the growing season.

Overall, for each field there are seven input attributes – accompanied by the respective current year's yield (2004 or 2006) as the target attribute. Those attributes will be described in the following. In total, for the F04 field there are 5241 records, for F131 there are 2278 records, for F330 there are 4578 records, thereof none with missing values and none with outliers.

2.1 Nitrogen Fertilizer – N1, N2, N3

The amount of fertilizer applied to each subfield can be easily measured. It is applied at three points in time into the vegetation period, which is the standard strategy for most of Northwest Europe [22].

2.2 Vegetation – REIP32, REIP49

The *red edge inflection point* (REIP) is a second derivative value calculated along the red edge region of the spectrum, which is situated from 680 to 750nm. Dedicated REIP sensors are used in-season to measure the plants' reflection in this spectral band. Since the plants' chlorophyll content is assumed to highly correlate with the nitrogen availability (see, e.g. [20]), the REIP value allows for deducing the plants' state of nutrition and thus, the previous crop growth. For further information on certain types of sensors and a more detailed introduction, see [16] or [33]. Plants that have less chlorophyll will show a lower REIP value as the red edge moves toward the blue part of the spectrum. On the other hand, plants with more chlorophyll will have higher REIP values as the red edge moves toward the higher wavelengths. For the range of REIP values encountered in the available data, see Tables 1(b) and 1(c). The numbers in the REIP32 and REIP49 names refer to the growing stage of winter wheat, as defined in [18].

---

[1] GPS: Latitude N 51 40.430, Longitude E 11 58.110
[2] We will call them *F04*, *F330* and *F131*, respectively

2.3 Electric Conductivity – EM38

A non-invasive method to discover and map a field's heterogeneity is to measure the soil's conductivity. Commercial sensors such as the EM-38[3] are designed for agricultural use and can measure small-scale conductivity to a depth of about 1.5 metres. There is no possibility of interpreting these sensor data directly in terms of its meaningfulness as yield-influencing factor. But in connection with other site-specific data, as explained in the rest of this section, there could be coherences. For a more detailed analysis of this particular sensor, see, e.g. [6]. For the range of EM values encountered in the available data, see Tables 1(a) to 1(c).

2.4 YIELD

Here, yield is measured in metric tons per hectare ($\frac{t}{ha}$) For the yield ranges for the respective years and sites, see Tables 1(b) and 1(c). It should be noted that for the F131 and F330 data sets the yield was reduced significantly due to bad weather conditions (lack of rain) during the growing season 2006.

2.5 TRACFORCE

The tractive force (or tractive effort) sensor measures the force that has to be exerted when a plough or similar (modern) devices are pulled along the field. Hence, it is assumed that the upper soil layer and its condition may have an effect on the final yield. This sensor is only available in the F04 data set.

2.6 Data Overview

In this work, we evaluate data sets from three different fields. A brief summary of the available data attributes for both data sets is given in Tables 1(a) to 1(c).

2.7 Points of Interest

It would be interesting to see how much the influencable factor "fertilization" really influences the yield in the current site-year. Furthermore, at the core of this article, we are interested in finding out which sensor data are actually useful for the purpose

---

[3] trademark of Geonics Ltd, Ontario, Canada

Table 1: Overview of the F04, F131 and F330 data sets

(a) Data overview, F04

F04	*min*	*max*	*mean*	*std*
YIELD03	1.19	12.38	6.27	1.48
EM38	17.97	86.45	33.82	5.27
N1	0	100	57.7	13.5
N2	0	100	39.9	16.4
N3	0	100	38.5	15.3
REIP32	721.1	727.2	725.7	0.64
REIP49	722.4	729.6	728.1	0.65
YIELD04	6.42	11.37	9.14	0.73

(b) Data overview, F131

F131	*min*	*max*	*mean*	*std*
YIELD05	1.69	10.68	5.69	0.93
EM38	51.58	84.08	62.21	8.60
N1	47.70	70	64.32	6.02
N2	14.80	100	51.71	15.67
N3	0	70	39.65	13.73
REIP32	719.6	724.4	722.6	0.69
REIP49	722.3	727.9	725.8	0.95
YIELD06	1.54	8.83	5.21	0.88

(c) Data overview, F330

F330	*min*	*max*	*mean*	*std*
YIELD05	4.64	14.12	10.62	0.97
EM38	25.08	49.48	33.69	2.94
N1	24.0	70	59.48	14.42
N2	3.0	100	56.38	13.35
N3	0.3	91.6	50.05	12.12
REIP32	719.2	724.4	721.5	1.03
REIP49	723.0	728.5	726.9	0.82
YIELD06	1.84	8.27	5.90	0.54

of yield prediction. There may be data attributes which are irrelevant and others which may be highly relevant. This *feature selection* problem will be described in the following section.

3 Feature Selection Approach

This section deals with the developed feature selection approach. First, according to the literature, some decisions have to be made regarding the type and general structure of feature selection. The ensuing section presents a suitable algorithm, of which the details will be presented. The feature selection algorithm incorporates a regression task, therefore regression models will be presented. Additionally, the details of error measurement are shown.

3.1 Approach Justification

In the data encountered here, the main reason for applying data mining techniques is that the interesting features are hidden in a search space of high dimensionality.

Reducing the dimensionality of the data could be done via sampling or otherwise discarding data records, but in our case this would render the precision agriculture approach useless. Therefore, the actual features of the data should be condensed to those that are most promising for a yield prediction task. Hence, feature selection eventually is a means of removing irrelevant and/or redundant features.

According to [15], the selection of features can be achieved in two ways. The first one is to evaluate and rank features according to some criterion. The other one is to select a minimal subset of features without deteriorating learning performance. The latter approach can usually be run automatically, while the first one provides reasonable guidance to an expert user. Since the data analysis task in this work is not aimed at the average user, but should preferably contribute insights into the data for professionals, the "evaluate-and-rank"-approach will be pursued in the following.

Once we have decided for evaluating and subsequently ranking features, there are still a multitude of options to select the most promising features. There are quite a few surveys which aim to categorise existing approaches, such as [1], [2], [8], [14]. One of the categories is usually how the search for features is conducted: *forward selection* starts with an empty set and keeps adding features until a stopping criterion is met. *Backward elimination* starts with a set including all features and subsequently keeps removing features. Obviously, both cases could also yield a ranked list of features. Since both approaches have their advantages and drawbacks, but backward elimination is computationally heavier, we decided to employ forward selection and leave backward elimination for future work.

A second category is how the feature space is traversed in the search for features to exclude or include. Doing a complete search is the straightforward option, but should usually be avoided due to computational constraints. Heuristic search may miss optimal subsets, but generates good solutions quickly with a certain probability depending on the heuristic used. Non-deterministic search randomly explores the feature space, obviously limited by the available computational resources. Since this work is the first to evaluate whether feature selection may be a successful approach to decide which agricultural sensor data are useful, we simply employ a complete search. This is possible since the number of features in the available data sets is small. In future work, different search strategies will be evaluated.

A third decision to be made is whether to use a *filter* or *wrapper* approach. The earlier one does not depend on the actual induction (regression) algorithm for evaluating the generated subsets. On the contrary, the wrapper approach explicitly uses the induction method (e.g. a regression tree) for evaluating the subset. For a more detailed explanation, we refer to e.g. [13]. In the following work, we consider the wrapper approach because it also enables a comparison of the used regression techniques. A similar approach is taken by, e.g. [12].

3.2 Selection and Regression Approach

As mentioned in the previous section, we decided to use forward selection. A possible implementation is given in Algorithm 1. The algorithm works in a straightforward way: starting with an empty list of features S, and a list of all features F, it repeatedly moves the *best* features for the regression task from F to S. This series of steps is repeated until a regression error goal is met or F is empty.

Algorithm 1 *forward selection* of features

1: $S = [\,]$, F ← features
2: **repeat**
3:    $E \leftarrow [\,]$
4:    **for** $j = 1 \ldots length(F)$ **do**
5:        $f \leftarrow F[j]$ {select j-th feature}
6:        $S_j \leftarrow S \cup f$ {add current feature to S_j}
7:        $M_j \leftarrow model(S_j)$ {generate regression model from data}
8:        $E_j \leftarrow evaluate(M_j)$ {calculate modeling error}
9:        $E \leftarrow E \| E_j$ {store error}
10:   **end for**
11:   $S \leftarrow S \| F[min(E)]$ {add best feature to S}
12:   $F \leftarrow F - F[min(E)]$ {remove best feature from F}
13: **until** min(E) $\leq$ threshold OR $F = [\,]$
14: **return** S {return list of features, best one first}

3.3 Regression Modeling

This subsection serves as an overview of different regression techniques which may be used on the agriculture data. A more thorough description can be found in, e.g., [26]. Since the focus here is on feature selection, two of the four models presented in [26] are chosen, namely regression trees and support vector regression. On the one hand, the latter technique turned out to be the one that performed best on different data sets. On the other hand, regression trees convey a lot of understandability which might yield further insights into the data, hence they have been chosen here.

The regression task can be formalized as follows: the training set

$$T = \{\{x_1,\ldots,x_n\},y_i\}_{i=1}^{N} \tag{1}$$

is considered for the training process, where $x_i, i = 1,\ldots,n$ are continuous input values and $y_i, i = 1\ldots,N$ are continuous output values. Given this training set, the task of the regression techniques is to approximate the underlying function sufficiently well. The quality of the approximated function can be measured by error values.

Regression trees have seen some usage in agriculture [7, 11, 17]. Essentially, they are a special case of decision trees where the outcome (in the tree leaves) is a continuous function instead of a discrete classification. Further details can be found in section 3.3.1.

A technique that has, to the best of our knowledge, not been used on similar yield data, but for similar regression tasks, is a derivative of support vector machines (SVMs). Similar to decision trees, if the target attribute is discrete, SVMs would solve a classification task, whereas in the case of a continuous attribute, a regression task would be solved. Hence, support vector regression (SVR) will be explained in section 3.3.2.

3.3.1 Regression Tree

Regression trees approximate learning instances by sorting them down the tree from the root to some leaf node, which provides the value of the target attribute. Each node in the tree represents a split of some attribute of the instance and each branch descending from that node corresponds to one part left or right of the split. The value of the target attribute for an instance is determined by starting at the root node of the tree and testing the attribute specified by this node. This determines whether to proceed left or right of the split. Then we move down the tree and repeat the procedure with the respective subtree. In principle, there could be more than one split in a tree node, which would result in more than two subtrees per node. However, in this application scenario, we do not consider regression trees with more than two subtrees per split node.

Regression as well as decision trees are usually constructed in a top-down, greedy search approach through the space of possible trees [21]. The basic algorithms for constructing such trees are CART [4], ID3 [23] and its successor C4.5 [24]. The idea here is to ask the question "which attribute should be tested at the top of the tree?" To answer this question, each attribute is evaluated to determine how well it is suited to split the data. The best attribute is selected and used as the test node. This procedure is repeated for the subtrees. An attribute selection criterion that is employed by ID3 and C4.5 is the entropy and, resulting from it, the information gain. Entropy is a measure from information theory that describes the variety in a collection of data points: the higher the entropy, the higher the variety. In an attribute split we would like to lower the entropy of the two resulting split data sets. This reduction in entropy is called the information gain. For further information we refer to [21].

However, if the addition of nodes is continued without a specific stopping criterion, the depth of the tree continues to grow until each tree leaf covers one instance of the training data set. This is certainly a perfect tree for the training data but is likely to be too specific – the problem of overlearning occurs. For new, unseen data, such a specific tree will probably have a high prediction error. Therefore, regression trees are usually pruned to a specific depth which is a trade-off between high accuracy and high generality. This can easily be achieved by setting a lower bound for the number of instances covered by a single node below which no split should occur. For our work we used the R implementation of `rpart`.

3.3.2 Support Vector Regression

Support Vector Machines (SVMs) are a supervised learning method discovered by [3]. However, the task here is regression, so we focus on support vector regression (SVR) in the following. A more in-depth discussion can be found in [9]. Given the training set, the goal of SVR is to approximate a linear function $f(x) = \langle w, x \rangle + b$ with $w \in \mathbb{R}^N$ and $b \in \mathbb{R}$. This function minimizes an empirical risk function defined as

$$R_{emp} = \frac{1}{N} \sum_{i=1}^{N} L_{\varepsilon}(\hat{y} - f(x)), \tag{2}$$

where $L_{\varepsilon}(\hat{y} - f(x)) = \max((|\xi| - \varepsilon), 0)$. $|\xi|$ is the so-called slack variable, which has mainly been introduced to deal with otherwise infeasible constraints of the optimization problem, as has been mentioned in [31]. By using this variable, errors are basically ignored as long as they are smaller than a properly selected ε. The function here is called ε-insensitive loss function. Other kinds of functions can be used, some of which are presented in chapter 5 of [9].

To estimate $f(x)$, a quadratic problem must be solved, of which the dual form, according to [19] is as follows:

$$max_{\alpha, \alpha^*} - \frac{1}{2} \sum_{i=1}^{N} \sum_{j=1}^{N} (\alpha_i - \alpha_i^*)(\alpha_j - \alpha_j^*) K(x_i, x_j) - \varepsilon \sum_{i=j}^{N} (\alpha_i + \alpha_i^*) + \sum_{i=1}^{N} y_i(\alpha_i - \alpha_i^*) \tag{3}$$

with the constraint that $\sum_{j=1}^{N} (\alpha_i - \alpha_i^*) = 0, \alpha_i, \alpha_i^* \in [0, C]$. The regularization parameter $C > 0$ determines the tradeoff between the flatness of $f(x)$ and the allowed number of points with deviations larger than ε. As mentioned in [9], the value of ε is inversely proportional to the number of support vectors. An adequate setting of C and ε is necessary for a suitable solution to the regression problem.

Furthermore, $K(x_i, x_j)$ is known as a kernel function which allows to project the original data into a higher-dimensional feature space where it is much more likely to be linearly separable. Some of the most popular kernels are radial basis functions (equation 4) and a polynomial kernel (equation 5):

$$K(x, x_i) = e^{-\frac{\|x - x_i\|^2}{2\sigma^2}} \tag{4}$$

$$K(x, x_i) = (\langle x, x_i \rangle + 1)^p \tag{5}$$

The parameters σ and p have to be determined appropriately for the SVM to generalize well. This is usually done experimentally. Once the solution for the above optimization problem in equation 3 is obtained, the support vectors can be used to construct the regression function:

$$f(x) = \sum_{i=1}^{N} (\alpha_i - \alpha_i^*) K(x, x_i) + b \tag{6}$$

In our experiments, we used the R SVM interface to libsvm [5] with the `e1071` R package.

3.4 Performance Measurement

The performance of the models will be determined using the root mean squared error (RMSE). For the RMSE, first the difference between an actual target value y_a and the model output value y is computed. This difference is squared and averaged over all training examples before the root of the mean value is taken, see equation 7.

$$RMSE = \sqrt{\frac{1}{n} \sum_{i=j}^{n} (y_i - y_{a,i})^2} \tag{7}$$

In [26] it has been established that model parameters set for one data set may be carried over to a different data set. Hence, it is assumed that the RegTree and SVR parameters may be fixed. Nevertheless, although computationally heavy, a *complete search* feature selection strategy with an automatic fine-tuning of model parameters for the SVR and RegTree model has been used.

For training the models, a cross validation approach is taken. As mentioned in e.g. [10], the data will be split randomly into a training set and a test set. The model is trained using the training data and after each training iteration, the error on the test data is computed. During training, this error usually declines towards a minimum. Beyond this minimum, the error rises – overlearning (or overfitting) occurs: the model fits the training data perfectly but does not generalize well. Hence, the model training is stopped when the error on the test set starts rising. We use a size ratio of 9:1 for training and test set. The data sets are partitioned randomly 20 times, the models are trained and the error values are collected.

4 Experimental Results

The three data sets presented in Section 2 are evaluated here for the purpose of establishing whether a particular feature (sensor) is useful for yield prediction. The target attribute to predict via regression techniques is the respective current year's yield.

Two techniques have been selected: regression trees and support vector regression. 10-fold cross validation was applied for both techniques.

4.1 Feature Selection with RegTree

Regression trees were created using an auto-prune approach, which is similar to the grid search in the following section. A minimum split value of 30 is used, therefore leaves in the final tree will not contain more than 30 data observations for which the yield shall be predicted. An additional complexity parameter $cp = 0.001$ was set, which determines that a split must at least yield a prediction improvement of cp, otherwise it is not carried out.

As can be seen in Table 2, the predictive error of the regression tree decreases steadily as more predictors are added. This behaviour should be expected, since the regression tree receives more information to improve its predictive performance. However, after adding three or four features, the error seems almost to have leveled, which would imply that the remaining features are unnecessary for yield prediction. Generally, the REIP49 feature seems to be the one best suited for prediction. This should also be expected, since the measurement of REIP49 occurs late into the growing season when the crop is nearing harvest. In two out of the three data sets, the respective previous year's yield also seems to play an important role. Again, this should be expected, since areas with high/low yield are (without special treatment) bound to generate high/low yield in the following years as well. The EM38 measurement ranks third or fourth for the prediction task, even better than the REIP32 feature, which is a novel and important result. Even more useful might be the conclusion that N1 and N2, the dressings of fertilizer early into the growing season, do not bear significant amounts of information in regard to yield prediction within this feature selection approach.

Table 2: Results for Feature Selection via Regression Tree

step	F04 error	feature	F131 error	feature	F330 error	feature
1	0.342	YIELD03	0.235	REIP49	0.279	N3
2	0.262	REIP49	0.136	YIELD05	0.246	REIP49
3	0.228	N3	0.104	EM38	0.223	EM38
4	0.215	EM38	0.104	REIP32	0.199	REIP32
5	0.210	REIP32	0.104	N1	0.189	N1
6	0.209	TRACFORCE	0.104	N2	0.187	N2
7	0.208	N1	0.104	N3	0.181	YIELD05
8	0.205	N2				

4.2 Feature Selection with SVR

For support vector regression, a grid search in the parameter space within reasonable bounds has been performed when searching for the optimal regression parameters, using the svm.best() R routine. The regularization parameter C was set to vary between 2^3 and 2^7, the ε parameter between 0.5 and 2, while a radial kernel was used.

Table 3 shows the results for SVR. In each feature selection step the best model from this particular step was chosen. Due to the *complete search* approach, the prediction accuracy may decline from one step to the next. Nevertheless, SVR agrees with the RegTree that the REIP49 feature is the one bearing most predictive power since it is chosen in the first or second step. It also agrees on the predictive power in the respective previous year's yield, which ranks high in F04 and F131, but low in F330. N1 and N2 do not improve the prediction significantly. In addition, the overall prediction error levels are higher than with the simple regression tree. This might be due to the grid search approach for selecting the best SVR model in each step. This grid search optimized the most important SVR parameters, while more may be chosen. Nevertheless, SVR tends to produce comparable results.

Table 3: Results for Feature Selection via Support Vector Regression

step	F04 error	F04 feature	F131 error	F131 feature	F330 error	F330 feature
1	0.557	YIELD03	0.469	REIP49	0.491	N3
2	0.509	REIP49	0.356	YIELD05	0.493	REIP49
3	0.466	N2	0.337	N2	0.469	EM38
4	0.483	REIP32	0.335	N1	0.519	N2
5	0.449	N1	0.303	REIP32	0.454	N1
6	0.471	EM38	0.333	N3	0.508	YIELD05
7	0.444	N3	0.285	EM38	0.439	REIP32
8	0.469	TRACFORCE				

5 Conclusion

In this paper we presented a novel application of a feature selection approach by using it on agriculture data. We were interested in evaluating the data attributes with regard to their utility for yield prediction. The presented approach employs *forward feature selection* and a complete search strategy. With it, two regression models (SVR and RegTree) were used to compare the yield prediction results for the different data sets. Both the SVR and RegTree regression models produced slightly different, but yet comparable results. Nevertheless, on the one hand both models returned understandable and explicable feature rankings, while, on the other hand, providing novel knowledge about the data sets and their features. Hence, the presented feature selection approach presents an immediately useful application of artificial intelligence techniques and may be developed further.

5.1 Future Work

Future work will focus on evaluating additional feature selection approaches like the reverse process of *backward elimination*. Additional regression models are to be included. Furthermore, different approaches to judging the importance of certain features may be used, such as principal components analysis or clustering.

Acknowledgements The results in this work were generated using R [25]. The scripts can be obtained from the author's research site: http://research.georgruss.de.

References

1. A. Arauzo-Azofra and J. M. Benitez. Empirical study of feature selection methods in classification. In *Hybrid Intelligent Systems, 2008. HIS '08. Eighth International Conference on*, pages 584–589, 2008.
2. Avrim L. Blum and Pat Langley. Selection of relevant features and examples in machine learning. *Artificial Intelligence*, 97:245–271, 1997.
3. Bernhard E. Boser, Isabelle M. Guyon, and Vladimir N. Vapnik. A training algorithm for optimal margin classifiers. In *Proceedings of the 5th Annual ACM Workshop on Computational Learning Theory*, pages 144–152. ACM Press, 1992.
4. L. Breiman, J. Friedman, R. Olshen, and C. Stone. *Classification and Regression Trees*. Wadsworth and Brooks, Monterey, CA, 1984.
5. Chih-Chung Chang and Chih-Jen Lin. *LIBSVM: a library for support vector machines*, 2001. Software available at http://www.csie.ntu.edu.tw/ cjlin/libsvm.
6. D. L. Corwin and S. M. Lesch. Application of soil electrical conductivity to precision agriculture: Theory, principles, and guidelines. *Agron J*, 95(3):455–471, May 2003.
7. S. F. Crone, S. Lessmann, and S. Pietsch. Forecasting with computational intelligence - an evaluation of support vector regression and artificial neural networks for time series prediction. In *Neural Networks, 2006. IJCNN '06. International Joint Conference on*, pages 3159–3166, 2006.
8. M. Dash and H. Liu. Feature selection for classification. *Intelligent Data Analysis*, 1:131–156, 1997.
9. S.R. Gunn. Support vector machines for classification and regression. Technical Report, School of Electronics and Computer Science, University of Southampton, Southampton, U.K., 1998.
10. Robert Hecht-Nielsen. *Neurocomputing*. Addison-Wesley, September 1990.
11. Chengquan Huang, Limin Yang, Bruce Wylie, and Collin Homer. A strategy for estimating tree canopy density using landsat 7 etm+ and high resolution images over large areas. In *Proceedings of the Third International Conference on Geospatial Information in Agriculture and Forestry*, 2001.
12. M. Karagiannopoulos, D. Anyfantis, S. B. Kotsiantis, and P. E. Pintelas. Feature selection for regression problems. In *Proceedings of HERCMA'07*. Athens University of Economics and Business, September 2007.

13. Pat Langley. Selection of relevant features in machine learning. In *In Proceedings of the AAAI Fall symposium on relevance*, pages 140–144. AAAI Press, 1994.
14. H. Liu and L. Yu. Feature selection for data mining. Technical report, Arizona State University, 2002.
15. Huan Liu and Hiroshi Motoda, editors. *Computational Methods of Feature Selection*. Data Mining and Knowledge Discovery. Chapman & Hall/CRC, October 2007.
16. J. Liu, J. R. Miller, D. Haboudane, and E. Pattey. Exploring the relationship between red edge parameters and crop variables for precision agriculture. In *2004 IEEE International Geoscience and Remote Sensing Symposium*, volume 2, pages 1276–1279, 2004.
17. David B. Lobell, J. Ivan Ortiz-Monasterio, Gregory P. Asner, Rosamond L. Naylor, and Walter P. Falcon. Combining field surveys, remote sensing, and regression trees to understand yield variations in an irrigated wheat landscape. *Agronomy Journal*, 97:241–249, 2005.
18. U. Meier. *Entwicklungsstadien mono- und dikotyler Pflanzen*. Biologische Bundesanstalt fr Land- und Forstwirtschaft, Braunschweig, Germany, 2001.
19. Iván Mejía-Guevara and Ángel Kuri-Morales. Evolutionary feature and parameter selection in support vector regression. In *Lecture Notes in Computer Science*, volume 4827, pages 399–408. Springer, Berlin, Heidelberg, 2007.
20. E. M. Middleton, P. K. E. Campbell, J. E. Mcmurtrey, L. A. Corp, L. M. Butcher, and E. W. Chappelle. "Red edge" optical properties of corn leaves from different nitrogen regimes. In *2002 IEEE International Geoscience and Remote Sensing Symposium*, volume 4, pages 2208–2210, 2002.
21. Tom M. Mitchell. *Machine Learning*. McGraw-Hill Science/Engineering/Math, March 1997.
22. Jacques J. Neeteson. *Nitrogen Management for Intensively Grown Arable Crops and Field Vegetables*, chapter 7, pages 295–326. CRC Press, Haren, The Netherlands, 1995.
23. J. R. Quinlan. Induction of decision trees. *Machine Learning*, 1(1):81–106, March 1986.
24. Ross J. Quinlan. *C4.5: Programs for Machine Learning (Morgan Kaufmann Series in Machine Learning)*. Morgan Kaufmann, January 1993.
25. R Development Core Team. *R: A Language and Environment for Statistical Computing*. R Foundation for Statistical Computing, Vienna, Austria, 2009. ISBN 3-900051-07-0.
26. Georg Ruß. Data mining of agricultural yield data: A comparison of regression models. In Petra Perner, editor, *Advances in Data Mining*, Lecture Notes in Computer Science, pages –. Springer, July 2009. (to appear).
27. Georg Ruß, Rudolf Kruse, Martin Schneider, and Peter Wagner. Optimizing wheat yield prediction using different topologies of neural networks. In José Luis Verdegay, Manuel Ojeda-Aciego, and Luis Magdalena, editors, *Proceedings of IPMU-08*, pages 576–582. University of Málaga, June 2008.
28. Georg Ruß, Rudolf Kruse, Martin Schneider, and Peter Wagner. Visualization of agriculture data using self-organizing maps. In Tony Allen, Richard Ellis, and Miltos Petridis, editors, *Applications and Innovations in Intelligent Systems*, volume 16 of *Proceedings of AI-2008*, pages 47–60. BCS SGAI, Springer, January 2009.
29. Georg Ruß, Rudolf Kruse, Peter Wagner, and Martin Schneider. Data mining with neural networks for wheat yield prediction. In Petra Perner, editor, *Advances in Data Mining (Proc. ICDM 2008)*, pages 47–56, Berlin, Heidelberg, July 2008. Springer Verlag.
30. M. Schneider and P. Wagner. Prerequisites for the adoption of new technologies - the example of precision agriculture. In *Agricultural Engineering for a Better World*, Düsseldorf, 2006. VDI Verlag GmbH.
31. Alex J. Smola and Bernhard Sch Olkopf. A tutorial on support vector regression. Technical report, Statistics and Computing, 1998.
32. Michael L. Stein. *Interpolation of Spatial Data : Some Theory for Kriging (Springer Series in Statistics)*. Springer, June 1999.
33. Georg Weigert. *Data Mining und Wissensentdeckung im Precision Farming - Entwicklung von ökonomisch optimierten Entscheidungsregeln zur kleinräumigen Stickstoff-Ausbringung*. PhD thesis, TU München, 2006.
34. Michael D. Weiss. Precision farming and spatial economic analysis: Research challenges and opportunities. *American Journal of Agricultural Economics*, 78(5):1275–1280, 1996.

SHORT PAPERS

Method of Combining the Degrees of Similarity in Handwritten Signature Authentication Using Neural Networks

Ph. D. Student, Eng. Eusebiu Marcu

Abstract This paper introduces a new method of combining the degrees of similarity for a hand-written signature (also known as holographic signature or biometric signature) using neural networks. This method is used for a biometric authentication system after the degrees of similarity between a signature and it's reference template are computed. The degrees of similarity are defined using Levenstein distance of the handwritten signature's features. Using this method we achieved the following biometric performance metrics: FRR: 8.45% and FAR: 0.9%.

1 Introduction

As technology is evolving, the security threats also are evolving. Security refers to the response of a system when different types of attacks are launched on to. Biometric technology or biometrics "refers to methods for uniquely recognizing humans based upon one or more intrinsic physical or behavioral traits. In information technology, in particular, biometrics is used as a form of identity access management and access control" [1].

We propose a new authentication method for a biometric technology (handwritten signature) and compare our method with other similar methods.

1.1 Biometric Security

There are two main biometric categories: **physiological** - refers to the shape of the body - and **behavioral** - related to the behavior of a person. In the first category, are included DNA, iris recognition, fingerprint, hand and palm geometry, etc. In the

Ph. D. Student, Eng. Eusebiu Marcu
University Politehnica of Bucharest e-mail: marcueusebiu@gmail.com

M. Bramer et al. (eds.), *Research and Development in Intelligent Systems XXVI*,
DOI 10.1007/978-1-84882-983-1_37, © Springer-Verlag London Limited 2010

second one are included voice recognition, gait, signature and others. Performance of a biometric system is defined by the FAR and FRR metrics. FAR or false match rate is "the probability that the system incorrectly declares a successful match between the input pattern and a non-matching pattern in the database. It measures the percent of invalid matches". FRR or false reject rate is "the probability that the system incorrectly declares failure of match between the input pattern and the matching template in the database. It measures the percent of valid inputs being rejected" [1]. These two performance metrics are the most important.

1.2 A Short Introduction to Neural Networks

Methods based on neural networks are used extensively in pattern recognition problems. One of these problems is biometric signature authentication.

The most easy way to define a neural network is that a neural network represents an attempt to simulate the brain and specific functions of living organisms. A general definition is : an artificial neural network (ANN) represents a system consisting of a large number of interconnected elementary processors (artificial neurons) that operate to solve some specific tasks. The process unit inside an ANN is the neuron. This artificial neuron tries to imitate the structure and the functionality of the human neuron. An artificial neuron has a number of **inputs**, each one having a **synaptic weight**, an accumulator, an activation function and an output.

Therefore, we have

$$u_k = \sum w_i \cdot x_i, \tag{1}$$

The value u_k is named **net input** and the **output** of the neuron is y_k. The function φ is called the **activation function** and the value θ_k is called the **threshold** value. When training a network we must provide a learning algorithm like back propagation learning.

2 Collecting a Base of Biometric Signatures

A biometric system is measured by its performance metrics. For computing the performance metrics of a biometric system a base of biometric samples must be acquired. Our base has a number of 2932 original signatures and 2773 forgery signatures from 73 subjects. An original signature is a signature provided by a subject and a forged signature is a signature provided by a subject A that forged other subject B having the graphical picture of subjects' B signature.

Each biometric system must have a device for capturing the biometric signals. Our device has two 2D MEMS accelerometers [2] and an optical navigation system - ONS - that gives the relative position. Therefore, our device produces six signals

(4 accelerations and 2 relative positions). These are the base signals. These signals are combined to produce new signals called **components** from which we extract the **biometric features**. The biometric features are the most important part of a biometric signature. Each individual has its own biometric features for its signatures. Based on these biometric features we compute the distance of two strings composed of biometric features using **Levenshtein distance algorithm**. We developed a number of algorithms that compares two sets of features strings that outputs the Levenshtein distance between them. Some algorithms are using only the acceleration signals, others only the ONS signals and one algorithm is using all six signals. We call these algorithms Signature Recognition Algorithms - SRA.

For a base of signatures using the SRA algorithms, we compute the distance between all signatures inside the signature base. These distances are stored in binary matrices (see table 1 - distance matrix between signature 3485 - as original - and 3480, 3481, 3482, 3483, 3484 - as samples on subject 85).

Table 1 Distance matrix for signature 3485 vs. 3480, 3481, 3482, 3483, 3484

Sign id	3480	3481	3482	3483	3484
SRA1	0.667383	0.638186	0.690937	0.696175	0.715465
SRA2	0.864226	0.846354	0.862053	0.845086	0.871723
SRA3	0.331611	0.48791	0.47794	0.546078	0.64832
SRA4	0.732921	0.734493	0.795157	0.653635	0.838952
SRA5	0.350115	0.380471	0.354693	0.329385	0.47436
SRA6	0.667741	0.645182	0.685711	0.689252	0.71225
SRA7	0.605706	0.596052	0.630995	0.586095	0.607647
SRA8	0.602377	0.596205	0.617832	0.616843	0.630798

3 Neural Network Architecture

Further we'll use a total interconnected feed-forward neural network. In our experiments, we used an artificial neural network that has an input layer, a number of hidden layers and an output layer containing only one artificial neuron.

When training the network, the output neuron gives us the average learning error for an input data and when evaluating the network the output neuron gives us the response of the network. If the response of the network is greater than a threshold value, we will say the the authentication was successful otherwise the authentication failed. The threshold value will be determined experimentally.

4 Training and Evaluating the Neural Network

The most important thing when using an artificial network is the training data. As we said earlier (in 2), when comparing two signatures we compute the similarity of these signatures computing the Levenshtein distance.

4.1 Signature Types

As said in 2, there are two types of signatures: originals and forgeries. One subject A has a number of originals and a number of trained forgeries (see 2), forgeries by other other subjects having A's graphical signature. The original and forged signatures that are not subject's A signatures, we will consider random forgeries for subject A. We will consider five from the original signatures (picked at random) sample signatures. Therefore, from only two types of signatures we will create four types: samples, originals, forgeries and random forgeries.

4.2 Implementing the Training and the Evaluation on a Base of Signatures

After collecting a base of signature, we computed a number of matrices for every SRA algorithm that contains the Levenshtein distances between all signatures.

These matrices will contain the distances between the samples and samples, samples and originals, samples and forgeries and samples and random forgeries. Using these distances, we will create the input data that trains the neural network - normalized distances. A **normalized distance** is given by following formula:

$$I_{M \cdot i + j} = \frac{d_{ij} - \Delta_{ij}}{\Delta_{ij}}, \tag{2}$$

where I is the input data array, d_{ij} is a distance in the Levenshtein matrix, Δ_{ij} is the minimum distance between samples signatures with them selfs, M is the number of sample signatures (in our tests M = 5), with $i = \overline{1,M}$, $j = \overline{1,N}$ where N is the number of SRA algorithms (in our tests N = 8). The number M of signatures was determined experimentally based a classical method of authentication - the threshold method: a signature is authenticated if the average value of distances was higher than the general threshold value; if the number M was grater than 5, the result was slightly better and if it was lower then 5, the results were worst (we also noticed that subjects preferred to offer a smaller number of signatures). Therefore, the input data is an array with $N \cdot M$ values ($N \cdot M = 40$). Each array was an input to each neuron in the first layer.

When training the network we will provide both the input data and the output data. There will be two kinds of input data and output data. The first type of input data will contain the normalized distances between the samples and originals and the output data will be an one element array containing the one (1) value. The second type of input data will contain the normalized distances between the samples and forgeries (and random forgeries) and the output data will be an one element array containing the zero (0) value. 1 stands for success (authentication succeeded) and 0 for failure (authentication failed). So, the response of the network when provided an original is the one value and when provided a forgery the response is the zero value.

The exposure is the rate of different types of signatures that will train the network. In our tests we set the 1.05 value for the originals, 2.00 value for the forgeries and 3.00 value for the random forgeries. This means that the network will learn more about forgeries than originals.

4.3 Results Obtained

Using this procedure, we obtained the results - see table 2. In this table we show the best results together with the network configuration that gave these results.

Table 2 Results Obtained - architecture 1

Parameter	Value
Learn rate	0.23
Momentum	0.5
Alpha	3
Threshold	0.9
Original exposure	1.05
Forgery exposure	3
Random exposure	2
Neurons in layer 1	100
Neurons in layer 2	100
Neurons in layer 3	1
Epoch	120
FRR	8.4451460142068%
FAR	0.948692956032%

4.4 Comparisons with other similar methods

Similar methods are using also a feed-forward neural network but also a RBF neural network. The table 3 contains the values of the FAR and FRR performance metrics.

Table 3 Comparison with other similar methods

Method name	FAR value[%]	FRR value [%]
Neural Network-based Handwritten Signature Verification [5]	2.0	1.3
Off-line Handwritten Signature Verification using Radial Basis Function Neural Networks [6]	4.89	6.94
Off-line Signature Verification Using Fuzzy ARTMAP Neural Network [7]	7.27	11
On-line Signature Biometric System with Employment of Single-output Multilayer Perceptron [8]	6.45	0

5 Conclusions

The paper introduces a method based on neural networks for authenticating handwritten signatures. In this paper we tried to minimize the FAR value and we considered only the values below 1%. In our tests we trained and evaluated diffrent types of NN architectures (increasing the number of hidden layers and the neurons inside them) but the best results were given by the 100-100-1 architecture.

The future works involves the creation of new algorithms SRA better defining degrees of similarity between original and forgery signatures.

References

1. http://en.wikipedia.org/wiki/Biometrics
2. (WO/2006/085783) SYSTEM AND METHODS OF ACQUISITION, ANALYSIS AND AUTHENTICATION OF THE HANDWRITTEN SIGNATURE, http://www.wipo.int/pctdb/en/wo.jsp?IA=WO2006%2F085783
3. International Committee for Information Technology Standards, 2007, Study Report on Biometrics in E-Authentication, 30 March 2007, INCITS M1/07-0185
4. Bai-ling Zhang, Min-yue Fu, Hong Yan.: Handwritten Signature Verification based on Neural 'Gas' Based Vector Quantization. 1051-4651/98 IEEE (1998)
5. McCabe, A., Trevathan, J., Read, W.: Neural Network-based Handwritten Signature Verification, JOURNAL OF COMPUTERS, VOL. 3, NO. 8, AUGUST 2008
6. Azzopardi, G., Camilleri, K.P.,: Offine Handwritten Signature Verification using Radial Basis Function Neural Networks
7. Murshed, N.A., Bortolozzi, F., Sabourin, R.: Off-line Signature Verification Using Fuzzy ARTMAP Neural Network, 0-7803-2768-3/95 IEEE 1995
8. Szklarzewski, A., Derlatka, M.: On-line Signature Biometric System with Employment of Single-output Multilayer Perceptron, Biocybernetics and Biomedical Engineering 2006, Volume 26, Number 4, pp. 91102
9. Radhika,K.R., Venkatesha, M.K., Sekhar, G.N.: Pattern Recognition Techniques in Off-line hand written signature verification - A Survey, PROCEEDINGS OF WORLD ACADEMY OF SCIENCE, ENGINEERING AND TECHNOLOGY VOLUME 36 DECEMBER 2008 ISSN 2070-3740
10. Katona, E., Kalman, P., Toth, N.: Signature Verification Using Neural Nets

Evolutionary Physical Model Design

A. Carrascal[1], **J.M. Font**[2] **and D. Pelta**[3]

Abstract Both complexity and lack of knowledge associated to physical processes makes physical models design an arduous task. Frequently, the only available information about the physical processes are the heuristic data obtained from experiments or at best a rough idea on what are the physical principles and laws that underlie considered physical processes. Then the problem is converted to find a mathematical expression which fits data. There exist traditional approaches to tackle the inductive model search process from data, such as regression, interpolation, finite element method, etc. Nevertheless, these methods either are only able to solve a reduced number of simple model typologies, or the given black-box solution does not contribute to clarify the analyzed physical process. In this paper a hybrid evolutionary approach to search complex physical models is proposed. Tests carried out on both theoretical and real-world physical processes demonstrate the validity of this approach.

1 Introduction

In order to understand real-world complexity, science tries to formulate world by means of a mathematical language able to model each of the observed physical processes. Mathematical representation allows quantify magnitudes and establish relations between variables involved. Once the physical model is built, it can be employed to predict the system state in the future whenever the initial conditions are known.

There is no physic model construction methodology beyond the scientist intuition, experience and intelligence [1]. The more complex the physical process

1 Fundación Fatronik-Tecnalia, Paseo Mikeletegi 7, Parque Tecnológico, 20009 Donostia, Spain.
acarrascal@fatronik.com

2 Dpto. de Inteligencia Artificial, Facultad de Informática, UPM, Madrid, Spain.
jm.font@upm.es

3 Dpto de Ciencias de la Computación e Inteligencia Artificial, Univ. Granada, Spain.
dpelta@ugr.es

M. Bramer et al. (eds.), *Research and Development in Intelligent Systems XXVI*,
DOI 10.1007/978-1-84882-983-1_38, © Springer-Verlag London Limited 2010

to describe is, the more difficult the construction process will be. Once a model is proposed, it has to be experimentally evaluated. When the obtained deviation between the model prediction and the experimental data is within reasonable error limits (arbitrarily determined), the model is considered valid. This inductive process assumes the model validity while there are no contradictory experimental cases found .

Other approach when building physical models consists of building process from data. When a model fits data it will be considered valid. There are several techniques based on this approach: regression, interpolation, finite element method, etc [2]. This approach can only be applied to simple physical process and frequently it provides black-box solutions that do not contribute to clarify the analyzed physical process.

Evolution-based algorithms have been considered to be the most flexible, efficient and robust of all optimization and search algorithms known to computer science. There are four main types of evolutionary algorithm currently in use: genetic programming (GP), genetic algorithm (GA), evolutionary programming (EP) and evolutionary strategies (ES). Besides, Memetic algorithm (MA) is a combination of GA and local search (LS) methods. These methods are now becoming widely used to solve a broad range of different problems [3].

Grammar-Guided Genetic Programming (GGGP) is an extension of traditional GP systems, conceived to always generate valid individuals (points or possible solutions that belong to the search space) [4]. To do so, GGGP employs a set of genetic programming operators such as grammar-based crossover operator (GBC), grammar-based mutation operator (GBM) and grammar-based initialization method (GBIM) [5]. Besides GGGP employs a context-free grammar (CFG) so that every individual in the population is a derivation tree that generates a sentence (solution) belonging to the language defined by the CFG [13]. A context-free grammar G comprises a 4-tuple $G = (\Sigma N, \Sigma T, S, P)$ such as $\Sigma N \cap \Sigma T = \emptyset$; where ΣN is the alphabet of non-terminal symbols, ΣT is the alphabet of terminal symbols, S is the axiom of the grammar and P is the set of production rules, written in BNF (Backus-Naur Form).

The well known GA is an evolutionary algorithm which explores search spaces by maintaining a population of individual genotypes and applying them a set of genetic operators (selection, crossover, mutation, etc.). After phenotypes are obtained from genotypes they are evaluated and fitness values are assigned them. Typically phenotypes consist of collections of domain dependent parameters. Genotypes consist of coded versions of these parameters, represented as genes [6]. Real coded genes need specific genetic operators. Inspired by the mathematical morphology theory, MMX is a real coded crossover operator with a low computational cost, able to modify the exploration and exploitation capabilities dynamically depending on a genetic diversity measure. It has been demonstrated that obtains better results against other real coded crossover operators: RFX, BLX-α or GBX [7].

The use of a local search procedure generally improves the performance and the exploitation capabilities of the evolutionary algorithm, speeding up the convergence of the algorithm. One of the most common LS methods applies little random perturbations to each genotype gene [8].

In this paper a combined evolutionary approach is proposed as automatic physical models generator. By means of a grammar describing allowed mathematical expressions syntax, a GP algorithm will search into the physical models search space. The grammar will allow the definition of constants whose values will be determined by using a GA together with a LS method.

2 Evolutionary Physical Model Design

The mathematical grammar defined in table 1 allows the creation of a great number of physical models. Thanks to both linear and non linear mathematic functions, a lot of physical processes can be modelled: kinematics, dynamics, thermodynamic, chemical models, etc.). Furthermore, by means of exponential functions a great number of simple linear differential equation solutions can be achieved.

Table 1. Simple math expressions grammar definition

$$P = \{ \ S ::= F \ ; F ::= + F \ F \ ; F ::= - F \ F \ ; F ::= * F \ F \ ;$$
$$F ::= {}^{\wedge} F \ F \ ; F ::= e \ F \ ; F ::= k_i \ ; F ::= v_1 \ ; F ::= v_2 \ ; F ::= v_n \}$$
$$\Sigma_N = \{ \ S, \ F \} \ \ \Sigma_T = \{ \ +, \ -, \ *, \ e, \ {}^{\wedge}, \ t, \ k_i, \ v_1, \ v_2, \ ..., \ v_n \}$$

The considered context-free grammar allows the definition of complex mathematical expressions. The number of constants is only limited by the maximum number of allowed derivations. t is the independent variable and n is the number of dependant variables v_n.

Figure 1 show the hybrid evolutionary system diagram composed of three modules: GP, GA and LS modules. GP module starts generating an initial mathematical expressions population (GBIM method). After each mathematical expression is evaluated, genetic programming operators (selection, GBC and GBM operators) are applied until the stop criterion is reached (typically model fits experimental data). A penalizing linear term, which is proportional to the mathematical expressions length, was added (Occam's razor principle). From a mathematical point of view, this term avoid obtaining complex interpolants.

GA module is called when each mathematical expression need to be evaluated. For this purpose a GA is executed with a population of real-coded individuals. Individual genes are formed with the mathematical expressions constants that need to be determined. After population random initialization each mathematical model is tested with available experimental data and a fitness value is obtained (absolute difference between experimental and predicted data). Then a set of genetic operators (roulette selection method, random mutation operator and MMX) is iteratively applied until an arbitrary number of iterations are reached.

Finally, an additional exploitation method is applied over GA descendants in the LS module. A traditional random best ascent LS method is employed. This step speeds up the convergence of the algorithm by adjusting the mathematical expressions constants values.

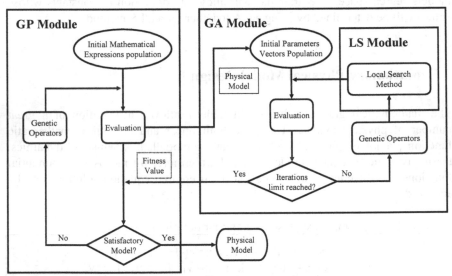

Figure 1 Combined Evolutionary System proposed.

The evolutionary hybrid system outcome is a physical model in which all the constants have been solved. Together with the physical model, a measurement of the given solution validity is provided.

3 Physical Models

The simple mathematical grammar defined in table 1 allows the creation of a great number of physical models. Thanks to both linear and non linear mathematic functions, a lot of physical processes can be modelled: kinematics, dynamics, thermodynamic, chemical models, etc.). Furthermore, by means of exponential functions a lot of simple linear differential equation solutions can be represented.

Thermodynamic Model

A real world thermodynamic scenario has been selected to test the evolutionary model generation system. A train unit bogie has been monitored during a randomly selected real world journey. The temperature T of the reduction gears area was monitored together with the surrounding environment temperature Ts and train velocity v.

The combined evolutionary system was asked to obtain the temperature variation of the reduction gears sensor dT/dt over the time with no more prior information about the system. With the grammar defined in table 1, the system obtained the next mathematical expression:

$$\frac{dT}{dt} = 0{,}0061 \cdot T_s(t) - 0{,}0063 \cdot T(t) + 0{,}024 \cdot v$$

This expression, whose behaviour can be seen in figure 2, fits data with a low mean absolute error (1,89°C).

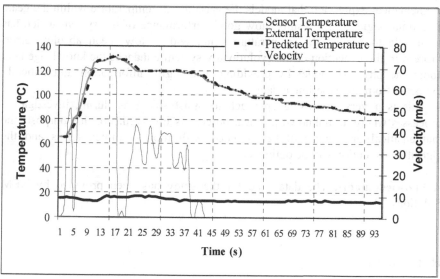

Figure 2 Predicted vs. real train temperatures.

If we relate mathematical expression obtained to Newton's Law of Cooling that describes heat transfer processes, we can deduce that there exists a heat focus U which is lineally proportional to the train speed with an approximate heat transfer coefficient k equals to 0,0062.

$$\frac{dT}{dt} = k[T_s(t) - T(t)] + U \approx 0{,}0062[T_s(t) - T(t)] + 0{,}024v$$

Beyond data regression, the solution given by the system provides physical information about the process.

4 Conclusions

A combined evolutionary system has been developed in order to tackle the physical model search problem. This evolutionary approach mixes Genetic Programming, Genetic Algorithms and Local Search techniques in order to obtain mathematical expressions which describe physical processes: the GP module generates individuals that codify well formed mathematical expressions, whilst GA and LS modules develop optimal parameter configurations for every generated individual. The system uses a basic mathematical context-free grammar that can be applied to model a great number of physical processes.

Experimental results have been retrieved from the application of the proposed system to a real world thermodynamic scenario, with the goal of shaping the mathematical expression that models the variation of temperature within the gears of a train bogie. These results show good performance of the system which has been able to predict the temperature value with a low mean absolute error. Moreover, the execution of the evolutionary system enhances the knowledge held about the physical model by providing meaningful information automatically extracted from the experiment data.

This is a very promising approach to assist scientists during investigation processes where an unknown physical process is involved. For this purpose, the mathematical grammar will be extended with more complex terms and the algorithm execution will be optimized.

Acknowledgments. The data used for the study has been provided by NEM Solutions S.L.

References

1. Langley, P.: Elements of Machine Learning. Morgan Kaufmann. (1995).
2. Meerschaert , M.M.: Mathematical Modeling. Academic Press (2007).
3. Dawkins, R.: Evolutionary Design By Computers. Peter J. Bentley Ed. (1999).
4. Whigham, P.A., Grammatically-based genetic programming, in: J.P. Rosca, (Ed.), Proceedings of the Workshop on Genetic Programming: From Theory to Real-World Applications.Tahoe City, California, USA, pp. 33–41 (1995).
5. Couchet, J., Manrique, D., Rios, J. and Rodríguez-Patón, A.: Crossover and mutation operators for grammar-guided genetic programming. Soft Comput. Vol. 11(10): pp. 943-955 (2007)
6. Rusell, S. Norvig, P.: Artificial Intelligence. A Modern Approach. Prentice-Hall. (2008).
7. Barrios, D., Carrascal, A., Manrique, D. and Ríos, J. Optimisation With Real-Coded Genetic Algorithms Based on Mathematical Morphology. Intern. J. Computer Math. Vol. 80(3), pp. 275-293, (2003).
8. Selman, B., Kautz, H., and Cohen, B.: Noise strategies for improving local search. In Proceedings of the 12th National Conference on Artificial Intelligence, pp. 337–343. (1994).

Decision Support in Designing with Polymers

U. Sancin and B. Dolšak[1]

Abstract Polymers are extensively applied and discovered acceleratory. As they are numerous, the mastery in plastic assortment is rarity and never complete. Experts in plastic products' design are mainly inaccessible to small and medium-sized enterprises (SMEs') due to their economic and personnel capacities. This paper presents a common plastic product development process and its deficiencies regarding material selection process, where engineer has to consider technical parameters along with customer's expectations. A decision support system for plastic products' design is proposed to offer intelligent advice or recommendation to young or inexperienced designers.

1 Introduction

Polymers are ubiquitous and living without them in present time is almost impossible to imagine. However, mechanical engineers are more used to designing with conventional materials than with plastics. The reason lies in classical mechanical education, extensive number of polymers on the market and lack of experience in plastic design, except in plastic product oriented enterprises.

Experiences play a key role in design. Economical status mainly does not allow SMEs' to hire expert's opinion so employed engineers have to rely upon their own knowledge. It is the same for the designers at the beginning of their career as their experiences are limited.

Design is computer dependent process and knowledge intensive engineering task. Mastery in Computer Aided Design (CAD) tools is crucial for every designer willing to design good and successful product. Within the design process, the engineer has to make many decisions whilst working with these tools. This is very important as product development process is a sequence of interdependent events and one decision at the early design stage would then exert influence on all successive events, and the final design solution.

1 University of Maribor, Faculty of Mechanical Engineering, SI-2000, Slovenia
email: {urska.sancin,dolsak}@uni-mb.si

M. Bramer et al. (eds.), *Research and Development in Intelligent Systems XXVI*,
DOI 10.1007/978-1-84882-983-1_39, © Springer-Verlag London Limited 2010

This paper introduces some basic ideas to develop a decision support system for plastic products' design. Section 2 explains why plastics are important in mechanical design and describes their advantages. Decision support systems and potential execution of proposed decision support system for plastic products' design are presented in Section 3.

2 Polymers in Design

2.1 Polymers

Today, conventional materials like metals and ceramics can be substituted by others, more suitable for certain types of product. Thus, plastics are reasonable alternative as they could offer better characteristics for noticeable lower costs. Some of the advantages such as less weight, lower material costs, cheaper mass production, recyclability, specific electrical, isolative or, corrosive, etc. features, easier part joining [1], higher aesthetic values (e.g. no dyeing is needed) or, easier production of precision products, are of major importance in product development process.

2.2 Designing with Polymers

Product development is complex engineering process. The designer is progressing though the process dealing with many design and manufacturing problems, while envisage the production process [2], product assembly, parts' maintenance, their influence on the environment or some other design aspect [3]. In addition, the engineer has to define the new product features like tolerances, type of surface or material, from which the product will be produced. To solve these dilemmas, he or she has to rely upon own knowledge or experiences as existing CAD application does not provide any recommendations or guidelines.

Material selection is one of these decisions, especially when the designer has to choose between approx. 120.000 different plastic materials [4,5]. It is of great importance as it influences technical and economical aspect of the product. To support this idea, an example of new product development process is described and illustrated in Figure 1.

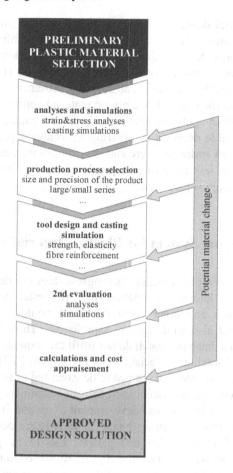

Figure 1 New product development process

After 3D computer model of potential product is finished, a preliminary plastic material selection is set considering strain and strength properties, product type (product's purpose, exposure to the high temperatures, etc.), customer's requirements and wishes, fashion trend, special restrictions (product's contact with food, toys, etc.) and material costs. At this stage, first strain/stress analyses and casing simulations could be performed. Some severe material changes could be done according to results and usage of reinforcement fibres is discussed.

Production process selection is next engineer's decision directly connected to plastic material selection as he or she has to consider products type, its size and precision, wall thickness, tolerances, surface roughness and even a size of production series. In case the manufacturer wants to use particular production machines or the series is large and the chosen polymer could be produced only with the production process suitable for small series, the need for material change is present again.

Next phase is tool design, followed by detail casting simulation. Due to the results, some parameters like strain, elasticity, fibre reinforcement or thermal resistivity may have to be adjusted. Furthermore, additional analyses and simulations are fired to approve or to disprove the last selected plastic. Final step before sealed approval is calculation and costs appraisement.

Evidentially from the Figure 1, the plastic material could be modified up to five times after preliminary polymer selection. In every phase, the designer has to make the best possible decision considering all relevant parameters, sometimes also contradictive. In order to overcome this bottle-neck and to make product development process less experience dependent, the decision support system for plastic products' design is proposed.

3 Decision Support System for Plastic Material's Selection

Product design is a complex process. Its progress does not depend on just solving problems regarding known information like requested technical parameters, standards, conditions and other constraints that could be resolved with one ultimate solution but also on designers' experiences. Thus, the regular computer programs based on a database search do not fulfil the requirements of the designer.

Development of intelligent decision support system [6,7] for plastic material selection [8,9] proposed here is expected to be executed in five phases, knowledge acquisition, decision support system shell selection, knowledge base construction, reasoning procedure definition, and development of an user interface.

First and most time consuming phase is knowledge acquisition as experts' cognition in the field of design and plastics has to be preciously collected, adequately processed, well organized, and properly stored in the knowledge base.

Before creating the knowledge base of the system containing human cognition, relations, and experiences, the decision support shell has to be selected. The generally accepted definition is that decision support systems are information systems supporting operational decision-making activities of a human decision maker. The decision support systems shall then help decision makers to compile useful information from raw data that are distributed in a potentially heterogeneous IT infrastructure, personal or educational knowledge, models and strategies. As long as the system can be designed in advance and the focus lays on data, in practice the application of decision support systems is often sufficient. However, according to Yilmaz and Oren [10] the versions of decision support systems are following:

- agent-directed decision support systems, used for rapidly changing environments where the system needs to be able to adapt;
- decision support simulation systems are used to obtain, display and evaluate operationally relevant data in agile contexts by executing models using

operational data exploiting the full potential of modelling and simulation and producing numerical insight into the behaviour of complex system;

- agent-directed decision support simulation systems are agent-directed simulations that are applied as a decision support system, whose focus is on processes, so the system can adapt to new requirements and constraints in the environment.

At this research phase the type of the decision support system for plastic material selection is not yet defined, however, it is expected the agent-directed decision support simulation systems to cover all requirements and wishes the most satisfactory.

After decision support system shell is selected, the knowledge base of the system will be build. It will contain human cognition useful for problem solving in the form of rules relating to modern plastic materials' selection and correlated manufacturing processes, assisted by Design for Manufacturing (DFM) strategies [11]. The presentation of knowledge will be of special importance. The potential for transparent and modular IT rules, whose advantage is neutral knowledge representation, uniform structure, separation of knowledge from its processing and possibility of dealing with incomplete and uncertain knowledge, is planned to be compared with more flexible knowledge presentation systems, such as fuzzy logic [12], where fuzzy sets and fuzzy rules will be defined as a part of an iterative process upgraded by evaluating and tuning the system to meet specified requirements.

Applying domain knowledge, including human cognition, relations and experiences in the knowledge base is the main goal for the system, as it will together with the data base, be serviceable for a complex reasoning procedure [13]. Reasoning procedure will behind the inference engine lead to qualified design recommendations and guidelines offered to the designer whilst designing plastic products.

Development of user interface will be the last phase in building the system as correspondence with the designer should be unambiguous and efficient. The system is anticipated to be designed as guiding mode. The first set of parameters should be provided to the system at the beginning but during processing phase the system may ask more questions to the user or require additional parameters. Graphic mode is anticipated to be used at the end of procedure to present final solution.

4 Conclusions

Unambiguously, we can designate plastic material selection as one of the knowledge intensive engineering tasks, where experts are precious and their knowledge domain esteemed. Engineers in small and medium-sized enterprises

(SMEs') or young designers are in an unenviable position as their knowledge domains and experiences are minimal. Plastics' design experts are able to use their expert knowledge and experiences, however, the new materials are discovered acceleratory. What is more, material parameters can be very diverse, even within one material family. Consequently, the possibility for failing to select the optimal polymer for the product is aggrandised.

Despite all available computer aid, the designer is still in an arduous position as no guideline computer support is at his or her disposal during plastics' material selection. The intelligent decision support system for designing plastic products proposed in this paper is an attempt to collect, organize and define human cognition as rules in a knowledge base, and as data in a data base, in order to build the foundation of an inference engine, which will, together with complex reasoning, be able to support the engineer's work.

References

1. Kim, I.S., Prasad, Y.K.D.V., Stoynov, L.A.: A study on an intelligent system to predict the tensile stress in welding using solar energy concentration. Journal of Materials Processing Technology. Vol. 153-154, pp. 649-653 (2004).
2. Vidal, A., Alberti, M., Ciurana, J., Casadesus, M.: A decision support system for optimising the selection of parameters when planning milling operations. International Journal of Machine Tools & Manufacture. Vol. 45, pp. 201-210 (2005).
3. Molcho, G., Zipori, Y., Schneor, R., Rosen, O., Goldstein, D., Shpitalni, M.: Computer aided manufacturability analysis: Closing the knowledge gap between the designer and the manufacturer. CIRP Annals - Manufacturing Technology. Vol. 57, pp. 153-158 (2008).
4. Ashby, M.F., Johnson, K.: Materials and design. Elsevier (2005).
5. Ashby, M. F.: Materials selection in mechanical design, 3rd Ed. Elsevier (2005).
6. Novak, M., Dolšak, B.: Intelligent FEA-based design improvement. Engineering Applications of Artificial Intelligence. Vol. 21, pp. 1239-1254 (2008).
7. Turban, E., Aronson, J.E., Liang, T.P.: Decision Support Systems and Intelligent Systems. Prentice Hall (2004).
8. Ullah, S.A.M.M., Harib, K.H.: An intelligent method for selecting optimal materials and its application. Advanced Engineering Informatics. Vol.22, pp. 473-483 (2008).
9. Đurić, M., Devedžić, V.: I-Promise—intelligent protective material selection. Expert Systems with Applications. Vol.23, pp. 219-227 (2002).
10. Yilmaz, L., Oren, T. (Eds.).: Agent-directed simulation and systems engineering. John Wiley & Sons (2009).
11. Sevstjanov, P., Figat, P.: Aggregation of aggregating modes in MCDM: Synthesis of Type 2 and Level 2 fuzzy sets. Omega. Vol. 35, pp. 505-523 (2007).
12. Zio, E., Baraldi, P., Librizzi, M., Podofillini, L., Dang, V.N.: A fuzzy set-based approach for modeling dependence among human errors. Fuzzy Sets and Systems. Vol. 160, pp. 1947-1964 (2009).
13. Benzmüller, C., Sorge, V., Jamnik, M., Kerber, M.: Combined reasoning by automated cooperation. Journal of Applied Logic. Vol. 6, pp. 318-342 (2008).

Cluster-Based Benchmarking of Universities as an Alternative to League Tables

Lars Nolle [1]

Abstract University rankings are used all over the world to compare the quality and the prestige of universities. These rankings are usually based on combinations of arbitrarily weighted performance factors. This method has a number of shortcomings. To overcome these shortcomings, a cluster-based approach to university performance evaluation is proposed. Different data mining techniques are used to analyse the performance of UK universities based on the same data used to compile The Sunday Times University Guide 2010 league table and the results are compared with the original ranking. It is shown that clustering techniques, such as Self-Organizing Map or the k-means algorithm, can be used to successfully classify universities in terms of performance.

1 Introduction

University rankings are used all over the world to compare the quality - and the prestige - of universities. Examples are the Times Good University Guide or the Academic Ranking of World Universities compiled by the Shanghai Jiao Tong University in China. These rankings are usually based on combinations of arbitrarily weighted performance factors [1]. However, it has been shown that reliable quality measures cannot be obtained from a weighted sum of quality attributes [2]. For example, the weighted sum does not take into account any possible correlation of the inputs [2]. It also does not take into account whether the attributes are inputs or outputs. If the weightings are known in advance, it is possible for a university to optimise its operational parameters in terms of league table rank rather than striving for real academic excellence. As a result, universities tend to play the league table game in order to use the league tables in their favour to attract students. In order to ensure a fairer comparison, alternative approaches are currently searched for, for example, profiling [3].

Another commonly used informal way of expressing the perceived quality of a university is to state its membership in certain groupings. Examples of those groupings are the 'Russell Group' in the UK or the 'Ivy League' in the US. Therefore, it might be more objective to express the quality in terms of group

1 Nottingham Trent University, School of Science and Technology, Clifton Lane,
Nottingham, NG11 8NS,UK
lnolle@theiet.ort

M. Bramer et al. (eds.), *Research and Development in Intelligent Systems XXVI*,
DOI 10.1007/978-1-84882-983-1_40, © Springer-Verlag London Limited 2010

membership rather than on a rank. These groupings should not be based on arbitrary groups, like the ones mentioned above, but on objective clustering of the feature space, i.e. quality measures space.

For example, one may wish to classify a particular university as 'standard', 'average', 'good' or 'excellent'. Therefore, it would be assumed that there are four clusters in the data and that each university could be assigned to exactly one cluster. This is very similar to the classification system used in the UK to evaluate the research performance of universities in 2001.

In this research, different data mining and clustering techniques are used to analyse the performance of UK universities based on the same data set used to compile The Sunday Times Good University Guide league table 2010 [4] and the results are compared with the original ranking.

2 Data Analysis

The data set employed [5] contained eight quality measures for 114 UK higher education institutions. To build the Sunday Times league table, the weighted quality measures were combined using a z-score transformation [6] and the totals were transformed to a scale with 1000 for the top score [7].

A common problem for statistical methods is the problem of missing values, i.e. the absence of data values for some of the variables of an observation [8]. In the Sunday Times data set, no data is available for Student Satisfaction for the University of Abertay, Edinburgh Napier University, Queen Margaret University, and the Robert Gordon University. Since clustering techniques are very sensitive to missing values, these records were deleted from the data set.

The data analysis was implemented in R [9]. Clustering algorithms depend on measures of similarity or dissimilarity. If the variables in a data set are measured in different units or if their ranges are not comparable, the data in the set should be standardized. Figure 1 shows a box plot of the original data. It can be seen that the ranges for Service & Facility Spend and Entry Standards differ significantly form the other variables. Therefore the columns of the data set were cantered and scaled, such that all variables have mean zero and variance one. Figure 2 shows the boxplot of the standardized data.

The next step in the data analysis was to plot the data with reduced dimensionality. For this, a principal component analysis (PCA) was carried out. The first two principal components explain 79% of the total variation in the data. Figure 3 shows a plot of the first two principal components. As it can be seen from the figure, the Russell Group universities are clearly located more towards the left side of the graph, the old universities are grouped in the middle of the graph, and former polytechnics and modern universities populate the right hand side of the principle component space.

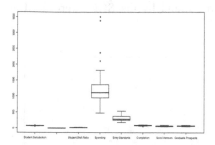

Figure 1 Boxplot of quality data.   Figure 2 Boxplot of data after standardisation.

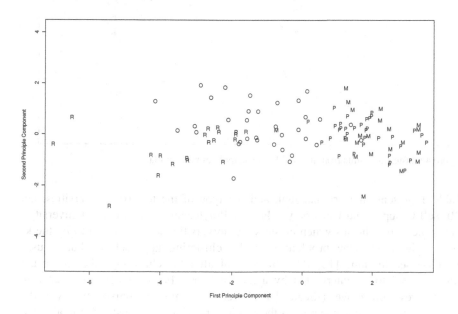

Figure 3 First two principal components: R – Russell Group university,
O – old university, P – former Polytechnics, M – modern university.

This indicates that there are clear clusters in the data, but because the first two principle components cover only 79% of the variation, a clustering on reduced dimensionality is not sufficient.

Next, a Self Organizing Map (SOM) [10] was used to cluster the standardized data set. It was assumed that there are four classes of universities and hence a SOM with four notes was used. The results are presented in principle component plane in Figure 4. It can be seen that there is a good separation of the clusters and also a strong correlation between members of the clusters and the type of

university. In a next stage the cluster centres found by the SOM were used as
initial clusters for the k-means algorithm [11].

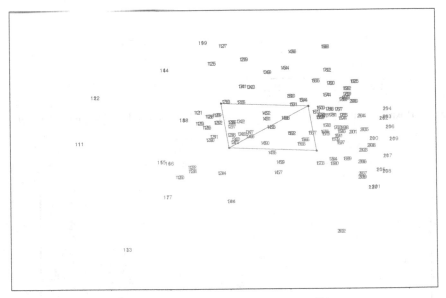

Figure 4 Clustering results from the SOM in principal component plane.

Table 1 presents the original rank and the type of the top 100 universities, i.e.
'Russell Group', 'Old University', 'Former Polytechnics' or 'Modern University'.
The table also indicates which clusters the universities were assigned to by the k-
means algorithm. One problem with the clustering approach is that it uses
unsupervised learning [12]. This means that after the clustering takes place the
clusters need to be interpreted by a human being. For example, the clustering
results presented above indicate that cluster 2 contains the universities with the
best performance, if compared to the original ranking, and cluster 4 contains the
worst performing universities. From the table it can be seen that cluster 2 is
predominately populated by universities from the Russell Group. However, some
old universities, like St Andrews or Durham, are also assigned to that cluster. This
is actually in line with the original Times ranking, in which these universities are
ranked in the top-ten. Cluster 3 is predominately populated by old universities, i.e.
pre 1992 universities. Interesting to see is that Dundee is also placed in that
cluster, despite being a modern university. Again, this is in line with the times
ranking, where it was placed on rank 41, right in between old universities. Clusters
4 and 1 again seem to correlate with the original ranks rather than differentiating
between former polytechnics and modern universities.

Based on these observations, it can be said that the cluster based approach is suitable to evaluate the performance of universities if it is possible to classify the clusters in a meaningful way.

Table 1 Comparison of University rank, type and cluster.

University	Rank	Type	Cluster	University	Rank	Type	Cluster
Oxford	1	R	2	City	49	O	3
Cambridge	2	R	2	Swansea	50	O	1
Imperial College	3	R	2	Oxford Brookes	52	P	1
St Andrews	4	O	2	Bradford	53	O	1
UCL	5	R	2	Ulster	54	O	1
Warwick	6	R	2	Bangor	55	O	1
LSE	7	R	2	Portsmouth	56	P	1
Durham	8	O	2	Nottingham Trent	57	P	1
Exeter	9	O	3	Bournemouth	58	P	1
Bristol	10	R	2	Chichester	59	M	1
York	11	O	3	Glasgow Caledonian	60	P	1
King's	12	R	2	West of England	62	P	1
Bath	13	O	3	Plymouth	63	P	1
Edinburgh	14	R	2	Northumbria	64	P	1
Leicester	15	O	3	Hertfordshire	66	P	1
Southampton	15	R	3	De Montfort	66	P	1
Loughborough	17	O	3	Gloucestershire	68	M	1
Sheffield	18	R	3	Sheffield Hallam	69	P	1
Glasgow	19	R	3	Brighton	70	P	1
Nottingham	20	R	3	Coventry	71	P	1
Newcastle	21	R	3	Bedfordshire	71	M	1
Birmingham	22	R	3	Winchester	73	M	1
Lancaster	23	O	3	Staffordshire	74	P	1
Manchester	24	R	3	Bath Spa	74	M	1
Aston	25	O	3	UWIC Cardiff	76	M	1
Cardiff	26	R	3	Birmingham City	77	P	1
Leeds	27	R	3	Central Lancashire	78	P	1
Liverpool	28	R	3	Lampeter	79	O	1
East Anglia	28	O	3	York St John	80	P	1
Royal Holloway	30	O	3	Worcester	81	P	1
Reading	31	O	3	Teesside	81	P	1
Queen's Belfast	32	R	3	Cumbria	83	M	1
Aberdeen	33	O	3	Salford	84	O	1
SOAS	33	O	3	Sunderland	84	P	1
Sussex	35	O	3	Lincoln	86	P	1
Queen Mary	36	O	3	Huddersfield	87	P	1
Surrey	37	O	3	Edge Hill	88	M	1
Strathclyde	37	O	3	Kingston	89	P	1
Kent	39	O	3	Manchester Met.	90	P	1
Heriot-Watt	40	O	3	Chester	91	M	1
Dundee	41	M	3	Roehampton	92	M	4
Keele	42	O	3	Northampton	92	M	1
Essex	43	O	3	Glamorgan	94	P	4
Hull	44	O	1	Arts London	96	M	4
Goldsmiths	45	O	3	Glyndwr	97	M	4
Aberystwyth	46	O	1	Canterbury Christ	98	M	1
Brunel	47	O	3	John Moores	99	P	4
Stirling	48	O	1	Westminster	100	P	4

3 Conclusions

This paper presented a cluster-based approach to university performance benchmarking as an alternative to the traditional ranking approach, which is usually based on combinations of arbitrarily weighted performance factors.

The cluster-based benchmarking method has the advantage that no arbitrary weighted factors need to be selected and hence any bias, intentional or unintentional, is removed.

In order to test the method, different data mining techniques were used to analyse the performance of UK universities based on the same data set used to compile The Sunday Times University Guide 2010 league table and the results were compared with the original ranking. It was shown that clustering techniques, such as Self-Organizing Map or the k-means algorithm, can be used to successfully classify universities in terms of performance. However, a disadvantage is that the classification, i.e. the interpretation, of the clusters had to be carried out manually after the clustering has taken place. This clearly is a shortcoming of the approach. However, possible ways of overcoming this will be studied during further investigations.

References

1. Turner, D.: Benchmarking in universities: league tables revisited, *Oxford Review of Education*, Vol. 31, No. 3, 2005, pp 353-371.
2. Kornbrot, D. E.: Misleading 'quality' measures in Higher Education: problems from combining diverse indicators that include subject ratings and academic performance and costs, *Radical Statistics*, Vol. 94, 2007.
3. Newman, M.: Pressure grows to replace league tables, *Times Higher Education*, 27 Aug-2 Sep, 2009, pp. 6-7.
4. O'Leary, J.: Big changes ahead in latest university rankings, *Times Online*, April 29, 2009.
5. Times Online, Good University Guide 2010,
    http://extras.timesonline.co.uk/tol_gug/gooduniversityguide.php, [accessed 2009].
6. Jury, E.I.: *Sampled-Data Control Systems*, John Wiley & Sons, 1958.
7. Times Online, Good University Guide 2010: How the tables work,
    http://www.timesonline.co.uk/tol/life_and_style/education/good_university_guide/article22
    35223.ece, [accessed 2009].
8. Rubin, D.B., Little, R.J.A.: *Statistical analysis with missing data* (2nd ed.), Wiley, 2002.
9. Dalgaard, P.: *Introductory Statistics with R* (2nd ed.), Springer, 2008.
10. Kohonen, T.: *Self Organization and Associative Memory* (2nd ed.), Springer, 1984.
11. McQueen, J.: Some methods for classification and analysis of multivariate observations, Proceedings of 5th Berkeley Symposim on Mathematics, Statistics and Probability, Vol. 1, 1969, pp 281-297.
12. Hopgood, A.A.: *Intelligent System for Engineers and Scientists* (2nd ed.), CRC Press, 2001.